REMEMBERING AMERICA

REMEMBERING AMERICA

A Voice from the Sixties

RICHARD N. GOODWIN

LITTLE, BROWN AND COMPANY BOSTON TORONTO

Permissions to quote from copyrighted material appear on page 544.

Library of Congress Cataloging-in-Publication Data

Goodwin, Richard N.
    Remembering America : a voice from the sixties / Richard N.
Goodwin.—1st ed.
      p.   cm.
    ISBN 0-316-32024-2
    1. United States—Politics and government—1961–1963. 2. United
States—Politics and government—1963–1969. 3. Kennedy, John F.
(John Fitzgerald), 1917–1963. 4. Johnson, Lyndon B. (Lyndon
Baines), 1908–1973. 5. Goodwin, Richard N. I. Title.
E841.G63 1988   88-15596
973.922—dc19   CIP

Designed by Robert G. Lowe

MV

*Published simultaneously in Canada
by Little, Brown & Company (Canada) Limited*

PRINTED IN THE UNITED STATES OF AMERICA

To My Wife, Doris

I acknowledge, first of all, my three sons — Richard, Michael, and Joey — who provided me with not unmixed, but life-sustaining joy during the preparation of this and other works. I am grateful to my close friend Michael Rothschild, who, from his artist's eyrie atop Tory Hill, bestowed hours of labor and his final blessings on this manuscript. And I owe much to the meticulously thoughtful suggestions of Pat Flynn, who took time from his own playwriting to help a needy friend. Linda Vandegrift's insightful and untiring research made it possible for me to revive and verify memories of events from the now-distant past. I have been enormously strengthened by the steady encouragement and constant flattery of Lindy Hess, while her husband, Bill Appleton, provided me with the energy needed to finish. Sterling Lord, my agent and friend for over twenty years, presided with his customary magisterial skill over the creation of this project, and continues to guide its progress through the labyrinth which leads the hopeful writer toward an ambivalent public. My editor Fredrica Friedman's belief in this book, before even a page had been written, gave me the necessary stimulus to initiate this story of my peripatetic years, and her sagacious editorial judgment at every single stage helped me to bring it to term. Mike Mattil, the acknowledged king of copyeditors, gracefully turned my textual obscurities into lucidly accurate prose. Nor would timely completion have been possible without the assiduous labors of Cynthia Stocking in translating my chaotic scribblings into a readable manuscript. And I owe most of all to my wife, Doris Kearns Goodwin, a most distinguished writer, whose love and critical intelligence have left their imprint on every page of this book.

Contents

REMEMBERING AMERICA

Prelude

Hello darkness, my old friend
I've come to talk with you again.

— Paul Simon, "The Sound of Silence"

AT NOON, January 20, 1961 — two and a half years after my graduation from law school — I became assistant special counsel to the president of the United States. My elevation took place simultaneously with that far more historic moment when John Kennedy took the inaugural oath before the aging hero of liberalism, Chief Justice Earl Warren. As I stood in that bitter-cold, iridescent day — sun glistening from the marble, the snow scattered from the unobstructed heaven — it seemed as if the country and I were poised for a journey of limitless possibility.

After the ceremony, I watched the inaugural parade from the presidential reviewing stand in front of the White House. It was emblematic of New Frontier heroics to come that I sat — along with the president, his family, and other officers of his administration — through the freezing hours of an interminable procession. Will it never end, I thought, shivering, or will the whole country pass in review?

When the parade was over I wandered into the West Wing of the White House to look at my new office. After inspecting my cramped but hugely portentous space, I walked along the first-floor corridor toward the Oval Office. Approaching me — having yielded to a similar impulse to inspect his chambers — I saw the figure with whom I had shared sixty days in the cramped cabin of a twin-engine Convair named *Caroline*, as we crossed and re-crossed the country during frantic months of campaigning.

Kennedy had changed from his formal wear to a dark business suit; moved with the same purposeful stride. He looks just like he always did, I thought, as if I had expected his ceremonial ascension to metamorphose his outward appearance — ennoble his features, enlarge his physical stature, ready him for immediate transport to Mount Rushmore.

"Dick," he called, beckoning me toward him. His voice hadn't changed either. As I approached him, I could see excitement in his eyes. And why not? I had been exhilarated at the sight of my own small office. He ran the whole place.

"Mr. President," I replied.

"Mr. President." What grandeur in the phrase, how lovingly it passed my lips. If there was such swollen warmth in saying it, what must it be like to hear?

"Did you see the Coast Guard detachment?" he asked.

Frantically I canvassed my memory of the parade.

Impatiently Kennedy interrupted my efforts at recollection. "There wasn't a black face in the entire group. That's not acceptable. Something ought to be done about it."

The observation was an order. It was a manner of command I had learned well over the brief period of my employment. I turned immediately. Struggling to maintain the dignity of office, I walked down the corridor until, turning the corner, I began to run up the stairs toward my office. The Coast Guard? I thought. Who ran the Coast Guard? The Pentagon, Bob McNamara. No, the Treasury Department. Doug Dillon.

Then it struck me: swift, accelerating elation. I was not to draft a statement or make a promise. Now we could do more than talk. We could change it! This was what it had all been about: the struggle, the fatigue, the fear, the uncertainty, the slim, fragile victory. It was the meaning, the essence of that abstraction — power. For a moment, it seemed as if the entire country, the whole spinning globe, rested, malleable and receptive, in our beneficent hands. "Here on earth God's work must truly be our own." I did not pause to reflect upon what I knew with philosophic certainty — that we were neither gods, not special intimates to His will. And why should I? We would do what men could do. And men — determined, idealistic, tough-minded, powerful — could perform great works, high deeds in Albion past all men's believing.

I picked up the White House phone. "Get me Secretary Dillon, please," I asked the White House operator. Dillon listened to my report of the president's comments. "Tell him I'll get right on it," he replied.

That summer the first black professor was hired at the Coast Guard Academy and the following year four black cadets entered the academy. The first irreversible steps toward desegregation had been taken.

We had made a difference. I had helped make a difference. It was, admittedly, a small problem, one resolvable by presidential authority alone. But it was successfully resolved. And the exhilaration of that achievement reinforced my belief that far larger dangers and difficulties could also be mastered; that it was a great country, but it would be greater.

Seven and one half years later I paced the fifth-floor corridor of the Good Samaritan Hospital in Los Angeles, California. Robert Kennedy was dying. The assassin's first bullet fired at Kennedy on the eve of his victory in the June California primary entered the head just behind the right ear and hit the spongy mastoid bone, scattering fragments of bone and metal through the brain. Six surgeons operated on the wound for three hours and forty minutes.

For twenty-five hours, a small group of family and friends kept vigil in the hospital. We ate sandwiches, went for occasional walks, looked at the crowd outside, and drank coffee while the accumulated weariness slowly dulled feeling.

For a long time the doctors told us to hope. So we did. Then they said it was hopeless. So we waited. I cried, and then, when it seemed I was too tired to feel anything, I cried again. And at the very end, Kennedy's boyhood friend, Dave Hackett, touched my arm and said, "You'd better go in now if you want to see him. It's almost over."

I entered Kennedy's hospital room, where a few minutes later, the doctors finally turned off the machines that pumped the lungs and blood of Robert Kennedy's corpse. My best and last friend in politics was dead.

A few months later I attended the Democratic convention in Chicago as a delegate from Massachusetts, pledged to Senator Eugene McCarthy. After Bobby's death, I had rejoined McCarthy's campaign, knowing that he had no chance of nomination, yet moved by some indefinable inward obligation to finish the year as I had begun it — in the ranks of those committed to an end of the Vietnam war. At McCarthy's request I drafted a "peace plank" for the party platform — the text approved by

McCarthy, George McGovern, and Edward Kennedy, and tentatively accepted by agents of Hubert Humphrey until a call from the White House commanded the Humphrey forces to reject any statement that hinted at the slightest doubt of Lyndon Johnson's policies.

Johnson himself had planned to attend the convention until his friends and lieutenants had advised him that a personal appearance would throw the convention into turmoil. "I can't guarantee what'll happen, Mr. President," explained Congressman Hale Boggs, a Johnson loyalist named to lead the platform committee. "You have a lot of friends here, but no one can control these delegates. Your enemies will stir things up." Coming from Boggs, these politic euphemisms could only mean that Johnson would be verbally abused, greeted with jeers, slandered from the floor; exposing the angry ferocity of a divided party to a watching nation.

So Lyndon Baines Johnson, president of the United States, titular head of the Democratic party, recalled the Secret Service agents who had gone to Chicago in preparation for his visit and stayed home. Sitting in a White House that was no longer the vitalizing center of the nation, but an exile's prison, he mourned: "I've never felt lower in my life. How do you think it feels to be completely rejected by the party you've spent your life with, knowing that your name cannot be mentioned without choruses of boos and obscenities? How would you feel? It makes me feel that nothing's been worth it. And I've tried. Things may not have turned out as you wanted or even as I wanted. But God knows I've tried. And I've given it my best all these years. I woke up at six and worked until one or two in the morning every day, Saturdays and Sundays. And it comes to this. It just doesn't seem fair."

It is impossible not to be moved by the poignancy of Lyndon Johnson's remarks — wholly sincere, totally honest — nor to realize that his personal tragedy of rejection was also a metaphor, a symbolic reenactment of what an entire nation — equally ambitious and hopeful — was also losing as Johnson's war destroyed Johnson's Great Society.

As the convention, subordinate to Johnson's will, proceeded to its ritualistic endorsements of the past, thousands of young people arrived in Chicago to protest the war, the nomination of Humphrey, the Democratic party's symbolic repudiation of what they had mistakenly thought to be the inevitably triumphant spirit of the sixties. As I stood outside the Hilton Hotel across from Grant

Park, I saw the student encampment transformed into a battle-ground, as members of the Chicago police, unleashed by Mayor Daley without opposition from the White House, mounted attack after attack, clubbing unarmed youths to the ground, dragging them brutally across the trodden grass, shoving them into police wagons.

For a brief moment images out of the past raced through my mind — Birmingham, the bridge at Selma, the flames of Watts. But this was different. It wasn't racial conflict; nor established privilege defending itself against some illusory fear of revolution. It was working Americans attacking young Americans simply be-cause they were young, or of different upbringing, or thought to be condescending, or, maybe, just because they were there. I re-called the words of a folk song: "Where have all the flowers gone?" Trampled, I thought, into the earth of Grant Park.

That November, Richard Nixon was elected president of the United States.

The sixties were over. A failure. Their ambiguous promise soon yielding to the drab withdrawal of the decades to follow. The twenty years since those final days in Los Angeles and at the Chicago convention have taken me along the paths of thought and literary creation toward which I was attracted, perhaps destined, from childhood. I have not missed public life. Nor have I written about my brief period of engagement. Not until now; moved to speak by an apprehension that the defeats of the sixties might be more than a temporary setback — that we are threatened with a loss of far vaster dimensions than the collapse of the New Frontier or the Great Society; of larger portent than the destruction and self-destruction of great leaders. The chronicles of great nations are not solely composed of alternating periods of stagnation and prog-ress. They also reveal the possibility of irrecoverable decline.

For the first time since we became a nation, America confronts that possibility. Yet decline, the progressive blight of self-seeking, protective fragmentation, is not inevitable, not necessary. Today, for the first time since our defeat in Vietnam, one senses large numbers of Americans emerging from an almost willed sleep to a repudiation of resignation and an awakening resentment of their loss of power over the direction of the nation and the conditions of their daily life. There is — or seems to be — an emerging desire to grapple with the country's ills. There is anger at political leadership that has forfeited its claim to confidence and trust. The sixties have passed into history, but the animating spirit of that time is not dead.

Much of what has been written about the sixties recalls the riots of urban blacks and the apotheosis of mind-twisting drugs; hippies and love-ins and communes; the violent furies that loosed citizen against citizen at Grant Park and Kent State; divisions so fierce and profound that the newly elected Nixon could tell us that his mission was to "bring us together again." But these were not the sixties. They happened, of course. Had occurred, or begun to emerge, before the final pages were torn from the calendar of the decade. But they came late, after the mad, voracious war had consumed our most expansive sense of possibilities, caused us to doubt "the better angels of our nature"; impenetrably sheathed our governing institutions against the just claims of our own people. Chronologically part of the decade, they were, in reality, its failure.

Dimly aware that society had lost its capacity to respond, many of those most ardently dedicated to liberating change lashed out in self-defeating fury, or turned to a vain search for some form of fulfillment — of freedom, as they conceived it — outside the larger society. But there can be no country within the country. The "new consciousness," the "counterculture," had barely emerged before they began to be accommodated, absorbed by the ascendant structures of American life.

The word "sixties" itself is a convenient label for a multitude of events and people. Yet every decade has its own characteristics, and the sixties were so different from the decades that have followed that its years seem like some faint and distant resonance from a half-alien America — like the Great Depression or the Civil War, the westward settlement or the onset of industrialism. Yet it happened only yesterday. It is within the living memory of every citizen over thirty. The great issues that were then debated have not been resolved. They have deepened, accumulated new and more formidable dimensions. Indeed, "my" sixties never happened. The decade contained a promise, an augury of possibilities, an eruption of confident energy. It was smothered and betrayed by a needless tragedy of such immense consequences that, even now, the prospects for a restorative return remain in doubt.

At the outset of that decade, aspirations deeply embedded in the country's history had begun to dominate the public dialogue.

A confident nation entered the longest sustained economic boom in its history. The ancient phrases — "opportunity," "justice," "equality" — seemed not ritualistic invocations, stock phrases from old Independence Day orations, but guides to action. Their achievement was within our grasp.

We were gifted with leaders of large dimension and capacity — John Kennedy, Martin Luther King, the Lyndon Johnson of the Great Society, Eugene McCarthy, Robert Kennedy. But their ascension was not a gift of fortune. Their qualities were also the creation of the people they led; their energy and direction a reflection of a people confident in their power to shape the future — their own and that of the country. If we believed in our leaders, it was because we believed in ourselves. If we felt a sense of high possibilities, it was because the possibilities were real. If our expectations of achievement were great, it was because we understood the fullness of our own powers and the greatness of our country.

This characterization of the sixties is not the product of long-delayed reflection. I believed it, felt it while I lived it, as did many, many others. In 1963, I gave a speech to a group of students from all parts of the world. I was speaking of the Peace Corps as an illustration of the conviction that "touches on the profoundest motives of young people throughout the world . . . tells them . . . that idealism, high aspirations, and ideological convictions are not inconsistent with the most practical, rigorous, and efficient of programs — that there is no basic inconsistency between ideals and realistic possibilities — no separation between the deepest desires of heart and mind and the rational application of human effort to human problems. . . . It will be easy," I concluded, "to follow the familiar paths — to seek the satisfaction of personal action or financial success. . . . But every one of you will ultimately be judged — will ultimately judge himself — on the effort he has contributed to the building of a new world society, and the extent to which his ideals and goals have shaped that effort."

Others might express it differently or better, but that passage contains, for me, the meaning of the sixties. If we have lost what it implies, then the sixties will have been more than an episode of failed ambitions. It will have been a watershed, a decisive turning point in the American story.

I cannot offer an objective history of the sixties. I lived them, with the arrogant, restless, romantic energy of youth. Nor has the passage of years provided detachment. My emotions remain as intensely engaged today as they were on that early evening in January of 1961 when I tumbled toward my office in enthusiastic obedience to John Kennedy's first presidential command.

I can, however, provide a rather special vantage. Chance, unexpected and, at first, unsought, placed me at the center of national politics: at the Supreme Court with Mr. Justice Frankfurter; in the White House with John Kennedy and with Lyndon Johnson; then in the vanguard of the presidential campaigns of Eugene McCarthy and Robert Kennedy. Present while many of the principal events of the sixties unfolded, I observed, participated, reacted, and remembered.

This book is a record of that experience of public life, recalled as honestly as fallible memory permits. It is not a history or a memoir; an autobiography or a critical analysis. It is an exhortation. It is an exhortation to remembrance, written in hope that by recollecting what we were, we may remember what we can be. For the America of such long and noble lineage, this athletic democracy — now dormant — needs only the touch of faith to awaken a strength and courage of imagination more than adequate to navigate beyond the stormy present toward a destiny, never precisely defined, but which, for centuries, has been not the goal, but the meaning of America.

I do not presume to think that this work can alter, even slightly, the contours of American beliefs and expectations. Yet it is the only instrument I have. And it is the truth. I know, even as I try to summon "spirits from the vasty deep," they will not come to me. Yet should a nation, an entire people, call on them, they will arrive — transported by the very act of invocation.

PART I / PREPARATION

The Child is father of the Man;
And I could wish my days to be
Bound each to each by natural piety.

— William Wordsworth

1 / Beginnings

SHINING BLACK CRYSTALS scattered along the sun-scorched stone. I had never seen, nor imagined, the abundance of black bodies that I saw when, aged ten years, I emerged from Washington's Union Station poised beneath the marble structures from which the country was governed.

Accompanied by my mother and younger brother, I had made the ten-hour train trip from our native Boston to join my father, who had come to work for the Maritime Commission a few months before the Japanese attack on Pearl Harbor. A trained engineer, he found his job had disappeared during the depression. He was forced to make his living as an insurance salesman until the god-like Roosevelt had need of men with his skills in the frantic effort to prepare the country for war. Until then, we had lived in a small apartment in a lower-income working-class section of Boston. One rarely saw a black face. The small black population of Boston lived somewhere else; distant from that world, bounded by a few dozen blocks of streets and apartment buildings, from which I was taken on occasional automobile trips to the countryside — my uncle's place on the lake at Wrentham, or Hood's farm, where one could watch real cows being milked.

A few months after my father's departure, an aunt interrupted my tenth birthday party. The Japanese had just attacked Pearl Harbor. I barely noticed the swift dissolution of my celebration, feeling a thrill of excitement, an exultation of awareness that great events had happened. And on my birthday. On Dick Goodwin's day. Ignoring my departing friends I rushed to the radio, listened to the confused tumble of announcements, took several pieces of paper, and penciled the news of the attack across the top of a dozen sheets. I ran down the street to the corner drugstore and offered my homemade broadsheet to passing motorists at the outrageous price of five cents a copy, selling out quickly for enough money to buy six comic books.

I had, for the first time, turned my engagement with language into profit. I could, my mother told me, talk before I could walk; had taught myself, with her help, to read before entering the first grade. By the time of this tenth birthday I was reading the works of James Fenimore Cooper and Mark Twain. I read at the table, propped books on the sink while brushing my teeth. Books, those fabulous frigates, were not only an escape from more unpleasant aspects of my life, but a source of delight, of pleasurable fulfillment. Perhaps my closest moments with my father, who loved and cherished books, were our walks together to the local public library, which contained a miraculous, unbounded store of tales and adventures. He would accompany me through the shelves, never interfering with my choices, and together we would return home where, stimulated by this tacit paternal blessing, I would turn eagerly from one work to another, embarked — although I did not know it then — on a lifelong love affair with language, its content, and the rhythmically cadenced interior sounds of words themselves. It was natural for me to react to Pearl Harbor by translating experience into headlines and sentences. I had already begun to think of words as the world made manifest.

I soon understood, or was told, that a terrible thing had happened. We were at war. But that reality was an abstraction compared to the fact that my father's job was secure — at least for the duration. And we were going to Washington, a city whose only known location was in pictures illustrating a few grammar school texts.

Perhaps it was because those photographs had only been accompanied by portraits of grave, dead, famous men, that — half expecting to encounter Abraham Lincoln — I was struck so forcibly by the sight of so many black faces. The sight had no large meaning, aroused no private emotion except astonishment at this first encounter with the wonders of a new world.

The very next day I walked from our new flat in a housing project in now-suburban, then rural, Maryland, to a small creek. Glimpsing a large turtle idling through the slow currents, I rushed home to tell my parents astounding news. I had witnessed, for the first time, a live animal in its natural surroundings.

Toward the blacks as toward the turtle, I felt no sense of apartness except for that part of me which was slowly maturing to a solitary identity, severing me from the universe. Blacks existed. They had been perceived and incorporated by my expanding interior imagination of the world. Later, while attending a segregated school in Washington, when I heard others parrot the catechisms of racial hostility they had picked up at the family table, it meant nothing to me. They were only fashionable expletives — like "damn," or "hell," or "shit" — which had no consequences for the real world of a ten-year-old.

There were, as I realized much later, other experiences that formed my attitudes toward the racial battles that were to dominate much of public life in the 1960s. Having grown up in a largely Jewish neighborhood in Boston, the anti-Semitism of Maryland came as a puzzling surprise, soon displaced by fear and, ultimately, defiance. I was frequently harassed and taunted — "Jew Boy," "kike" — and occasionally beaten up by older boys.

Among my circle of friends, members of a neighborhood club we named the Terrible Turtles, there was a boy named Fuzzy Hayes. Bigger than I and stronger, he would occasionally use anti-Semitic phrases in my presence. But he was careful not to press his hostile gibes, and I was afraid of him. One day, when the fresh-laid sod of the housing development was still soaked with spring rains, Fuzzy and two of my friends took a ball from my younger brother. They began to throw it to each other, challenging me to recover it. It was only a game. The ball was caught by Fuzzy, who held it as I ran toward him, but, instead of relaying it, he held on and shouted as I approached, "Come get it, Jew Boy." Something in my brain exploded, the entire world was drowned by a torrent of darkening blood. I remember nothing that happened until, a few moments later, some of my friends were pulling me away from Fuzzy Hayes, who lay on the ground, struggling as I held his face in the strangling mud. He was suffocating. And for many years — perhaps even now — my only regret was that I had not killed him.

From that day forward Fuzzy never said an offending word to me. My fear of him was gone. And I noticed that when a group of us walked together, he kept some distance from me, slightly out of reach. I even felt an occasional twinge of affection, quickly suppressed, toward a boy who had managed to make me feel so good about myself.

For almost the first time, the world — not my parents or teachers — had taught me a moral lesson. I did not learn not to be afraid, for I have experienced many moments of fear, far more intense and more firmly grounded in reality. But there is a time when one must yield forever, or hurl oneself at the source, without calculation of probabilities. And in later years when, on television, I watched the bodies of protesting blacks battered by the firehose in the hands of a Birmingham sheriff or club-wielding policemen, I often imagined I saw in their expression of rage the face of Fuzzy Hayes.

In August of 1945, as I sat quietly reading in our apartment, an elongated spherical casing tumbled from a solitary plane toward tranquil, unsuspecting Hiroshima, and the world shuddered. Hearing the news on the radio, I rushed to the kitchen. "Mom, they've dropped some kind of superbomb on the Japs. The radio says the war is probably over. Does that mean we'll be going back to Boston?" For me, the atomic age meant just that. We moved to Brookline where I completed high school, and then went to Tufts University in Medford, where my performance earned me a full scholarship to Harvard Law School.

That first year at law school was the most intense intellectual experience of my life. College had been the pursuit of grades, largely achieved by temporarily mastering large amounts of course material in the few weeks before examinations. At law school there was no possibility of mastery. The boundaries of understanding were infinite, achievement measured solely by comparison with the performance of five hundred other students — competitors for marks that meant, for those at the top, an invitation to join the *Harvard Law Review* and a secure path to the highest citadels of the legal profession. Since the results of that competition were determined by a single set of examinations at the end of the year, there was no limit to one's labors, no possibility of completion. There was always more to know, a deeper level of understanding. For the first time I felt pressed to the limit of my capacity, driven by the "unseen hand" of competition with men and women whose abilities were unknown.

Later, Supreme Court Justice Frankfurter told me that he still remembered the moment of awed, silent reverence as he stood in a law school corridor while a fellow first-year law student pointed to the back of a young man a few yards away and whispered, "That's the president of the *Law Review*." The future justice's attitude may seem slightly ludicrous to our more egalitarian age, but one should not totally disdain (the tribute mediocrity pays to achievement) a post sought and won by both Alger Hiss and Dean Acheson. Moreover, in practical terms the position opened the door to employment in the most affluent and prestigious law firms, even if you were Jewish.

Late that spring in the crowded silence of Langdell Hall, I sat furiously scribbling lengthy answers to the essentially unanswerable questions posed by my professors. Then I returned home to await the verdict. The completion of the year marked my eighteenth year of incarceration in the American educational system. The state of the world, to which I was largely indifferent, was relatively tranquil. Although Eisenhower had ended the Korean conflict, the wartime draft was still in effect, although as a student I was temporarily exempt from conscription.

In the summer of 1954, a letter from Harvard Law School with a report of grades astonishing to me, my family, and friends arrived at our small Brookline apartment. It was followed by a notice that my performance meant that I — along with the other members of the top twenty-five — was now an editor of the *Harvard Law Review* and that I was to return several weeks early to begin work on the first issue.

Sometime that August, I drove to the initiating *Law Review* dinner in my battered Chevrolet convertible — purchased with the residual earnings of my summers as a fry cook (clams, french fries, and onion rings) at nearby Revere Beach, an amusement area for the lower classes (now gone to condominiums). I had spent my summers there since high school, having become semipermanently ensconced behind the scorching Frialators after operating kiddy rides, a Loop-the-Loop, the Virginia Reel, and the fun-house controls, which sent jets of air to lift the skirts of women customers as they crossed a passageway exposed to delighted sidewalk spectators. (I always viewed slacks, then rare, as the greatest challenge to my coordination. If successfully penetrated, the passageway between leg and fabric yielded pleasure of lustful imaginings more gleefully obscene than the sight of still another pair of underpants.)

At the dinner, my classmates and I were congratulated on our ascension into the elite by the president of the *Harvard Law Review*, who then gave us our first assignment: to verify, for accuracy and relevance, the footnotes of articles scheduled for publication in the first issue of the *Review*, the country's leading publication of legal scholarship.

The next morning, manuscript in hand, I entered the cavernous stacks of the law school library. Interminable shelves of books in towered stacks, the volumes multiplied far beyond the precious handful that had yielded the most enraptured moments of my young life. The air was musty, redolent of old bindings, each breath stained with the accumulated dust of the long summer stillness. Commanded from level to level, I had been going to school forever. I reached for a volume of court reports. I couldn't. It was a prison. I turned, moving swiftly into the bright August heat, entered my car, and drove directly to the Brookline town hall, where I waived my draft deferment.

For years thereafter I explained that I had been conscripted involuntarily by a draft board that had run out of nonexempt candidates; that I had not appealed since I would have to serve when I graduated, and so I "might as well get it over." I lied because the truth would have made others regard me as mildly insane or, even worse, as a fool.

Yet, looking back, it seems to me there was in my action some augury of "the sixties." Mine was a purely personal act, similar to the mini-revolts of many young people in other times and places. Words like "the establishment," "the system," had not assumed a pejorative aura, indeed, were rarely heard. Yet there was in what I did something of defiance — not for a cause, not to protest injustice or oppression, but against a structure of rational expectations. I was not motivated by inability or unwillingness to meet the demands of an established order. Quite the contrary. I had conformed my energies to the demands of the structure that opened the path to worldly success. And I had met them. Yet, I had to get away. Some vacancy at the heart demanded response.

A few years later it would have seemed a strange kind of defiance to enter the army, even in peacetime. But I knew no alternative. I was aware of no causes, no movements in which to enlist. There were such possibilities, even then, but they lay beyond my horizon. It was also true my choice virtually eliminated the risk that ordinarily accompanies rebellion. Any suspicion of instability was dispelled by the masquerade of dutiful acquiescence to law. I could always return to Harvard, an honorable veteran of his nation's service. Yet diluted as it was, it was a reflection of discontent, an undefined act of protest, although I was the only one who knew it.

That same year Elvis Presley was beginning to horrify the respectable with the suggestive gyrations of his hips, and the Supreme Court overturned the precedents of three-quarters of a century in *Brown v. Board of Education.* In May, while I was preparing for my examinations in property and contract law, a French army surrendered Dien Bien Phu, liberating forces destined to more mightily scar and transform American life than any event since Colonel Anderson led his troops out of fallen Sumter.

Something was in the air. There had to be, although I could not hope to sense it as I sat outside my basic training barracks at Fort Dix alongside a company of other recruits — exhausted, sweat stained after a long bus ride and a night spent half-dozing on the dirt outside still unassigned barracks — while a huge, black, unsmiling sergeant informed us, "Your ass is grass, and I is a lawnmower."

A child of the neon and concrete, having never traveled outside the urban centers of the Northeast, I felt excitement approaching the intensity of disbelief as — my training over — I boarded the propeller-driven military transport that in a mere twenty-two hours would carry me to Frankfurt, from which a train would take me to my assigned station at an ordnance depot located in the forest of Braconne, just outside the town of Angoulême, only sixty-four miles northwest of Bordeaux.

Europe! Through the Looking Glass. Land of Oz. Crystalline fountain of the mythology contained in my history books, progenitor of those adored volumes that had engaged and enlarged my maturing passions. Later I would lie on Wenlock Edge staring at Housman's "woods in trouble," walk the lakes where Wordsworth had seen the human soul mirrored with the Divine, search out the street in which defeated Stendhal had shared the fate of Julien Sorel, watch bulls fall to the swords of Hemingway's matadors. And Stratford, of course, to sit upon the grass, but not to "tell sad stories of the death of kings." Not yet. That time would come years later, and on American soil.

I had no trace of the expatriate longing that had persuaded both Henry James and the writers of the twenties to escape phil-

istine America for a more enriching and appreciative culture. I
was quintessentially American, irrevocably rooted in the turbulent
energy of my homeland. And Europe was over. It had torn itself
apart in some magnified version of the Pelopennesian wars. My
anticipation was that of a child's visit to the circus, a student's
approach to the Louvre, or the excitement I have seen in my own
boys as they enter Disney World.

During my eighteen months in France I traveled extensively
throughout Western Europe; saw much, experienced much, learned
much. Great wine tasted like the musty interior of an old cathedral (so much for Manischewitz), the sight of the Pyrenees sloping
into the Atlantic along the road south of Biarritz moved me to
tears, dinner at a good French restaurant gave taste a dimension
more wondrously alien to my perceptions than Riemannian ge-
ometry. I lost a few dollars amid the cathedral hush of a Biarritz
casino, caught a distant glimpse of Eisenhower and Khrushchev
conveyed by limousines to their Geneva summit, traced the Rhone
glacier to its source. And I unmasked, in somewhat obsessive pursuit, the varied exhilarations of sex. But this belongs to my private
biography.

If memory of the white clustered villages on green-sloped Pyrenees, or the multihued fall vineyards near Carcassonne, exercised
some influence in the formulation of Lyndon Johnson's program
for natural beauty, my European experience was most often of
practical use at state dinners and other presidential functions in a
tedious exchange of animated banalities with often rich and worldly
fellow guests.

My experience in the army had more direct influence on the
attitudes I would bring to high politics and the White House. I
despised it, of course. Not the army itself, or the idea of the army,
or the purpose of the army, but my condition of military servitude: a lowly private, ordered and organized and arranged; compelled to prepare myself and my belongings for innumerable in-
spections, assigned on regular rotation to scrub the kitchen pots
and floor. My distaste, therefore, was largely a matter of rank,
and could have been transformed into something approaching enjoyment had I been promoted to general or, even better, commander of NATO. (Not too many years later I visited the Pentagon to brief the Joint Chiefs of Staff on our policy toward Cuba.
As I confronted the array of spangled shoulders, shined and crowded
stars reflecting the bright fluorescents with a terrestrial Milky Way

of light, there was a moment of exultation — a child's fantasy come true — which was intensified by my intuition from across the room of surly resentment at having been ordered into the presence of this kid, ex-Corporal Goodwin.)

In what then seemed a natural response to discontent, I began, tentatively at first, then systematically, to find ways of evading military discipline. And with enormous success. In my entire overseas tour, I never stood an inspection, avoided all company duties, manipulated the excessive passes and leave time that enabled me to tour most of Europe, and managed an early discharge — quite honorable — which allowed me to return home for the entire summer preceding my second year of law school. Indeed, I was technically AWOL during my entire overseas tour.

Shortly after being assigned to a barracks, but before my face and name were fixed in the mental landscape of platoon leaders, I managed a three-day pass from which I never returned to my designated corner of the company. Reentering the camp on a Sunday night, I stole a mattress, which I kept rolled in the locker in the small wooden structure housing the Troop Information and Education Office to which I had been assigned. Every evening, after sunset, I carried my mattress and blanket in search of an empty bunk — a man on leave or in the hospital. At reveille I rushed to the quarters assigned to a company of Polish guards, who soon gave up their occasional queries directed at the eccentric young American who came to wash and shave among them.

I was on the base for duty, appeared regularly at company formations, but, a man without a home, I did not appear on any duty rosters, left no unexplained vacancy when I failed to stand inspection.

I ingratiated myself with my superiors — thus lowering the threshold of potential suspicion, and ensuring a lenient disregard of my late return from passes and leaves — by putting my imagination at the service of their professional needs and apprehensions.

My most impressive triumph took place when, just before a major headquarters inspection, it was discovered that we had one more two-and-a-half-ton truck than the total (almost a thousand) recorded in the shipping manifests. For days we counted and recounted, but the discrepancy remained. The possibility of some error in the records was unthinkable or, at least, inadmissible —

to us and, more importantly, to headquarters. But the truck was
there. Observing the captain's mounting panic, I suggested that
the only escape from this dilemma was to bury the truck. Working
at night, a handful of trusted men, under my supervision, dug a
large pit far back in the forest, drove the truck in, and covered it
with earth, where, I assume, its rusting remains still repose. The
inspectors found everything in perfect order, the captain was delighted, and I went to Paris on a special pass.

My success in exploiting the vulnerabilities of bureaucracy left
me with a dangerously incomplete understanding. About a week
before I was to return to the United States, I encountered my
platoon commander, ROTC Lieutenant Lloyd, while walking from
my office to the mess hall. Confronting me directly, he said, "Well,
Goodwin. I hope you're all ready for the big inspection Saturday."

"Yes sir," I replied.

He didn't move. I could sense, behind his acutely attentive gaze,
a puzzled struggle of recall. Had he ever seen me at an inspection?
When? My facial muscles tensed, my rigidity of expression a mask
for fear. Disobedience of orders. Court-martial. Disqualification
for the bar. Leavenworth. The silent moment seemed interminable. He knew. To this day I believe that at the surface of awareness he knew he had never seen me at any inspection. But his
upbringing on a midwestern farm, the arduous routine of chores
fulfilled, had left his imagination without the reach to encompass
so heinous and prolonged a defiance of orders. Miss one inspection, default on a single assignment — of course. Readily noted,
quickly punished. But never; not once in eighteen months. It was
not to be grasped. "I'll look for you, Goodwin," he said, turning
to leave.

"Yes, sir," I replied, the fear draining away. I had just seen the
other face of bureaucracy — not the amiable bumbling of institu-
tionalized mediocrity, but the coercive force by which authority is
sustained. Defiance of established institutions, of "the system,"
was not a game for children, but a hazardous course where failure
or defeat could impose large and serious consequences. I had
learned a lesson. But not completely. For despite the fearful nar-
rowness of my escape I would not attend Lieutenant Lloyd's last
inspection. Using stratagems far too labyrinthine for description,
I managed to have myself sent by official order to another post
for my final weekend. It was not an act of principle, a "statement" of moral courage. I had a no-hitter going. It was the last

of the ninth. Two outs. I couldn't lose it now, not if I could help it, whatever it took.

In December of 1955, while I was trifling with authority in the forests of France, a black seamstress in Montgomery, Alabama, undertook to defy an entire, deeply rooted culture of injustice when she refused to obey the driver's order that she move to a seat in the rear, or colored, section of the bus; and with that single act of courageous defiance began — not chronologically but spiritually — the period we now know as "the sixties." Rosa Parks's disobedience to established order crystallized a mass of resentments and desires into a new struggle for black freedom, and propelled Martin Luther King, Jr., from the anonymity of his Atlanta pulpit to a national leadership that transformed him into the most towering figure of the decade. That single act initiated an unprecedented period of protest, aspiration, conflict, and progress, which was, in defiance of events, to be formally dated from the election of John Kennedy in 1960.

I returned from my army assignment for my final two years at Harvard Law School, unaware that I was also returning to a country on the edge of tumultuous change; or that I would play a part in the events of change. I was going back for a law degree, and then . . . well, I wasn't sure.

2 / The Justice

YOU ARE NOW on the *cursus honorum*." The speaker was Professor Abe Chayes, standing beside me at the buffet table of a cocktail party to honor the graduating members of the class of 1958 who had served as editors of the *Harvard Law Review*. I instantly understood his meaning, "the way of honor." I was first in my class of five hundred, president of the *Harvard Law Review*, and on my way to serve as a law clerk to Supreme Court Justice Felix Frankfurter. Thence, following a well-marked, oft-trodden path, I would serve in the "real world," most probably as an associate with a Wall Street mega–law firm, and then become a professor at "the law school."

"Fuck that" were the words I didn't say, as I nodded in seeming acquiescence. I had already concluded that big-time law — i.e., corporate law — was an occupation for skilled servants of business; distinguished from accountants, secretaries, and chauffeurs only by the historic prestige of their professional status and the size of their fees. Yet I did not have an alternative. I had thought of returning to Boston and opening my own one-man law office. But who would my clients be?

Several months before my graduation, Sumner Kaplan, a neighbor in Brookline, who was also a representative to the state legislature, had taken me to a small, upper-floor apartment in downtown Boston where Senator John F. Kennedy maintained his Massachusetts residence. A man called Frank Morrissey took our coats. Morrissey had served as a kind of personal factotum to Joseph P. Kennedy and, for years, had been assigned to keep watch on young John's activities so the father could be alerted to any hazards — personal or public — that might obstruct the career of his swiftly rising son. The outer room was crowded with a variety of politicians and lobbyists, for whom the senator's appearance in Boston was a chance to advance a favored project or impress a lucrative client. I knew none of them either by sight or name.

In about twenty minutes we were taken to a small sitting room, where the senator, already standing, greeted my friend Sumner, shook my hand, and said, "I understand you're going to work for Frankfurter." As I nodded in confirmation, he added, "He's not my greatest fan. Give me a call when you get there." He then waved briefly toward three men who were entering the room behind us, smiled warmly in our direction, and strode toward his new visitors. With a skill whose exercise was totally concealed from my understanding, without the slightest sign of dismissal or termination, our encounter was ended. And, in milliseconds, lest there be any confusion, Morrissey had Sumner by the arm. "It was so nice of you to come. I know the senator appreciates everything you've done."

That was it. I had made my first contact with national politics. As I headed for the subway, I looked at my watch, calculating the time I had remaining to study for an approaching exam. It was back to reality. More than a year passed before I realized that something had happened. I — a hater of organization and contemner of bureaucracies — had taken a first, essential step toward a career in the most monumental, complex, and overpopulated of all American institutions: the government of the whole, frigging United States of America.

Liberated from the schoolhouse, I prepared to return to Washington, unaware my education was to begin. I had gladly accepted the clerkship with Mr. Justice Frankfurter — an unrefusable honor and, not incidentally, a way to postpone career decisions — not knowing that in the brief year with the justice I would have found not an employer, but a mentor, whose beliefs and intensity of engagement with life would irrevocably fortify and shape my own beliefs and values.

Though I had studied some of his opinions, the arid discourse of the classroom had not prepared me for my first personal encounter. In April of my graduation year, on a visit to Cambridge Frankfurter had asked to meet with his new law clerk. Seated in a small sitting room adjoining the offices of Dean Erwin Griswold, I indifferently scanned the morning papers, when the door opened and a small, almost tiny man strode through the door and approached me with hand outstretched, moving swiftly, seeming to bound slightly off the floor with every step, like a gliding kangaroo. "So you're Goodwin," he said, placing his hand on my arm with that strong, fierce grip I was to come to know well. "Yes, Mr. Justice," I replied, suddenly conscious of my rumpled suit, the overlong hair tumbling across my forehead. "Good," he responded, not, I was later to learn, as a signal of approbation (there was little in my appearance to inspire praise), but a sign that with his fraternal grasp I was being welcomed into that honored group of clerks, now reaching back over a generation, that constituted the justice's extended family, the formidable substitute for the children he never had.

"They tell me you're very bright," he said. I had no response. "Well," he said, "we'll find out soon enough," the smile removing the sting from his words.

"I'll be down just as soon as the school year is finished."

"Take a vacation first," he admonished. "August will be soon enough."

"I don't need one. I'd like to get right to work."

His voice suddenly became solemn, a tone adopted for lessons to be remembered, his finger outstretched; "Young man, there's something I want you to remember for the rest of your career. The laws of physiology are inexorable."

What had such laws to do with me, in my twenties, exuberant with anxious vitality? But his manner seemed to convey some undecipherable wisdom. And, he was the boss. (As it turned out, my vacation, even though later abbreviated, could not have been better timed, for early that summer I married Sandra Leverant, a Vassar graduate whom I had known since high school.)

Then, as swiftly as he had entered, the justice relaxed his grip, headed for the exit, turning at the door to repeat in stentorian tones: "Remember, take a vacation." Then he laughed and was gone. I stood there half-expecting to hear the sound of sleigh bells on the roof of Langdell Hall. It had been a totally unexpected encounter: not an interview, but a kind of laying on of hands, a symbolic initiation. Despite the abruptness of our meeting, I was moved. He cared. Not about my credentials (those had been established) but about me — a child and a stranger — wanted me to understand something, not about law, but a principle of personal life: that the process of life was ironbound by limits that neither the eager energy of youth nor the highest gifts of maturity could rupture or transcend. He was talking about health, but I later understood that the way he said it — "the laws of physiology" — was a clue to a less banal faith — that the well-being of the democracy he so dearly loved, as well as that of the individual, depended upon fierce obedience to the principled process from which its vitality flowed.

In a few brief moments, what had been a job had been transformed into a relationship. I quickly repaired to the library stacks, anxious to know more about the man I was about to serve.

Frankfurter was an incarnation of the American dream. Born to Jewish parents in Vienna, Austria, he had arrived in New York at the age of twelve, unable to speak a word of English. A few years later he had plunged into the melting pot of City College and then gone to Harvard Law School, graduating with the highest honors. Although he was to be one of Harvard's most honored teachers of law, his energies overflowed the confines of academic life into a continual and fervent engagement with the issues and passions of his time.

Frankfurter had accompanied Secretary of War Henry Stimson to Washington, worked under Woodrow Wilson during World War I. ("A self-righteous pedantic snob" was his verdict on Wilson.) And despite his ambitions for public office, he had not hesitated to engage in some of the most controversial issues of the interwar period: fighting against the anticommunist "red hunting" of Attorney General Mitchell, becoming an eloquent advocate for the condemned Sacco and Vanzetti. These were all "liberal" causes, but at the heart of Frankfurter's indignation was the transgression of limits on democratic power by public officials.

During this period he formed a close friendship with Franklin Roosevelt, who, upon election to the presidency, turned to Frankfurter for recruitment of many of the bright young men who staffed the New Deal. "Felix's hot dogs" they were often called, either in scorn or sardonic admiration; and they were among the leaders of an entire generation of gifted young Americans who helped reconstruct the depression-torn nation. In 1939, in recognition of Frankfurter's abilities and in gratitude for his services, Roosevelt appointed him to the Supreme Court.

From the immigrant gates of New York to the High Court: an

American story, which had given Frankfurter a profound love for the country that had made possible his dreamlike passage. To the end of his life he remained an almost childlike patriot, his labors a profound love affair with the nation — not a sightless admiration, but one illuminated by an intelligent understanding of the principles that sustained American freedom, and a worldly knowledge of how easily men of power were tempted to violate those principles. "Nature," he once told me, "is the great democrat," bestowing its gifts of intelligence and vitality on the poor and well-born alike. But it was the structure, the elaborately designed process of American freedom, that allowed those gifts to find fulfillment. The Supreme Court was, for him, not a substitute for the institutions of representative government, not endowed with power to impose its own shifting views on the nation. It was the protector of democracy against itself, the guardian of the Constitution against the abuse, the overweening exercise of power by men and institutions that ignored the carefully constructed confinements of the Founding Fathers — from the red-baiting Attorney General Mitchell, to southern governors resisting desegregation, to William Casey and Oliver North and Ronald Reagan.

Although this wisdom was to become embedded in my own view of public life, I was compelled to begin my term with Frankfurter by disobeying his very first command, cutting my vacation short and going to Washington in early August to attend a special term of court called to consider the cause of *Aaron v. Cooper*. A lower court had granted the high schools of Little Rock, Arkansas, the right to delay implementation of a desegregation program because of mounting public opposition to integration. Hastily summoned into session, the Supreme Court was called on to consider whether such opposition was a sufficient cause for delay. The answer, of course, had to be no. Permitting public opposition to justify the denial of constitutional rights would destroy those rights, amount to a virtual reversal of the Supreme Court's historic decision in *Brown v. Board of Education*.

The lower court was unanimously reversed, although Justice Douglas did not attend the special session, being content to have the opinion dropped to him from a plane into some mountain wilderness where he was enjoying his usual strenuous vacation. Frankfurter was furious, viewing Douglas's failure to return as a contemptuous degradation of the judicial process. "That man," he told me, "is an opportunist and a malingerer. He's more concerned about his public personality than the work of the Court. In fact, he doesn't do his work. He just decides who he wants to win and then votes — a lazy, contemptible mind."

I can still recall entering the small, somber courtroom to attend the oral arguments in *Aaron v. Cooper;* shown by smiling, indulgent guards to the special seats flanking the paneled benches which were reserved for law clerks and guests of the justices; hearing the crack of the gravel, a signal to rise as the black-robed justices, led by Earl Warren, filed silently to their seats. Then the voice of the clerk — "Oyez! Oyez! Oyez! All persons having business before the Honorable, the Supreme Court of the United States, are admonished to draw near and give their attention, for the Court is now sitting. God save the United States and this Honorable Court." I felt an unanticipated chill, awareness that I was at the margins of the long flow of history, old as the Republic, amid which men had presided over the shaping events of a nation. John Marshall had sat on this same court and Roger Taney had returned Dred Scott to slavery and moved the country toward civil war; the New Deal had been demolished by the Nine Old Men and then revived by the men of Roosevelt, including my own employer.

The very case I was attending was a consequence of the latest shaping period in American judicial history — one of those rare times when the magisterial legal pronouncements of the Court reach out to modify the life of the country. The Supreme Court had not, in some aberrant convulsion of arrogance or ideology, designated itself the agent of social revolution. It did not simply convene on its own initiative to decree the end of segregation. That was not within its power, nor its circumscribed role in the democratic structure. Black students, their parents, and attorneys compelled the Court to decision. They sued.

To decide that suit the Court must either uphold its antique precedents, thus ignoring the blatant reality that the doctrine "separate but equal" had become a disguise for American apartheid, or it must decree an end to segregation. Even then, the Court, aware of the enormous and unforeseeable import of such action, delayed until its decision could be made unanimous. Justice Robert Jackson, formerly chief prosecutor at the Nuremberg war trials, was — Frankfurter told me — the last holdout. Once he had been persuaded — more by the necessities than the legal merits of the case — the Court, in 1954, made its decree in *Brown v. Board of Education*. The opinion was delivered by Chief Justice Warren, on behalf of what was thenceforth to be known as the "Warren Court." But the true leaders of the Court, the two men whose intellect and personal force were to shape its course, were Justice Black and Justice Frankfurter: southern populist and northern intellectual, fierce adversaries, sharply divided in philosophy, principle, and temperament. But not on this matter. Once it was clear that the case had to be decided, only one outcome was possible.

Enforcement was more difficult. The Court could not — even if it had the power — overturn rooted social structures in a single, sweeping decree. It was the responsibility, the obligation, the power of the president and Congress to implement the Fourteenth Amendment as reinterpreted by the Court. And they did nothing. Thus implementation was left to the district courts, instructed to proceed "with all deliberate speed." The other institutions of government would let the judges take the blame, and the political heat. They would, with forceful rhetoric, praise or condemn, but not act.

The southern resistance to integration, successful at first, had a wholly unforeseen consequence. Black Americans would no longer leave enforcement of their rights to the white rulers who decreed them. They would fight. Enormous social changes during and after World War II had transformed black temperament, fortified black possibilities. The Court had simply cast a tiny, but necessary, spark of hope on the swelling and flammable contours of black expectations. They would have freedom; peacefully if possible, with blood if necessary. This demonstration that individual citizens — the hitherto impotent and anonymous — could struggle for moral justice and, occasionally, attain it began to fissure the complacent, self-indulgent façade of American innocence. It was an energizing impulse for a multitude of battlegrounds, many of them remote from racial conflict, which were to make the sixties a time abundant with life-enhancing possibilities. "Every man can make a difference," said Robert Kennedy; but not until Rosa Parks and Martin Luther King and Thurgood Marshall had already given us proof.

Thus, the gradually accumulating forces whose undammed pressures were to shatter the national tranquillity and give special meaning to the decade known as the sixties had established their first Washington outpost in that most unlikely sanctuary, the Supreme Court of the United States.

I did not foresee that America and I were already embarked on so tumultuous a course, as I walked up the stone steps of the

Supreme Court each morning, crossed the broad marbled plaza chipped from the quarries of icy Vermont, moved past the three Fates patiently weaving the thread of life — their frozen labors ironically flanked by the figure of Justice sternly unaware that its upraised sword and scales were feeble armor against the gossamer fabric of the adamantine ladies — into my modest office separated by a door from the chambers of the justice.

Seated at my desk in the first days of my employment, reading through the flow of petitions and briefs that inundated the Court, I heard a door open and, almost simultaneously, looked up to see Justice Frankfurter standing before me, his outstretched hand holding a single sheet of paper covered with his cramped, semi-legible handwriting. When the justice wanted to communicate with a clerk, he did not call for you or make a normal entrance, he simply materialized. The illusion was not a trick but a philosophical creation: Life was too short to allow a wasted moment of labor, pleasure, or intimate companionship. The justice lived as if each day might be his last. Much later, as I battled fatigue, struggling through the early-morning hours to perfect a presidential speech or prepare a White House program, I would recall his example — the essential truth of his insatiable grasp for life's possibility — send for another cup of coffee, shake off my weariness, and resume my labors. I didn't have it right. Not yet. Not exactly. There would be time to sleep soon enough.

Handing me the paper, the justice waited, shifting his weight impatiently as I struggled to decipher in the scrawled sentences his reasons for denying a petition for appeal to the Supreme Court. "Well," he said, "what do you think?" The case seemed trivial, a matter of statutory interpretation that did not merit a full review. "I agree with you," I responded, starting to return the scrawled page. "Don't agree with me!" he interrupted, refusing to take the page from my hand. "I don't need to hire the best students from Harvard Law School to agree with me. Anyone can do that. Argue. Tell me what's wrong with my decision. There must be something wrong. I'm not perfect. That's the only way you can be of any real service."

"All right," I answered, somewhat pedantically, "I think the Court should hear the case. The meaning of a federal statute is in dispute, and if it's not resolved by the Supreme Court, the lower courts will give it different readings, leaving the meaning of the law in confusion."

"So!" he said triumphantly, "you think we should take the time of this Court to resolve every insignificant ambiguity in the federal laws. Look at those shelves," he said, pointing toward the innumerable volumes of federal statues that lined my office. "If we tried to decide what every law means, we'd have to sit until doomsday, and the really important issues could never be considered or resolved with the care they demand."

The unanticipated debate went on, each new argument demolished with stern ebullience, until, satisfied at last, the justice turned back to his own office. "I'm right," he said as he left. "Don't you see that I'm right?" Of course I saw it, had thought him right from the beginning. But I had learned an important lesson: One did not serve a powerful master by flattering accommodation to his views. I would bring this belief with me to the White House, where my contradictions were not always so warmly received.

At the close of my first day at work, the justice took me for an automobile tour of Georgetown, pointing out restaurants suitable for a young couple of modest means. Weeks later, while trying to gnaw through a badly overdone steak, it occurred to me that the justice himself had probably not set foot in a "cheap" restaurant for decades. Yet his evident concern for my digestion was the beginning of awareness that my appointment as a clerk was not merely a job but initiation into a fellowship. The justice sustained an almost paternal relationship with his clerks, past and present; their presence an opportunity to continue, in microcosm, the teaching career he had abandoned for Roosevelt's appointment to the Court.

On that same ride the justice pointed vaguely toward a Georgetown street which, he told me, had been the residence of Justice Oliver Wendell Holmes, a man he had revered in life and apotheosized in death. "I brought Franklin Roosevelt there," he told me, repeating a story that had been told to successive law clerks for a generation. "Roosevelt was already president-elect, not yet inaugurated, and he told me he'd like to meet Holmes." (Then in his nineties, and retired from the Court.) "They talked for several minutes and after accompanying Roosevelt back to his residence, I returned to Holmes's residence.

" 'What did you think?' I asked Holmes.

" 'A third-rate intellect but a first-rate temperament.'

"I was a little disappointed," Frankfurter continued, "but Holmes was right. Temperament. There was the secret of Roosevelt's greatness. He had the ability to recognize intelligence, wanted bright people around him, but he had the instincts to understand the difference between good ideas and practical possibilities. He knew the limits of his power, and, most of all, he loved being president. No one has ever been a good president who didn't love his job."

It was recollection of this incident that led me, six years later, to suggest that President Lyndon Johnson visit the mortally ill Frankfurter, who, to the chagrin of his doctors, left his bedroom and demanded he be suitably dressed to receive the president of the United States.

Twice each year all the Frankfurter clerks — a line that reached back almost twenty years from my tenure — would assemble: once for a celebratory dinner, and once again for a sherry party on the occasion of the justice's birthday. Among the guests, my predecessors in office, were men who then or later would advise the White House, serve in presidential cabinets, lawyers of national reputation, judges, and the merely successful.

At the dinner that year I was seated next to Phil Graham, who had deserted the law to take over the *Washington Post*, and was in the course of establishing a publishing empire that has continued to flourish in the years since he blew his brains out in the bathroom of a family house, the victim of a manic-depressive psychosis. My conversation with this man of immense charm and exuberant vitality turned to literary subjects. I was surprised to discover later that he had informed friends — Joseph Alsop, Dean Acheson — that the justice had a clerk who actually read books. But that was before I realized that Washington was a company city: its business politics; its leaders and aspiring juniors largely ignorant of literature, history, philosophy, and all other realms of thought and discourse not directly related to the most mundane and practical concerns. People read memos, not books, hire professors, not acquire learning.

My acquaintance with my predecessor clerks and others in the justice's large and eclectic network of friends was to have no immediate practical consequence. But it marked me in the minds of many "who counted" as a young man with possibilities, perhaps even a young man on the rise. One day Congressman John Lindsay of New York — stunningly handsome, already exuding an ambience of almost presidential density — was brought into our office by the justice. "These are the kind of people," he told Frankfurter, waving vaguely in our direction, "I'd like to have around me." Presumably he meant in the White House, or some other exalted office.

Of far more enduring import than these "contacts" were the lessons learned through continued exposure to the justice's mind and memory. Large, even historic, public figures — Wilson, both Roosevelts, Eisenhower, Acheson, Truman — were disenthroned from my textbook world, and set upon the level as objects for analysis, gossip, criticism, and personal judgment. The distinctions between men of power were not between nobility and baseness, or virtue and corruption, but that balance between strengths and flaws, beneficent works and ruthless betrayals which coexisted, of necessity, in all men of action — and whose relative measure divided greatness from mediocrity. The necessities of public ambition were hard on virtue. Circumstances constantly challenged conviction. Frankfurter himself, anxious to please his great patron, Franklin Roosevelt, had occasionally violated the boundaries of judicial integrity through direct participation in political conflicts. Purity and power are constant companions only in fairy tales and legends, and even there the fate of their fellowship is the death of Arthur.

Yet, on balance, the justice was the most principled public figure I have known. From his tutelage I would acquire certain fixed guides that — though occasionally transgressed — prevented me from blind compliance with the volatile and unpredictable demands of political life; allowed me to challenge the childish, very American, belief that acts were to be judged by their consequences, that desirable results retroactively blessed the method of their accomplishment.

Two of the cases during my term of court emerged from the final spasms of the anticommunist witch-hunts that had accompanied the growing hostility and fear of Armageddon known as the Cold War. In one case, a college professor, one Mr. Barenblatt, had been convicted of contempt by a federal court for refusing to answer congressional questions about his communist affiliations. While in distant New Hampshire, Mr. Uphaus had been convicted of the same offense for refusing to give a list of his guests at a summer camp suspected of being a "communist front" by the attorney general of New Hampshire, who was zealously enforcing the legislature's command that he forestall a communist overthrow of that patriotic state. Neither the triviality nor the absurdity of the allegations was before the Court. The issue was the power of government to investigate and expose. One could not question the right of a government to guard against threats to its survival. On the other hand, there was no power to expose and slander those with unpopular opinions. It was — to oversimplify the legal issues — the Court's job to balance government's power to protect itself against the individual's freedom to choose and safeguard his associates.

To me, the "right" decision was plain. Professor Barenblatt was not engaged in subversive activities. He had committed no crime. The congressional committee was simply out to castigate, expose, and slander in its unremitting pursuit of political gain. Nor was the state of New Hampshire endangered by a communist conspiracy emanating from the Uphaus summer camp.

This much seemed obvious. Not just to me, but to all my fellow clerks and, probably, to all the justices. Clearly the convictions should be reversed. There was, however, one obstacle to this otherwise obvious course. Congress and the legislature of New Hampshire had authorized these investigations on the premise that the danger from communist conspiracy was real and its extirpation required far-reaching, virtually unrestrained inquiry. Thus the Court was being asked, indirectly, to overrule these legislative determinations, at least as applied to the particular cases before us. This, Frankfurter, and four other justices, refused to do.

On his return from the regularly scheduled Friday conference where the members of the Court met privately to make their decisions, Frankfurter informed me of his vote. Shortly thereafter I entered his office, and, at his invitation, launched into my carefully prepared argument against his position (always subject to change until the actual opinion had been drafted, circulated, signed, and announced). After a few minutes of patient audience, he interrupted. "Your difficulty, Dick, is that you don't understand democratic government. And you don't know the role of this Court."

"I do know that is up to the Court to protect individual liberties," I replied.

"Wrong!" he exclaimed in sharply raised tones. "Is that what they teach you up at Harvard now?"

"I think, Mr. Justice, that I read it in one of your opinions."

"Misread! Our job is to enforce the law, including the Constitution. We have nothing to do with your abstract notions of justice or liberty. Only with what the law provides."

"I believe —"

"I'm not interested in what you *believe*. What do you *think?*"

"I think the Constitution protects freedom of association."

"You're begging the question."

"How?"

"That's the issue, not the answer — whether these associations
are constitutionally protected. You wouldn't argue there is a constitutional right to join a gang of murderers?"

"Murder is against the law. A danger to society. Barenblatt and
Uphaus are not dangerous, and they haven't broken any law."

"The Congress and a state legislature have decided there is a
danger, and assigned power to investigate it."

"But they're wrong. At least in these cases."

"I agree with you . . . but not on the main matter. You think
they're in error. I think it. But that doesn't mean we can substitute our opinion for theirs."

"If they have violated the Constitution, it is the duty of the
Court to overrule."

"It depends."

"On what?"

"On a great many things. On precedent, on the recorded intent
of the law, on the facts that are presented to us, not what we read
in the papers."

"But here the only motive —"

"We have nothing to do with motives. We are not a court of
mind-readers. It is not up to us to decide why a legislature acted,
only what they did. On the record. If there is a real danger of
subversion, a real conspiracy against government, there is power
to prevent it, and that includes investigation. I know what you
want. You want me to say they're wrong, that there is no danger,
that they're just out to get votes by scaring the public no matter
who gets hurt."

"That's just what they are doing. And you agree with me."

"Privately, perhaps. But as a justice I have no right to substitute my judgment for that of a legislature. Not on a matter like
this. Or perhaps you think we should have our own investigation,
appoint a special master to examine all the evidence of the last
decade to decide whether there is a conspiracy."

"Of course not. But when the case is clear."

"To you. Not to Congress or the New Hampshire legislature. It
is beyond us. Beyond our capacities and thus beyond our power."
Then, lowering his voice, speaking in almost avuncular tones: "I
was appointed when this Court almost wrecked the country and
itself by trying to substitute its economic views for those of the

president and Congress. I am not going to impose my views about communism on the rest of the government."

Then, as I turned to leave, only half convinced, but the argument clearly lost, he interrupted my exit, almost musingly. "It is what we mean by democratic government. I don't believe that when the Founding Fathers wrote the Constitution they meant for basic questions of social and political policy to be decided by nine men meeting in a secret conference on Friday afternoon."

The contempt convictions would be affirmed by a vote of 5–4.

Reentering my office that day, I sensed, in the justice's words, a resonance, only vaguely apprehended, from some awakening truth at the heart of understanding. I, whose still inchoate politics were to mature into "Kennedy liberalism" and, later, to far more radical, if nameless, form, was becoming an institutional conservative. And have so remained.

Yet it would take years of experience, roaming the highest echelons of public power, before I would fully understand the meaning and wisdom of the justice's cryptic, almost metaphorical, injunction. He was talking about his beloved Court. But behind his argument was the principle that reconciles democratic freedom with all the institutions that govern a nation. "I have never known a man of power," he once told me, speaking of Roosevelt's plan to pack the Supreme Court, "who did not resent any obstruction to its exercise." His observation was only a slightly modernized version of Jefferson's assertion that the basis of democracy was not "confidence" but "jealousy"; meaning that we could not entrust our liberties to men of power — however beneficent their intentions — that their will and ambition had to be hedged and confined by other repositories of power: institutions, laws, and, ultimately, the people themselves.

Those who drafted the charter for a new nation understood the central dilemma of democracy: No man, and no group of men, can be trusted with power. Yet no organized society can function without public authority. They tried to resolve this contradiction by writing a Constitution that fragmented public power — among the institutions of the federal government, between state and nation, between the people and those who governed them. Whether called "checks and balances" or "separation of powers" or "federalism," it reflected a wisdom derived from two millennia of Western history: that the guardians must be guarded, that the often frustrating, occasionally paralyzing, clash of will and desire between men and institutions was the necessary foundation of a lasting democracy. We could maintain our freedoms only by making sure that no one was strong enough to take them away. They would use the impulse toward self-aggrandizement, so firmly embedded in human nature, as a protection against excessive power, by contriving a structure that made every assertion of authority by one a threat to the authority of others.

In our time this conflict has been most dramatically manifested in the tendency of the presidential institutions to overflow their bounds, to pursue goals heedless of the desires and prerogatives of the Congress and, by indirection, the people who elect it. There was no discussion of constitutional limits at the meetings I attended in preparation for the Bay of Pigs. I heard no expression of deference to the clear congressional authority over questions of war and peace as Lyndon Johnson led us, secretly, deceptively, into an undeclared war in Southeast Asia. The enormous cost of these disruptive failures only confirms the Founders' apprehension, and should remind us that democracy is not an artifact but a process, not a form of power — like dictatorship or monarchy — but a continual, unresolvable struggle against the restraints that make men free.

Of all the constitutional institutions, the Supreme Court alone cannot be checked or overruled by other institutions or by popular dissent. Their decisions cannot be vetoed or overruled in an election. That is the theory. The reality is that the power of the Court itself rests on popular consent or, at least, acquiescence and would swiftly dissolve were that support withdrawn. Frankfurter often referred to the "self-inflicted wounds" of the Court — meaning decisions that so exceeded its mandate that they jeopardized the Court itself. The *Dred Scott* decision did not legitimize slavery — although it purported to do so; nor could the Nine Old Men obstruct the reforming impulses of the New Deal. By trying to exercise such power, attempting to impose, by judicial fiat, the justices' own views of important social and economic questions, the Court undermined its own authority. It transgressed the boundaries of the judicial power, and, as a result, almost ended its own.

Those boundaries are not laid down in the written Constitution but in the doctrine known as "judicial self-restraint," which must also be understood as "judicial self-preservation." It is not an easy doctrine to define. But behind it is the democratic faith that the people, acting through the institutions of representative government, must be trusted to resolve the great moral and social issues of the day. The Supreme Court can guard against excesses, protect the helpless individual, but on the large issues it must respect the process of democracy. For the reality is that even though it can pronounce on issues that divide the nation, it cannot enforce its pronouncements. Even the decision in *Brown v. Board of Education,* a necessary exercise of power by the institution that had itself validated segregation, would have been a nullity had it not touched the conscience of the country and helped stimulate long-suppressed black anger.

In the sixties, although I approved the result of the Warren Court's decisions, I found myself at odds with many liberals, being convinced that the Court was exceeding its proper bounds, that its members were seeking desired results despite precedent and constitutional tradition. "This transformation of the Court's role," I wrote in 1967, "will come back to plague us when, as they inevitably must, judicial personnel and attitudes change." They are changing. And if the Rehnquist Court takes as spacious a view of its role as did its predecessors, we may find that the net result of judicial activism has been a diminution of personal liberty, and the dissolution of established restraints on economic power.

Midway through my year at the Court I called Senator Kennedy's secretary, Evelyn Lincoln, told her of the senator's earlier invitation to "call on him," and, shortly thereafter, received an appointment to visit his Senate office located only half a block from the marble temple of the judicial branch.

With the exception of a couch or two, and some narrow passageways left free for human traffic, all the space in the small outer offices was covered by desks, each virtually concealed by a sprawl of papers, and behind which sat a human being whose ear was firmly attached to a telephone receiver. The ambience of confused, cacophonous vitality signaled a world far different from the judicial sanctum from whose ordered tranquillity I had walked. It was my first visit to a Senate office since, as a twelve-year-old boy, I had roamed the legislative corridors on occasional forays from my junior high school, surreptitiously descending to the basement monorail that connected the office buildings with the Capitol across the street. There, I and my companions would ride the train until a guard, noticing our frequent reappearances at the entrance, informed us that "this isn't an amusement park." Perhaps not. But it was the closest a boy could come to one in the District of Columbia.

The harried animation of the cubicled offices testified to the rapidly mounting intensity of Kennedy's four-year campaign for the presidency, already — by early 1959 — more than halfway to the time of decision. As a secretary closed the door to the senator's private office behind me, I was abruptly in an enclave of deceptive serenity. The tall, handsome Kennedy rose from behind his desk, shook my hand, and, smiling warmly, his eyes never leaving my face, showed me to a soft leather chair and resumed his seat. Quickly, with some trace of nervousness, I told him that I would like to be of help in the campaign, but, of course, could do nothing until my year at the Court was finished. (Lest I inadvertently breach the constitutional separation of powers.)

"I appreciate your offer," he said, his smile friendly but noncommittal. "Your boss is not one of my supporters." The remark was not a question but a statement of fact, intended, perhaps, to elicit a reaction that might tell him whether I had absorbed some of the justice's well-known hostility to his candidacy. I did not tell him of Frankfurter's remark to me that his father, Joseph P. Kennedy, was "the most wholly evil man" the justice had ever known; their early New Deal friendship having been transformed into intense animosity rooted in the older Kennedy's anti-Semitism, opposition to American involvement in the struggle against Nazi Germany, and, perhaps, to other conflicts of principle and ambition of which I knew nothing. "He said," I responded, "that no one was ever a good president who didn't really enjoy his job." "You tell him," the senator replied, his tone slightly sharper, "that I'm going to have a hell of time."

Then, softening, he asked about my work on the Court, what I had thought of Harvard Law School; the casual amiability of our conversation belied only by the probing intensity of his eyes. His curiosity — about me and the Court — was genuine, but he was also taking my measure. This intense but unthreatening concentration was, I later learned, among the most consistent traits of his character. Even in a crowded gathering, he made his companion of the moment feel as if they were joined in solitary fellowship. The curiosity was real, as was the calculation.

After ten or fifteen minutes he rose. "Let me introduce you to my staff," he said, motioning me to accompany him to the outer offices, where I met some of the men with whom I was, little more than a year later, to join in close, often uneasy, association. "Keep in touch," he admonished as he turned back to his office, and the more important business of the day.

No promises had been made, even implied. My brief interview had been only one among a multitude of encounters through which — every day of every week — Kennedy was extending his reach, preparing for the days of combat ahead. The wasted time, the meetings without consequence, were an inescapable element of an endeavor in which one did everything, talked to everybody, in hopes that something would have results. Politics, like war, is waste. I had been given no reason to think my visit might irrevocably alter my life. I had, however, been reminded that I was halfway through the year, and must act soon if I was to find an alternative to the jobs offered by major law firms, which were arriving in such abundance. At the same time, somewhere in Kennedy's office, my name was being entered in a large card file of "bright young men" who might someday, somehow, be of some use in the approaching campaign.

A few months later, during the spring of 1959, I received a letter from the placement director at Harvard Law School. The House Subcommittee on Legislative Oversight — an adjunct of the Committee on Interstate and Foreign Commerce — was looking for young lawyer-investigators, and Harvard Professor Clark Byse had suggested my name. This was the committee that had recently conducted an investigation of Sherman Adams, Eisenhower's chief of staff, its disclosures forcing the resignation of the second most powerful man in government.

Sensing an opportunity to avoid, or at least postpone, a decision to practice law, motivated also by a nascent fascination with public life and the vaguely sensed, still unformed spirit of the decade just ahead, I paid a visit to the chief counsel of the committee, Robert Lishman. "The committee has jurisdiction over all the administrative agencies," Lishman explained. "All of them?" I interrupted wonderingly. "Every one," he replied. "Of course we can't do everything at once." Even so, the choices seemed virtually limitless. The committee was empowered to investigate the entire fourth branch of government, bureaucracies established over decades to supervise almost every substantial activity of American commerce — railroads and trucks; the stock market and the banks; advertising and drugs; telephones, radio, and television. Often heedless, even defiant, of the public interest they were established to defend, all of them, with age, had moved toward partnership with the interests they regulated. What a gold mine! What fun it would be!

"I'd like to try it," I told Lishman, and he, somewhat astonished to find a former president of the *Harvard Law Review* among his applicants, offered me a job on the spot. My work was to begin immediately after the Supreme Court's summer recess terminated my one-year appointment.

3 / Investigating the Quiz Shows

My NEW OFFICE was only a two-block walk from the Supreme Court, but a continent apart in process of decision and action. Reasoned interpretation, reliance on precedent were submerged by the clash of political aims and ambitions. Law was to be forged, not by application of judicial principles, but from the shifting inclinations of the public and pressures from the powerful. The principles of judicial restraint had no place here. We could do what we wanted, within wide and poorly defined limits we were free to pursue "the right," to enforce the needs and interests of the people. Or so — at first — it seemed.

That same summer a New York grand jury, looking into possible consumer fraud, had completed a nine-month investigation of accusations that the television quiz shows — which had engaged the eagerly watchful interest of the population for several years, whose contestants had become national heroes, living exemplars of American genius — had been a fraud; that questions and answers had been given to the winners in advance. A few weeks after beginning work with the committee, I saw a report in the *New York Times* that the presiding judge had impounded the results of the grand jury sessions (known as a "presentment"). There were to be no indictments, no charges of wrongdoing, and no public disclosure of the evidence. Excited, I went to Lishman. "There must be something here," I said. "If there was nothing wrong, then why keep it secret?" "It's worth looking into," he replied. "We have jurisdiction over the FCC [Federal Communications Commission], and that's television. And we're not restricted to investigating violations of law if the public interest is involved. Why don't you go to New York and see if you can get that presentment."

Returning to my desk, I called for an appointment with the New York district attorney, Frank Hogan. The next day I was on a plane, bringing, in my person, the power of the American Congress to the labrynthine, parochial, suspect corridors of Manhattan justice. My departure went unremarked, except by my wife and the slightly inconvenienced hosts of a dinner party I was to attend. But within a few months the consequences of that trip would explode into headlines across the country, give me a succulent but also disquieting taste of public recognition, and unfold a moral tale that, to this day, engages the energies of aspiring authors.

The quiz shows were the most extraordinary phenomenon in the history of television. Neither before nor since has any contrivance of the tube so absorbed the fascinated contemplation of the public.

The first great triumph was called "The $64,000 Question," the creation of Lou Cowan, who, years earlier, had devised and produced "The Quiz Kids." Presumably he took the concept of a long-expired radio show, called "The 64 Dollar Question," and multiplied by a thousand. This simple act of arithmetic imagination was to sweep the airwaves. In the mid-1950s, sixty-four thousand dollars was a great deal of money; the reward for knowledge was not simply admiration, but wealth. Viewers were invited to watch the American dream come true before their eyes, not in the chance fortune of a lottery, but through the hitherto secluded brilliance of fellow citizens.

Each contestant on "The $64,000 Question" selected a particular area of expertise — opera or American history or boxing — and was asked a succession of increasingly difficult questions: "Who sang the lead roles in the first La Scala production of *Rigoletto*?" or "What nineteenth-century middleweight champion lost his title in the second round?" It was a kind of genius version of Trivial Pursuit. With each correct answer the stakes were doubled until a reward of sixty-four thousand dollars was offered for the final answer. And because the contest was prolonged, viewers developed a familiarity with the contestants, regarded them with friendly, almost personal, admiration. Only contestants likely to arouse empathetic fondness were selected. But this took time. Unknown individuals were not transformed into lovable and/or admirable characters overnight. It was, therefore, important that the more promising contestants reappear on the show for several weeks. That was possible only if they gave the right answers. And so, conceived in the necessities of entertainment, the cheating began.

At one point, British producers started a London counterpart of the quiz shows. After a few weeks they called New York. "How," they wanted to know, "do you find all those brilliant Americans? Our contestants keep missing questions. We can't keep them on the show." The New York producer mumbled something about "testing procedures" and swiftly terminated the call.

"The $64,000 Question" was an unprecedented smash. On Tuesday night America slowed down to watch the CBS show. It was almost impossible to find a cab in Manhattan because the drivers were at home or in a bar. Theater owners lamented the disastrous decline in Tuesday attendance. And the personalities of contestants, their prospects of victory, were the frequent topic of dinner-table conversations during the six-day interlude between performances.

Faced with the triumph of a competing network, NBC developed a show of its own. They would meet the challenge by increasing both the stakes and the difficulty of the game. On "Twenty-One," there were no categories. Questions were drawn seemingly at random from every field of human knowledge. The amount to be won was theoretically unlimited. (Although, in reality, carefully controlled. The shows had budgets.) As long as a contestant kept answering correctly, his earnings would mount.

"Twenty-One" matched its rival, becoming one of the most-watched programs on television. The big winners on "Twenty-One were transformed into instant celebrities. The titanic Charles Van Doren, young scion of a famous literary family, won $129,000 and became a national hero. He graced the cover of *Time* magazine. And after his appearance was completed, he was designated a consultant to NBC at a yearly fee of $50,000, and given his own spot on a popular morning show. Students at Columbia, where Van Doren taught English, put up signs directing visitors to "the smartest man in the world." He was our answer, a symbol of our answer, to the shocking launch of the Soviet Sputnik and its implied message that American technological and intellectual superiority had fallen into "the dust-bin of history." Although intellec-

tuals and psychologists fiercely debated whether the capacity to
recall an immense volume of unrelated information was a manifestation of real intelligence or some genetic aberration, the admiration of the public was unqualified.

While the nation was absorbed with its newly created heroes,
the sponsors and networks were getting rich. Revlon, which sponsored "The $64,000 Question," found it necessary to send out large
advance shipments of the particular product it intended to pro-
mote — lipstick or eye shadow or rouge — in anticipation of a
buying surge following each Tuesday's performance. The company itself enjoyed unprecedented growth (its sales went up from
thirty-three million to eighty-five million dollars), while sales of
Geritol — a sponsor of "Twenty-One" — soared beyond all expectations, projection, and common sense. As for the networks,
their earnings depended on ratings, and the ratings were never
better.

The networks and sponsors made many millions. The producers made a few million. The contestants made thousands. And all
was right with the world.

On arriving in New York, I was surprised that Assistant District Attorney Joe Stone seemed pleased to see me. Diligent, experienced, incorruptible, he had labored for months to construct
a case for the grand jury. And now I appeared, an eager parvenu,
barely out of law school, never having uncovered so much as a
traffic violation, ready to take over. Yet there was no sign of resentment at my unasked intrusion, no hint of that condescension
which mature experience owes to youth. Stone was that rarest of
public servants, concerned with uncovering and disclosing the truth,
wherever credit might go. Although he had found much to indicate that the quiz shows had been rigged, he was hampered by
lack of resources, limitations on his jurisdiction, the absence of
any criminal statute prohibiting television fraud, and — most in-
furiating — the decision of Judge Mitchell Schweitzer to impose a
seal of secrecy on the grand jury proceedings. Since grand jury
reports in New York had been customarily issued and made public since colonial times, Schweitzer's decision was not only unusual, but suspect. (In the early 1970s Schweitzer was forced to
resign from the bench as a result of charges of corruption against
him by the New York City Bar Association.)

Stone told me that his own progress had been blocked, but Judge

Schweitzer would almost certainly release the minutes at the request of a congressional committee. If there had been a bargain,
it could not have included resistance to the wishes of Congress.
The next morning, after Judge Schweitzer had been informed of
my request, I was taken to a New York City courtroom by one of
Stone's assistants to make the first and last trial court appearance
of my soon to be aborted legal career. I knew we would get the
record. But the formal procedure of acquisition was less familiar
to me than the mysteries of Dionysus. I didn't know what to do,
and I was not qualified to do it. I was not even a lawyer, having
just taken the still-ungraded Massachusetts bar exam. The judge
asked if there were any motions. My companion jostled me: "Now,"
he whispered. "How about you?" I said. "It's okay," he said,
"you don't have to be a member of the New York bar." It hardly
seemed the place or time to explain that I did not belong to any
bar. And so, rising, somberly clad in a dark pin-striped suit, I
intoned, with an air of feigned confidence, that "On behalf of the
Subcommittee on Legislative Oversight of the House Committee
on Interstate and Foreign Commerce, I request release to the
aforesaid committee of the grand jury records in the case of . . ."
I had not watched all those movies for nothing. The judge lowered his gavel. He would accept and consider the motion, meaning, as happened shortly thereafter, they would be released to the
committee.

Once the records were released, I returned from Washington to
retrieve them. Flying home, I looked through the voluminous pages
of testimony, pausing intermittently to sit back, staring exultantly
at the crowded drifts of dazzling clouds. With a single sentence, I
had overturned the intentions of the New York judicial system.
True, the power was borrowed, derived from my employers. But
since its exercise was mine, it also belonged to me. Or so it seemed
in that time before I had learned how easily public power could
be dissolved or turned upon the wielder. No such sensation had
accompanied my work on the Supreme Court. Law clerks may
have influenced other justices in their decisions. But not Frankfurter. His vote was wholly shaped by inner deliberations steeped
in decades of intimacy with history and constitutional law. We
might help sharpen a point or two, accumulate some additional
arguments and precedents for an opinion whose conclusion and
reasoning were his own. But this was different. I had suggested
the course, planned the action, performed it. To the legal func-

tionaries of New York, I was the Congress. It was a heady feeling, the onset of an addiction from which only years of experience, and harsh recurrent trauma, would free me. And even now, it still lingers, its resurgence a constant threat to the more quiescent labors of my present life.

I found the grand jury records crammed with contradictions. But there was enough to convince me, as it had persuaded Joe Stone, that the quiz shows had been fraudulent. The evidence did not yet meet the rigorous standards of legal proof. But I knew. Now we must make the case.

Armed with the credentials of a special investigator, I spent most of the next few months in New York — with an occasional foray to Hollywood — talking to contestants and producers, gradually moving up to advertising agencies, sponsors, and the networks themselves.

I first met Charles Van Doren at breakfast in the NBC cafeteria following his daily appearance on Dave Garroway's popular morning show. Van Doren's function was to add a few minutes of cultural seasoning to the hourlong concoction of gossip, news, and humor. He might read a brief poem, comment on some painting being exhibited at the Metropolitan Museum. Not much, just enough to add a touch of class. Absolutely calm, with friendly but never overeager amiability, he answered my questions about the quiz shows. A century of breeding had prepared him for this encounter. He could not, of course, speak for other contestants, he told me, but his own appearance had been exactly what it seemed. Gifted with an extraordinarily retentive memory, widely read, he had been able to answer questions whose content was never revealed until the show was under way. Yes, it was possible that other contestants had been given answers. How could he know? But the producers were such decent, honest men. He couldn't believe they would do something like that. "And look at the result," he said. "Not the money, although it certainly came in handy. At least I could buy my own house. But I'm the only person who reads poetry on television. I'm a teacher, you know, and now I can reach millions. All because of the quiz shows."

Sincerity, honesty, integrity — pick your term — infused his manner. Courtesy without submission, exposition without resentment. I liked the man; began to doubt my own conviction that he was lying. I had accumulated a great deal of evidence that contradicted him. Not conclusively. Not beyond doubt. But very substantial. Yet, dammit, I wanted to believe Van Doren. He was so forcefully sincere. He seemed to believe, must believe, what he was saying. And perhaps he did. The depths of the human mind have hiding places for the most contradictory recollections and beliefs; desires whose powerful surge can overpower conscious knowledge and awareness.

After the meeting I was shaken. Maybe we were wrong. Maybe those who had implicated him were mistaken, or lying for their own purposes. Then I went to interview Herbie Stempel, and under the assault of his vengeful brilliance, Charles Van Doren's life began to unravel.

Of moderate height, his features bearing a dark, Semitic stamp, illuminated by eyes of flickering intensity, ceaselessly loquacious, Herb Stempel seemed to have been designed as Van Doren's antipode. He had come from a working-class background, a family in the anonymous lower reaches of the social structure, whose otherwise unremarked history had contained some dormant code of DNA gifting Stempel with a remarkably spacious memory, which he had furnished with an extraordinary collection of information.

A chance encounter at one of the Greenwich Village cocktail parties from which the ever-alert television producers recruited so many of their contestants brought him an invitation to take the examination administered to aspiring quiz show guests. The test consisted of questions designed to uncover knowledge of miscellaneous obscurities — e.g., Name the man who led the American forces at the battle of Lexington (John Parker). Stempel's score was astonishing, the best — he proudly told me — ever attained by any quiz show contestant, including Van Doren.

The purpose of the test was not to ensure a good performance. The producers would take care of that. But exposure on national television would inevitably attract press attention to these new-made heroes of intellect. Undoubtedly, some skeptical reporter would try to test a contestant and find out if he was for real. Therefore, it was important that the subject of inquiry be credible, able to display, on demand, remarkable retentive powers. The test scores were the producers' guarantee against accidental exposure of ignorance.

The coincidence of a cocktail party discussion and his surprising test performance changed Herbie Stempel's life. He was selected to be the first big-money winner on "Twenty-One," with prize earnings of just under a hundred thousand dollars. Throughout the week preceding each show, prime-time "promos" would exhort listeners to watch the newly discovered genius, Herb Stempel, as he rose from poverty to wealth. Could he keep it up? Would he? Each week millions of viewers tuned in to watch the drama unfold. This unknown, unappreciated, unprivileged young man became an instant celebrity. He was stopped by strangers on the street, saw his name in the papers and his face on the tube. Stempel defeated all challengers until, one melancholy day, the producers told him the show needed a change. They had selected a replacement hero named Charles Van Doren. It was all over for Herb.

Week after week, Stempel watched as the victorious Van Doren transcended mere celebrity to become a national folk hero, his triumphs, as measured in dollars and publicity, far surpassing Stempel's own achievement. This man who, in Stempel's lucid, fevered imagination, had everything — privilege, breeding, aristocratic birth and manner — who seemed to possess every advantage that life had so cruelly and capriciously denied him, had now stripped Herb of his only public distinction. It was unfair. Why, he was smarter than Van Doren. Much smarter.

Unable to contain his mounting anger/envy/frustration, Stempel was determined to tell his story, to expose this overprivileged fraud even at the cost of admitting his own. Two years after his appearance, well after the shows had been dropped from the networks, Stempel — his resentments unabated — went to the newspapers. But they wouldn't touch the story, refusing to risk multimillion-dollar lawsuits based on the unsupported tale of this disgruntled, disheveled, unstable individual. Next Stempel went to the district attorney's office. As Joe Stone explained to me: "I get a dozen nuts a week with crazy stories. He had no evidence. I did not dismiss his story, but it was only after we received additional, unrelated information that we even began a grand jury investigation. And that didn't go anywhere." Stone's reaction was justified. Stempel was a "nut," so obviously in the grip of an obsession that any reasonable man would doubt him. Stone would come to believe his story, at least most of it. But it wasn't proof, just the allegations of a man who could not be expected to fare well on a witness stand. Then I came along. A congressional investigator, unfettered by rules of evidence or the necessity to meet judicial standards of proof.

I called Stempel. Did he want to see me? He could hardly wait. Here was his chance. For what? Vindication or vengeance? It hardly mattered, not to me.

At our first meeting we talked for hours, and, in the weeks to come, he would call me on the telephone, arrange meetings, turn up unexpectedly at my Washington home. Long after I had learned, and verified, everything he had to tell, he continued his pursuit, fearful that through negligence or the intervention of mysterious higher powers, his despised adversary might escape. And he was right to be apprehensive. Van Doren almost got away. I wanted him to. And his downfall, when it came, was not Stempel's doing, but the consequence of Van Doren's own self-destructive stupidity.

During a series of conversations, useful information embedded in long rambling digressions, Stempel's account gradually congealed into a narrative, paraphrased thus:

"After they picked me, the producer, Dan Enright, took me in hand. He told me that we would go over the questions and answers before each show. He would be my coach. He told me not to worry. I wasn't doing anything wrong. It was just entertainment, show business, and everyone knew that was make-believe. But don't tell anyone, or you'll get into a lot of trouble.

"They made sure I always worked with the same man. It was the same with all the other contestants. They thought if something went wrong, if someone complained or said he had been fixed, it would just be one person's word against another's. Nothing could be proved. They didn't realize, or didn't care, that as the show went on, a producer would have to fix several contestants. They thought they were protecting themselves. But even that was make-believe.

"My producer didn't just give me the answers, but told me how I should behave. If the question had four parts, for example, I was to hesitate on part three, pretend to be puzzled, ask if we could return to it after I had given the answer to the fourth part. Jack Barry [the on-air quizmaster] would agree and, after my correct response, would say, 'Now, Herbie, let's try that third one again.' I was supposed to pause, appear as if I was straining, laboring to recall, and then look up toward the camera with the right answer.

"It was all done to increase suspense. The contestants were put into an isolation booth, supposedly to prevent coaching from the producers or the audience. Sometimes they shut off the air conditioning in the booth so that I would sweat while pretending to concentrate. We all had a role to play. I was the poor boy from Brooklyn." (Stempel wasn't poor, and he was from Queens.) "I had to call him Mr. Barry. Everyone else called him Jack. I was supposed to wear the same old suit every week, and a shirt with a frayed collar. Once I wore a new suit. Producer Dan Enright got mad. 'You're not doing your homework, Herbie,' he complained.

"The contests were usually close. Each question was worth a certain number of points, and the first contestant to reach twenty-one was the winner. The prize money was scaled according to the point spread between you and your opponent. So they wanted to keep the difference small. But as long as you kept winning you stayed on the show.

"After several weeks, they told me I was going to lose. They had picked someone else to be the next big winner. I was very upset. I had done a great job. The ratings were up. Everyone was watching me. They told me not to worry; that they'd give me a job with the show. But later, when I asked for my assignment, they kept putting me off, stalling, acting as if I was pestering them. Like I was some kind of ignorant, pushy slob.

"But the worst thing was the question I was supposed to miss. It called for identifying the movie that won the Academy Award in 1955. I had seen *Marty* three times. I knew the answer. I had to pretend that I didn't know. It was humiliating.

"I can't prove that Van Doren was fixed. I didn't hear them give out the answers. That's not the way they worked. But if they told me I was going to lose, then they had to know he was going to win. And they couldn't be sure of that unless he had been coached.

"The whole show was a fraud. Remember how they made a big thing of keeping the questions in a bank vault? Every week a bank official would come on the show and hand Barry a sealed envelope to be opened in front of the audience. Of course, the producer had a copy of those questions in his desk all week. They're the ones who wrote them."

I found Stempel's reasoning inescapably persuasive. The story was coherent, the supporting detail elaborate. His willing, even eager, partly naïve disclosure of events that exposed unflattering, petty, self-seeking aspects of his own character added to the credibility of his tale. Listening to him, I knew — however abject his motives — he was telling the truth. I had only to prove it. The key to proof would be the testimony of Albert Freedman, an associate producer in the Barry-Enright organization, and Van Doren's personal coach.

When Frank Hogan announced his grand jury investigation, Freedman had met with Van Doren at Longchamps restaurant at 59th and Madison. "You have nothing to fear," he reassured the agitated Columbia instructor, "I'm not going to tell. Not even torture could make me reveal the truth."

It was one among dozens of similar conversations in which frantic producers cajoled and coerced contestants to commit perjury. Having seduced them into fraud, they now persuaded them to crime. After being indicted for perjury, Freedman fled to Mexico City. The committee had the U.S. embassy in Mexico inform Freedman that his only alternative to permanent exile was to testify before the Congress. This timid, gentle man, suddenly deluged by powers and dangers beyond his fantasies, hastened to betrayal. No one had warned him about something like this. He was in show business. It was all make-believe. The whole world was make-believe. You turned off the set, and it faded away. ("After all," another producer once told me, "didn't everybody cheat on his income tax?") But this — a grand jury, the Congress of the United States, jail — was from another planet, tangible, beyond the sorcerer's reach, unsympathetic, even hostile, to the showman's creed.

"I met with Van Doren every week," Freedman told us (as he had told the grand jury). "We went over the questions and answers for the next show, practiced his delivery. He was usually cooperative, but he had some eccentricities. Once in a while he would insist I only give him the questions. He would look up the answers himself. It worried me. Suppose he made a mistake. But he never did. After he became famous, you could see he was getting uneasy. He told me he wanted to get off the show. I kept persuading him to stay on; told him that he was doing more for education on the show than he could accomplish at any college. He was making learning respectable, more than that, something heroic. I showed him the letters we got from parents and teachers, thanking us, saying all their kids wanted to know as much as he did. But finally he insisted. Probably all the attention was scaring him. It was so much bigger than anyone had imagined. So we had him lose." (It was like finding yourself in the middle of a huge arena, Van Doren later told me. Everyone was cheering you. Your own family was right in front. There was no way to escape.)

I took the transcript of Freedman's testimony to Van Doren's Greenwich Village house. We sat in his living room, not alone this time, but in the presence of a lawyer. I read Freedman's testimony aloud. Cautioned by his attorney, Van Doren did not respond. As I began to depart, he insisted on accompanying me down the narrow staircase to the street. Shaking my hand, he said, "Someday I'll be able to tell you why they're lying to you."

Although the evidence was conclusive, I was troubled. Compelling Van Doren to testify at a congressional hearing would destroy his reputation, severely damage his life. Only a few months before when I participated in the Supreme Court's deliberations on the Uphaus and Barenblatt cases, we had struggled with these same issues. Although the Court's decision had been divided, all the justices and clerks — the horrifying excesses of McCarthyism still fresh in memory — had agreed that a legislative committee had no power to expose for the sake of exposure, destroy reputations and careers for publicity and political gain. There had to be a genuine legislative purpose. The issue that had split the Court was whether it should override the decisions of Congress and the New Hampshire legislature that such a legitimate purpose existed.

I had no such constitutional doctrine to comfort my own decision. Since most of the contestants, confronted with our accumulating evidence, had admitted complicity, we had plenty of witnesses willing to testify. Their evidence would expose the fraud and provide an ample basis for legislative and judicial action. We didn't need Van Doren. So there was no reason to call him, no necessity of legislation or complete disclosure. And he was only a quiz show contestant, whose paltry earnings were insignificant compared to the profit of networks and sponsors, who still continued their righteous, improbable denials of knowledge. Should we destroy the pilot fish, while the leviathan was left unmolested? Of course, it was not up to me. The committee, not some novice investigator, would decide. With the complete support of Chief Counsel Lishman, I presented my arguments, and, to my relief, the congressmen, acting on principle, voted to omit Van Doren from the list of witnesses.

The week before the hearings were to begin, I asked Van Doren to visit my home in Georgetown. Since our small rented house had no enclave secluded from family and houseguests, we talked while touring Georgetown in Van Doren's rented car. "The committee's not going to subpoena you," I informed him. He betrayed no sign of relief, maintaining the same sober, thoughtful expression that had enthralled a nation. "I know you're lying, Charlie," I said, "we can prove it."

"I'm sorry you feel that way, Dick," he responded.

"Never mind," I continued. "But after the hearings begin, you must make no statements. Don't say anything. Go hide in the country if you have to. Because if you defend yourself publicly, you'll force the committee to call you."

The following week the House hearing room was jammed to hear our prize witness, Herbie Stempel. In the days preceding his appearance, Stempel had called me constantly. "When are you going to call Van Doren?" he asked, "You are going to call Van Doren, aren't you?" and finally, as the import of my continual evasions aroused his direct suspicions: "You've got to call Van Doren."

A few weeks earlier I had asked Stempel: "Herbie, why do you hate Van Doren?" "I don't hate him," he objected. "Come on, Herbie," I replied, "you've been after him from the beginning."

"I did get mad about one thing," he explained. "We were on some kind of a benefit show together. You know, a quiz show rematch for charity. After the show, he was talking to some people behind stage, and I went over to shake his hand, and he completely ignored me. It was like I wasn't even there."

The story was an illuminating metaphor. Whatever Van Doren's flaws, he was not a snob. He was much too well bred to spurn a handshake. He just hadn't seen Stempel, and Stempel had interpreted that momentary inattention as confirmation of his most painful misconceptions. Even if the incident never happened at all — and perhaps it didn't — the telling reveals a most relentless motivation.

Stempel's testimony was a well-staged sensation, headlined across the country. After he described being coached, we showed tapes (kinescopes) of his appearances. At his pretended labors of concentration, the jubilant excitement of Jack Barry at each successful prodigy of recall, the committee members and the audience burst into laughter. Yesterday's high drama had been transformed into today's hilarious farce. Stempel concluded with the story of his defeat, adding, gratuitously, with carefully rehearsed assertion, that Van Doren must have been fixed; that it was a logical certainty. A week later, on October 26, *Life* magazine would write that "the nationwide hubbub about Charles Van Doren gathers force. He was discussed everywhere by millions of people. . . ."

The day after Stempel's testimony, the committee received a public telegram from Van Doren, asserting that he had never been supplied with any questions or answers during his appearances on "Twenty-One." I later learned that NBC executives had informed him that unless he made a public denial, he would have to sever all ties with the network — his consultancy and his spot on the Garroway show. He could have walked from the meeting in feigned indignation. Instead, dutiful to the end, he sent the telegram.

I was stunned. He had been warned. He knew what evidence we had. The man must want to destroy himself.

In the next few days the committee was flooded with letters and telegrams, many of them bitterly excoriating the congressmen's "persecution" of that "nice Charles Van Doren." There was no choice, no politically rational choice. I was given a subpoena and instructed to serve it on Van Doren in New York.

Troubled, ambivalent, I went to see Justice Frankfurter and recounted the circumstances. "He brought it on himself with that suicidal telegram," I explained, "but still there's something wrong; a congressional committee is going to destroy a man's life to protect itself against criticism. We don't need his evidence. If only he had kept quiet." The justice listened patiently to my confession of conscience, then replied. "This isn't the Supreme Court. It's a committee of Congress. They have a lawful right to investigate the quiz shows. Once they began, the rest was inevitable. To the public Van Doren is the quiz shows. It would be like playing *Hamlet* without Hamlet. You're not pursuing an innocent victim, but a willing participant. The fact others may have done worse doesn't make him guiltless."

Having received my reassuring absolution, subpoena in hand I flew to New York. On my arrival, I called Van Doren's lawyer. There was no need, I told him, to start some kind of public search for Van Doren (who had left the city for a country house) if he would agree to appear voluntarily before the committee and tell the truth. A few hours later the attorney called me back. Charlie would be there. For the next few days I sat in my New York hotel room, while journalists speculated on Van Doren's disappearance ("Where's Charley?" the *New York Journal American* headlined).

The night of November 1, his testimony scheduled for the following morning, knowing from his lawyer that Van Doren was finally going to tell the truth, I invited Van Doren, his wife, Gerry, his father, the Pulitzer Prize–winning poet Mark Van Doren, and Joe Stone to my home for a quiet dinner to go over the details of the next day. To the last, Mark Van Doren had refused to believe his son's fraud. Now, pale and clearly shaken, he somehow managed to summon a flow of conversational pleasantries from his reservoir of breeding and wisdom. I was glad when the evening ended.

The next day, Van Doren admitted that he had been rigged from the time of his first appearance and confessed that he had lied to the grand jury and investigators in an attempt to cover up the fraud. I listened to the statement from my seat at the counsel table just below the dais where committee members sat confronting the witness and the audience behind him. As Van Doren talked I looked down, casually thumbing through documents. The sight was too painful. His boyish face was drawn and his eyes were bloodshot. "I would give almost anything I have to reverse the course of my life in the last three years," he began.

As Van Doren continued his testimony, I saw Herbie Stempel enter the hearing room. He had flown down from New York to be present on this day of days. Unable to see Van Doren from the audience benches, he carefully, almost on hands and knees, crept up to the side of the elevated committee dais so he could watch Van Doren's face as he spoke the words that would devastate his life.

The next day Van Doren wrote me a letter.

Dear Dick:

The dinner was superb, the accommodations splendid, and the conversation even at times uncharged with passion and danger. What an extraordinary evening it was. I will of course never forget it.

Hunters used to say that the stag loved the hunter who killed it . . . thus the tears, which were tears of gratitude and affection. Something like that *does* happen, I know. And Raskolnilov felt the same. But I hope that's not all that's involved. Thus Gerry and I do extend an invitation to you to come and wish you would come. There are a number of things I'd like to talk to you about — none of them having to do with quiz shows.

I made the mistake of reading the papers. I should have taken your advice. I wish the next six months were already over.

There have been many hard things. But I am trying to tell you that we will live and thrive, I think — I mean I know we will live and I think we will thrive — and that you must never, in

any way, feel any regret for your part in this. Perhaps it is nonsense to say that, but I thought it might be just possible that you
would.

Charlie

And I always have. A little. Although it was the right thing
to do.

The other big-money quiz shows were not as meticulously
scripted, but none was honest, just slightly more indirect. Producers of "The $64,000 Question," for example, would spend hours
with prospective contestants probing their particular area of expertise — music or sports or American history. From these sessions they were able to frame questions they were certain the contestant could answer. If they were subtle enough, and the contestant
sufficiently naïve, it was possible that an individual might win
without even knowing the show had been fixed. But this was rare.
Most understood and tacitly accepted the fraud, more easily because, after all, they did know the answers. Such refined indirection, it was thought, made exposure less likely. It also resulted in
an occasional mishap.

After flying Randolph Churchill to New York, the slightly over-
awed producers of "The $64,000 Question" took him to dinner
before the show. His category was to be the English language —
an infallibly intriguing juxtaposition of man and matter. For his
first appearance, they had prepared one simple question, something he was sure to know. There would be plenty of time for a
detailed exploration of his knowledge in the weeks to come as he
marched through successively more difficult questions toward the
planned sixty-four-thousand-dollar triumph. After all, one didn't
fix an unsuspecting English aristocrat the minute he got off the
plane. Unfortunately, the genial Churchill, as was his custom,
downed three or four martinis before going to the studio, and stood
wordlessly, swaying slightly before the camera, as he was asked
the origin of the word "boycott" (from the despised Irish land-
lord, Captain Boycott). The expectant silence continued, all eyes
fixed on the silently smiling Churchill, until the master of ceremonies, his disappointment obvious, was forced to give the answer. The next day Churchill's return ticket to London — first
class — was waiting at his hotel desk.

A young, impoverished, poorly briefed Greenwich Village poet
realized, in the middle of his appearance, that he was being asked

the identical questions put to him during an earlier private session with a producer. On air, watched by millions of people, he felt compelled to answer, but immediately afterward he accused the production team of fraud and angrily refused to return for his next appearance. He wanted no part of their phony quiz show. The producers were stunned. And they had a right to be. For in my entire investigation, I found no other individual who refused to participate. A man of principle, or a fool, he alone sailed against the wind. I don't even remember his name, but I owe him a debt of gratitude, living proof that at least one man could cling to moral principle amid the wonderland of fantasy and greed.

On "The $64,000 Question," as on the others, the criteria of showmanship and popular appeal governed the choice of contestants. An obscure cobbler was showcased as America's leading authority on opera. But since he had an Italian name, nearly all the questions were confined to Italian opera. A jockey shined as an expert on art. When the psychologist Joyce Brothers came for an interview, she requested, naturally enough, that her category be psychology. It wouldn't do. "A psychologist on psychology? Too boring. Obvious." However, she was an attractive lady with a sympathetic personality and an almost photographic memory. "Why not try something else," they suggested, "like boxing?" A young woman professional on boxing would be a natural. Taking the producers' casual suggestion seriously, Brothers began a systematic study of *Nat Fleisher's Ring Book*. (Fleisher was a friend of her father's.) Not long afterward, Joyce Brothers astonished the nation with her command of boxing history and statistics — all contained in Fleisher's encyclopedic work — won sixty-four thousand dollars and a position of national prominence, which was to yield her a public career as soothsayer to the troubled multitudes which she still enjoys.

Sitting at her small kitchen table, I interviewed Ms Brothers in the presence of her friendly, protective husband. As I inquired into the details of her performance, she began to cry, envisioning public humiliation, the crumbling of reputation and career. How could this happen? She had done nothing wrong. She had memorized the book, absorbed the complete and definitive record of boxing lore. She had never been given any questions in advance, had answered from her own, newly acquired knowledge. I believed her. We never had any contradicting evidence. She was never called to testify.

However, the testimony of those who had produced the show was essential to our case. And they had to talk. The accumulating admissions of contestants meant that denial by the producers would, almost certainly, precipitate indictments for perjury. Bewildered by their unexpected predicament, never understanding why others might question the morality of their act, oblivious to the fact that the public — which they had so handsomely entertained — might feel itself the offended, even indignant, victim of fraud, they reluctantly revealed the details of their spectacular contrivances. However, even in their hour of distress, their shows canceled, their future careers bleak, the producers refused to implicate the networks or sponsoring corporations in their fraud. "Look, Dick," one of them explained to me, "if I even hinted that the networks knew — and they didn't know — I'd be all through. They'd never let me through the door again."

"But you're already through," I objected in my naïveté, "they'll never take you back. They can't afford to. Why should you take the whole guilt on yourself, when they're the ones who made the big money."

"Maybe you're right," he replied, "but maybe not. Public memories are short, but corporations never forget, or forgive. Hell, television is my whole life; if there's any chance of getting back, I don't want to throw it away now." He paused for a long moment, avoided my gaze. "Anyway, they didn't know a thing. Understand, we did it on our own."

"You're making a big mistake," I responded futilely.

But the mistake was mine. After a suitable period of exile, many of the producers did return and prospered, their renaissance perhaps not wholly unrelated to their loyal insistence on the innocence of the powerful

Initially, the networks and sponsors ignored the committee investigation. Then the hearings began, and exposure of the quiz show fraud took on monstrous proportions. One national publication asserted that "not since the Black Sox scandal had there been such a betrayal of public trust." Another solemnly editorialized about "public concern over a deepening mess that had exposed a nation's sagging moral standards." The unanticipated storm changed everything.

The networks, with considerable justice, had no fear of politicians, but the awakened disapproval of the great American public stripped strong men of their sleep, made corporate corridors shake, the skyscrapers themselves to tremble. The executives of Revlon and Geritol, of NBC and CBS hastened to condemnation of those who, they asserted, had deceived them as well as the public. They had bought the shows and left their conduct to the producers. They were merely interested spectators, like everyone else in the television audience, with the single, irrelevant exception that they had many millions of dollars at stake.

One by one, voluntarily, with seeming eagerness, the television and corporate executives came to testify before the committee. Frank Stanton, president of NBC, testified that they had no knowledge of the fix, but stalwartly and without evasion admitted that in principle networks should have a moral responsibility for their shows. (Although, as it happened, in this particular case, they had none.) Charles Revson, the meticulously attired tryant of a flourishing cosmetic empire, admitted that since the quiz programs had such an enormous impact on his sales, his company had made occasional suggestions, but he "never, never imagined that the producers would tamper with the honesty of the shows."

With the big executives present, the atmosphere in the committee room changed. Not for them the finger-wagging, inquisitorial manner reserved for contestants, producers, and other culprits whose notoriety exceeded their power and wealth. They were greeted with deference, made their statements, answered a few mild questions. Their records and memos were not subpoenaed, nor were we instructed to investigate the precise extent of their involvement more rigorously. Some stones were better left unturned.

Frantically concerned to protect themselves from the gathering storm, to dispel mounting public distrust, the networks fired anyone — innocent or guilty — whose name was publicly associated with the quiz shows. (On learning their intent to discharge the head of CBS television, Lou Cowan, who was lying in a hospital bed with a life-threatening embolism, I informed the CBS president that we had no evidence of his involvement. It made no difference. He had originated "The $64,000 Question," was associated with the show — not in reality, but in the "public mind." And so he had to go.)

It was my amazed first glimpse of the cowardice at the core of this electronic prodigy endowed with the capacity to influence an entire nation. After our hearings had ended, the country's most distinguished television critic, John Crosby, wrote that "the moral squalor of the quiz show mess reaches through the whole industry.

Nothing is what it seems in television . . . the feeling of high purpose, of manifest destiny that lit the industry when it was young . . . is long gone."

And what of the ranking corporate executives? Did they know? I believed then, as I believe now, that they knew; must have known — from Stanton and Kintner and Revson down. Perhaps not everything, probably not the details, but enough to arouse the suspicions of any man who had the slightest interest in uncovering the truth. The world of television is small, filled with gossip, rumors, secret communications, and hidden plots — for power, for attention, for money. And these shows were not insignificant morning commentaries or late-night documentaries. They were the centerpiece, the stellar performers, hugely profitable, discussed in the press, watched by unprecedented multitudes. If they went unscrutinized, if the corridor gossip, the rumors, the occasional revelatory mishaps and accusations went unheeded, then who was guarding the store? Did Nixon know about Watergate? Reagan about Contragate? Denial strains credibility. But deny it they did. And no man — witness or congressman — dared contradict. They continued, untarnished, their long and prosperous careers.

The quiz show investigation provoked a reaction far beyond any expectation of committee or staff or the television industry itself. "Even if the hoax they perpetrated breached no law," the *Washington Post* editorialized, "it nevertheless robbed people of a kind of faith which it is dangerous to destroy in a democracy." "It is a melancholy business," Ralph McGill editorialized in the *Evening Star,* "and it is the more so because it is a reflection on all of us and on our national character. The quizzes revealed our deep psychological lust for material 'things,' and greatly stirred the wish, if not for easy money, then for an isolated booth in which to find it. I keep remembering a conversation with Carl Sandburg," McGill wrote. " 'Time,' he said, 'is the coin of your life. It is the only coin you have and only you can determine how it will be spent. Be careful lest you let other people spend it for you.' Those who faked the quiz shows spent a lot of it for a great many million Americans."

To a nation since grown accustomed to public deception it may be difficult to understand the public outrage provoked by the television quiz show scandals. But we were more innocent then. The deception violated our misplaced trust in the guardians of the swelling electronic media, and mocked our libidinous urge to believe in their newly revealed breed of intellectual heroes. We had been mind-fucked on an enormous scale. And we didn't like it.

Some writers later reflected that the quiz show scandals marked the beginning of our loss of innocence. But it was not so. The intensity of indignation, the extent of public outrage, was testimony to an American innocence of belief strong enough to survive this and graver challenges to come; an innocence that was to quicken the public movements and private rebellions of the sixties until it dissolved in the futilities of Vietnam. For innocence is a strength. It supports the animating will to believe which nourishes protest against deception and injustice, gives courage to the oppressed and discontented. The hopeless do not revolt. The cynical do not march. Only when what we call "innocence" is also a reality — success a seeming possibility — are we strong or courageous enough to assault the ramparts of established order.

We were nearing such a time. The assault on television deception was only a trivial, early fissure in the foundation of complacency and apathy which seemed to have hardened its hold on American life. Even as Van Doren testified, far to the south small groups of black college students were meeting secretly to voice indignation at their exclusion from "white only" lunch counters in drugstores and five-and-tens. While on the other side of the capital a young Massachusetts senator was sketching out a theme for a presidential candidacy based on an intuitive belief that his fellow citizens were dissatisfied, that they expected more from their society and themselves, that they wanted to "Get America Moving Again." Although we didn't know it in that fall of 1959, "the sixties" were already stirring. And I was going to be part of it. The quiz show investigation, so heady and dazzling an experience for a young man who had never before even read his name in a major newspaper, was only an overture.

Midway through the investigation, I received a call from Ted Sorensen, Senator Kennedy's principal assistant. "How would you like to try your hand at writing a speech?" he asked. "I would," I replied instantly, even though I had never drafted a speech for anyone. He explained that Kennedy's speeches had three severable sections. The first part was a tribute to the Democratic party, an exposition of its majestic principles. The second was a "substantive" section, which discussed some issue of the day — farm policy, arms control, Medicare, and so on. And the third section

was an invocation of American greatness, the dazzling prospects
of our nation, its responsibility to sustain the torch of freedom.
The three parts were interchangeable, different beginning and
ending sections would be attached to a particular substantive discussion, making it possible for the senator to give different speeches
on the same subject (or discuss different subjects in the same
speech).

Sorensen suggested a topic and I worked on a draft during a
lengthy, pre-jet flight to California for an interview with Leonard
Bernstein's sister, a former associate producer of a major quiz show.
I had, unaware, been entered in an undisclosed essay contest. The
mounting demand of Kennedy's still-unannounced candidacy for
"issue" material — speeches, articles, pamphlets — had become
too burdensome for even the astonishingly productive and hardworking Sorensen. The systematically assembled card file of prospects had been culled for potential assistants. I was one, among
many, who were being tested; the purpose, even the existence, of
competition undisclosed. Soon after submitting my first draft I
was asked to try another, then one more, and — the quiz show
investigation still under way — I was invited to join the staff in
Kennedy's Washington office. My job, I was told, would be working with Ted Sorensen on "issues," meaning Kennedy's presidential campaign, which, unofficially pursued for three years, was soon
to be formally proclaimed. "Will you accept?" Sorensen asked.

Would I? Of course. Who wouldn't? Wow!

I was to begin working for Kennedy as soon as the quiz show
investigation was completed. But my political career almost ended
before it had begun. *Life* magazine asked me to write an article
describing the conduct of the quiz shows. It appeared on November 16, 1959, under the headline "Committee Investigator Reveals
How Fixers Seduced Innocents." A few days later I awoke to read
a *Washington Post* editorial condemning me for profiting from public service.

I was devastated. It was my first taste of public criticism. Although only a gentle hint of what future years would bring, it then
seemed the end of the world. Painful shock yielded to almost disabling depression. I did not go to work that day; could not. Late
in the morning, I received a call from the intuitively prescient
Frankfurter. "Some pains," the justice reassured me, "are like
stomach infections, which stay for months. Others are like tooth-
aches, which you can't even remember after you leave the dentist.
This kind of thing is like the toothache." He was right. Although

his wisdom did not dispel my fierce morning ache, it did help dispel my senseless fear that the whole world would now turn against me.

It seemed so unfair, I thought. The article had been approved in advance by Robert Lishman, my immediate superior, and by Oren Harris, chairman of the committee. It contained no insider information, nothing unavailable to a diligent student of the public record. Other committee investigators had written of their exploits without public censure. Yet these exculpating facts were irrelevant. Some anonymous hand had reached out and, moved by a sudden attack of moral indignation, a dinner party comment, a difficulty in meeting his daily quota of comment, or even indigestion, had struck a casual, indifferent, but very painful blow.

After my initial shock at the *Post* editorial had dissipated, I remained apprehensive that my involvement in this mini-controversy might jeopardize my job with Kennedy. It was never mentioned. My desk was waiting for me. Yet my *Life* magazine adventure had not gone unnoticed. Years later, Robert Kennedy told me: "I was a little worried about hiring you. I thought you might write about us. And you're the only one who never did."

True enough, Bobby. I never did. Not until now.

Once reassured that my job was secure, I walked from the House Office Building, across First Street, into the familiar pillared sanctuary of the Supreme Court. Since the Court was in session, I took a seat in the courtroom section reserved for law clerks and, by custom, available to former clerks. I asked a court messenger to deliver a note to Frankfurter at the bench. "Mr. Justice, I am going to start working for Senator Kennedy next week." The justice took the note, looked toward me, scribbled something on a notepad, and summoned a messenger, who made his way past the droning lawyers, whose tedious formality seemed suddenly to have grown so distant from my own tumultuous, thrill-promising prospects, and handed me the paper. "I wish you a great deal of success and happiness in your own career," he had written, "but not in the main thing," meaning, of course, Kennedy's run for the presidency.

No half-truths or politic omission for the justice. Consistent to the last, his note was a token of my now-completed transition from one world to another; from the quiet, protected arena of reflection to the thronged, turbulent arena of action. I was a politician now, and my purpose was victory.

PART II / THE KENNEDY YEARS

Shall hearts that beat no base retreat
   In youth's magnanimous years —
Ignoble hold it, if discreet
   When interest tames to fears;
Shall spirits that worship light
   Perfidious deem its sacred glow,
   Recant, and trudge where worldlings go,
Conform and own them right?

                — Herman Melville

4 / The Nomination

ONE EVENING near the end of the thronged, ceaseless journey toward election day, as we sat on the *Caroline* — the small twin-engine propeller-driven plane that carried the candidate and his staff — Ted Sorensen, who had spent years of unremitting labor helping chart the Kennedy course, turned and said to me, "Your timing was awfully lucky. You missed all those years of work, and got on board just in time for the victory."

He was right, although I hadn't planned it that way. For three years Kennedy and his staff had been traveling to endless meals of cooling meat and overdone potatoes, while I had been absorbed by law school exams, Justice Frankfurter's demands, and the quiz show investigation. Nor were the rewards yet certain. I was personally sure that Kennedy would win, but my excessive confidence rested more on faith than knowledge of politics. In fact, we would tremble at the edge of defeat until the very end, and, had we lost, I would have been just another young ex–campaign assistant looking for a job. Still, I was very lucky, at least as judged by the parameters of Sorensen's own spacious aspirations. I had been selected to accompany the Democratic candidate in a presidential campaign. Should he be elected, I was virtually certain of a position with responsibilities larger than those ordinarily entrusted to a youth just two years out of school.

As Sorensen reminded me of my good fortune, the *Caroline* suddenly began to shudder, striking turbulent air as it descended toward its landing somewhere over the Great Plains. Although I was vulnerable to fear of flying, there was no rush of anxiety as I leaned over to pick up a few papers scattered by our drop through an air pocket. Imprisoned in this tiny capsule of hollowed metal piercing the storm thousands of feet above the desolate, corrugated earth, I felt as secure as though I were in my Georgetown living room. Kennedy was on board. And we all knew that nothing could happen to him. He was destiny's child, our talisman against outrageous fate. Throughout the plane the normal sounds of conversation, immune to the dangerous sweep of air, demonstrated that my companions shared my belief — this blind, irrational faith that, for a while, we were protected by the candidate's immortality.

I still have Kennedy's reading copy of a speech from that trip. The text, after reciting a litany of national goals, pronounces that "all this will not be accomplished in the first 100 days," a reference to the opening months of the New Deal. On that page the candidate has carefully crossed out the number 100, and changed the phrase to "1000 days." Merely a rhetorical flourish and, perhaps, a more calculated effort to avoid too clear an identification with Roosevelt's revolutionary program. Nevertheless, with a single cramped movement of the pen, the mere addition of a cipher, Kennedy had drawn the boundary of his presidency and of his life. Thus the gods cryptically mocked the arrogant faith that provided such false sustaining comfort.

It was not a traditional first day on the job when in the fall of 1959 I entered Kennedy's Senate office to begin my labors. There would be no period of orientation, no introductory lectures, but only the briefest of greetings — little more than acknowledgment of my existence — before Ted Sorensen handed me a folder crammed with memos, saying, "The senator is doing a two-thousand-word article on arms control, this is some background stuff on our position, we need it by tomorrow," showed me to a desk, and disappeared behind a partition. Of course I didn't know anything about arms control. But that didn't seem to matter. The folder contained information from publications and academic advisers, along with previous Kennedy speeches. My job was not to make policy, not to create, but to translate the ponderous mélange of fact and opinion into a brief, readable piece suitable for a moderately ignorant public.

In the early evening, Sorensen, having completed whatever urgent task had absorbed him through the daylight hours, came over to my desk, read through the four or five pages I had completed. "Not bad," he said and then, assuming the mantle of editorial revision, showed me where cuts could be made, complicated structure shortened, and, most important, where I might have deviated from the senator's established position.

It was, at first, through Sorensen that I came to know the "Kennedy style" — the ordered structure of his analysis, the somewhat ordered cadences of his formal speeches, the general themes ("A great country that can be greater," "Democrats lead while Republicans preside," "The country's sinking but it'll swim again") — which would frame the discussion of specific issues. Later, I would form a more directly personal view of Kennedy's thought and manner of speech. But now, at the beginning, Sorensen was indispensable. He had worked closely with Kennedy for years, knew Kennedy's ambitions and mind as well as any man. (No one ever really knew John Kennedy.)

Later I would have my differences with Ted Sorensen, but those old resentments have long since faded, leaving me with the memory of the exciting dawn days of my career when he was both model and mentor to the young apprentice politician. He was described by Teddy White as "self-sufficient, taut, purposeful, a man of brilliant intellectual gifts, jealously devoted to the President and rather indifferent to personal relations." All true. But we were not a fraternal organization, or a group of college chums. Our relationship was shaped by the common commitment of our energies to a single goal, a bond that — until the goal was achieved — would be far stronger than mere friendship, if, ultimately, far more fragile.

I learned a lot from Ted about the craft of politics and political speechwriting. And he always appeared grateful at having found someone to share the burdens of his work, even if he seemed to look upon me less as a discovery than a creation. "I was talking to Steve Smith [Kennedy's brother-in-law] the other day," Sorensen said to me during my second month at work, "and I told him how remarkably you had managed to master our way of doing things. He said it was probably because you were working with me on a daily basis. That any bright young man who got the same kind of direct, personal instruction would have done the same thing." He related the anecdote without a smile, looked toward me as if expecting some expression of gratitude for what, to me, hardly seemed a compliment.

Through the fall and winter of 1959 and early 1960, as I toiled to help meet the boundless flow of requests for speeches, articles, and brochures, I discovered that the demands of politics were insatiable; that the notorious saying "when the going gets tough, the tough get going" was misleading bravado. Either the going was always tough — which is partly true — or you kept going whatever the conditions — which is also true. Arriving at Kennedy's office in the Senate Office Building, I and my handful of colleagues worked well into the night, our labors arrested only by a rational calculation of the need for sleep. While, in another building, the larger campaign structure was being constructed under the leadership of Robert Kennedy.

Late at night, leaving the office, we would stand for a moment, clearing our lungs of the stale office air, staring at the unlit office buildings, and, across the street, at the somnolent Capitol. The darkened windows, blending into the night-gray of the gargantuan stone structures, testified to the absence of the other guardians and leaders of the nation's well-being. All but one. No matter how late we left the office, from across the street the night was pierced by a single lighted window from the office of the Senate majority leader. No one could outlast Lyndon.

My understanding of the campaign — of presidential politics in general — evolved gradually, through conversations, observations, experiences. Years later Justice Frankfurter told President Johnson in my presence, "That boy has politics in his blood." I did not know whether the remark was intended as a compliment or a prescription for emergency dialysis. In any event, even if I had a natural talent for politics, understanding of the process, knowledge of "how it works," comes only through experience, and I had entered that most exclusive and intense classroom of all — a presidential campaign.

"I don't mind sticking it to old Ike," said the senator as we sat on a bench in the deserted Butler Aviation terminal at Washington's National Airport. It was a cold January day in 1960, and Ted Sorensen and I had come to meet him on his return from still another trip to the heartland, bringing with us a draft of the speech that was to be the informal inauguration of Kennedy's presidential campaign. He had made the formal announcement of his candidacy twelve days earlier, to a crowd of reporters, family members, and staff gathered in the Senate Caucus Room. I was only in my third month with the senator's staff, and this was my first participation in a major campaign event.

Scheduled for delivery at the National Press Club, the speech was intended to describe Kennedy's view of the presidential office, a foundation for the message he would carry into the primary elections. Weeks of preparation, memos from presidential scholars, Kennedy's own statements and private reflections had been distilled into a dozen pages, which asserted, in a litany of forceful clichés, that the role of the president was to lead, morally and in action, to take initiatives and not just react to crisis, to revive a flagging America and draw the nation to new heights of grandeur. Wreathed with quotations from legendary heroes and scholars of repute, the address was not an exercise in political science. It was intended as contrast and rebuke to the Eisenhower presidency — then perceived as a time of listless drift, presided over by a man unwilling to intervene against a gradual deterioration of American strength and spirit.

I had participated in shaping this draft with considerable enthusiasm, sharing, as I then did, the fashionable liberal contempt for this "do-nothing" man, with his confused syntax, who had somehow mesmerized huge numbers of people into thinking him half great. Gallup polls showed him to be the most popular incumbent since Roosevelt. In late 1959, during a presidential trip to a dozen nations, huge crowds stood in the drenching Italian rain and under the blazing sun of India to hail a triumphant Eisenhower. I and my colleagues tried to find reasons for this "unjustified" popularity, and, naturally, we found them: "He was the conquering hero of World War II"; "He was a benign, unthreatening person," a kind of "father figure to the world." Only much later, after years of turbulence and rivers of blood, did I come to understand how much I had underestimated Eisenhower.

It was true that his failure to deal with emerging domestic problems, particularly his reluctance to intervene in the growing racial crisis, had deepened the difficulties that his successors would have to confront. But it was also true that he brought the Korean conflict to a swift conclusion, and throughout his term he sent no Americans into combat. He was the first president since Hoover of whom this could be said, and he was to be the last for a long time. This was not merely good fortune. In Hungary and Cuba, Indochina and the straits of Formosa, Eisenhower resisted pressures for forceful intervention to which other presidents might have yielded. He kept the military under firm civilian control for the last time, warned of the alliance between big business and big defense that threatened the health of our economy, and strove, desperately but futilely, to bring an end to the Cold War. George Kistiakowsky, Eisenhower's science adviser, once told me that after the collapse of his scheduled summit meeting with Khrushchev, Eisenhower, in tones of melancholy reflection, had told him: "My entire administration has been a failure. The one thing I wanted, thought I could achieve, to move from the arms race toward peace, is a shambles. The whole thing is a wreck." Clearly the masses of India and Brazil, Italy and the United States understood something that those of us who were closer and more sophisticated failed to grasp. Eisenhower was a man of peace. He was infused by an essential goodwill toward his companions of the earth. They knew it. And they loved him for it. There were worse things than inaction. Much worse.

But this wisdom, so bitterly acquired, lay far in the future on this cool night as I watched the weary young senator scrutinize the pages that would form the foundation of his approaching campaign. Despite evident fatigue and the grotesque hour, no phrase was carelessly skimmed, no idea allowed to pass without reflection and judgment. I was struck by his attention to the smallest details of expression, a characteristic he was to manifest throughout the campaign. I was not then aware of how few politicians so meticulously guard themselves against the errors of subordinates.

Even though I and, I assume, Sorensen, firmly believed that Eisenhower deserved the most severe censure for the inadequacies of his leadership, his personal popularity was also a fact. The polemic we might have written, the one that conveyed our true opinion, had been tailored to the political realities of the day. The speech did not mention Eisenhower by name. One could not attack "old Ike." Not personally. But the implications of Kennedy's address were clear. His call for new leadership to lift America from its corrosive complacency was an implicit but harsh accusation of Eisenhower failures.

Sorensen and I, our manuscript in hand, felt compelled to warn the weary candidate that the speech would be so interpreted. He did not even look up from the draft. Our admonitions were superfluous. The man could read. The man was smart. And his laconic rejoinder, the reflection of a course already set.

What choice did he have? A Democratic candidate had to run

against the Republican record. His opponent would be Richard Nixon, whose greatest strength would be the popularity of his predecessor. Although Eisenhower was contemptuous of Nixon, whose own animosity toward the president who never wanted him was widely known, the two men were joined by the most powerful of political ties: self-interest. For Eisenhower, the election of a Republican successor would be a vindication of his leadership; and Nixon, like some infertile bride, had to rely on Eisenhower's teeming allurements to nurture his own fortunes into flower. (This was a reality that Nixon — in a now-familiar habit of self-delusion — would deny, until in the last desperate days of the campaign, he would, at the price of some inward humiliation, ask Ike to campaign for him. Until then he had been determined to make it on his own, while the proud Eisenhower sat in the Oval Office waiting for the request that came only after it was too late. The enormous response to Eisenhower's last-minute emergence — ticker-tape parades, cheering crowds — made it clear that an earlier intervention would have put Nixon in the White House.)

For the next year, in hundreds of speeches, in continual assaults on the Republican party, on the Republican record, and on the Republican candidate, the name of Eisenhower was omitted. We even managed to find a way to accuse Nixon of having personally "lost Cuba" to Castro. On an earlier trip to that now-hostile island, the vice-president had praised the doomed Batista. That misguided support of a repressive dictatorship had fed the fires of anti-American revolution. Or so we said. Much later in the campaign, sitting in a hotel room during a trip to the barrens of Ohio, I handed Kennedy the draft of a detailed "documented" assault on the Republican loss of Cuba, the negligent establishment of a "communist base only ninety miles from our shores." Kennedy read the speech in silence, looked up, and remarked, musingly, "Of course, we don't say how we would have saved Cuba." Then, handing the speech back, unamended: "What the hell, they never told us how they would have saved China."

With his speech on the presidency Kennedy had staked out his claim, presented the terms of the message on which his candidacy was based, and which he must now carry to the handful of primary voters whose judgment — on the man and what he stood for — would be decisive.

The first of the contested primaries was to take place on April 5 in Wisconsin. (Kennedy was an unopposed "favorite son" in

New Hampshire.) In late March, sitting at a counter in some small Wisconsin diner, cradling an early-morning cup of coffee in his cold-numbed hands, Kennedy turned and gestured to workers approaching the factory gate where he would soon take his stand. "You think I'm out here to get votes," he said to his companion. "Well, I am. But not just their votes. I'm trying to get the votes of a lot of people who are sitting right now in warm, comfortable homes all over the country, having a big breakfast of bacon and eggs, hoping that young Jack will fall right on his face in the snow. Bastards." Then, reluctantly getting off the stool: "What the hell. They'll take me if they have to. Let's get started."

The preceding fall, just before joining the Kennedy staff, I had attended Justice Frankfurter's annual sherry party for his law clerks, past and present. In his customary dialectic fashion, the justice asked each of the more than twenty men who he thought would win the Democratic nomination. Adlai Stevenson and Lyndon Johnson were the clear preferences. I was the only member of this august company to select Kennedy, and my opinion was already hopelessly compromised by inexperience, desire, and ambition. But I was not merely getting myself "on the record." I believed it. To me, Kennedy represented a new generation of believers. The others were politicians rooted in the past, out of touch with the reawakened aspirations of the nation. How could he be denied?

Quite easily, as it turned out. A single significant failure for Kennedy, an act of political daring by one of his opponents, would probably have been enough to keep him from the nomination.

"Let's get this over quick," Kennedy said just before the long campaign for the nomination was about to begin, "before they all find out how little they want me."

Kennedy was right. They didn't want him. "They" being the political leaders who would control most of the delegates to the national convention. The Democratic party as such did not exist. (Nor does it now.) It was simply a convenient label for a collection of state parties, which would assemble every four years to nominate a presidential candidate. There was the Unruh party in California, the Lawrence party in Pennsylvania, the Daley party in Illinois, the Johnson party in Texas, the Kennedy party in Massachusetts. And for those states not blessed with a single dominating leader, the party was guided by a handful of local leaders able to influence some significant portion of the state delegation.

The foundations of this traditional structure were already beginning to weaken. But in 1960, it constituted, for purposes of the nomination, the Democratic party, although the Kennedy campaign would prove, over time, to have accelerated a process of terminal decay.

Now, of course, the old bosses are gone. Lest we be too quick to exult in their demise, remember that this departed system nominated Roosevelt, Truman, Stevenson, John Kennedy. Not such a bad record compared to the current process whose selection is dictated by primaries, television, and, above all, by organization and money.

In the late winter of 1959, as the first presidential primaries approached, Kennedy had already spent four years traveling the country, campaigning for local candidates, attending party functions — piling up obligations, creating loyalties, charming and impressing the locals. But the most important leaders, those with power to decide the convention, still stood aside — waiting, calculating. Although most of them were New Deal liberals — and Kennedy was suspect to the party's liberal wing — their hesitation was not predominantly ideological. They wanted a winner. And John Kennedy was too young, too inexperienced, and, above all, too Catholic. "Look at Dave Lawrence" (governor and boss of Pennsylvania), Kenny O'Donnell, Kennedy's most trusted adviser, explained to me; "he loves Adlai, but Adlai's not running. At least that's what he says. He's a Catholic himself, and he's thinking of the next election. He doesn't want Jack running all over the country stirring up the Catholic issue. It can only hurt him. And he doesn't think Jack can make it anyway."

Most of these leaders liked Jack Kennedy. Several of them, especially Mayor Daley of Illinois, owed something to the senator's father, Joe Kennedy, obligations incurred during their own rise to power. But politics was their business. And business was business. They would go along — willingly or with reluctance — only if Kennedy could make their choice appear reasonable or, even better, inescapable.

Early in the primary season, I expressed some doubts about a particularly vicious attack on Kennedy's opponent, Hubert Humphrey. Hubert had a strong following in the liberal wing of the party, I objected, and if we got too mean then, it might hurt us in the election. "Fuck the election," Larry O'Brien — calm, sagacious, long-time political counselor — instructed me. "There won't be any election, not for us, if we don't get nominated. That's all we can think about. If we make it, then we can worry about Hubert." Political lesson No. X: "Keep your eye on the ball. Don't risk the present for the sake of the future. Save statesmanship for the White House."

There was no master plan, no grand strategy such as — it is reputed — Hamilton Jordan prepared for the aspiring Jimmy Carter. In 1956, Robert Kennedy had accompanied Adlai Stevenson's campaign to, in his father's words, "See how it was done." And also, we might add, to see how it shouldn't be done. "No wonder people thought Adlai was speaking over their heads," said John Kennedy in the middle of his own campaign. "That's just what he was doing." Kennedy himself had spent four years campaigning within the party. He knew the players, those who counted and those who blustered; understood the levels of power, who controlled them, what could move them, how they might be influenced to his support even against their internal inclinations.

And he knew that the trail to the prize lay inexorably through the thicket of the presidential primaries — in New Hampshire, Wisconsin, West Virginia, Indiana, Nebraska, Massachusetts, Maryland, and Oregon. So, with the exception of Ohio and California, he threw his hat into every single binding presidential primary where no legitimate favorite son was running.

Meanwhile, three of the leading contenders — Stuart Symington, Lyndon Johnson, and above all, Adlai Stevenson — waited for the prize to come to them. In physical appearance, Missouri Senator Stu Symington probably came closest to everybody's idea of what a president ought to be. At fifty-eight, he was strikingly handsome, a large, athletic man with piercing blue eyes, an easy smile, and a ruddy, healthy complexion. He was favored by a poll of House Democrats, by a large number of labor leaders, and by many of the best-known professional politicians. And his biggest supporter was former President Harry Truman. But Truman, who viewed primaries as civil wars that tore the party organization apart, was one of the voices who persuaded Symington to eschew the primary route in favor of positioning himself as the perfect compromise candidate at a convention they all assumed would be deadlocked.

Meanwhile, in Washington, Lyndon Johnson, like Symington, assumed that the primaries would produce no clear-cut victor and that the Senate majority leader would then be able to cash in on the enormous accumulation of political debts his Washington leadership had earned him. He believed mistakenly that the leaders of the Senate would also command the state delegations. Favored by a poll of Senate Democrats, by most southern leaders, and by many professionals, Johnson sat back and waited.

Meanwhile, in Springfield, Illinois, Adlai Stevenson also waited. "Deep down he wants it," a close friend said in the winter of 1959–60. "But he wants the convention to come to him, he doesn't want to go to the convention." Having endured a brutal string of primaries in 1956, he had no desire to go through it again and didn't feel that he had to. If the people didn't know who he was and what he stood for after two presidential races, then they would never know.

With Symington, Johnson, and Stevenson waiting in the wings, only one Democrat followed Kennedy's lead into the primaries. Thank God — or fate — for Hubert Humphrey! The impassioned, intelligent senator from Minnesota, a leader of the party's liberal wing, supported by followers of unmatched intensity, was also compelled to enter the primaries in pursuit of his presidential ambitions. He did not have the same problems as Kennedy. He had become firmly identified with the more ideological segment of the Democratic left, and had antagonized the South with his heroic plea for civil rights during the 1948 national convention. He could not expect to be nominated unless he proved that he could win elections outside his home state of Minnesota. And by taking on Kennedy, he transformed the primaries. If Kennedy had won without significant opposition, his victories would have been meaningless. Against the formidable Humphrey, they were to be decisive.

One should not wonder that some candidates ignored the primaries of 1960 in the expectation that the convention would ultimately turn to them. Until 1960 no Democrat had ever won the nomination because of the primaries, although a few had been driven from the field by defeat. There were only a handful of states that even conducted presidential primaries, and in some of those the results were not binding on the delegates. Until Kennedy, the most successful contestant in primary elections had been Estes Kefauver. And he never came close to the nomination. The primaries were largely symbolic exercises, interesting but inconclusive tests of a candidate's skill and appeal. But that was just what John Kennedy needed: a symbol. A demonstration that — contrary to the established wisdom — people would vote for a young, inexperienced Catholic candidate for president of the United States. And even this demonstration would not have been enough except for the huge, largely unnoticed, growth of national media — corporate journalism and the unprecedented reach of television — which would bring local contests in places like Wisconsin and West Virginia into the consciousness of the nation, mini-Superbowls of politics. Now the Kansas farmer and the California commuter alike would follow the distant sounds of our favorite national sport, witness the victory, absorb enduring impressions of the victor. Political leaders in states remote from the campaign could sense their own constituencies' response to the Kennedy candidacy, and knew that they could ignore it only at a price. And possibly, just possibly, if sentiment was strong enough, the price might be very high. It would be an overstatement to claim that the primaries forced the bosses to choose Kennedy. But, for many, it tipped the balance.

Wisconsin was supposed to be the knockout blow. Humphrey, decisively and humiliatingly defeated in the state neighboring his native Minnesota, would be forced to withdraw, allowing Kennedy to sweep through the remaining primaries. Sorensen and I, along with other staff members, toiled urgently, sleeplessly in the Washington office, unleashing a prodigal burst of energy as if entering the final lap and not — as it proved — only the beginning of a difficult marathon. But the center of the campaign was in the wintry cities and towns of Wisconsin; in Madison and Milwaukee, in Ashland and La Crosse, and in hundreds of other places, where Kennedy and his "machine" began at dawn to shake hands, speak to voters in auditoriums and small groups gathered at rural crossroads, distribute leaflets and bumper stickers, consume time on radio and television. Our job was to provide the fuel, a continual flow of statements and issue papers incorporated by the candidate into his incessant talks.

"This is awfully boring stuff," I said to Sorensen as I handed him still another manuscript detailing the woes of the Wisconsin dairy farmer. Replete with facts, statistics, quasi-technical proposals for reversing the decline in farm income, I was describing a problem that I — a child of city streets — knew nothing about. "I don't think people, even farmers, can follow all this stuff," I told Sorensen. "I can hardly understand it myself, and I wrote it." "That's not the point," Sorensen explained. "They don't follow

it. But at least they know he's talking about something." (Later
in the campaign, as we worked together on a major farm speech,
Kennedy turned to me, saying, "Tell me, Dick, have you ever
seen a cow?" As a matter of fact, I had. Ten or twelve of them at
the model Hood's Milk Company farm, where my parents had
taken me on infrequent visits to Boston's rural outskirts. But I
had not paid much attention to the livestock, being drawn to the
playground swing and slides that the Hood Company had
thoughtfully provided for grammar school tourists.)

Of course, I thought, reflecting on Sorensen's comment. Kennedy's second greatest handicap (next to Catholism) was the perception — carefully cultivated by his opponents — of a millionaire
playboy, a young second-term senator who had cleverly combined
money, glamour, the PT-109, and, one was forced to admit, hard
campaigning, to thrust himself into the race for an office he was
unqualified to occupy. This censure — subsumed under the code
word "inexperience" — was to impair his candidacy until the debates with Nixon convinced the voters he could more than hold
his own against the incumbent vice-president. The purpose of the
speeches was not simply to inform, but to demonstrate Kennedy's
command of national issues. The words were dense and difficult,
but the music was plain. He knew what he was talking about.
He knew about them. And that's what they wanted to know
about him.

So I wrote about dairy price supports, condemned the callous-
ness of the Republican Department of Agriculture, discussed the
manifold distresses of the wheat market, and — in one memorable
thrust of exposition — promised to clean up the harbor at Ashland, Wisconsin, which — I assumed, on the advice of experts —
was in serious trouble. (Ever since, even now, I occasionally feel
stirrings of desire to visit those troubled waters whose name is so
firmly graven in memory.)

Wisconsin was not easy territory for Kennedy. "The Wisconsin
farmer is a very reserved person," one reporter observed. "Day
after day, Kennedy would walk along the street and shake hands
with the people, but their response was never very enthusiastic. It
was pleasant but just sort of a grunt and a nod of the head." In
one trip through the rural farms in the north he traveled two
hundred fifty miles without seeing nearly that many eligible voters. In contrast, Humphrey found himself at home among the
farmers of Wisconsin, declaring that he was "riding a wave of

support" that could carry him to victory. "I never felt so sure of anything in my life," Humphrey told a luncheon audience at Boscobel, a little river town in southern Wisconsin. "I feel like I just swallowed two tons of vitamins."

Yet despite Humphrey's public optimism, the reports coming back to the Kennedy office from Wisconsin were encouraging. Gradually the tireless, omnipresent Kennedy campaign was taking hold. Not only were the crowds larger, but their composition was changing to include younger people and others not normally drawn to political rallies. Shortly before the election, a Wisconsin political leader called me in Washington to report that more than four thousand people had turned out to cheer Kennedy at the Shroeder Hotel in Milwaukee. "It was great," he enthused, "and the amazing thing was that I didn't recognize half of them and I know nearly all the Democrats in this district." Later, Humphrey would complain about Kennedy's superiority of money and manpower. It was true, but not the whole truth. Kennedy also outworked his opponent.

"Whatever other qualifications I may have had," Kennedy would later say after winning the presidency, "one of them at least was that I knew Wisconsin better than any other president. My foottracks are in every house in the state. . . . I know the difference between the kind of farms they have in the 7th District and the 1st District. . . . I don't think it's a bad idea for a President to have stood outside of Maier's meat factory at 5:30 in the morning with the temperature at 10 above."

Sensing defeat, reading the predictions of a Kennedy avalanche, a desperate Humphrey stepped up his attack. The campaign became more vicious, more personal. "Beware of these orderly campaigns," Humphrey said. "They are ordered, bought and paid for. . . . I feel like an independent merchant competing against a chain store." Humphrey supporters spread accusations of Kennedy's admiration of Joe McCarthy, and about his father's contributions to Nixon.

Returning to Washington for an important Senate vote, Kennedy talked to us about the new Humphrey "smear tactics" with mounting rage. "It's just one fucking lie after another. First I'm some kind of a witch-hunter because I was in the hospital when that censure vote on McCarthy was taken. Then it's the money Dad gave to Nixon ten years ago. Hell, he's a businessman. He gave to everybody. Then it's Bobby out buying votes. Do you know how many voters there are in Wisconsin? I know we're rich, but not that rich. He talks about me, about my family, about my friends, the only thing he won't discuss are the issues. Son-of-a-bitch."

"We've got some pretty good stuff on Humphrey," a staff member interrupted, "we could put it out, try and get him on the defensive." Kennedy's demeanor changed with astonishing swiftness, the infuriated tirade immediately replaced by the clipped, modulated tones of political calculation. "I don't think so. I'm winning this thing on my own terms, and if we start exchanging smears the whole campaign will become an issue of credibility. Whose lies do you believe? I'd rather have people make a judgment about who can lead the country, and who can win." Kennedy paused, smiled. "And if I'm wrong, there'll be other primaries. You better hold on to that stuff, just in case."

As the primary election approached, each staff member put five dollars into an office pool, the money to go to the person who most accurately predicted the result. I was the only one to prophesy a close election — my undeveloped intuition combined with the gambler's knowledge that the odds of winning were increased if one selected the lowest or highest set of figures. And I won.

Kennedy was victorious, but it was not the expected knockout. Six of ten Wisconsin congressional districts went for Kennedy, and he received a decent but not overwhelming majority of the state-wide popular vote. Given the expectations of the national press, the results were, at best, ambiguous; and the religious issue had been given new life.

A disappointed Kennedy received the returns in his third-floor suite at the Pfister Hotel in Milwaukee. Slowly sipping a bowl of chicken noodle soup, he knew instantly from the way the votes had split — with Humphrey winning the predominantly Protestant districts while he had swept the Catholic areas — that the results would be interpreted in religious terms. 'What does it mean?" one of Kennedy's sisters asked. "It means," he responded bitterly, "that we have to do it all over again. We have to go through every primary and win every one of them — West Virginia and Maryland and Indiana and Oregon, all the way to the convention."

Kennedy was right to worry. "Religion is a big factor in Kennedy victory" ran the front-page story in the *New York Times*. "Senator Kennedy's drive for the Democratic Presidency gained new momentum today . . . but the voting also poses perils by emphasizing the religious issues. Politicians contended that a hardening of this issue in a country that is predominantly Protestant would in the long run make it more difficult for Senator Kennedy to get the nomination."

In the meantime, a jubilant Humphrey — miraculously unburdened of his nightmare visions of humiliating cataclysm — proclaimed a moral victory that he intended to transform into a numerical majority in the next primary — in West Virginia, where less than 5 percent of the population was Catholic.

"Here is where fate intervened," Pierre Salinger observed, "for had Humphrey given up the campaign then and there and not run in West Virginia, Kennedy might never have been able to demonstrate that he could overcome the Catholic issue. Had he faced no opposition, any victory there would have been meaningless in terms of bargaining with big-city bosses."

So the campaign moved on to West Virginia. Several months earlier Kenny O'Donnell had met with West Virginia county and political leaders. "There's nothing to worry about," they reassured him, "Jack will murder Hubert. Humphrey's liberalism just won't take down here." As soon as the Wisconsin votes were in, Kennedy sent O'Donnell to talk with the same group. The minute he walked into the room, he sensed the change in atmosphere. "We don't know." "It'll be close," a "tough fight." "Wait a minute," O'Donnell objected, "a few months ago you told me it would be a landslide." There was a pause, an almost embarrassed silence, until a boss of Charleston broke the silence: "That's right, but we didn't know he was Catholic."

O'Donnell left the meeting and called Kennedy.

"Tell me, Kenny," Kennedy asked, "is there any way we can win down there?"

"Yes," responded O'Donnell, "you can convert."

If there was anything I knew less about than milk, it was coal. But coal it was. This economically downtrodden Appalachian state was out of time with most of affluent America. Proud of their war heroes and of Chuck Yeager, who had broken the world speed record for terrestrial travel, their patriotism was not an icon withdrawn for display on the Fourth of July but a temper of the mind. They were poor — many of them — but not broken. Their pride demanded only the chance to work, to make a decent life for their families; and they had worked — many of them in the painful, life-threatening depths of the mines — until distant, mysterious, indifferent forces had taken the tools from their hands and sentenced them to a struggle for subsistence.

So I read the memoranda sent by our experts, studied books on mining, on the state itself, and consulted the guidebook to West Virginia prepared by the New Deal Writers Project during the depression. And I wrote about coal: how to revitalize the mines, the industry. We proposed "coal by wire," burning fuel in West Virginia generating plants to transmit electric power to other parts of the country. There were other subjects, of course, ranging from a program to industrialize the state (we had a program for everything), to rhetorical panegyrics about West Virginia's heroic contribution to America.

There was one subject I did not write about: Kennedy's Catholicism. We were instructed never to mention, even by implication, the question of religion. We did not prepare answers to the ominous rumors and charges, assert that he would not ban contraception, take orders from the pope and Cardinal Spellman, or construct a transatlantic tunnel between Washington and the Vatican. Yet it was the biggest issue. West Virginia was white, and very Protestant. Not only did most of the residents know little about Catholicism, they didn't know any Catholics, thus lacking personal experience to counter even the most grotesque rumors and bizarre accusations.

Humphrey and his staff were equally taciturn. The decision for silence was not dictated by some aberrant intrusion of moral principle on what was becoming a brutal, bitter, "no holds barred" campaign. Humphrey refrained because, after all, everyone knew Kennedy was Catholic; those hostile to his faith required no reminder. They would vote their prejudices. But a direct assault would leave Humphrey vulnerable to charges of inciting bigotry, perhaps arouse a backlash that would harm his candidacy not only in West Virginia, but throughout the party. (In 1970, on a visit to Montgomery, Alabama, I asked George Wallace how he would handle the issue of Chappaquiddick in a campaign against Ted Kennedy. "I'd never mention it," answered the skilled campaigner with a smile.)

Kennedy did not discuss his Catholicism for fear he would "only stir things up." So, still ignoring the most important issue of his campaign, perhaps hoping he could dissolve it by the mere force of his presence, John Kennedy, indefatigable, in continual pain from his injured back, his Addison's disease held in check by cortisone, spent interminable days driving from town halls to poisonous luncheon gatherings to run-down farms. He sat on a convenient log to chat with a group of curious, suspicious miners, then descended into the shaft where they spent their midnight days. They liked him. He was direct, his discussion stripped of rhetoric — he used words they could understand and answer; and he was curious, seemingly more interested in their way of life, the rigors of their job, even the mechanics of mining, than in trying to persuade them of his own merit. It was Kennedy at his best, because it was, in part, the real Kennedy. I never met a man so able to make an individual or a small group feel as if they and he were alone together, confined by the contours of a tiny world, bound by his quest to know, to understand, what others were like, what they were.

At another coal mine a week earlier Kennedy had come within six inches of being electrocuted. He was joking with miners at the Itmann operation of the Pocahontas Fuel Company when his head nearly touched a high-voltage line. "Look out for the wire," shouted a group of miners. Kennedy ducked and then resumed his conversation. "That wire sure would have lit up your lights," one miner said with a grin.

It was the natural efflorescence of Kennedy's lifelong search for information, for knowledge to feed that protean comprehension whose changes enhanced his capacities to lead, to win elections, to satisfy an insatiable curiosity, to enhance the charm that, ever since he was a small boy, had won him a unique place in his rivalrous family. Kennedy was in West Virginia to win an election. But in that struggle he was learning more about America; about that underside of American life which he had never experienced so personally, intimately. Midway in the campaign, returning to Washington for a crucial Senate vote, he strode into the office, proclaiming to no one in particular: "You can't imagine how those people live down there. I was better off in the war than they are in those coal mines. It's not right. I'm going to do something about it. If we make it." Then, ironically: "Even if they are a bunch of bigots."

These were not people living in India or Africa, he later said. They were fellow Americans, thrown out of work, hungry in a country that stores food and lets it rot. Nearly 15 percent of the population was unemployed. One out of every eight people, more than one hundred thousand families, found it necessary to line up every day for handouts from the federal government's stockpiles of surplus lard, rice, and cornmeal. He was particularly upset by the conditions in the hollows, where children took their free school lunches home to share with their starving parents.

By every customary standard of political judgment, the campaign was going well: The candidate was favorably received, said the right things, had assembled a good organization. But this was not a customary campaign. Beneath the surface, one still sensed the great, silent, resistant issue. It would not go away. Gradually Kennedy, his familiarity with the state and its people increasing, came to the inward judgment that most West Virginians did not hate Catholics, but they had fears — sensing in the Church some undefinable threat to their personal independence, to freedom. Thus, on April 19, in Wheeling, West Virginia, without warning, spontaneously, much to the surprise of his advisers, Kennedy spoke directly to the "Catholic issue" in an answer to a question from the audience. "I am a Catholic," Kennedy responded, "but the fact that I was born a Catholic — does that mean that I can't be president of the United States? I'm able to serve in Congress and my brother was able to give his life, but we can't be president?" Feeling a positive reaction from the crowd, Kennedy decided then and there to bring the issue up himself wherever he went and to answer it as fully as he could. "Is anyone going to tell me that I lost this primary forty-two years ago when I was baptized?" he demanded of an applauding crowd in Fairmont. Then later in Clarksburg he told his audience that the real issues in West Virginia were unemployment, coal miners, and jobless glass workers, "not where I go to church on Sunday."

"I will not allow any pope or church," he told audience after audience, "to dictate to the president of the United States. There is no conflict between my religion and the obligations of office; should one arise I would resign. I refuse to believe that the people of this state are bigots, guided in this most important choice by prejudice."

That message, repeated throughout the remainder of the campaign, began to erode the Catholic issue. West Virginians were not bigots, by God, and they would prove it!

The very fact that had seemed such a handicap — the almost total absence of a Catholic population — made the job easier. Prejudice is stronger, more virulent where the majority lives alongside a disliked minority. Proximity breeds fear, provides tangible objects for hostility, gives voice to dinner-table gossip and the ignorant fables of the local bar. Perhaps they didn't like Catholics in West Virginia, were apprehensive, but it was the idea of Catholicism that fed their prejudice, not its tangible presence. And so, it could be met on the level of ideas.

In the closing days, the campaign became more bitter, the tone more personal. "I don't think elections should be bought," Humphrey told a cheering crowd in the heart of the coalfields of southern West Virginia. "I can't afford to run through with a checkbook and a little black bag." (Presumably full of cash to bribe voters and local chieftains.) "Bobby said if they had to spend a half million to win here they would do it. . . . Kennedy is the spoiled candidate and he and that young, emotional, juvenile Bobby are spending with wild abandon. . . . Anyone who gets in the way of . . . papa's pet is going to be destroyed."

Kennedy decided it was time to hit back. From an anonymous source in Minnesota, the Kennedy camp received copies of correspondence between Humphrey and his draft board, letters revealing that Hubert had tried on several occasions to postpone his military service. It was decided that the material should be made public by Franklin Roosevelt, Jr., who was campaigning for Kennedy throughout the state, drawing large crowds. To the people of West Virginia President Roosevelt was a god. In the smallest mountain cabin, in the most dilapidated shack, there would be a single picture on the wall — a portrait of FDR. It was an important asset to have his son and namesake campaigning on our side, and if retaliation was needed, young Roosevelt was the perfect person to launch it.

No sooner had Franklin Roosevelt, Jr., made his charge that Senator Humphrey had sought a deferment during the war (that he was, in other words, a "draft dodger") and that he had documents to prove this, than Kennedy immediately disavowed any knowledge of the incident. "Any discussion of the war record of Senator Hubert Humphrey was done without my knowledge and consent, and I strongly disapprove the injection of this issue into the campaign," Kennedy said. "I have campaigned on the issues in West Virginia. These are issues of today and of the future and not of matters twenty years ago." But the damage was done.

On May 10, a wet, drizzly day, the voters in West Virginia went to the polls. By 10 P.M. it was clear that Kennedy had scored a triumphant victory, sweeping Humphrey in every part of the state — in the cities of Charleston and Wheeling, in the suburbs, in the hill country, in the hollows.

Desiring to hear the returns in the privacy of his Georgetown home (afraid that he would lose), Kennedy had flown home earlier that day. The moment his victory was clear, however, he chartered a plane to fly back to West Virginia. At 1 A.M. Humphrey's telegram of concession arrived at the Kennedy headquarters in Charleston. Minutes later, Bobby Kennedy, representing his brother, who was still en route from Washington, walked through the rain-soaked streets to pay a call on Humphrey. Senator Humphrey's eyes gleamed with tears as he spoke to his followers, many of whom were weeping. "I have a brief statement to make. I am no longer a candidate for the presidential nomination." Bobby Kennedy walked over to Humphrey and put his arm around his shoulders. Then they walked out together to meet the victorious John Kennedy, who was just then arriving back in Charleston.

"The religious issue has been buried here in the soil of West Virginia," Kennedy told a jubilant crowd. "I will not forget the people of West Virginia, nor will I forget what I have seen or learned here."

That night, the Senate office was in an uproar as the returns revealed a Kennedy landslide, and later, we broke into cheers as Humphrey conceded defeat and withdrew from the presidential fight. Across the street, in his Capitol Building chambers, the Senate majority leader was also watching. Whether he knew it or not, his last chance for the nomination was gone. Johnson might have done very well in West Virginia had he entered the primary. It was his kind of state: half southern, afflicted with rural poverty similar to that of his native west Texas. Among such people, and in such an atmosphere, Johnson could be a potent campaigner. He had proved that in Texas. A victory in West Virginia would have eliminated Kennedy, and brought him close to the nomination. But he did not choose to run. Thought it unnecessary. Was afraid to risk defeat. And so it was over — this time.

Only one obstacle remained. Adlai Stevenson was the personal favorite of the party's liberal wing. And there was still time for him to enter the Oregon primary — a state that was little more than one giant suburb, a Stevenson stronghold. A victory in Oregon might well be enough to transform party sentiment — admiring, nostalgic, almost romantic — into the more substantial currency of delegate votes. "I always knew," Kennedy said later, "that Adlai was the only one who could beat me. He was the one they wanted. But he just wouldn't go for it." Still, in the spring of 1960, after West Virginia, aware of Adlai's potential threat, Kennedy offered to make Stevenson secretary of state in return for his support. Stevenson declined, hoping that, in the end, the convention would reject this young usurper. But all he did was hope. He did not enter the late primaries. He did not work to enlist the delegations of crucial states. He waited for fortune to come to him. So he lost; and, afterward, was never considered for the State Department appointment he desired. The delegates may have loved Adlai, but they voted for Kennedy. He had demonstrated that neither youth, inexperience, nor Catholic faith were insuperable obstacles to victory. And even though one could argue in the abstract that Wisconsin and West Virginia were not "typical," the entire country had watched Kennedy's arduous, thrilling struggle to victory. To reject him now would appear a blatant defiance of the popular will, and, even more ominously, a nasty affront to the Democratic party's huge Catholic constituency. Doubts remained — about the man, about his ability to defeat Nixon — but there was no choice. He had to be nominated.

It was years before the dimensions of Kennedy's achievement were fully understood. He had used the primaries — hitherto symbolic — to capture the Democratic party, setting in motion an irreversible change in American politics.

During the Democratic convention in Los Angeles, those of us who remained in Washington prepared for our takeover of the Democratic party. By inviolable tradition, the party machinery — the National Committee, its records, and staff — belonged to the presidential nominee. As soon as Wyoming's votes gave Kennedy the nomination, we left the Senate office, descended to the darkened street below, where waiting automobiles carried us across town to the K Street headquarters of the Democratic National Committee. As we entered, the members of the committee staff, watching a television broadcast from Constitution Hall, turned, startled by this unannounced invasion, their surprise soon yielding to awareness, as we filed through the offices, placing briefcases and cartons of papers on nearby desks. The old party was gone. The Kennedy party had come. Just like the movies! A coup — swift, silent, and successful. Except there was no opposition. After all, we were all on the same side. At least, we were now.

5 / Seed Ground of the Sixties

WITH KENNEDY'S NOMINATION I had passed through the first stage of my political education. Unlike my earlier experiences — the Supreme Court, the quiz show investigation — the objective was not to find rational justice or uncover the truth, but to win elections. It was difficult, confused, often vicious combat. And I loved it.

There were no references then to the "well-oiled Kennedy machine" or the political "brilliance" of the candidate and his advisers. That came later, the gift of victory. When you win an election, everything you did was right; everyone is a genius. Monumental careers are spawned by such mythology. If you lose? What can be said? You're a loser; at best, unfortunate, probably inept. Amid that campaign, not yet seduced by the accolades that success would bring, we were aware that, like all the other contestants, we improvised, responded hurriedly to unforeseen events, made mistakes. Ill fortune and miscalculation disrupted carefully devised plans. We had intended to deliver the knockout blow in Wisconsin and failed. We had fervently desired to avoid that confrontation in West Virginia which proved necessary to Kennedy's nomination. That victory itself was largely due to the candidate's impromptu decision — against the agreed counsel of his advisers, in defiance of his own considered judgment — to confront the religious issue directly. Anger, frustration, some sudden illumination of intuition, whatever the impulsive source, it worked. Successes born of such inward solitary decisions are more than luck.

They are the mark of a great politician. Yet they are also good luck; no one gets to be president without it.

It was during the primaries that I first experienced the seductive power of advocacy. What began as a political tactic — attacks on our opponent's record, his qualities, even his honesty — were transformed into fierce conviction; while we thought Humphrey's attacks were unfair, dishonest, below the belt. Justice Frankfurter once told me how he disliked lawyers who weren't satisfied to win their case, but who also wanted to be told they were right. So, too, the unremitting ferocity of political combat compels one to believe in the righteousness of the cause, the treacherous injustice of the opponent. How else could one sustain the necessary energy and passion through the long months of conflict? Yet when the West Virginia battle was over, unburdened by triumph, Robert Kennedy had walked across the street to shake Humphrey's hand, praise his passionate devotion to the good, and begin a process of forming an alliance for the battles ahead. He was a good man, Hubert, and still retained an impassioned group of supporters. One of John Kennedy's favorite aphorisms was that "in politics, there are no friends, only allies." And the converse is also true — no enemies, only adversaries. Most of the time.

The practitioners of politics are bound together by interest, dispersed when interests diverge. This observation is not as cynical as it might seem. Politics is not love, and it is not a game. It is a deadly serious struggle for public position and influence over the lives of others. The "interest" that draws men to power has many forms: the desire for material gain, some inner need to command. But it can also be compounded of shared convictions, mutual values, a common belief about the purpose to which political power should be directed.

And, if at first it seemed a long way from the strains of "America the Beautiful" to the rancorous clamor of the political arena I had entered, the seeming disjuncture was mostly due to my own ignorance. (As my own later assimilation of the country to its government was due to ignorance of another kind.) The lobster is the scavenger of the sea, indiscriminately devouring the foulest refuse of ocean floor, yet transforming it into the most succulent of flesh. Out of the cheating and lies of politics, out of the deals, the "image-making," the slanders, the getting and spending, the freedom of a nation is nourished, sometimes diminished, occasionally enlarged.

Kennedy had gambled that through the largely symbolic conquests of the primaries he could force a reluctant Democratic party to accept his leadership. He had won that gamble. Now he must play for larger stakes. He must not only overcome national resistance to his youth, his inexperience, and his religion, but persuade the country to abandon seemingly secure, if unadventurous, Republican rule and reject the chosen successor to an immensely popular president. No artfully contrived combination of political forces could achieve that. He had to touch the secret fears and ambivalent longings of the American heart, divine and speak to the desires of a swiftly changing nation — his message grounded on his own intuition of some vague and spreading desire for national renewal.

Although Kennedy himself formulated the themes of his campaign, they were an efflorescence of the times, and the events of the decade which immediately preceded his campaign. I myself was a child of the fifties — graduating from high school as the decade began, leaving law school for Washington as, in 1958, it neared its end. We were known as "The Silent Generation," although I never thought of myself or my friends as particularly quiet. When I entered college in 1953, *Life* magazine, then the acknowledged weekly diary of the American dream (a title since usurped by the *Wall Street Journal,* a token of our progress toward increased candor in the admission of greed), editorialized that "the one thing we can count on is that we seem to have a good system for making hard work worthwhile for anybody who wants to try it." Sure, some folks were down on their luck, but "for those whose plight is really bad we now have all manner of relief measures and free services."

During my sophomore year, the same magazine headlined that in America, "Nobody Is Mad With Nobody," an assertion that was unintentionally consistent with the assertion of Jack Kerouac's new book, *On the Road,* that "This is the story of America. Everybody's doing what they think they're supposed to do." Unlike *Life,* Kerouac's description was not meant as praise. But they were talking about the same thing; as was Malvina Reynolds, who was writing a song that captured the amused attention of my generation:

> And the boys go into business
> And marry and raise a family
> In boxes made of ticky tacky
> And they all look just the same.

During my first year in law school, I read what was then thought a supreme intellectual synthesis of the evolution of contemporary America — William Whyte's *The Organization Man* — describing a smoothly working social machine, headquartered in the mushrooming suburbs, whose inhabitants cultivated the attributes of personal conformity and hardworking devotion to the company that led to advancement.

In retrospect it seems apparent that the self-congratulatory rhetoric, the muted, angry — more often sarcastic — responses, all of which assumed the same description of the country, were a sign of impermanence, of emerging challenge to the seemingly established order. People are not moved to analyze, praise, or satirize universally held and deeply rooted values. They are a given — like the belief in God in Puritan Massachusetts, or the patriotic devotion that followed Pearl Harbor. At the source of discussion is a fear of challenge, the desire for challenge, the hope of challenge. And the challenges soon began to come; their significance unclear at the time, each one seemingly confined to a particular, restricted aspect of American life. And even when coalescing events began to fissure the entire façade of complacency, the leaders of opinions were among the last to know.

In the early sixties I was invited to have cocktails with Hedley Donovan, the editor of *Time* magazine, and his principal minions, to discuss a new presidential program for the cities. We mounted to the top of Rockefeller Center, where a small, tastefully decorated cocktail lounge looked out through ribbed glass walls over the magnificent metropolis stretching to the East River and beyond. I began to talk about the "problem of the cities," when an editor interrupted me, and with an expansive gesture toward the vista below, objected, "There is no problem of the cities." And he was right. There was no problem. Not from there.

I was already serving as president of the *Harvard Law Review* when, in 1957, American receivers picked up a single repetitious tone, coming mysteriously from the upper atmosphere; the Soviet Sputnik was orbiting the earth. In every continent men watched the night sky for a view of this awesome achievement, man's first conquest of space. The news was a bombshell. Stephen King, the best-selling horror novelist, remembers the lights going on as he watched a movie so the theater manager could grimly announce the staggering news to his audience of teenagers. The ten-year-old King was stunned. It couldn't be. They couldn't have beat us. Across the country this reaction was multiplied a thousandfold.

With a single, immense leap, the Soviets had undermined our confidence in the divinely bestowed preeminence of America. Voices were raised to challenge the quality of our education, our laboratories, our very way of life. Had we — we asked ourselves — become soft, complacent, begun to decline?

The year I graduated law school — 1958 — newspapers were crowded with accounts of anti-American riots that, within the next two years, would spread to embassies and missions in dozens of countries. In France, a tomato was splashed into the windshield of an American tourist's car; in Morocco, a bitter dispute was raging over air base rentals; in Germany there were increasing outbursts of popular resentment against American GIs, who had come as occupiers and stayed on in the role of defenders against the new communist menace; in Okinawa the U.S. Air Force was under attack for appropriating highly productive land to expand air fields. *The Ugly American,* a devastating fictional critique of American policy in Asia, written by two Americans, became a best-selling book.

What had gone wrong? The liberator of World War II, the guardian of freedom, the beacon's of man's hope, was being spat on and reviled — not in communist countries, where all was peaceful, but in Europe and the continents of the third world. That same year Vice-President Nixon was almost killed by angry anti-American mobs in South America. And not long afterward, Eisenhower himself was forced to cancel a trip to Japan because his safety could not be assured.

We had thought of ourselves as a symbol of freedom, exemplar and guardian of man's desire for justice and relief from oppression. Now it seemed that substantial numbers in many countries had another opinion. They thought of us as the selfish rich aristocrats of the globe, modern imperialists who wished only to protect their own interests, indifferent to the misery and discontent of those in other lands. The accusations were true only in part. Yet they could not be disregarded as the agitations of communists. They reflected an opinion more widely held then we had ever suspected. Americans — preserved from irrational response by a certain native honesty — didn't like the impression we were making on the world. And worse, it was dangerous. For enmity toward America was, ultimately, in some indefinable sense, a victory for the Russians in a cold war that became more ominously intense as the decade was ending.

In 1955 and 1956, Eisenhower had proposed that the skies over both the United States and Russia be open to reconnaissance aircraft from the other country, and rejected the use of force to resist the brutal Soviet invasion of Hungary. The Soviet Union rebuffed the "open skies" proposal, and blatantly reaffirmed their right to use force against rebellious satellites. A year later there was Sputnik, and its corollary, a Soviet preeminence in long-range rockets capable of intruding earthly as well as stellar space. The Russians were on a roll. And they intended to make the best of it.

In May of 1959 Khrushchev instructed the Western powers that if they were not out of Berlin in six months he would throw them out. The ultimatum was mere rhetoric. Neither we nor the Russians made a move. But the threat reflected an ominous Soviet intention to drive the Western powers from their irritating sanctuary deep inside the frontiers of East Germany. In September of that same year, Fidel Castro — whose revolutionary victory in January had been hailed by Americans as a victory for democracy — was calling the United States "a vulture . . . feeding on humanity," establishing close relationships with the Russians, and daring "the Yanquis" to invade.

By the time Kennedy announced his candidacy, on January 2, 1960, Eisenhower and Khrushchev were preparing a summit meeting to discuss the increasing tensions between their two countries. But four months later, on May 2, while Kennedy — the disappointing Wisconsin primary behind him — was campaigning through the rural valleys of West Virginia, the Russians shot down an American spy plane, the U-2, launched a verbal assault against this American aggression, and threatened to shoot rockets at any country that permitted the use of its territory for airborne espionage. The early torrent of threatening Soviet indignation omitted personal censure of Eisenhower, seemingly a tacit intimation that the Russians still would deal with a president betrayed by overzealous subordinates. But Eisenhower took full responsibility. He had known about the U-2 missions. He had approved all of them. While commentators and politicians debated the wisdom of Eisenhower's admission, Kennedy had no doubt. "He had no choice," the candidate told us on a brief return to Washington. "He's the president. He's in charge. If he denied knowing, they'd think he was a liar, or that someone else was running the country. Either way he loses. We all lose."

Six days after West Virginia had brought Kennedy to the verge of nomination, Khrushchev stalked out of the Elysée Palace in

Paris where the world leaders had assembled, accused Ike of "treachery" and "bandit acts," canceled both the summit and his invitation for an Eisenhower visit to Russia.

If there was any hope that a possibility of détente or reconciliation remained, it was dissipated two days later when Khrushchev, still in Paris, declared he would solve the "Berlin problem" by signing a separate peace treaty with East Germany; an act that would have allowed East Germany to block access across its territory, confronting the West with a choice between withdrawal or forceful penetration. Khrushchev's declaration, later repeated, was to present Kennedy with the most dangerous decision of his first presidential year.

Racial turbulence, assaults on American confidence, the progress and mounting hostility of the Soviet Union were, it could now be seen, harbingers of the fast-approaching sixties. Even as we mourned or praised — each according to his own inclination — the apathetic materialism, the retreat into opportunism and personal self-indulgence, the seeds of change were being nourished toward maturity in the newly fertile soil of a changing America.

> Gold in the mountain
> And gold in the glen,
> And greed in the heart,
> Heaven having no part,
> And unsatisfied men.

In the fifties, our population rose more rapidly than during any decade since the great waves of immigration came to a halt a half century before. Two-thirds of this growth was in the suburbs. The new suburbanites had made it. But the result was not satisfaction, only a redirection of discontent toward new objects, toward whatever was wrong, incomplete, with their lives, their communities, their country.

In that same half century we had experienced the largest internal immigration in our history. In 1910, 90 percent of American blacks lived in the states of the Old South, most of them in the rural countryside. By 1960, half of our eighteen million blacks had moved to northern cities, while many of those who remained left the harsh, unprofitable soil to live in the larger southern cities. Racial conflict had come north, where its eruptions would be witnessed by a different and larger audience. While in the South, freed from rural isolation, blacks could more easily band together in organized expressions of hope and anger. They could no longer be ignored; refused to be ignored; and could now force awareness of their oppression on white America.

And the economy itself, the source of affluence and outlet for ambition, was changing. By 1960, there were, for the first time, more workers in white-collar jobs than in manufacturing. In every city, the closed and boarded fronts of small shops — the corner grocery, the neighborhood butcher — signaled the encroachment of giant chains, poignant revelation of the fact that proportionately fewer Americans were self-employed than at any time in our history.

These changes were both signal and cause of a disruption in the astonishing growth of postwar America. Throughout the fifties, our rising production of wealth and personal income began to slow to less than half that of the previous quarter century, its progress more seriously impeded by recurrent recessions — one of which, at the end of the decade, helped to elect John Kennedy.

The decade of the fifties had begun with an illusion, which events, at first, had seemed to verify: We were destined to grow in wealth and power; our citizens, all our citizens, would enjoy an ever-improving life, and bequeath an even more golden future to their children. In all the world we were first — in affluence, in freedom, in power, in knowledge — and would dedicate our preeminence not only to ourselves, but to guarding the "free peoples" of the world toward their own aspirations.

As the decade ended, this conviction had begun to fade. There was not anything impossible about this destiny. But it was not inevitable. History would not make itself. It had to be made and remade, and by us. It was the oldest lesson of civilization, one we had known and lived, and seemed somehow, for a time, to have forgotten.

Kennedy had sensed that subterranean pressures were already beginning to fissure the illusions of the fifties, that national discontent was mounting. Or so it seemed. He was to derive the theme of his campaign from that belief: that his fellow citizens would respond to an injunction to "get America moving again." The discontent was already manifest. The only question was whether it was rising fast enough. Kennedy thought so, and staked his hope for the presidency on that calculation. Thus he sought to transform a political struggle into a cause: a movement that transcended the satisfaction of merely personal desires. And it worked. By little more than one-half of one percent.

"The United States looks tired," Kennedy repeated again and again. "My campaign for the presidency is founded on the single assumption that the American people are uneasy at the present drift in our national course, that they are disturbed by the relative decline in our vitality and prestige and that they have the will and strength to start the U.S. moving again. If I am wrong in this assumption, and if the American people are satisfied with things as they are, if Americans are undisturbed by approaching dangers and complacent about our capacity to meet them, then I expect to lose this election. But if I am right, and I firmly believe I am right, then those who have held back the growth of the U.S. during the last years will be rejected in November and America will turn to the leadership of the Democratic party."

None of us, not even Kennedy, could distinguish with any certainty the apprehensions of our intuition from wishful desire. But we were on our way. And, meanwhile, outside the curiously insulated domain of self-important policies, other movements were being formed. From a hundred different centers of energy, belief, frustration, anger, and will, people were beginning to move, gathering determination to force America closer to its own idea of freedom. What a wonderful battle. What joy to be in the middle of the fight.

6 / The Election

> The time you won your town the race
> We chaired you through the market place.
>
> — A. E. Housman, "To an Athlete Dying Young"

ON SEPTEMBER 4, at Detroit, I boarded the *Caroline* to begin sixty-eight days of nonstop campaigning for the Kennedy-Johnson ticket.

That improbable ticket had been conceived in miscalculation and brought to term by Kennedy's swift, sagacious reaction to the consequences of his only partially intended action. Prior to the convention, we would occasionally divert our labors in Kennedy's Washington office by discussing the vice-presidential nominee. Naturally, Lyndon Johnson was among those mentioned. But discussion rarely passed the threshold objection: Lyndon would never accept. Why would the most powerful majority leader in the history of the United States exchange his post for the puerile office of vice-president, whose sole constitutional power was the right to cast the deciding vote should the Senate be deadlocked? Nor was the office a promising step toward higher office. No vice-president in the modern era had been elected to the White House from that office. (Nixon was trying to be the first.)

I had no rational rejoinder to this formidable argument. Yet I vaguely sensed something in Johnson's temperament that told me otherwise. He had sought the nomination and been defeated by a junior and not terribly effective member of that body he ruled so forcefully. How could he now return to that Senate chamber, endure the consoling remarks of his colleagues, imagine their unexpressed satisfactions, their sardonic whispers, their questioning glances? It would be an almost unendurable humiliation. Much later, my almost daily contact with President Johnson confirmed this uninformed guess. He was a man who never retreated. To resume his place in the Senate would have been — as seen through the prism of his turbulent ego — a submission to disgrace.

In Los Angeles, Kennedy, accepting the powerful logic of a near certain refusal — as if Johnson was a creature of logic, of Kennedy's kind of logic — offered him the nomination. Johnson accepted the Kennedy proposal, and remained adamant as the Kennedy camp, confounded by his unanticipated acquiescence, tried to influence him to withdraw. Robert Kennedy — John Kennedy's other voice — was dispatched on this unpleasant task, only to find that if it were done, it would have to be done by the candidate himself. And he couldn't do it without antagonizing those whose support he had intended to cultivate — southern leaders, moderate democrats, the vital state of Texas.

"Don't worry, Bobby," Kennedy told his brother, still upset by the failure of his mission to Johnson, "nothing's going to happen to me."

Politically, the decision proved an unintended masterstroke. Johnson helped to hold together for one final effort the fading remnants of the southern organizations that, for a hundred years, had delivered the "solid South" to the Democratic nominees (Lincoln's legacy to liberalism), freeing Kennedy to campaign for the increasingly crucial northern black vote. Historically the decision may have been the most important single act of Kennedy's public life; he had unknowingly named the man who would reshape the decade to whose leadership Kennedy himself so urgently aspired.

In years to come, Johnson would blame Robert Kennedy for having tried to oust him from the ticket. He knew better. But he could not admit — perhaps not even to himself — that Robert Kennedy must have been his brother's emissary. Anger that could not be acknowledged must be displaced. Thus were planted the seeds of unremitting hostility, which were to culminate in the confrontation of 1968.

So Kennedy and Johnson it was. But to us, as to the country, there was only one candidate and one opponent, as I joined the small traveling staff that would accompany Kennedy on his arduous struggle to present himself and his message to almost every state of our undecipherable continent.

Sorensen and I were the only two speechwriters on the plane for the entire campaign, although others would make occasional contributions. Accompanying our travels was the bustling, talka-

tive press secretary, Pierre Salinger, whose shrewdness and calculation were concealed by an almost clownlike, accommodating
amiability intended to create an ambience of warmth and welcoming respect for the press corps, which conveyed our daily efforts
to the nation. Dave Powers, friend and companion since John
Kennedy's first campaign for Congress, called on a limitless store
of anecdotes and street wisdom to provide the candidate with necessary diversion from the demands of the campaign, and his advice, never offered unless asked, was often decisive. Perhaps closest of all was the dour, taciturn Kenny O'Donnell — politician,
personal confidant, Robert Kennedy's college roommate — who
had no ambitions, no desires, no purpose that was not Kennedy's.
One day, talking with Teddy White, Kennedy pointed to O'Donnell, stretched out sleeping across the seats: "You see Kenny, there.
If I woke him up and asked him to jump out of this plane for me,
he'd do it. You don't find that kind of loyalty easily."

Our entourage also included the political counselor Larry
O'Brien; John Bailey, the Connecticut boss who had been among
the first to support Kennedy's presidential hopes and would be
rewarded with the chairmanship of the Democratic National
Committee; and others whose names and roles have been amply
recorded in the voluminous accounts of this most profusely recorded making of a president. If we were not exactly a "band of
brothers," free from all jealousies, enmity, and the clash of ambitions, we had this in common: The candidate came first. Nothing
could be done to disrupt his cause; no energy directed to any purpose but his. That was the one unforgivable sin.

We all knew it wouldn't be easy, but believed if we worked hard
enough, refused all respite of body and mind, the reward was certain. We were convinced that our candidate was the best man, his
summons a trumpet of truth, his cause infused with the moral
imperatives of America. And on the other side was Nixon: treacherous opportunist, visionless, disliked even by the president he
served.

In the beginning — in September — according to Doctor Gallup, Nixon had a lead of 49–46. After the first debate, on the
twenty-fifth of that month, Kennedy was ahead by the same margin; Kennedy gained another few points toward the end of October, then saw his lead narrow as the election approached. At 7
P.M. on election eve the united wisdom of CBS and IBM foretold
a Nixon landslide, and, by midnight, another corporate alliance

with different initials announced an easy Kennedy victory. When it was all over, less than one percentage point separated victor from vanquished; a shift of a few thousand votes in two doubtful states would have thrown the election into the House of Representatives.

The poll numbers, which were to form the backbone of so many dramatic tales, were all fiction. At least, they might have been. Small numerical differences are meaningless. We publish and read them out of our yearning for an illusion of certainty. Did Nixon begin his campaign ahead by three points? Who knows? It could have been even. Or, perhaps, Kennedy held a lead. Ask any mathematician who does not depend on polls for a living.

The numbers yield only one certainty: From beginning to end the election was a tie. The campaign, the entire prodigious, extravagant, debilitating struggle, was for the allegiance of that small handful of voters who had not made their choice even before it had begun. But there was also another objective: to keep from losing votes, to forestall the abandonment of those unmeasurable numbers whose preferences — volatile, ambivalent, liquid — might shift under the slightest pressure of . . . what? Events? A mistake by one candidate, a favorable impression made by the other? An upward movement in the economy? Renewed truculence by Khrushchev? The intervention of Eisenhower or his reluctance to intervene?

Even today it is impossible to know how much, or whether, the campaign influenced that mysterious, mute leviathan — the American people. But at least we got their attention. The turnout was the largest in American history.

"There are more Democratic votes out there than Kennedy votes," the candidate laconically instructed us in a guiding assumption of his strategy. Although he proclaimed himself the herald of a "new generation of Americans," the country was only eight years removed from Roosevelt and Truman, the voters' memories softened by nostalgia for the leadership that had taken us through the Great Depression and the great war. He would emblazon this tradition upon his banners. Only by running, continually, forcefully, as a Democrat could he overcome the perception that he was too young, too glamorous, too Catholic, an outsider of alien breed without claim to the heritage of the party that had nominated him.

Arriving in Los Angeles in the first week of the campaign, I presented the senator with a proudly drafted discourse on civil rights. Ten thousand people jammed the Shrine Auditorium that night as Kennedy strode to the rostrum, acknowledged the tumultuous reception with a slight nod of his head, and launched into an eloquent extemporaneous exposition of his candidacy with my prepared text (also eloquent) still in his pocket. It was as if all that he had learned in his miles of campaigning had come together that night on the rim of the Pacific.

"I think the record of the two parties," he began, "and its promise for the future, can be told pretty well from its record of the past. Mr. Nixon and I, the Republican and the Democratic parties, are not suddenly frozen in ice, or collected in amber since the two conventions. We are like two rivers which flow back through history, and you can judge the force, the power and the direction of the rivers by studying where they rose and where they ran throughout their long course. . . . Just contrast the slogans of the two parties . . . what the two parties stand for. 'Stand Pat with McKinley.' " The crowd laughed. " 'Retain Normalcy with Warren G. Harding.' 'Keep Cool with Coolidge.' " The crowd laughed even harder. "Had enough?" Kennedy asked, his face breaking into a broad grin. "The weakest slogans in the history of American politics. Contrast the slogans of which we are proud: Woodrow Wilson's 'New Freedom,' Franklin Roosevelt's 'New Deal.' " The crowd roared. "Harry Truman's 'Fair Deal.' " The crowd roared again. "I ask your help in this election, not just in a contest with Mr. Nixon but in a contest for the future of this country."

He then went on to take up a small part of my draft, outlining what he would do as president to move forward in civil rights. Then, putting the draft away, he ended on a powerful note, saying that he wanted historians at a later date to say: "These were the years of the American life, the 1960s. Give us those years."

The tumultuous response confirmed his judgment; the theme was set. That night, returning to the plane, he looked toward me as he entered his compartment and said — with friendly irony — "Nice speech, Dick." "Both of them, Senator," I replied.

The appeal to party tradition coexisted in a somewhat uneasy tension with Kennedy's claim to represent "a new generation of Americans who fought in Italy and Europe, who fought in the Pacific for freedom in World War II." He was to be both traditional and different, devotee of the past and marketeer of the future. Not a contradiction. Not even improbable. How else did one defend old principles, except by fighting new battles? Appeals to the past were necessary to diminish apprehension about Kennedy himself; promises of a changing future were to tap mounting discontent, a sensed national decline, recent injuries to patriotic pride.

At the start of the campaign, sitting in the Senate office, Kennedy read a memo from economist John Kenneth Galbraith, describing the eight-year deterioration of economic growth and the present slide toward recession and unemployment. As he returned the last page to his desk, Kennedy looked up, grinning, and asked: "Do you know how I tell what is monetary and what is fiscal? Monetary begins with an M, and so does Martin of the Federal Reserve Board. How about that, Professor Galbraith?"

There would be plenty of experts eager to steer the candidate through the technical structures of economic policy, but it was the coal miners of West Virginia, not the professors of Harvard, who taught him that economic dissatisfaction derived from harsh realities. Four years of journeying to every part of the country had informed his intuition that confidence and pride in America had been undermined — by recession, by Khrushchev, by Castro, by an inchoate awareness of a vacancy in the soul of America. If the people loved Ike, it was partly because he was a personal emblem of a more glorious past, thus set apart from the incapacities of his administration.

Nixon's own campaign was — had to be — the mirror image of Kennedy's. He would run as the legitimate Republican heir to a popular Republican president. His large experience — senator, fierce adversary of communist conspiracy who had brought Alger Hiss to justice, vice-president for eight years, world traveler on comfortable terms with heads of foreign nations, tempered by personal debate with the volatile Khrushchev — was an imposing contrast to the greenhorn senator who had never held an executive office, whose own travels, with the exception of his service in the Pacific, were but the wanderings of a wealthy dilettante.

We disliked Nixon at the beginning, despised him by the end. "He's a filthy, lying son-of-a-bitch, and a very dangerous man," was among our candidate's kinder descriptions of his opponent in the closing weeks of the election. In part, Kennedy's remark was a natural reflection of a brutal political battle, but, obscenities aside, Kennedy had also come to sense that the man was truly dangerous, that his unique blend of intelligence and amorality might have devastating consequences for the country. As a result of our hostility we underestimated Nixon. Admittedly, he was clever, certainly he understood politics, the art of acquiring votes and power. But, we thought he did not know, thus could not reach, the country he aspired to govern. We were wrong. He knew a lot about America. He could reach, with uncanny intuition, the buried doubts, the secret dreads, the nightmare panic of the threatened soul (the foreclosing banker, insurrectionary blacks). And he also understood, less mystically, with unwavering clarity, his own greatest asset: He was the Republican candidate in a normally conservative country.

Nixon's greatest difficulty — at least at the beginning — was, like Kennedy, to accommodate his reliance on the past (in his case, Ike) with his awareness of rising national discontent. He did the best he could: He would carry the magnificent Eisenhower era toward new realms of achievement. Everything was already wonderful, but it would stay that way only if we devised new approaches to new challenges. And all this with the ever-watchful Ike, or his staff, carefully monitoring for any signs of disloyalty.

Thus from the beginning, for both candidates, circumstances and conditions combined with sensible calculation to dictate the themes and strategy of political combat. Then, as opening day approached — traditionally the beginning of September — fortune intervened, and on Kennedy's side.

On August 24, at an Eisenhower press conference, a reporter asked the president, "What presidential decisions of your administration has the vice-president participated in?" A smiling Eisenhower replied, "If you give me a week I might think of one," then signaled the conference to an end before other questions could be asked. Ah! The gentle, affable Ike — who would have thought to cast him as Richard III who could "smile and smile and murder while I smile." Later, we are told, he called Nixon to explain he had merely been speaking facetiously. Of course: We always knew Ike was a great humorist, a master practitioner of black comedy.

Eisenhower's comment was not fatal. But it hurt. It did damage to the most important prop of Nixon's campaign — his invaluable, trusted, intimate service as vice-commander of the nation. How much Ike must have disliked him!

Two days later, the discomfited Nixon was cheered by huge, raucous, admiring crowds that greeted him in Atlanta and other cities of the traditionally Democratic South. Not since Jefferson Davis forcibly rejected the leadership of Lincoln had any Republican candidate for president received such warm southern hospitality. Nixon loved it. What politician wouldn't? But it was a curse in disguise. It persuaded Nixon that he might actually carry the South. To do so, however, he would have to mute his advocacy of civil rights; despite the fact that his careful cultivation of black leaders, his espousal of measures directed toward racial equality, had given him stronger support in the black community than any Republican since Roosevelt. Kennedy, by contrast, was suspect. He had never been among the Democratic leaders in the struggle for racial equality, had defeated the adored Humphrey, and his ideological devotion to liberalism was doubted.

Nixon's pursuit of southern votes was to erode his support among northern blacks. Kennedy, by contrast, went all out in pursuit of the northern black vote — yielding place to no man in his demands for racial justice — while counting on Johnson and other political leaders to hold the southern Democratic organizations together for one last shot. Nixon's decision was wrong. Kennedy's was right — politically. A large part of the South, held together by fading bosses and a crumbling structure of party control, stayed with the Democrats, while black voters made the difference in many northern cities.

In a close election, everything is decisive. But I always thought we owed a special debt of gratitude to those marvelous people of Atlanta who braved the scathing sun of a Georgia summer to stand up and cheer for Richard Nixon.

Next to riding a motorcycle alongside Dennis Hopper, there is no better way to see America than from the cabin of a twin-engine prop plane. That first week, having landed at Pocatello, Idaho, during the night, I walked out from the Bannock Hotel before breakfast to stare toward the stone towers that rose from the edge of surrounding fields: a northern edge of the fabled Rocky Mountains. Pocatello! A week before I had not known of its existence. Now, here it was. The beauty mine, a sparkling edge of my multifaceted country; the people, not merely friendly and casual, but somehow linked in those bonds of affection which, Lincoln proclaimed, mystically fused the inhabitants of a large and diverse continent.

Three speeches later, the *Caroline* rumbled out of the flat basin bound for Spokane, Washington, only to receive word from Pierre Salinger that the press plane that followed us was missing one of its most important members. Exhilarated by the unaccustomed freedom of mountain air, a reporter — whose byline often adorned the front page of a leading eastern journal — had spent the night in an Idaho bar and, thus sedated, never heard the wake-up call. Already behind schedule, we could not return to pick him up, and flights from Pocatello to Washington State were nonexistent. For two days, while the pain-stricken journalist labored to catch us, his colleagues filed dispatches under his name, concealing his absence from editors who never would have understood the powerful seductions of remote Pocatello.

Flying over the Seattle harbor, I looked down at a collection of naval ships, scattered like a child's toys across the sheltered recess of sea. Glancing across the aisle I saw Kennedy watching through his window, and remarked impulsively, "Just think, Senator, in a few months they'll all be yours." "Thanks a lot," he grimaced, immediately returning his attention to a speech draft which had been resting on his lap. I had tempted fate, and he would distance himself from this hazardous exchange.

Less than a week later, sitting in a bus that carried us toward a rally somewhere in the harsh ranch country of west Texas, I struggled to put the finishing touches on a speech setting forth Kennedy's Latin American policy. The fall of Cuba and the disastrous Nixon trip had transformed Latin America — customarily neglected by candidates and public alike — into a major arena of foreign policy debate. It was not enough to condemn the Republican (not Eisenhower, of course) "loss" of Cuba; we also needed an affirmative statement of Kennedy's hemispheric intentions. The major elements were self-evident: The United States, confronted by the reality of rising discontent and the certainty of turbulent change, would place itself on the side of the democratic left; those who sought not only growth, but social justice — the elimination of tax systems and land ownership that enriched a few while relegating most of the population to brief, brutal lives of unremitting poverty.

To dramatize the policy, we needed a name — at least I thought we did — something that would establish Kennedy's proposals as a coherent successor to the Good Neighbor policy of Franklin Roosevelt, who was the last of our presidents to give serious attention to the Western Hemisphere. It should be in Spanish, I thought, to demonstrate that we envisioned not another exercise in generous paternalism, but a partnership, a joint venture in democratic reform. Unfortunately, my search for a ringing slogan was handicapped by my almost complete ignorance of Spanish. Looking down at the empty seat beside me, I saw a magazine published by a Mexican-American society in New Mexico, serendipitously discarded by an earlier passenger, and entitled *Alianza*. Perfect. At least it sounded right. An alliance. What else could it mean? Yet, in any language, the most obvious meanings could conceal unanticipated connotations; perhaps even subtle sexual implications. (In English, for example, *liaison* can mean more than a communication between officials.)

At the next stop I rushed to a phone to call my friend Karl Meyer in Washington. Then a novice reporter with the *Washington Post*, Karl had an intense personal interest in Latin America, and among his friends were several members and functionaries of Washington's Latin community through whom I had acquired some knowledge about the labyrinthine transformations of that hitherto mysterious continent. I asked Karl if there was any danger in the word. He thought not, but would check it out, and in fifteen minutes called back: "Ernesto [Betancourt] says there's no problem. But he thinks it should be an alliance for something." "Like what?" I asked. "He thought 'development' would be good," Karl replied.

"What's that in Spanish?"

"*Desarrollo*."

"He'll never be able to pronounce it," I objected. "How do you say 'progress'?"

"*Progreso*," Karl informed me.

"Perfect." And I wrote the phrase "*Alianza para progreso*" (omitting the necessary *el* until later, in the White House, the correction was made by Spanish-language grammarians) into the speech scheduled for delivery that afternoon outside the Alamo in San Antonio. By that time Kennedy, giving six or seven speeches a day, had been warned by Dr. Gould — his throat specialist — to conserve his voice between stops. So, after quickly reading through my suggested draft, Kennedy scrawled a note on his lined yellow pad, "Let's not waste this one. The ministers is the big one for today." (That night he was to confront the "Catholic issue" directly before the assembled Protestant ministers of Houston, Texas.) So it was that more than a month later, on October 18, in Tampa, Florida, Kennedy first proclaimed the Alianza para Progreso, which was to be among the keystones of his foreign policy.

By consensus — of staff, traveling press, and editorial commentary — Kennedy's confrontation with the suspicious ministers in Houston on that night of the Alliance for Progress's anonymous birth was a great success. "We have far more critical issues to face in the 1960 election," he began, "but because I am a Catholic and no Catholic has ever been elected president, the real issues in this campaign have been obscured . . . so it is apparently necessary for me to state once again — not what kind of church I believe in, for that should be important only to me — but what kind of America I believe in. I believe in an America where the separation of church and state is absolute . . . where no religious body seeks to impose its will. . . . I want a Chief Executive whose public acts are responsible to all groups and obligated to none. . . . This is the kind of America I believe in and this is the kind my brother died for in Europe. And this is the kind of America for which our forefathers died when they fought for the Constitution and the Bill of Rights."

Kennedy had rarely been more impressive. His exposition, woven from appeals to constitutional principle and passionate assertions of personal belief, was more than enough to overturn any rational apprehension that his Catholic allegiance might menace Protestant and/or secular America. We were elated. We had met the enemy on his home grounds, and we had won. But, of course, it was not so simple. Neither reason nor honest passion could overcome fears rooted in childhood, absorbed from parents and neighbors who had themselves been shaped by the folk wisdom of earlier generations. In the country, as in West Virginia, people would overcome embedded prejudices only after they came to have confidence in the man, not his arguments.

Much later, in 1968, Eugene McCarthy told me that "if I'm elected, I'll be the first Catholic president"; meaning that Kennedy was only a nominal Catholic, born into a faith whose moral authority was ignored in the conduct of his daily life. "I remember on Fridays," Dave Powers told me, speaking of a time when Catholics were forbidden to eat meat on Friday, "Jack and I would wait till everyone was asleep and then sneak out for a hot dog." If true, it was a venial transgression, a trivial manifestation of a much larger truth: Jack Kennedy was among the most secular of men, his values derived not from his catechism, but from the mainstream of Western thought, Christian and pagan.

Yet he had been baptized at a Catholic font, faithfully observed the prescribed rituals of his Church, and thus had thrust upon him the burden of representing all of Catholic America — the legitimacy of their claim to a place of equal honor and dignity in the larger society. It was partly ironic. But no one was better suited to break the barrier. However, he would never completely overcome the issue of his religion. An upsurge of anti-Catholic sentiment in the closing days of the campaign turned most of the American heartland against his candidacy.

(Shortly after his election, riding down Fifth Avenue, Kennedy leaned out of the car window as he passed St. Patrick's Cathedral and waved toward the church. "Thanks," he said, "thanks a lot.")

The campaign, like any national campaign, was a war of attrition — no swift overwhelming stroke, but constantly chipping away small fragments of doubt and distinterest in hopes that the total of these gargantuan labors would reach a figure impressive enough to win and/or retain the support of a majority.

No one speech, no single performance, however brilliant, could dispose of the Catholic "issue," or any other significant personal issue — excessive youth, inadequate experience, apprehensions that this almost exotically glamorous man might wander from the safe mainstream of American political life. Words were easily found, the appropriate formulas of intention readily crafted, but trust in the man came with slow, painful hesitation. Each day, many times each day, in every corner of the country, new audiences listened and observed — a handful in direct attendance, the rest absorbing fragmentary accounts filtered through the typewriters of hurried, exhausted journalists, diluted by the mechanical revision of a hundred rewrite desks.

In the beginning, apart from the big occasions when the crowd or the special challenge seemed to pump him up, Kennedy's voice was rapid and rushed; he appeared unsure as to the proper manner and posture of a man who was seeking the presidency. He was uncomfortable pausing for applause or engaging his audience in rhetorical questions. For several days his sense of privacy prevented him from mentioning that Jackie was not with him because she was pregnant. When he finally got around to it, he spoke with characteristic humor, telling his pre-ultrasound audience: "My wife is at home. She is going to have a boy in November." This inevitably led to a question from the audience: "There are a lot of expectant fathers who would like to know your secret of knowing that it is going to be a boy." "She told me," Kennedy said with a broad grin. "You have to ask her." There was much laughter.

In every state the candidate would buy television time for a brief speech before a local assembly followed by a period of questions from the audience. But who was watching? And what did they hear? Not many, and not much. "Listen, Dave," Kennedy said to Dave Powers, "would you leave the bar in Charlestown [Massachusetts] to go watch a political speech? I sure as hell wouldn't." And the ratings confirmed his assertion. Even when we commandeered a national network, the average audience was less than ten million, most of them, we assumed, among the politically interested citizens who had already made up their minds.

"There's only one way we can break through the paper curtain," Kennedy had told us. "Television. At least people can listen to what I say, not what some reporter says I said. . . ." But we had already discovered that buying television time was not enough. We needed an audience. And, miraculously, Richard Nixon assured us an audience large enough to satisfy the most insatiable politician.

To Nixon, the decision to debate Kennedy must have seemed unavoidable, and perhaps it was. He had a lead, but a narrow one. A refusal to meet his adversary in personal combat might have been turned against him, used to cast doubt on his claims to superior knowledge, wisdom, and manly courage. Moreover, Nixon had, inevitably, been seduced by his own assaults on Kennedy's incapacities. ("Kennedy," Nixon told an intimate, "speaks over people's heads. I did pretty well with Khrushchev. I'll murder Kennedy.") He would beat him, and thus win the election on his own. Without Ike.

The debate was scheduled for September 26. The day before, the "issue team" — Ted Sorensen, Mike Feldman from our Washington office, and I — descended on Chicago to begin preparation. Since only two writers traveled with Kennedy continually, and I was by far the junior, it was my task to maneuver safely a large nylon suitcase and a footlocker — both crammed with memos, reprints, drafts, and reference material — from hotel room to plane and back again, each day of the campaign. To supplement our traveling files, Mike had prepared a ponderous volume fixed in a black binder, cataloging by issue virtually every recorded Nixon comment over the last several years. Fondly known to us as the "Nixopedia," the work was to supply material to attack the vice-president's frequent deceits and contradictions.

In the use of this reference material we were guided by a handful of instructions and comments scrawled on a note pad by Kennedy (still obedient to his throat doctor) during the preceding days: "We've got to recognize," he exhorted, "that he's just going to move from lie to lie about us in the next eight weeks. And we've got to get ours about him. I haven't yet said anything about him that's in error, except that he favored flexible price supports." Or, "We ought to have the quote of Nixon or some Republican about being 'a conservative at home — a revolutionary (liberal) abroad.' Then we say it can't be done. Wilson — Roosevelt — Truman succeeded abroad because they succeeded at home."

We worked through the night preparing index cards with single-sentence statements of Kennedy's position on a wide variety of domestic issues, some supporting facts, Nixon's probable position, and suggested rejoinders. As we labored, Kennedy was completing a campaign swing through nearby Ohio, where a perceptive listener might have guessed the candidate's mind was elsewhere. "It is possible for us to win Ohio and it is possible for us to lose Ohio," he told a partisan crowd at the Hotel Hollenback. (Kennedy, his brilliant political intuition still intact, was right as usual: We lost Ohio.)

The next morning, our unrested minds partially restored by several cups of coffee, we brought our heap of cards to Kennedy's suite, where the candidate, braced by a pair of pillows, sat in bed, alone, a discarded breakfast tray beside him, awaiting his assistants. With a voice-saving gesture he greeted us and reached for the products of our labor.

Throughout the morning he read the cards, stopping only to question the accuracy of our statements, substitute a more congenially phrased summation of his own, or ask for additional information. "Get Flemming's statement on medical care," he instructed (Arthur Flemming was Eisenhower's secretary of health), "and show how ours would have cost less. We tied ours to a tax increase. He didn't." Every request sent one of us rushing from the room to search the files or, if necessary, to telephone our "issue section" in Washington, captained by later Solicitor General Archibald Cox.

I was learning what it meant to be a professional. Tonight was it; the whole ball game. At least it might be. Yet there was no outward sign of tension, no reference to the import of the occasion, to disturb our subdued concentration on the particulars. We might as well have been preparing for a press conference in Albuquerque, except for the occasional appearance of family members who had, to this point, been pursuing their separate tasks. Bobby entered the suite, sat for about twenty minutes, left silently to check out the details of logistics and studio arrangements. Eunice, children in hand, came in, turned her cheek for a kiss, and then — "Come, children, Uncle Jack is busy" — left the room.

At lunchtime we returned to our rooms to revise the cards, fill in gaps, rephrase statements — all in compliance with the candidate's laconic directions. As we left, I saw Kennedy pick up the morning papers, looking — I presume — for late news reports that might be mentioned during the evening's discussion. On our return, we again reviewed the range of possible questions, Kennedy silently absorbing our work and explanatory comments, rehearsing only in the privacy of his own mind.

Ted Sorensen handed him the draft of a suggested opening statement. "Too rhetorical," he said, "let me give it a try," motioning us to leave the room while he dictated to Evelyn Lincoln, his personal secretary; recalling us about forty minutes later to take the newly typed draft with instructions to "clean it up"; and then, the debate only a few hours away, announcing, "I'm going to take a nap; be back here around seven." On returning to my room, I found that I had left some of my notes in the candidate's suite. I returned, entering on tiptoe — candidates did not then have Secret Service guards to obstruct intruders; that protection was provided only after Robert Kennedy's assassination — and walked to the oval glass table where the debris of the day's work was strewn. The suite was silent. He's actually sleeping, I thought wonderingly, then glimpsed Eunice and her children entering behind me. A whispered maternal comment triggered a sudden, loud exchange between the children. There was a roar from the inner bedroom — "What the hell's going on out there?" I ran, never looking back. The sister could take care of herself.

Meanwhile, on another Chicago street, Richard Nixon spent the day in his hotel room, alone with his thoughts. He too was a professional, unwilling to reveal outward signs of strain, but choosing to protect himself from observation not through inner discipline, but by seclusion behind closed doors. In the studio that night, Nixon would pace along the slightly raised stage in short, nervous steps, occasionally arousing himself to a forced, barely comprehensible, attempt at humor.

The debate less than a hour away, we reentered the candidate's suite. Bobby was already there, along with Kenny O'Donnell and

Dave Powers. We handed him a freshly typed, "cleaned up" copy of his opening statement. "How about makeup?" Bobby asked. "There's a man here." "I don't think so," Kennedy replied, "just some talcum," and entered the bathroom to brush some Mennen over his naturally — or pharmaceutically — sanguine features.

I sat with a small group of staff members before a television set, elation mounting as the debate unfolded. Our man was, as we had anticipated, in command of his material, calm, his serious intensity of conviction occasionally interrupted by flashes of humor. He could have been talking to a small group in a friendly living room. And he was. To millions of groups in millions of rooms.

But Nixon!

Admittedly he knew his answers, was quick to prod Kennedy's presumed vulnerabilities. But the camera showed something else: a man strangely severed from his own shrewd, reasoned discourse. Facial muscles tensed, sweat appearing on brow and cheeks, lips occasionally forced into a smile unrelated to his words, Nixon appeared more like a losing football coach summoned before the board of trustees than a leader of the free world. Afterward analysts and apologists would blame Nixon's dismaying appearance on his makeup, the lighting, the erroneous advice of technicians. But we knew better. The country sensed it. What we saw on Nixon's face that night was the panic in his soul.

As the moderator signed off, our small band erupted in cheers. I was jubilant. It was over! We had won! Not just the debate. We had won the election!

Leaving the studio, Kennedy departed for the airport where an ebullient campaign staff greeted him with applause as he boarded the *Caroline* for a flight to Hellriegel's Inn in Painesville, Ohio, where he was to give a breakfast speech pledging full employment for the workers of that industrial state. Relaxing with a beer and a bowl of tomato soup, Kennedy, although physically and mentally exhausted, was clearly satisfied with his night's work. Almost compulsively, as if unwilling to admit the debate was over, he rehearsed his answers and those of Nixon with almost total recall. "We'll need something better on education," he said, as if already preparing for the next debate or, just as likely, inwardly trying to reedit the hour that had just passed. To me it all seemed too subdued, too matter-of-fact. We had beaten the bastard, hadn't we; nothing could stop us now. Yet we all restrained our shared elation in deference to Kennedy's own behavior. Finally, unable to hold back, I blurted, "We've got it won now." Kennedy looked up, smiled. "It was all right," he said and returned to his soup.

He knew what I was too inexperienced, too partisan to realize. It was far from over. Whatever lead the debate had produced would gradually diminish toward virtual extinction by election eve. But the campaign had entered a new dimension. The attacks on Kennedy's youth, immaturity, and inexperience had been answered and destroyed as the cameras revealed, in Teddy White's words, a man who, "obviously, in flesh and blood . . . was the Vice-President's equal." And not just equal; more authentic, more American as Americans would like themselves to be.

The campaign had been stripped of deceptive irrelevancies, except for the indestructible issue of religion. Nixon had forfeited his most telling issues. From now on it would be Democrat against Republican, Kennedy's summon to hazardous greatness against Nixon's assurance of progressive continuity, man against man. You paid your money and took your choice, or, rather, you cast your vote and took your chance.

And though we had not yet shredded the "paper curtain," the debate had made a substantial tear. The crowds that lined the streets and filled the halls swelled in numbers, responding to the candidate with mounting, often near-hysterical intensity. In a single night, television had created its first political celebrity. Riding in a motorcade through Chicago, I watched an uncountable mob break through the fragile police barriers, flowing toward and, it seemed, over our tiny vessels like the unbound walls of ocean rushing toward Pharaoh's legions. In a Buffalo auditorium I was forced to cover my ears against the high-pitched screams that greeted Kennedy's entrance. Then, looking toward the stage, I saw Kennedy wave to the shouting audience before taking his seat. Another breakthrough. Until now the candidate had walked quickly to his place, refusing to acknowledge the shouts of supporters until he had been introduced; a refusal which was part of the same style that impelled him to continue speaking through interrupting bursts of applause, and to decline to put on the varied headgear — ceremonial Indian headdresses or a construction worker's hard hat — presented by his hosts. Milking the crowd for applause, engaging in traditional political horseplay, clearly made Kennedy uncomfortable. Perhaps he felt it an impairment of his dignity, a contradiction to the seriousness of his intent, the majesty of the high office he pursued. Or perhaps some shrewdly calculated judg-

ment — one wholly compatible with his temperament — warned
him that people were not looking for a leader who was also "just
one of the boys."

"For God's sake, Jack," John Bailey told him, "you don't have
to stand up there and take bows. But they're yelling for you. They
came just to see you. At least you can wave." Kennedy didn't
answer Bailey. But that night in Buffalo he smiled and waved. I
saw it myself.

As Kennedy gained confidence, his humor became more evident. In the midst of the campaign Nixon was hospitalized for
several days and Kennedy announced that he would refrain from
all criticism of Nixon while the vice-president was ill. Later, asked
when the moratorium would end, he replied, "Well, I said I would
not mention him unless I could praise him, so I have not mentioned him." When a group of young Republicans kept interrupting his speech with loud chants of "We Want Nixon," he said,
with a cheerful grin, "I don't think you're going to get him, though,"
and the crowd cheered. When Michigan's governor, Mennen Williams, introduced him as potentially the greatest president in the
history of the United States, he suggested that perhaps the governor was overstating it one or two degrees. "George Washington
wasn't a bad president and I do want to say a word for Thomas
Jefferson." The audience loved it.

Aware that he had overtaken Nixon, Kennedy moved swiftly to
conciliate those large and substantial groups who might have some
reason to suspect a candidate who could ignite such emotions,
whose doubts about his responsible moderation would not be stilled
by an impressive television performance. (Was he also his father's
son?) "On our speech to the businessmen Monday," Kennedy
scrawled on his note pad, handing me his instructions across the
narrow aisle of the *Caroline*, "it should be carefully done. And don't
forget to check with the staff of the Joint Committee. Although it
is primarily to mail to a wide business list, it could be very important. It might mean the *Times* support. We should indicate
indirectly that we are not in labor's pocket."

In accordance with the candidate's clearly implied wishes, I
omitted from the "business speech" Kennedy's comment, earlier
that day, when, having finished reading a memorandum detailing
exorbitant defense industry profits, he threw the pages toward the
empty seat beside him and exclaimed, unsmiling — "That's what
makes me anti–big business, they're just as big bastards as my

father said they were." As for the *Times* support, perhaps the speech
made a difference. In any event, wavering until the closing days,
and then only with evident reluctance, the *New York Times* magis-
terially endorsed John F. Kennedy for president. "I'm one of those,"
he later said, referring to a well-known *Times* promotional ad, "who
can truthfully say, I got my job through the *New York Times*."

Day was nullified by night and then restored as we labored
through the unmarked hours of the weeks that followed the debate
to sustain, perhaps extend, our lead. It was not so much the inconclusive polls, but something in the air, intangible but still sensible — the responsive crowds, the warmth of local political leaders, the subtle undertone of respect among the press corps — that
told us the White House was coming closer.

But any danger of overconfidence was swiftly dissipated as we
moved through the industrial heartland into the farm belt. This
was Nixon country. The Kennedy glamour, the youthful assurance blended with thoughtful eloquence, only intensified suspicion. As our caravan moved across the Midwest, its soil-hardened
citizens sensed, somewhere in the hidden depth of folklore and
memory, the "Music Man," the "City Slicker," the ghost of those
pin-striped easterners with their big words and false cordiality who
had slain the beloved William Jennings Bryan.

"Get some of Nixon's quotes on agriculture and compare them
to what Benson said, show the similarities," Kennedy instructed
me as we sat together in his hotel suite, through whose windows
stretched the late-evening moonscape of desolate Nebraska. It was
my job to prepare The Farm Speech — a major exposition of ag-
ricultural policy that was a compulsory exercise for any presidential candidate. It was scheduled for delivery in less than forty-
eight hours at the annual South Dakota Plowing Contest. Ezra
Taft Benson was Eisenhower's acutely unpopular secretary of agriculture; by tying him to Nixon, we would, the theory ran, persuade discontented farmers that Kennedy offered a more abundant future. It was, we both knew, a doomed exercise; no eloquence
of his or mine could persuade the skeptical, deeply conservative
tillers of the soil that this slick, sophisticated urban youth with the
strange accent and foreign faith knew the pains of their labor,
could respond to their distress. But we had to try. It was a mandatory tradition for one who sought to be president "of all the
people."

"I've got all the material right here," I said, patting a file folder crammed with memos from farm experts, "but tell me one thing, Senator, what's a plowing contest?"

The senator's broad grin momentarily dissolved his weariness. "Don't worry, Dick, you don't have to enter. And I've got a bad back. They'll do the plowing, you just worry about the speech."

"After we blast Nixon, I assume you want to give your program."

"Do I have one?" He smiled, then more seriously: "Give them the whole thing from our position on parity to Food for Peace. They may get a little bored listening, but not as much as I will saying it. They're not the jolliest bunch in the world."

I retreated to my own room, working to piece together a comprehensive statement of farm policy from the recommendations of assorted farm state politicians and academic experts who had contributed their thoughts to our traveling files. The next night I brought the completed draft to Kennedy. He read it in silence, and with the same degree of understanding I had brought to my writing. After finishing, he looked up. "Just think, Dick, here we are, a couple of Brookline farmers, preparing policy for the entire country. Isn't politics wonderful?" (Kennedy had been born in Brookline, the Boston suburb where I had gone to high school.) "Let's go with it." As I took the draft from his hand and walked toward the door, the candidate called out after me, "Remember, Dick, I don't want to make policy, I want to make votes." (As it turned out, we didn't make either.)

At 3 A.M. my phone rang. It was Kennedy. "Look," he said, "about that speech. I want to be sure I don't fall on my face. Call Hubert [Humphrey] in the morning and read it to him. Make sure it's right."

Shortly after dawn, the plowing contest only hours away, I telephoned Hubert and read him the speech. "Wonderful, Dick," he said, "it's just what I would have said myself." (Of course it was. The program memos had been prepared for us by Hubert's staff.) "It's okay with Hubert," I told the candidate at breakfast. He grunted unresponsively, took the speech, put it in his coat pocket, and resumed his inward meditation over the ordeal that lay ahead.

Later that afternoon Kennedy stood in a South Dakota fairground, presenting his "farm policy" to a huge crowd of dour, unresponsive farmers who listened to him with all the animation of a wheat field rooted to the earthen plain. "Well, that's over," he said, as we boarded the *Caroline* for the next stop. "Fuck the farmers after November."

"They loved it," I said in false reassurance.

"They've got a funny way of showing it," he answered. "Now where's my speech on how peace can be maintained?"

Late on the evening of October 13 we flew into Ann Arbor, Michigan, where Kennedy was to begin the next day of campaigning. As our bus entered the Michigan campus we saw a large group of students who had abandoned books and bed to witness the candidate's arrival. Sorensen turned to me: "He won't just let them stand there; he's going to speak. Maybe that'll give us a chance to get something to eat. I'm starved." (In a campaign, never knowing when the next meal might arrive, one eats at every moment of opportunity, which is why most of us were gaining weight.) Fortunately the school cafeteria had stayed open in anticipation of Kennedy's late arrival. As we entered, we could glimpse Kennedy mounting a stone staircase beneath which students were hastily assembling. Ted knew his man.

I had just passed from the overdone Salisbury steak to a soggy piece of lemon meringue pie when a member of the press staff rushed in, sat down facing us across the table, and wearily announced, "You know what he just did? He proposed a Peace Corps."

The concept of a Peace Corps — a group of young Americans sent to work among the citizens of underdeveloped lands — had been mentioned by other liberal democrats, Hubert Humphrey among them, but had never developed into a serious possibility. Now, this very night, Kennedy had adopted the idea and made it his: not a piece of Senate rhetoric, or an obscure plank in an unread party platform, but a specific promise, a pledge to action, from a man who was about to become president.

Within two days after Kennedy's extemporaneous advocacy, seven hundred students at the University of Michigan had signed up for service in the nonexistent agency, and in subsequent days, at nearly every stop, we saw groups of young people with placards and leaflets proclaiming their desire to serve.

The unexpected magnitude of response was not the result of some chemical connection between the youthful candidate and his even younger audience. Inadvertently, intuitively, Kennedy had tapped into a still-emerging spirit of the times. "Give us the sixties," he had said at a time when the decade had not yet acquired its metaphorical meaning of tumultuous change unleashed by the desire to transform the nation. It was one thing to tell young people that "they could make a difference," that together "they could change the world." It was something else — much more — to offer a tangible, specific instrument for the fulfillment of those vague exhortations. The Peace Corps was such an instrument, and the almost instantaneous, excited reaction was proof that the hopeful assumption that lay behind the Kennedy rhetoric was grounded in an emerging reality. Later he was to exhort Americans to ask what they could do for their country. Tonight, in the cold air of Michigan's fall, he was telling them what they could do. A challenge that was also a promise. And they loved it.

There were no such generously peaceful impulses in Atlanta, Georgia, that same week, when, on October 19, police arrested Martin Luther King for refusing to leave the all-white restaurant of a department store. Taken immediately to court, King was sentenced to four months at hard labor.

The morning after King's imprisonment, resting in his motel room, beginning to prepare for his fourth and last debate with Nixon, Kennedy was interrupted by a telephoned suggestion from his brother in Washington, that he "might want to intervene" directly on behalf of King. Kennedy turned to the handful of staff members who had already assembled to begin the day's work. "What do you think?" he asked. The political advisers, led by Kenny O'Donnell, expressed opposition. "You have no legitimate right to interfere with the judicial system of Alabama"; "It's a local concern"; "Our position in the South is already precarious, and this can only antagonize the white political leaders whose organizations are essential to electoral success."

As the discussion continued, I saw Sarge Shriver standing at the entrance to the room. He silently motioned me to join him. "Listen, Dick," he said, "do me a favor. I'll wait outside. You come and tell me when Kenny and the others have left."

In a few minutes, having made their argument without any response from the candidate, mistaking silence for acquiescence, the staff members departed. Lingering a moment, until I heard their departing footsteps at the end of the hall, I went to Shriver: "Now's your chance, Sarge." He entered the candidate's bedroom where I could hear sounds of a brief, intense exchange. I could not make out the words. Shriver left the room smiling. Kennedy, now alone, picked up the phone and placed a call to Coretta King, told her of his shock and outrage at her husband's mistreatment, promised to "do all I can." The next call went to Robert Kennedy. We had friends in Georgia, and more important, allies among politicians whose own ambitions were linked to Kennedy's increasing likelihood of success. Someone called someone. Someone called the judge. And that day Martin Luther King was released from confinement in the Atlanta jail. Reverend King and his wife gave Kennedy public credit. Martin Luther King's father — also a minister — announced that he would put love of family above religious principle and cast his own vote for a Catholic. ("Well, I guess we've all got fathers," Kennedy said on hearing of the elder King's renunciation of his anti-Catholic convictions.)

More than all the speeches, the eloquent assertions of support for civil rights and racial equality, the rhetorical demands for an end to black oppression, that single act — the calculated impulse of a late October morning — persuaded large numbers of blacks that Kennedy had within him the right answer to the only question that matters amid fierce social conflict: Which side are you on?

> Down in Harlan County
> There are no neutrals there,
> You either are a union man
> Or a thug for J. H. Blair.

As the King story spread through northern ghettos, black support for Kennedy — hitherto ambivalent or disinterested — began to solidify, acquired the added enthusiasm necessary to persuade black Americans that their choice at the polls might make a difference, that Whitey was still Whitey, but some more so than others. In an election decided by a handful of votes in a few key states, that political reward was of enormous consequence. Joseph P. Kennedy's most insightful political aphorism had again proved its wisdom: "When in doubt," the old man said, "do right."

Two days later, on October 21, on the edge of his final debate with Kennedy, his pride drowned by panic, a humble Nixon asked Eisenhower to intervene; and the tide began to move against us. For the next fifteen days we would fight to hold a diminishing lead.

Eisenhower's appearances transcended politics. Tumultuous

throngs crowded city streets to cheer their final glimpse of the departing leader — admired for himself and as living symbol of America's most glorious triumph. We were being hurt. And we knew it. But how much? The questions would only be answered at the polls.

Kennedy, himself, responded to the situation with a metaphor. "While we meet tonight," he told an audience in California, "the rescue squad has been completing its operation in the city of New York. Governor Rockefeller, Henry Cabot Lodge, the vice-president, and President Eisenhower all rode up together. We have all seen these circus elephants complete with tusks, ivory on their head and thick skins, who move around the circus ring and grab the tail of the elephant ahead of them." The crowd laughed and then broke into cheers. "Dick Nixon grabbed that tail in 1952 and 1956, but this year he faces the American people alone. We are choosing a president of the U.S. President Eisenhower is not running. Mr. Nixon is. And the American people have to choose between Mr. Nixon and the Republican party that he represents and the Democratic party and progress."

It was quintessential Kennedy. The challenge blunted by humor, the avoidance of direct attack on Eisenhower, the issue restored to perspective — a contest between parties, a call to reject Nixon. Yet the repetition of this same rejoinder at nearly every campaign stop was itself evidence of the candidate's mounting apprehension. But it was the best we could do. Ike was in the field. He could not be censured for supporting his party's chosen successor. We could only hope that Eisenhower had come too late.

As we accelerated our efforts in the final weeks, forcing our energies through the deepening quagmire of fatigue, thoughtful judgment was displaced by instinct. It was all we had left. "The mornings are the worst," Kennedy told me. "It's like a pitcher." (Meaning that an overworked pitcher must somehow manage to survive the hazardous early innings before regaining his groove.)

Nixon demanded a fifth, and unscheduled, debate. Although we immediately expressed our own ardent desire for a last confrontation, privately we wanted to avoid it. In the three debates that followed his initial victory, Kennedy had at least held his own; thus fortifying the favorable impression he had made on the country. The debates had already served his purpose. A fifth debate offered little prospect of further gain, and carried the hazard of some unintentional error by the tiring Kennedy, or some novel

Nixon attack that the few remaining days would give us little chance
to answer. Since we could not — politically — refuse the vice-
president, we negotiated instead. Representatives of the candidates argued about the subject matter, the format, the timing —
while both Kennedy and Nixon accused each other of fearful unwillingness to reach agreement. (The technique is not novel; it has
been demonstrated at arms control conferences for decades.) There
would be no fifth debate.

It was a mistake.

Until now, the attention of the electorate had been focused on
the drama of personal confrontation, nullifying the Republican
advantage of superior resources — money for television, radio, literature, organization. Liberated from the equalizing distraction of
another debate, the Republicans poured money into television and
radio ads. While we were actually canceling scheduled appearances for lack of funds, they multiplied their effort, culminating in
Nixon's four-hour national broadcast the day before election. The
mounting, largely unanswered, barrage of media hurt us. The dimensions of that damage could not be measured, but much of it
could have been prevented had we allowed a fifth debate to dominate the final week.

There was to be one more mistake. It was a beaut. And I
made it.

Our precipitous, interminable journey through America taught
us that Cuba was a dominant issue of foreign policy. (All foreign-
policy issues were thought less important than domestic concerns;
which is why I so often composed drafts about external affairs
while Sorensen dealt with the "bread and butter.") The unexpected emergence of an anti-American, pro-Soviet dictator "only
ninety miles from our shores," "only eight minutes [by air] from
our coast," had done more than Khrushchev could to anger and
alarm the American people. At every major evening stop members
of the audience would submit written questions to be answered by
Kennedy. Later that night, reclining on the *Caroline*, I would read
through the multitude of queries, most of which — for lack of
time — had gone unanswered. Everywhere — in the Dakotas as
well as Florida — there were more questions about Cuba and Castro
than about any other matter of foreign policy.

Informed by our totally nonscientific sample, we made the "issue of Cuba" a major staple of our campaign. In dozens of speeches
we assailed Nixon and the Republicans for losing Cuba to our

communist adversaries. ("Ike didn't lose it," Kennedy scribbled
in the margin of one of these speeches, "he gave it away.") We
censured the feeble Republican response to this new danger; proposed further sanctions, a step-up of propaganda, action to "quarantine" the Cuban revolution, increased support for those Cubans, in exile and elsewhere, who opposed the Castro regime.

As our rhetorical assault mounted in the closing weeks of the
campaign, Kennedy was careful to strike from my drafts any implication that we would act forcibly to overthrow Castro. We would
observe international law, and act in concert with our fellow
members of the Organization of American States.

The reasons for Kennedy's caution were more than political. As
a presidential candidate, he had received secret briefings by the
CIA, some of which revealed that we were training a force of Cuban exiles for a possible invasion of the Cuban mainland. Kennedy felt it imperative that he not reveal, even by indirection, the
secret knowledge with which he had been entrusted. The rest of
us, of course, were not briefed, had no knowledge that a U.S.-
sponsored attack on Castro was being prepared.

In late October, en route to New York, Kennedy told me to
"get ready a real blast for Nixon." Later that evening, sitting in
the crowded staff room of the Biltmore Hotel, I typed out still
another assault on the administration's Cuban policy. The statement was little more than a rephrased version of what we had
said a dozen times. Or so it seemed to me. Buried in the third
point of a lengthy series of proposals was the exhortation: "We
must attempt to strengthen the non-Batista, democratic, anti-Castro
forces in exile, and in Cuba itself, who offer eventual hope of over-
throwing Castro. Thus far these fighters for freedom have had
virtually no support from our government." "Strengthen," "support," were vague injunctions, a harmless rephrasing of earlier
rhetorical flights. I called Kennedy at the Hotel Carlyle to read
him the statement. He was asleep. I consulted with other staff
members. None of us had the heart to wake the weary candidate
for this trivial restatement of his position. Yet it had to be released
almost immediately if we were to meet the morning paper deadline. Others read it and — our concentration obscured by fatigue
and the press of other business — we saw no danger. So we released it. It was the only public statement by the candidate in the
entire campaign that he had not personally reviewed.

And the next day the roof fell in.

We were wildly irresponsible, Nixon proclaimed, the advocates of an American-sponsored revolution, possibly even an invasion, contrary to all sound foreign policy, in violation of our international agreements, certain to cripple our interests throughout the world. (Nixon, of course, knew all about the tentative invasion plans.) Kennedy, he said — more in feigned sorrow than in pretended anger — was too inexperienced, too impulsive, to understand the horrifying consequences of his ill-conceived proposals.

Establishment columnists and stately editorialists, although speaking, as they always do, in more subdued and equivocal language, joined the censure. "Senator Kennedy made what is probably his worst blunder of the campaign," James Reston wrote in the *New York Times* the following Sunday. "His statement this week on Cuba, publicly calling for government aid to overthrow Castro, is a clear violation of the Inter-American treaty prohibition against intervention in the international affairs of the hemisphere republics." We were quick to reply that the malevolently deceitful Nixon had deliberately misinterpreted our words, that the use of American force was neither called for nor contemplated. Unfortunately Kennedy could not violate the trust of his secret briefings to expose Nixon's hypocrisy in so violently denouncing the use of force which he, personally, was already engaged in preparing.

Finally, the furor subsided, leaving behind some small residue of distrust, some slight stirring of almost abandoned apprehensions.

Would it have made a difference had we shown the statement to Kennedy? Probably. With his knowledge of CIA planning, my language would have seemed too militant, too close to disclosure of top-secret possibilities. Although I did not know of the CIA's activities, just the same, my usual meticulous caution of phraseology had deserted me. "It was the words 'freedom fighters,'" Kennedy later said to me, "that's what caused the problem."

The next night, on the *Caroline,* the candidate pointed toward me and Sorensen: "If I win this thing, I won it; but if I lose it, you guys lost it." There was no other reproach. Never. One could love a man like that.

It was almost over. In one last Herculean surge, in the final five days, Kennedy carried his message from California to Phoenix and Albuquerque, to Amarillo and Oklahoma City, Roanoke and Toledo, as if we could enfold the entire gigantic continent in one final embrace.

"Kenny, what am I doing here?" the candidate asked O'Donnell as the *Caroline* touched down in New York for a final two days of campaigning before he would go north through New England toward home. "During the day you've got a motorcade through the different boroughs," O'Donnell responded, "then tonight is the speech at Madison Square Garden."

"I don't mean what," Kennedy said, his voice rising in obvious irritation, "I mean why. I've already got New York. I should be out in California right now, that's where it might make a difference. Who approved this schedule anyway?"

"You did, Senator," O'Donnell replied. Kennedy did not respond. His question was rhetorical, born of weariness and mounting concern over Nixon's unexpectedly strong final drive. The trip to New York — a grand climax to the long campaign — had been planned long before. Yet Kennedy's acute political instincts were wholly accurate. New York was safe. California was on the edge. (He would lose that state by the narrowest of margins.) But it was too late. The ponderous machinery of a presidential campaign could not be abruptly thrown into reverse, sent racing back across the continent.

That afternoon, as the Kennedy motorcade inched through the streets of Queens and the Bronx, I sat with Dave Powers in the senator's suite at the Carlyle Hotel making some final revisions in the speech he was to deliver at the Garden to a sell-out audience of Democratic leaders and party faithful. Kennedy was scheduled to return to the Carlyle in the late afternoon, go over his speech, and then proceed to a pre-speech reception for party dignitaries and large donors at the Biltmore Hotel. I finished my work, chatted amiably with Dave, watched as the early November dusk darkened the Manhattan streets. But Kennedy did not arrive. Uneasily I turned to Dave. "Are you sure he's coming here first?" Dave checked the schedule. "That's what it says." Now it was almost 6 P.M., the candidate was to give a major address in only two hours, and his speech — unedited and unread — was sitting on the coffee table between us.

"Looks like you'll have to give the speech, Dave," I said. "We seem to have lost the candidate." Powers went to the phone and called the Biltmore, where an agitated aide responded: "Where the hell are you guys?"

"We're right here," Dave answered calmly.

"Well the candidate's here, and he's raising hell about his speech."

Grabbing the draft, Dave and I immediately took a taxi to the midtown Biltmore. A frantic O'Donnell greeted us at the door to the senator's suite. "The motorcade got lost," he said; "we spent the whole afternoon riding around the Bronx trying to find some crowds. They were supposed to call you from the car."

"No one called," I said. "Where is he?"

"Inside," said O'Donnell, pointing to a closed door which opened to a small side bedroom. The suite was already crowded with dignitaries, many in formal dress, including the legendary leaders of New York's badly divided Democratic party — former Senator Lehman and Eleanor Roosevelt, Carmine De Sapio and Mike Prendergast — along with an assortment of wealthy contributors and the liberal social elite of Manhattan.

I followed O'Donnell into the bedroom where Kennedy, dressed only in his undershorts, sat in front of a table on which a waiter had placed a large metal canister containing his dinner. Standing beside him, an agitated Pierre Salinger was absorbing the brunt of the candidate's fury. "It's that fucking De Sapio," Kennedy said, "he screwed the whole thing up. It's bad enough that I'm in New York when I should be in California," directing a piercing glance at O'Donnell, "but then to waste the whole day riding around in the boondocks. I'll take care of those guys after Tuesday, when I don't need them anymore. I don't know how we let these things happen."

As the senator continued his enraged monologue, O'Donnell and Salinger valiantly exited the room, leaving me alone with Kennedy. "Where's my speech?" he asked me. "I've got to give the damn thing in less than two hours." I handed it to him silently. This was no time for explanations. "I better eat first," he said, placing the draft on the table, opening the metal food warmer, and grabbing a plate. "Shit," he said, pulling back his hand and shaking it — the plate was very hot. "You get it," he said, pointing to the food and turning to look at the speech draft. I was committed, but not that committed, and went to the bathroom for a towel that would let me withdraw the food without burning myself. Already immersed in the draft, Kennedy began to make changes and insertions while I stood there cutting his steak into bite-sized pieces. Well, if we lose, I thought silently, I'll always be able to get a job as a waiter.

"Thanks," he said, and turned to his food, his rage returning as he began to eat. "Who the hell was leading that motorcade?" he erupted. "I'd like to find the son-of-a-bitch who was driving."

"I don't know, Senator," I replied; "he's probably outside."

With that, Kennedy leaped from his chair, strode to the door, and still clad in underpants, walked through the suddenly silenced assembly of stunned guests and headed straight for a nondescript man standing on the far side of the room. "Are you the driver?" Kennedy asked. 'Yes, sir." "Well next time get a road map." Then, his anger abated, seemingly oblivious to the unbelieving stares of his reception guests, Kennedy returned to the bedroom, closed the door, and began to revise his speech.

Less than thirty minutes later, clad in evening dress, the tall, handsome senator emerged and began his rounds of the suite, greeting each guest with a friendly handshake and a quip, totally controlled, his calm, amiable presence dominating the room.

About an hour later, Kennedy stood in front of an audience brought to attentive silence by his eloquent summation of the campaign, making only occasional references to the prepared text whose themes he seemed somehow to have mastered amid the turbulence of his still-undigested meal, relying on his own command of language and sense of the audience to impart renewed vitality to my carefully crafted prose. As usual — at least on large occasions — Kennedy made the speech written by someone else into his own — a powerful emanation of his own passions and ideas.

"If I am elected next Tuesday," Kennedy proclaimed, "I want to be a president who does not speak from the rear of the battle but who places himself in the thick of the fight . . . a president who fights for great ideals as well as legislation . . . a president who cares deeply about the people he represents . . . to share in the benefits of our abundance and natural resources. . . . I want above all else to be a president known as one who not only prevented war but won the peace — as one of whom history might say: He not only laid the foundation for peace in his time, but for generations to come.

"I run with the view that this is a great country, but it can be greater . . . to see us build a strong and vital and progressive society that will serve as an inspiration to all those people who desire to follow the road of freedom . . . in 1960 the cause of all mankind is the cause of America.

"I am not promising action in the first 100 days alone — I am promising you 1000 days of exacting presidential leadership."

Then the journey home, through Connecticut and Rhode Island, where large crowds waited late into the night for a sight of

their fellow New Englander, finally entering Boston Garden to be
cheered by a tumultuous, adoring crowd, liberally scattered with
admiring politicians — Massachusetts' only indigenous crop —
wondering how he did it; and if him, why not me? It was a great
day for the Irish.

And then the silence.

What had begun as a confident adventure had ended in fatigue
and doubt. Toward the end of the campaign, I would be startled
into wakefulness by the ring of the hotel wake-up call. I lay there
for a moment, my first thought "if only it was over," and then
stumbled toward the window looking for a sign to remind me where
we were — what city? which state? "The Albuquerque Trust," that
meant New Mexico; or "The Minneapolis Register," yes, the dairy
speech was ready. Yet in all that time I never doubted that Kennedy would win. Not until election day.

The Monday before election Tuesday, Nixon had spent four
hours on national television answering telephoned questions from
viewers across the country. As I stood in a long line before my
polling place in Brookline, Massachusetts, I overheard two women
discussing the Nixon telethon. "He was very impressive," one said.
"I think I'm going to vote for him," responded her companion.
My heart sank; maybe he had done it after all, maybe the bastard
had caught us. Only yesterday it had seemed impossible. How
could Nixon — a man like Nixon — defeat our hero?

My mind instantly recalled an image of the day before. Sitting
on the *Caroline*, the staff crowded toward the front seats where a
television set was precariously balanced on the edge of a bench,
showing the Nixon performance, I walked to the back of the plane,
where Kennedy sat behind a closed door in his small private compartment containing a narrow bunk and lounge chair to provide
him with occasional rest and privacy from his bustling, talkative
crew. "Nixon's on television, Senator," I said, "if you want to
watch." "I don't think so," he replied, his calm, almost indifferent
air betrayed by the rhythmic rapping of his hand along the arm
of his chair; a rare display of inner stress, which he nearly always
kept so perfectly concealed, even from his closest colleagues. He
had known then, I thought as I neared the voting booth; he could
feel it slipping away.

On the afternoon of election day, Ted Sorensen, Mike Feldman,
and I drove through the ugly, unkempt southern fringe of Boston,

entered the tree-walled corridor of Route 3 that concealed the towns
of the South Shore, crossed the high-arched bridge over the Cape
Cod Canal; and sped down the Mid-Cape Highway, to Hyannis — its semirural ambience still resistant to the ravaging development that has since destroyed its restorative tranquillity.

For the first time in what seemed forever, we had nothing to
do — no speeches to prepare, no information to gather, no public
issues or political strategy to debate. The intensities of the long
campaign had so compressed our memories that it seemed as if
our lives had spun into an unanticipated vacancy. We were disengaged, irrelevant; judgment had now fled to other hands. The
liberating release dissolved our weariness. (It would return.) We
sang, joked, played word games. One of us would give a phrase
that was the answer to a question which his companions must
guess. Teddy White would later immortalize this game, citing as
illustrations of our youthful brilliance an exchange in which the
answer was Nine W; the correct question, "Do you spell your
name with a *V*, Professor Wagner?" (Nein! W — get it?) Unfortunately for historical accuracy, although the "answer" was proposed, none of us could guess the question. On several occasions
during the quarter century that followed I have been asked, admiringly, to verify White's account. And I always complied. No
one wishes to destroy a legend, especially when he is part of it.
But the hell with it.

That night I awaited the returns in the Yachtsman Motel overlooking the cold, November waters of Buzzards Bay, I read, watched
television, restlessly walked the corridors talking to other staff
members, had a few beers with the reporters who had become
friends during the long journey. As the approach of dawn brought
the near-certainty of victory, I may have been the only person in
the motel with ambivalent feelings about the future. For years,
chance, ambition, and a certain weakness of will had postponed
my intention — dating from high school — to be a writer. First
there was law school, then Frankfurter, the quiz show investigations, the campaign. Now I would almost certainly, at the age of
twenty-eight, be asked to join the White House staff. How could
I refuse? The opportunity was extraordinary — to participate in
the power of the presidency at so young an age. Yet I also was
afraid — tormented by the prospect that further postponement of
my inner ambition would irretrievably fracture the edge of possibility.

I had a talent for politics; understood it by instinct; loved the combat of mind and physical energies; believed that we could — would — accomplish great things for the country I loved. Yet it might be a trap — inextricable, decisive. And perhaps it was. One cannot be both in the world and out of it. But even as I wrestled with conflicting passions I knew there was no choice. Whether from weakness or ambition, conviction or attraction to the manifold pleasures of public life, I would stay with Kennedy.

For now I would put aside my doubts; rather, I felt them dissolve in the almost sensual thrill of victory — not a culminating triumph, but the promise, almost limitless in dimensions, of enormous possibilities yet to come. I felt it. Certainly Kennedy felt it. And, I was sure, on that fresh new morning, that the people we had wooed and won — even the doubters and the reluctant — sensed that this was something different from an ordinary presidential election; that the nation had begun to move and they were moving with it. At least I thought they felt that way. They should have, dammit. It was true, wasn't it? And what did it matter? We had world enough and time to transform this election into a day the future would remember.

> Plodding feet, tramp, tramp
>   The Grand Old Party is breaking camp
> Blare of bugles, din, din, din
>   The New Frontier is moving in.
>   (modified from Robert Sherwood)

Thus I, the reluctant suitor, yielded with surprising ease to the exultant arms of victory. Naturally there was, in this ready acquiescence, something of personal ambition. I had cast an occasional longing eye as I passed the White House on my way to work. But it was more than that. I was going to help change America. Me. Dick Goodwin. A kid from Brookline. And not through solitary thought and pronouncement, but by action. The goals were vaguely defined; would be modified by fate and uncontrollable events. But there was greatness in it. I was sure of that. At least I was sure that morning as I watched the westward-moving sun crimson the familiar waters of Buzzards Bay, signaling the approach of Kennedy's early-morning drive to the auditorium from which he would graciously assent to the power he had so tenaciously pursued.

7 / To the White House

DURING the interlude between election and inauguration known as the "transition," I worked in the Senate office while other staff members and family companioned the president-elect as he shuttled between Palm Beach and his Georgetown home. The center of decision was — as it had been during the campaign, and would remain in the White House — with Kennedy himself. Yet the staff was small, the interchange of commands, ideas, and gossip frequent; and so, even in the comparative isolation of our "lame-duck" office, we were told, or heard, of the discussion which accompanied judgments that would populate and give direction to the approaching administration.

By December we had compiled a formidable list of campaign promises, eighty-one in all, ranging from a promise to build the Rampart Canyon dam (Promise No. 2), use all the "authority and prestige" of the White House to assemble a conclave of Israeli and Arab leaders (Promise No. 47), and issue an executive order ending discrimination in federally supported housing, thus abolishing racial barriers "with a stroke of the pen" (Promise No. 52), Later Kennedy, under mounting pressures to make good on this last pledge, asked Ted Sorensen, "Who the hell wrote that?" "I didn't," Sorensen disclaimed. "Well then," Kennedy replied, "I guess nobody wrote it." In fact, the promise was contained in my draft speech for our campaign trip to Los Angeles, and delivered by Kennedy without the slightest hint of doubt or equivocation; another demonstration that politics is to governing as a cartoon is to an etching.

My principal assignment was to help set up a series of task forces, committees of experts on a wide range of issues — including national security, agriculture, natural resources, Latin America, Africa, and foreign economic policy — to make policy recommendations to the new president. "Just get the best people you can, Dick," Kennedy instructed me. "I don't care who they were for." This did not mean that we were to balance liberals with Goldwater conservatives, but that we should seek useful counsel from those in basic agreement with Kennedy's world view, regardless of their formal political allegiances.

By this time I had decided that I didn't want to be a speechwriter, let alone an assistant speechwriter (under Sorensen). Writing speeches had allowed me a significant role in the pursuit of office. That goal attained, I wanted to be involved — not just in talking about policy but in making it, sharing in the substance of government. As a step toward that ambition, I put myself on the task force on Latin America, headed by redoubtable Adolf Berle, a Wilsonian liberal, whose experience went back to Roosevelt's Good Neighbor policy, and who still remained in touch with a wide range of Latin American leaders and thinkers. The other members included Harvard economics professor Lincoln Gordon, Robert Alexander, an economist at Rutgers who was an expert on the Bolivian revolution, Arturo Morales Carrion, a brilliant "young Turk" of the Muñoz government in Puerto Rico, and Teodoro Moscoso, head of Puerto Rico's successful development agency, Operation Bootstrap.

My own qualifications were much slimmer — a layman's interest in the area, preparation of the candidate's speeches, a short Berlitz course in Spanish. But I had one overriding credential: I was making the choices. And the other members of the task force — most of whom went on to serve in responsible positions as ambassadors, administrators, even assistant secretaries — seemed pleased to have in their ranks one who had direct access to the president-elect. For me, the lengthy, serious discussions were an intensive education; my participation a kind of casting session for the part I would play in the Kennedy presidency. For, unknown to anyone, including me, I was insinuating myself into a very large role in Latin American policy.

I was also drawn into discussions of the most important, controversial, and difficult appointment of all. Who would be secretary of state? Foreign policy was both Kennedy's greatest interest and the source of the most urgent difficulties he would confront. In many ways, Kennedy was our first (and last) foreign-policy president. He had lived in England, the European continent, and very briefly in Argentina (recovering from a youthful ailment on an Argentine ranch); had been in the Pacific during World War II; traveled widely to most other parts of the globe; covered, as a journalist, the birth of the U.N. in San Francisco. Notable citizens from a wide variety of nations had been guests at his family's dinner table; his father's business interests spanned the continents.

Kennedy realized that the leaders of other nations were also politicians, their freedom of action, even under nominal dictatorships, constrained by the circumstances of their national life — the need to retain some measure of popular support, the demands of their military, the influence of those who dominated economic life. The leaders of the Middle East and Asia, like the boss of Chicago, could not defy their constituencies — not completely — without undermining their own authority. Once, after the State Department had objected to his conduct of a personal correspondence with Nasser of Egypt, Kennedy explained: "Nasser's got his problems. I've got my problems. I'm not going to persuade him to act against his interests. I won't even try. But it can't hurt down the line if we understand each other a little better."

This informed tolerance was infiltrated, sometimes distorted, by his personal experience, as observer and participant, of the Second World War. The man who, as a student, had written *While England Slept* did not intend to allow hope of peace to enfeeble our capacity to make war. The son of a notorious appeaser, personal witness to Chamberlain's folly, was not likely to withdraw before the demands of our Soviet adversary. The fighting sailor of World War II, like many of his generation, derived from his participation in American military exploits a heightened, almost naïve confidence in the country's ability to match any foe, bear any burden necessary to victory. His was a generation of winners. In toppling the formidable military empires of Germany and Japan, they had been imbued with the belief that America possessed reserves of will and strength adequate to any threat. Like many of his fellow veterans he did not fully appreciate — at first — how nuclear weapons had changed the nature and possibility of war; or that obscure, murky, and inconclusive battles within the third world could not be translated into the kind of contest between Western powers that had directed, scarred, and degraded the most bloody century in human history.

For a man so naturally drawn to the arena of global politics, the choice of a secretary of state was crucial. The first choice for this job was Senator J. William Fulbright of Arkansas: intelligent, principled, familiar with the machinery of foreign policy, and as cosmopolitan in outlook and experience as Kennedy himself. But the appointment was politically impossible. Just before Christmas, at her home in Palm Beach, Rose Kennedy confided to her diary, that "on Thursday, Senator Fulbright here for lunch. Had rather hoped to be Secretary of State, but was not chosen because colored people do not like him. . . ." The opposition to Fulbright came not only from blacks who could not abide the elevation of a man who had signed the infamous "Southern manifesto," but from Jewish groups who suspected his oft-displayed warmth toward the Arab states. Kennedy would not begin his administration by antagonizing some of the most loyal and ardent elements of his fragile political coalition. "Why can't I have Fulbright?" the president-elect said to a friendly *Time* magazine correspondent. Then, quietly, "I guess I can't."

Gradually others on the short list of possibilities were eliminated. Adlai Stevenson had refused his chance to secure the position during the campaign, and although that objection was not insuperable, Kennedy didn't like him and was delighted to find, on a visit to Hyde Park, that Eleanor Roosevelt had lost enthusiasm for her former favorite. Bypassing Adlai would not, as Kennedy had feared, antagonize the liberal wing of the party. Chester Bowles was too ethereal, too loquacious, too inclined to lecture the new president about geopolitical morality. David Bruce was "too old," Averell Harriman was a defeated politician who had not yet ingratiated himself with the new administration. That left the virtually unknown Dean Rusk, recommended by Dean Acheson and Walter Lippmann alike. Rusk had been a Rhodes scholar and a professor of government; he had served with the army in the Far East during the Second World War and had ended up at the Rockefeller Foundation, where he was in charge of a variety of programs of health, education, and technical assistance for the underdeveloped countries.

Only later did I understand the often decisive principle of presidential appointment: The deficiencies of those one knows are also known; relative strangers, being remote from experience, appear

unblemished. Neither Kennedy nor those closest to him knew of
Rusk's inadequacies. His credentials were impressive, his sponsors
men of high reputation. And so, through a half-blind process of
elimination, Rusk's name had risen to head the list. There was,
however, one possible obstacle. Rusk had been assistant secretary
of state for Far Eastern affairs during the Korean war. Had he
said or done anything during that period that might jeopardize
his chances of Senate confirmation? Kennedy instructed me to
"check it out." I waded through dozens of tedious articles in foreign-
service journals, read newspaper summaries of Rusk's speeches in
the early fifties, talked to some of his former colleagues at State.
There was nothing, I reported to Kennedy at the end of my labors. Nothing controversial, no sentence or sentiment that might
make him vulnerable to even the most militant defender of pure,
hardheaded patriotism. In retrospect, I was to realize that for a
man to be in charge of the Far East during Korea and never once
utter a controversial sentiment, to evade completely identification
with the numerous miscalculations of that war, evidenced a talent
for avoidance of responsibility, a capacity for bureaucratic survival, which, however admirable in an underling, should have
aroused serious doubts about his ability to occupy the second-
highest position of decision and command.

On a plane ride to New York, I showed the president-elect a
recent copy of *Foreign Affairs,* in which Rusk had written a lengthy
article asserting that the president should be, de facto, his own
secretary of state; that he and he alone should make foreign-policy
decisions. Kennedy's thought exactly. He wanted no Acheson or
Dulles. He would seek counsel, weigh the views of others, but the
judgments were to be his and, once made, faithfully to be obeyed.
Just as Rusk had written.

The decision was taken. Rusk was appointed. And from that
mistake grew the power of National Security Adviser McGeorge
Bundy and the White House foreign-policy staff (as well as my
own, more transient authority), essential to compensate for the
deficiencies of the cautious and inept secretary; while during
Johnson's presidency this initial misjudgment was to have even
more serious consequences. Much later I sat in the White House
mess with Allan Whiting, a State Department specialist on China,
who told me how, during the Korean war, he had gone to inform
Rusk that his analysis of new intelligence indicated an imminent
Chinese intervention against the American armies that had swept

through North Korea toward the Chinese border. "They wouldn't dare," was Rusk's only reply. Whiting would be exiled to a listening post in Hong Kong, while Rusk would become secretary of state.

Aside from occasional, marginal involvements in the appointment process, my time was consumed with the policy task forces. I took more than a week drafting and circulating the report of the Latin American task force, finding my interest and attention increasingly drawn to that infinitely varied, turbulent continent. Finally the cabinet was in place, dozens of lesser positions filled, reports and memos drafted and ready for presidential attention. It was time to take over.

For me, and for most of the Kennedy staff, entering the White House was not merely a transition from seeking power to exercising it, but more as if we had entered an unsuspected space warp, been suddenly translated to a different world. No longer a "band of brothers" joined in a single mission, we now occupied divided spheres of responsibility, liberated to pursue, within limits, often fierce rivalries for presidential favor, public recognition, and power. The intimate camaraderie of the campaign dissolved, displaced by the harsher reality of divergent ambitions, a muted struggle between strangers, cast together by the coincidence of mutual service to Kennedy's pursuit. The war was over. The occupation had begun.

Just before entering the White House, Ted Sorensen — my constant companion, friend, intimate confidant of months on the *Caroline* — decided that since he was to be special counsel to the president, those who had worked with him (Lee White, Mike Feldman, and myself) would be designated as his assistants. Lee White voiced the objection all of us felt: We were in the White House to work for John Kennedy and no one else. Sorensen acquiesced, and so, in a change that would appear trivial only to those who have been deprived of personal encounters with the subtleties of life at court, we were given the title of Assistant Special Counsel to the President. (Not, as was first intended, Assistants to the Special Counsel.)

This episode strengthened my own conviction that I did not want to work for Sorensen, helping in the preparation of speeches, memoranda, and so on — a kind of continuation of my campaign role on a larger scale. I went to the new secretary of state, Dean Rusk, and asked if there might be a position in the State Department where I might be of service. Rusk was amiable, seemed favorably inclined, but made no commitment. He would never, I later realized, simply take on a member of the White House staff, one of Kennedy's own men, without the explicit approval of the president, and the acquiescence of others — Bundy, Sorensen, et al. — with whom he would have to work. And he was right to hesitate at my unusual proposition, being far wiser in the ways of bureaucracy than I was ever to become.

Kenny O'Donnell, now the president's appointments secretary, heard of my job search. Seeing me in a White House corridor, he put his arm over my shoulder in a totally uncharacteristic gesture, and asked if he could be of any help. I explained my predicament. Kenny was delighted. He disliked Sorensen, regarding Ted as a less stalwart loyalist than himself, and saw an opportunity to do some minor damage. He reported my questing perambulations through the upper reaches of government to President Kennedy. The president called me into his office: "I hear you don't want to work here, Dick," he questioned. "I don't think I can work well with Ted," I explained, "and since he's far more valuable to you than I am" (disingenuous but true), "I thought I'd try something else." Kennedy listened silently, then commanded, "You know how we do things. I think you better stay on here for a while."

So I stayed in the White House but — and not by coincidence — began to receive my assignments directly. Immediately after my interview Kennedy told Sorensen of my discontent and its source; perhaps hoping to heal any breach. It had the opposite effect. Sorensen never forgave me. (Four years later, according to Johnson adviser Jack Valenti, he vigorously opposed President Johnson's intention to return me to the White House staff, and, in fact, I was not appointed until Sorensen had departed.)

My growing immersion in Latin American policy, the steady accretion of authority until I became — for a while — the president's principal assistant for hemispheric policy, is only comprehensible — could only have happened — in a staff system much different from today's monolithic and multitudinous White House. We were few in number. McGeorge Bundy with a handful of assistants (the number would multiply) occupied the basement floor of the West Wing — that section of the White House prized for its geographical proximity to the Oval Office. On the second floor sat Larry O'Brien and those who worked with him to cultivate and coerce the Congress on behalf of the president's programs.

Sorensen had his own office down the hall from Kennedy, and worked closely on legislation and messages with White and Feldman, whose second-floor offices adjoined my own. On the other side of the mansion, in the East Wing, Arthur Schlesinger had his more luxurious, but more remote domain. While a handful of other important advisers — budget director Dave Bell, science adviser Jerry Wiesner, among others — were situated across a narrow, paved, completely enclosed roadway, in the Executive Office Building. Although physical closeness to the Oval Office was thought a symbol of power, the most important adviser of all was located far down Pennsylvania Avenue, in the office of the attorney general.

There was no chief of staff; no general among the colonels. The president's own office was flanked on one side by O'Donnell and, on the other, by his personal secretary, Evelyn Lincoln. When Kennedy wanted something, he often called us directly, or had Kenny relay the message. (Kenny could be relied upon not to impart any unintended, personal nuance to a presidential directive.) Nor did any of us hesitate to approach Kennedy directly on matters we thought of presidential interest or concern. If, as he often did, O'Donnell protectively barred the formal entrance to the presidential chambers, we simply walked over to Evelyn Lincoln, who amiably gossiped with us while we awaited the inevitable appearance of the president, the door to his office swinging open as Evelyn entered with letters to be signed, or to signal Kennedy's brief foray to give an instruction, or glance at the daily papers kept on a table in his secretary's office.

Seeing a staff member, Kennedy — unless totally preoccupied — would invariably ask, "What is it, Dick?" and I would tell him briefly as he stood there or, if the problem was more complex, would enter his office behind him for a longer discussion. Nor was this "management style" limited to members of the immediate staff. The State Department bureaucracy was often disrupted by a presidential call to a country desk office to ask how the economic mission to Bolivia was progressing, or to seek the opinion of the person most immediately engaged in monitoring the latest overturn of a Brazilian government.

Kennedy wanted the facts — not conclusions, but the details that had led to conclusion — and sought them from those most intimately engaged in the matter that concerned him. He wanted opinions directly, not as mediated and homogenized through a hierarchy of committees and subordinate chieftains. How else was he going to know what was going on in his government? How else accumulate the information relevant to decision? Naturally, the enormous span of presidential authority limited this kind of direct contact to more pressing matters of decision and policy. Yet even as narrowed by necessity, the range of direct presidential involvement was impressive. More than once my special White House phone would ring at home, and the familiar voice would ask if our delegation to the next OAS meeting had been selected, who was on it, why had we omitted a particular official. Indeed, during that first year in the White House, I spoke to Kennedy about some aspect of Latin American policy on the average of once a day — even during the crises over Berlin, Laos, the brutal assaults on freedom riders in Montgomery. If nothing else, it kept you on your toes.

Nor did the president reach out only to officials. He was a voracious reader of newspapers and journals. And frequently an interviewer would find that Kennedy was interviewing him. "How do they think we're doing in California?" he asked a reporter for the *Los Angeles Times*. He would seek the opinion of a British correspondent on the political strength of the Macmillan government; talked with Tad Szulc of the *New York Times* — the best-informed Latin American correspondent in the business — about "pressures" on him to sanction Castro's assassination. (Tad said he thought it was a very bad idea.)

Undoubtedly some would criticize the Kennedy approach as an unwise dissipation of energy; the same philosophers of management who thought it unnecessary for the president of General Motors to visit an assembly line or explore the manufacturing techniques being developed in distant Japan. It is the complaint of those who do not understand the nature of bureaucracy — the desire to avoid decision and, especially, the responsibility for decision; to refrain from firm assertions of opinions lest they be contradicted by later events; to sift information as it moves up through the hierarchy until it is stripped of the detail, the subtleties of nuance, which, alone, allow one to understand fully what is being said and its relevance to final judgment. Nor should one underestimate the immense impact of direct presidential contact on morale. He was interested in what you knew and thought, shared your concerns if not always your opinions, received your comments with respect — at least outwardly. The result was to instill

a fierce loyalty among those who served Kennedy, a personal dedication toward this rather detached, friendly but essentially im-
personal leader who rarely complimented a staff member but never
treated him with indifference or contempt. (Occasionally when a
Sorensen speech draft was unsatisfactory, Kennedy would give it
to Arthur Schlesinger with the injunction: "Rework this a little,
but don't tell Ted I asked you.")

Inevitably the president's style influenced the conduct of his
staff. A secretive, inward president breeds a secretive, remote staff,
who disseminate his mood and manner to the outermost limbs of
the executive branch. The same structural imperatives guided us —
most of us — in the other direction, toward contact with department officials, members of the press, individuals outside of government — Martin Luther King, Joan Baez, Ralph Nader, and
James Baldwin, literary critics and Ivy League economists, those
who were leaders of opinion, and many who simply had strong
opinions. This openness had its hazards. One day I received a
call in my White House office from a young attorney, who, without preliminary courtesies, launched into a lengthy exhortation
about the injustice of present sugar import quotas, and the need
to readjust them for the benefit of certain Caribbean states. I listened politely for a while, before interrupting to inform him that
it was all very interesting, but I had nothing to do with sugar
quotas, that he should call Ted Sorensen or Lee White. He thanked
me abruptly "for my understanding," and hung up. Later I realized he must have been sitting with a sugar-producing client whose
astonishment at the attorney's instant access to the White House
justified a very high fee. But a few instances like this were enough
to dispel naïveté about the ubiquity of greed, and our vulnerability to those who could contrive ways of making money from totally meaningless White House contacts.

The hazards of openness were trivial compared to the enrich-
ments, both of personal experience and, more substantially, of
government. In some of our more critical overseas missions and
in a few Washington buildings, a soundproof, steel-walled chamber is physically suspended within a larger room; a warranty of
privacy from intrusions, personal or electronic. The White House
itself can be such a room, an isolated sanctuary within which men
debate issues of high national policy closed off from the nation
and the world whose course they seek to alter. Within the protective luxury of those walls — occasionally infiltrated, with permission, by other Washington insiders (favored columnists, congres-

sional leaders) — it is easy to indulge, and then believe, the delusion that you are the country; that a vast, sprawling continent has been miraculously compressed within the tiny frame that contains your labors. It is a hallucination bred of sensory deprivation and fed by a continual stream of flattery, respectful attention, and well-meant invocations of patriotic reverence. It is intensified by the natural tendency of all power — even the most democratic — to resent any impediments to its exercise. What better way to achieve this than to close oneself off from dissent or to pretend it does not even exist.

The pressures toward such dangerous and misleading isolation are so powerful — so pervasive in that company town called Washington — that they can only be resisted by a continual, conscious effort to reach out, personally and with a critical intelligence, to people and ideas apart from government, to the ceaseless movement of an elusively complex society.

The president does not rule America. He does not even lead it, except within limits defined by the society itself. John Kennedy's exuberant vitality and his expansive rhetoric concealed a cautious awareness of the limits of his leadership — the restraints imposed by other political leaders, by public sentiment and belief. Some would censure him for timidity — the failure, for example, to move swiftly enough against racial oppression. Yet the most serious misjudgments of his presidency — the Bay of Pigs, growing involvement in Vietnam — emerged from secret, incestuous councils unrestrained by political debate and public temper.

Although the forces that would shape "the sixties" were already beginning to impinge on the mood and awareness of the nation, they had not yet disrupted the relatively moderate course of society. The southern sit-ins of 1960, provoking outbursts followed by forcible federal intervention, were not yet understood as auguries of a growing black revolt, had not yet touched the conscience and aroused the indignant energies of white Americans. Domestic conservatism — shared by Congress and a large popular majority — fortified Kennedy's natural inclination to turn toward the overtly urgent difficulties of foreign policy. He did request the legislation he had promised to remedy the blatant inequities of national life — Medicare, relief for depressed areas, immigration reform, a stimulus for economic growth. But, for the most part, these measures failed to win a significant popular constituency, languished in Congress.

But the rising tensions of the Cold War, the fear of Soviet encroachment, the erosion of American preeminence, both moral and material, provided a natural arena for the new president. Anti-American feelings had spread across the underdeveloped continents. Fourteen days before Kennedy took office, on January 6, Khrushchev declared that the Soviet Union would support "wars of national liberation" anywhere in the world, and proclaimed his intention to sign a peace treaty with East Germany that would effectively block American access to Berlin, adding, ominously, that any attack on the frontiers of East Germany would be treated as an attack on the entire Warsaw Pact, i.e., the Soviet Union. In distant Laos, communist insurgents slowly accumulated power. While in April of 1961, an amazed planet looked skyward hoping to catch a glimpse of the satellite that carried Yuri Gagarin in triumphant orbit through regions of outer space which no American had yet penetrated.

To Kennedy, as to the swollen, bellicose Castro, Latin America was destined to be a principal battleground between systems of government, a test of the prospects for democracy against the ambitions of the totalitarians. This was our hemisphere, protected against Old World incursion since the Monroe Doctrine of 1820, populated by men and women who shared the values, the culture, the religion, of our common Western ancestry. From the time Alexander Hamilton had secretly dispatched gunboats to assist revolutionaries against Spanish rule, we had, intermittently, engaged ourselves in the affairs of our Good Neighbors to the south; an intervention that was not always benign, was sometimes violent, and was often intended to protect our immediate economic interests.

No part of the globe — with the exception of immediate crises in Berlin and Laos — was to have precedence over the formulation of a policy toward Latin America. Decades of self-serving neglect, indifference to the turbulent changes of an aroused continent, had already led to the creation of one Soviet ally and the rise of communist insurgencies in a dozen other countries.

Because of this presidential concern — shared by few others in his government (Europe and Southeast Asia being the traditional contenders for establishment attention) — I became a principal actor in the Kennedy foreign policy. Having detached myself from the "Sorensen group," I was a kind of staff member without portfolio. But in the Kennedy White House, authority and responsibility depended less upon formal titles and assignments than on the inclinations of the president. If you were the person he called for information or to relay an order, you then became the president's man, legitimate conduit of his authority. And when it came to Latin America, Kennedy called on me. I didn't know a great deal about Latin America, but by the beginning of 1961 I knew much more than I had.

8 / Alianza para el Progreso

SOMETIME TOWARD THE END of January a call from Kennedy summoned me to the Oval Office. As I entered, I saw the president standing inside one of the glass doors that opened onto the grounds and garden behind the White House. Glancing up as I entered, he beckoned — "Look at this, Dick" — and pointed toward the floor. Joining him, I looked down to see a series of small, pitted indentations. "You know what that is?" he asked. My mind raced: Some new security device? Unlikely, too visible. The site of microphones implanted by the nefarious Hoover? He wouldn't dare, not so obviously. "It's from Ike's golf shoes." Kennedy grinned. "He put them on at his desk, then walked out here to practice his putting. Maybe we ought to put a rope around this piece of floor and leave it as an Eisenhower memorial." He paused, then smiled. "Well, I guess we all have our way of relaxing from the burdens of office; at least I won't leave any marks on the floor." (Soon thereafter the spike marks were sanded away.)

Walking over to his desk, Kennedy picked up a folder crammed with papers. "Telegrams from Latin America," he explained. "There's even one from that bastard Somoza saying my election has given him new hope for Nicaraguan democracy. Draft an answer saying that's my hope too — democracy for Nicaragua. That ought to scare him." He drew another document from the file. "This is what I want to talk about. It's from Betancourt." (Rómulo Betancourt, after leading the movement to overthrow the Venezuelan dictatorship, had been elected president of his country and was the acknowledged leader of the forces of liberal democracy in Latin America.) Kennedy read from the message: "Your statements during the campaign have aroused great hopes among the leaders of progressive democracy. We await your actions as President with immense joy and expectation that your great democracy will join us in the struggle against all forms of totalitarianism which strangle the lives of our people."

Looking up, Kennedy said, "I'd like to get a major statement on our Latin policy soon. Next to Berlin it's the most critical area, and will be for a long time. The whole place could blow up on us. You remember those people who threw rocks at Nixon. I'd like to believe it was just Nixon's personality, but they were sending us a message. We can't embrace every tinhorn dictator who tells us he's anticommunist while he's sitting on the necks of his own people. And the United States government is not the representative of private business. Do you know in Chile the American copper companies control about eighty percent of all the foreign exchange? We wouldn't stand for that here. And there's no reason they should stand for it. All those people want is a chance for a decent life, and we've let them think that we're on the side of those who are holding them down. There's a revolution going on down there, and I want to be on the right side of it. Hell, we are on the right side. But we have to let them know it, that things have changed."

"If you want them to believe you," I said, "we'll have to back it up with action, and that means a very large commitment. It's a big continent."

"I'll make a big commitment," Kennedy answered abruptly. "I don't know if Congress will give it to me. But now's the time, while they're all worried that Castro might take over the hemisphere. I'm worried myself. Not about Castro particularly, although we have to do something about him, but if people think they have to choose between communism and not eating, they'll go for communism. Wouldn't you? I would. Do you think we can have something ready in a month?"

"We already have your campaign statements," I replied, "and the task force on Latin America has done a helluva job. It's just a matter of putting it all together. If we can get everyone to agree."

"I don't care if everyone agrees," Kennedy replied. "You know what our thinking is. That's the only agreement you need — with me."

At these words, I felt a surge of exultation. He really meant it.

During the campaign Kennedy had approved and delivered the call for a new Alliance for Progress. But that was politics, a rebuke to Republican failures in Latin America. Now we would transform the polemics of domestic combat into the official policy of the United States. And although the ideas came from many sources, the task of translation — of reaching to the hopes of an entire continent — had been entrusted to me. I had a mandate from the president himself to override bureaucratic dissent. Naturally the new policy would have its opponents among those who believed America's interests were best protected by authoritarian governments of the right, and the use of our influence to ensure the prosperity of American companies. But we had won the election. Our views — Kennedy's and mine — were shared by many "expert" advisers and the most progressive democratic leaders within Latin America. And the shield of presidential approval was more than enough to protect my efforts against enemies on the right. Or so I thought, being, in those early days, equally naïve about the resilient determination of public bureaucracy joined with private wealth, and the extent to which a president could defend a controversial assistant.

As I turned to leave the Oval Office, Kennedy said, "One more thing, I don't want this to be an anti-Cuban speech. Just throw Castro in with the other dictators. I don't want them to think the only reason we're doing this is because of Cuba." (We both understood that it was at least part of the reason, at least an important catalyst.) Then, as I neared the door: "Latin America's not like Asia or Africa. We can really accomplish something there."

And we will, I thought, as I walked back to my office. It was the opportunity of a lifetime — not just for Kennedy or me, but for the United States.

The countries of Latin America were not emerging from the confused strife of postwar colonial revolutions. They had been independent for almost two centuries. But not totally. The great power to the north had shadowed, sometimes dominated, their evolving societies. Setting ourselves up as the protector of the continent, we had frequently intervened with private capital, or, occasionally, with military force to advance our own interests. The United Fruit Company had virtually owned Guatemala. Wilson had invaded the same Mexico from which, in the preceding century, we had stripped half its territory to form new American states. Prolonged marine occupations of the Dominican Republic and

Nicaragua had compelled those countries to collect taxes and pay debts owed to American entrepreneurs.

Resentment, fear, hostility were accompanied by often grudging respect bordering on admiration for the northern giant's ascendancy to unprecedented wealth and world power. If there was anger, there was also an untapped readiness to respond should America demonstrate a respectful attention toward the concerns of its continental neighbors. The impact of Roosevelt's Good Neighbor policy was proof. Later, in 1961, after Kennedy had motored through cheering mobs in Bogatá, Colombia, and while he was sitting in a luxuriously outfitted drawing room of the presidential palace awaiting a state dinner, the president of Colombia, Alberto Lleras Camargo — himself an enlightened, cultivated member of the ruling oligarchy — asked Kennedy, "Do you know why those people were out there cheering for you today?" and then as Kennedy sat silently, expectantly, "Because they think you're on their side against the oligarchs. You had better keep it that way."

The future of Latin America, its success in fulfilling the "revolution of rising expectations" that had swept across the third world after the Second World War, was inescapably linked to the actions and attitudes of the United States. Hate us or like us, they could not leave us. Nor could we afford to ignore the reality of newly liberated desires and energies which were beginning to shatter the ruling structures of long-settled societies. The rise, and CIA overthrow, of the leftist Arbenz of Guatemala, and the ascendancy of Castro were tangible warnings of the dangers in our self-serving neglect. Yet a Western culture rooted in centuries of historical evolution was resistant to alien ideologies from the remote Soviet Union or from China. The Alliance for Progress was to provide an alternative. We would put ourselves — our wealth, our power — on the side of change, become the ally of justified discontent, a spokesman and weapon for the oppressed and impoverished against the unjust social structures — the landed wealthy, the brutalizing military — that barred the way to a better life. At least we would try. For in Latin America, as elsewhere, we could not govern, only influence. The wealthy and powerful of other countries would not meekly yield up their domination because of a speech — or a hundred speeches — by the president of the United States.

Later in 1961, in a letter to former President Kubitschek of Brazil, Kennedy summarized his conviction "that no program which is restricted to the technicalities of economic development can fully answer the needs of the Americas. Only an approach to economic progress and social justice which is based on a wide acceptance of the fundamental ideals of political democracy and human dignity can hope to conquer the many ills of our hemisphere and respond fully to the aspirations of our people. . . .

"Such an effort requires more than dollars. . . . [W]e are embarked on a political task in the highest sense of that term, a task which requires determined national leadership in order to enlist the mind and effort of each individual citizen and group in the pursuit of our common goal."

To Latin Americans these words from a president of the United States had a ring of revolution. For us, the rhetoric had a more familiar resonance — the extension of the spirit of the New Frontier to an entire hemisphere. In retrospect, our expressed intentions may appear naïve, grandiose, even arrogant. But not in 1961, when it appeared that the common effort of men of goodwill could enhance the lives of the most oppressed among us — from the Mississippi Delta to the altiplano of Bolivia. We believed it, and so, ultimately, for a while, did the masses of Latin America. And that belief — the overcoming of disbelief — was the crucial first step toward fulfillment.

Thus, because the danger appeared so immediate, the opportunity so great, Latin America would receive the immediate attention of the New Frontier.

And there was another reason for haste. For almost a year, the CIA had been training a group of Cuban exiles for a possible invasion of Cuba. If that attack was to go forward (the issue was still unresolved), it should take place in the generally benign and progressive context of a new American policy, lest it appear merely the latest in a long line of self-serving military interventions. Most of the nations of Latin America were hostile to communism, unsympathetic to Castro, but would be repelled by the United States' use of force to impose its will on a fellow American state. Unless Kennedy first clarified his intentions toward a continent that had already seen his election as an augury of hope, inevitable disillusionment would be followed by an aggravation of anti-American feelings. Instead of improving relations, reducing the danger of newly hostile regimes, we might make things worse.

Responding to the urgency of Kennedy's direction, I convened a series of White House meetings to discuss and refine the work of the Latin American task force. Our objective was to distill the lengthy, detailed recommendations into a major presidential address. The conferences were conducted with a confused informality that would have been inconceivable a year later, when bureaucratic lines had hardened. Ten to twenty people crowded around the conference table in the "fish room" of the White House (so called because it had once contained Franklin Roosevelt's aquariums). Career officials apprehensive of their future mingled with new Kennedy men uncertain of their still-inchoate authority, joined by others who had no official position and whose only credentials were their knowledge of the hemisphere and the contributions they had made to campaign pronouncements. The lone representative of the State Department (no Rusk, no Bowles, no Ball, not even a Bundy) was the assistant secretary of state for Latin America, Tom Mann, a holdover from the Eisenhower administration, who sat in wordless acquiescence as we condemned and prepared to overturn the policies he had so faithfully administered.

The president's speech was scheduled for March 13, five weeks away. We were agreed that the policies of recent years had been an abysmal failure. They must be explicitly rejected. That was a given, a starting point for discussion. Most of those who attended the meetings had been critics, public or academic, of the self-destructive neglect of recent years, and understood the structures of political and social oppression that obstructed the tumescent aspirations of the Latin masses. All of us — nearly all — were in agreement with Kennedy's campaign pledges, and were emboldened by the new president's buoyant, confident desire to make a comprehensive break with the past.

My own chairmanship of these meetings went unchallenged. I was the president's representative, charged with drafting his address. Kennedy himself conferred with me almost every day, interjecting his own ideas, responding to my accounts of our progress. Kennedy alone among the top officials of his government understood the importance of Latin America, the extent to which our interests were linked to its emerging social revolution, the imperative need to rank it among the foremost subjects of concern and action. In three years as president, Kennedy would make three trips to Central and South America, and was planning a fourth, to Brazil, in 1964. He involved himself not merely in the formation of policy, but its implementation, constantly reshuffling officials who seemed unable to get results, receiving a continual stream of Latin visitors — not only heads of state, but leaders of dissent, journalists, private citizens of substance in their own countries.

Later that year, I sat in Kennedy's office while he told Assistant Secretary of State Robert Woodward that if the Alliance for Progress conference failed, "You're out of a job."

"I'm expendable, Mr. President," Woodward replied.

"I appreciate your offer," Kennedy interrupted, "and I'd like to take you up on it. But that's not the way thing work. There are people walking around here involved in the Cuba thing" (the Bay of Pigs) "up to their ears, who nobody ever heard of, advancing their careers, while the Cuba thing sits on my desk like a sack of wet potatoes. It all comes back here. Since I'm going to be held responsible for all these things, I'd like to have something to do with them."

On Tuesday, March 7 — six days before the president's scheduled address — I conducted a series of meetings that may help illuminate the accelerating momentum of the administration's involvement with Latin America, and my own.

At 10 A.M. I met with Adolf Berle to discuss the deteriorating situation in the Dominican Republic. Recent cables had told of increased brutality by the Trujillo regime. Following an almost successful attempt by Trujillo to assassinate President Betancourt of Venezuela, who had provided sanctuary for the enemies of the Dominican dictatorship, all the nations of the Organization of American States, including the United States, had broken diplomatic relations with the Dominican regime. Trujillo had responded to his forcible isolation by intensifying repression of dissident groups who might be stimulated to action by his exile from the community of states. (Trujillo systematically murdered potential middle-class opponents; his son, Ramfis Trujillo, was reported to have a refrigerated room at the rear of his house where, suspended from meat hooks, the bodies of slaughtered adversaries were kept for viewing by dinner guests.) Believing that Trujillo's overthrow was inevitable, Kennedy wanted to be prepared to guide the transition to a friendly democratic regime, and had asked that a contingency plan be drafted.

At ten thirty, Arthur Schlesinger and Walt Rostow came to my office to discuss a special economic mission to help arrest the ominous deterioration of the Bolivian economy. On both nights of the preceding weekend, Kennedy had called me at home, expressing his concern about the threat of chaos in Bolivia, demanding that we "get going on this matter," and commenting on the qualifications of those being suggested for the rescue mission. Fortified by this presidential direction, we decided that our emissaries should ignore proposals by both the International Monetary Fund and State Department that Bolivia needed a good dose of an antiinflationary austerity, and instead should offer immediate economic assistance. Bolivia was one of the most impoverished countries in the hemisphere; the life expectancy was thirty-six years. Most of the population had been reduced to the margin of subsistence. Things were grim enough without calling for further sacrifice from those who had nothing to give.

At 11 A.M. I turned my attention from a right-wing dictator to our enemy on the left, as a group of men from the Defense Department and the CIA discussed the desirability of setting up a revolutionary government should the still-conjectural invasion of Cuba be successful.

At eleven thirty I met with my fellow members of the Latin American task force to discuss which components of a new policy deserved explicit presidential endorsement. The task force report was almost a hundred pages. Kennedy would speak for thirty minutes.

At two thirty a call from Bobby Kennedy diverted my attention from global meditations to the mounting domestic turmoil of another struggle for social justice — the demand for integration of public facilities, which had sent the freedom riders on their bloody trip to the heart of the South. The attorney general was angry. "Too many people are getting involved in this thing" (civil rights), he complained. "We have to decide whether we are going to have an administration position and what it's going to be." Although I had been given some responsibility for White House policy on civil rights, the conversation left me with little doubt that the attorney general would soon take full command. And he needed no liaison with the president.

My own activities in civil rights would diminish and then disappear as my responsibilities for Latin American policy increased — not by design, but as a consequence of Kennedy's insistent intervention in the details of policy. He did not intend to leave things to the State Department, or to anyone else; and, as the resident staff authority on Latin America, maintaining his involvement and enforcing his will soon became my full-time occupation.

At five that afternoon, more than twenty people attended a final conference in the "fish room." Twice during the meeting Kennedy summoned me across the narrow West Wing corridor that separated us from the Oval Office. "Will the speech be ready?" he asked. "Yes, Mr. President." "I don't want it on television. I can't go to the well too often. This is not for the American people, it's a message to Latin America. Let's save our television for something like health or education. Make sure the speech is beamed to Latin America. Keep repeating it the next day."

The evening of March 7, in the isolation of my West Wing office, I began translating Kennedy's directive into a presidential speech. I did not lack for material. Arthur Schlesinger describes seeing me virtually concealed behind a desk piled with memos, reports, economic studies, and books. Nor was there any lack of suggestions from administration colleagues. Ted Sorensen thought the program should be set forth as a series of distinct points, in the Kennedy campaign style. (It was.) Dean Rusk proposed a concluding point inviting Latin America to "contribute to the enrichment of life and culture in the United States" through a program of educational and cultural exchange. (It was included.)

Overwhelmed by the voluminous and often discordant mass of material, constantly interrupted by further suggestions from colleagues — I finally retreated to the privacy of my Georgetown home. There, I began the task of synthesis and selection. The formation of a coherent policy was less formidable than I had feared. The major problems of Latin America, summed up in the then fashionable phrase "revolution of rising expectations," were clear and must be directly addressed.

It was easy to say the right thing, but more difficult to convince the people of Latin America that the United States, so often hostile to liberating change, was now prepared to embrace and assist the forces of social and economic revolution. The text must reflect Kennedy's own vitality and confidence, demonstrate an honesty of intention combined with mutuality of respect. It must not only signal a change in the policy of the United States, but try to vitalize the progressive, democratic forces in each Latin American country upon whose efforts and achievements the success of the Alianza para el Progreso would depend. And there were deep and well-founded suspicions to overcome.

Later, many would complain that the Alianza stimulated hope

beyond practical possibility. And perhaps it did. But nations, whole peoples, are not stirred to difficult, revolutionary deeds by the careful studies of engineers or the cautious projections of economists. Only those who provide a large vision, a noble goal, the prospect of a bright future — not just for the unborn, but for the living who must bear the battle — can raise a standard that others will follow. Promises must be grounded in reality. But hope must reach to the bounds of possibility if there is to be any hope at all. That is the lesson which bureaucracy rejects, and leadership understands.

After a few days of work in the comparative solitude of my home, I brought a finished draft to the White House. As I entered the Oval Office, Kennedy asked, "Do you have the speech? Hell, I've got to give it in two days." I handed him my effort, and, for the next couple of hours, he carefully reviewed the text, making editorial revisions, offering suggestions (i.e., commands). There was no need to make substantial changes. The speech was Kennedy. It had been drafted to suit his natural cadences and forcefulness of delivery, to express his convictions — both about Latin policy and the role he envisioned for a renascent America. I had worked to give voice to his ideas, persuasive force to his intentions. And he was satisfied with the result.

After completing his editorial review, Kennedy leaned back: "Good job, Dick." I was surprised and gratified. (Kennedy's working relation with his staff did not include exchanges of flattery. He didn't offer it, and did not expect it from others; with the result that the mildest of compliments was equivalent to a deluge of approval.) "But do I really have to say these words?" He pointed to a place in the text where I had placed certain phrases in Spanish. "It will make a difference," I replied. "The whole idea is a partnership, and if you use some Spanish words it will be taken as a sign of respect."

"Do you know any Spanish?" he replied.

"Not much."

"Well I don't know any."

"They're simple words to pronouce."

"For you, maybe. I do know some French, but every time I try to use it no one can understand a word. Maybe it's my accent."

I did not contradict the president, but a Boston twang did not explain the fact that Kennedy's pronunciation of foreign words was atrocious. He turned every syllable into English. "It doesn't matter if you get it just right," I said, "it's the idea of it that's important."

"It would be nice if they could understand what I was saying." Then, pausing: "Maybe I'll get Jackie to help me."

The speech was scheduled for the evening of March 13. That afternoon I entered Kennedy's office to find him pacing the floor of the Oval Office reciting aloud — "*techo . . . techo; trabajo . . . trabajo . . . obero* [sic] *. . . obero.*" Seeing me, he stopped. "How's that?" "Pretty good," I said, "except that it's *obrero* with an *r*, not *obero.*" "*Obrero,*" he repeated — "*obrero . . . obrero . . . obrero.*" "That's perfect, Mr. President," I said, and retreated hastily, being unwilling to take any further responsibility for Kennedy's mangled Spanish.

At five that afternoon the Latin American diplomatic corps began to assemble in the East Room of the White House. Accompanying the Latins was a specially invited bipartisan group of congressional leaders. A dazzling Jacqueline Kennedy, exchanging greetings in perfect Spanish, led the diplomats and their wives on a tour of the mansion. As the 6 P.M. hour of delivery approached, the guests took their seats, the camera lights went on, there was the sound of "Ruffles and Flourishes" from the marine band, followed by the resonant strains of "Hail to the Chief," as Kennedy entered smiling, strode to the lectern, and began to deliver the first major foreign-policy speech of his administration.

After greeting his guests, the president invoked the hope expressed more than a century earlier by the great Latin liberator, Simón Bolívar, "to see the Americas fashioned into the greatest region in the world, " 'greatest' " he said, quoting Bolívar, " 'not so much by virtue of her area and her wealth as by her freedom and her glory.' . . .

"We meet together as firm and ancient friends," he proclaimed. ". . . Our continents are bound together by a common history, the endless exploration of new frontiers. Our nations are the product of a common struggle, the revolt from colonial rule. And our people share a common heritage, the quest for the dignity and the freedom of man."

Reminding his audience that all the countries of the Americas had begun in revolutions which are "not yet finished," Kennedy defined "our unfulfilled task" as a mission "to demonstrate to the entire world that man's unsatisfied aspiration for economic progress and social justice can best be achieved by free men. . . .

"[L]et me be the first to admit," Kennedy continued, "that we North Americans have not always grasped the significance of this common mission, just as it is also true that many in your own countries have not fully understood the urgency of the need to lift people from poverty and ignorance and despair."

At this, a slight rustling disturbed the silence of the East Room: An American president was acknowledging his own country's errors and implicitly rebuking the oligarchs of the south.

"Throughout Latin America," Kennedy continued, ". . . millions of men and women suffer the daily degradations of poverty and hunger. . . . And each day the problems grow more urgent . . . discontent is growing. In the words of José Figueres, 'Once dormant peoples are struggling upward toward the sun, toward a better life.'

"If we are to meet a problem so staggering in its dimensions, our approach itself must be equally bold . . . therefore I have called upon all people of the hemisphere to join in a new Alliance for Progress — Alianza para Progreso — a vast cooperative effort, unparalleled in magnitude and nobility of purpose, to satisfy the basic needs of the American people for homes, work and land, health and schools — *techo, trabajo y tierra, salud y escuela.*"

To give content to this Alliance, Kennedy proposed a "vast new Ten Year Plan for the Americas . . . a decade of democratic progress."

The success of the Alliance, Kennedy stressed, will depend on the "efforts of the American nations . . . to . . . mobilize their resources . . . and modify their social patterns so that all, and not just a privileged few, share in the fruits of growth. . . .

"[I]f the countries of Latin America are ready to do their part . . . then I believe the United States . . . should help provide resources of a scope and magnitude sufficient to make this bold development plan a success — just as we helped to provide . . . the resources adequate to help rebuild the economies of Western Europe."

The analogy to the Marshall Plan was deliberate. In Latin America as in Europe we could provide resources; but direction, planning, social change must be the responsibility of the Latin republics themselves.

Kennedy then sketched out a ten-point program including a special fund for social development, stabilization of commodity prices, and the development of a Latin American common market. He called for a meeting of all the countries of the hemisphere to "begin the massive planning effort which will be at the heart of the Alliance for Progress."

"With steps such as these," Kennedy proclaimed, "we propose to complete the revolution of the Americas. . . . To achieve this goal political freedom must accompany material progress. . . . Therefore let us express our special friendship to the people of Cuba and the Dominican Republic — and the hope they will soon rejoin the society of free men. . . ." It was Kennedy's only reference to Cuba.

"This political freedom," Kennedy continued, "must be accompanied by social change. For unless necessary social reforms, including land and tax reform, are freely made . . . then our alliance, our revolution, our dream and our freedom will fail."

This was the heart of Kennedy's policy. It was a call to uproot those social structures which, in almost every Latin country, had allowed a handful of wealthy oligarchs and generals to prosper while the mass of the population was imprisoned in hopeless poverty. Our help would not go to enrich the few, would be denied to those unwilling to establish a framework of social justice. Coming from an American president, it would appear as a summons to social revolution, and, after the first glow of Kennedy's speech had faded, the Alliance for Progress would meet its most determined opposition not from the communists, but from the wealthy, the privileged, and the powerful.

"[O]ur greatest challenge," Kennedy asserted, "comes from within — the task of creating an American civilization . . . where, within the rich diversity of its own traditions, each nation is free to follow its own path towards progress. . . . But the efforts of governments alone will never be enough. In the end the people must choose and the people must help themselves."

It was the essence of that which was best and most noble in Kennedy's public philosophy: the acceptance of diversity, the responsibility of each individual to accept the burden of creating the future. He had addressed the same message to the United States in his inaugural.

"Let us once again," Kennedy concluded, "transform the American continent into a vast crucible of revolutionary ideas and efforts — a tribute to the power of the creative energies of free men and women — an example to all the world that liberty and progress walk hand in hand. Let us once again awaken our American revolution until it guides the struggle of people everywhere —

not with an imperialism of force or fear — but the rule of courage and freedom and hope for the future of man."

For a moment the East Room was silent. Then the ambassadors rose and began to applaud, the applause mounting in intensity, prolonged, until Kennedy himself stilled the gathering by descending into the midst of his guests to shake hands. Looking at the faces around me, I was inwardly exultant (and outwardly restrained). We had reached them. I was, of course, relieved that my effort had been successful. But mostly, I was happy because I believed every word of that speech — those I had written and those Kennedy had added. My feeling was not only gratification at personal achievement, but also, strangely enough, love — not for Kennedy, but for those desperate millions I had never seen whose lives would, as a consequence of this day's work, be less painful, more touched with hope. For we would do what we promised. I did not doubt it then. And though history would betray my faith, it was not beyond our reach.

Stopping for brief greetings with the Latin diplomats, Kennedy saw me as he neared the exit of the East Room. Placing his hand on my shoulder, he whispered, "How was my Spanish?"

"Perfect, Mr. President," I said.

"I thought you'd say that," he answered, and left the room. Coming from a Boston Irishman, the gesture was a positive show of affection.

The occasion had been a smash.

After the speech, waiting for their cars under the canopy of the south entrance to the White House, the Latin diplomats talked excitedly about Kennedy's performance. "*Es magnifico, magnifico,*" repeated Juan Bautista de Lavalle, Peruvian ambassador to the OAS, grabbing the arm of a Brazilian colleague, "El Plan Kennedy, that's the name for it." "Yes," responded the Brazilian, "this glorifies Operation Pan-America" (an earlier proposal for hemispheric development by President Kubitschek of Brazil). "This is what we need — strength now, with leadership. This is what we wanted."

Fernando Berkemeyer, ambassador from Peru, his dark, expensively tailored suit reflecting his birth into one of Peru's wealthiest families, beamed. "Excellent, excellent. . . . Currency and credits are necessary, but the priorities involve social legislation in my country. These social problems must be dealt with. Yes, above all." Then, aware of his own somewhat ambiguous qualifications

as a leader of the masses: "My own family is prepared to help in
any necessary way . . . we pay our taxes under the law of Peru."

Over the next forty-eight hours the success of the evening was
confirmed by a flood of commentary from Latin America.

El Debate, the official government daily of Uruguay, summarized: "There is too much connectedness of thought, too much
harmony between the means and the ends, too close a rapport
between the reality we know and the theory presented us to doubt
the sincerity of the young President. Furthermore this is the policy
we have been asking of the U.S. There it is. Let us trust in its
fundamental truth."

Other commentary was even less restrained. "Kennedy has
spoken," said Venezuela's leading leftist daily, "with greater understanding of the reality of Latin America than any other previous U.S. Chief of State, including Franklin Delano Roosevelt."
While, to another Caracas commentator, it was "a rock flung
against the forehead of the communists." Brazil's most respected
journal called the speech "an American Marshall Plan . . . destined to transform the 1960s into an historical period of democratic progress." While a more suspicious Rio paper sardonically
announced that "Kennedy issues a decalogue to free Latin America from misery in ten years."

Within the United States the reaction was equally positive. In
an editorial entitled "The Unfinished Revolution," the *Washington
Post* concluded: "President Kennedy's address on Latin America
yesterday was worthy of the great problem to which it was directed. Not since the late George C. Marshall held out a hand to
the devastated countries of Europe in 1947 has the U.S. made so
stirring an appeal to a distressed region of the world."

Even before the initial flood of praise could recede, the lines
were being drawn. From persecuted, pillaged Haiti, there was only
silence. A shameless Trujillo claimed that the speech meant nothing to him since "the Dominican Republic in the Trujillo era had
already attained and surpassed all the goals set for Latin America." Within weeks, right-wing newspapers in Chile were referring
to the "naïve" Kennedy as an "unwitting ally of the communists." And Fidel Castro soon withdrew from his castigation of
the Alianza as "a calculated plan for buying Latin America and
turning it against Cuba," and proudly took full credit for the
American initiative: "Cuba and Cuba alone is responsible for this
so-called Alliance," he blustered. "Without our revolution there
would be no Alliance and without us it will not continue."

The attacks from the right were expectable. As for Castro, he was only partly right — less than he liked to think and more than we were willing to admit.

Occasionally, those involved in the preparation of a major presidential address would give a "backgrounder," explaining to carefully selected journalists just how the document was created — premises, intentions, prospects for success, and (most mysterious of all) the inward churnings of the presidential mind. Such briefings were sometimes fairly accurate, sometimes part fiction, occasionally complete fabrications — all were designed not so much to inform as to advance the interests and image of the president. (And, in part, our own.) The favored journalist, given such an "inside," "off-the-record," "exclusive" account — essentially unverifiable since the president himself was not available — had little choice but to print it and receive the envious congratulations of his less fortunate colleagues. Thus, when it worked, did the "official story" become the common wisdom.

I did not conduct a background session after the Alliance speech. But now the address and the man who made it are part of history, can only be understood in the context of history. Admittedly twenty-five years is a long time to wait, but if the passage of time distorts memory, it also confers advantages. I no longer need to justify either the president or myself. In many cases premises and predictions no longer need be debated. They have been tested by events.

In El Salvador, for example, the Latin American task force recommended that "a capable ambassador should be sent at once. The country is in the throes of almost inevitable social revolution (over-populated, tremendous concentration of wealth in a dozen extremely high families . . .)." In Nicaragua, we urged the removal of the current American ambassador, "widely believed to have been in Somoza's pocket," and his replacement by one capable of assisting the transition to "a democratic and economically progressive forward-looking government, capable of maintaining itself against continuing attacks both from the Army and from the Castro-supported left — an extremely difficult task." Difficult indeed, especially since, after Kennedy's death, it was not even tried. Instead we continued to support the dictator, held hands with the forces of reaction, and the "Castro-supported left" moved into power. Now we are multiplying the consequences of our past failure, heaping error upon irretrievable error, by opposing the

Sandinistas with just enough force to help them consolidate power and solidifying the alliance between democratically inclined Nicaraguans and Soviet-leaning Marxists. For me, it is like watching the rerun of a very bad movie — much worse the second time around.

And I know more about Latin America now. In March of 1961 I had never set foot south of the border (aside from one orgiastic night just beyond the Texas border during the campaign, which had little to do with high policy, but which an exceptionally imaginative psychiatrist might conclude had planted the seed of my love affair with Latin America.) In the next few years I would travel in twenty of the twenty-two countries of Latin America. That experience would enrich my understanding, and give tangible material content to the abstractions of Washington discussion. ("You can always tell underdevelopment by the women," a Brazilian explained as we walked through an impoverished village. "See," he said, pointing to a woman bent under a load of kindling, "she is only twenty-three and looks about fifty. In the rich villas of Rio the fifty-year-olds look thirty.") But nothing I saw or observed or felt — no revelation or exigent passion — caused me to discard the essential judgments of those first months. It is possible that, bent on self-justification, I was drawing selectively on experience to confirm already hardened preconceptions. But I don't think so. I was twenty-nine then, my mind that of the quester, and the few years, which then seemed a compressed lifetime, now appear briefer than the sigh of a child. To an amazing extent, the appraisal of 1961 remains accurate in the circumstances of 1988.

Certainly, it is as misleading now as it was then to speak of a policy for Latin America, as if the dazzling diversity of a continent and a half could be subsumed under a single label. "Latin America" is just a convenient geographical expression for countries, whole civilizations, that are as different from one another as they are from the United States. There are nations whose populations are dominated by the descendants of devastated Indian civilizations, and others whose people are of European descent — not only Spanish, but Italian and German, and even some of the fecund, ubiquitous Irish. There is Argentina, whose resources so richly bestowed by nature have been wasted by man, and the barren lands of the Andean plateau, where the most arduous labors can yield little more than subsistence. There are countries whose armies are, for the moment, obedient to civilian control, like Venezuela; or with no army at all, like Costa Rica; or under the brutal rule of military despotism, like Chile. There are the pious poor of officially anticlerical Mexico who creep on bloodstained knees across the rough stone plaza leading to the Church of Our Lady of Guadalupe, and the Catholic blacks of northeast Brazil praying to voodoo gods who were, under compulsion of the converters, given the names of saints.

But traveling through Latin America is not merely a pilgrimage to a staggering display of societies, cultures, governments. It is a voyage through the centuries. The fourteenth century is frozen in time on the altiplano of Peru, where I watched men tilling a field, bent over a piece of blunt iron bound to a wooden staff, compelled to work three days a week for their overlord; their entire world bordered by the surrounding hills. They knew nothing of a President Kennedy or the country he ruled. The eighteenth century inhabits a suburb of Lima, where a generous host served brandy in a house stocked with servants, walked me through a garden stocked with domesticated deer, to an underground vault stocked with a priceless collection of ancient gold and silver — the fruits of land he hardly ever visited. Our own century is São Paulo, men fighting through traffic jams along concrete corridors between towers of metal and glass, on their way to build, invest, pursue the rewards of modern business success. And in Brasília, a science-fiction city on a desert plain, its ribbed steel and concrete structures towering in isolation from all human concerns, can be found, perhaps, the century that is coming to all of us.

This description, while accurate, is also incomplete; a reality but also a metaphor. It is a truism that no one escapes history, that all of us — men and nations — are prisoners of their own time. Even the most defiant, those who would violently sunder the structures of a hated society, must define their anger in terms of what exists and what is possible. And for all their wondrous diversity, the people of Latin America were also inhabitants of the postwar world; creatures of the modern conditions that both fired their passions for human fulfillment and confined its attainment. Long neglected, thought almost irrelevant, in the multipower struggles of earlier years, they had become, at least marginally, caught up in the conflict between the United States and the Soviet Union known as the Cold War.

Not since Macedonia confronted Persia — Alexander against

Darius — had the civilized world been so clearly polarized. That earlier division led to war, which, almost certainly, would also have been the form of our own resolution had not the technology of atoms made universal defeat the most likely outcome of direct conflict.

As the Soviet desire to expand its empire, enlarge the hegemony of its ideology, became manifest, and the futility of a direct military contest more obvious, the United States was compelled to move from its traditional isolation and, reluctantly at first, then with greater enthusiasm, embrace its role as leader and ally of those nations, and groups within nations, unwilling to submit. The world was — or seemed — as Robinson Jeffers predicted, "Two bulls in one pasture."

But this is not the place for an analysis of that changeling monster, "the Cold War." For Latin America it meant the seductive appearance of an alternative ideology of development: not socialism, whose adherents had been plentiful for decades, but "Marxism," translated into social reality by concentrated and self-perpetuating power, and linked to the Soviet Union by natural sympathies and the need for a counterweight to United States hostility. The handwriting was already on the wall, or rather scribbled across the cement façades of a hundred bridges and barrios — "Cuba, sí, Yanqui, no." "Latin America was dividing into two groups," the task force report asserted: "those that pin their faith on a communist solution . . . and those that hope to maintain freedom, achieving at the same time social justice and improved economic conditions. We must make certain . . . that the latter group prevails."

Accompanying the Cold War, and equal in importance, was the technological flowering that provided a new dimension of reality for the hope of enriched life for the Latin masses. "It all began with the transistor radio," a Latin diplomat once told me. And perhaps it did. But somehow, irresistibly — through the Andean passes, across the Amazonian basin to the sugar plantations of northern Brazil, down the coastal fringe of Brazil's immensity to the River Platte and Buenos Aires, upward along the Chilean littoral — there moved the message of new possibilities. The word, once made manifest, could not be recalled. People who live with almost unbearable toil, resigned either to fate or the decrees of Providence, lack the essential condition of progress — the belief that man can master his own environment. Hopeless men do not

make either modern nations or modern social revolutions. "Dream
the impossible dream," sings the man of La Mancha. But it is the
possible dream that summons the armies of discontent. And the
impossibility that was once a reality, a fact of life, had become a
lie, a deception imposed by the few who wished to ride the many.
And, once exposed, it had forever lost its persuasive force. The
ruling groups of Latin America — the handful of wealthy industrialists, the generals, the landowners — were increasingly, and
correctly, perceived as obstacles to awakened aspirations.

It was on the basis of these realities — not some ideal construct — that the Latin American task force formulated the observations and proposals that were an important foundation of Kennedy's Alliance for Progress.

"Since World War II," the report explained in an analysis from
which much of Kennedy's policy was drawn, "Latin America has
been largely ignored by the United States. . . . [T]he great
American corporations have been too influential in the Department of State policymaking offices. . . ." Our stress on "private
enterprise" had, in practice, "meant encouraging further enrichment of wealthy Latin industrialists who were untaxed, and unresponsive to the needs of the nation, while allowing American-
owned companies to accumulate their Latin profits in New York
banks."

As a result, "instead of seeking to identify ourselves with internal elements in those countries whose political aspirations and
economic objectives are similar to our own, the United States has
become associated in the Latin American mind with the oligar-
chies, the ruling classes, who have only their own interests at heart
. . . the forces of freedom have had little support from us and
have been unable to establish themselves as effective forces for
growth."

Of course, we could not occupy the continent, or command its
leaders. But the great influence of the United States was undeniable, and could be decisively fortified by the desire of the Latin
American majority — contoured by rooted values of culture, religion, and a common Western origin — to secure the fruits of
progress without sacrificing democratic freedoms. Even Castro, from
his base in the Sierra Maestra, had found it desirable to proclaim
devotion to democracy, lest his revolution be drained of popular
support or be aborted by American intervention. ("Fidel was always a communist," Che Guevara told me later in the summer of

1961, "but if he had admitted it you would never had let us reach Havana.")

"Popular enthusiasm for Cuban social reforms," the task force wrote, "helps to explain why the majority of Latin Americans do not share our concern with the growing communist orientation of that country. . . . Castro . . . is today a symbol of hope to millions of Latin Americans. . . . The objective of excluding Soviet influence is attainable by a closer identification with the needs and aspirations of the people, particularly with the need for social reform." Nor was this a painful necessity forced upon us by Cold War exigencies. "We are agreed," the report asserted, "that the great social transformation already going forth is desirable as well as unavoidable. . . . The hemisphere is large enough to have diverse social systems . . . which work together in friendship."

This diagnosis of the Latin condition, the report concluded, dictated a foreign policy founded on three principles. "First, the principle of human freedom and maintenance of humane standards of dealing with individuals. Second, that governments take their legitimacy from the free assents of their peoples . . . and third, that governments do not become either prisoners or tools of big power politics."

But the assertion of benign ideals was not enough. "Instructions should go forward," the report recommended, "that our embassies in Paraguay and Nicaragua (and elsewhere) should maintain correct but cool relations with the regimes — taking care not to become identified with the dictators there. Countries that have non-representative governments may be tolerated but are not candidates for special cordiality."

Yet representative government could not be sustained, would not survive, where impoverished masses toiled for subsistence while a handful of the fortunate enjoyed the resources of the nation. "[L]and hunger is at the heart of Latin America's political and social unrest. . . . We should consider the active steps that might be taken to push reluctant governments into making land reform (i.e., the redistribution of land to those who worked it)."

Although "American investment can be helpful, we should make it clear that private investment . . . is not the primary or determining element of American policy, nor even a major objective." Indeed, the U.S. should prevent "an excessive domination of U.S., private capital . . . and liquidate or reduce such domination where it exists." As token of this dramatic reversal of earlier policies we should provide a tin smelter for the nationalized mines of Bolivia, and offer financing, hitherto denied, to State-run oil companies"; even if Standard Oil and David Rockefeller objected, as they soon did, and not without effect.

Most important, we should make it clear that the Alliance for Progress was not an American plan to be forced on the weak and unwilling. "It is imperative," Kennedy was advised, "that in all our dealings with Latin American countries we treat them as partners, not as dependents. A 'father knows best' attitude has been the cause of much of the ill will directed toward the United States in recent years."

It is reported that when Karl Marx saw the steam locomotive on display at the great Victorian Exposition of 1851, he turned to his companion and joyously proclaimed, "The revolution is already here. The only question is its direction." Looking southward from the Kennedy White House, one could see that the Latin American revolution was there — had been gaining force and urgency for several years. The issue of its direction, and that only, was still unresolved; remains unresolved. It was in recognition of this fact — this self-evident perception of actual and irresistible conditions — that the Alliance for Progress was conceived. Those who seek, in the face of change, to perpetuate the past are the true romantics. Proclaiming themselves to be tough-minded pragmatists, they are destined to drown in the waxing tide they seek to arrest. And they may take many down with them. The tangible, realistic interests of the United States — prevention of Soviet incursion, the growth of progressive nations capable of sustaining their own independence, a continent whose development would enrich and strengthen the entire Western community — could be advanced only through a policy that placed us firmly, militantly, on the side of those who demanded that all were entitled to share in power and the fruits of growth. "And how fortunate we are," I wrote later in 1961, "to live at such a time, when necessity and self-interest merge with the deepest and most ancient beliefs of the American people."

"All right," Kennedy said to me the morning after his address to the Latin diplomats, "that's the easy part. I made a speech. Now let's show we mean it. Starting today." Fired with enthusiasm I returned to my office, only to find that a ten-year, multinational multibillion-dollar program could not be started that afternoon. In fact, it was almost three weeks before I embarked for Rio de Janeiro, where the leading Latin economists had convened for a meeting of the Inter-American Bank. My own purpose was not banking, but to draw up plans for the hemispheric conference which Kennedy had called to establish the Alliance for Progress. An alliance, after all, required allies — bound by formal agreement to common goals.

On the morning of my departure, I called on Secretary of State Rusk. I wanted to discuss my concerns about a certain issue that had been considered during the preceding weeks, but would be finally decided during my absence. It was the plan to sponsor a U.S.-trained group of Cuban exiles in an amphibious invasion of Cuba at a place known as the Playa de Giron, the "Bay of Pigs."

9 / The Bay of Pigs

A WEEK OR TWO after the inauguration (long enough for me to receive a top-secret clearance), Cord Meyer, a young, affable, wellborn, outwardly gentle officer of the CIA, called on me in my White House office. "We," he said (ah, that mysterious "we"), "thought you should know about some of the things we have been doing." He then proceeded to reveal to my wondering ears a tale of the CIA's eclectic adventures: mastery of the National Student Association (explained as our deterrent to communist youth groups), sponsorship of various intellectual and literary publications in Western Europe (explained as our deterrent to the philosophical ideologues of Marxism), contributions to noncommunist political parties from Italy to Peru (explained as our effort to achieve a democratic balance in election fights with Moscow-aided politicians). He obliquely referred to the brilliantly planned, virtually bloodless CIA overthrow of Guatemala's leftist government, and, of course, made casual reference to that pièce de résistance of CIA operations, the reestablishment in power of the shah of Iran. He did not mention the U-2. We had all read about that in the papers. Nor were the plans for a U.S.-sponsored assault on the Cuban mainland discussed. That would come a few weeks later, and from other sources. No security clearance bestowed the right to that information; only a "need to know," and my need had not yet been established.

Although these were only fragments of information, hinting at vast and wondrous operations still unrevealed, I was overwhelmed. Not dismayed or repelled. Far from it. I felt like an underprivileged child taken from the ghetto streets to tour the largest Toys 'R Us in distant suburbia. That president of the National Student Association I had met — on the CIA payroll; the *Encounter* magazine whose essays had absorbed my curious attention — a CIA production!

The briefing had achieved its purpose. I was impressed, even excited. The veil had been lifted on the alchemical magic of the clandestine, its power to transform the most innocent-seeming reality into an instrument of freedom's struggle. As Meyer unraveled his tale, I felt the first stirrings of that seductive power — the invisible child wandering unseen through the grown-up world: "Who knows? The Shadow knows" — which only time, reflection, and harsh experience would purge from the vulnerable soul.

Realities would clash with pretensions soon enough, reveal the small, weak, terribly limited congregation concealed beneath the dark billows of the wizard's cape. Yet that first encounter has, ever since, allowed me to understand how intelligent men, confronted with insuperable facts and arguments, despite a record of disaster heaped upon disaster, can still act as though in possession of some secret power to manipulate the destinies of men and whole nations. It is, after all, merely a subcategory of desire; the will to believe, from which none is wholly exempt, which can send men of brilliance and experience tumbling confidently toward the gale-tossed, advancing tides. It happened to the astonishing guardians of Periclean Athens, when they hurled their dwindling power against irrelevant Syracuse. It was to happen to America as it wasted the energies of a great nation — carved self-inflicted, still unhealed scars on the moment of its highest hopes — in a futile struggle over a remote stretch of populated jungle called Vietnam. And it was about to happen to John Kennedy in Cuba.

On March 17, 1960, while Kennedy was campaigning through the terminal snows of a Wisconsin winter, Eisenhower had approved a plan to train a group of Cuban exiles for possible use against the Castro regime, either to be infiltrated as guerrillas or to be used in direct assault against the Cuban mainland.

That August, as Kennedy completed his preparations for the campaign, the "Special Group" of the National Security Council had decided that the "guerrilla option" was "untenable"; that if the Cuban force was to be used, it would be for an invasion.

Later, in the spring of 1961, after we had made our own disastrous use of the fighting force bequeathed by Eisenhower, I wrote a memorandum to the president concluding that although Eisenhower did approve the training of Cuban exiles for what was later to be the Bay of Pigs, there was no decision to go ahead. On the basis of Eisenhower's general record (i.e., of nonintervention), we have to give him the benefit of the doubt and assume he would not have invaded; a conclusion strengthened by the fact that preparations were scheduled so as to avoid actions during his presidency, and his adamant resistance to pressures to speed up the process in order to attack before the election. Nor was anyone more insistent on immediate action than Vice-President Richard Nixon, who, while pleading with Ike to go ahead, had attacked Senator Kennedy's "shockingly reckless" encouragement to anti-Castro revolution. ("It's too bad it wasn't done then," Kennedy later remarked.)

It may well be true, as Clark Clifford has said, that at a meeting with Kennedy the day before the inauguration, Eisenhower said that it had been the "policy of [his] government" to help the exiles "to the utmost" and that this effort should be "continued and accelerated." But these vague and ambiguous exhortations did not constitute a recommendation for an invasion which Eisenhower himself had not approved, and which the Pentagon had said could not be successful without back-up support from the American military. The wily Ike was not going to let the new president off the hook — not after having been attacked for "losing" Cuba. If Kennedy should decide against using force, he would not be able to cite Eisenhower as justification. It wasn't Ike's problem anymore. He was going home.

During his final weeks in office, in January, Eisenhower severed diplomatic relations with Cuba, a step provoked by Castro's harassment of the American diplomatic mission and his increasingly open, more fiery attacks on the United States and all its works. "We will make the Andes into the Sierra Maestra of the revolution," Castro announced to admiring throngs. Freed from the uncomfortable, potentially subversive U.S. presence, Castro went to Moscow, where television cameras recorded his loving *abrazo* of Chairman Khrushchev, who returned the embrace, exultant, if somewhat surprised, at this unanticipated defection of a Caribbean state. Soon after, Che Guevara, revolutionary extraordinaire, now economic minister of Cuba, arrived to negotiate agreements for trade and economic assistance with the Russians, who were slightly puzzled, occasionally irritated, by this bearded, romantic revolutionary — a figure out of the communist past. "Guevara was impossible," Soviet Ambassador Dobrynin told me years later; "he wanted a little steel mill, an automobile factory. We told him Cuba wasn't big enough to support an industrial economy. They needed hard currency, and the only way to earn it was to do what they did best — grow sugar." I reflected that Dobrynin sounded exactly like an official of the State Department; the bureaucrat and the dreamer, enemies the whole world round.

Within a week of taking office Kennedy was briefed on the invasion plan by CIA Director Allan Dulles — a figure of awesome reputation dating back to modestly successful espionage activities during World War II, author of the successful CIA interventions in Iran and Guatemala, and Kennedy's first appointee to high office. Other members of the White House staff involved with foreign policy, myself included, were soon informed and engaged in deliberations.

The president was tempted. ("There are two people I'd like to get out," he had said during the campaign. "Jimmy Hoffa and Castro." Then, "Why doesn't he take off those fatigues? Doesn't he know the war is over?") However, he would need time, he told Dulles, to consider the plan, discuss it with advisers, think through the implications, the possible consequences. "That's understandable, Mr. President," the courteous Dulles responded, "but there isn't much time."

Kennedy was told — we were all told — that the Cuban brigade had been in training for almost a year, its morale was high, its fighting spirit at its peak. The Cubans wanted to go now. If we delayed much longer, the men would become dispirited, suspicious of our intentions; the brigade would dissolve, its members returning to Miami to report of a failure of American will — a failure of Kennedy's will. Inside Cuba there was an active underground, a few guerrilla groups, and increasing anti-Castro feeling among middle-class Cubans threatened by the transition to a socialist economy. (Cuba, relatively affluent, was one of the few Latin American countries with a substantial middle class.) However, Castro was moving to consolidate his power; the regular army was being displaced by a loyal militia. If we did not act swiftly, we would lose not only the brigade, but our last chance to overthrow Castro quickly, easily, and without direct military intervention. It was soon or never. At least that's what we were told by the CIA.

One of my law school professors, a distinguished authority on

the law of property, had told us, "If you let me frame the question, I will get the answer I want." Dulles and his acolytes had
framed the question: "Will you act now or forfeit, perhaps forever,
this golden opportunity?" And we all succumbed. Even those who
opposed the plan (except for Arthur Schlesinger) failed to challenge the imperative of a swift decision.

Admittedly we were new to government, unfamiliar with the
institutions of military and foreign policy, reluctant to challenge
the assertions of men who had helped conduct the Cold War since
its inception. But beneath the uninformed acquiescence, there was
also arrogance — the unacknowledged, unspoken belief that we
could understand, even predict, the elusive, often surprising, always conjectural course of historical change. Indeed, this false
certainty underlay the belief — on both sides of the Iron Curtain — that the United States and the Soviet Union were engaged
in a titanic, global struggle between communism and democratic
capitalism for the allegiance of the world's people. That assumption dominated, and helped explain the first of the Kennedy years;
only later would it yield to a more sophisticated awareness that
the multitudinous globe could not be crammed into simple categories — friends and enemies, communists or anticommunists —
that the world would go its own, unforeseeable way, not on one
road or two, but along a myriad of divergent paths.

Of course there was some justification for the rush to decision.
We were not fools. Undoubtedly a prolonged delay would have
brought dissolution of the Cuban brigade, an end to the glittering
possibility of a swift, decisive strike. Our error — our first error —
was the conviction that a reasoned decision was possible, blind-
ness to the reality that any conclusion was nothing more than a
guess built upon desire.

But there was another, more decisive, essentially inexplicable
error: The plan never had a chance. It was doomed from start to
finish. In retrospect it could be seen for what it was — not a mere
miscalculation but an absurdity. The plan called for sending twelve
hundred men on an amphibious invasion of a country defended
by a fairly well equipped army of over two hundred thousand.
Our own bountiful experience of island invasions in the Pacific,
where John Kennedy had commanded a PT boat, demonstrated
that a successful assault required overwhelming strength. Our val-
iant invaders would be outnumbered well over a hundred to one.

After the event there were frequent, self-justifying references to failed air strikes, poor communication, presidential indecision. Yet a few more bombs, better logistics, more detailed plans would not have made more than an hour or two's difference to the inevitable outcome. It was a handful against an army. In retrospect, it is clear that the invasion could have succeeded only if supported by direct U.S. military intervention. Yet Kennedy explicitly ruled this out, publicly and privately, in the weeks before the attack. At a press conference on April 12, asked about rumors of an impending U.S. attack on Cuba, Kennedy pledged, "There will not be, under any conditions, an intervention in Cuba by United States forces. . . . The basic issue . . . is between the Cubans themselves."

Privately he was even more forceful. Before the press conference, at a high-level council of war, a staff member — who had already sent the president a memorandum against the plan — tentatively suggested that if the invasion succeeded, and if the exiles proclaimed a revolutionary government, and if we recognized them, and if they were having trouble, and if they asked for help, then, and only then, we might have to send in some supporting forces.

"Under no circumstances," Kennedy exploded. "The minute I land one marine, we're in this thing up to our necks. I can't get the United States into a war, and then lose it, no matter what it takes. I'm not going to risk an American Hungary. And that's what it could be, a fucking slaughter." He paused. "Is that understood, gentlemen?"

"Yes, Mr. President," chorused the deputy director of the CIA and the representative of the Joint Chiefs of Staff.

"And you think they can make it on their own."

"Yes, Mr. President."

That could only mean — again in retrospect — that the invaders would be met not with guns, but brass bands, enthusiastic *abrazos*, and banners proclaiming "Welcome to the Liberators of Cuba."

At a meeting at the State Department that same week, the CIA operations chief, Richard Bissell, went over final plans for the attack he had nurtured so long and lovingly. A cultivated man with impeccable credentials — good school, good family, good war — a social acquaintance of many Kennedy intimates, including the president's own family, Bissell was best known as the originator and handler of the U-2 spy plane which had given us much useful information about Soviet troop and weapons deployment; and

which, bad luck, old chaps, had destroyed the Eisenhower–
Khrushchev summit when the Russians shot it down. On balance,
however, it was viewed as a triumph of Bissell's imaginative in-
genuity. Perhaps it had made prospects for peace more remote,
but at least we knew about the enemy. (After he was fired, Bissell
spent much of his time contriving ingenious justifications — the
occupation of a professional lifetime, after all — for his ardent
sponsorship of the Cuba adventure. As obsessively as the Ancient
Mariner, he recounted his sad tale of promises broken, decisions
not taken, fatal hesitations — all fabricated to divert attention from
his own fabulous staggering miscalculation.)

The plan, as Bissell described it, was for the exile force "to
establish a beachhead, establish a revolutionary government, and
rally the oppressed army and people of Cuba to the banner of
liberation."

"Suppose they can't establish a beachhead?" he was asked.

"It's unlikely," Bissell responded, "but we have a contingency
plan." He turned to his uniformed military aide, who drew a document from his briefcase and handed it to Bissell, who then pointed
to a large map of the targeted section of Cuba coastline. "If they
can't hold on here," he said, pointing to the Bay of Pigs, "they'll
move into the mountains here," pointing to a spot about forty
miles away, "and form guerrilla units which we can resupply by
air. That's the worst that can happen."

Unfortunately it was not a topographical map, and thus did not
reveal that the terrain between the landing spot and the mountain
haven consisted largely of impassable swampland. Nor did he ever
inform the brigade leaders of this "contingency plan." They knew
Cuba better than we, and might have had second thoughts about
an operation that provided so suicidal an alternative.

Finally, rather timidly, I asked about a problem which, as an
amateur in these matters, seemed to me of legitimate concern.
"How do we know the Cuban people will support the rebels, why
do we think they want to overthrow Castro?"

Without a moment's hesitation, Bissell turned again to his bemedaled colleague: "We have an NIE [National Intelligence Es-
timate] on that, don't we?" The officer nodded in affirmation.

It was an unforgettable moment. I was stunned. Looking around
the room I saw my colleagues sitting silently, seemingly unaf-
fected, perhaps quieted, as I was, by a fear of appearing foolish. I
had no experience of covert activities or military planning, had

never shared in decisions of such complex magnitude. And across the room were the men who had done it all.

A National Intelligence Estimate is simply an intimidating label for a document prepared by a few government employees, its conclusions no better than the analytic powers of its drafters and the accuracy of their sources. It is a rather slender support for a commitment to invade another country. Moreover, I doubt that such a document existed. In the interests of secrecy, the intelligence arm of the CIA — that section charged with the preparation of intelligence estimates — had been excluded from the Bay of Pigs planning. It would have been a miraculous display of intuitive genius, or a coincidence of unprecedented magnitude, had they prepared a document in support of an invasion they didn't know about. (Except, of course, for what they read in the *New York Times.*) The president's own task force had concluded that Castro enjoyed the overwhelming support of the Cuban people. Every independent observer — American and Latin alike — had come to a similar conclusion: Certainly there was discontent, unrest, even shock at the sudden turn toward Moscow, but Castro had cast out the old order, returned the natural wealth and beauty of the country to *campesinos* and workers, and, in return, still enjoyed the expectant support of his people. There was no basis whatsoever for the belief that Cuban unrest had reached the point of desperation where multitudes would risk their own lives by rushing to support a small group of rebels struggling to maintain a foothold on a remote beach.

Yet the CIA, and other proponents of the plan, kept insisting that Cuba was a tinderbox, ready to spring into flame at the first spark of insurrection. Why did they say this? There was no evidence, no auguring incidents of rebellion, no examples of growing resistance. They said it because, without the prospect of an alliance with internal rebels, the invasion would have been revealed for what it was — a preposterous, doomed fiasco.

Just prior to the week of final decision I was scheduled to leave for Rio for several days of meetings with leading Latin economists to plan the Alliance for Progress conference, scheduled for August. Fearful that our still-unborn hemispheric policy — the grand Alliance for Progress — might be aborted on the beaches of Cuba, I had breakfast in the White House mess with Schlesinger, Walt Rostow, and McGeorge Bundy to discuss whether the mounting momentum toward presidential approval could be arrested.

"Even if the landings are successful," I argued, "and a revolutionary government is set up, they'll have to ask for our help. And if we agree it'll be a massacre. Castro's forces won't just surrender. The Spanish are willing to die. We'll have to fight house-to-house in Havana. It'll be an American Hungary."

As, somewhat overwrought, I drained my final cup of coffee, Bundy advised, "Listen, Dick, I have an idea. Why don't you go over to see Rusk before you leave."

Brilliant. That's just what I would do. Only later did I realize that the suggestion was little more than a device to get rid of this irritating young man — a mere stripling — who had no business meddling in such lofty matters, but who could not be simply dismissed because, after all, the president seemed to like him, was known to listen to him on occasion.

I went almost immediately to Rusk's office. He listened patiently to my monologue, then — I'll never forget it — leaned back on his chair, pressed his fingertips together, hovered for a moment in this pose of thoughtful concentration, and then, slowly, pausing between each phrase: "You know, Dick, maybe we've been oversold on the fact that we can't say no to this thing."

That was it. And there went the ball game. If the secretary of state believed he "couldn't" say no, who could, except the president, who was himself surrounded by men who were saying "yes." I was beginning to understand the secret of Rusk's extraordinary staying power — say little, and, above all, go with the flow.

Mine was not the only discordant voice, nor the most important. Senator Fulbright had written the president that the venture was "ill-considered," that it would be impossible "to conceal the U.S. hand," that "to give this activity even covert support is of a piece with the hypocrisy and cynicism for which the United States is constantly denouncing the Soviet Union." Moreover, the senator asserted, "If the exiles meet resistance and ask for our help, it will mean the use of armed force," which would undo "the work of thirty years in trying to live down earlier interventions." Leave Castro alone, Fulbright concluded; "the Castro regime is a thorn in the flesh but it is not a dagger in the heart."

Arthur Schlesinger, at Kennedy's request, wrote a long and equally forceful memorandum in opposition to the CIA plans. In the State Department Undersecretary of State Chester Bowles expressed his own vigorous objection in a memo that Rusk did not bother to send on to the White House.

However, the dissenters were all on the outer fringes of deliberation, excluded — with rare exceptions — from the small inner circle to which deliberation had been confined in order to ensure "maximum security" for the operation. Robert Kennedy and Ted Sorensen did not participate, presumably because they had no formal responsibilities for foreign policy.

From the window of the plane carrying me to Rio I looked down upon a continent whose staggering reality seemed indifferently related to the intensely absorbing concerns of Washington debate. The tiny island of Cuba appeared over the left wing tip and was gone; the entire Caribbean — like some accidental lake set amid a shoreless wilderness — traversed in what seemed like minutes, before we crossed the northern coastline of Venezuela, and I saw the interminable stretch of forests, a huge swatch of undifferentiated green laced with shining crooked threads of blue leading to the legendary Amazon, which appeared a slash carved by some angry divinity across the face of a continent. As we approached Rio — our descent monitored by the hopefully benign, outwardly expressionless, Christ of the Andes — Cuba seemed very far away, was far away, our fear almost absurd, the bombastic pretensions of a Castro muted, stilled, and dissolved by the multiform immensity of a world ample enough to accommodate, scorn, and discard the jostling claims of a hundred petty pretenders. For a moment I allowed the heretic thought that all of us — Americans, Cubans, transient tyrants, hopeful leaders of infant democracies — were playing our children's games at the foot of a tolerant giant careful, sometimes, not to crush us as it walked, with ponderous, unknowable certitude, toward its own destination.

The plane touched earth, the small, impermanent welts swollen into a towering conglomeration of concrete buildings; creatures invisible from the air become life size, rushing to meet us, take our bags, speed us past smiling officials, restoring our inward sense of importance — our own, and the importance of the work we had come to do. From the air and from the ground — two views, two visions, two dimensions of thought. Which was true? Or, which was closer to the truth? It didn't matter. This was our moment, our small portion of energy and mortality plucked from the passage of millennia. And we would use it as best we could.

And then there was Rio: of all cities the most hostile to dark contemplations, the very air an aphrodisiac, its warm, odored moisture at once calming the mind and arousing the flesh with promise of sensual pleasure. I attended long meetings with Latin American economists, discussed the proper formulation of a ten-year plan of development, drank with journalists long past midnight while they imparted information and opinions that embassy officials had ignored or prudently withheld from the enigmatic emissary of a still unfamiliar president, and enjoyed, in the time remaining, the girls of Ipanema.

Although rumors of an attack on Cuba had circulated throughout the hemisphere, the subject rarely arose. One diplomat, a banker from Argentina, advised me, "If you're going to invade, and, of course, my government cannot condone unilateral intervention, for God's sake make sure you finish him off." I asked a Colombian ambassador — a man of distinction and experience — "Why don't the Russians pump a lot of money into Cuba and make it a model of development that would strengthen the communist cause in other countries?" Slightly surprised at my seeming innocence, he hesitated, then, smiling benignly: "Because you don't feed the lamb in the mouth of the lion."

To those bordering the Caribbean, Cuba was a real danger. They were apprehensive that Castro — either by example, or by direct material help — might strengthen nascent communist movements in their own countries. However, these same countries — especially Mexico and the nations of Central America — had themselves felt the weight of American intervention most heavily and could not support action that might be precedent for later interference with their own affairs. At least not openly. ("Get rid of Trujillo, first," President Betancourt of Venezuela had advised us, "then you can do something about Castro.")

For the larger countries of the south, Cuba was an American problem. What had they to fear from some small, militarily insignificant island in the remote Caribbean — as far from Buenos Aires, for example, as Berlin was from Washington? Nor would it have occurred to them to jeopardize the great promise of the Alliance for Progress by opposing us on so trivial a matter. "Do what you think you have to do," was the attitude, "and then proceed with more serious matters."

By the time I returned to Washington, the invasion had been approved. When I entered the Oval Office to report on my trip, Kennedy took me by the arm, led me to a window overlooking the Rose Garden — presumably so no one could overhear him — and said, "Well, Dick, it looks like we're finally going to put your

Cuban policy into action," meaning, of course, my ill-begotten campaign statement about the need to support the "freedom fighters." John Kennedy, I thought, had a great sense of humor. But it was the last laugh we would have for some time.

The invasion was scheduled for April 17. It collapsed almost as quickly as it began. A few days later a grim State Department circular to all diplomatic posts reported: "A volunteer force of some 1200 Cuban freedom fighters" (my old campaign phrase) "landed on south coast Cuba for declared purpose liberating their country from communist dictatorship Fidel Castro . . . they had received support from American sources" (our government's sponsorship was obvious and already admitted) ". . . actual operation badly mauled by heavy air and tank activity . . . beachhead was overrun on afternoon April 19 . . . casualties severe."

When it was all over, Kennedy was furious — furious at the advisers whose persuasions were mingled with misjudgments so grotesque as to constitute misrepresentation; furious at Castro, who had humiliated his fledgling administration; furious, most of all, at himself for having approved and commanded this comic-opera fiasco whose failure, in the new clarity of retrospect, was quickly seen to be inevitable. He should have seen it. He didn't see it. Why hadn't he?

The anger and confusion that suffused the White House was not conducive to clear thinking and sober analysis. The day after the invasion collapsed, Kennedy delivered the most truculent statement of his administration. He would let Castro go this time, he said (what choice, what sensible choice did he have?), but "our restraint is not inexhaustible," we will act "alone, if necessary . . . to safeguard our security . . . and should that time ever come we do not intend to be lectured on intervention by those whose character was stamped for all time on the bloody streets of Budapest."

It was a threat of possible U.S. invasion, in the most bombastic Cold War tradition. Fortunately, he didn't mean it. Having exorcised his anger, Kennedy repelled all further suggestions of military action and proceeded, sensibly, to cut his losses.

In the White House, a few hours after his speech, I walked into the Oval Office and told Kennedy that I thought his statement about unilateral intervention was unwise. It just sounded like a kind of vague threat in the face of defeat, I said, when we have no intention at all of intervening in Cuba.

He looked toward me, unangered, replying in mild, barely distinct tones. "I didn't want us to look like a paper tiger. We should scare people a little, and I did it to make us appear still tough and powerful." He got up, lay his paper aside, shrugged his shoulder. "Anyways, it's done. You may be right, but it's done." My notes of that day comment that "this was the first time I had made an ex post facto criticism of the president."

By the next day the reemergence of rational discussion signaled the dissolution of shock. The morning of April 21, Kennedy opened the breakfast meeting that preceded his scheduled press conference by remarking, "The happiest people in government today are the ones who can say they didn't know anything about it." Then, after a brief discussion: "I'll make a short opening statement designed to cut off questions about Cuba, and not take any more questions on the subject." According to my notes: "He was concerned that the entire blame for this not be placed on the CIA. His concern was based on the newspaper stories this morning, especially James Reston of the *New York Times*, indicating that the operation was not properly staffed, and that there had been no National Security Council meeting. The president pointed out that this had been given careful consideration by all the responsible people of the NSC with the exception of Ed Murrow, Doug Dillon, and Frank Ellis. It was decided to leak the story that this operation had been carefully studied by the Joint Chiefs of Staff, and approved — which was true. There was talk about remedial measures. The president said he 'could fire Allen Dulles — and Dulles was the kind of guy who would go quietly' — but he did not think that was advisable, because Dulles, as a conservative and a Republican, 'helped keep the Republicans off his back. As long as he was there, they couldn't criticize.' "

"In my experience," Kennedy told us, "things like this go along for a while, but memory is short, and if we just sit tight for about three weeks, things will cool off and we can proceed from there." Whom was he trying to reassure? Himself, perhaps. And he was right. Although scars remained, the president's popularity went to an all-time high of over 80 percent. ("The worse you do, the better they like you," Kennedy remarked on seeing the poll results.) There was no strengthening of communist movements throughout the hemisphere, and at the Alliance for Progress Conference four months later, not a single Latin nation — with the exception of Cuba — made any reference to the Bay of Pigs. In terms of global politics and the strength of Kennedy's own presidency, it came to be regarded as an aberration, swiftly forgotten. But not by Cuba, and not by the embittered and abandoned exile groups who now dominate Miami politics.

There was, however, an augury of the turbulent years to come, in the unanticipated flurry of domestic protest. Members of the "Fair Play for Cuba" committee — including many individuals who had supported Kennedy's election — organized to denounce the American "aggression." The violent Cold War rhetoric of John Foster Dulles, the destruction of our U-2 spy plane, had elicited little more than muted cocktail-party dissent. Now people — white, middle-class people — were in the streets. They had expected something more, something different, from Kennedy and, fueled by the anger of damaged illusions, carried placards, made speeches, marched. The protesters were small in number, their actions marginal, their organization quickly dissolved. But they were the first faint tremor of a shift in the foundation. The suppressing fears of McCarthyism, the muting complacency of the Eisenhower era were disintegrating, liberating new energies of discontent, a refusal of resignation; a change which — ironically in this instance — had been an important source of Kennedy's appeal. "Every man could make a difference," even in opposition to presidential power itself. It was an early symptom — insubstantial and isolated — of a time when millions would begin to feel that their futures, the shape of life in America, the decisions of remote Washington potentates, could be influenced, perhaps decisively, by the shared purpose, the united energies of aggrieved, determined individuals.

Meanwhile Kennedy acted to salvage what he could, to put the event behind him, to reshape his government and reexamine his own inward failures of analysis. "We're not going to have any search for scapegoats," he instructed a meeting of the National Security Council; and swiftly made a public declaration (ungrammatically) that "the final responsibilities of any failure is mine, and mine alone." The president's assertion — no reference to Eisenhower's "plan," no veiled hints of staff inadequacy or agency misrepresentation — was received with relief, thought courageous, began the restoration of confidence. It was a wise decision. And it was absolutely true. He had listened to the briefings, heard all the arguments, and given the order that was his alone to give.

Why?

The literature of the Kennedy years is replete with justifying explanations. When he took office, the attacking forces were trained and ready to go. He and his staff, new to government, were told by leaders of the CIA and military — men of long experience and high reputation — that the operation would probably succeed in getting rid of Castro. ("One cannot be certain in this business, Mr. President, but this is as close as you come.") He was reassured that the Cuban people would rise against Castro, the Cuban militia would not fight, the U.S. identification kept secret. All wrong. Probably not lies, but the product of wishful thinking by arrogant men, intoxicated to the point of delusion by their command over the arcane mysteries of "covert" war; their judgment distorted by the intensity of their desire to prove themselves, to cut away this communist growth that had been insidiously intruded upon the chaste body of the Americas. To protect both secrecy and certainty of judgment, analysts familiar with Cuba — within our own government, and from allies — were excluded from deliberations. ("In spite of . . . alienation of the middle class," the British Joint Intelligence Committee informed the CIA before the Bay of Pigs, "the hard core of fanatical support for the regime, backed by an efficient propaganda and security apparatus, is likely to be able to resist attempts, from within or from outside Cuba, to overthrow the regime.")

Still, beneath the assurances, the distortions, the grotesque miscalculation, was the fact that twelve hundred men were to attack an army of two hundred thousand, with no evidence that anything but armed hostility would greet them. That fatal, decisive reality could have been exposed had Kennedy more forcefully probed, questioned, analyzed the expositions of his advisers; had he talked to those outside the operation who were not blinded by emotional commitment or professional hubris. Yet he did not do so. He abandoned his characteristic method of operation: the search for divergent views, the forceful challenge of expert opinion, the refusal to be restrained in interrogation by either the reputation or record of those he confronted.

How can it be explained? Kennedy himself didn't have the answer. "How did I ever let it happen?" he asked rhetorically, "I know better than to listen to experts. They always have their own agenda. All my life I've known it, and yet I still barreled ahead." Then, turning to Arthur Schlesinger and referring to his memo in opposition, he said, "Well, Arthur, at least you've got a good piece of paper for your book on 'Kennedy — the Only Years.' That is if you dare publish it while I'm still alive."

But I don't believe it was simply bad advice or some inexplicable mental lapse that led Kennedy into the Bay of Pigs. Years before, as an army private stationed in southern France, I had visited a casino in Biarritz to try my luck with the dice. After an hour or two I had won several hundred dollars, a huge sum to one of my meager means, and departing with my winnings — imagination fired with images of purchasable pleasures — I passed the roulette table. With a single bet I could double my winnings. I placed all my money on the black, and the ball came to rest on the red.

From his survival in the Solomons when the Japanese had split the PT boat in two, John Kennedy had been on a roll. Against all the odds — in defiance of expert political opinion — he had challenged and defeated Senator Henry Cabot Lodge, the titans of the Democratic party (Humphrey, Johnson, and Stevenson), and, finally, Richard Nixon, chosen successor to one of the country's most popular presidents. "They said it couldn't be done, and he did it." Now it was Castro's turn. What difference did odds make, if you were fortune's child?

Kennedy would not make that mistake again. He continued to believe in himself — capacities, judgment, goals — but the fates could not be counted on.

It would be absurd to pretend that the Bay of Pigs was somehow a "blessing in disguise," an inexpensive lesson in the limits of newly acquired presidential power. The first adventure of the New Frontier had been a failure, and not an ordinary failure, but one that reeked of incompetence, of naïve and therefore dangerous militance; one that weakened the new president's pretension, so eloquently proclaimed just a few months before, to leadership of the free world.

But all this could be overcome. The agonies of this beginning could tutor the long journey that lay ahead. The president had learned — as had Lincoln and Roosevelt before him — that the use of power, the decision to use it, could not be entrusted to those whose professional lives had been devoted to the management of force. They were believers by necessity, compelled to assert the effectiveness of the instruments they had spent a lifetime to master.

Kennedy would become much more cautious, more aware that the immense power he commanded was a blunt and often untrustworthy instrument, ill suited to the achievement of precisely limited objectives, rendered impotent when shackled by the restraints imposed by political necessities.

It is said that the young Oliver Wendell Holmes, having written a college paper "disproving" the philosophy of Plato, brought the completed work to Ralph Waldo Emerson, a family friend. Emerson read carefully, and then, addressing the young, expectant Holmes, handed it back with the remark that "when you strike at a king you must kill him." The armed might of the United States is bound by a similar imperative; unsuited to limited objectives, unforgiving of failure, its only response to frustration is more of the same — larger numbers, increasingly destructive force — until the enemy is destroyed. This lesson, one that inheres in the nature of modern military might, is not that every adversary must be pursued to extinction, but that in loosing such power you may well be compelling yourself to a choice between total destruction or defeat; that the equivocal accommodations of the pre-nuclear age are no longer a practical tool of statesmanship, that war is not an extension of politics, but the end of politics.

And there was another lesson, never articulated — at least not within my hearing — never discussed in the many of documents that proposed and discussed, argued and rebutted. In the language of diplomatic analysis, the Bay of Pigs was a "failure," a "setback" leaving the "problem of Castro" unresolved. But there was blood in the water. Blood on the beach. Metal-torn bodies. The shackled limbs of a thousand prisoners. In the White House there was no blood. Only fit and prosperous men, conservatively attired in the dark expensive suits of democratic nobility. It had all seemed so respectable in the ordinarily quiet, occasionally heated, words of debate: reasons examined, objections met and surmounted, neatly typed plans carefully stacked on shined mahogany tables, the well-barbered heads nodding in acquiescence to decisions, the orders carried at light speed on the abstract chastity of electromagnetic waves to ships waiting to embark and a handful of eager pilots.

It is true that decisions of state are difficult, even agonizing. But it is even harder to die.

In the months that followed, John Kennedy and his brother devoted extraordinary efforts to securing the release of those taken prisoner at the Bay of Pigs. It soon became clear that Castro would make a deal. He would sell prisoners for medical supplies or food or farm implements or other goods needed by his badly strained economy. (Ah, those stingy Russians.) He wanted ransom. And we had, the president thought, no choice but to pay. "Let's see if it can be done privately, Dick," he told me. "Bobby can get some businessmen to contribute. We'll give them a tax write-off." Then, more intently: "But whatever it takes, let's do it. I put those men in there. They trusted me. And they're in prison now because I fucked up. I have to get them out."

With that conversation, the curtain of my understanding closes. Presidents don't lament or cry, at least in front of subordinates. But Kennedy had seen men perish in combat. He knew that the long chain of command terminated in a fearful reality. Did the fate of his Cuban "freedom fighters" influence him, affect the course of future decisions? Were they one of the lessons of the Bay of Pigs? I do not know. But never again would he seem to be at ease with the idea of sending men out to fight.

"The tumult and the shouting die," the President had candidly accepted blame, the warm Caribbean tides gently stroked the now unperturbed sands of northern Cuba. But behind the majestically expressionless facade of the White House there was turbulence. The United States has been defeated, the president humiliated. Castro's hegemony over his island nation became virtually invulnerable, while half a world away the delighted Krushchev thought he perceived naïveté, inexperience in the temperament of his youthful adversary, a fatal weakness of will behind the soaring rhetoric.

Within a week of the Bay of Pigs, Kennedy called a meeting of his advisers to discuss the next stages of our Cuban policy. Around the table in the Cabinet Room were the familiar faces of the national security apparatus, but accompanying them were the Kennedy men: Ted Sorensen and other members of the domestic staff, and McGeorge Bundy, who, without change of title, had been given charge of the White House Situation Room and would, it was understood, now be Kennedy's principal assistant — conduit for information and directive — on almost all matters of foreign policy. Most significant of all was the presence of Robert Kennedy, whose energies, previously absorbed by the multiple responsibilities of the Justice Department, would now be directly engaged in the president's conduct of foreign policy.

The agenda for the meeting was "A review of the U.S. policy toward Cuba." The unspoken issue was What Next? — i.e., How could we enfeeble, perhaps eliminate, the communist rulers of Cuba? The question itself reveals the weakness of the pragmatic liberalism that we so ardently professed. It implied that if a problem can be stated it can be solved.

Of course the assumption is a fantasy. Some "problems" cannot be solved — e.g., the "liberation of Eastern Europe." A problem that has no solution is not a problem at all, but a reality — an historical fact that must be regarded as an assumption, not an object of action. This was to prove true of the "Cuban problem."

At the meeting, Undersecretary of State Chester Bowles, substituting for the absent Dean Rusk (who often found a reason to avoid meetings certain to be heated and controversial), read aloud the recommendations of the State Department. The tedious, bureaucratic verbiage, although crowded with qualifications and contingencies, essentially concluded that nothing could now be done; that Castro's power was secure from anything except an American invasion. (An accurate estimate.) When Bowles finished, Bobby exploded: "That's the most meaningless, worthless thing I've ever heard. You people are so anxious to protect your own asses that you're afraid to do anything. All you want to do is dump the whole thing on the president. We'd be better off if you just quit and left foreign policy to someone else. . . ." As the embarrassing tirade continued, the president sat calmly, outwardly relaxed, only the faint click from the metallic pencil cap he was tapping against his almost incandescently white, evenly spaced teeth disrupting his silence — a characteristic revelation that some inner tension was being suppressed. I became suddenly aware — am now certain — that Bobby's harsh polemic reflected the president's own concealed emotions, privately communicated in some earlier, intimate conversation. I knew, even then, there was an inner hardness, often volatile anger beneath the outwardly amiable, thoughtful, carefully controlled demeanor of John Kennedy.

After Bobby had finished, the group sat silently, stunned by the ferocity of his assault, until the president — without comment on his brother's accusations — named a "task force" to develop a new Cuban policy from which the State Department was pointedly omitted. Shortly thereafter Bowles was fired.

To my surprise, I was named vice-chairman of the group (under Paul Nitze of Defense), and, a few weeks later, when Nitze went on to more promising endeavors, I became chairman. I was excited, gratified, almost jubilant at this indication of presidential confidence. It was probably the most significant appointment of my Kennedy career. And the most meaningless. Our objective was to contain the spread of Castroism and unseat the communist government in Cuba. And although Castroism would be contained, it was not because of anything we did.

There was, however, no dearth of recommendations for action. My desk was soon heaped with CIA and Defense proposals for a variety of covert activities; for the escalation of propaganda aimed at the Cuban mainland; for the formal expulsion of Cuba from the OAS. It looked like action. It sounded like action. It satisfied, partially, the need for the illusion of action. But it all came to very little.

The Defense Department assigned Ed Lansdale to work with me to devise measures for the overthrow of Castro. (Lansdale had an almost legendary reputation as the man who had helped defeat the communist insurrection in the Philippines.) Together we called upon the National Security Agency, the CIA, even the Joint Chiefs of Staff, exhorting the chieftains of American power to conjure plans that might lead to Castro's undoing. After the first week, while we sat in my office preparing another in a series of endless memoranda, Lansdale looked toward me. "You know, Dick, it's impossible."

"What's impossible?" I asked.

"There is no way you can overthrow Castro without a strong, indigenous political opposition. And there is no such opposition, either in Cuba or outside it."

He was right, of course. And although we kept trying, it was hopeless from the beginning. Within two weeks I drafted a memorandum for the president, which came to much the same conclusion that had unjustifiably discredited Bowles: that our most effective "immediate" steps would be an effort to organize collective action, help democratic parties in other countries, and — most important of all — accelerate the Alliance for Progress. "This program," I wrote Kennedy, "with its emphasis on social and economic advance is the real hope of preventing a communist takeover."

As for more immediate threats, I concluded that the spread of Castroism was a very real danger, but that "in the last six months there has been a significant decline in Cuban effectiveness . . . because of the growing isolation of communist-fidelista elements from the Democratic left as Castro's pro-Soviet bent has become more apparent" (most communists in Latin America were essentially nationalists, with no desire to substitute Soviet mastery for American) ". . . in fact, most of the greatest danger spots . . . do not owe either their existence or their strength to Castro, but to local and independent leadership. *This danger would continue to grow if our only anti-communist move were to knock out Castro.*"

There was, however, one possibility that had not occurred to me, which I heard for the first and only time at a meeting of the Cuban task force sometime around the middle of May. About twenty people were gathered at a conference table in the State Department, when Secretary of Defense McNamara, having sat through an hour of inconclusive discussion, rose to leave for another appointment and, firmly grasping my shoulder with his right hand, announced, "The only thing to do is eliminate Castro." I listened, puzzled, thinking, Isn't that just what we have been talking about for a month? when the CIA representative looked toward McNamara and said, "You mean Executive Action." McNamara nodded, then, looking toward me: "I mean it, Dick, it's the only way." I had never heard the phrase "Executive Action" before. But its meaning was instantly apparent. Assassination. Two divergent thoughts raced through my mind. Could he really mean it? Did we do such things? And: It's absurd — even if you killed Castro you would accomplish nothing. His brother Raul or Che would take his place, both, if anything, more fanatic, more devoutly pledged to international communism, than Fidel.

After McNamara left I continued the meeting without reference to his remark, although the CIA representative, on his return to Langley, carefully prepared a memo "for the files" recording the "suggestion" of the secretary of defense. It was the first and only time that I heard a serious suggestion of assassination, although, with the dissolution of the task force and the establishment of a more permanent anti-Castro operation, my own involvement in anti-Cuban actions came to an end. (In 1966, while traveling through Latin America with Bobby Kennedy, he remarked, "I'm tired of all these Latins attacking me for going after Castro. The fact is that I'm the guy who saved his life." What did he mean? I don't know. For just at that moment we were approached by a mutual friend who wished to introduce us to two very beautiful Latin ladies.)

I do not know if we tried to kill Castro — and there is much evidence that we did — but, if so, the effort is only added testimony to the futile vanity of "covert operations."

10 / Meeting with Che Guevara

A FEW WEEKS after the disaster in Cuba, Kennedy called me. "Let's get moving on the Alliance for Progress," he directed, "before they think I didn't mean it, that all we care about is Castro."

"We are moving," I replied. "We have an agenda" (prepared in my Rio meetings) "and the conference is set for the beginning of August." There was no reply. Semi-apologetically I went on: "There are more than twenty countries involved and we have to talk to them first to make sure everyone understands what's supposed to happen; otherwise we'll just end up with two weeks of speeches."

"It ought to be tomorrow," Kennedy replied.

"It's not just the Latins, I can't even get the State Department to agree on a position."

"We already have a position. Tell them to read my speech." He paused. "Never mind. I'll talk to Dillon." (Treasury Secretary Dillon was to head the U.S. delegation.)

At the beginning of August a thirty-three-man U.S. delegation boarded one of the special presidential jets for the long flight to Montevideo, Uruguay, from which we would proceed to the conference site at Punta del Este — a popular seaside resort in summer, virtually abandoned during the chill of the subequatorial winter. The shuttered hotels and restaurants had been reopened for the use of the economic ministers and their advisers, who were gathering for what was hoped would be an historic meeting; a few hundred delegates assembled in luxurious isolation, encouraged by the physical setting to form personal relationships, to continue the discourse of the day over meals and into the nights. For recreation we would take walks along the deserted beaches littered with the bodies of penguins cast ashore by the Antarctic currents. The formal sessions themselves were conducted in a remodeled gambling casino, which had been wired for simultaneous translation in English, Spanish, Portuguese, and French.

The delegations, coming from every American republic, represented a staggering diversity of political and economic structures — dictatorships and democracies, entrenched privilege and populist aspiration. The finance ministers themselves were, for the most part, drawn from the more intelligent and enlightened members of the oligarchy; hopeful, suspicious, apprehensive. From the beginning attention was focused on the dramatic conjunction of the men who led the delegations from the United States and Cuba. C. Douglas Dillon was imposing in appearance as he moved confidently through the conference hall, meticulously attired in a dark pin-striped suit. Millionaire investment banker turned public servant, he was now the personal representative of the president of the United States. Che Guevara, of prosperous Argentine parents, was a medical doctor turned professional revolutionary. Hero of the Sierra Maestra, Castro's closest confidant, now czar of the Cuban economy, he wore the battle fatigues of revolution, combat boots, and a black beret, his bearded face dominated by the intensity of his restless, questioning eyes. (The dress was as practical as it was symbolic. In the stifling conference chamber, Guevara was the only comfortably dressed man in the room.)

However, the contrast between the two men was merely symbolic of a rooted hostility which made any accord between the United States and Cuba inconceivable. Our task was to reach agreement among all the other American states on a program of economic development that would require a commitment to large changes in the distribution of power and wealth within their own societies. From the moment of our arrival it was clear that such agreement was possible only if the United States was also willing to make a specific and substantial pledge.

The night before the conference opened I sat in Dillon's hotel room along with other members of the American delegation as we discussed our fear that the conference might degenerate into a series of rhetorical exchanges without agreement on tangible and

specific goals. "We're asking them to make a very difficult effort,"
I objected, "and all we're giving them is words. They won't be-
lieve it." Listening quietly to the discussion, Dillon interrupted:
"I'll pledge a billion dollars a year." The representative of the
State Department, Assistant Secretary Ed Martin, was horrified.
"We can't do that. Nobody has approved it. It hasn't been cleared.
At least we have to consult the secretary of state."

"What do you suggest?" Dillon asked. "That we all sit on the
beach in Uruguay for a month or two while the people in Washington discuss it?"

"We don't have the authority," Martin responded.

"Of course I have the authority," Dillon pronounced. "I'm the
personal representative of the president of the United States . . .
Plenipotentiary. It says so on my credentials. And I'm going to give
them a billion dollars."

The next day, August 5, after the delegates had assembled for
their opening session, Dillon rose from his chair at the conference
table, announced that he had a statement from President Kennedy, and began to read: "Only an effort of towering dimension,
an effort similar to that which was needed to rebuild the economies of Western Europe, can ensure the fulfillment of our Alliance for Progress. To that end, the United States will allocate at
least one billion dollars in development assistance to Latin America in the first year of the Alliance."

The room suddenly came alive; delegates stirred, turned and
whispered to their colleagues, then fell politely silent as Dillon
continued to read.

"The tasks before us are vast, the problems difficult, the challenges unparalleled. But we carry with us the vision of a new and
better world and the unlimited power of free men guided by free
governments. And I believe that our ultimate success will make
us proud to have lived and worked at this historic moment in the
life of our hemisphere."

The delegates — sophisticated men of affairs, tinged with the
cynicism generated by years of frustrating experience with the
Yanqui colossus — began to applaud, politely at first, and then
with mounting enthusiasm. The sense of relief was palpable. Kennedy really meant it. Maybe. This was not propaganda. This was
dollars. (When we returned to Washington, Kennedy's only comment was to say, "Well, Doug, I guess I'm going to have to find
you your billion dollars.")

Across the room I watched Che Guevara as he sat crouched over the table, listening intently through his headset. His expression did not change, and, when Dillon finished, he sat back in his chair with folded arms and silently watched the applauding delegates. "We will see," he told a reporter after the session. "Messages are words. The facts are stubborn."

The ambience of rising optimism was fortified when Dillon next proceeded to make his own opening statement — promising that if the Latin American countries truly committed themselves to land and tax reform, they could expect to receive twenty billion dollars more over the decade.

One after another the Latin American delegates rose to respond. "Speed is of the essence," said our host, the president of Uruguay, "both in the provision of loans and in the adoption of peaceful but at the same time revolutionary reforms." We must "put into immediate operation," exhorted the premier of Peru in more cautiously ambiguous terms, "the most efficient and concrete means of substantially raising the standard of living of our peoples." There was, however, no outpouring of pledges to specific measures of social reform. We were, after all, asking the establishment to disenthrone itself; and, even among those who shared our belief in the need for "peaceful revolution," there was caution, awareness that powerful interests in their own countries would resist change, that their own positions might be at risk.

The conference broke into a series of working groups to draft the proposals that would be assembled into a comprehensive agreement. For the next few days, I moved from one group to another, a roving delegate without any formal position, whose only authority was the general assumption that I was "Kennedy's man." It was more than enough, especially when joined to Doug Dillon's unwavering support. (Dillon, then and later, was far more committed both intellectually and emotionally to the Kennedy policies than any officer of the State Department.) I did nothing to modify the impression that my words carried the imprimatur of the highest authority. Nor was it a deception. Admittedly Kennedy had not designated me his spokesman. He didn't have to. I understood his policies and objectives, knew what he wanted from the conference: a hemispheric rallying to the principles of his Alliance for Progress. Our job — my job — was to accomplish his purpose. Lines of authority, titles, formal sanction for specific acts were, I believed, unimportant, should not be allowed to obstruct Kenne-

dy's overriding mandate: "Get the job done." I might be wrong
about the president's objectives, or I might fail in their achievement. But that was a risk I was willing to take. More than willing.
Eager. Full of passionate intensity.

Most components of the Alliance were easily agreed upon. Economic assistance would be acceptable. Our leadership in stabilizing the prices of Latin American commodities — coffee, sugar, tin —
would be welcomed. The Latin American common market was a
good idea. It was Kennedy's insistence on a Latin commitment to
social reform that provoked opposition. (Not of course from countries such as Venezuela who had already instituted their own social revolution.) Everyone was willing to profess a need for "social
reform" or "social justice" as an abstract ideal. But we wanted
more: specific pledges to land redistribution, progressive taxation,
the allocation of resources to projects most immediately beneficial
to the impoverished masses — health care, education, housing. I
spent hours with delegates explaining cajoling, persuading. "Social reform is not an abstraction," I told one Latin group. "It is
made up of concrete programs, land for the landless, fair taxation.
If we don't include these, the whole commitment to social reform
will seem like a deception," and, I added more ominously, "President Kennedy will look like a fool."

Gradually, the draft was modified, hardened, made more specific. Only afterward did I realize that much of the reluctance was
the consequence of disbelief. It might be good politics, but we
couldn't really mean it. Decades of history denied it. Much later,
Eduardo Frei, the leader of Chile's progressive Christian Democratic party, who was to be one of Chile's last elected presidents,
wrote that the "Latins were astonished that this young Yankee
was trying to force them to agree on radical social change. It was
as if the positions of decades had been reversed." And after the
conference Frei wrote me a letter saying, "If it had not been for
the work of the United States delegation, and you in particular,
the essential social reforms would never have been adopted." I
framed the letter, and hung it in my White House office.

Finally, the last obstacles to agreement overcome, the labors of
the working groups were synthesized into a single document: the
Charter of Punta del Este — the constitution of the Alliance for
Progress. My own sense of achievement, almost triumphant, would
in the next few years prove to have been naïve. The Kennedy
insistence on "peaceful social revolution" would enormously en-

hance the popularity of the new American president among the masses of Latin America; result almost, by the time of his death, in his apotheosis. But Guevara was also right: Words were easy, "the facts are stubborn." At Punta del Este the diplomats were supreme. They would return to societies dominated by the possessors of wealth and power and military force who would not easily yield their long-entrenched power to paper promises. Change would come slowly, if at all. As President Lleras Camargo later explained to me, "It took Latin American leadership a year to read the charter and understand there was more to it than promises of United States assistance."

Throughout the working sessions Che Guevara had been unfailingly courteous, said little, his manner amiable. He was, after all, merely there as an observer, and had no intention of trying to obstruct what he regarded as an exercise in futility. He was, he believed, watching the doomed efforts of the past to save itself against the future which he embodied. He also understood that to most of the larger Latin American nations Cuba was irrelevant, a distant Caribbean island (geographically farther from Argentina, for example, than the newly independent nations of West Africa), which had achieved a totally unwarranted eminence by arousing the hostility of the United States. "Cuba is your problem," a Brazilian delegate told me. "We have nothing to do with Cuba. They don't even speak Portuguese."

Although there was no direct contact between the Cuban and American delegations during the conference, Guevara had noticed that I was continually smoking cigars throughout the lengthy meetings. "I see Goodwin likes cigars," he remarked to a young member of the Argentine delegation. "I bet he wouldn't dare smoke Cuban cigars."

When the Argentine repeated this to me, I told him that I would love to smoke Cuban cigars but that Americans couldn't get them. (In fact, we did have a few, since the members of Guevara's revolutionary bodyguard were selling them to the hotel clerks for resale — principally to North Americans — at a sizable markup.) The next day, a large polished-mahogany box, hand inlaid with the Cuban seal amid swirling patterns in the national colors, flying a tiny Cuban flag from a brass key, and crammed with the finest Havanas arrived at my room. With it was a typewritten, signed note from Guevara, reading, in Spanish, "Since I have no greeting card, I have to write. Since to write to an enemy is difficult, I limit myself to extending my hand."

Guevara's gesture of generosity was not without motive. He had important matters to discuss with the United States, and had singled me out as one of the "new Kennedy men," with direct access to the new president, and unlikely to be confined by the restraints and prejudices of the traditional diplomat. The day after I received the cigars, I was informed by the same Argentine intermediary that Guevara would like to talk to me informally; that after the conclusion of the conference a small private party had been arranged to take place in a nearby villa where, Guevara hoped, we might have a chance "to exchange views." I told Dillon of the arrangement. "I don't see what harm it can do," he replied.

But Dillon soon retracted his agreement. On the final day, as all of the ministers (except Guevara) filed to the center of the conference table to sign the Charter of Punta del Este, Guevara took off the gloves. The new Alliance, he said, was an "instrument of economic imperialism," doomed to failure, for "one cannot expect the privileged to make a revolution against their own interests." Then, in a lengthy polemic, he asserted that the play of historical forces was working on behalf of communism, that in one Latin American country after another, there would be either leftist revolutions or rightist coups leading to leftist takeovers.

Responding angrily, Dillon said the United States would *never* recognize the permanence of the present regime in Cuba, for to do so would betray thousands of patriotic Cubans. After this bitter emotional confrontation, a friendly party no longer seemed appropriate. I canceled my plans to attend. The conference was over.

The next day, a few of us slept late before driving through the rich, green countryside to Montevideo, where we were to stay the night before boarding the presidential jet for Washington. After we had arrived at Montevideo's crowded Hotel Victoria Plaza, and while we were eating in the dining room, a young Brazilian delegate accompanied by the correspondent for *Figaro* stopped at my table to ask if I would like to go to a birthday party being given for the Brazilian delegate to the Latin American Free Trade Association. Having no better way to spend the evening, I accompanied the two men to a small apartment in a quiet, dark, residential neighborhood. The party was sedate as Latin American parties go; men and women dancing to rather moderate samba and tango records while many of the guests who had been at the conference, including some journalists, stood around debating the week's events.

What happened next was a mystery to me until years later when an account of the party by the French journalist was published in *Le Figaro littéraire*. He and a Brazilian friend, both of whom had been involved in the unsuccessful effort to arrange a meeting between Guevara and myself on the last day of the conference, decided that this was their opportunity. They called Guevara at his hotel, told him I was there, and invited him to come. He asked for someone to come and bring him. Meanwhile, the French correspondent joined me and, without mentioning the call, said he could introduce me to Che Guevara. To what seemed casual banter, I replied, "We don't need the French to mediate."

Twenty minutes later, at the early Latin hour of 2 A.M., Guevara entered, accompanied by two bodyguards, still garbed in the well-pressed olive-drab combat fatigues that he had worn throughout the conference and that had helped make him the romantic hero of the Punta del Este girls, who gathered around him admiringly every time he walked through the streets. Although I was surprised, I had no doubt he had come to talk with me. Had I been wiser and more experienced, I would probably have left.

But what the hell, I told myself in the highest tradition of Kennedy-style machismo, an American didn't have to run away just because Che Guevara had arrived. Anyway, I rationalized, this wasn't a meeting, it was just a "chance encounter" that could not be construed as a defiance of instructions. However, underlying these justifications — my real motive for remaining — was curiosity about this romantic figure of revolution. I wanted to talk with him.

Guevara and his two bodyguards slowly circled the buffet table in the outer room, sampling the heavy cream cakes that are the Uruguayan equivalent of the eggs and coffee that often appear in the early morning at one of our own parties. Guevara then turned to an Argentine and a Brazilian, both of whom had been delegates to the conference and were casual friends of mine, and told them he would like to speak with "Goodwin." They guided Guevara toward me as I was talking with three journalists, including Juan de Onis, who was then the Rio de Janeiro correspondent for the *New York Times*. We were introduced, shook hands, and stood silent for a moment — suddenly in the center of an arena. Then

Guevara said he would like to say something to me. At that time, my Spanish was good enough so that I could understand much of what he said, but throughout the discussion each of us spoke in his own language, with the Brazilian and the Argentine alternating as interpreter. I replied that I had no authority to negotiate or discuss anything but that I would be glad to listen and report what he said "to others." That satisfied him. However, a crowded room and samba music didn't seem an appropriate setting, so the host led our diverse little group to a small sitting room. Responding to a faint murmur of inner caution, I asked Juan de Onis to come with us, so he could later testify that I had not bargained the Western Hemisphere away to Khrushchev. I soon discarded even this skimpy protection, when Guevara indicated that he could not talk comfortably while there were newspapermen in the room. The Argentine and Brazilian officials stayed throughout.

The room contained a small couch and a chair, three seats for the four of us. Guevara immediately sat down on the floor. What the hell, I thought, I wasn't going to let him "outproletarianize" me and followed his example, leaving the furniture to the diplomats, who insisted — naturally — that we should take the comfortable seats, and joined us on the floor. We both rose, Guevara settling into the couch while I faced him from a heavily upholstered chair.

From a distance, as he had walked purposefully through the conference rooms and the streets of Punta del Este, the slightly stocky, erect man in fatigues, with his untrimmed beard, had seemed rugged, even tough. Now, as I looked at him across a distance of a few feet, his features seemed soft and slightly diffuse, almost feminine. At the start, he appeared to be nervous — more nervous than I was — looking from person to person, shifting in his seat, and talking slowly and uncertainly, as if every word had to be carefully considered not only for its content but for its effect on the audience. As we talked, he relaxed. But gradually his manner grew more intense, and for the next three hours his eyes rarely left mine. He spoke with an air of detachment. What he said was free of polemics, insults, and obvious propaganda, and he was willing to interrupt the flow of discussion for an occasional humorous exchange. There was never any question about his complete confidence that he spoke for the Cuban government. His remarks were well organized — had been carefully thought through — and rarely did he distinguish between personal opinion and Cuba's official position. Although at that time some hemisphere experts were still debating whether Castro was truly a communist, Guevara left no doubt of his own adherence to communism and used the word frequently in referring to himself and to Cuba. My recollection of our conversation is based on lengthy notes that I made immediately after the meeting and that I later transcribed into a memorandum for the president (and, in 1966, used as the basis for an account published in the *New Yorker*).

Guevara began by saying he wished to thank us for the Bay of Pigs.

I said he was welcome.

Their hold on the country had been a bit shaky, he explained, but the invasion allowed the leadership to consolidate most of the major elements of the country behind Fidel.

Perhaps, I answered, they would return the favor and attack Guantánamo.

Oh, no, he said, with a laugh. We would never be so foolish as that.

Even though the Bay of Pigs was not dangerous, he continued, it did reveal the most dangerous factor in the relations between our two countries: the American failure to understand the Cuban revolution. Then, alternating between pride and admonition, Guevara began a lecture on the Cuban revolution. That revolution, he asserted, is irreversible. We intend to build a socialist state. Our ties with "the East" (Russia) will continue, since those ties stem from natural sympathies and from common beliefs about the proper structure of the social order. You in the United States, he warned, must not act on the false assumption that you can rescue Cuba from the claws of communism. Nor should you believe that Fidel is a moderate surrounded by a bunch of fanatic and aggressive men, and might conceivably be moved over to the Western side. He is one of us and always has been. It will not be possible to overthrow the revolution from inside, since there is diminishing support for such an effort and the internal opposition will never be strong enough. The Cuban revolution, he said, is gathering strength, not losing it, and is influencing liberal thought all through Latin America.

Guevara spoke with growing intensity of the impact of the Cuban revolution throughout the hemisphere in demonstrating that a popular socialist revolution was possible in the Americas. However, he continued emphatically, in building our communist state we do not intend to repeat the aggressive and repressive acts of the East. There will be no Iron Curtain around Cuba. Rather, we will encourage technicians and visitors from all countries to come to our country and to work.

Guevara then went on to discuss the difficulties of the Alliance for Progress, and asked if I had listened to his speech at the closing of the conference.

I assured him that I had listened to his speech very carefully.

He said he wished to add that there was an intrinsic contradiction in the Alliance — that by encouraging the forces of change and the desires of the masses we might loose forces that would be beyond our control and would end in a Cuban-style revolution.

I noticed that neither at this point nor at any other did he imply that Cuba might play a more direct role in advancing the march of history.

Now that he had discussed America's difficulties, Guevara continued, he would like to discuss Cuba's problems, and he would do so very frankly. We have, he explained, several rather serious problems. There is still a disturbing amount of counterrevolutionary sentiment, with armed men trying to undermine the government, and there is considerable sabotage. The small bourgeoisie are hostile to the revolution, or, at best, are lukewarm. Then, there is the Catholic Church. Here he just shook his head in dismay. Most of our factories, he said, have American machinery and equipment, and sometimes, when it breaks down, an entire assembly line, or even a factory, is paralyzed until we can get what spare parts are needed through Canada or until we can retool with Soviet or European equipment. Completing the catalogue of ills, Guevara admitted: We have accelerated the process of development too rapidly and our hard-currency reserves are very low. Thus, we are unable to import consumer goods and meet the basic needs of the people. (This was one of the first solid indications of the Soviets' reluctance to invest enough in Cuba to make it a model of socialist development in the hemisphere — a failure that was surely one of communism's great lost opportunities in Latin America.)

After thus balancing the problems of the United States and Cuba, Guevara proceeded to the core of his purpose. We don't want a true understanding with the United States, he said, because we know that that is impossible. I would like a modus vivendi. Of course, it is difficult to put forth a practical formula for such a modus vivendi. I myself, he said, know how difficult it is, because

I have spent a lot of time thinking about it. However, it is better and easier for Cuba to propose such a formula, because your country has public opinion to worry about, whereas we can accept anything without worrying about public opinion.

Guevara paused and waited.

I remained silent, aware of my own lack of authority, and unable to think of any response that would not — at least in the mind of Guevara — signify American receptivity to the idea of a modus vivendi with Cuba.

After a moment or two, Guevara broke the silence, saying that, in any event, there were some things he had in mind. He then began to outline what was evidently the Cuban negotiating position. We cannot, he said, give back the expropriated properties — the factories and banks — but we can and will pay for them in trade. We could also agree not to make any political or military alliances with the East, although this would not affect our natural sympathies. Free elections can be held, but only after a period of institutionalizing the revolution has been completed.

I asked him if this meant a one-party system.

He replied that it did. We will also agree not to attack Guantánamo, he continued, laughing, as if such an assurance were absurdly self-evident. Then he touched on the most sensitive point of all. We are willing, he said, to discuss an agreement limiting the activities of the Cuban revolution "in other countries." Here, almost for the first time, he became cautious and oblique. Clearly, he could not affirm that Cuba was promoting revolution in other countries — even though he knew I had access to the facts about such activity — while he was in the presence of the Argentine and Brazilian officials, whose countries, after all, were somewhere on the list. Yet, although he was indirect, Guevara made clear his awareness that any possibility of a modus vivendi would depend on Cuba's willingness to refrain from revolutionary activity in other countries; and he was telling me that Cuba was willing to discuss such a prohibition as part of an overall understanding. In return for these agreements by Cuba, the United States was to stop any effort to overthrow the Cuban government by force, and was to lift the trade embargo. I know it will be difficult to discuss these things, he said, but perhaps we can begin by discussing subordinate issues, such as the hijacking of airplanes to Cuba. Once such talks begin, more important issues can be brought into the discussion.

By now, almost three hours had passed. (Interpreting required more than half the time.) Having completed his exposition, Guevara could not resist the satisfaction of once again gently expressing his gratitude for the Bay of Pigs. It was not only a great political victory for the Cuban revolutionary leaders, but had also transformed Cuba from an aggrieved little Caribbean country into an equal antagonist of the United States. He closed by saying he would tell no one about the substance of this conversation except Fidel. I said I would not publicize it, either.

It was almost 6 A.M. when we rose, shook hands, and went back into the main room of the apartment, where a diminished number of couples were still doing the samba. I asked the journalists to treat the fact of the discussion as off the record. They agreed, and all three honored their pledge. (Even when the encounter became front-page news, about ten days later, Juan de Onis observed his commitment with a punctiliousness rare in journalism, and never wrote a word on the subject, although the two other men considered themselves released from their pledge.)

I returned to my hotel immediately, leaving Guevara to the cream cakes, and made notes of what he had said until it was time for breakfast and the delegation's departure. In eleven hours, the presidential 707 carried us two-thirds the length of the hemisphere, to Andrews Air Force Base, in Maryland, where members of the delegation boarded helicopters for the familiar trip past the Washington Monument to the White House lawn. After President Kennedy had greeted us with a brief statement of congratulation, I walked into the mansion with him and told of the meeting with Guevara.

There was no sign of annoyance from the president, no hint of reproof, only curiosity about Guevara and interest in what he had said. "Write up a complete account," he instructed, "and circulate it to Rusk, Bundy, and the others." Then, pointing to a small package I was holding, he said, "What's that?" It was the still-untouched box of Cuban cigars that Guevara had sent me. I handed the box to Kennedy, who put it on his desk and promptly opened it. "Are they good?" he asked. "They're the best," I replied, whereupon he took one from the box, lit it, and took a few puffs, before suddenly turning to me, exclaiming. "You should have smoked the first one."

"It's too late now, Mr. President," I responded. He grimaced slightly, and then resumed smoking.

Two epilogues ramify from this unplanned and unexpected encounter: my own, and the epilogue of Che Guevara.

My memorandum to the president went to his foreign-policy advisers in the White House, the State Department, and the Pentagon. I also sent the president another memorandum, giving my views on our future policy toward Cuba, in the light of both the Punta del Este conference and the conversation with Che Guevara. "Pay as little attention as possible to Cuba," I recommended. "Do not allow them to appear as the victims of U.S. aggression. Do not create the impression we are obsessed with Castro — an impression which only strengthens Castro's hand in Cuba and encourages anti-American and leftist forces in other countries to rally round the Cuban flag."

Meanwhile, Guevara had left Punta del Este for a visit to his native Argentina, and a supposedly secret meeting with President Arturo Frondizi.

It is difficult to understand how the extremely intelligent Frondizi succumbed to the illusion that such a meeting could be hidden, especially since he knew that the Argentine military had a group of men on guard at the presidential palace whose sole mission was to spy on the president's activities. The Argentine generals were getting increasingly restive and were seeking a pretext for bringing off one of their periodic coups (which occurred several months later). Almost immediately, there was a storm of accusation in Buenos Aires, suggesting that Frondizi was seeking an accommodation with the communists. In defense of his president, the Argentine foreign minister, Adolfo Mugica, claimed that it had been perfectly all right for Frondizi to talk with Guevara, because I had been negotiating with Guevara in Montevideo. In most Latin American countries, a United States precedent is an almost perfect defense against charges of being pro-communist.

The minister's statement was picked up by the American press — much to my discomfort, for the clear implication was that some sort of secret formal negotiation had been conducted. I called the Argentine ambassador and pointed out that the statement was inaccurate and disturbing, and the White House denied that we had made any deals with Castro. The story lapsed for a few days, until Frondizi sacrificed his foreign minister to the demands of the military. Then that determined gentleman, in the course of announcing his resignation, proclaimed that what he had said about "Goodwin" was true just the same, and that the Goodwin–Guevara conference demonstrated that Castro's regime sought better relations with the United States.

This was enough to thrust the story onto the front page of the

Washington Post, and to persuade Senator Wayne Morse to convene his Latin American subcommittee to hear my story. I duly appeared, explained how the meeting had come about, and was rewarded with a public statement by Senator Morse that neither I nor the government had sought a meeting with Guevara or entered into any negotiations.

But the incident did not go away. For months I had been the target of frequent criticism from those who regarded me as an iniquitous "leftist" influence on policy, or who believed I was usurping the rightful role of the State Department, or who considered me insufficiently attentive to the legitimate interests of private enterprise, or who found me too arrogant or too abrasive or too young. David Rockefeller had joined with the right-wing Iowa senator, Bourke Hickenlooper, to express their misgivings over my role in Latin American affairs. Reporting on the Punta del Este conference, *The Vision* (an American newsletter on Latin American development) wrote that "neither U.S. nor Latin American businessmen took kindly to indications by Richard Goodwin, the President's chief Latin American Adviser, that he thought private enterprise had a bad connotation in Latin America because it is associated with U.S. imperialism."

I did not answer these criticisms. Indeed was not even aware of most of them, was naïvely oblivious to expressed resentments that were reaching the Oval Office. I continued to assert my views forcefully, even angrily, often bypassed or defied traditional procedures, overrode bureaucratic hesitations. There was an element of arrogance in my behavior, but it reflected my conviction that I was acting as the agent of Kennedy's intentions, the mirror of his own urgent desire for action. Had I known then how the combination of youth and assertiveness had stirred hostilities both outside and inside the government, I might have altered my behavior. But I didn't know; was, in my judgment, just doing my job. And never once did Kennedy himself ask me to modify my conduct, or direct me to withdraw from the aggressive pursuit of the policies I was interpreting and attempting to implement. Still I had made mistakes, unnecessarily antagonized important people with the zealousness of my approach. The public revelation of my meeting with Guevara fortified the objections to my conduct, provided the multisourced opposition with a tangible weapon of attack.

A Republican congressman from New York, Steven Derounian, made a speech on the House floor that denounced my "so-called chance meeting" with Guevara, said I was a "kid playing with fire," and argued that I was running a one-man State Department on Latin America. "The American people," he said, "have a right to demand that the President put his house in order and one way to do that is to squelch these puerile undertakings by Mr. Goodwin and let Secretary of State Rusk be in fact the Secretary of State." Goodwin should be "summarily dismissed," Derounian concluded.

Aware of mounting criticism against me not only in the Congress but in the conservative bastions of the State Department as well, I wrote a memo to President Kennedy. "As you know," I began, "I am very deeply involved in the day-to-day conduct of Latin American affairs. This involvement is inevitable as long as I am acting as an agent of yours in your effort to re-energize a long dormant and ineffective area of our policy. But such involvement is bound to create some difficulties . . . [and] I am bound to be the object of some criticism and even personal abuse. I do not mind this in the slightest. It does not bother me or affect my work. I only point it out as a possible potential source of some embarrassment to you. I also get word that the Tom Dodd–HUAC–*Human Events* crowd has been 'looking into my background.' Fortunately I was born too late to join anything incriminating."

I had hopes this would close the matter, but I was wrong.

Following our meeting in 1961, Che Guevara's own career took a far more abrupt and fateful course than did my own. Remaining minister of the economy, he became the target of mounting hostility from the Russians, who disliked him for what they regarded as his stubborn inefficiency in economic matters. His revolutionary beliefs demanded that Cuba be made an industrial state, relieved of dependence on its sugar crop. Soviet economists tried, with limited success, to persuade him that economic facts would not yield to ideological commands, and that it was far more efficient for Cuba to sell sugar and buy goods with the income than to manufacture everything it needed. The economists were right, of course, and as the Cuban economy lagged, Guevara was gradually relieved of his control. In addition, it is almost certain that Guevara's relations with Castro were marked by periods of violent strain alternating with periods of renewed intimacy. Perhaps there was just not room enough in Cuba for both of them.

Whatever the reason, in 1965 he abandoned his position of high authority in Cuba and set out, single-handedly, to lead a still non-existent revolution in the forsaken wretchedness of Bolivia. "Dear Fidel," he wrote, "I leave here the purest of my hopes as a builder, and the dearest of those I love. And I leave a people that received me as a son. That wounds me deeply. I carry to new battlefronts . . . the revolutionary spirit of my people, the feeling of fulfilling the most sacred of duties. . . . This comforts and heals the deepest of wounds. . . . Ever onward to victory! *Patria o muerte!*"

Less rhetorically, but with more illuminating self-revelation, he wrote to his parents in Argentina: "Dear folks, . . . Once again I feel between my heels the ribs of Rosinante; once more I hit the road with my shield upon my arms."

He was off to battle, not against windmills, but against real enemies armed with mortal weapons. But the choice of language, the analogy to the fabled man of La Mancha, hinted an awareness that his quest might be equally futile.

It is hard to think of a place where a guerrilla war would have been more certainly doomed than the Bolivia of the mid-1960s. Everyone in Bolivia was poor. The oligarchy had been driven from the country in the revolution of 1952 and the land redistributed to the *campesinos*. The most important industry, the tin mines, was largely owned by the state. Thus the revolutionaries had no oligarchs to terrorize, no wealthy businessmen to hate, and no large landowners from whom the soil could be wrested. Poverty alone does not fuel ideological revolution, but the visible coexistence of poverty and privilege.

Moreover, Guevara's type of guerrilla war demanded an army that shared his passionate expectations, comrades in a cause that could sustain the revolutionary spirit against danger and adversity. The Indians of the Andean plateau could not be easily shaped into such an instrument. Since the Spanish conquerors smashed the empire of the Incas and reduced its people to servitude, the descendants of the conquered had heard many unmeant promises, would not easily believe the rhetoric of redemption, whether it came from the Bolivian governments, the United States, or Che Guevara. Nor were the stocky brown Indians of Bolivia likely to follow a romantic white Argentine suddenly materializing from a place as foreign to them as New York City or London. "The inhabitants of the region," Guevara wrote shortly before his death, "are as impenetrable as rocks. . . . You talk to them, and in the depths of their eyes it can be seen that they don't believe."

The outcome was inevitable. Outside the protective citadel of the Cuban island he became an open target. The United States dispatched a Special Forces group to find Che and to kill him. But they were unsuccessful. It was the Bolivians themselves who captured and wounded Guevara, took him prisoner, and shot him. "It is possible," he had written his family, "that this may be the finish. I don't seek it, but . . . [i]f it should be so, I send you a last embrace."

In death Che Guevara became a romantic symbol of the revolutionary struggle, not only against "Yankee imperialism," but the efforts of the dispossessed everywhere to shatter the ancient sources of oppression. But what he wrote was true: He did not seek death. I had seen enough of his personal vitality, his love of life, to believe that he would have preferred survival — even as a prisoner — to martrydom.

Before he left Cuba, a female television correspondent interviewing Guevara asked him why he didn't like any Americans. "I like one," he said. "Who?" she asked. "I won't tell you," was the generous answer. "It might hurt his career." The correspondent persisted, however, until she hit on my name. Guevara nodded, and said, "That's the one."

Hearing the story at a Washington cocktail party, I telephoned the correspondent. "He's right," I said, "it'll make me a target for every right-winger in Congress." She obligingly cut the segment. I have regretted my timid request ever since.

In the note that accompanied the cigars, Guevara had referred to me as an enemy. He was right. Had I been in office, I would have joined in recommending that we assist the Bolivian government to subdue Che's guerrillas. Just as he would have struck at me if — under some set of unimaginable circumstances — I had stood between him and the success of his revolution.

Yet I was glad, even proud, of Che's comment to the journalist. And I like to think that I would have done what little I could to prevent Guevara's execution. We were both trapped in the contending forces of a world we had not made; passionate adversaries in the struggle to control the future. Yet I liked the man. He had humor and courage, intellectual gifts and an unmistakable tenderness of spirit. I understood that he also contained ruthlessness, self-defeating stubbornness, and a hatred strong enough to cripple the possibilities of practical action. It is the paradox of the revolutionary that such divergent feelings must coexist in the same man. "The true revolutionary," Guevara once wrote, "is moved by strong feelings of love. . . . Herein lies what are perhaps the great dramatic challenges to a leader. He must combine an impassioned spirit with coolness of mind; and he must make painful decisions unfalteringly." The statement is both true and an impossibility. He is describing a man at war with himself, who must either withdraw from revolution, grapple the cruel and ruthless instruments of successful violence, or die.

My own life, my own hope that human life might be enriched by my efforts, took a far different form. I was, after all, an American liberal; still idealistic enough to believe in the power of reason and the capacity of democracy to overcome resistance to injustice. Yet just the same, as we sat together in the small sitting room of a shabby Montevideo apartment, I could sense shared passions fruitlessly struggling to cross the barrier of irreconcilable loyalties and beliefs. With this difference: In Che Guevara's quest, he was, in E. E. Cummings's words, "more brave than me, more blond than you."

Looking back over a quarter century it seems — something that never would have occurred to me at the time — that Che Guevara was also a child of the sixties. He was one among many leaders who believed that society could be changed from within, that the energy and commitment of multitudes could be linked to compel the enrichment of human life. It is the belief that binds the very different figures who dominated the time: both Kennedys, Martin Luther King, Lyndon Johnson of the Great Society, the student organizers of the SDS, the early leaders of the peace movement. And in other countries there were de Gaulle of France, Mao of China, Haya de la Torre of Peru. We may, and we should, view the goals and methods embraced by some of these leaders as foolish or tyrannical or even reprehensible. But that is not the point. They did not emerge by some accident of chronology. They were the creations of a time when the world seemed more plastic, subject to modification by human will. They were not the leaders and creators of the sixties, but drew their own stature, power, and direction from the conditions of the time. That is why, as the times changed, they would have no successors. There would be no place for romantics in the triumphant ascendance of bureaucracy.

11 / From the Inside Out

I was so much older then, I'm younger than that now.

— Bob Dylan

IN THE LATE FALL of 1961, having seemingly survived the Guevara mini-uproar, I was again seated in my White House office relaying commands over the telephone, holding meetings, conferring with the president on an almost daily basis.

There were continued rumblings of criticism about my anomalous role as the president's agent for Latin America. I had no position in the established agencies of foreign policy — the State Department or Bundy's National Security staff. My only source of authority consisted of the telephone that linked me to the Oval Office. And I used it freely. The affronted bureaucracy stuck back. There were newspaper articles referring to the "anarchy" in the conduct of Latin policy. One foreign-service officer, a Mr. Smith Simpson (whose name alone qualified him for the diplomatic corps), told reporters that "since President Kennedy saw in the Alliance . . . one of the more promising advances in foreign affairs . . . he had his staff push on it. Unfortunately the willingness of his staffers" (me) "exceeded their experience and maturity." (True enough: I was young, inexperienced and very "willing" to "push.") "Lines of authority became . . . fuzzed up . . . confusion was generated . . . office directors in State did not know which way to look for orders. . . ."

Although annoyed by such criticism, I did not feel endangered. I was, after all, just doing what the president wanted; an assumption of safety that rested on an incredible naïveté, itself the product of ignorance about the nature of institutions and the men who led them. Presidents wanted many things — among them contented lieutenants and a smoothly functioning bureaucratic apparatus.

In late October, at a press conference, Kennedy was asked about the "criticism of our handling of inter-American affairs" caused by "advisers in the White House duplicating and sometimes overriding people in the State Department."

"My experience in government," Kennedy said, in the midst of a long and semiapologetic reply, "is that when things are noncontroversial, beautifully coordinated, and all the rest, it may be that there is not much going on. . . . So if you really want complete harmony and goodwill, then the best way to do it is not to do anything. . . . So we are attempting to do something about Latin America, and there is bound to be a ferment. If the ferment produces a useful result, it will be worthwhile. . . ."

Right on, I thought. But my enthusiasm was premature.

The following afternoon I stood in the Oval Office, waiting for McGeorge Bundy to complete a conversation with the president, so that I could inform him of my recent discovery that the CIA had been engaged in covert operations in the Dominican Republic, had actually transferred some small weapons to a group that wished to overthrow Trujillo by assassination. Looking toward me, Kennedy said, "You know, Dick, maybe we'd be better off if you were in the State Department, closer to the action." He paused for a moment, then waved his hand as if brushing the idea aside. "Hell," he said, speaking to some undefined space between me and the attentive Bundy, "if Dick goes over there, we'll never hear anything about Latin America."

After Bundy left, I told Kennedy what I had learned. He reacted angrily. "Tell them no more weapons. The United States is not to get involved in any assassinations. I'd like to get rid of Trujillo, but not that way."

Although he had dismissed the idea of my departure, I was now aware that it was on his mind. So I was not wholly unprepared that November day in 1961 when I stood on the porch outside the Oval Office of the White House watching Kennedy walk across the South Lawn toward the helicopter that awaited his departure for a weekend at his Virginia estate. Glimpsing me as he neared the steps of the helicopter, Kennedy beckoned toward me. As I approached him, he smiled, leaned over, spoke loudly into my ear over the noise of the spinning rotors. "You know, Dick, I think you'll be more effective in the State Department." I did not reply.

"I'm going to announce it next week." Then, mounting the steps, he shouted, "We'll talk about it when I get back."

But there was nothing to talk about. The decision had been made. My White House days were over. For now. And although I would have many conversations with Kennedy in the future, the promised discussion never took place.

> . . . they talk for a while about whether [Big Nurse is] the root of all the trouble here or not, and Harding says she's the root of most of it. Most of the other guys think so too, but McMurphy isn't so sure any more. He says he thought so at one time but now he don't know. He says he don't think getting her out of the way would really make much difference; he says that there's something bigger making all this mess and goes on to try to say what he thinks it is. He finally gives up when he can't explain it.
>
> — Ken Kesey, *One Flew Over the Cuckoo's Nest*

Trying to recall the emotions of my brief, decisive encounter with Kennedy is like taking an archaeologist's pick to the surface artifacts of an ancient community, hoping to penetrate through the time-mantled layers — city heaped upon city, each carefully, hopefully, constructed on the ruins of its predecessors — to reach the primeval settlement that was the predecessor of all to come. I am a different person from the young man who, on that uncommonly mild and brilliant November afternoon, was told of his exile from a man he admired, and more than admired. Were the same situation to recur, I would feel differently, respond differently, behave differently. At least I think so. The perverse elusiveness of emotional recollection, further distorted by the irrepressible desire for self-deception, makes all memoirs, including this one, a partial misrepresentation; and, incidentally, makes great poetry possible. "Memoirs," Justice Frankfurter once told me, "are the most unreliable source of historical evidence. Events are always distorted by refraction through the writer's ego." (I.e., the spectrum is not the light.)

Having unburdened myself of this admission, let me tell you exactly how I felt. I was saddened; not stunned, but suffused with a milder melancholy more like that of a rejected lover. It was not a defeat. At least it didn't appear to be. As a deputy assistant secretary of state I would have direct, daily authority over the implementation of Latin American policy; my ties to the president would remain intact; I would possess direct, commanding influence over the ponderous instrumentalities of foreign policy. My regret had its source not in reason, but in the pain of severance — from that small band of colleagues with whom I had made the intense, uncertain journey to the White House; from the leader whom I admired almost to the point of hero worship.

Yet the moment of melancholy evoked a revelation. Walking back to my office, self-pity gave way to resentment — not toward Kennedy, but toward myself. Why did I feel sad, rejected? Then, in a moment of memorable illumination, I understood. Not the answer, but the absurdity of the question. Politics was not love. The ties that bound men of power were not compounded of affection, or even compassion. In Norman Mailer's phrase, politics was property; an exchange, value given for services rendered. I was not in the White House because John Kennedy liked me (although he may have) but for my contribution to his ambitions and objectives. In return I received a title, a significant office, and the opportunity to help shape the course of public power. If my presence caused difficulties, if my value declined, then I must go. It is a simple matter of transaction; not ruthless at all, but rational, the inevitable deduction from the syllogism of power. Should one desire more forgiving bonds, there is always marriage and lots of children.

Fueled by this new awareness, renewed vitality reawoke habitual passions. I had not been fired, I told myself. I would not take it as a defeat. My responsibilities for Latin America had not been ended. I knew what Kennedy wanted, what I wanted. Our policies were not just official doctrine. They were right. They were profoundly, passionately devised to advance the interests of the United States and to alleviate the violent injustices that imprisoned millions in poverty and fear. The course had been set, but the sailors were still holding meetings on the beach. It was my job to get them on board, order them into the riggings, leave the tranquil harbor of indecision behind. I would go to the State Department, not to find a warm spot in the belly of the beast, but to kick the huge, somnolent, indifferent monster in the ass. And so I did. For a while. Until its lethargic, but unexpectedly potent immune system — unable to incorporate my alien intrusion — expelled me.

On November 17, Kennedy announced a major shakeup in the State Department, including my appointment in a list of high-level changes. I treated it as a promotion; the president called it "putting the right man in the right job"; and the press, for the most part, went along. *Time* magazine reported that it "was hardly a shift at all. . . . President Kennedy's No. 1 man on Latin America in the White House became Kennedy's No. 1 man on Latin America at the State Department . . . his unmistakable authority was succinctly put by a White House staffer: 'The President likes him.'" In the *Washington Post* the headline announced: "JFK Ignores Complaints: Goodwin's Power Continues to Rise."

Unfortunately, for me, the *Washington Daily News* got closer to the truth when it reported that my transfer should remove "a major irritant" in Latin American policy since I had been "a sort of free-wheeling operator in the White House," much to the annoyance of that section of the State Department responsible for Latin America. Now, presumably, I would be under control.

As I prepared to enter the State Department, Chester Bowles was on his way out: the first major casualty in the top ranks of the New Frontier. Frustrated by the department's failure to transform itself into an intelligently active instrument of his foreign policy, the president had centered his discontent on the somewhat tendentious and pedantic undersecretary. There may well have been reason to regard Bowles as ineffective, but, as Arthur Schlesinger confided in a memorandum to the president, he was also "the one champion of fresh ideas and the New Frontier in the top command of State. His removal . . . will be regarded by the most stuffy and hopeless elements as a vindication of their own stuffiness and hopelessness. . . . It is ironic that Bowles is being removed for his failure to overcome the entrenched complacency of the foreign service pros — and that these very pros, who are the basic source of State Department inertia, will regard his removal as their victory."

Ironic indeed, I thought on reading Arthur's memo; little suspecting that I would soon be on the losing side of a similar irony. Moreover the underlying assumption — the hopeless inertia of the State Department — was Kennedy's opinion exactly. "I'm only the president," he said sardonically, "why should they pay any attention to me." My own transfer, although in part a response to public criticism of my anomalous authority, was also another in an intermittent series of efforts to make the department his.

They didn't work. Kennedy was never able to get the State

214 The Kennedy Years

Department to behave as he wished. But he kept trying right up until his death.

Things seemed to go smoothly at the State Department at first: I got along surprisingly well with my formal superior, Assistant Secretary Robert Woodward. And my lines were still open to the White House.

That December Kennedy was scheduled to make a trip to Venezuela and Colombia. Ignoring, as was his presidential prerogative, the new lines of authority, he called me to ask my opinion. "Most of the people over here don't think I should go. The Secret Service says it's too dangerous." (There had been a great deal of terrorist activity by communist groups in Venezuela.)

"The risk is up to you," I replied, "but I think the trip will be a triumph; it'll prove just how much the Alianza has changed things, and it'll help show them that you really care."

"So you think I should go," he commented.

"Yes," I answered.

Of course Kennedy wanted to go, was looking for an affirmative response, thought the security danger exaggerated.

"What about security?" he asked again.

"Betancourt will have the whole army out," I replied. "Nothing's certain, but I think you'll be as safe in Caracas as you are in the United States."

That December I accompanied Kennedy on the flight to Venezuela and drafted all his speeches. (I was to do the same on each of Kennedy's three trips to Latin America — to Mexico City in 1962, and Costa Rica in 1963 — despite my growing distance from any formal involvement with Latin America.) As the plane taxied to a stop at the Venezuelan airport, Kennedy — always the first to exit — walked up the aisle toward the door, touched me briefly on the shoulder, and, smiling, said: "Listen, Dick, if this doesn't work out, you'd better keep on going south."

The visit was a triumph. Mammoth, unprecedented crowds cheered the young, Catholic American president with his beautiful wife who had come to represent such bright new hopes. On our next stop, in Bogotá, Colombia, at least five hundred thousand people — more than half the population of the city — greeted Kennedy's arrival.

It soon became obvious that my move to the State Department had not accomplished its intended purpose — to end my authority in Latin American affairs. It wasn't my fault. Not completely. But Kennedy, it seemed, was incorrigible. Two or three times a week, ignoring my superiors, he would call me with instructions or questions which I dutifully relayed to the assistant secretary but which, because of their origin, could not be denied.

In March of 1962 I accompanied Teodoro Moscoso — director of the economic component of the Alliance for Progress — on a special mission to Chile. The right-wing Alessandri government was in desperate needs of funds to meet a growing economic crisis. We wanted to help, but were seriously concerned by the failure of Chile to embark on the badly needed social reforms — including redistribution of land — which they had pledged at Punta del Este. We would commit 140 million dollars, Moscoso and I told the government, only if they promised to begin the reforms. The debate was fierce. At one meeting I said that "if you don't do something about these changes soon, Allende [leader of the Communist party] will win the next election." Looking at me across the table the young minister of finance said reproachfully: "The problem is that you just don't understand Chile."

Undersecretary of State George Ball took the moment of my absence from the country to strike. He fired Assistant Secretary of State Bob Woodward (making him ambassador to Spain) and replaced him with the tough, hard-bitten Ed Martin — a veteran of many bureaucratic wars, and personally loyal to Ball. According to newspaper accounts, whose accuracy I later confirmed, Ball told Woodward he was being moved "because you haven't been able to control that boy." Woodward replied, "How can I control him? He's a White House man."

Ed Martin knew how. And he did.

I could not, of course, be fired or demoted. The president himself had bestowed the title. But bureaucracy has far subtler means of eroding unwelcome interference. And Ed Martin knew them all. I was, for example, simply not invited to meetings where important matters of policy were being discussed. My secretary was approached and asked to keep a record of my phone calls, even to monitor my conversations with the president, and report my activities to Martin. (Without telling me, of course.) Loyally, she refused, but when she told me of the request I realized how determined Martin was to avert the fate of his predecessor. Decisions were made and communicated without my knowledge. There was no formal change in my status. I was simply bypassed. I had my office, a resounding title, a continual flow of routine busywork, but responsibility for significant policies was simply drained away. The situation was intolerable. I had not come to work in Washington in order to occupy a spacious office, my name and title inscribed on the door, while puttering around the fringes of high events. Nor did I have any stomach for the bureaucratic battles (or the skills to fight them). So I left. Not formally, of course, but without resigning or even asking permission.

In the summer of 1962 I walked the few blocks that separated the State Department from Peace Corps headquarters, where Sarge Shriver was constructing one of the most successful operations of the New Frontier, and offered my services. Sarge welcomed my offer of assistance, gave me an office, and treated me as a personal assistant and adviser across the entire spectrum of Peace Corps activities — projects, recruitment, negotiations with other governments. I discussed my new undertaking with no one — not the State Department, and not the White House. Fuck them all, I thought; they could fire me if they wanted, but I wasn't going to let them cut off my balls.

Naturally Kennedy soon learned of my work at the Peace Corps. Shriver, after all, was a member of the family. And I hadn't asked him to keep my activities secret. I assume that when Kennedy learned, he knew that my departure was not a temporary indulgence, the result of some transient fit of anger. I had changed jobs, a fact that would not be formally recognized until January of 1963. Until then my State Department office would remain unoccupied, my absence unexplained. Nor did Martin or Ball ask where I had gone. Inquiries might arouse press interest, and queries from reporters were not to be encouraged. Anyway, I am sure they didn't miss me.

On July 3, 1962, Kennedy called me; "Bobby told me yesterday about your work in the Peace Corps. Whatever you feel like doing is okay with me" (not quite) "but I want you to wait until after the Brazil trip" (later postponed). "I want you to go down in the advance party, and also there is the problem of speeches." There was a pause. I made no reply. I would, of course, do as he asked, but I was not in a genial mood. "Anyway," he continued after a momentary silence, "if we ever do put out any announcement on your Peace Corps assignment I think we ought to emphasize the Latin American part of the work."

Arthur Schlesinger explained Kennedy's acquiescence to the State Department with his usual generosity of spirit, both toward Kennedy and toward me. "The incident [my movement to the Peace Corps] reminded one of the limits of Presidential power because, though Kennedy retained his special fondness for Goodwin and often called upon him for special jobs, he could not, without cost to other objectives, preserve Goodwin's usefulness in a department that did not want to use him. The government lost, however, the imagination, drive and purpose Goodwin had given so abundantly to the Alliance."

Perhaps. Perhaps Kennedy could not have intervened without "cost to other objectives," or perhaps he didn't want to. As for my contributions, the loss, if any, would prove to be minimal, since, at the end of 1963, the Alliance for Progress would come to an end.

In mid-October of 1962 I received a request from the White House to work with Arthur Schlesinger on the draft of a speech to be delivered by Adlai Stevenson at the United Nations. Meeting with Arthur, I discovered that the subject of the address was to be our discovery that the Soviet Union was installing nuclear missiles in Cuba. Thus, although I did not participate in the secret White House deliberations, I was aware of the approaching confrontation between the United States and the Soviet Union now known as the Cuban missile crisis. Once the speech was completed, I was scheduled to accompany Douglas Dillon to Mexico City, where a meeting of Latin American foreign ministers was in progress. We were to arrive at the meeting before Kennedy announced his naval quarantine of Cuba, so we might explain the president's action to the other countries of the hemisphere. In Washington the sense of impending disaster — the possibility of a nuclear exchange — was palpable.

In retrospect, it seems highly unlikely that the Soviet Union would have gone to war to assert its right to place missiles in Cuba. But at the time the danger seemed real. And it was not impossible. Backed into a corner, seeing that our own nuclear force was on full alert, the Soviets might well misjudge our intentions, suspect that our actions were a prelude to a full-scale attack, and decide that their best hope of survival was to strike first. It would have been insanity, but history contains many illustrations of wars initiated as a result of such grotesque misjudgments. A few days before going to Mexico City I called my wife, who was vacationing in Puerto Rico, and told her to meet me in Mexico City. "Why don't you just come over here, after the conference, and we can have a short vacation," she responded. "No, you've got to go to Mexico City," I said, "I can't explain over the phone but you have to go there." I couldn't tell her my real reason: If war came, Puerto Rico was doomed, but Mexico City might survive.

As everybody knows, there was no war. The story of the missile crisis has been amply documented in dozens of histories and memoirs. The confrontation — the most dangerous of the postwar period — was to have transforming consequences — for Castro, for Khrushchev, and for Kennedy.

Fidel Castro's influence in Latin America was severely diminished. He had become a hero, a role model, to leftist forces whose ideology, though Marxist and anti–United States, was intensely nationalistic. During the crisis it became clear that the fate of Cuba was being decided not by the Cubans, but between Kennedy and Khrushchev. To Latins it appeared that Castro had exchanged one master — the United States — for another. As a Peruvian youth leader later told me, "We were for Fidel until we heard the balalaika."

For Khrushchev, the missile crisis marked the beginning of the end. Like Kennedy at the Bay of Pigs, he had believed the intelligence experts who told him that the missiles could be emplaced in total secrecy (although our reconnaissance capabilities should have been well known), listened to the advisers who assured him that the Americans might protest but wouldn't act, and yielded to the military chieftains who urged the necessity of restoring the nuclear balance, which, they argued, had shifted to the United States. He would pay for his misjudgment, the product of a Soviet version of secret government, with his job.

Kennedy's reaction would change the course of his administration. He had seen over the edge of the pit, glimpsed the indifferently consuming flames, which were obscured by the rhetoric of the Cold War. "Contest," "confrontation," "deterrence" were — or could be — euphemisms for death. "It is insane," I heard him say at a small White House meeting, "that two men, sitting on opposite sides of the world, should be able to decide to bring an end to civilization." Accompanying the shock of recognition was a sense of triumph. Whatever John Kennedy felt he had to prove — determination, courage, will, the skillful use of power — he had proved it: to the world, the country, and to himself. Like some fever that reaches its life-threatening height as the night moves toward dawn, and then begins to break, the Cold War had mounted toward its moment of final agony, hovered for a fear-filled moment, and then had begun to recede. Never again would John Kennedy use the fierce rhetoric of the dedicated Cold Warrior. The next year would bring the test-ban treaty and the American University speech — an invitation to peaceful coexistence based on mutual understanding. And by the end of 1963, Kennedy would begin secret discussions with officials of the Cuban government, hoping to lay the foundation for a meeting with Castro and a peaceful solution to the "Cuban problem."

Following the missile crisis, I formally resigned from the State Department for a post with the Peace Corps. Although the announcement stated the assignment was "temporary," Radio Havana knew better, announcing that "actually Goodwin has been eliminated from the 'brain trust' which supposedly advises Kennedy on the policy that should be pursued in each of the Latin American countries."

Moving from the State Department to the Peace Corps was like emerging from the Cretan labyrinth. The minotaur had managed a bite or two. But now I could again breathe the fresh air of open country. Although my work with the Peace Corps would take me to every continent of the world, I had returned to America. The America of the sixties.

Away from the center of power I became aware of, felt part of, the liberating forces outside government that were working to change America. Thousands of men and women — white and black — went south to enlist in the civil rights revolution. Young Americans were seeking a new politics, not only in academic discussions, but through the formation of organizations complete with platforms and manifestos. In Michigan the Port Huron Manifesto became the founding document of the Students for a Democratic Society, whose goal was nothing less than the spiritual enrichment of American society — not through prayer or love-ins, but by diminishing the power of dominant economic institutions and the materialistic obsessions that obstructed individual fulfillment. On the other side of the political spectrum appeared the Young Americans for Freedom, whose libertarian goals were often amazingly convergent with those of their counterparts on what was called the "left," but which lay outside the framework of traditional labels.

These movements were not then identified with bitter division, or hostility — sometimes violence — toward the established sanctuaries of democratic rule. On the contrary, they reflected, and openly proclaimed, their dedication to the traditional ideals of American freedom, asserted their intention to return the nation to those principles which it had distorted or abandoned. It was, wrote Nan Robertson, in the *New York Times,* "[t]he bright promise of 1962, that peaceful, simple protest — a sit-in, a boycott, a picket line — could change, indeed had already changed, deeply rooted institutions and prejudices. . . ." The government of John Kennedy was not at war with these movements; indeed, Kennedy's own questing vitality, his obvious openness to divergent views — listening even if he rejected — had helped to stimulate the quest for change, the sense of large possibilities. "In 1962," Harvard professor Stanley Hoffman observed, "some students were disaffected with their government, but it was still their government. They had the basic trust of people brought up to believe it was really theirs." And not only students, but black men in Alabama, coal miners in Appalachia, peace activists gathered in middle-class suburbs.

"Ask . . . what you can do for your country," Kennedy had exhorted, and many took up the challenge; often finding answers he did not agree with, could not accept, but which he had helped to provoke. He had asked people to work to change America, and if their labors took unforeseen, even objectionable forms, it should not have been surprising. If you "let a thousand flowers bloom," you're not going to end up with a neatly cultivated rose garden.

The Peace Corps volunteers and the men who organized them — Bill Moyers, Bill Josephson, the formidable idealist/supersalesman Sarge Shriver, and dozens of others — were more closely attuned to this indefinable and still undefined spirit of the sixties than were the vast bureaucracies that surrounded them — from which they had been liberated only because the State Department wanted nothing to do with a harebrained, doomed scheme that had emerged from the irresponsible rhetoric of politics.

At the Peace Corps I assumed the position of secretary-general of the International Peace Corps Secretariat. The purpose of the secretariat was to encourage and assist other industrialized countries to establish Peace Corps of their own. The idea — wholeheartedly approved by Shriver — was mine; the organization was my invention, and both the job and its grandiose title — secretary-general — were creatures of my restless imagination. (I was one of only three secretaries-general in the world, the other two being the chiefs of the United Nations and the Organization of American States.)

During my stay with the Peace Corps I traveled frequently — usually in Shriver's company — to every part of the world, looked for crocodiles in East Africa, narrowly missed an airplane crash in the desert of southern Iran, and drove the length of Afghanistan from Kabul to the Khyber Pass. Nor was my severance from the center of power complete. I maintained my social contacts with the Kennedy family, continued to accompany Kennedy on his trips to Latin America, and was called upon to draft all his speeches on the Alliance for Progress.

In March of 1963, for example, I went with Kennedy to Costa Rica for a "summit" meeting with the leaders of all the Central American countries. The reception, as usual, was large and enthusiastic. The night of arrival, I sat in Kennedy's hotel room with Kenny O'Donnell and Dave Powers talking idly with the president, who, his jacket off, his shirt open at the neck, would occasionally walk to the window and wave at the crowd that had gathered in the streets below, and would remain through the night. Each appearance was greeted with cheers and shouts of *Viva Kennedy*. Returning from one of his cameo appearances, Kennedy said, "If we could only move them all to Ohio, just for the election. I might carry the damn state." Pointing to some cables that had arrived from our beleaguered missions in Southeast Asia, Kennedy remarked, "Think of all the energy and time we're putting in over there. This is where we should be putting our attention. It's all going to be decided down here." Then: "It's going to be the biggest foreign-policy issue in the election, Latin America." A little later, having returned to the window, Kennedy waved me over. "Look down there, Dick . . . no, near those cars. Now that's one hell of a woman. . . . Why don't you . . ." His voice trailed off. I was never able to figure out what he was about to ask me. Perhaps he wanted some changes in the next day's speech.

Yet the enlightening satisfactions of my work with the Peace Corps and my intermittent assignments for the president could not mask the fact that I had descended rather precipitously from Latin American chief in the White House to a relatively minor post. I began to wonder if I might not accomplish more on the outside — working with civil rights, perhaps. There was a lot going on out there.

Indeed, only obstinate pride had kept me in the government; I was damned if I would leave when I was down, give my adversaries the satisfaction of mumbling, "Goodwin's gone" over Georgetown dinner tables. It wasn't much of a reason. But it wasn't self-deception. Then, unexpectedly, in the fall of 1963, at Schlesinger's suggestion, Kennedy asked me to become his special consultant on the arts, a position that would return me to the White House. I accepted, not because it represented a significant upward move ("Why the hell does Dick want that job anyway?" Kennedy asked Schlesinger) but out of a personal fascination with the artistic world that dated from my pre-political youth, and because it would bring me back to the White House where, with a presidential campaign less than a year away, other things were possible. Unlikely, perhaps, but possible — which, for a habitual risk-taker, was good enough.

It was agreed that before the White House announced my appointment I should assemble a special Council of the Arts to be composed of persons prominent in theater, music, dance, motion pictures, art, and architecture, whose names could be announced simultaneously with mine.

Organizing the council was not my first involvement with government and the arts. That had come early in the administration when Jacqueline Kennedy sent a memorandum to her husband asking if something could be done to help save the monuments of ancient Egypt threatened by the construction of the Aswan Dam.

In the late fifties, engineers foresaw that floodwaters from the dam would drown many of Egypt's most precious antiquities, including the mammoth Abu Simbel. (If he had to choose between the pyramids and Abu Simbel, André Malraux had written, he'd save Abu Simbel.) The United Nations set out to raise the funds necessary for preservation, but the Eisenhower administration refused to contribute. (Dulles was enraged at Egypt's acceptance of Soviet aid for the dam project.) In return for contributions, Egypt had offered to give some of the monuments to the donating countries, including, if the donation was large enough, a small temple. Approached by European friends in an effort to reverse America's position, Mrs. Kennedy had written the memo, which the president then sent on to me "for possible action." After a brief investigation it became clear that without American help the monuments would perish — not only Abu Simbel, but a large number of statues, temples, and artifacts centered around the island of Philae. I had no doubt about the merits of the project. I was less certain that Kennedy could be persuaded to ask Congress for an appropriation of thirty or forty million dollars to save Egyptian antiquities. With the help of Jerome Wiesner, I carefully prepared my presentation to the president — a large book with pictures of the monuments, summaries of artistic opinion, even a film of Abu Simbel. Finally I entered the Oval Office to make my pitch. Kennedy examined the book, while I explained that the treasures were unique, priceless, part of humanity's most noble heritage, etc. "That's all fine," Kennedy said, "but what do you think Rooney's going to say when I ask him for forty million dollars to save a bunch of rocks in the middle of the Egyptian desert?" (Congressman Rooney from Brooklyn was chairman of the committee that would decide on this project.) "I know what he'll say," Kennedy continued. "He'll say, 'Jack, you must be out of your mind. There's not one Egyptian voter in the whole country.' " I wasn't going to argue politics with the master. Naturally, Rooney wouldn't think much of the idea, but he was a Kennedy loyalist. Instead I told Kennedy of the Egyptian promise to give some of the antiquities to contributing countries. "Imagine, Mr. President," I concluded, "Napoleon only brought an obelisk back to Paris. You can bring an entire temple to Washington." He looked at me for a moment, those steel blue eyes unwavering, enigmatic. I've gone too far, I thought. Then Kennedy leaned back in his chair as if pondering a difficult decision, and smiled broadly — "Let's give it a try."

Kennedy talked to Rooney. Rooney said, "Jack, you must be out of your mind, but if that's what you want, I'll try it." The money was appropriated. And the preservation was successful.

Now all I had to do was pick the temple. I asked a group of Egyptologists to meet me in New York, where we examined pictures of the dozen or so temples from which we could choose. The experts quickly narrowed the selection to three or four. One of them, I noticed, had a long stone walkway leading up to the façade. "What is that?" I asked. "It led to the banks of the Nile," one of the experts explained, "so the temple could be approached by boat." It'll be perfect for the Potomac, I thought to myself; we can reconstruct the walkway and do what has to be done to protect it from the climate. "Let's take that one," I said aloud. There was no objection. But by the time the temple of Dendur was ready for shipment, I had left the government; and the energetic Thomas Hoving had persuaded a then indifferent government to let it go to the Metropolitan Museum, where it can be seen today; an in-

congruity of place only partially redeemed by its nearness to the
New York apartment of Jacqueline Kennedy, whose intervention
brought it to America.

The weekend of November 16, I flew to Palm Beach to work on
a speech on the Alliance for Progress that Kennedy was to give to
a convention of publishers in Miami. Unfortunately, the audience
was composed of fairly conservative publishers (i.e., businessmen), who were not very enthusiastic about our "leftist" Latin
policies; and a tired Kennedy was not in his best form.

Tuesday, November 19, I was standing in Evelyn Lincoln's office when the president walked in, saw me, said he thought the
speech went well. He then picked up a copy of the *Washington
Daily News*. The headline read, "Kennedy Gets Mild Response
from Publishers." Kennedy was infuriated. "Imagine a guy like
Scripps, or was it Howard, was sitting right there and then lets a
story like this appear. It serves me right to talk to publishers. I
don't want to talk to publishers again. It doesn't do any good.
What about that dinner in New York? Do I have to do that?" He
started to reenter his office, then turned toward me, saying, "Come
and see me tomorrow."

Wednesday, November 20, the day before Kennedy was scheduled to leave for Texas, I accompanied a group of Latin American
artists and intellectuals to the White House. They urged him to
appoint his brother Robert Kennedy as head of all Latin American affairs — a kind of hemispheric superchief.

"It's a good idea," Kennedy responded. "I understand you're
going to see the attorney general later in the day. Why don't you
ask Bobby if he'll take the job." (Bobby was receptive, but noncommittal.)

That afternoon, Arthur Schlesinger and I went to the president's office with the names of some people I wished to add to the
Council of the Arts. Before we began our discussion of the arts,
we suggested — again — that Kennedy create the special post of
undersecretary of state for Latin America (thus elevating it above
the other geographic regions) and, to ensure that a higher title
would mean higher authority, appoint a relative to the job — if
not Bobby, then Sarge Shriver.

"Dammit," Kennedy replied, "I've told Rusk three times that
I thought we should have an undersecretary for Latin affairs. All
I get back is that it's being studied. Arthur, you and Dick write a

memo for me to sign. Say that I already know the reasons why I can't do it. Now I want the reasons why I can do it."

Kennedy then looked at my list of suggested names for the arts council, said, "Fine," then asked if we could "put on James Fleming of Indiana. He's been very helpful to us." I agreed, of course. I said that the more I'd thought about the arts council, I realized it really could be something far more than a public relations thing — worrying about who came to dinner at the White House. That it should concern itself with the entire problem of the aesthetics of our society — the way our cities looked, the beauty of our environment as well as the general encouragement of the arts. I said that I thought this whole business of the aesthetics of our society could be to him what conservation was to Teddy Roosevelt.

"It's a good idea," he said, "let's work on it," and then, preoccupied, walked toward the door, saying, "I never want to talk to those damn publishers, never!"

I left, never to see Kennedy again.

The morning of Thursday, November 21, I received a call from Milton Esterow of the *New York Times*. He told me he was writing a story for the next day's paper, revealing Kennedy's intention to appoint me presidential adviser on the arts. There would be a profile on me as that day's "Man in the News." (The forgotten morning edition of November 22 carried the feature. It was something more than ironic.) I told him nothing was definite, but he ignored this. He obviously had the story pretty cold. He asked me some personal questions for the profile and I answered them. If he was going to write it anyway, I wanted it to be as good as possible. I was convinced Esterow's story would be fairly favorable since he would be dependent upon future contacts with me for stories and information in his assignment covering arts and Washington for the *New York Times*.

After speaking with Esterow, I called the president's party in Texas, talked to the assistant press secretary, and told him about the Esterow story. In less than an hour he called me back and said the president wanted me to prepare a statement on my appointment and send it down for release on Friday afternoon, November 22. That night I went to a party for a group of Latin American intellectuals and artists, where I danced, ate, drank until 4 A.M. And I could easily write the announcement in a couple of morning hours.

> The distance that the dead have gone
> Does not at first appear;
> Their coming back seems possible
> For many an ardent year.
> — Emily Dickinson.

I did not ordinarily keep a diary, being too weary for writing at the end of a twelve-hour workday. Yet there were occasions when I yielded to an inner compulsion to record — not for history, but to clarify my experience, or simply as catharsis. I made such notes more often than usual toward the end of November in 1963 — and use them here in an effort to convey the immediacy which time has blurred. They are repeated as written, slightly edited for clarification, with any present amplifications clearly identified.

Friday morning, November 22. I woke up late, head pounding from the revelries of the night before, went to my typewriter to prepare the statement of my appointment, sat there looking through the morning paper waiting for my head to clear. The story was very favorable, without the snide cracks that usually accompanied articles about me (brash, inexperienced, arrogant, etc.). The picture was nice and the whole thing had a good tone and ring. With a sense of excitement about my new job, I set to work on the statement.

It was midafternoon before I finished. After the statement was completed, I called Kenny O'Donnell's White House office, telling the secretary that I had some more names for the arts council and would she make sure that they went to Kenny in Texas.

At this point, her voice broke: "Oh! Mr. Goodwin. Don't you know? The president is dead! He was killed in Texas. Somebody shot him."

"He's dead," I said.

"Yes, oh yes."

I knew by the tone of her voice there was no doubt.

I ran into my bedroom where my wife Sandra was napping. "Sandra, the president's dead. He was shot in Texas." "You're kidding," she said sleepily. "No," I said, "it's true, he's dead." I sat on the floor, shaking, my body rocking involuntarily: "No, oh no." "It can't be true." "It is true." I was crying. It was unbelievable, stunning. An awful feeling of helplessness — nothing could be done, no recall. It — he — was over, done, finished. My only instinct was to dress and go to the White House. I knew I couldn't stay home. I dressed quickly, unseeingly, dazedly. I drove to the White House in tears, sobbing in the car. I clung to the wheel and watched the road with a ferociously forced concentration of energies. I had to make it. The city was quiet. There was traffic. Nothing seemed very different. A maze of thoughts. Jackie, Bobby . . . Johnson was president . . . My future. But under it, over it, swarming anguish . . . loss. He was dead. My God, he couldn't be dead. A line repeated insistently, an involuntary drumbeat in my mind: "Full fathom five my father lies, of his bones are corals made."

There was no parking in the avenue beside the West Wing, so I parked illegally on the street. I was not to return until 6 A.M. the next morning. I went up to Ralph Dungan's office. There was a meeting going on. Sarge Shriver was in charge. Mac Bundy, Sorensen, many others, were there. I felt I couldn't go in — curious insider/outsider that I was. I felt that walking in might seem as if I was asserting my right to belong when no assertion was right, or could be made — at a time when ego or the signs of ego had to disappear forever, or at least for now. I slumped in the chair in the outer office, controlling myself, sitting quietly, looking down. Others came by — Bill Wirtz, Celebrezze sat in the next chair. We said nothing. Nothing could be said. Tears had to be stopped, controlled, passion hidden. Bundy went in and out.

We began to work on the arrangements for that evening. The body would arrive in the early evening, after dark. Johnson would be there. He had been sworn in on the plane. Kennedy's body would lie in state. Would the casket be open or closed? It should be closed. Everyone agreed. But it would be up to the family. Arthur Schlesinger came in followed by Ken Galbraith and Kay Graham. Arthur was crying. Ken had tears and his face was streaked with feeling. Kay sat quietly on the couch, sorrowing. Arthur said — What kind of a country is this? Those who preached hate and violence, the far right. This was their doing. Our fault was that we had never taken them seriously. I couldn't listen. I nodded agreement, moved away.

I heard the helicopters landing on the South Lawn. The staff was flying to the airport to meet the incoming plane. I didn't want to join a greeting party, a masquerade, a delegation to meet flesh empty of life, of meaning. I went to the rear entrance of the White House toward the helicopters, torn, uncertain. I couldn't go . . .

went back to see if I could help Sarge, who remained. We slumped
in chairs, talked for a moment or two. He said little; his face was
drawn but he maintained control of himself, of the situation.

People began returning. They had seen the casket come off the
plane — Jackie behind it. Soon word came that the casket had
gone to the Bethesda Naval Hospital, would be brought back later
that night to lie in state in the East Room. Jackie wanted the East
Room to look as it did when Lincoln's body lay there. I grabbed
the Sandburg biography from the Cabinet Room. It had a description which I brought over to Bill Walton (a family friend and
artist who had been asked to prepare the room). Bill was already
at work. Arthur got someone to go to the Library of Congress.
They returned with a contemporary sketch and newspaper description of Lincoln lying in state in the East Room. It had been
open to the public. Sarge said there wouldn't be time for that.
The public would view it at the Capitol Rotunda.

We learned that Jackie and Bobby had gone to the hospital
with the casket. We were told the body would be prepared there;
we could tell the man from Gawlers undertakers to leave. Someone did. We worked on the East Room. We got an upholsterer,
the same man who had upholstered the White House furniture for
Jackie. We needed a catafalque and were told there was one over
at Fort Myer like the one used for Lincoln. We sent for it. We
were told everything should be ready by 12:30. I went over, said
the middle chandelier would have to come down. Walton said,
"Let's wait and see how big the catafalque is." I said, "It was
done for Lincoln . . . look at the picture." He said, a little irritated, "Let's see." We were all a little frantic, concentrating on
details, controlling our feelings, trying not to get annoyed by minor disagreements, keeping absorbed in the work. Sarge said he
wanted an honor guard along the curved entrance, and lights to
light them. The White House man said TV lights would do it.
Sarge said no. They were too bright. Much discussion about small
150-watt spots: Could they be put in trees? Not possible. Finally,
we went to the D.C. police department for small flares which they
used in streets. Shriver said troops would come to form an honor
guard inside the White House, and along the outside walk. We
worked to decorate the East Room with black crepe. It was going
slowly. Much debate as to whether the folds around the chandelier were deep enough. I said I didn't think so — it looked a little
ludicrous, like a black brassiere or short panties. The symbolism

of women's underwear kept popping into my mind. I thought it would look a little absurd, perhaps obscene. Walton disagreed. I was upset. It seemed terribly important. It wasn't.

The time had been postponed to 1:30. The catafalque had not yet arrived. I called the military office, asked where it was. It was getting late. They put a tracer on it, sent men out looking for it as it had left the fort. I was harsh. We need it right away, hurry up. It shortly arrived. It had no superstructure and so the chandelier didn't have to come down. We set it up in the middle of the room. Black stand in black base.

The candlesticks were too big and ornate, metallic. We got four others, simpler, with glossy wooden arms. We tested them to see if they would light. I lit one with a match. They did light. The priests arrived and sat around. Four small stands for kneeling were set up. Two on the side of the catafalque facing entrance for priests. Two other at foot of casket for mourners. We needed a crucifix. The one they had was too big. Sarge sent out to his house for his crucifix, saying, "Of course, I'd be honored if they used mine. It was given to me by Cardinal Gibbon" (his godfather, I think).

Time of arrival kept getting postponed. I walked out many times into the front entrance of the White House. It was crisply cool. Along the driveway, toward the gates, the bright TV lights shone. A crowd of people silently gathered along the front fence and across the street. I had gone down to Janet Travell and gotten some Dexamil and took one. She asked me to lie down for five minutes. I said I couldn't, "Thank you very much, Janet," took pills with me, and went. We kept drinking coffee. It was brought out to us. And then sandwiches. Over in Dungan's office we had eaten hamburgers. I went in the kitchen a couple of times for coffee as the night wore on. The troops for the inside honor guard had come in. We debated their placement. The troops who were to line the driveway had not arrived. I spoke harshly to Shepard (a military aide), as did Sarge. Shepard ordered the troops to come from the marine barracks at 8th and I. They arrived a few minutes before the coffin. There were only about fifteen of them. Instead of stationing them along the walk, we decided they should form a double column and march up the driveway ahead of the hearse. They were brought down to stand at the gate. They double-timed up from the rear and through the front entrance, where they went into formation and were told what to do.

I walked inside. Arthur and Bill Wirtz were talking in the Blue

Room. Pierre Salinger had arrived, looking haggard. His plane with Rusk had been an hour and a half out of Honolulu when the word came. They turned around, refueled in twenty-five minutes, and flew straight back. In the plane all had been quiet, no one moved or said anything for half an hour. Then people played bridge, talked softly, read papers as the came. Rusk had a quiet talk with those in the plane. Pierre looked very distraught and went off.

I stood on the front portico, out of sight of reporters and cameramen. I wanted to see the car enter. It came in, black, dark, headlights, the guard began its march. I rushed through the back entrance to the far corner of the East Room, where we had agreed to stand. Pierre was there, and Arthur and Bill and Ralph, and the others who had worked there that night. We waited in silence, grief. The casket slowly came in the door. I tried, but could not stop sobbing. He was there, in that casket. They placed the casket on the catafalque. Mrs. Kennedy stood there beside Bobby. Kenny and Larry came in behind them and moved to the side.

She had on a pink dress, some said it was bloodstained but I didn't see the blood. Her face was fixed straight ahead, lovely, painful to see. A small altar boy, wearing a cassock and carrying a forked metal taper, went to light the candles. They lit with great difficulty. He stood in front of one for several seconds. It finally lit. He went to the last one. It wouldn't light. Finally his taper went out and he took out a match to relight it, but, as he did, the candle started up into life and he walked away. We were all immobile, every attention fixed on the boy and his efforts to light the candle, let it light! Yet not caring. Time seemed to stand still. The priest said a short prayer. Mrs. Kennedy walked over to the coffin, knelt on the base, turned her head away from where we were standing, rested her cheek along the flag which draped the coffin. Her hands went up over it, embracing the casket for a moment. She got up. Bobby held her by the arm as she walked out. The rest of us stood there for a moment, weeping.

Then we all started to go. I moved a little from room to room. I saw Sarge and Jean Smith come in and kneel in prayer on the two stands beside the casket. Bobby came down. He opened the casket and asked Bill and Arthur to look. They were debating whether it should be open. But, Arthur told me, the reconstructed face was white and waxy. It didn't look like him. It was open for 5–10 minutes and then closed forever. It would be closed for the funeral and while lying in state at the Capitol.

I stood way down the corridor. I couldn't talk to anyone. Fi-

nally Arthur and Bob McNamara left and I followed them out to
my car. It was about 5:15. I took Joe English home and then
drove to Arthur's house in Georgetown. He was seated in front of
his typewriter. I sat, we drank, consoled each other with our talk.
We mentioned Oswald briefly but it was the dream talk of fatigue
and grief-ridden men. I left as the sun was rising, went to bed
about 6:30, to rise the next day at 8:30.

Saturday, November 23: I woke at 8:30, dressed, and returned
to the White House — to Dungan's office. We waited there, working on more details. Sandra arrived at about 11:30. We went over
to the line to pass in front of the casket. We filed slowly through
the Blue and Green rooms and into the East Room. The line went
across the room and past the coffin. There were tears and the
contorted features of controlled anguish everywhere. Sandra passed
by crying. I paused a moment in front of the casket — it was unimaginable that he lay in that box. I tried to picture it but I
couldn't. I tried to think the right profound thoughts about destiny . . . blighted hope . . . freshness decayed . . . all that was
wanted, that could have been. But the thoughts were unreal. I
could not escape from myself. There were tears. They came from
another part of me of which I was not then aware, or was too
tired to be aware. We went past and down and back to Arthur's
office. Marion Schlesinger and the children came in. We said hello,
subdued, trying not to look at each other, struggling to recapture
poise. They left and went to view the coffin. Sandra and I sat
there, silently, trying not to think, yet struggling to imagine. Arthur and Marion returned. We sat and talked. Arthur said how
he wanted to leave now, it had all gone for him. He had come to
Washington not in search of a job but to work for JFK. He had
planned to leave after the election anyway. It was not yet time to
argue our intentions. Passion had to drain away before discussion
could begin. Sandra came back. A little later, I left. I would see
everyone at the Occidental Restaurant. In the West Wing I met
Sarge with Joe English, Bill Haddad, and others. Sarge began to
tell anecdotes about the Peace Corps. Our loud conversation, even
laughter, contrasted with the muffled atmosphere around us. Sorensen came and sat down by himself at a table — quiet, unsee-
ing, only his drawn pale features betraying emotion.

Then there were the ceremonies of mourning and burial. There
is no need for description. The long silent lines outside the Capitol, the ritual mass, a riderless horse, the roar of jets overhead in

the formation of death, a meticulously folded flag placed in the widow's arms, all implanted in the memory of the living, later exposed to the half-comprehending perceptions of the then unborn. For a moment a turbulently discordant America was fused in a single sentiment, joined by an irrecoverable departure.

And not just in America. Young people grieved in the streets of Moscow. On the plateau of the Andes, *campesinos* knelt in the fields. On a remote river in the Sudan, a young American stopped at the single store in a small village to buy food. The old man behind the counter slowly wrote down the prices on a piece of scrap paper and, after he had calculated the total, he carefully, slowly, scraped a dark penciled border around the bill. The American watched patiently and, when it was finished, asked why he had done that. "Haven't you heard?" the old man said evenly. "The greatest man in the world is dead today."

It was the first worldwide mourning in history. And perhaps the last.

12 / Coda

I cease from my song for thee
From my gaze on thee in the west, fronting the west, . . .
O comrade lustrous with silver face in the night.

— Walt Whitman

JOHN KENNEDY was president of the United States for two years and ten months. Had their terms been similarly truncated, Franklin Roosevelt would be remembered as an inspiring failure; Woodrow Wilson as an accidental interlude in decades of Republican rule and American isolationism; Abraham Lincoln as the man who allowed a peaceful separation to become a bloody dismemberment of the Union.

One cannot apply customary canons of historical judgment to so abbreviated a span; although many have done so — pedantically balancing achievements and failures, Cold War militance with peace-protecting acts. John Kennedy's presidency was not an artifact, a fixed construction of goals and deeds frozen in ice or preserved in amber, but a metamorphosis. The John Kennedy of 1963 was not the John Kennedy who took office in January of 1961. The man was the same but the intensities, the conduct, the destinations were not the same. If this is so — and it was so — one must grant him the capacity to change, to revise settled conceptions under the tutelage of external events and inner experience. It may seem a minor tribute, until one reflects how few among the world's leaders have possessed it, how few of us, in our own lives, combine the strength of mind and ego to question and revise the settled convictions of maturity.

It does not detract from my admiration to acknowledge that the private Kennedy was flawed, his admirable strengths mingled with less commendable fragilities. That only tells us that he was a man

like the rest of us. I could, were that my purpose, try to describe
his inner contradictions, attempt to find their source in the manifold pains and rejections that were so carefully concealed, and
partially overcome, by a carefully cultivated charm and a very
real yearning to understand and grasp the possibilities of life. But
such revelations are not part of my story. John Kennedy was a
public man, a leader of men, and, as such, must be judged by his
public acts and the consequences of his leadership.

I am not among those whose own lives were so fused with his
that they are compelled to act as guardians of his memory. He
trusted me. Within limits. He often exposed his private thoughts
and intentions in my presence. Again, within limits. He valued
my services and rewarded them with large responsibilities, yet he
was willing to allow, to author, my separation from the luminous
center when he felt it necessary to other, higher, imperatives of
power. Nor did my understanding of his reasons eliminate a certain personal resentment, a feeling of mistreated loyalties. Yet I
never lost the belief that he was an extraordinary leader; that his
death was an immense, perhaps irretrievable, loss.

Historians and others have criticized his militant response to
the challenges of Soviet power, his cautious reluctance to assault
racial injustice, the moderation of his efforts to help the deprived
and helpless. Some of these criticisms are just. But it must also be
remembered that the Cold War was real, that the Soviet Union
had proclaimed its intention to "bury" America and extend its
power to the third world through "wars of national liberation."
While within America the conservatism of the Eisenhower years
was still dominant. For the most part Kennedy's efforts to attack
the most blatant inequities of American life — through Medicare,
relief for depressed areas — languished in Congress, and failed to
win a significant popular constituency. A president does not run
America. He leads it, and cannot compel it in directions it is unwilling to take — not without forfeiting his ability to lead at all.
Perhaps he could have acted more forcefully. I thought so at the
time. But the judgment was his.

I do believe that by 1963, John Kennedy had begun to alter the
direction of his leadership and was intent on a process of accommodation that might end the Cold War; that he had recognized
the urgency of black aspirations and was prepared to use his office
toward their fulfillment; had decided to assault the obscene persistence of poverty in a country that, under his leadership, had

entered the largest sustained economic boom of its history. Nor are these beliefs based on faith alone. He had already begun.

One can debate the magnitude of his concrete accomplishments, debate the wisdom or courage of his actions, argue about his future intentions, speculate on the extent of his commitment to combat in Vietnam. (Would he have . . . ?) But the largest question — what he meant to the country he governed, and what he has come to mean — cannot be answered or argued with the sterile platitudes of rational discussion. It is not an issue of reason.

Shortly after the assassination, one of Kennedy's closest friends lamented that his brief rule would soon be forgotten, eclipsed by the ascendant Johnson, his memory consigned to the abyss of semioblivion occupied by most American presidents. "He'll be remembered," I reassured her, speaking more out of a desire to comfort than any historical foresight. Yet today, a quarter century later, he is remembered far more vividly than many of his successors. My children's grammar school classmates know his name, think of him — obscurely, vaguely — as among the somewhat arbitrary pantheon of our history's more heroic leaders. His voice and figure reappear with amazing frequency on televised documentaries and docudramas. And the mention of his name can still arouse emotions, stir debate among those who lived while he governed.

One can multiply justifying nouns: youth, energy, critical intelligence, rationality, glamour, charisma, and more. But one does not understand a man, explain the force of his leadership, by reducing him to component attributes. Still less do they tell us why his memory endures.

I have often reflected on the source of Kennedy's impression on the country he led and on the historical memory of the country which has survived him. I think — without being at all certain — it is that he seemed to embody the idea of America. Not the nation itself. That would be presumption. But the idea by which we have defined America, and, by extension, ourselves as Americans.

The assertion requires some elaboration. A country is more than a place, an organized society through which we derive wealth and power. It is also an idea, and it is that idea which forms the most decisive bond between its citizens, which makes it possible to speak of the American "community." And for each nation the idea is different. Frenchmen, for example, can be sustained and elevated by the invocation of glory. "Ye sons of freedom awake to glory," exhorts the first line of the "*Marseillaise*"; while in modern France de Gaulle rose to power on the same appeal. But Americans are not moved by a call to glory; that call being too intangible, too dependent on the inspiration of a lengendary past.

Conscious of a long and dazzling rise to sovereignty and then to empire, the English have been linked by their responsibility to a brilliant heritage. ". . . we must speak / That if tonight our greatness were struck dead / There might be left some record of the things we said," wrote Tennyson in 1852; his exhortation echoed almost a century later when Winston Churchill inspired his war-torn nation to act so that future millennia would look back and say, "This was their finest hour." Americans are more likely to be vitalized by more immediate goals — "Beat the Japs"; "Put a man on the moon" — than by the quest for a place of honor in the chronicles of history.

This does not mean that the American idea is a practical one. In many respects it has been the most romantic of all; given its unique form and force by the unique circumstances of our birth and growth. To be French or British, Chinese or Egyptian is to be part of a cluster of events and beliefs transmitted across centuries. Such comforting continuity was not possible to Americans. The wilderness had sheltered no Roman legion, no Peter and Constantine, no Renaissance or Elizabethan Age. We could not reflect on that interminable procession of rulers and artists which provides a Frenchman with his proudest moments. Nor could we anchor ourselves in a fixed territory and population — a place occupied by a people of shared origins. We moved from our colonial fringes to occupy a continent, our population constantly changing its composition; individuals and families always moving on.

Thus we formed — could only form — a stabilizing continuity, an idea of what it meant to be American, from a common belief in the purpose and direction of a nation. We were William Bradford's "city on a hill," Washington's "great experiment," Jefferson's "chosen country," Lincoln's "favored land," and from there, in a direct line, to Wilson's Fourteen Points, Roosevelt's Four Freedoms, and John Kennedy's declamation that "the same revolutionary beliefs for which our forebears fought are still at issue around the world. . . . We dare not forget today that we are the heirs of that first revolution."

This American idea differed from that of others in a crucial quality. It had to be constantly renewed, always contemporary. It could not be sustained — could not sustain us — by recalling that

we had once been a land of opportunity, that we had once possessed a great purpose, that there had been a time when we stood
for the freedom of man. "Justice," "freedom," "opportunity,"
"model and exemplar to the world" are either present realities or
the idea is dead. Indeed, discontinuity, freedom from ties of the
past, was expressed as a moral principle by men like Jefferson,
who said that no generation should be allowed to bind the next;
informed Lincoln's claim that "the dogmas of the quiet past are
inadequate to the stormy present." Each generation must measure
and adapt its own performance against the changing requirements
of the American idea — that we were a nation constantly moving
toward some large and worthy future purpose; not in search of
some safe harbor or final resting place, but adventurers with a
cause, each achievement only a prelude to those still grander and
more noble destinations that lay beyond a constantly receding
horizon.

This idea contains no claim of moral superiority. Still less does
it encompass the realities of American history and modern life.
Our behavior has often contradicted faith, belief, and principle.
But it is the American idea; forced upon us by history and certain
moments of illuminating vision. It has provided us with a sense of
shared worth and social purpose. Even our most unholy depar-
tures have sought justification in that idea. We may have had
warlike majorities, destructive majorities, or greedy majorities, but
we have never had a majority of cynics. At least until now.

John Kennedy expressed — in words, in action, in manner —
his own belief in America's possibilities; that we were a nation
with a large purpose, a mission, perhaps dangerous, certainly difficult but within our powers. It all sounded so fresh and contemporary, but it was a reaffirmation of the idea that was the nation — that had come on the *Mayflower*, was thriving before the
first settlers crossed the Alleghenies, had been bred into every
generation. Many citizens disagreed with Kennedy's policies, his
actions, his direction. But his presence helped to revitalize our
belief in ourselves — as individuals and as Americans. Some would
join the Peace Corps. Others would march on Washington. He
was cheered, and he was denounced. But he would be remembered, because he made others remember — what we were as a
people, how strong we could be, how proud. Call it "style," dis-
dainfully if you will. But style is the archway through which power
enters into historical memory: the judicious, dignified Washing-

ton, the poetic Lincoln, the ebullient Franklin Roosevelt. Kennedy
has not yet won a place in that company, but if he does it won't
be because of the space program or the missile crisis. It will be
because what he was helped remind us of what we could be.

John Kennedy was not the sixties. But he fueled the smoldering
embers, and, for a brief while, was the exemplar who led others
to discover their own strength and resurgent energy; their own
passion, love, and capacity for hate.

As for the man himself, he remains, in part, a mystery. My own
efforts at understanding and explanation are incomplete. The recognition of history, which he so badly wanted, is still undeter-
mined. Yet . . .

> The man Flammonde, from God knows where,
> With firm address and foreign air
> With news of nations in his talk
> And something royal in his walk
> With glint of iron in his eyes,
> But never doubt, nor yet surprise,
> Appeared, and stayed, and held his head
> As one by kings accredited
>
>   .   .
>
> He never told us what he was.
>
>   .   .
>
> To play the Prince of castaways.
> Meanwhile he played surpassing well
> A part, for most, unplayable;
> In fine, one pauses, half afraid
> To say for certain that he played
>
>   .   .
>
> What was he, when we came to sift
> His meaning, and to note the drift
>
>   .   .
>
> Why was it that his charm revealed
> Somehow the surface of a shield.
>
>   .   .
>
> Rarely at once will nature give
> The power to be Flammonde and live.
> We cannot know how much we learn
> From those who never will return,
> Until a flash of unforeseen
> Remembrance falls on what has been.
> We've each a darkening hill to climb;

And this is why, from time to time
In Tilbury Town, we look beyond
Horizons for the man Flammonde.

— Edwin Arlington Robinson

PART III / JOHNSON

CHORUS: Did you perhaps go further than you have told us?
PROMETHEUS: I caused mortals to cease foreseeing doom.
CHORUS: What cure did you provide them with against
    that sickness?
PROMETHEUS: I placed in them blind hopes.
CHORUS: That was a great gift you gave to men.

                   — Aeschylus, *Prometheus Bound*

13 / An Unexpected Return

THE FLOW OF TIME is intractable. Although the living continued to mourn the dead, the Kennedy men had to respond to the events, the need for decision, which were swiftly engulfing them. Johnson was now in command, his intentions still a mystery, failure to consider the future would be unnatural; perhaps even fatal to ambitions which must now move into obscurely perceived, unmapped paths. For me the possibilities were simple and, thus, easily decided. Or so I thought.

I hardly knew Johnson, my contact limited to occasional pleasantries over the past three years. He was unlikely to confirm my appointment as adviser on the arts. So I convoked my Peace Corps staff, assured them that the secretariat would continue its work, and, privately, began to give serious thought about my departure from government.

In the weeks that followed the assassination small groups of Kennedy liberals — Galbraith, Schlesinger, Secretary of Labor Bill Wirtz, White House staff members — grieving, disoriented, old suspicions rearoused, met in small informal groups to discuss whether Johnson could be denied the party's nomination at the convention, now little more than half a year away. Some may have been motivated, in part, by a foreseeable loss of personal influence or position. But not many, and not much. The gatherings were suffused by a sense of disbelief, an unwillingness to accept what they thought to be true — that the hardly won Kennedy renaissance, the liberal renewal, had been so abruptly, arbitrarily cut short; the fruits of progressive victory transferred to this "conservative" Texan, this master political manipulator, peerless "boss of the Senate," personal protégé of Georgia's Richard Russell, whose values and convictions (if he had any) were remote from their own.

Not only had Camelot dissolved, but Mordred was in command — or at least so it seemed, and was often expressed in those early weeks of incoherent grief and shock. "What does he know about people who've got no jobs," Robert Kennedy told me, "or are undereducated? He's got no feeling for people who are hungry. It's up to us."

Bobby, and others no less vehement, were mistaken; had misjudged the gargantuan figure who would emerge from the humiliating shadows of the vice-presidency to dominate American public life for almost half a decade; who would make himself — personality, actions, ambitions — a national focus for admiration, anger, fear, and derision to an extent unrivaled by any president since Roosevelt. The mistakes, the furious misjudgments, were understandable, amid what seemed the shattered castle of dreams and intentions. Bobby and others would revise their judgments, but, for the moment, were inwardly compelled toward resentment at the alien usurper. "The king is dead, long live the king" is a slogan for subjects, not for princes.

Although my own partial expulsion from the inner circle had not — judging by the intensity of my sorrow — lessened my feelings for Kennedy, it restrained me from making instinctive judgments about a man whose capacities and thoughts were unknown. I did not know Johnson and would not judge him. Not until later. Not until I had come to understand him more profoundly, in more intimate detail than I would know any person in public life. Except, perhaps, for Bobby.

Before I would have that opportunity, within weeks of Kennedy's death, I experienced another blow, less personal, but directed at the heart of my own involvement in public policy.

In late November 1963, at Johnson's request, I had sent a memorandum to the White House on the Alliance for Progress. After detailing the myriad difficulties that beset the still-sluggish Alianza, I concluded that "We have only eleven months [before the election] to demonstrate that the Alliance is going ahead full steam. . . . The Alliance had an enormous asset in the person of President Kennedy. Latins felt that they could count on him to cut through the morass of the bureaucracy. . . . You need someone in over-all charge who will be a symbol of your personal concern and determination. . . ." Rather naïvely I suggested Sarge Shriver or Robert Kennedy for the job.

In about two weeks I had my answer. On Saturday, December 14, press secretary Pierre Salinger announced the return of Thomas Mann to the job of assistant secretary of state for inter-American affairs to which he had first been appointed by Eisenhower and later removed by Kennedy. Arthur Schlesinger sent me a copy of the briefing transcript, to which he had affixed a note on which was scrawled "R.I.P."

The next morning, I received a call from Pedro San Juan, who had served Kennedy as interpreter and adviser on trips to Latin America. "I am going to write an obituary," Pedro said; "the Alliance for Progress, born October 1960, died, December 14, 1963." My diary entry that Sunday reads: "San Juan's call reflects the general mood of the Kennedy crowd over the appointment of Tom Mann. . . . There is real gloom among the advocates of the Alliance for Progress. Mann is a colonialist by mentality who believes that the 'natives' — the Latin Americans — need to be shown who is boss. He is a tough-line man — a man who feels the principal job of the United States in Latin America is to make the world safe for W. R. Grace and Company. He is not much of an administrator but is tough, arrogant, and opinionated. In other words, he has all the worst qualities coupled with a basic lack of belief in the Alliance for Progress. Unless a miracle occurs we can expect a process of deterioration of the U.S. position to begin. It may not be visible for quite a while, but it will come. Well, it was a good try. At least that is my today's mood."

But it was more than a mood — the transient merger of grief with frustration. Obedient to an atavistic disposition — action stripped of vision — we returned to the policies which, only a few years before, had been so clearly perceived as the source of certain decay. We would, with certain honorable exceptions, support the status quo — any status quo — outwardly allied to our Cold War aims and respectful of American business. The consequence was, over a quarter century, to validate the prophecies of the Latin American task force and the premises of the Alliance for Progress. Economic aid continued, but, stripped of the insistence on social justice — *techo, trabajo y tierra, salud y escuela* (homes, work, land, health, schools) for the masses — it could not halt, indeed would accelerate, the polarization between the authoritarian right and the anti-American left. It would also, more importantly, destroy the alliance between the United States and the desire of the Latin multitudes for their "inalienable rights" to life, liberty, and the pursuit of happiness. Those rights, we seemed to say, in contradiction to Jefferson, had been reserved by God to Americans. As Kennedy predicted, the failure of peaceful revolution has now awakened the forces of violence — by the state and against it. The precise consequences are unforeseeable. But they will not benefit — materially or morally — the objectives or the spiritual wellbeing of the United States.

On Monday, December 16, 1963, Arthur Schlesinger and I entered the spacious office of the attorney general — its walls decorated by the multicolored, scribbled drawings of small children — ostensibly to discuss plans for the Kennedy Library, but, more urgently, in search of a fellow spirit to share our futile laments over Tom Mann's appointment.

Bobby Kennedy motioned us to sit, poured some bourbon; idly we discussed politics, the projected Kennedy Library, the value of recording reminiscent anecdotes while they were still fresh. The ringing of a phone on his desk brought the attorney general to his feet. He listened in silence then responded: "He's dead. Let him be dead. . . . Come and see me next week."

He turned toward us, the forced geniality drained from his face as Arthur continued to express our distress; staring intently at us, past us:

"The Alianza isn't just important to Dick Goodwin or Arthur Schlesinger. It's important to me and Ed Henry and a lot of people. Averell Harriman said to me last night, 'I didn't come down here to work for George Ball or Dean Rusk; I came to work for John Kennedy.' Well, I don't want to see Averell Harriman get screwed, or anybody else. Harriman's got his faults. I've got my faults. We've all got faults. But I don't want to see him get screwed. . . . There are hundreds of guys around here in positions of influence. We're important to Johnson. I'm the most important because my name happens to be Kennedy. But we're all important, if we act together. I haven't thought it through yet. But we are."

Then standing rigidly by the phone, hands clenched, facial muscles tensed against an unseemly show of grief: "I've lost a brother. Other people lose wives." His voice trailed off into an instant of silence. "I've lost a brother, but that's not what's important. What's important is what we were trying to do for this country. We got a good start; we had a committee working on poverty, a juvenile delinquency study. You can't do a lot in three years, but we'd gotten started. We could have done a lot in five or more years. There's a lot of people in this town. They didn't come here just to work for John Kennedy — an individual. But for ideas, things we wanted to do. I don't want people running off. . . . A lot of people could scramble around now, get themselves positions of power and influence. But that's not important. What's important is what we can get done. . . . Remember after November fifth [the presidential election] we're all done. We won't be wanted or needed. We're not going to do what the ADA says or anyone else, but what's good for America."

As we left, I glimpsed a column by Samuel Lubell in the morning paper, reporting that southerners were opposed to Robert Kennedy for vice-president, and Negroes were for it (the term "blacks" not yet born). I showed it to Bobby, who studied it intently, then, musing, with analytical detachment, "Well, he's [LBJ] already got the Negroes. . . . He's already got the Negroes."

"Thanks, Dick," he said, as we left.

Bobby Kennedy's monologue that day in December was a cry of pain: judgment and desire distorted by disconsolate deprivation, a vain desire to recreate — in some undecipherable fashion — that which had been extinguished by a malign fate. Those who had come to labor for the New Frontier were not linked by common, crusading ideals (although there were idealists and crusaders among them), but by John Kennedy — personality, will, and the magnetic radiance of power that drew men toward it for a variety of motives — ambition, rank, prestige, or the mere pleasure of nearness to the source. That bond was now gone, the companions of the past could not be rallied to influence or coerce the new president, to accept Robert Kennedy as some kind of a surrogate leader, if that's what he he had in mind. They retained life, energy, ambition and would — must — pursue their own values and career within the framework of a new reality. As Bobby himself would do, after time had muted his grief.

In early January, Johnson sent Robert Kennedy on a goodwill visit to the Far East. Glad to get out of the country, away from that Washington where every sight and encounter abraded his destitute spirit, accompanied by his family, he visited six countries in thirteen days. On his return in late January, he reentered the now-alien Oval Office to report. After a brief discussion on the trip, Johnson abruptly told him, "I want you to get rid of that Paul Corbin" (one of Kennedy's political staff whose loyalties Johnson distrusted). "I don't think I should," Bobby replied; "he was appointed by President Kennedy, who thought he was good."

"Do it. President Kennedy isn't president anymore. I am."

"I know you're president, and don't you ever talk to me like that again."

"I did you a favor sending you to the Far East."

"A favor! I don't want you to do any more favors for me. Ever." And with that, Robert Kennedy rose, and without looking back, stalked angrily out of the Oval Office.

Brutal? Not really. An inevitable encounter between two strong-willed men, one still unable to accept the irretrievable, the other feeling compelled to assert his rightful authority over this living reminder of the now almost mythical predecessor whose memory seemed likely to overshadow and depreciate his own authority and achievements. (In 1965, Johnson, to dramatize his War on Poverty, went to visit an impoverished household in Appalachia. "They had seven children, all sick and skinny," he recounted. "They seemed real happy to talk with me and I felt real good about that. Then as I walked out, I noticed two pictures on the wall. One was Jesus Christ on the cross. The other was John Kennedy. I felt as if I'd been slapped in the face.")

Although Johnson might have been more gentle with Bobby (and vice-versa), he was right. The order was his to give. He was the president. Within the year, Robert Kennedy, practical rationality having resumed control, would ask Lyndon Johnson for a favor: support and endorsement in his campaign for the Senate in New York. And Johnson responded — made television commercials, accompanied Bobby on a campaign tour. It was just good politics, of course, but it must have given Johnson a special satisfaction to grant needed help to this man who had so disdained him. It must have felt even better when, in the fall elections, Johnson carried New York by a landslide, while Bobby barely made it.

Although I had been moved and impressed by Robert Kennedy's plea to stay on and "continue the fight," I was under no illusion that it might somehow be possible to mount a guerrilla insurgency against the Johnson White House, or, if it was, that I could play an important role. And thus I began, metaphorically, to pack my bags. Outside the government men and women of my generation were working to change the country; the constructive social movements of the sixties had begun to spread from living-room meetings and libraries, to campuses, underground journals, and the struggles for black freedom. If I had lost connection with the New Frontier in Washington, perhaps I would find it out there.

Then, in January, an obscure incident in Panama began a train of events that ended with my appointment to President Johnson's White House staff. While I was still deliberating my departure, fierce anti-American rioting in Panama, directed at United States control of the Canal Zone, virtually compelled the president of that country, then approaching a national election, to sever diplomatic relations with the United States and demand a complete revision of the Panama Canal Treaty.

We reacted as predictably as a bear stung by a bee: We roared. "I'm not going to be pushed around by a country no bigger than St. Louis," Johnson told intimates. Faced with his first foreign-policy "crisis," only nine months away from his own election campaign, the president refused to negotiate while the violence continued, and announced that even if peace was restored he had no intention of negotiating a new treaty, although he would be willing to "discuss" the "possibility" of a new treaty. Senate Republican leader Everett Dirksen, sensing a political issue in the making, offered the statesmanlike counsel that "To give an inch would be equivalent to telling every small country that all they had to do was break off relations, attack our embassy, and demand whatever they wanted." He did not explain what other small countries he had in mind or what they might demand. But surely there were others, and they all must want something. Didn't everybody?

The intermittent exchange of rhetoric continued until the middle of March, when a team of OAS negotiators announced that President Chiari of Panama and the United States (acting via Tom Mann) had agreed to name ambassadors to begin discussions and/or negotiations. Radio Panama proclaimed a victory, whereupon an irritated Johnson disowned both his own assistant secretary and the Organization of American States. The agreement, he said, was a figment of many imaginations. And on March 16, speaking at a ceremony to commemorate the third anniversary of the Alliance for Progress, Johnson departed from his prepared text to say that there had been absolutely no meeting of the minds, that we hadn't given an inch.

Now everyone was mad. The Latin diplomats told reporters that Johnson was transforming the Alliance for Progress into a weapon of old-fashioned imperialism. The European press was almost uniformly critical of the new president's ineptitude in the first test of his foreign-policy skills. Leading members of the Democratic party — men whom Johnson had carefully cultivated as protection against any challenge to his nomination — openly censured American actions.

Until the "Panama affair" Johnson had received nothing but warm and virtually unqualified praise for his skillful transition to the presidential office. Now the "honeymoon" was threatened, and all because he had escalated a trivial dispute over words into a clash of high principle. The Panamanians had withdrawn from their insistence on "negotiating" a new treaty, and agreed with us and the OAS simply to "discuss" the possibility of a negotiation. But our breach of this agreement had made even "discussion" seem like a coerced concession. In other words, we had painted ourselves into a corner. We could go to war, which was out of the question. We could do nothing, which meant the continuation of riots and a mounting rhetorical battle. Or we could talk, which, it seemed, we had refused to do. As a result, a trivial dispute, easily soluble by the appropriate manipulation of verbal formulas, had become a confrontation, a "mini-crisis" for the new president.

Around March 17, I accompanied Sarge Shriver to a meeting in the "fish room" of the White House, where he had gathered the heads of various government departments to discuss the use of Peace Corps volunteers in a variety of overseas programs. After about one hour of politely obtuse discussion, it was becoming clear that the chieftains of professional bureaucracy had faint enthusiasm for introducing a bunch of young, enthusiastic amateurs into their carefully crafted and scheduled projects. We could, Sarge explained, help them accomplish more and faster, not realizing that his mounting eagerness only increased the apprehensions of those for whom ordered planning and totally controlled execution — at least on paper — were far more important than results, were their protection against future scrutiny by superiors or, God forbid, by the Congress. Seeking momentary relief from the litanies of evasion, the interminable non sequiturs, the tedious, fearful rejection masked in the language of appreciative rationality (Sarge, after all, was being mentioned as a candidate for vice-president), I stepped outside the room into the West Wing corridor. As I stood there, surveying the scene of past glories, the door to the Oval Office — about thirty feet down the hall — opened and Lyndon Johnson stepped out.

Seeing me, he motioned. "Dick, can you come here for a minute?" I walked toward him, exactly as I had approached a similar summons from John Kennedy on that January day three years before. "Come on in," he said, following me into the Oval Office and carefully closing the door. I turned to find the gargantuan figure (Had he actually grown since becoming president — or was it my imagination?) standing less than a foot away. Leaning toward me, his eyes locked into mine, his physical closeness designed to put me on the defensive (a characteristic maneuver; not a trick, but derived from an intuitive understanding of human discomfort, vulnerability, a violation of the insulating space that separated each individual from others). "Tell me, Dick," he demanded softly, "what do you think we should do about this Panama thing?"

"I haven't been involved, Mr. President," I replied, maneuvering for time to frame my answer to the unexpected question. "And I'm not sure I know all the issues involved." The president stood silent, intense, gaze unwavering. "But from what I know, it doesn't seem too difficult." Then, more forcefully, old passion returning: "We're a great big, powerful, rich country. Panama is tiny, weak, poor. They know we could just come in and take what we want, and they'd be helpless. All they've got is their pride, and if we make threats and demands, they can't give in. They'd lose their dignity."

"So what would you suggest? That we give them whatever they want?" Though harshly phrased, it was not a question, but an invitation to continue.

"Tell them they're a great country, our allies in the fight for freedom, that they've fought beside us in war and been our friends in peace, that we're grateful, glad to have them as friends, anxious to keep a small misunderstanding from damaging such a valuable relationship."

The president's expression did not change. "Can you write me a statement?"

"Of course."

"Send it over to Jack Valenti. He'll make sure it gets right to me." The intensity drained from his posture. Smiling, he placed his huge arm over my shoulder, silently walked me back into the corridor, turned, and disappeared into his office.

Much later I realized that, inadvertently, without calculation, I had communicated with the heart of Johnson's genius — that capacity for manipulation and seduction bred by his extraordinary intuition of other men — their ambitions, needs, weaknesses, pride — which was the foundation, the inward core of his political mastery in the Senate and, for a while, in the White House. Panama and Congress, President Chiari and Everett Dirksen; an equation he perceived instantly, naturally, and which he could use without any sacrifice of dignity. He had been doing it all his life, and knew that in exchange for words — only words — many men would make concessions, yield their will to his, enhance his power.

I returned to my Peace Corps office, completed a statement by early evening, and called Valenti, who sent a messenger for my ill-typed draft. (No secretary could be allowed to see it.) For four days there was no response, not even an acknowledgment. Then, on March 21, Johnson, without notice, walked into the office where his new press secretary, George Reedy, was conducting the morning press briefing. "Is it all right with you folks," he asked, "if I monitor your press conference?" And without waiting for acquiescence began to read a marginally amended version of my statement, which, he said, would be sent to the president of the OAS that afternoon.

"The present inability to resolve our differences with Panama is a source of deep regret . . . we have long been allies in the struggle to enhance democracy . . . Panama has unhesitatingly come to our side . . . when we were threatened by aggression . . . we have also had a special relationship with Panama (in maintaining the canal). . . . All free nations are grateful for the effort they have given to that task . . . the claims of . . . Panama . . . do not spring from malice or hatred of America. They are based on a deeply felt sense of the honest and fair needs of Panama. It is, therefore, our obligation as allies and partners to review these claims and to meet them, when just and possible. We are prepared to review every issue . . . at any time and at any place. . . . As soon as he is invited . . . our ambassador will be on his way . . . his instructions will not prohibit any solution which is fair. . . . For despite today's disagreements, the common values and interests which unite us are far stronger than the differences which now divide us."

On March 24, President Chiari of Panama welcomed Johnson's "constructive evaluation." "During the two great world wars," Chiari declared, "Panama and the United States united their efforts, and each in proportion contributed to the victory of the democratic cause. . . . Rightly does President Johnson recognize . . . that there is no malice or hate in the demands of Panama because they are just and sincere. . . . [O]ne can see his purpose that relations be reestablished and that special representatives be designated to solve these matters. . . . I am willing to act in this way."

The "Panama problem" was over. (A formal agreement was signed on April 3.) The Panamanians got their discussions (now called a "review"). Johnson got an end to the rioting without a new Canal treaty. And I got a job in the White House. My beloved Latins had, inadvertently, restored me to the center of power where, over the next two years, I would share more substantially in presidential authority and policy than ever before.

Within a day or two of the president's statement, and the favorable press reaction that followed, Valenti asked me if I would prepare a speech for a Democratic party gathering.

Before working on the speech, I read through a half-dozen of LBJ's previous speeches and decided that the mistake so far had been the effort to make Johnson a rhetorician, a turner of ornate phrases. Believing that speechwriters cannot make a man something he is not — that it will not ring right, will always come out a little off-center — I decided to write the speech in simple, straightforward, unadorned language.

The next day I brought my draft to Valenti. He listened to the speech with enthusiasm, saying it was just the sort of thing he wanted for LBJ. "LBJ's way of speaking," he explained, "is a lot closer to Roosevelt than to Kennedy. Kennedy's stuff might have been fine for him, but not for Johnson." He then said he was going to recommend that the president bring me to the White House. He asked how I had worked with LBJ before. I told him I hadn't. After asking a few questions about my background, he said, "I want to be honest with you; it's the only sensible way to be. Some of the people in the Kennedy coterie were not your friends . . . some who are no longer here." (I knew better. Some were still there, but Jack, prudently, did not want to jeopardize any potential future relationships.) "They didn't want you to do anything for LBJ. I don't try and keep useful people from the president like some do. I want him to know who can help. . . . I'm going to take the speech up as it is and see that he reads it in its pristine form, before others get their hands on it."

I did not doubt Valenti's sincerity. He wanted me in the White

House. But his expression of intent was not, could not be, the product of solitary reflection. The matter must have been discussed — with Bill Moyers (a close personal friend of mine who had already moved from the Peace Corps to the top rank of Johnson aides) and, in all probability, with the president himself. Jack, after all, had only one loyalty and it is unlikely that he would disclose his recommendation to me unless he had first cleared it with Johnson, making sure that it would be approved. His job was to protect the president, not expose him.

That night, I talked to Robert Kennedy and asked him what he thought of the offer. Did he think I should take the job if it materialized? He thought for a while, then said, "Well, from the selfish point of view — you can think selfishly once in a while — I wish you wouldn't. But I guess you have to. After all, if any one of us is in a position to keep him from blowing up Costa Rica, or something like that" (Costa Rica! Of all unlikely places!) "then we ought to do it. So I guess you should do it. If you do, you have to do the best job you can, and with complete loyalty. There's no other way." Of course. It had never crossed my mind that there was any other way; that one could work for a president of the United States without a complete commitment to serve his objectives, interests, and the office of which he was the personal embodiment.

The next morning I walked from my Peace Corps office to a small drugstore located a block from the White House in search of a cup of midmorning coffee. As I crossed Pennsylvania Avenue, I encountered McGeorge Bundy. I had not talked with my once-intimate colleague for almost a year — no dinner invitations, not even a telephoned exchange of pleasantries — and thus was somewhat (not completely) surprised when he hailed me and, approaching, said in vigorous tones: "We really miss you at the White House, Dick." (Had he just noticed my absence after almost two years?) "We could really use someone of your abilities."

"Thanks, Mac," I replied and continued toward the coffee counter. That's it, I thought. It's been decided. Johnson's going to bring me back to the White House.

That same afternoon the offer was made and accepted.

During this, my second tour of duty in the White House, my rseponsibilities were to be limited almost exclusively to domestic affairs. It was fine with me. For that was now where the action was. Or so it seemed. ("Those fellows over at State really have something against you," Johnson later delighted in telling me, "but I just let them know your president is with you all the way"; a classic example of the Johnsonian technique — divide and dominate — with which the president tried to maintain direct personal control over not only his own staff, but all the institutions of government. "Now that Fulbright tells me, George," he once told Senator George Smathers, "that you just don't bother to come to committee meetings; that you just can't be counted on." "That's not true, Mr. President," Smathers responded. "I'm always there when it's important." "I believe you, George, but that's what he tells me.")

After joining the Johnson staff, I moved first to a secluded office in the Executive Office Building and, within a month, was transferred to a second-floor office in the precious West Wing of the White House: the very same chamber I had claimed with such innocent exultation only three years before.

The next time I left, the choice would be mine.

14 / The Master at Work

ONE MORNING in late March 1964, I arrived at my office to find an urgent summons: The president wanted to see me. He was in the mansion. Handing my briefcase to a secretary, I walked through the West Wing, past the empty Oval Office, along the narrow corridor to the mansion flanked by the Rose Garden and the swimming pool on whose walls, at John Kennedy's direction, there had been painted a mural of the harbor at St. Croix, up the staircase of the presidential home, where a guard waved me toward Johnson's bedroom. "Go right in, the president's expecting you." Knocking once to signal my entry through a door already partly ajar, I strode decisively into the bedroom. It was empty, the bed still unmade, three television sets — one for each network — beaming the day's commentary to an empty room. I stood for a moment, puzzled, uncertain, when I heard the already-familiar voice. "That you, Dick? Come on in." The sound came unmistakably from the adjacent bathroom. There, seated upon the toilet, apparently in the midst of defecation, was the president of the United States.

Johnson stared at me intently, looking for any sign of embarrassment. There was none. My years in the army, countless visits to locker rooms, and occasional stayovers in the boudoirs of uninhibited ladies had long since destroyed any vestige of childhood chagrin at watching the performance of normal bodily functions. Although, admittedly, I had never before seen a president taking a shit. (Kennedy's intimacies with me were restricted to receiving communications while taking a bath.) I remained standing, of course — Johnson had the only seat in the room. He continued to look at me, calculating my reaction ("You can tell what's in a man's heart," he later told me, "by looking into his eyes"), and then, seemingly satisfied, began to talk.

"I wanted you to work for me," he asserted. "Some folks around here, some of your *Kennedy* friends, were against it. They said you were too controversial; brilliant but controversial. Well, I'm controversial too. Someone who isn't controversial, well, that usually means he's satisfied to sit around on his ass" (a strange metaphor for the occasion) "and get nothing done. Don't bother yourself about the critics. I never do. You just do your job and no one can touch you. The president will always be there to back you up."

Then, lowering his tone, forcing me to approach more closely: "Look, Dick, I need you. I need you more than Kennedy ever did. And you need me. I loved Jack Kennedy, just like you, but he never really understood the Congress. I do. And I'm going to pass all those bills you cared about. It's a once-in-a-lifetime opportunity, for you, for me, for the country."

"I'll do everything I can, Mr. President," I replied.

"You're going to be my voice, my alter ego, like Harry Hopkins." (Characteristic Johnson hyperbole, meant to be understood as such — at least five staff members had already been promised the Hopkins role.) "What the man in the street wants is not a big debate on fundamental issues. He wants a little medical care, a rug on the floor, a picture on the wall, a little music in the house, and a place to take Molly and the grandchildren when he retires. I'm going to get my War on Poverty. Of course, we can't have it all in one gulp. We'll have to make some concessions, make a few compromises — that's the only way to get anything. But that's this year. I have to get elected, and I don't want to scare people off. Next year we'll do even more, and the year after, until we have all the programs. But no compromises on civil rights. I'm not going to bend an inch, this year or next. Those civil rightsers are going to have to wear sneakers to keep up with me."

He looked toward me, expectantly, seeking a sign of skepticism, finding none.

"Those Harvards think that a politician from Texas doesn't care about Negroes. In the Senate I did the best I could. But I had to be careful. I couldn't get too far ahead of my voters. Now I represent the whole country, and I have the power. I always vowed that if I ever had the power I'd make sure every Negro had the same chance as every white man. Now I have it. And I'm going to use it. But I can't if people like you go running off." (Running off, I thought, hell, I had just arrived.) "Why, I never had any bigotry in me. My daddy wouldn't let me. He was a strong anti-Klansman. He wouldn't join the Methodists. The Klan controlled the state when I was a boy. They threatened to kill him several times."

Just as I began to apprehend that Johnson was risking a severe case of hemorrhoids, the president reached for the toilet paper. I made my exit to the bedroom where, a moment later, clad in his pajamas, Johnson approached, glanced briefly toward the televisions, then turned toward me. "I'm sick of all the people who talk about the things we can't do. Hell, we're the richest country in the world, the most powerful. We can do it all, if we're not too greedy; that's our job: to persuade people to give a little so everyone can be better off. We can do it if we believe it. It's not a matter of twisting arms like those reporters say. What convinces is conviction. Logic and reasoning won't win your case for you. You just have to get full of your subject and let it fly. I was successful with people in the Senate because I was convinced that I was right — intensity of conviction is the number-one priority."

Johnson turned to get dressed, and, not having said a word, yet conscious that I had passed some kind of mysterious test, I left the mansion for my office and the day's work.

The unusual setting for my interview — for interview it was — was not an accident but, like almost everything Johnson did, a calculation. His display of intimacy was not gross insensitivity, or an act of self-humiliation, but an attempt to uncover, heighten, the vulnerability of other men — the better to know them, to subject them to his will. I realized this much later when Johnson delightedly described a similar mise-en-scène with McGeorge Bundy, "one of the delicate Kennedyites," who "came into the bathroom with me and then found it utterly impossible to look at me while I sat there on the toilet. You'd think he had never seen those parts of the body before. For there he was, standing as far away from me as he possibly could, keeping his back toward me the whole time, trying to carry on a conversation. I could barely hear a word he said. I kept straining my ears and then finally I asked him to come a little closer to me. Then began the most ludicrous scene I had ever witnessed. Instead of turning around and walking over to me, he kept his face away from me and walked backwards, one rickety step at a time. For a moment there I thought he was going to fall into my lap. It certainly made me wonder how that man had made it so far in the world.''

I didn't know, then or later, what impression Lyndon Johnson had formed of me, into which category of his enormously subtle intuition I had been fitted. But I knew my own reaction. Lyndon Johnson had "let it fly." At me. And it worked. Putting aside — not wholly — the obvious flattery, the hint of unmatched rewards to come (the president's "alter ego"), I sensed the enormity of the man's will, the intensity of his intent, not just to pass the Kennedy programs, but to go far beyond his predecessor's reach, to leave a mark on the country that would equal, even surpass, that of his youthful hero, Franklin Roosevelt. He wanted to out-Roosevelt Roosevelt.

Johnson, unlike Roosevelt, had inherited a country of mounting prosperity, could not draw energizing power from despair and distress. So he took another course, the only one open to him, the one most congenial to his character. He would persuade everyone — businessmen, union chiefs, bankers, politicians — that his goals were in their interest; not only their economic self-interest, but the interest that he, perhaps naïvely, thought was buried somewhere in every man — to contribute, to leave behind a mark of which he could be proud. "A rising tide lifts all the boats," noted John Kennedy, except, he omitted to say, for those boats stranded on the beach beyond the water's reach. And for those, Lyndon Johnson would simply reverse the command of King Canute. He would summon the tides themselves to greater heights.

In his pursuit of consensus, Johnson was obedient to the lessons of his earliest days in public life, when, as a young man, he fought to bring electric power to the impoverished homes of his native Blanco County. "The man who had the most influence over me, more than anyone," Johnson told me, "was Texas Senator Alvin Wirtz. Wirtz was trying to persuade the local power companies to put in lines that would reach out to rural areas and make electric power available to small farmers. After considerable effort, he organized a meeting at which the big power companies and potential consumers were represented. The power representatives were a bit difficult. At a certain stage an ardent populist — me — blew off, and gave them hell. There was great excitement and enthusiasm for my performance. However, the meeting broke up without a decision, and I noticed that my friend and mentor Wirtz did not

look toward me as enthusiastically as some of the others. 'You
better come into my office,' he said. We got behind closed doors.
'Lyndon,' he said, 'it took me more than a year to get this meeting
organized. You've got to realize that the power companies own
the power, and we're not going to get it unless they agree. You
undoubtedly feel good about the ruckus you raised, but I want
you to remember some advice — you better not tell a man to go
to hell unless you can make him go there.'

"And that," said Johnson, concluding the anecdote, "is the essence of democratic politics. Things get done only by agreement
between opposing forces. The best decisions are neither bought or
sold. Before you do anything, your last thought ought to be 'I've
got to live with the son-of-a-bitch.' "

In 1964 and well into 1965, it seemed as if Lyndon Johnson's
energy and will might impose itself on the course of an entire
nation, return the country to the most generous and spacious elements of a liberal tradition dormant since the New Deal. A willing
Congress acted on an unprecedented volume of presidential requests with a dispatch not seen since Roosevelt's "hundred days,"
passing dozens of new programs and liberating important social
legislation that had been debated and refused for more than a
generation. Hitherto unyielding opposition dissolved before a
president who was in continual communication with leaders of
public opinion — Roy Wilkins of the NAACP, union presidents
Walter Reuther and George Meany, Rockefeller of New York and
the automobile chieftains of Detroit. While, closer to home, he
labored, often far into the night, telephone constantly in hand, to
persuade, seduce, coerce congressional leaders, committee chair-
men, and, it seemed, most of an entire membership whose individual predilections and desires seemed as familiar to Johnson as the
scores of Verdi or Puccini were to Toscanini. "I never saw anybody work with Congress like that," an awed Larry O'Brien told
me. "The man's a genius." Yet there was no reason for astonishment, not if one had known the earlier Johnson, the majority leader,
before confinement in the vice-presidency had drained his energy,
blunted his will, reduced him to an almost paralyzing despair. He
had simply brought to the larger scale of national leadership those
skills which had made him master of the Senate. "When you're
dealing with all those senators," Johnson explained, "the good
ones and the crazies, the hard workers and the lazies, the smart

ones and the mediocres — you've got to know two things right away. You've got to understand the beliefs and values common to them all as politicians, the desire for fame and the thirst for honor, and then you've got to understand the emotion most controlling that particular senator when he thinks about this particular issue."

At the beginning of 1964, Johnson's most urgent task was to consolidate and demonstrate his command of both party and country. The nomination was only months away, and in November, a presidential election. Although he seemed almost certain to be the party's choice, there were always Bobby Kennedy and his liberal coconspirators ready — in Johnson's mind — to attack at the slightest show of personal inadequacy or unfaithfulness to the Kennedy legacy. Nor was victory over some still-unnamed Republican candidate a certainty. He would have to prove himself to the country, become not just Kennedy's accidental successor, but a leader worthy in his own right of the highest office.

Johnson chose the Kennedy tax cut proposal for his initial battle. Languishing in a mildly hostile Congress, the tax cut had been designed by the engineers of Keynesian economics to stimulate economic growth, and thus increase income and reduce unemployment. The principal beneficiaries of this reduction — the "business community" — were also among its fiercest opponents, their ideological devotion to a balanced budget not yet having been overwhelmed by the prospect of short-term profits. (Ah, those days of innocence, once violated, never recoverable.) And their opposition was strengthened by Kennedy's then-staggering proposal to spend 101.5 billion dollars, the first peacetime budget in history to break the magic 100-billion-dollar mark. "You can defend the 101.5 billion," economics adviser Walter Heller told Johnson. "It is an irreducible minimum." "I can defend 101.5 billion," Johnson responded sardonically, "but *you'll* have to take on Senator Byrd. If you don't get it down to 100 billion, he won't pee one drop."

Whereupon, Johnson took over personal management of the budget — cut and patched, invoked the infinitely varied subtleties of accounting legerdemain, which, by postponing expenditures, seemed magically to eliminate them.

But no general exposition of tactics — however colorful — can yield an accurate appreciation of Johnson's skills. Fortunately, at the close of each day's business, a trusted secretary would type his secretly transcribed conversations, and a few of those more revelatory records are among my personal papers. (The rest, an immense volume, are entombed in the Johnson Library whence they may, in some distant future, emerge to confound an amazed posterity.)

Late in January, Johnson called finance committee chairman Byrd into his office. "I've got a surprise for you, Harry," he announced, brandishing a thick file of figures. "I've got the damn thing down under 100 billion . . . way under. It's only 97.9 billion. Now you can just tell all your friends that you forced the president of the United States to reduce the budget before you let him have his tax cut." Although Byrd was delighted with the lowered budget, he was still opposed to a tax cut. However, he agreed not to use his power as committee chairman to keep the measure from a vote. And that's all Johnson needed. He would get the votes.

And when the Senate Finance Committee convened on the morning of January 23, the votes were there. Passage of the tax cut seemed assured until Senator Russell Long introduced a surprise amendment to repeal excise taxes, amounting to about 450 million dollars, on a variety of luxury items — jewelry, furs, handbags, luggage, and other products dear to the hearts of conservative wives and wealthy campaign contributors of both parties. The passage of Long's amendment was an augury of disaster, threatening to stimulate a multibillion-dollar orgy of tax-cutting on the Senate floor, stripping the bill of its carefully balanced economic justification, and guaranteeing its defeat.

At 12:34, according to the transcripts, while Johnson was having lunch, Senator Smathers reported that because of Long's amendment, Senator Williams would vote with Gore and Douglas to cut out 455 million of revenue.

Johnson responded instantly. (In the next couple of hours he was to call nearly all seventeen members of the finance committee.) "Now listen, George," he told Smathers, "Clint Anderson is the key to this whole thing. I begged him last night not to come unglued on this."

"Well, it worked," Smathers responded, "at least partway. Anderson didn't show up for the meeting."

"That's not what I was asking," Johnson replied. "Look, George, why don't you see if you can get Abe Ribicoff and Paul Douglas together on this. I'll take care of Anderson."

At 1:05, the president called Senator Anderson: "I know you

got mad, and I can't blame you. But we can't help what Russell Long does. Get in there and get Ribicoff. He's got to vote with me once."

Anderson: "He won't do it. He won't go with anybody."

Johnson: "You get that meeting. Take the leadership. I know you can win if you fight for it."

Responding to the presidential plea, with its flattering implication, Anderson agreed to "try," and, putting down the phone, Johnson instructed his secretary to reach Senator Vance Hartke of Indiana.

"Vance, can't you help me on this excise thing? You're going to wreck this damn bill. Now they're all going to get together this afternoon" (an unnamed, still-unrecruited "they") "and try to make a motion to keep all excise taxes in there. And we need your help. They all got mad yesterday because you all screwed up that oil vote. All of us are going down in defeat if we can't operate better than that. Anderson says he'll change if you'll change." (Anderson had made no such bargain; but who would ever know?)

Hartke: "One thing I wanted was to eliminate the tax on musical instruments." (Music, presumably, being especially dear to the hearts of Indiana.)

"What's important is the big credit to the Democratic party. The goddamned band and musical instruments, they won't be talking about them next November. They're going to be judging us by whether we can pass a tax bill or not, and whether we got prosperity. We just want a general vote, so you won't have to vote on each special tax." (Patriotism, party, and a way to avoid a stand on music.)

Hartke: "Let me try to get that done."

A few minutes later, at 1:28 P.M., the president called Senator Ribicoff of Connecticut, a former member of Kennedy's cabinet.

"Abe, can't you go with us on this excise thing and let us get a bill? We were all ready to report this bill to the Senate, and now we got it just good and screwed up." ("We," not "you," spoke the diplomat.) "Why can't you meet at two o'clock, and let's leave this excise like you had it before you met this morning. Anderson is going to help us. Hartke will help us. And if you'll help us, we'll have it over." (It's all up to you, Abe.)

Ribicoff: "Well, one of my problems is that one of the amendments in there is something for my home state that's already been announced."

"I know it. But it's the same for everyone. They've all got one of those 'home state' cuts in there . . . my friend."

Ribicoff: "Well let me see how I can save my face."

"You save my face this afternoon and I'll save your face tomorrow. You just work it out. I don't give a damn about the details. I just want you to work it out. Will you?"

Ribicoff: "I'll do my best. . . ." (pause) "Okay, Mr. President."

Having, somewhat precariously, brought back enough straying senators to initiate — with some hope of success — a motion for reconsideration, Johnson turned, at 1:47 P.M., to the all-important finance committee chairman, Harry Byrd.

"Listen, Harry. They're going to offer a motion this afternoon to take all these excise repealers out. I hope you can help them, because it will just throw everything out of caboodle if we lose 450 million on this thing. If you'll go along with me on that, we can do it. You can do this on general motion. You can tell them you voted with them on the individual, but when a general motion came along you just can't justify losing 450 million to the Treasury." (By suggesting and organizing a general motion to eliminate all excise repealers, Johnson was making it unnecessary for any senator to go on record against his own special interest, or one dear to the heart of a colleague.)

Byrd: "I'll do the best I can."

That afternoon the finance committee met and voted, 9–8, to reconsider and defeat the excise tax cuts they had passed that morning.

At 4:30 that afternoon, Johnson called Senator Anderson: "I want to congratulate you. You did a fine job. When you lead, you lead."

Anderson: "We didn't lose a vote on the Democratic side."

"I'm proud of you, and I'm proud of Ribicoff, and Russell was just fine, and Smathers worked hard." (Notice the subtle gradations of gratitude.) "And thank you, Clint. I'm proud of you."

At 5:36, Ribicoff received a presidential call:

"You did a great service for your country, and a bigger one for your president, and I appreciate it. They would have riddled us if it wasn't for you. You're a team man, and I'll bet on your team." (I.e., I'll be for your team, if you'll play on mine.) "I need you. And I want to talk to you. Come on down for a little discussion."

Ribicoff: "You're doing great. And I'm going to work my head

off for you the next time." (Ribicoff, one of John Kennedy's earliest supporters, had just made a political commitment.)

A final call, at 5:40, went to Harry Byrd:

"You're a gentleman, and a scholar, and a producer, and I
love you."

Byrd: "Well it was only one vote. We got by."

"I know it. That Harry Byrd though, he can do anything. You've
learned to count since I left up there. I used to do your counting.
But when you can beat them nine to eight, you're doing all right."

Byrd: "I'm glad you called about it."

With the removal of this final obstacle, the long-awaited tax cut
passed the Senate by a vote of 71–21, and was signed into law on
February 26. "It is," a jubilant Johnson told the television audience, "the single most important step that we have taken to
strengthen our economy since World War II."

Johnson explained that the tax cut would benefit everyone:
Businessmen would have more money for investment, members of
the middle class would have more money to spend, and millions
of the poor would be exempted from the tax rolls; while for those
more ideologically inclined there was budget reduction for the
conservatives and Keynes for the liberals. Nor should gratification
be marred by any sense of guilt: The beneficiaries of lower taxes
were the agents of true patriotism, for "by releasing millions of
dollars into the private economy the tax cut will encourage the
growth and prosperity of this land we love." Thus, everyone was
free to enjoy their newfound income with a clear political conscience, to admire their cake and eat it too.

It was true. Most of it. Certainly Johnson believed it as did
most of the American public — not just the voting masses, but
economists, businessmen, legislators. Indeed, it became a matter
of dogma to credit the Kennedy–Johnson tax cut for the economic
boom that followed its enactment and that continued until, like
all domestic progress, it was swallowed up in the insatiable jungles of Southeast Asia.

In retrospect, it is less clear that the tax cut was the engine of
prosperity. Our economy had grown steadily since 1960 and, although there were signs of faltering, it may well have resumed its
upward course without help from Lord Keynes. I never believed
that the massive American economy had been launched into even
higher orbit by such a tiny nudge from the Treasury. However,
we did have a tax cut, and we did have a boom, and, although

coincidence is not causation, it was enough that nearly everyone believed that we had found the alchemists' formula for mounting national wealth. On the basis of that belief, the trustful expectations it excited, Johnson would build the "consensus" necessary to accomplish his almost unlimited projects of change and reform.

15 / The Great Society

ONE AFTERNOON in early April of 1964 I went for a non-aerobic but historic swim. Bill Moyers, whose office sat just below mine in the spacious splendor (by government standards) once occupied by the departed Sorensen, called me up. "Come on, Dick, the president wants to see us."

"In his office?"

"Nope, in the pool. He's swimming and so are we."

"I don't have a bathing suit."

"You don't need one."

An involuntary pang over the fate of my only good business suit faded almost instantly as I realized I was being summoned for a skinny-dip.

Bill Moyers was at this point my closest friend and ally in government. A close association with Johnson, predating the Kennedy years, had elevated him from deputy director of the Peace Corps to the top level of the White House almost immediately upon Johnson's accession. "You're my number-one man," I heard him tell Bill in my presence, then confiding after Moyers had left, "That boy's like a son to me, even if he did go to work for those Kennedys." More skillful than I in navigating the mine-strewn labyrinth of bureaucratic survival and advancement, he shared with me the romantic idealism of the true believer, became a staunch ally, a kindred spirit, in the internal struggles to shape enlightened domestic policies. His closeness to Johnson, Johnson's dependence on him, can be measured by his continuation in office and in power long after he had manifested his opposition to our

escalation in Vietnam, the one subject that was to become Johnson's decisive litmus test for loyalty.

We entered the pool area to see the massive presidential flesh,
a sun-bleached atoll breaching the placid sea, passing gently,
sidestroke, the deep-cleft buttocks moving slowly past our unstar-
tled gaze. Moby Dick, I thought, being naturally inclined to literary reference. "It's like going swimming with a polar bear,"
Moyers whispered, being of a more naturalistic bent. Without
turning his body, Johnson called across the pool: "Come on in,
boys. It'll do you good."

We stripped on the spot, the nearby dressing rooms being reserved for the abnormally squeamish. (You could use them, of
course, but not without eliciting a sarcastic glance.) Moyers dived
into the water while I, untrained in aquatic sports, slid, half-falling,
over the guttered side and into the water — a bit tepid for New
England tastes, just right for Texas.

Johnson turned, and the three of us slowly spiraled, paddling,
around the circumference of the pool while the president began to
reveal his reflections and intentions about the future of the country — the future of his leadership of the country.

My presence in the pool was an acknowledgment of my new
status. From that day until I left the White House in late 1965, I
was to draft every major presidential address. And in those days,
as in preceding administrations, a speechwriter was not just a
speechwriter — a remote and secluded wordsmith whose relationship to the substance of policy was that of a Hollywood script-
writer to the final print of a multimillion-dollar epic. Like Sam
Rosenman with Roosevelt, Clark Clifford with Truman, Emmet
Hughes with Eisenhower, Ted Sorensen with Kennedy, even my
own relationship to the Alliance for Progress, the chief presidential speechwriter was expected to have a voice in the formation of
national policy, to attend meetings of the cabinet and National
Security Council, maintain constant communication with the
president.

The two roles — writer and policymaker — were symbiotic: Active participation made accurate articulation likely; personal contact with the president made it far easier to ensure that his public
statements reflected his thoughts and philosophy, the natural cadences of his voice, and his distinctive mannerisms of expression.
(Only later, under Nixon, was the speechwriter — or, rather, a
committee of speechwriters — exiled to the Executive Office

Building, cut off from the deliberations of policymakers, condemned to churn out endless prose for the consideration and zealous editing of staff members higher in rank, until the final product, homogenized, stripped of all fresh phrasing, devoid of distinction, was placed, eunuchlike, on the president's desk. Thus the spoken memo replaced the speech, and eloquence, once nourished by intimate association with action, entered its terminal decline. While individuals of considerable political-literary talent had some of their most dazzling efforts ignored or dismantled.)

As we sluggishly bobbed around the pool, the president began to talk as if he were addressing some larger, imagined audience of the mind.

"There's a Gallup poll coming out; says that seventy-five percent of the American people approve of what you boys are doing. It's really your work, you and the rest of the staff. I'm just a conduit." (As a volcano is merely a conduit for ash and flame.) "I want you to know how much I appreciate it. The transition hasn't been easy. It's like getting used to a new wife; there are a lot of frustrations and difficulties.

"Now, I've got two basic problems — get elected, and pass legislation the country needs. Kennedy had some good programs, but they were stalled in Congress. I had to pull them out of the ditch. That was my first priority. We already have the tax cut, and the civil rights bill is coming — with a little high-priced help from my good friend Dirksen [Republican leader Everett Dirksen of Illinois]. He's not going to have his party blamed for standing in the way, not in an election year. That's one issue I won't compromise. And he knows it. Now that Medicare might take a little longer. Those rich doctors are a little slow, they're afraid some politician — me — is going to pick their pockets. Well, I wouldn't mind. They've got too much money already, but Medicare is just going to make them richer. Once they understand it, they'll be lined up outside the Capitol cheering us on. Hell, if I were a young man today I'd get myself a medical diploma and then find an investment broker to handle the profits. But we've got to give them that. It's more important that old folks get taken care of. It's a national disgrace in a rich country like this that sick people don't get taken care of.

"But it's not enough to just pick up on the Kennedy program and try to do a better job. The fact you get a few bills is not important. Keeping Congress, everybody, fat and happy is not important. We've got to use the Kennedy program as a spring-board to take on the Congress, summon the states to new heights, create a Johnson program, different in tone, fighting and aggressive. Hell, we've barely begun to solve our problems. And we can do it all. We've got the wherewithal. This country was built by pioneers with an ax in one hand and a rifle in the other. There's nothing we can't do, if the masses are behind us. And they will be, if they think we're behind them. Everyone, deep down, wants something a little better for his children, everybody wants to leave a mark, something he can be proud of. And so do I. You too, Bill, and you, Dick. Well now's your chance. I never thought I'd have the power. Now, some men, like Nixon, want power so they can strut around to 'Hail to the Chief'; some, like Connally, want it to make money; I wanted power to use it. And I'm going to use it. And use it right if you boys'll help me."

Then, turning directly to me, the eastern stranger, the intellectual and the Jew: "You would have loved my father. He was a liberal, almost radical, Democrat. He hated the KKK. The day after I was elected to Congress he told me to go up there, support FDR all the way, never shimmy and give 'em hell. My own hero was Sam Houston, and my favorite was Andrew Jackson. He was tough, hard, a man of his word and he loved people. Woodrow Wilson talked a lot about it, but he never did much for the masses. That's why Princeton never appealed to me. Lincoln — he's a kind of storybook president, I try to think about him, but I can never bring him to life in my mind. Why, the thing I'm proudest of in my life is not being majority leader, but helping those kids when I ran the National Youth Administration, and getting public power for Johnson City. Electricity changed those people's lives, made things easier, brought light into the darkness."

Suspended almost motionless in the water, oblivious to the incongruity of my nakedness, I felt Johnson's immense vitality — intense, forceful, direct — focused on my receptive mind. I felt uncomfortable, almost dimensionless, could not feel, sense, my body, the slow sustaining movement of my arms. There was only the powerful flow of Johnson's will, exhorting, explaining, trying to tell me something about himself, seeking not agreement — he knew he had that — but *belief.* And he knew his man. Momentary unease, even the more judicious judgments of my rational self, was gradually displaced by excitement, some prospect of limitless possibilities — for me, for Johnson, for the America that had lifted me from a small Boston apartment to such dizzying heights. I agreed with Johnson that it could be done. I still do. Now I was beginning to believe that, perhaps, probably, almost certainly, this was the time and Johnson the leader who could move us, move an entire country, toward some distant vision — vaguely defined, inchoate, but rooted in an ideal as old as the country. "The citizens of America," wrote George Washington, "are . . . to be considered the actors of a most conspicuous theatre, which seems to be peculiarly designed by Providence for the display of human greatness and felicity."

Although I remained expressionless, somewhere in the depths of that incredible intuition — the genius of an unconscious that lay almost at the surface of awareness — Johnson realized that he had reached me, touched the core of my own ambitions. ("Once you've made your point," Johnson later advised me, "stop talking. If you keep going, you'll just unpersuade them all over again.") Johnson broke from our small triangle, paddled toward the far end of the pool, turned. "Now, boys, you let me finish the Kennedy program. You start to put together a Johnson program, and don't worry about whether it's too radical or if Congress is ready for it. That's my job. And I hope you won't think I'm being arrogant to tell you I'm a little better at that than you. And I'm not worried about the press either." (Not much. Johnson scrutinized the daily papers like a playwright for whom each night of his life was a new opening.) "The only presidents they haven't attacked are the presidents who haven't done a damn thing, like Coolidge. They sure let FDR, Truman, and Jackson have it. Ike was a war hero, all he had to do was smile, and he got away with real murder. They let Kennedy have it too. He became a great hero only after his death; he was not one on his way to Texas."

The swim was over. As we followed Johnson out of the pool, standing there on the cool stone, toweling our water-wrinkled bodies, Johnson mused softly, facing the blank, unresponsive stillness of the deserted water: "They're trying to get me in a war over there: It will destroy me. I turned them down three times last week." Where? I wondered silently. Not Cuba. Laos or Vietnam, perhaps. It was probably one of those. But it didn't matter. We had other, more important work to do. We had a mandate, an assignment, which within two months would enter public life as the Great Society.

* * *

The somewhat grandiloquent phrase — "Great Society" — was not initially contrived as a summarizing caption for the Johnson administration. It first appeared as little more than a fragment of rhetorical stuffing in a speech I had prepared for a relatively trivial occasion. ("In our time we have the opportunity to move not just toward the rich society or the powerful society, but toward the great society.") The phrase caught Johnson's fancy and he used it on two or three other occasions until the press — ever-alert for the simplifying slogan — began to insert it in their efforts to analyze and describe the new administration. By the time of our swimming-pool meeting, capital letters had been substituted — the Great Society — and, inadvertently, the embryonic Johnson program had a name.

Over the next month, obedient to the president's mandate, consulting frequently with Moyers, talking with Johnson, seeking ideas from a widening circle of advisers, I worked toward a more distinct definition of goals and values that would be consistent both with Johnson's own beliefs and his desire to expand the programs of his progressive predecessors into new and more monumental dimensions. Our self-imposed deadline was May 22, when the president was scheduled to address the graduating class at the University of Michigan, the campus where, in 1960, John Kennedy had proposed the Peace Corps.

Finally, discussion ended, the deadline near, I sat in front of my typewriter, the desk strewn with reports, recommendations, memos containing a multitude of proposals, programs, suggested laws, and executive actions. Many of them had merit, and would later be embodied in presidential messages. But my objective — my mandate as I understood it — was not to produce a catalogue of specific projects, but a concept, an assertion of purpose, a vision, if you will, that went beyond the liberal tradition of the New Deal, whose contemporary expressions were proposals for Medicare and Johnson's own War on Poverty.

That liberal tradition was derived from historic American ideals enshrined in such familiar phrases as "equality of opportunity" and "social justice," was reflected in Lincoln's assertion that the object of democratic government was "to elevate the condition of men — to afford all an unfettered start in the race of life." It asserted that all citizens should have a chance to share in American abundance, and accepted a common obligation to provide the necessities of life to the old and those otherwise disabled from rewarding labor.

That purpose was still incomplete; remains incomplete. To go beyond it was not to deny the urgency of its continued pursuit but to acknowledge the truth — the revelation of our modern world — that private income, a decent standard of living, was only a foundation; that private affluence, no matter how widely distributed, could not remedy many of the public conditions that diminished the possibilities of American life.

Yet I knew one could not impose on a living nation some utopian construct, an ideal state framed in philosophic isolation. Nor was that the intention. Johnson's goals, like Roosevelt's, must emanate from distinctively American values, look toward a future that was also an invocation of the past.

That tradition existed, as venerable in its origins as the quest for equality and the freedom from material want. It was the Continental Congress that had substituted the "pursuit of happiness" for "property" in the traditional trio of inalienable rights. To Jefferson, our democracy and its economic prospects "would liberate citizens to pursue the arts and refinement of manners . . . that harmony and reflection without which liberty and even life itself are but dreary things." For Walt Whitman, although acknowledging our genius for "materialistic development, . . . democracy [was] only of use that it may pass on and come to its flower and fruits in the highest form of interaction between men and their beliefs." While, at the height of World War II, Robinson Jeffers, a pessimistic poet-patriot, admonished: "And you, America . . . You were not born to prosperity, you were born to love freedom / The states of the next age will no doubt remember you, and edge their love of freedom with contempt of luxury."

Yet historic values, however noble, traditions, however indigenous, cannot give life to presidential purpose. Political leaders cannot impose new direction on a resistant or indifferent nation. Change, the possibility of change, always comes from beneath: Awareness of deficiency turns into desire, desire into protest, protest into — well, it depends on the strength of resistance, the capacities and inclinations of leadership, the disposition of chance. Johnson's Great Society must be defined in response to the discontents, the movements for change of his time.

And as I labored over Johnson's speech in May of 1964, the country was alive with change: ideas and anger, intellectual protest and physical rebellion. Without this ferment the formulation of the Great Society would not have been possible, not even conceivable. My office was not an armed barrier to rising protest and discontent. Nor was my mind. There was, among the converging demands of the day, much that was unacceptable. But many of the "movements" voiced liberating aspirations that were close to my own; that, more importantly, corresponded to Lyndon Johnson's own impulses, could help to define and fuel the large purpose he wished to pursue.

Although protest and activism were taking many paths, the ramifying impulse to defiance was the eruption of black fury and frustration, molded into a movement that had assaulted the barriers of a century. The civil rights revolution demonstrated not only the power and possibility of organized protest, but the unsuspected fragility of resistance to liberating change.

"Awareness," Camus writes, "no matter how confused it may be, develops from every act of rebellion: the sudden, dazzling, perception that there is something in man with which he can identify himself, even if only for a moment." That "awareness," transmitted swiftly, powerfully, by the new media of mass communication, would lead many white Americans from identification with the black cause toward an identity with other centers of active protest — some transient, some frivolous, some seemingly destined to change the contours of American life.

The year before Johnson had outlined the intentions that were to result in the Great Society, I had read — everybody had read — Betty Friedan's *The Feminine Mystique,* a work that had done much to initiate first the consciousness, then the revolt, of American women against the repressive denial of their human possibilities. By 1964 the women's movement was growing, proliferating; it was already clear that a powerful new force for social change was emerging.

In the same spring that Johnson went to speak at Ann Arbor, Ralph Nader — a law school classmate of mine — moved to Washington, hired by Assistant Secretary of Labor Pat Moynihan to "advise" the government on automobile safety, an assignment that he would later expand into a passionate and well-documented assault — *Unsafe at Any Speed* — against the callous disregard of the entire auto industry for the safety of those who bought its cars. Congress held hearings to consider Nader's charges, giving him a national platform. General Motors, enraged by this presumptuous deviation from the reverential admiration to which it was accustomed, hired detectives to discredit Nader by investigating his private life. Their conduct — managed with the same care they brought to building cars — was quickly exposed. Congress and the press were indignant. Nader became a hero, not so much because of his revelations, but because a single individual, without power or position, had taken on the giant of American industry and won — at least for now. The powerful, it seemed, were not invulnerable to the truth. And moved by Nader's example, dozens of consumer groups were formed to address a wide variety of business derelictions — from inadequate meat inspection to faulty natural gas pipelines to, eventually, the hazards of nuclear power.

These, and other, "movements of the sixties" were different forms of rebellion against oppression or exploitation. I agreed with their objectives. Johnson intended to align himself with the cause of blacks and women and consumers. And I saw them as evidence that the country was ready for leadership committed to social change.

But these movement did not provide a description for the Great Society. Johnson was looking for something different, less confined to particular grievances, a statement of national purpose, almost prophetic in dimension, that would bind citizens in a "great experiment." And which would, not incidentally, give him his place of honor in history. The observation is not intended as irony. What else can a president — having already achieved the highest place — aspire to? Moreover, a president concerned over the verdict of history is far more likely to serve the Republic well than one who measures his success by the comments of an anchorman, the praise of a columnist, or numbers in a poll. Nor were my own ambitions modest. Naturally, writing this or any speech would not make me a world-historical figure. But it was a chance to help make history. At least I felt that way in those heady days of 1964. And even if wrong, the sentiment was understandable, perhaps essential. For so strenuous a reach of energy and imagination is possible only to one who believes in its significance. I could not have written about a Great Society without believing it both worthy and possible.

The sixties had also produced "movements" that were critical not just of specific wrongs, but of the entire direction of modern America. These voices came largely from the margins of society — the New Left or the New Right, literary intellectuals and social thinkers, groups of little power or political weight. Yet I had collected some of these critical expressions in my files and, while trying to frame the speech in my mind, glanced through the folder — not to borrow ideas, but to stimulate my own thinking. For buried among the screaming and invective, the nonsensical and utopian, the outrageous and the impractical, there were opinions and insights that seemed to emanate from a more pervasive discontent; one shared by a great many Americans who knew nothing of these groups, their manifestos, essays, and polemics.

"We are people of this generation" (no controversy there), "bred in at least modest comfort, housed now in universities, looking uncomfortably to the world we inherit," began the Port Huron Manifesto, issued in 1962 by the newly formed Students for a Democratic Society. "Some would have us believe that Americans feel contentment amidst prosperity — but might it not be better be called a glaze above deeply-felt anxieties about their role in the new world? . . . Loneliness, estrangement, isolation describe the vast distance between man and man today." Despite the exaggerated prose, the commentary contained a truth. There was anxiety among middle-class Americans, a sense of estrangement from their neighborhoods and communities, and from the ties that linked them to their fellow citizens.

"The economic boom has continued unabated for at least two thirds of the nation's people," wrote another journal of dissent, "but along with it has come the dawning realization to many that wealth and comfort are not enough to justify life, that the nation is spiritually empty, without any long-term purpose aside from the extension of economic prosperity to all its citizens." I had no intention of calling for a spiritual rebirth; indeed, I believed that the extension of economic prosperity to all our citizens was itself a worthy, even "spiritual" purpose. However, I did agree that wealth and power were not enough, even if the opinion wasn't novel, having been asserted more eloquently by Jefferson two centuries before.

Reading these phrases I knew they were not at all radical. They were vague and incomplete expressions of a much larger, though largely inarticulate discontent; the frustrated expectations of many middle-class Americans, a realization that despite their increased standard of living, many aspects of their daily life had become harder, more constricting. The liberal assumption that rising wealth more widely distributed would liberate Americans for the "pursuit of happiness" had proven not false, but inadequate. Indeed, the very engine of prosperity — growth, development, technology, the golden liberators — were themselves corroding the spiritual and material conditions of American life.

Private income could not prevent the deterioration of urban life or the dissolution of community. It could not restore our contact with the natural beauty that had been stripped from our urban areas. It could not assure us that the intelligence and talents of our children would be skillfully cultivated. It could not prevent the erosion of sustaining human values — fellowship and shared compassion. Nor could it return from increasingly concentrated centers of authority that power over the conditions of our existence which is essential to freedom — which *is* freedom.

Naturally, government cannot bestow happiness or eliminate anxiety. But I believed that government, acting as the agent of a collective will, could change the circumstances of our daily life — our cities and environment, the quality of education, the restoration of "power to the people."

As I worked to phrase some of these ideas, I realized this was not simply a choice among directions. It was, in 1964, the only possible direction for liberating, progressive change. Johnson, and I, and the rest of Washington, were not just officers of government. We were citizens of the age. The currents of contemporary distress, the afflictions of our time were contained in our own consciousness, an internal guide to the necessary direction of progress. One could, of course, simply refuse to act. But that refusal — as the dismal experience of a quarter century has now proved — does not arrest the forces of decline and deterioration. They compose the machine of the world — a machine that men can chose to run but, if left untouched, is admirably constructed to run without us.

"A political speech," Teddy Roosevelt once said, "is a poster, not an etching." Thus I worked to compress a description of the Great Society into general and, I hoped, moderately memorable phrases. An almost metaphoric statement of principle was followed by brief indications of some specific objects of concern. I chose, as illustration, the enhancement of urban life, the restoration of natural beauty, and the improvement of education — because they were problems about which the president had expressed concern, and because they would satisfy the president's passing passion for alliteration (city, countryside, and classroom).

Finishing the speech the night before it was to be delivered, I brought it to Moyers. He was enthusiastic. The next morning, accompanied by Moyers, I brought the speech to Johnson. Sitting behind his Oval Office desk, he read it slowly, making occasional penciled changes. Having finished, without saying a word, he picked it up and began to read it again, even more slowly. I looked nervously at Moyers. "It's very different from Kennedy, Mr. President," I said hopefully. He did not look up. I waited as several minutes passed. "It's a whole new direction for the Democratic party," I said. "But it's not radical," Bill Moyers swiftly interjected. "I think it's going to surprise a lot of people, and please most of them." There was no response, not even an acknowledgment that our voices had been heard. Finally, after pausing on the last page to change a word, Johnson put down the draft and looked up, questioningly, as if surprised to find us standing there. "It ought to do just fine, boys. Just what I told you." Then, turning his head: "Jack!" Valenti approached the desk. "What time's that damn plane leave? And why are we always running out of Fresca?"

Later that day I stood on the South Lawn of the White House and watched the president climb the steps to the helicopter which would take him to Andrews Air Force Base for the flight to Michigan. I had decided not to go. He was scheduled to arrive, speak, and return immediately. The Signal Corps would return with a videotape of the occasion. I could watch it tomorrow. I needed sleep.

On May 22, 1964, standing before the graduating class at the peaceful Ann Arbor campus, speaking for thirty minutes, interrupted constantly by applause, the president left the almost completed Kennedy legacy behind and struck out on his own.

"The Great Society . . . demands an end to poverty and racial injustice. . . . But that is just the beginning. The Great Society is a place where every child can find knowledge to enrich his mind and enlarge his talent . . . where leisure is a welcome chance to build and reflect, not a feared cause of boredom and restlessness . . . where the city of man serves not only the needs of the body and the demands of commerce but the desire for beauty and the hunger for community.

"It is a place where man can renew contact with nature . . . which honors creation for its own sake and for what it adds to the understanding of the race . . . where men are more concerned with the quality of their goals than the quantity of their goods."

Johnson then began to sketch out the application of these principles to some specific afflictions of American life.

Quoting Aristotle — "Men come together in cities in order to live, but they remain together to live the good life" — Johnson said that in our rapidly expanding urban areas "it is harder and harder to live the good life." The central cities are in "decay," the suburbs being "despoiled." "There is not enough housing . . . or transportation. . . . Open land is vanishing and old landmarks are violated.

"Worst of all, expansion is eroding the precious . . . value of community with neighbors and communion with nature. The loss of these values breed loneliness and boredom and indifference. Our society will never be great until our cities are great . . . where future generations can come together, not only to live, but to live the good life."

Outside the cities, Johnson proclaimed, "America the beautiful . . . is in danger. . . . The water we drink, the food we eat, the very air we breathe, are threatened with pollution. Our parks are overcrowded, our seashores overburdened.

"[W]e must act now . . . for once the battle is lost, once our natural splendor is destroyed, it can never be recaptured. And once man can no longer walk with beauty or wonder at nature his spirit will wither. . . ."

In the schools of America, "our society will never be great until every young mind is set free to scan the farthest reaches of thought and imagination."

Eight million adult Americans, Johnson told the Michigan students, had not finished five years of school, more than a quarter of the entire population had not completed high school, and more than one hundred thousand high school graduates, "of proven ability," failed to enter college for lack of money. There was an urgent need for more classrooms and decently paid teachers. "Poverty must not be a bar to learning, and learning must offer an escape from poverty.

"But more classrooms and more teachers are not enough. We must seek an educational system which grows in excellence as it grows in size. This means better training for our teachers . . . preparing youth to enjoy their hours of leisure as well as their hours of labor . . . exploring new techniques of teaching, to find new ways to stimulate the love of learning and the capacity for creation.

"I do not pretend," Johnson said, "that we have the answer" to the difficulties of moving the country toward a Great Society. "But I do promise . . . to assemble the best thought" for "a series of White House conferences and meetings on the cities, natural

beauty, the quality of education, and on other emerging challenges"; and from these "begin to set our course toward the Great
Society.

"The solution," he cautioned his audience, "does not rest on a
massive program in Washington, nor . . . on the strained resources of local authority. They require us to create new concepts
of cooperation, a creative federalism, between the national capital
and the leaders of local community.

"Your generation," Johnson told the now-cheering students, has
"the chance never before afforded to any people in any age . . .
to help build a society where the demands of morality, and the
needs of the spirit can be realized in the life of the nation."

Then, addressing his audience directly, Johnson shouted a litany of questions from behind the massive podium, across the
crowded spring-green graduation grounds, each question being
answered with mounting applause, mingled shouts of affirmation,
as if the mammoth Texan had, for the moment, transformed the
worldly northern university into a Baptist meeting.

"Will you join in the battle to give every citizen the full equality
which God enjoins and the law requires . . . ?"

(Yes, we will.)

"Will you join in the battle to build the Great Society, to prove
that our material progress is only the foundation on which we will
build a richer life of mind and spirit?"

(Yes, yes, and yes, and yes again.)

Then, with the cheers, at first muted as if the audience were
surprised at their own response, than mounting toward unrestrained, accepting delight, Johnson concluded: "There are those
timid souls who say . . . we are condemned to a soulless wealth.
I do not agree. We have the power to shape civilization. . . . But
we need your will, your labor, your hearts. . . . So let us from
this moment begin our work, so that in the future men will look
back and say: It was then, after a long and weary way, that man
turned the exploits of his genius to the full enrichment of his
life."

Watching the film in the White House basement, almost involuntarily I added my applause to the tumultuous acclaim coming
from the sound track. I was not applauding myself. Certainly I
felt personal pride, satisfaction in my work. But it was also as if I
were hearing the words for the first time, experiencing the exhil-

arating revelation of suddenly widening horizons. It was not self-deception. The carefully crafted, familiar draft had been transmuted by the voice of the president, his display of passionate determination — the word made manifest. What had left my hands as an idea had become a reality. So I clapped for the president, and for our country.

The speech was a triumph. Johnson had struck a resonance, touching, perhaps, some fragment of those "mystic chords of memory" invoked far more eloquently by Lincoln a century before.

Not original, derived from the manifest currents of contemporary discontent, themselves traceable from significant strands of the American dream, the Great Society was also Johnson — the legacy of a mother, herself imaginatively linked to the genteel tradition of the Old South, who struggled to persuade her son of the superior worth of ideas, refinement, moral values over the raucous grubbing for money or political office that suffused the atmosphere of Blanco County and the Johnson household.

This element in Johnson was submerged by the gargantuan manipulator, the tireless practitioner of political skills, for whom leisure truly was a "feared cause of boredom and restlessness." Yet it was there, even though he himself would often deny it. And he was aided in his concealment by the inability of academicians and opinion-makers to reconcile his native crudity with his stated aspirations. "I always knew," Johnson later told me, "that the greatest bigots in the world lived in the East not the South. I knew they wouldn't tolerate a Texas Johnson any more than a Tennessee Johnson. Economic bigots, social bigots, society bigots. Whatever I did, they were bound to think it was some kind of a trick. How could some politician from Johnson City do what was right for the country?"

Yet, even if Johnson was right to suspect the condescending disdain of the "eastern establishment," there was, in the first years of his presidency, an almost universal suspension of disbelief, as the country witnessed, first with relief, then with gathering acclaim, the unexpected emergence of a new leader who seemed both formidable and benign. "When Kennedy was killed," Averell Harriman told me in mid-1964, "I was discouraged. I felt that Johnson was not up to the job, that he and I were not in agreement on the issues. But he surprised me. The man has great instincts, and he knows how to make government work. I think he might make a great president." To which his wife added, "We felt the same way about Truman, remember, Averell, and look how he turned out."

A few days after returning from Ann Arbor, Johnson summoned me to his office. As I entered, he was sitting in a small anteroom adjoining the Oval Office, where the president could seclude himself for relaxation, private conversation, a drink with friends.

"Come on in, Dick," he beamed, "sit down. Try some of this scotch." I accepted all three invitations. "Henry Luce called me this morning. Old man Henry himself. He said he'd support me on the basis of the Great Society speech alone. You helped get me *Time*'s support, and I want you to know I appreciate everything you've done since you came here."

I relaxed against the back of my armchair, crossed my legs with a casualness intended to mask my self-satisfied pleasure, casually sipped the unwatered whiskey — "just one of the boys" — when Moyers and Valenti joined us. "Let me tell you, boys," the president continued to his enlarged audience, "the Washington press are worse than a wolfpack when it comes to attacking officials, but they are like a bunch of sheep in their own profession, and they will always follow the bellwether sheep, the leaders of their profession. The only two newspapermen practically all of them admire are Lippmann and Reston. As long as these two are for LBJ, he will, on the whole, get a good press from the rest of them. You certainly have Lippmann and Reston in your pocket now. I hope you don't lose them." (Translation: I've got them in my pocket, and I don't want to lose them.)

"Now just listen to this," he continued, and, reaching for a file beside his chair, like the proudest of authors, Johnson began to read us his reviews.

"Here's what Reston says about us: 'In his first six months LBJ has produced a period of reconciliation, raising three hopes. That he may be able to ease the tension between the North and South, between the legislative and executive branches, between the White House and the business community. His relations with the diplomatic community and the intellectual community at home are still insecure.' Hell," Johnson interrupted himself, "those last two don't matter a damn, not a bushel of votes between them. Now listen to this: 'The general feeling is that the President has done better in his first six months than either his enemies or even his friends expected on that tragic day. The basic question is: What is the end and purpose of all this political skill? This is the question LBJ answered at the University of Michigan.'

"That's good, but Arthur Krock is even better, and don't forget he was one of the Kennedys' closest friends. Hell, he used to write Jack Kennedy's college papers. 'The product of LBJ's first six months has been extraordinary in volume, in the scope of his aspirations, the expenditure of energy and tangible accomplishment. . . . There is a nationwide belief in the sincerity of Johnson's expressed wish to be the best President in history for the people as a whole!'

"He's right about that," Johnson interjected, "I not only mean it, but we're going to do it. They're already bragging on us getting a few little bills through. Wait till they see what's coming.

"They're even beginning to think I might know something about foreign policy," he said, picking up still another clipping: " 'The President hit it off beautifully with Chancellor Ludwig Erhard of West Germany,' " Johnson read, commenting, "That Erhard was all over me. He was ready to go in the barn and milk my cows, if he could find the teats. There's only one way to deal with the Germans. You keep patting them on the head and then every once in a while you kick them in the balls.

"Here's a *U.S. News,*" Johnson announced, reaching for a magazine lying on the floor at the foot his chair, already opened to the appropriate page: " 'In barely six months as President, Lyndon B. Johnson has stamped the LBJ brand all over American affairs. The new President dominates politics. He has command of the front pages of newspapers much of the time. Nobody matches him on the airwaves.'

"You see," Johnson explained, "I always said that charisma stuff was a bunch of bullshit," then continued to read, " 'Congress has moved. . . . Voices are heard comparing the President to Andy Jackson or to Teddy Roosevelt . . . !'

"They're two of my personal heroes," Johnson commented, "and they're right about the polls." He reached into his inside pocket and extracted several sheets of paper. "We've got our own polls. They're even better than I thought. If the Republicans nominate Goldwater, and it looks like the damn fools are going to do it, we'll sweep every part of the country, even New York." (They did, and he did.)

"This one surprised even me," Johnson said, abruptly returning to his collection of clippings, "the *Wall Street Journal*, greediest bastards in the world." Then reading: " 'Many industry leaders are pleased beyond their initial expectations at the President's attitude toward business and his conduct of the Presidency.'

"One thing you've got to understand about businessmen. Like the rest of us, they want to have some pride in what they do, to be proud of the country . . . as long as it doesn't cost them any money. Every time a poor person gets off welfare, starts to make a decent living, there's someone else to buy what they make. It's in everybody's interest. They can understand that, if you explain it to them properly."

Johnson returned his newspaper cuttings to the floor beside his chair, leaned forward, his eyes fixed on us with the now-familiar intensity that always accompanied his exhortations of persuasion. "I'm a dreamer," he announced, "always have been. My mother taught me that unless you had a dream, your life wouldn't amount to a hill of beans. She could have been a great novelist. You boys are dreamers too. Every American has a little bit of dream in him. But it's not like those Harvards think. It's not enough to sit around and dream, and criticize things you don't like. You've got to do something about it, in the real world. That's why we're here.

"We got a pretty good start. But now we've got a new Johnson program, the beginning of one, the skeleton. Now it's time to put some flesh on those bones. I'm counting on you. I can't do it alone. Let's get to work, bring in all those experts and put it all together. And don't worry about the politics. I'll get it done."

Then rising from his chair, signaling that our visit was at an end: "We've got a great opportunity here. Let's not waste it."

We didn't need a pep talk. We were more than ready, already aware and excited by our awareness that we — destiny's accidental children — might be able to redirect the course of American life. Nor did Johnson himself really think we needed to be persuaded. It was more like a rehearsal, a preliminary tuning of the energy and will that he intended to exert on a myriad of audiences — powerful individuals, interest groups, an entire country.

"We are," pontificated the *Washington Post*, "entering a new era of good feeling, and Lyndon Johnson is the gargantuan figure making it all possible."

In that spring and summer of 1964 the possibilities were dazzling, as we struggled — office lights burning far into the night —

to translate the Great Society into practical, tangible programs, give reality to the vision, confident that Johnson, within the necessary limits of political compromise and accommodation, would persuade the Congress and the country to his will.

In little more than a year, until the drumbeat of progressive reform was stilled by the trumpets of war, a cascade of programs and proposals, presidential messages and executive orders, unmatched in volume and sweep since the early days of the New Deal, was loosed upon a receptive Congress, moved to action not just by the manipulative skills of the president, but by the awakening enthusiasms of the larger constituencies on which their power and ambitions depended.

Over that period Johnson shattered the paralysis of decades. It seemed that whenever we began the labor of designing new messages and laws, we were interrupted by a summons to a signing ceremony for those previously submitted.

The results of that effort are contained in the voluminous *Public Papers of the President,* published by the Government Printing Office, freely accessible to the curious. They read today like some antique artifact of ambition, the remnants of an almost-forgotten past, consigned by the changes of history to an undeserved oblivion. But not completely. Some of Johnson's work — Medicare, federal aid to education — became an enduring part of the American landscape. Other achievements — the Voting Rights Act — permanently altered the political process. Still others, even now, in 1988, are being rediscovered by politicians in their anxious quest for "new ideas" whose appeal might draw the support of voters to their ambitions.

Designing the Great Society was a multilayered process. The task forces that Johnson promised were assembled, bringing together not merely experts and specialists, but the philosophical explorers of American public life (Robert Wood of MIT, who was later to become secretary of HUD, along with Jane Jacobs, author of *The Life and Death of the American City*). From their discussions (attended by members of the White House staff) we attempted to extract a coherent program of public policy, then to make necessary compromises to accommodate the demands of "interest" groups that had the power to obstruct, perhaps defeat, our proposals. The title of our new Department of the Cities, for example, had to be changed to the more prosaic "Housing and Urban Devel-

opment," because of the adamant insistence of the entrepreneurs
and unions of the housing industry that they be given explicit
recognition. Similarly, by providing aid to parochial school students, we were able to blunt the opposition of the Catholic Church,
which had helped to defeat all previous attempts to enact federal
aid to education.

If some of these compromises threatened to disrupt our long-
term design — well, the important thing was to get the laws on
the books, get things moving. The work of purification could come
later. That's how the democratic process works, when it works
. . . if it works. However, far more significant than the concessions to which we were compelled, was the astonishing reach of
ambition and action permitted by the great, if temporary, Johnsonian consensus built upon the twin pillars of relative peace and
increasing national prosperity.

In proclaiming his War on Poverty, Johnson said it was "not a
struggle simply to support people, to make them dependent on
the generosity of others. It is a struggle to give people a chance.
It is an effort to allow them to develop and use their capacities
. . . so that they can share, as others share, in the promise of this
nation."

Although the War on Poverty was, in part, a renewal of traditional remedies for inequality of opportunity, it contained elements that were distinctively Johnsonian, which would be among
the guiding principles of the Great Society. It recognized that a
"cure" for poverty did not consist so much in a redistribution of
wealth but a redistribution of power — to individuals and communities alike. An array of new programs, and innovative educational institutions, would allow the young to acquire the skills that,
if matched to ambition, would allow them to become productive
members of society. Knowledge was power — the strength to force
open the door to American life. And this transfer of power was
not limited to individuals. A Community Action program asked
the citizens of every community to prepare their own local plans
for an attack on poverty "based on the fact that local citizens best
understood their own problems," and promised federal financing
to implement these plans. Moreover, the assault on the causes of
poverty would be supervised by a brand-new government agency,
the Office of Economic Opportunity, on the very sound principle,
a legacy from Roosevelt, that a new bureaucracy has more energy,
more willingness to innovate, than an old one. (Indeed, there is

no doubt that we would have a more efficient and productive government if every government department were required to self-destruct after a couple of decades — a rather modest proposal compared to Jefferson's belief that the preservation of a vigorous democracy required a total political revolution every generation or two.)

In calling for a "war . . . not only to relieve the symptom of poverty, but to cure it, and, above all, to eliminate it," Johnson reiterated a theme congenial to his character, typical of his approach to leadership, and essential to the "consensus," which, alone, could move the nation to action. Although the elimination of poverty was a moral imperative, the right thing to do, it was not merely an act of altruistic compassion. It was an "investment in the most valuable of our resources — the skills and strength of our people . . . which would return its cost manyfold to our entire economy. . . . Our history has proved that each time we broaden the base of abundance, giving more people the chance to produce and consume, we create new industry, higher production, increased earnings and better income for all."

The assertion was more than political sagacity. It was also true. And our current economic stagnation, our lost preeminence in global trade, owes much to the abysmal and self-destructive failure to incorporate the multiplying impoverished into the productive structures of American life. In the War on Poverty, Johnson claimed, we would all be winners. So, too, in defeat we have all become losers, except, of course, for those at the very top of the ladder of affluence from Orange County, California, to Beacon Hill in Boston.

On July 2, 1964, Johnson appeared on national television to sign the Civil Rights Act of 1964, proposed by John Kennedy the year before, and enacted after Johnson had, for the first time, broken the southern filibuster led by his closest political friend, Richard Russell. Then the culminating achievement of the civil rights revolution, the act was to prove only a prelude to equally significant assaults on racial injustice, which were to be the most substantial achievements of the Johnson administration.

Within the next year, the president signed the Economic Opportunities Act, establishing the War on Poverty, and put his signature on the Food Stamp Act. He went to his boyhood classroom in Texas to sign the law, which, for the first time, provided federal funds to elementary and secondary schools, and did so on a scale even larger than the proposal Congress had soundly defeated in 1961. He journeyed to Independence, Missouri, so that Harry Truman could sit beside him as he signed Medicare, a tribute to the former president who had tried, and failed, to establish some form of national health insurance. Less than two weeks later, Johnson approved the congressional enactment of much of his program for the cities, including the new cabinet department. And sometime amid this dazzling display, Johnson established a National Endowment, which, for the first time in American history, would give federal funds to help support humane and artistic activities, those gentler arts that were, naturally, also part of a Great Society.

In early 1965, I sat with Bill Moyers and complained, "We're running out of laws. He's passing everything, and there'll be nothing left, unless we get some new ideas."

"Don't worry, Dick," Moyers wisely enjoined, "we've still got plenty of problems. And where there's a problem, there's going to be an answer." He was right, of course. But not completely. Problems don't automatically create answers, sometimes they only bring more problems, and some problems have no solution — no public, political solution. But that cast of mind, call it what you will — romantic illusion, fighting spirit, Panglossian optimism — is the carrier of the energy and will necessary to any progress, to even a modest, partial resolution of public distress.

But the design, the practical possibilities and soon-shattered hopes, of the Great Society can be more easily glimpsed not in the laws that were passed, but in the expansive presidential messages that undertook to challenge some of the biggest and most resistant obstacles to the fulfillment of American freedom. They were — with some fragmentary exceptions — to go dead in the water almost as soon as they were launched. But the problems they describe have not gone away, have, indeed, been made more serious, far more formidable by a quarter century of indifference, neglect, and deliberate self-seeking aggravation.

A small sampling from some of these messages may help illustrate not the full scope of Johnson's program, but the truth that resolution of even the largest, seemingly intractable problems can be approached through realistic diagnosis and tangible action.

In a "Special Message on Conservation and Restoration of Natural Beauty," Johnson observed:

"The storm of modern change is threatening to blight and diminish in a few decades what has been cherished and protected for generations. . . . A growing population is swallowing up areas of natural beauty. . . . Modern technology also has a darker side. Its uncontrolled waste products are menacing the world we live in, our enjoyment and our health. The air we breathe, our water, our soil and wildlife, are being blighted by the poisons and chemicals which are the by-product of technology and industry. The society which receives the benefits of technology must . . . take responsibility for control.

"Our conservation must be not just the classic conservation of protection and development . . . its concern is not with nature alone, but with the total relation between man and the world around him. Its object is not just man's welfare but the dignity of man's spirit. This means that beauty must be part of our daily life. It means not just easy physical access, but equal social access for rich and poor, Negro and white, city dweller and farmer.

"Beauty is not an easy thing to measure. It does not show up in the gross national product, in a weekly pay check, or in profit and loss statements. But these things are not ends in themselves. They are a road to satisfaction and pleasure and the good life. Beauty . . . is one of the most important components of our true national income, not to be left out simply because statisticians cannot calculate its worth.

"We have been careless, and often neglectful," Johnson told Congress. "But now that the danger is clear and the hour is late this people can place themselves in the path of a tide of blight which is often irreversible and always destructive."

Today, after a quarter century, the hour is still later, perhaps beyond recall. The multitude of programs and shared effort then proposed to arrest the "tide of blight," intended as first steps toward that goal, became casualties of the changing national mood — defeated, diluted, ignored, transgressed. The result: Look around you, breathe deeply, take a drink of chemical-saturated water, go for a swim in the urban rivers, which were to be made playgrounds for the many. The state of beauty, now called the environment, has, as Johnson predicted, steadily deteriorated; much of the damage is, in fact, irreversible; and new dangers to our well-being, of an immensity inconceivable a few decades ago, are now upon us.

In a later "Message on the Cities," Johnson told the Congress that "within the borders of our urban centers can be found the most impressive examples of man's skill . . . as well as the worst examples of degradation and cruelty and misery to be found in modern America. . . . Our task is to put the highest concerns of our people at the center of urban growth and activity. It is to create and preserve the sense of community with others which gives us significance and security, a sense of belonging and of sharing in the common life. . . . The modern city can be the most ruthless enemy of the good life, or it can be its servant.

"There are a few whose affluence enables them to move through the city guarded and masked from the realities of the life around them . . . for the rest of us the quality and nature of our lives are inexorably fixed by the nature of the community in which we live. Slums and ugliness, crime and congestion, growth and decay inevitably touch the life of all. . . .

"The American city should be a collection of communities where every member has a right to belong . . . where every man feels safe on his streets and in the house of his friends . . . where each individual's dignity and self-respect are strengthened by the respect and affection of his neighbors . . . where each of us can find the satisfaction and warmth which come only from being a member of the community of man. This is what man sought at the dawn of civilization.

"We are," the president confessed, "only groping toward solution. . . . This message, and the programs it proposes, does not fully meet the problems of the city. We need more thought . . . and knowledge as we painfully struggle to identify the ills, the dangers and the cures. . . . We need to reshape at every level of government, our approach to problems which are often different than we thought and larger then we had imagined.

"The federal government will only be able to do a small part of what is required. The vast bulk of resources and energy . . . will have to come from state and local governments, private interests and individual citizens. But the federal government does have a responsibility [to] be sure that its efforts serve as a catalyst and a lever to help and guide state and local governments toward meeting their problems."

Despite the modesty of disclaimer, the message was more than exhortation. It proposed an astonishing array of new programs and institutions to help improve the quality of urban life. Old housing agencies were to be swallowed up in a new cabinet-level department. Their programs — many of which had persisted de-

spite almost unanimous recognition of failure — were to be reduced or eliminated as soon as "new and more flexible instruments have shown they can do a better job." (Yet many of them —
although inadequate, even destructive — would persist; a tribute
to the intransigence of an entrenched bureaucracy buttressed by
its own constituency in Congress and in the housing industry.)
The federal government would take responsibility for training urban planners and help finance the development of long-term programs through a new Institute of Urban Development — a West
Point for creative construction. There were proposals touching upon
almost every aspect of city life — zoning codes, the acquisition of
open spaces for city parks, the construction of neighborhood centers for health, education, and recreation. But Johnson had no
intention of simply opening the doors of the federal treasury. The
cities would, for the most part, be required to earn federal assistance by providing funds of their own, and, most important, by
devising long-range development programs, not only for the central city, but for entire metropolitan areas. Had "Metropolitan
Area Planning" been pursued, it might well have averted, at least
diminished, the devastating consequences of divisions that have
created a country within a country, the incarceration of the poor
and the black within an iron ring of affluence, which has led not
only to the doom of school integration but to a physical separation
that has condemned many to lives of corrupting despair, outcasts
in the land of opportunity.

It has now become fashionable for politicians to exalt the benign virtue of community, to bewail its loss. Community, of course,
is an abstraction — like justice or freedom, faith or morality. It
cannot be imposed by the powerful, resting as it does on our willingness to enact the more spacious and generous qualities of individual nature. But the possibilities of community can be destroyed, aborted by an environment that discourages, even prohibits,
a mutuality of interest, a shared responsibility; which leaves —
appears to leave — the more fortunate untouched by those struggling for breath in an inner "sea of troubles."

But the rhetoric, which today seems so hollow, not because it is
untrue, but because it is unaccompanied by action, shadow without substance, seemed then — as the decade of the sixties neared
its midpoint — a description of possibility, a manifesto of intent.
And, however foolish or arrogant the speeches and messages of
the sixties sound, they are authentic, like faded daguerrotypes, a

reminder to our more cynical age of that time when public service, the turbulent energies of a whole nation, seemed bursting with possibilities — conquer poverty, walk on the moon, build a Great Society.

16 / Lyndon's Landslide

IN THE MIDDLE of all this we won a presidential election.

In retrospect it was an astonishing performance. This "accidental" president, who could never have reached the presidency from the outside, without any natural constituency beyond his home state of Texas, by the spring of 1964, from within the Oval Office, had blended the powers of his position with the immensely persuasive force of his personality to achieve complete command over the party that had rejected him only three years before. And, before the year was over, he so dominated American public life and had won the approval of the nation on so large and varied a scale, that the election was over even before the votes were counted. The sardonic nickname "Landslide Johnson," bestowed when, in 1948, he had won a Senate seat by ninety-six disputed votes, became a description of reality as he attained the most crushing majority over a Republican opponent since Roosevelt buried Alf Landon in 1936.

From the moment of his succession to the presidency, Johnson knew the only threat to his nomination came from that same liberal wing of the Democratic party which had mounted an unsuccessful rebellion against his nomination as vice-president. And so almost from his first day he acted — not to assault his potential opposition, but, more characteristically, to reassure and seduce them. The humiliations of his years as vice-president were put aside, seemingly forgotten (but not really, never truly forgiven), and those he supposed to be the authors of his degradations, whose contempt — real or imagined — had so poisoned his days that his physical health was endangered, were embraced as treasured companions. "I understand how you feel," he told many a Kennedy aide, placing his huge arm over the shoulder, drawing him closer to tones of whispered intimacy, "I feel the same way. I loved Jack Kennedy. I need you now. I need you more than he ever did. You have to help me."

He summoned Adlai Stevenson (unforgettably and unfairly characterized by Johnson with the remark "He squats when he pees") from New York where he was enjoying an honorable exile as ambassador to the United Nations: "Listen, Adlai, I know these folks in Washington haven't been paying much attention to you. . . . I want you to be right at my side whenever I have to make an important decision, and I don't care what those fellows over at the State Department think." A relieved and delighted Stevenson returned to New York to inform his acolytes and former supporters that the country was in very good hands indeed.

Reaching out to established party constituencies, Johnson counseled Roy Wilkins, head of the NAACP, on how black pressure could be most effectively exerted on the Congress to pass the civil rights bill, and, as a bonus, encouraged Wilkins to suggest a black candidate for a vacant federal judgeship, whom Johnson then promptly nominated. The warring titans of organized labor — George Meany and Walter Reuther — were, separately, assured by Johnson that he intended to see the antiunion legislation of the past reversed — "Hell, I was a laborer myself" (having worked on the railroads as a teenager) — and that if they ever needed anything from the president, no appointment was necessary: "You just come on over, my door is always open." (Presumably, precautions would be taken to make sure they didn't meet inadvertently in the corridor to the Oval Office.)

More important than the careful cultivation of powerful individuals and interest groups were Johnson's actions to reassure the country that the stunning, dislocating events in Dallas would not be allowed to divert the ship of state from the enlightened course charted by its now dead captain. He embraced the Kennedy program ("Let us continue") without qualification or exception, promised to extend and strengthen it, and, in fact, began to deliver on his pledges. Legislation began to move, the War on Poverty was launched, presidential concern extended to new constituencies. The women's movement, for example, was still in its infancy when, in early 1964, Johnson announced the appointment of dozens of women to significant government posts, declaring that discrimination against women was "the equivalent of closing male eyes to female facts," that the society needed the "skill and intelligence and capacity for leadership" which women possessed, "that their neglect was society's loss but equally, the women whose gifts are suppressed . . . are losers too."

Within months of his ascension Johnson had convincingly established his devotion to the "Kennedy legacy," demonstrated his commitment to extend the progressive intentions of his predecessor, and displayed the skills and energies necessary to fulfill his pledges. All opposition, all talk of opposition, to Johnson's nomination died away. The only remaining political issue was the selection of a vice-presidential candidate.

Almost from the beginning, Robert Kennedy — refusing to let passion distort his political acuity — accepted the inevitability of Johnson's nomination, and the virtual certainty of his election. Yet, in mid-December, less than a month after his brother's death, amid confused grief, he refused — could not make himself acknowledge — how swiftly, completely the Kennedy years had passed, telling me, "We're very important to Johnson now. After November third . . . we won't matter a damn. But between now and then he needs us. I haven't talked to Johnson yet. I'm not mentally equipped for it, or physically. The vice-presidency may be the key job. But not just because someone wants to be vice-president, not just to hold the office. When the time comes we'll tell him who we want for vice-president."

What Robert Kennedy did not realize, could not then have foreseen, was that "when the time came" there would be no "we" — no band of Kennedy loyalists with the power to "tell" the president what to do; that Johnson's domination of the party would be so complete, his popularity in the country so widespread, that he wouldn't "need" anybody. However, in the early months of 1964, while he was consolidating his hold over the varied factions of the Democratic party, Johnson had no wish to arouse unnecessary antagonisms by arbitrarily excluding the former president's brother from consideration. It would inevitably seem a vindictive act, and the president was far too skillful a politician to indulge his personal enmity at the cost of possible damage to his still-uncertain, not yet established, domination of party and public. He would wait, labor to assemble his forces, and then act. Until then, why of course Bobby must be considered, and also — he let it be known — Sargent Shriver, the Kennedy brother-in-law whom he had selected to head the War on Poverty — thus succeeding, as he intended, in creating a schism between Bobby and Sarge.

It was, of course, all nonsense. Barring the most dire of unforeseen necessities, Johnson had no intention of putting Bobby Kennedy, or any Kennedy, or any relative of any Kennedy on the ticket. ("Just remember, Bill," he told Moyers, who was futilely pleading the Shriver cause, "blood is thicker than water," ignoring the fact that Shriver was not a blood relative at all, merely an in-law, but that was close enough — far too close — for Johnson.) Moreover, it was obvious that the personal hostility between Johnson and Kennedy would have made any working relationship impossible. Nor do presidential candidates choose running mates who have followings and constituencies of their own, who might, therefore, be capable of independent action, even become rivals. Still, the unusual circumstances of Johnson's accession, the short time that remained until election, might, it seemed, suspend the natural laws of selection — an understandable illusion to which Bobby Kennedy clung.

If I shared in this illusion, it vanished once I went to work in the White House and came to understand the depth of Johnson's hostility toward Bobby Kennedy, the intensity of his desire to establish himself not as heir to Kennedy, but as master and architect of a new Johnson administration.

In my diary notes of March 1, 1964, I wrote: "Up to now, I had thought Robert Kennedy would be the running mate, especially if he carries out his implied intention to pressure LBJ, and threaten to challenge his legitimacy as a successor to JFK. I had thought this might be decisive." (A foolish and naïve belief.) "But LBJ probably hates Bobby so much that he won't take him under any circumstances." (A sensible and sagacious belief.) "Moreover, Bobby will, in the last analysis, not be able to make good on his implied threat without hurting himself irrevocably." (It would have been political suicide.) "Sarge seems more and more likely to me — as a Catholic, as one who carries much of the JFK image, and as someone LBJ likes and trusts." (Wrong again.) "Of course Johnson would rather have Hubert, a successful senator, whom he understands and respects because he is successful in the same arena in which LBJ had his own triumphs."

A few days after this was written Bobby invited me to join him and a few friends for dinner at the Jockey Club. "Bob told me,"

I noted, "that I ought to go away, make money, and then come back. You can afford to stay when you are young, but after that you need to be independent." (Words I have since filed under "Best Advice I Never Took.") "I asked him whether he could take a relaxed life. He said, yes he could, that he would like to relax, read, take a couple of courses; that he could do this and not be restless. 'Well, if that's what you want,' I said (not believing it for a minute), 'you'll probably have the chance. I don't think it's at all likely that LBJ will give you the nomination. A politician can usually persuade himself to believe what he wants to believe, and LBJ will want very strongly to believe that he doesn't need you.' " (In the end no self-deception would be necessary. Johnson wouldn't need him.)

By spring, it had become apparent to Robert Kennedy that he was unlikely to receive the vice-presidential nomination. He still wanted the job, had not completely conceded hope, but could sense his prospects slipping away as Johnson's tightening hold on the party eroded his potential leverage. Sentiment is not power, and although he would be the personal favorite of many in the Democratic party, their affection, even admiration, could not be expressed in opposition to presidential wishes. "No friends, only allies," as John Kennedy said. Surely Bobby understood that; he was a politician too. "You know," he told me musingly as Washington slipped toward summer, "I might just take a year off, take the kids, go live in Europe. I've got to get out of Washington."

"It would be the best thing to do," I replied. "Washington is a company town, and it's no fun when someone else owns the company."

"I could run for governor of Massachusetts in 1966," he reflected, "but I've had a study done, and that job doesn't have any real power. It's all divided up with the legislature and the governor's council. The other alternative is to go to New York and run for senator. There's no residency requirement, but it has all the messiness of the arrogant outsider coming to take over. Don't you think I'm arrogant, Dick?"

"Probably," I answered, "but so am I. When do you plan to leave?"

"By the summer. I can't take much more of this."

For months, however, Johnson deliberately, and for sound political reasons, refused to close the vice-presidential door to anyone, including Bobby. He had all the cards, and was under no obligation to show his hand until it was called by events. The uncertainty of others only augmented his strength, a principle of rule which predated the Medici.

Then, on July 15, 1964, the Republican party nominated Barry Goldwater for president, effectively destroying any case for a Kennedy candidacy. Every liberal, every member of a minority, every union man would be for Johnson against this newly anointed apostle of the right. The only contest — if there was any — would be for the votes of moderate conservatives, to whom Bobby's presence on the ticket would be a deterrent. Of course, Johnson would not have picked Robert Kennedy even if the Republicans had nominated a ticket of Communist party chief Earl Browder and Martin Luther King. But now the inevitable exclusion would not appear a purely personal rejection. It would be supported by solid political reasoning.

On July 29, Johnson, in what must have been an act of purest delight, summoned Robert Kennedy to the White House to tell him the news.

Shortly after Kennedy had arrived, Bill Moyers called me. "Lyndon's telling Bobby that he can't have the nomination." Saddened but not surprised, I left my office and walked out to the drive that separated the West Wing from the Executive Office Building. As I paced, I saw a dark limousine driving toward me from the White House entry. Robert Kennedy was in the back seat, and, seeing me, told the driver to stop, rolled down his window, and sat there wordlessly, not knowing if I knew, aware that it would be inappropriate for him to break the news. That prerogative was reserved to the president.

"It's too bad," I said. He looked at me, lips closed tightly in a slightly pained expression that I would not see again until the night we lost the 1968 Oregon primary. "That's okay," he replied. "Well," I commented, "I suppose there's nothing to be done about it." Not a question but a statement of fact. He shook his head in agreement and drove off, on his way out of the administration and toward a successful race for the U.S. Senate in New York.

I had not come to know Robert Kennedy very well during the Kennedy years. I saw him socially at those New Frontier parties where even the less agile among us discarded restraint and dignity in clumsy, whirling, swirling, twirling imitations of the Twist, lately imported from New York City's Peppermint Lounge to the "fun" parties of "Camelot after-hours." During our business encounters, privately and in larger meetings — on Cuba, the Dominican Republic, the Alliance for Progress — he was always helpful, and more than helpful: an aggressive, unqualified spokesman for his brother's policies as both he and I conceived them. But such meetings were infrequent. Yet even on the basis of such slim evidence I detected — or thought I did — a similarity of outlook, and even of temperament. Except, of course, that he could get away with it. I was less attracted by what I then perceived as a kind of moral righteousness, rooted in a primitive Catholicism, that did not seem to influence unduly his approach to public policy, but would have made me very uneasy had he been given the power to censor books and movies, or use electronic eavesdropping without restraint of law.

In early 1964, just before joining the White House staff, I was invited to the Venezuelan embassy for an announcement of that government's gift to the Kennedy Library. That night I wrote: "Bob Kennedy came in during the ceremony and extemporized a little speech of thanks about the common enemies of us all — hunger and illiteracy. It is curious. He doesn't have the intellectual depth of his brother" (an error of judgment it took me years to correct) "but he has a feeling for the needs and mood of other people which few politicians possess. I am constantly wavering in my opinion of RFK. He is, after all, only where he is because of birth. He has a great tendency to divide the world between the good guys and the bad guys. On the other hand he has intuitive understanding of the complexities and subleties of other people's motivations. His weakness is probably to act quickly, from emotion — to have too emotional a response to events, although when he has thought them out he is very good."

All these were then incomplete impressions, based on fragments of acquaintance, and would change — become more complete, more subtly modulated in the years ahead as, after I left the government, Bobby and I became much closer, became friends. But that day, as I watched his car leave the White House, although I felt sympathy with his pain, would have been pleased at his selection, I reflected that Kennedy would have other opportunities to demonstrate his qualities, pursue public leadership. This setback had been inevitable. He was a good man, but he never had a chance.

Later that same day, unwilling to single out Bobby for special rejection, Johnson told a startled press corps that he had excluded from vice-presidential consideration all members of the cabinet and those who met regularly with the cabinet, eliminating at a single stroke McNamara, Shriver, and Adlai Stevenson, all of whom had hopes of selection. Presumably any high-level experience in the executive branch of the government automatically disqualified an individual from holding the second-highest office in the executive branch. Or something like that. Although the reasoning was hard to follow, it was a brilliantly eccentric way to eliminate, seemingly impersonally, those candidates, mentioned by the press and privately encouraged by the president, whom Johnson had no intention of selecting: Shriver because of his Kennedy family ties; McNamara because he was unacceptable to organized labor, having rejected George Meany's candidate as assistant secretary for manpower; and Adlai Stevenson because he was Adlai Stevenson.

It is almost certain that well before the convention Johnson had decided to select Hubert Humphrey as his running mate. But Humphrey was to be the last to know. Johnson went out of his way to stimulate and nourish the hopes of others — Gene McCarthy of Minnesota, Tom Dodd of Connecticut — extolling the personal qualities and political advantages that a variety of political figures would bring to the ticket. There was a marginal political justification for this pretense of uncertainty: to inject some semblance of suspense that might attract viewers to a Democratic convention whose main business would be completed long before it met. But the primary target of these maneuvers was Hubert himself — the longer and more painful his uncertainty, the greater his relief and gratitude when the final blessing of his great benefactor was bestowed. Johnson, to whom secrecy was an essential ingredient of power (as the country would soon learn), now used it to dramatize his total command of the party, and to increase his tightening hold on the mind of Hubert Humphrey.

The convention in Atlantic City was not a deliberation, but a celebration: a tribute to Lyndon Johnson. His huge pyramid-size portraits flanked the stage from which the chairman pronounced the presidential will — rules, credentials, platform — and gaveled them into near-unanimous approval. On the second day of the convention, wishing to sustain the mystery of Humphrey's future, Johnson sent a plane to bring a somewhat puzzled Senator Tom Dodd to Washington; the summons clearly designed to imply an urgent wish to discuss the vice-presidential nomination with the Connecticut solon.

The day before his own nomination, Johnson broke with prec-

edent and flew to Atlantic City, where he told the convention and
the country that he intended to recommend Senator Hubert Humphrey for the vice-presidential nomination. A month before, I had
noted a discussion of political strategy with Bill Moyers and Larry
O'Brien: "We debated whether the president should stay in
Washington or Atlantic City while the convention was in progress. Decided that Washington would be better for image, but he
wouldn't be able to resist coming to Atlantic City." And he didn't
resist. Why should he? This was his moment, the culmination of
a political lifetime. The party to which he had devoted three decades of labor, which had rejected him four years earlier, was now
at his feet — admiring, obedient, the instrument of his personal
will. So he came to the convention hall, nominated Humphrey,
went home, and returned on the next evening to accept the nomination that was his by acclamation.

Having helped draft both speeches — along with the party platform — I accompanied the president on both his round trips to
Atlantic City. I had never seen him in a better mood, his exuberance manifested by a continual outpouring of flattery and praise,
being so totally, congenitally political a creature that he praised
himself by praising others. On the journey to nominate Humphrey, the interior of the aircraft had become a place of celebration. "You know," Johnson said as he held his glass up to the
light, sparkling points of amber gleaming through the whiskey,
"every family has a certain thread that runs through it. In the
Kennedys it was women. All those town houses and all those
women, in Joe's and all his sons' lives. Like an animal need, the
need for women. . . . For other families it's money, or skiing, or
meat. In ours it was alcohol." And with that he finished the drink
and extended his arm for a refill. It was an exaggeration, of course.
The Kennedy family history was not untouched by alcohol, nor
Johnson immune to the "animal need" for women (to say nothing
of "meat"). But there was — as with all of Johnson's hyperbole,
even the most grotesque of his prevarications — something to it.
I took it as I supposed it was meant — a Texas tale. Anyway, I
saw no need to impose such sharp divisions of desire. I liked both.

The second flight, the night of the acceptance speech, was slightly
more businesslike as Horace Busby and I labored to modify —
according to last-minute presidential directions — the draft he was
to deliver, within hours, to the convention and a nationwide television audience. Looking toward the president, who was chatting

with a few old political friends from Texas, I remarked, "This may be the last time you'll have to leave Washington. With Goldwater as your opponent you can run the entire campaign from the White House."

Johnson turned toward me, his manner suddenly serious: "You fellows ought to stop talking about being happy about Goldwater. Suppose there is a heart attack or something. Goldwater is a mean, vindictive little man. After I accepted the vice-presidency he wrote me the worst letter I have ever received. He said it was demeaning of me to accept an office under someone who was my inferior, who didn't have my ability or my experience. He is nasty and petty, with a warm handshake, and a pleasing façade." Then he paused, smiling warmly to reassure me he had meant no rebuke. "Let's get that speech finished, boys, the whole world is waiting for you." And so it was. But not for us.

The campaign itself was a politician's dream. From the beginning, the only issue was not victory or defeat, but the size of the inevitable triumph. Absent a scientific miracle — i.e., the rejuvenation of Eisenhower with glandular transplant — it is unlikely that any Republican could have defeated Johnson. Not only was the country at peace, but Kennedy in his last year had reduced Cold War tensions to their lowest point since World War II. We were in the middle of a sustained economic boom, and without inflation. Moreover, Johnson had not only inherited the Kennedy constituency (at the time of his death, JFK had the approval of about 70 percent of the electorate), but had expanded it to the doubtful and disaffected with the impressive performance of his first year in office.

Adding to the abundance of our advantages, the Republican party — seemingly determined to forfeit whatever slim chance it had — nominated the leader and hero of the semi-ideological right, whose views were far from what was then the mainstream of American politics. We watched the Republican convention in delight as the delegates, determined to exile the once-ruling moderate eastern wing of the party, shouted a cacophony of hate and disapproval at Nelson Rockefeller; and we could hardly contain our pleasure as the candidate himself confirmed the country's worst fears by proclaiming that "extremism in the defense of liberty is no vice," demonstrating that even a cliché — in the wrong place and from the wrong man — could be powerfully self-destructive.

Moreover, Goldwater's path to his party's leadership was strewn with statements (partly careless, partly calculated to win the allegiance of the Republican right, which now was in control of the party structure) that, if properly incorporated into our arsenal of attack, were certain to frighten away large numbers of moderate voters. He had, for example, proposed virtually to dismantle social security; observed that the country would be a better place if we could saw off the Eastern Seaboard and send it out to sea; and discussed nuclear weapons as if they were merely magnified hand grenades, advocating that the decision to use them be entrusted not to the commander-in-chief alone, but to combat commanders in the field. As a result, the issue of the campaign was not the Democratic record, not liberalism, not Lyndon Johnson — but Barry Goldwater himself. It was an incumbent's dream, and a challenger's nightmare. (George McGovern was to place himself in a similar position in 1972, and with the same result.)

Every morning a group of us — Bill Moyers, Jack Valenti, myself, Clark Clifford, Larry O'Brien — met on the first, or presidential, floor of the West Wing to discuss campaign strategy, issue instructions to the field, prepare responses to the latest Republican tactics. Upstairs Mike Feldman presided over a parallel meeting of what we called, in those days of innocence, the "Department of Dirty Tricks," whose energies were devoted to finding ways of confronting the Republican candidate with his own more damaging statements and positions — planting questions, providing placards for demonstrators, etc. — trying to make every campaign stop an arena for Goldwater v. Goldwater. In retrospect our efforts to keep the Feldman operation secret, even the name bestowed on his activities, seem amusingly naïve. It would take Richard Nixon to teach us what "Dirty Tricks" really meant.

At one of our earliest meetings, toward the end of August, Johnson entered unannounced and took a seat at the end of the table, facing his close and trusted friend Clark Clifford: "Now, boys, let's hear what you have in mind for me." For about twenty minutes we continued to debate a variety of proposed strategies, until Johnson interrupted. "You fellows are the experts," he said, "but this is how I see it. I'm the president. That's our greatest asset. And I don't want to piss it away by getting down in the mud with Barry. . . . My daddy once told me about the time a fire broke out in a three-story building in Johnson City. Old Man Hutchinson was trapped on the third floor and the fire ladder was too

short to reach him. So Jim Morsund, he was one of the volunteer
fire chiefs, grabbed a piece of rope, tied a loop in it, threw it up
to Mr. Hutchinson, and told him to tie it around his waist. . . .
Then he pulled him down.

"Now Barry's already got a rope around him, and he's knotted
it pretty firm. All you have to do is give a little tug. And while
he's fighting to keep standing, I'll just sit right here and run the
country."

And so we had a strategy. Translated into more conventional
political terms it meant that we would open the campaign with
an assault designed to put Goldwater on the defensive, and then,
as he struggled to extricate himself, withdraw to the high ground
of constructive statesmanship. And that's exactly what we did. It
was the only political campaign, among the dozens I have worked
in, that pursued to the end a design devised from the beginning;
that was not required to modify and improvise in response to events
or changes in the mood of the electorate.

Obviously the president himself — the leader of the entire free
world — could not demean himself by descending to personal attacks on the senator from Arizona. (During the entire campaign
Johnson almost never spoke Goldwater's name.) Nor was it necessary. Television, which during the 1960 campaign had demonstrated an unsuspected power to influence the electorate, by 1964
had metastasized to almost every American home. So we prepared, in collaboration with a New York advertising agency, a
series of brief television "spots" (I refused to call them "commercials," a doomed semantic resistance to the president as product)
aimed at Goldwater's most egregious, self-imposed political weaknesses. And by Labor Day, the traditional opening of a presidential campaign, we were ready to unleash our planned attack.

One example will suffice, especially since it was, according to
the *New York Times*, "probably the most controversial TV commercial of all time."

We had instructed the advertising agency that Goldwater's casual approach to the use of atomic weapons, together with the
militance of his Cold War rhetoric, was to be a major theme of
our television campaign since it undermined public confidence in
that "wise restraint" which was the most important quality expected of a president in the atomic age. ("It's a very big bus,"
Johnson told us, "and we're all in it. People want to be sure that
the man at the wheel isn't going to drive it over a cliff.") At the

end of August, our small "council" assembled in the White House to view the final product, created by the agency after consultations with Moyers and myself. We watched with mounting jubilation as the screen showed a small girl with wind-tossed hair, plucking the petals from a daisy as she stood, in innocent solitude, amid a golden field of flowers. As the girl counted each discarded petal — one, two, three — a strong masculine voice could be heard behind the girlish tones, reciting the now-familiar "countdown" — ten, nine, eight . . . When the ominous cadences reached zero, girl, field, and flowers dissolved, replaced by the blossoming mushroom cloud of a nuclear explosion. The male voice reentered: "Vote for President Johnson on November third. The stakes are too high for you to stay home." (That was the twenty-second spot; in longer thirty- or sixty-second versions, Johnson's voice, unidentified but unmistakable, preceded the final exhortation: "These are the stakes. To make a world in which all of God's children can live. . . . We must either love each other, or we must die." I preferred the abbreviated rendition — the message was more cleanly powerful without the president's voice.)

After the viewing-room lights went up, the advertising executive looked with anxious uncertainty toward his momentarily silent and expressionless audience. Finally, a voice was heard — I think it was Bill Moyers's — "It's wonderful. But it's going to get us in a lot of trouble." He was expressing what we all knew. The spot was a winner, but it would almost certainly be attacked as "unfair," even "dirty politics," by establishment pundits and publications. James Reston wouldn't like it, nor the editorialists for the *Washington Post* and *Time* magazine. But their reach and influence were insignificant compared to a medium that entered the home of almost every voter in America. Yet they could not be totally ignored. A few objections were meaningless, but a sustained attack on our campaign tactics would ultimately be taken up by the rest of the media — including television commentators, whose views were invariably derived, after some time for reading and discussion, from the "bellwether sheep" of their profession.

So we evolved a strategy. We would saturate prime-time viewing hours for a few days (or more, if we could get away with it) and then respond to the inevitable protests by withdrawing the spot. "It seems fine to us, but if that's how you feel about it, Mr. Reston [or Mr. Sulzberger . . . or Mr. Bradlee], we won't use it anymore."

It worked beyond our grandest expectations. The *New York Times* reported that "within days of its first showing . . . Newspapers were bombarded with letters from angry Republicans. . . . Mail piled up in the offices of the Democratic National Committee. . . . The little girl became part of the rhetoric of the campaign. . . . Vice-Presidential candidate Hubert Humphrey said he thought the commercial was 'unfortunate.' " (His statement, of course, was cleared by the White House; after all, who could help it if an advertising agency occasionally went wild.) The little girl of our campaign commercial was part of a *Time* cover on "The Nuclear Issue."

"If that's your judgment," we answered objecting journalists in private, "we'll take the spot off the air. Not that it's unfair, but we want to avoid even the appearance of unfairness"; and we even received, with appropriate humility, the congratulations of a few commentators on our "responsibility." But the damage we intended was done — the image of the small girl, the nuclear blast, indelibly engraved on the American mind. Goldwater spent the rest of the campaign not only attacking our tactics, but, more significantly, trying to refute the implication that his election would increase the danger of nuclear war, never successfully eliminating the doubt that we had not created — that was his own doing — but had so dramatically cultivated.

I did not think the commercial spot was unfair — a little extravagant perhaps, but within the bounds of legitimate political debate. In dozens of statements, Goldwater had expressed his willingness to use military force in the protection of "American interests," had indicated that nuclear weapons were not unique but merely another weapon in the arsenal, referred to the Soviet Union as an implacable enemy bent on the destruction of freedom. If one took him seriously — and it is always a mistake not to take a man's statement of convictions seriously — then he was a very dangerous man. And this impression was not mine alone. For the most important feature of this notorious spot was what it didn't say. Barry Goldwater's name was not mentioned. It was unnecessary. Everyone who saw it knew what it meant, and whom it meant.

Our television bombardment of the early weeks had many other targets. In one spot a disembodied hand (presumably Barry's) was seen tearing up a social security card; in another a woodsman's arm (presumably Barry's) carefully sawed the Eastern Seaboard from a wooden map of the country until the completely detached fragment fell into a pool of liquid and slowly drifted in the direction of the British Isles. (This spot was only shown east of the Appalachians, on the very sound premise that it would bring cheers of approval in every western bar.)

While Goldwater struggled to wave away the swarm of killer mosquitoes which absorbed his energies and obscured his message, Johnson — ignoring his opponent, insulated by the dignity of the Oval Office — spoke of the now and future glories of the nation over which he unmistakably presided: growing national abundance and personal prosperity in a country where even the sky was no longer the limit but merely a passageway to the galaxy beyond. There was no talk of the "limits of liberalism," only the spacious vision of a Great Society, founded on the extension of opportunity to all its people — Negroes and women, the poor and sick — and destined to enrich the lives of all its citizens.

Does it sound utopian? Perhaps. But I believed it, believed that it was possible, that we had the resources and skills if we knew how to use them, wanted to use them. Nor was I alone. The Johnsonian platform had the support of the American majority, would receive their overwhelming endorsement — a mandate, if you will — on election day.

That mandate was not restricted to Johnson's intentions for our own society. It also expressed the public's desire for peace; an approving response to the presidential pledges to pursue accommodation with the Soviet Union, to reduce the burden of the arms race, and to avoid the use of American military force, with the necessary qualification that we would resist direct threats to our own security. I wrote many of those pledges, provided the words that expressed, gave content to, our intention to pursue peace. I meant everything I wrote, and so, I thought then, did the president, who praised and delivered the campaign statements without significant alteration. It was only later that I realized that I might have been wrong, may have unwittingly participated in an inexcusable deception; that the dangers of conflict were certainly far greater, more complicated, and closer, than I had supposed them to be.

As we moved into the pleasant early weeks of autumn in Washington, Johnson — now certain of election, sensing swelling popular approval of his candidacy — abandoned the White House, the protected majesty of his seat in the Oval Office, and took to the road. In every part of the country, his appearance drew admiring, cheering crowds of unprecedented dimension. Traveling with Kennedy in 1960 I had been impressed with the numbers who had waited to see the candidate as he made his final swing through New England on the way to Boston and Hyannisport. No one could remember anything like it. Not until 1964. As the presidential jet taxied to a halt, at the end of every runway we could see mammoth crowds waiting behind flimsy rope barriers to greet the buoyant candidate. In the cities of New England unprecedented crowds, dwarfing the Kennedy receptions of four years earlier, cheered Johnson's every statement, were seemingly moved to unrestrained approbation by his very existence, there, on the platform, right in front of them. They had come to see not only a candidate, but the president of the United States, and the next president of the United States. Men held small children on their shoulders, so their sons or daughters might, in future decades, remember, or pretend to remember, the day they had seen President Johnson, in person, right in their own hometowns.

Johnson loved it, of course. What politician wouldn't? He plunged into every crowd, shaking hands, embracing, shouting unheard flatteries — returning love for love, or what he thought was love. ("The people loved me," he later told me, "and I loved them. I could see it in their faces. It was only when the press began to talk them up against me, that they became suspicious. They felt the same thing as before, but sort of felt they shouldn't, because some newspaper whore had told them I wasn't to be trusted. But even then I knew they really loved me. They were just confused.")

And so in the final weeks, we flew from crowd to crowd, as this formidable man strove tirelessly to absorb the love of thousands into the insatiable, bottomless reservoir of his need. I have never understood the public concern over the desire of a politician to make love to a few women. Lyndon Johnson wanted to make love to an entire nation; an appetite of awesome and terrifying dimensions.

On election day, November 3, 1964, I awoke in my Virginia home to the realization that for the first time in any political campaign, I felt no apprehension, no tension or uncertainty. Johnson had flown to his Texas home, bringing with him a draft of the victory statement. Most of the White House and campaign staff had remained in Washington. I went to the White House, chatted with Bill Moyers, discussed life at Harvard with Bundy, roamed the deserted White House gardens, and awaited the returns, wondering whether Goldwater would concede quickly or make us wait until after the peak television viewing hours had passed. It was over early. We gathered with our wives for a party in a White House mess uncharacteristically festooned with streamers and posters. We talked, exchanged campaign stories, laughed at the customary political anecdotes, watched Goldwater concede and Johnson humbly accept his mandate.

Lyndon Johnson had been elected by over 60 percent of the vote, then the largest margin in American political history. He had won all but six states. No longer the accidental successor, for the first time he was really the president. It was his victory and his alone, no fraction of his immense margin owed to any other man. It was the crowning glory of a lifetime in politics. It was the realization of ambition, not an ordinary ambition even for one who seeks the presidency, but a desire rooted in his Texas childhood, which had haunted him for forty years and more, which, miraculously, had been realized just when it seemed destined to elude him forever. To Lyndon Johnson, his election was the fulfillment of a dream, and more than a dream, the swift, surprising transformation of fantasy into reality. Boy, he must feel good, I thought, watching him, not yet understanding that fantasy was different from ambition, more pervasive, more dangerous; that, once attained, it could take command, reverse the process, transform and absorb reality itself into the form of fantasy.

So I had a few drinks. Too many. Joined in the slightly inebriated jubiliation of my friends and colleagues, sang a song or two, and, very late at night, stumbled toward my waiting White House car. "Well, I guess I get to keep you for a few more years," I said, gently patting the Ford on the fender, then slumped into the rear seat as the driver headed toward my home. Tomorrow, it's back to work, I thought, and then, speaking aloud, "Onward and Upward to the Great Society."

17 / We Shall Overcome

LITTLE MORE than sixteen months after the election, on the evening of March 15, 1965, in Selma, Alabama, tears rolled down the cheek of the Reverend Martin Luther King, Jr. He was sitting before a television set in the living room of Mrs. Jimmie Lee Jackson watching Lyndon Johnson instruct the Congress that urgent and immediate action to secure voting rights for all Negroes was a moral imperative, that all the authority and energy of his presidency would be used to overcome any obstacle to full political equality, and that — in the words of the now-familiar protest hymn — "we shall overcome." "Martin told us," one of King's aides later informed me, "that no speech by a white man had ever moved him, but now he felt the Negro cause was actually going to succeed." A few hours after the speech I was sitting with Johnson in the upstairs sitting room of the mansion when the phone rang. Johnson listened silently, then: "Thank you, Reverend, but you're the leader who's making it all possible, I'm just following along trying to do what's right." He put down the phone, looked toward me, smiling broadly. "That was King. He said it was ironic that after a century, a southern white president would help lead the way toward the salvation of the Negro." Johnson paused, visibly moved. "You know, Dick, I understand why he's surprised, why a lot of folks are surprised, but I'm going to do it. . . . You just keep giving me the music" (I had written the speech) "and I'll provide the action. Hell, we're just halfway up the mountain. Not even half."

The Voting Rights Act was the second major stride toward

Lyndon Johnson's largest and most enduring achievement — the virtual elimination of legal barriers to black equality; the end to officially sanctioned segregation, to Jim Crow and apartheid in the South; and the enfranchisement of millions of black Americans. It is true, as Johnson said, that he only went partway; that racism and its painful consequences were to persist long after Johnson had gone, and still remain one of the most resistant and enduring sources of injustice in American life. But it is also true that no president — before or since — acted more firmly or with greater commitment to the cause of black equality than Lyndon Johnson. Until, like all domestic progress, pursuit of that cause was swallowed up in more dubious battle.

The initiating impulse for the civil rights revolution, which shaped the sixties, did not come from Washington. It came from southern streets: the bus boycott in Montgomery, the freedom riders of Mississippi; the confrontations with governors Barnett of Mississippi and Wallace of Alabama on university steps; the violent assaults — police dogs and fire hoses — on protesting blacks by Bull Connor of Birmingham. That "black revolution," the manifest justice of its demand for equality, the vicious, venomous resistance of white officials had ignited the empathetic imagination of millions of white Americans, aroused spreading national support for the cause of racial justice.

Sitting with Arthur Schlesinger in his Georgetown living room in the early days of the Kennedy administration, we often criticized what we regarded as the president's excessive caution on civil rights. We did so without any feeling of disloyalty. Our admiration of the president was a premise of discussion, and not least among Kennedy's admirable qualities was his willingness to tolerate dissent — private dissent — both among the members of his staff, and in direct debate in the Oval Office. He had made clear his judgment that neither Congress nor the public would move faster or more decisively, that a futile crusade "might look good in the papers," but would result only in defeat and probably jeopardize the rest of his program. Where federal law was challenged directly, he acted decisively, sending federal marshals or troops to dispel resistance to court-ordered school desegregation. But the events of 1963 — the assaults on segregation not only of schools, but of lunch counters and stores, of southern life itself, followed by the often bloody resistance of white citizens and offi-

cials — convinced Kennedy that the legal abolition of segregation
was a moral and political necessity. On June 19, 1963, he had
sent a bill to Congress outlawing segregation in all forms of public
accommodation, a bill that, at the time of his death, still lingered
unenacted, seemingly doomed by the opposition of the southern
leaders who controlled the Senate.

Four days after taking office, on November 27, 1963, Lyndon
Johnson told a somewhat surprised Congress that "no memorial
or eulogy could more eloquently honor President Kennedy's memory than the earliest possible passage of the civil rights bill. . . .
We have talked long enough . . . about equal rights. We have
talked for one hundred years. . . . It is time now to write the next
chapter, and to write it in the book of law."

Did he mean it? Was he serious? The southern senator, the Texas
moderate, the personal protégé and close companion of Georgia's
Richard Russell — principal defender of the Old South, who had
been the most powerful man in the Senate until displaced by the
ascendant Lyndon Johnson.

Damn right he was serious. More serious than anyone yet suspected. Except, perhaps, for Russell himself.

The combination of national revulsion at southern white violence, and the horrified shock that followed Kennedy's murder
had created a clear congressional majority for the civil rights bill,
which Congress, prodded by Johnson, soon strengthened with
provisions against job discrimination and a grant of authority to
the Justice Department to intervene in private civil rights actions.
However, many earlier civil rights bills had commanded a similar
majority, only to collapse before a southern-led filibuster in the
Senate. Russell, assisted by Senator Robert Byrd, prepared to talk
this latest alien imposition on the South to death, or, as in 1957,
to prevent its passage until it had been seriously, even fatally,
diluted by compromise.

There was only one way to overcome the southern resistance,
and, although tried many times before, it had never succeeded. In
the spring of 1917 Woodrow Wilson had condemned the "little
group of willful men" who had "rendered the great government
of the United States helpless and contemptible" by a twenty-three-
day filibuster that prevented passage of Wilson's bill to arm
American merchant ships in the days before our entry into World
War I. In response, the Senate changed its rules to allow two-
thirds of all senators present and voting to impose "cloture" —

i.e., to cut off debate and force a vote. In almost half a century, there had been twenty-seven cloture votes, and only five had succeeded — none of them involving civil rights. Eleven times civil rights proponents had tried and failed to halt the filibuster, which had become the South's most effective weapon.

For Johnson, therefore, a majority was not enough. He needed the support of two-thirds of the Senate, and that would require help from the Senate Republican leadership, particularly Everett Dirksen of Illinois. Johnson could not coerce Dirksen to support cloture, but he might be able to seduce him — directly, through special "pork barrel" dispensations (a dam or a bridge or a national park), and indirectly, through others.

A phone transcript of January 6, 1964 — a couple of months before I reached the White House — illustrates an effort that was unremitting. It was a call from Johnson to Roy Wilkins, head of the NAACP.

LBJ: "When are you going to get down here and start civil righting?"

Wilkins: "As soon as I get rid of my board of directors annual meeting."

LBJ: "Well you tell them that I think they've got a mighty good man. I don't know of a better, fairer, or abler man in the United States. What I want you to do though is to get on this bill now. Because unless you get twenty-five Republicans you're not going to get cloture. Now you can't quote me on this, but Russell says he's already got enough commitments to prevent cloture. I think you are going to have to sit down with Dirksen and persuade him this is in the interest of the Republican party, and you think that if the Republicans go along with you on cloture, why you'll go along with them at elections. And let them know that you're going with the presidential candidate that offers you the best hope and the best chance of dignity and decency in this country, and you're going with a senatorial man who does the same thing. I'm no magician. Now I want to be with you, and I'm going to help you any way I can. But you're going to have to get these folks in here, and the quicker you get them the better. If we lose this fight we're going back ten years."

By the time I had moved into my White House office, in the spring of 1964, the filibuster had begun. It was to last for seventy-five days. As the scheduled cloture vote approached, virtually every doubtful or reluctant senator picked up his phone to hear that familiar drawl: "This is the president," or "This is your president," or "This is Lyndon," followed by a lecture, a plea, a promise, or all three — whatever it took. Senator Fulbright was asked to go on a special overseas mission, a critical matter of foreign policy that just happened to coincide with the date of the cloture vote. (He refused, but "with great reluctance." The political cost in Arkansas would be too high.) California Senator Clair Engle's doctors were persuaded to allow their patient, recovering from brain surgery, to make a quick visit to the Senate chamber, accompanied, of course, by "the best doctors in the United States." If the call was made at night, and the senator himself wasn't at home, Johnson spoke to his wife — "Now, honey, I know you won't let your husband let his president down. You tell him this is a chance to be part of history, something his family will always be proud of." And if neither senator nor wife was home, Johnson would speak to one of the children: "Now you tell your daddy that the president called, and he'd be very proud to have your daddy on his side." As I listened to these calls in the small anteroom adjoining the Oval Office, it seemed as if Johnson had a mental dossier on every member of the United States Senate — his family, the desires of his constituency, the unspoken ambitions of the senator himself.

On June 10 — the day of the cloture vote — Richard Russell, sensing defeat, protested that "the bill simply involves a political question and not a moral issue." To which Everett Dirksen eloquently responded that "civil rights is an idea whose time has come . . . we are confronted with a moral issue."

After two southern amendments to weaken the bill were swiftly defeated, at precisely 11 A.M. the clerk began to call the roll. As Senator Engle's name was called, there was a sudden hush as he was pushed into the chamber in a wheelchair, tried futilely to form the word "aye," and then, succumbing to his paralysis, simply nodded his head. "Senator Engle of California votes aye," intoned the clerk. "As the clerk reached the name of John J. Williams of Delaware," the *New York Times* reported, "and a soft 'aye' was heard, a sigh swept across the floor from the opponents of the bill." It was the sixty-seventh and decisive vote. (The final vote was 71–29.) After that, the *Times* reported, "it took just ten minutes to make history . . . to shut of a Southern filibuster against the most far-reaching civil rights bill since Reconstruction days."

It was not only the first victory for civil rights over the filibuster, it was also the final and decisive battle. For what was not then apparent, what the passage of time has demonstrated, is that the vote of June 10 irrevocably shattered the weapon of the filibuster, took from the hands of the South its last weapon of congressional defense against resistless change.

Everyone congratulated everyone. Johnson applauded the "heroic labors and dauntless courage" of senators from both sides of the aisle. Humphrey gave credit to Dirksen. Dirksen accepted, and returned the credit, while Senator Mansfield said, "Today the credit belongs to the fine labors of Senator Humphrey and Senator Dirksen." (After the bill had passed Dirksen told Johnson, "You left me upset for a hundred days on that civil rights." "Why, you got yourself in my debt on that one," Johnson replied. "You are the hero of the hour now. They have forgotten that anyone else is around. Every time I pick up a paper, it is Dirksen in the magazines, the NAACP is flying Dirksen banners and picketing the White House tomorrow." Neither man mentioned the Corps of Engineers project for Illinois, which Dirksen had requested and Johnson had granted.)

But the defeated Richard Russell knew better. "Lyndon Johnson," he said, "had more to do with this than any one man." And Anthony Lewis, liberal *New York Times* columnist and personal friend of the Kennedy family, agreed with him: ". . . Lyndon Johnson, this country's first Southern President since Reconstruction, made it all possible by his outspoken commitment to Negro Rights. . . . Nearly everyone has . . . forgotten the chaos and bitterness into which civil rights legislation had fallen last autumn. It seemed then that only a miracle could save it. . . ."

Following the Bay of Pigs, Kennedy had quoted the Chinese proverb that "victory has a thousand fathers, but defeat is an orphan." In the aftermath of the failed invasion, the quotation was sardonic. But the civil rights victory of 1964 did have many fathers: the civil rights movement and its leaders; John Kennedy, the man and the memory; the aroused will of a national majority; members of Congress, those of long conviction and the recently converted. But even though it can be argued, is almost certain, that an end to legalized segregation was inevitable, it would not have happened in June of 1964 — ten inexcusable years after the Supreme Court had spoken — had it not been for Lyndon Johnson.

In late June of 1964 I went to the president's office with the draft of a statement to be used at the signing of the Civil Rights Act of 1964. The president read silently for a few minutes, then looked up: "That'll do just fine, Dick. Maybe you could add something to show I understand that a law doesn't change people's feeling." ("Maybe" being presidential jargon for "make these changes.") "But it's a beginning. It shows the way."

Then he sat silently for a minute, staring with characteristic unblinking intensity. I had only been on his staff for a few months and he didn't know me very well, or so I thought, not yet aware of the man's astonishing capacity to penetrate the recesses of weakness, need, ambition, doubt, in other men. And he certainly knew that I didn't yet understand him very well, and that I was a Harvard, an easterner, a Kennedyite, but also — a saving grace — from a poor background and a member of a despised minority.

Then he turned and began to speak, not at me directly, but toward the empty office, a gesture intended to avoid the impression that he was trying to persuade me, that I — one of his own men — needed persuasion. "I know a lot of people around those Georgetown parties are saying that I wasn't much of a crusader for civil rights when I was in the Senate. Hell, I got through the only civil rights bill since Reconstruction" (the Civil Rights Act of 1957), "the only thing Eisenhower ever did for the Negro. And he didn't even want to do that until [Attorney General] Brownell and those others told him he had to. He didn't even like Negroes, would have fired the whole Supreme Court if he could have. But on balance they're right about me. I wasn't a crusader. I represented a southern state, and if I got out too far ahead of my voters they'd have sent me right back to Johnson City where I couldn't have done anything for anybody, white or Negro.

"Now I represent the whole country, and I can do what the whole country thinks is right. Or ought to. We've kept the Negro down for a hundred years, and it's time we let him up. It's wrong for the Negro and it's bad for the rest of us. In every southern state there are people who are poor and ignorant, they don't have jobs and their kids don't learn anything, and all they hear at election time is 'Negro, Negro, Negro.' They're keeping themselves down. I can't make people want to integrate, but maybe we can make them feel guilty if they don't. And once it happens, and they find out that the jaws of hell don't open, and fire and brimstone doesn't flood down on them, then maybe they'll see just how they've been taken advantage of.

"I'm going to be the best friend the Negro ever had. And I want you to help me. I don't expect any gratitude." (He did, of course; abundant, unquestioning gratitude.) "There's no reason for people to be grateful if you give them what's already theirs by right. I tell you, Dick, I've lived in the South a long time, and I know what hatred does to a man." The president paused, halted either by memory of his own past or because some unacknowledged objective had been accomplished. He pressed a button on his desk, and, miraculously, a Filipino mess boy appeared bearing a glass of Fresca. "Like one, Dick?" he asked.

"No thank you, Mr. President."

"Can't say I blame you, but it's too early in the day for anything stronger. Get that statement in shape; then let's you and me go make a little history."

Lyndon Johnson signed the Civil Rights Act of 1964 into law on July 2, thirteen days before a raucous Republican convention nominated Barry Goldwater, forty-nine days before a Senate resolution endorsed American military action in a body of water, halfway around the world, called the Gulf of Tonkin. That fall, while the White House turned its energies to the campaign, the Justice Department, acting on presidential instructions, began to prepare a series of alternative proposals to ensure blacks the right to vote, including a constitutional amendment that would have prohibited states from imposing qualifications for voting in all elections — state and federal — other than age, residence, felony conviction, or proven mental incapacity.

By the time I read the attorney general's memo, it was the winter of '65, for those of us in the White House — most of us — the "best of times," the days filled with the exhilaration of achievements realized, the energizing expectation of achievement soon to come. Yet there were no plans for immediate action on voting rights. We were consumed with the preparation and enactment of Great Society legislation ranging from the War on Poverty to highway beautification. ("Let's get as much as we can as fast as we can," Johnson told us. "I know all about these mandates. Roosevelt had one in 1936, and then he came up with that foolish court-packing plan. Hell, I was the only one to run for Congress on court-packing and he didn't even endorse me.")

Moreover, we thought, it would take time to digest the 1964 act, time to gear up the machinery of implementation, time for the southerners to absorb their defeat, accept their diminished power to halt the inexorable. Voting rights were to be Johnson's next major step on behalf of civil rights. It was clearly on his agenda. ("The right to vote is the meat in the coconut," he had told me. "They can get the rest themselves if they've got this — and they can get it on their own terms, not as a gift from the white man.") But action would come later in 1965, perhaps, or early in 1966. But now events were in the saddle and began to ride.

Martin Luther King and Governor George Wallace of Alabama, captains of the armies of black freedom and white resistance, were not bound by a White House schedule. Their followers were on the move, and they could either lead them or be swept aside.

Dallas County, Alabama, was typical of much of the South. Ninety-five hundred whites, 66 percent of those qualified, were registered to vote, while only 2.2 percent of voting-age blacks — 335 men and women — had been allowed to register. The population center of Dallas County was a town called Selma. In Selma, as throughout the South, a system of coercion combined with arbitrary disqualification had kept blacks from exercising rights granted them ninety-five years earlier by the Fifteenth Amendment.

On March 7, 1965, King initiated a southern-wide drive to compel black registration by leading a protest march from Selma to the state capital at Montgomery, fifty-four miles away. Sympathizers — white and black — came from all over the country to join the protest. Ignoring Wallace's warning that the march was illegal and would not be allowed, the protesters, two and three abreast, assembled in the center of Selma and began to walk, singing the words of the old Baptist hymn — now the anthem of black protest — "Oh deep in my heart . . . I do believe . . . we shall overcome someday."

Like millions of Americans I left my desk to watch on television as the marchers, approaching the Pettus Bridge, were confronted by Sheriff Jim Clark, backed by a mounted posse and a contingent of state police sent by Wallace. I watched as the marchers refused the order to turn back, were overrun by state troopers wildly swinging nightsticks, clubs, bullwhips; saw blood streaming from the faces of the unarmed marchers, the hate-filled ferocity on the face of a trooper as he swung his booted foot into the side of a black man lying semiconscious on the pavement.

For a century the violence of oppression had been hidden from the sight of white America, an abstraction — a few of its most egregious manifestations reported in the papers — but, for the most part, as distant from the American imagination as a flood in China or a famine in India. But now the simple invention of a cathode ray tube, transforming light into electrons, registering their impact on magnetic tape, had torn the curtain away. And America didn't like what it saw. Neither did I. And neither did Lyndon Johnson, who witnessed not a revelation (he had grown up in the South), but an unacceptable affront to the sensibilities and moral justice of the country he now led.

In Montgomery George Wallace was distressed. He had not ordered the unprovoked attack, anticipated neither the brutality and bloodshed nor the wave of revulsion that followed. The governor had national ambitions. It was one thing to block entrance to the University of Alabama, standing alone confronted by the power of the entire federal government; another to be seen as the hand behind the club, the absent author of beatings inflicted on peaceful people, some of them even white people. A few nights after the attack at Pettus Bridge, the Reverend James Reeb was beaten to death while onlookers chanted "nigger lover" as accompaniment to the mortal blows. Wallace knew he had to act. The protesters would not disappear. In fact their numbers were increasing as sympathizers made their way to Selma. He could not back down and simply permit the march without risking the hard core of his support. Yet continuation of the violence would irrevocably mark him as a harsh and vicious leader; destroy the pretense that he was not an enemy of the black man, but defender of the states against the intervention of the federal government. ("I made the government the issue, not the Nigras," Wallace told an associate when it was all over. "I couldn't get elected on a national Nigras platform. People everywhere are tired of the government telling them when to get up and when to go to bed.")

Trapped in an indefensible position, Wallace would turn for help to the only person who could help him — the president of the United States.

Meanwhile, in Washington, Lyndon Johnson waited. Black leaders and white congressmen called on him to dispatch troops to Selma. Angry pickets marched in front of the White House demanding immediate action. At a White House meeting convened to consider alternative courses of action, Johnson explained: "If I just send in federal troops with their big black boots and rifles, it'll look like Reconstruction all over again. I'll lose every moderate, and not just in Alabama but all over the South. Most southern people don't like this violence; they know, deep in their hearts, that things are going to change. And they'll accommodate. They may not like it, but they'll accommodate. But not if it looks like the Civil War all over again. That'll force them right into the arms of extremists, and make a martyr out of Wallace. And that's not going to help the Negroes, to have to fight a war — unless we're going to occupy the South. I may have to send in troops. But not until I have to, not until everyone can see I had no other choice."

"We have to do something," interjected an aide.

"We will," Johnson replied. "Keep the pressure on. Make it clear we're not going to give an inch. Now that Wallace, he's a lot more sophisticated than your average southern politician, and it's his ox that's in the ditch, let's see how he gets him out. Meanwhile, Nick [Attorney General Nicholas Katzenbach], let's have that voting rights bill ready to go to Congress just as soon as we give the word."

On the afternoon of Thursday, March 11, Lee White — a colleague on the White House staff — told me he had been informed that Wallace was sending a telegram to Johnson requesting an immediate meeting to discuss ways of maintaining law and order in Alabama.

On the morning of March 12, without waiting for the text to arrive (or pretending to), thus avoiding any necessity of responding to Wallace's rhetoric, Johnson wired Montgomery: "Television reporters have informed me that press tickers indicate" (Say it again, George, more politely this time) "you have sent a wire requesting an appointment at the earliest possible moment. I want you . . . as well as every other governor, to always know I am willing to see you on any matter of mutual interest and concern. I will be available in my office at any time that is convenient to you." (Nothing special, George. Everyone knows my door is open to the governor of a sovereign state — any governor — anytime he wants to come.)

The trap was set. The next day, Saturday the thirteenth, Wallace arrived at the Washington airport, where a limousine waited to speed him into the warm and waiting embrace of Lyndon Johnson.

I was present in the Oval Office during part of the three-hour meeting, and listened to Johnson's accounts that same evening.

Only a complete transcript could do justice to the encounter; a few brief recollections can, however, convey some of the flavor of what might have been Lyndon Johnson's finest performance.

In the Oval Office, as then furnished, low, plush couches were set out at right angles to a fireplace. Facing the fireplace and flanked by the couches was an unpadded, wooden rocking chair from which the president could comfortably view his visitors. Taking the short-statured governor by the arm, Johnson led him to the couch cushion nearest the rocking chair, where he immediately sank to a position barely three or four feet from the floor. The six foot four Johnson sat in the rocking chair and leaned toward the semi-recumbent Wallace, his towering figure inclined downward until their noses almost touched.

"Well, Governor, you wanted to see me."

Wallace shifted uneasily, eyes darting as if seeking some distance from the massive bulk ominously poised only inches from his face, sank as far back as the couch allowed — there was no dignified escape — and, unnerved, faltering, launched into the set-piece that he and his aides had outlined in Montgomery and refined on the plane trip to Washington. (Protection of law and order . . . a state responsibility . . . no federal intervention . . . outside agitators . . . must be stopped, etc.) Johnson listened wordlessly, expressionless, unmoving, his eyes rigidly focused on the governor's face. After about fifteen minutes, which must have felt like an hour, Wallace finished: "Finally, Mr. President, I'd like to thank you for the opportunity to let me come here and explain things to you in person."

There was a moment of tremulous silence. Then Johnson disengaged, sat back in his rocking chair, and began to speak as if George Wallace had not said a word, his own southern accent deepening as it usually did when exerting his powers on a fellow citizen of the South — no Washington alien, but one of the boys.

"Now, Governor," he said, "I know you're like me, not approving of brutality."

"Of course, Mr. President, but they were just doing their duty."

Johnson signaled to an aide, who, by prearrangement, brought him a newspaper that displayed the picture of an Alabama trooper kicking a recumbent black. He handed the paper to Wallace.

"Now that's what I call brutality."

"Well, it was just an isolated —"

"Don't you agree?"

"Sometimes things get a little out of hand. They didn't start it."

"Maybe. But it's still brutality. Don't you agree?"

"Yes, but they were just trying —"

Johnson took the paper from Wallace and put it aside.

"Now, Governor, you're a student of the Constitution. I've read your speeches, and there aren't many who use the text like you do."

"Thank you, Mr. President. It's a great document, the only protection the states have."

"And somewhere in there it says that Nigras have the right to vote, doesn't it, Governor?"

"Everyone in Alabama has the right to vote."

"Then we agree on that. Now tell me, Governor, how come the Nigras in Alabama for the most part can't vote?"

"They can vote."

"If they're registered."

"White men have to register too."

"That's the problem, George; somehow your folks down in Alabama don't want to registra them Nigras. Why, I had a fellow in here the other day, and he not only had a college degree, but one of them Ph.D.s, and your man said he couldn't registra because he didn't know how to read and write well enough to vote in Alabama. Now, do all your white folks in Alabama have Ph.D.s?"

"Those decisions are made by the country registrars, not by me."

"Well then, George, why don't you just tell them county registrars to registra those Nigras?"

"I don't have that power, Mr. President, under Alabama law . . ."

"Don't be modest with me, George, you had the power to keep the president of the United States off the ballot." (Johnson had not been listed as the Democratic candidate on the 1964 presidential ballot in Alabama.) "Surely you have the power to tell a few poor country registrars what to do."

"I don't. Under Alabama law they're independent."

"Well then, George, why don't you just persuade them what to do?"

"I don't think that would be easy, Mr. President, they're pretty close with their authority."

"Don't shit me about your persuasive power, George. Why, just this morning I was watching you on television. I've got three TVs right at the foot of my bed so I can watch all the networks at once. And if I see something that looks interesting, I've got a little control I can press to turn up the sound. You can be sure the minute I saw you, I pressed it. And you was attacking me."

"Not you, Mr. President, I was speaking against federal intervention —"

"You was attacking me, George. And you know what? You were so damn persuasive that I had to turn off the set before you had me changing my mind. Now, ordinarily I'm a pretty strong-minded fellow, just like them registrars. Will you give it a try, George?"

The colloquy continued, an outgunned Wallace grudgingly giving ground. Finally, after more than two hours had passed, Johnson sat upright in his chair, stared intensely at Wallace: "Now listen, George, don't think about 1968; you think about 1988. You and me, we'll be dead and gone then, George. Now you've got a lot of poor people down there in Alabama, a lot of ignorant people. You can do a lot for them, George. Your president will help you. What do you want left after you when you die? Do you want a Great . . . Big . . . Marble monument that reads, 'George Wallace — He Built'? . . . Or do you want a little piece of scrawny pine board lying across that harsh, caliche soil, that reads, 'George Wallace — He Hated'?"

And without staying for an answer, Johnson rose and strode from the Oval Office, leaving a subdued, partially stunned Wallace to absorb the Johnsonian barrage. (Later Wallace told the press, "Hell, if I'd stayed in there much longer, he'd have had me coming out for civil rights.") Johnson had accomplished his objective — not the conversion of George, but convincing Wallace that he had no intention of letting him off the hook, that Johnson would support the protests while holding Wallace responsible for keeping the peace . . . unless, of course, he asked for help.

A few minutes later Johnson returned and held a relatively brief private conversation with Wallace. The deal was made. Wallace would ask for federal help, using whatever justification was necessary, and Johnson would help him save his political ass by accepting the subterfuge.

Taking the Alabama governor by the arm, Johnson walked him through the White House lobby where over three hundred reporters, startled by the unexpected appearance, crowded around for an account of the meeting. As Johnson began to read a statement prepared in advance of the meeting, one could hear the muffled chant of pickets — "Freedom Now, Freedom Now" — continuing their walking vigil on Pennsylvania Avenue, just beyond the White House gates.

"The governor," Johnson said, "expressed his concern that demonstrations are a threat to the peace and security of the people of Alabama. I expressed my concern about the need for remedying those grievances which led to the demonstrations. . . . He repeated his belief that all eligible citizens are entitled to exercise their right to vote. . . . I said . . . that when all the eligible Negroes of Alabama have been registered . . . the demonstrations, I believe, will stop. . . . He agreed that he abhorred brutality. . . . [His] expressed interest in law and order met with a warm response . . . if local authorities are unable to function, the federal government will completely meet its responsibilities."

Then, turning to Wallace: "Now you folks let the governor speak."

"I am very hopeful we can reach a solution," Wallace said. "The president was a gentleman, as he always is, and I hope I was a gentleman too. . . . Although he does not agree with me on a variety of issues — and I can assure you of that —" (something for the home folks) "it was still a friendly meeting."

Having endured the "impromptu" press conference, Wallace left for his flight to Montgomery, and Johnson, reentering the Oval Office, instructed the attorney general to have a completed draft of a voting rights bill on his desk by the next morning. A few minutes later I was in the Cabinet Room for a scheduled, high-level meeting on foreign policy, listening to Johnson describe the meeting, mimicking with hilarious accuracy the agitated physical motions, the tones — alternately pleading and submissive — of his just-departed visitor. It was not a completely fair or accurate account — as much satire as report — but it contained the truth.

On Sunday, March 14, while my wife and I were spending a quiet day at home, Johnson summoned congressional leaders to an impromptu late-afternoon meeting. The ostensible purpose of the meeting was to fix a time for submission of the voting rights bill; the hidden intent was to have Congress invite the president to present it in person. After Speaker of the House John McCormack and Vice-President Humphrey had reviewed the events

in Selma and the status of voting rights legislation, Johnson remarked, "The problem is that people just don't know what we've
been doing."

"I think the president should go over to a joint session," said
McCormack, "and explain the bill and tell why it's urgent."

"Now let's not panic," responded Dirksen, who had no pressing
desire to give his old ally/nemesis a national platform. "This is a
deliberate government. Don't let these people say, 'We scared them
into it.' Don't let it look as if we're circumventing Congress."

"You started this arm-twisting label, Everett," Johnson sharply
rejoined. (Dirksen had not used the phrase.) "I don't arm-twist
anybody." Then, in more judicious tones, "I wouldn't think of
circumventing Congress. But people don't know the facts — that
we are doing everything we can to solve this. We must tell the
people to give us time to work this out — whether it's through
television, the papers, or Congress."

"I don't think your coming before Congress would be a sign of
panic," observed Carl Albert, House Democratic leader. "I think
it would help."

"It would show bipartisanship," said the Speaker.

"I think we ought to calm the waters," said the vice-president.

Dirksen fell silent, as Humphrey dictated the formula to a waiting secretary: "The leadership of Congress has invited the president to address a joint session of Congress on Monday night to
present his views and an outline of the voting rights bill."

That evening, unaware of the president's decision, my wife and
I went to a dinner party at Arthur Schlesinger's home. As we
were finishing our coffee, a Schlesinger friend entered and told us
he had heard a radio announcement of the president's intention
to address a joint session of Congress on Monday night. I was
surprised, and a little apprehensive: Was I supposed to write the
speech? If so, it would mean an all-night working session for which,
having just consumed an ample meal and several drinks, I felt ill-
prepared.

After a leisurely postprandial brandy, I left Schlesinger's and,
on arriving home, picked up the White House phone to ask the
operator if there were any messages. "We have nothing, Mr.
Goodwin." My slight disappointment outweighed by relief —
somebody else was going to write it — I went gratefully to bed,
prodded by alcohol into almost instant sleep.

The next morning, I arrived at my customary gentleman's hour of nine-thirty to find an obviously agitated Jack Valenti waiting at the door to my office: "Good morning, Dick, the president's speaking to Congress tonight."

"That's what I heard," I replied.

"He needs a speech from you . . . right away."

"From me! Why didn't you tell me yesterday? I've lost the entire night."

"It was a mistake. My mistake. He wants you to do it. Can you do it? You have to do it."

Of course I'll do it, I thought to myself. If the president needed a speech in ten hours, then I'd have to give him a speech, the best I could do in the time allowed — not as good as it should be, perhaps, but something. However, I was not about to let Valenti off so gently. "I don't know, Jack. It's pretty short notice. I'll do the best I can."

"We'll need it by the middle of the afternoon to put it on the TelePrompTers."

"I told you. I'll do the best I can." Wait'll he tells Lyndon, I thought, that Dick says he'll do the best he can to see that he has something to say in front of Congress and the whole country. I wonder if I'll be able to hear the explosion from here.

"Just be sure, Jack," I continued, "that I'm not disturbed by anyone — including you. If you want to know how it's coming, you can ask my secretary." Valenti left for the mansion, and I entered my inner office, stacked some blank paper in front of my typewriter, and began to think — not wondering what had happened, why I hadn't been told the night before, nor about the high historic drama of the event I was preparing (there was no time for that) — but what the hell to say, and how.

Later that evening Bill Moyers told me that Valenti, being the senior White House officer at the Sunday meeting, had asked another staff member to prepare a draft. The next morning, appearing, as he always did, in time for the presidential awakening, Valenti entered the bedroom where Johnson, lying in bed in his pajamas, simultaneously reached for his television remote control and asked Jack: "How's Dick coming with the speech?"

"He's not doing it," Valenti replied, "I assigned it to Horace Busby."

Johnson sat upright, his voice raised in sudden anger: "The hell you did. Don't you know a liberal Jew has his hand on the pulse of America? And you assign the most important speech of my life

to a Texas public relations man? Get Dick to do it. And now!"
Then the president, disdaining further discussion, turned to his
television sets — the morning news crowded with reports of Selma,
Wallace, and the president's scheduled address. Jack rushed from
the room to find me, abruptly realized that the late winter dawn
had barely appeared, and, despite the imperative command, he
could only await my arrival, that even a call to my house would
not have brought me any sooner.

As I sat before my typewriter, the constraint of time, the pressures of an impatient president began to dissolve, dissipated by
awareness of a rare and precious occasion. Even now, almost a
quarter century later, I can recall the mingled, swiftly mutating
images tumbling through my mind — black bodies on the Pettus
Bridge, Fuzzy Hayes strangling in the mud, the ferocious eyes of
James Baldwin as he sat across from me at lunch in the White
House mess, the fear of my youth and the horrified terror of adult
experience at the approach of muscular men whose faces were
contorted by bigotry — "kike," "nigger." By the purest chance,
an accident of time and place, I had been given an opportunity to
strike back, not from bravery bred of vulnerability, but from the
crenellated ramparts of great power. I could, that is, if my craft
was equal to my passion.

There was, uniquely, no need to temper conviction with the
reconciling realities of politics, admit to the complexities of debate
and the merits of "the other side." There was no other side. Only
justice — upheld or denied. While at the far end of the corridor
whose entrance was a floor beneath my office, there waited a man
ready to match my fervor with his own. And he was the president
of the United States.

A speech is not a literary composition. It is an event, designed
not to please the exegetes of language, but to move men to action
or alliance. Effective eloquence is born of great occasions, requires
such an occasion. If Patrick Henry had proclaimed "give me liberty or give me death" to a meeting of the Chamber of Commerce,
the phrase would have disappeared from memory as soon as it
dropped from his lips; instead, because it was spoken at a time of
momentous decision, it entered history. This was also a great moment, perhaps not equal to the colonial decision for independence,
but the culminating event — though not ultimately decisive — of
a century-long struggle for black freedom.

Although the time for preparation was short — each page, as it was completed, taken from my typewriter and carried to the president for review — every paragraph, every sentence, every word of every sentence was slowly shaped in my mind to the furthermost limits of my faculties and energy, before being reluctantly released from my fingers. There would be no time to edit. Indeed, there was to be no opportunity even to reread what I had done, cutting repetition, substituting more felicitous phrases. It was not until the last page was completed that I looked at my watch, shocked to find that it was 6 P.M., that the timeless, unfelt minutes — all experience of their passing suspended by concentration — had consumed almost eight hours. It was like falling from an unexpected precipice — at one moment imbued with seemingly limitless energy, the next on the edge of collapse. I was, I realized, very hungry. I could use a drink — at least one. But it was done. And, it was good — not great, but good. It would do the job, have an impact. At least I thought so — although I no longer had a copy of the text. In any event, my evaluation was now irrelevant. Final judgment belonged to others.

Although I had written the speech, fully believed in what I had written, the document was pure Johnson. For over a year I had met with the president, talked with him at length, observed him as he dealt with others — in his office, on the campaign trail, at the mansion dining table, during long weekends at the ranch, where I had been assigned my own small farmhouse for writing. I had come to know not merely his views, but his manner of expression, patterns of reasoning, the natural cadences of his speech. All that accumulated knowledge and intuition (defined by the Greeks as the meditation on concrete experience) had informed my day-long task. It is not the prerogative of the speechwriter to insert his own ideas, mannerisms, and sensibilities into the president's mouth, to make him something other than what he is. Indeed, it can't be done. Not well. Not without sacrificing all hopes of effective eloquence. The gap between the man and his expression cannot be concealed and, inevitably, degrades the quality of the performance to the memolike prose that is now so dominant in American life. On the other hand, my job was not limited to guessing what the president might say exactly as he would express it, but to heighten and polish — illuminate, as it were — his inward beliefs and natural idiom, to attain not a strained mimicry, but an authenticity of expression. I would not have written the same speech in the same way for Kennedy or any other politician, or for myself. It was by me, but it was for and of the Lyndon Johnson I had carefully studied and come to know.

Throughout the long day of work, I was, as I had directed, left undisturbed. Jack Valenti would appear at regular intervals to take, wordlessly, the latest page as it came from my secretary's typewriter. I have no doubt that it was one of his more unpleasant days in the White House, that he was continually subjected to the frustrated, anxious anger of a president who, in a few hours, must appear before the country to deliver a speech not yet written. Continually reminded of his "mistake," urged by Johnson to "hurry up, and get that damn thing written," yet unable to accelerate the process, Valenti was wise enough to understand that I could not produce any faster, would reject any additional pressure, and that all the power of the presidency could not make the typewriter keys move by themselves. Jack was, I like to think, somewhat solaced by the knowledge that I was a professional who understood that deadlines must be met, that the most eloquent message completed too late for delivery was a worthless scrap of paper. Johnson certainly understood it. All during a day filled, as I was later informed, with continual eruptions of wrath and shouted commands, he never called me, realizing that to transmit his anxiety would only increase my own and disrupt the concentration necessary to production. With one exception. About three o'clock in the afternoon my secretary told me the president was on the phone. "You remember, Dick," he said, the softly modulated, familiar drawl betraying not the slightest sign of concern about the rapidly dwindling hours, "that one of my first jobs after college was teaching young Mexican-Americans down in Cotulla. I told you about it down at the ranch. I thought you might want to put in a reference to that." "Yes, Mr. President," I replied. "I just wanted to remind you," he said gently, and hung up.

And I did remember how, a few months before, Johnson had described his experience in Cotulla. "I invested half my first month's salary in sports equipment," he explained. "I wanted them to learn the values of competition. But I knew that no matter how hard I tried, it wouldn't do any good if their families didn't encourage them to work. So I went around to every home in the district, trying to persuade the parents to participate, to help me out. Those little brown bodies needed so much and had so very little. I was determined to spark some ambition in them."

After the final page had gone to the mansion, I sent out for sandwiches, browsed through the papers, and waited. Around seven-thirty the president called: "I'd like you to ride up to the Hill with me tonight. . . . We'll be leaving around eight-thirty, but you ought to get here a little earlier."

"I'll be there, Mr. President." There was no comment or question about the speech from either of us. None was expected. It was beyond revision; indeed, had been finished too late for the TelePrompTers and would be delivered from a typed text. I had done my job. Now he must do his. Congress and the country would tell us how well we had worked. And if the last eight hours had been the finest moments of my life in politics, the next few would be Lyndon Johnson's.

Sometime after eight, freshly shaved, my suit still rumpled from the day's work, I walked over to the mansion, talked of trifles with Moyers and Valenti, until the Secret Service alerted us to enter the presidential limousine, its dark, metal-clad mass precisely defined against the gray night sky. A few minutes later, the president emerged, gently settled his massive bulk into the cushioned seat — without word of recognition or greeting — and began to read through the notebook that contained the text of his speech. A few code words were heard on the car radio, there was the sound of doors closing, as our motorcade — flanked by motorcycles, three Secret Service cars leading the way, still others following the president's vehicle — eased through the White House gates and, gathering momentum, moved like some black-hued hinged reptile through the empty Washington streets, from which the customary evening traffic had been excluded for the few minutes of our passage. This is how the making of history begins, I thought, watching the absorbed Johnson, in the silence of a single man's mind.

A few minutes later we arrived at the Capitol, and entered — conforming to long tradition — the chambers of House Speaker John McCormack, where the leaders of Congress and members of the designated welcoming committee awaited our arrival. Closing his notebook and handing it to an aide for safekeeping, a metamorphosed Johnson strode into the group, shaking hands, exchanging greetings, distributing accolades and appreciation: "I want to thank you, Mr. Speaker, for letting me come up tonight. . . . You were mighty kind, Everett, to invite me."

An assistant to the Speaker guided me and other members of the president's staff toward the House chamber to await the pres-

ident's formal arrival, instructing us to stand in the House well —
the small vacant space between the speaker's rostrum and the
completely occupied chamber, above which loomed the galleries
already filled beyond capacity.

In a few minutes, over the rustle of a hundred whispered conversations, I heard the resounding formal tones of the official
doorkeeper of the House — "Ladies and gentlemen, the president
of the United States" — and then a gradually mounting crescendo
of applause as Johnson, entering from the rear of the chamber,
accompanied by his congressional escort, slowly made his way to
the rostrum. I felt a charge race through my body — love, patriotism, some identity more deeply fused — at the precisely struc-
tured unfolding of this most dramatic ceremony of democracy.

John McCormack, the ascendant son of Boston's Irish streets,
born a few blocks from the poor East Boston neighborhood where
my own father had spent his childhood, looked at the tall man
from the hill country of Texas, faced the chamber, and spoke the
ritual formula: "The president of the United States."

As the applause resumed, Johnson walked to the rostrum, acknowledged the introduction, the presence of Senate leaders and
the vice-president, carefully placed his notebook on the rostrum,
slowly opened the black leather cover, looked out, unsmiling, across
the chamber. Silently he surveyed his audience — the entire Congress, members of the cabinet, the justices of the Supreme Court,
the galleries filled with invited guests. He knew nearly all of them,
knew much about them — old friends and past adversaries, those
he had led or manipulated, and those who had resisted his ambitions — all of them now looking upward, awaiting his words,
compelled to react, to shape their future actions, in response to
his exhortations. And, most important of all, on each side of the
rostrum were the cameras that, on this night, would carry his
words and presence to over seventy million Americans — the largest audience of his life.

There were a few introductory sentences. Then: "At times history and fate meet at a single time in a single place to shape a
turning point in man's unending search for freedom. So it was at
Lexington and Concord. So it was at Appomatox. So it was last
week in Selma, Alabama."

There was no applause, only a soft murmur something like a
sigh — of relief by many, of defeat by some — at the phrases which
had already made manifest the president's intent.

"There is no cause for pride in what has happened in Selma," the president continued. "But there is cause for hope and for faith in our democracy in what is happening here tonight . . . the cries of pain and the hymns and protest of oppressed people have summoned into convocation all the majesty of this great government. . . . Our mission is at once the oldest and the most basic of this country: to right wrong, to do justice, to serve man."

There was no sound or movement in the chamber, the audience seemingly fused into intense, attentive stillness.

"In our time we have come to live with moments of great crisis. . . . But rarely in any time does an issue lay bare the secret heart of America itself . . . a challenge, not to our growth or abundance, our welfare or our security, but to the values and the purposes and the meaning of our nation.

"The issue of equal rights for American Negroes is such an issue. . . . [S]hould we defeat every enemy, should we double our wealth and conquer the stars, and still be unequal to this issue, then we will have failed as a people and as a nation.

"For with a country as with a person 'what shall it profit a man, if he shall gain the whole world, and lose his own soul?' "

Someone in the gallery began to clap, and the applause swept across the chamber. You can always count on the Bible to get them going, I thought. It was the first of thirty-six cheering interruptions; twice the president would receive prolonged standing ovations.

His expression somber, his audience's approval unacknowledged, Johnson waited for the applause to fade.

"There is no Negro problem. There is no southern problem. There is no northern problem. There is only an American problem. And we are met here tonight as Americans to solve the problem.

"This was the first nation in the history of the world to be founded with a purpose. The great phrases of that purpose still sound in every American heart . . . 'All men are created equal' — 'government by consent of the governed' — 'give me liberty or give me death.'

"These words are a promise to every citizen that he shall share in the dignity of man. This dignity . . . rests on his right to be treated as a man equal in opportunity to all others . . . [to] share in freedom, choose his leaders, educate his children, and provide for his family according to his ability and his merits as a human being.

"To apply any other test . . . is to deny America, and to dishonor the dead who gave their lives for American freedom."

The "right to choose your own leaders," the president said, was "the most basic right of democracy," now denied to millions of citizens "simply because they are Negroes." He detailed the myriad barriers — the web of falsely contrived tests and qualifications used to prevent black registration. "For the fact is that the only way to pass these barriers is to show a white skin.

"Experience has clearly shown," Johnson said, explaining a reality already known to every person in the chamber, "that the existing process of law cannot overcome systematic and ingenious discrimination . . . ensure the right to vote when local officials are determined to deny it."

Therefore, the president announced, in the next forty-eight hours he would send Congress a bill striking "down restrictions . . . which have been used to deny Negroes the right to vote . . . establish a simple, uniform standard" for registration, "send federal officials empowered to register Negroes wherever state officials refuse to register them . . . and ensure that properly registered individuals are not prohibited from voting. . . .

"The last time a president sent a civil rights bill to Congress," the president reminded his audience, ". . . the heart of the voting provision had been eliminated." But the time for temporizing was past. "This time, on this issue, there must be no delay, no hesitation, and no compromise. . . . We cannot . . . refuse to protect the right of every American to vote . . . must not wait another eight months. We have already waited a hundred years and more, and the time for waiting is gone.

". . . For from the window where I sit with the problems of our country I am aware that outside this chamber is the outraged conscience of a nation, the grave concern of many nations, and the harsh judgment of history on our acts."

Having fulfilled the formal purpose of his appearance, the president looked beyond the issue of voting rights, describing the events at Selma as only a part "of a far larger movement, one that reached North as well as South — the effort of American Negroes to secure for themselves the full blessing of American life."

Then, looking straight out at his audience, speaking in loud but deliberate tones, in what was among the most dramatic single moments of the sixties, Johnson proclaimed: "Their cause must be our cause too. It is not just Negroes, but it is all of us, who must overcome the crippling legacy of bigotry and injustice.

"And we . . . shall . . . overcome."

The president paused. There was an instant of silence, the gradually apprehended realization that the president had proclaimed, adopted as his own rallying cry, the anthem of black protest, the hymn of a hundred embattled black marches. Seventy-seven-year-old Congressman Manny Celler — a lifetime of vigorous, often futile, fights for freedom behind him — leaped to his feet, cheering as wildly as a schoolboy at his first high school football game. Others quickly followed. In seconds almost the entire chamber — floor and gallery together — was standing; applauding, shouting, some stamping their feet. Tears rolled down the cheeks of Senator Mansfield of Montana. Senator Ellender of Louisiana slumped in his seat. In distant Alabama, Martin Luther King cried; while grouped around thousands of television sets in university halls and private homes, millions of people, especially the young, felt a closeness — an almost personal union — with their government and with their country, which exposed the masquerade of fashionable cynicism, unveiled the hunger for love of country, not as an abstraction, but as the binding force of a community whose largeness magnified each of its members. Standing in the well of the house, I felt it too — the urge toward tears which was not the edge of grief or of some simple pleasure, but some more profoundly human need to be a part of something greater and more noble than oneself.

God, how I loved Lyndon Johnson at that moment; how unimaginable it would have been to think that in two years' time I would — like many others who listened that night — go into the streets against him.

Waiting for the cheers to subside, his audience again attentive, the president admonished his national audience: "Let none of us look with prideful righteousness . . . on the problem of our neighbors. There is no part of America where the promise of equality has been fully kept. In Buffalo as well as in Birmingham, in Philadelphia as well as Selma, Americans are struggling for the fruits of freedom.

"The real hero of this struggle is the American Negro. His actions and protests . . . have awakened the conscience of this nation. . . . He has called upon us to make good the promise of America.

"We will guard against violence," the president promised, for "it strikes from our hands the very weapons with which we seek progress — obedience to law and belief in American values. But," he warned, "we will not seek the peace of suppressed rights, or the order imposed by fear, or the unity that stifles protest. For peace cannot be purchased at the cost of liberty."

The message was clear. Protests and marches would now receive the full protection of the federal government. "All Americans must have the privileges of citizenship." Nevertheless, civil rights legislation was not enough, for "to exercise these privileges takes much more than just legal rights. It requires a trained mind and a healthy body . . . a decent home, and the chance to find a job, and the opportunity to escape from the clutches of poverty."

In that sense, Johnson explained, the entire Great Society was a civil rights program, designed "to open the city of hope to all races." And, even more, not merely to "open the gates of opportunity. But . . . to give all our people, black and white, the help they need to walk through those gates."

Johnson then related to the nation the experiences he had reminded me of during our midafternoon telephone conversation: "My first job after college was as a teacher in Cotulla, Texas, in a small Mexican-American school. Few of them could speak English . . . and they often came to class without breakfast, hungry. They knew, even in their youth, the pain of prejudice. They never seemed to know why people disliked them. But they knew it was so . . . I saw it in their eyes. I often walked home . . . wishing there was more that I could do. . . . [Y]ou never forget what poverty and hatred can do when you see its scars on the hopeful face of a young child.

"I never thought then, in 1928, that I would be standing here in 1965 . . . that I might have the chance to help the sons and daughters of those students . . . and people like them all over the country.

"But now I do have that chance. And I'll let you in on a secret. I mean to use it."

Nearing the end of his address, Johnson declaimed his spacious ambitions, his philosophy of office to the intensely receptive, hopefully approving, audience: "The might of past empires is little compared to our own. But I do not want to be the president who built empires, or sought grandeur, or extended dominion. I want to be the president who educated young children to the wonders of their world. I want to be the president who helped to feed the hungry . . . who helped the poor to find their own way . . . who protected the right of every citizen to vote. . . . I want to be the president who helped to end hatred among his fellowmen . . . who helped to end war among the brothers of this earth."

The tragedy — the terrible, irrevocable tragedy — is that he meant it. The grandiosity of expression, the assertion of ambitions beyond the reach of any mortal, should not be allowed to deny the reality that he might have gone a long way toward his intent had his passage not been swept up in the turbulent eddies that so violently disrupted his public course and his own mind, mercilessly sweeping the journey toward unforgiving rocks.

"Above the pyramid on the great seal of the United States," Johnson concluded his address, "it says — in Latin — 'God has favored our undertaking.' God will not favor everything we do. It is rather our duty to divine His will. But I cannot help believing that He understands and that He favors the undertaking that we begin here tonight. . . . Thank you."

As Johnson made his way through the throng of enthusiastic congressmen, we hurried through a side entrance into the waiting limousine. We didn't want to miss our ride. A few minutes later, the towering figure emerged from the crowd, which had flowed over the walk, and slid into the seat facing the accompanying members of his staff. The door closed, the radio spoke, and we began to move toward Constitution Avenue. The car was silent. No one wanted to be the first to speak. Only two opinions mattered now: one man's, and all men's. And we were neither. Midway in passage, Johnson turned to Valenti: "Well, Jack, how did I do?" Didn't he know, I thought, it had been a glorious success, certainly on the Hill, and, I was sure, across the country? But I hadn't understood the question. Valenti did, however, and, immediately pulling a notebook from his jacket pocket, read: "The total delivery time was forty-five minutes, twenty seconds. You spoke for thirty-six minutes and forty seconds, and applause took eight minutes and forty seconds. Your rate of delivery was 96.35 words per minute, and there were thirty-six interruptions for applause."

Unable to restrain myself, I interjected, "Thirty-seven, Jack, I counted thirty-seven interruptions." Then, seeing the president glare at Valenti (on this night I could do no wrong), I quickly amended, "Just kidding. I didn't keep count." The president's facial muscles relaxed, and Jack smiled. Valenti, among his manifold duties, was the official statistician of presidential oratory, bringing to that task the same precision with which I now measure the daily hitting performance of Wade Boggs — the last task of pleasure and consequence left to a star-crossed fan of the Boston Red Sox.

Nothing more was said. Nor could I discern what the president was feeling. Clearly he must have experienced the exultant approval of his audience, felt the unprecedented surge of warmth (was it love?) flowing toward the insatiable reservoir of his desire. Yet like any dramatic troupe on opening night, we would have to sit and wait for the reviews.

No sooner had we reached the upstairs sitting room of the White House, than the reactions began to come. The White House switchboard was, we were informed, jammed beyond its capacity, almost all of the calls expressing enthusiastic approval. The sitting-room phone began to ring, as those select few allowed direct access to the president — congressional chieftains, acknowledged leaders of private life — began to call. "Thank you, Dick," I heard him say, "I understand. And I want you to know that no opinion in the world means as much to me as yours." Hanging up, the president broke into a grin: "That was Dick Russell. Said that though he can't be with me on the bill, it was the best speech he ever heard any president give." (Proving that liberal southerners had no monopoly on hyperbole.) "Let's have a little whiskey, boys, looks like we've got something to celebrate."

There were more calls, all of them effusive, and the first telegrams began to arrive. Holding the blue wireless forms, Johnson read aloud: " 'As someone else whose roots lie deep in the South I thought your speech historic. Everyone must have the right to vote.'

"That's from Bernie Baruch," Johnson said; "it must have hurt like hell for the old codger to admit that anyone could do anything right without him."

There were others, far too many to include in this account: "Thank you for taking such a courageous stand for all Americans. I pray that God will continue to give you strength and protection. I remain yours in Christ." — Mahalia Jackson. "The greatest speech you have ever made. And you are so right." — Edmund G. Brown, governor of California.

There were similar messages — by wire and telephone — from every major black leader, a multitude of labor chiefs, governors, businessmen, and private citizens; the tone and content of their response was fully consistent with Tom Wicker's summary in the lead story of the next day's *New York Times:* "No other American President," Wicker wrote, "had so completely identified himself with the cause of the Negro. No other President had made the issue of equality for Negroes so frankly a moral cause for himself and all Americans."

As the hour passed midnight, the happy, expansive president drew on his store of endlessly fascinating tall Texas tales in which fact and fiction, time and place were skillfully manipulated to absorb, entertain, and edify the listener. Like the lectures of Mark Twain — the spiritual predecessor of the presidential fabulist — the stories transcended petty, pedantic standards of accuracy; seeking, instead, a verisimilitude that would engage the amused sensibilities of the listener, yield, almost subliminally, a message, an enhanced impression of Johnson, or the childlike pleasure of a story well told. (And it was all free. It would take Stephen Spielberg to demonstrate that huge fortunes could be built on such a gift.) As we moved into the early morning, the complexity and intensity of his narration were undiminished by the gradual dissolution of his audience. First the members of his family, then other members of the staff took their leave and went to bed, until there were only three of us — Johnson, myself, and a young woman assistant to a member of the staff.

I listened as we refought the battles of the Alamo and San Jacinto, relived the avuncular eccentricities of Sam Rayburn (standing in imitation, Johnson seemed magically to shrink his own six foot four inches into Mr. Sam's diminutive figure shuffling slowly across the House floor), watched as glass after glass of scotch disappeared into a seemingly bottomless well, matched him drink for drink as if engaged in some illusory test of manhood. (Thank God for my White House driver, I thought as the disorienting haze enveloped awareness, if only I can make it down the stairs.)

Johnson didn't want to go to bed. And neither did I. Neither of us wanted the night to end, to consign the immediacy of triumph to the muted recesses of memory. The next day I would — as my profession required — refuse to admit that I had written the speech, retreat to the required formula: "I did some work on it." But tonight I could indulge, inwardly, my mingled arrogance, pride, excitement at authorship of words that had touched, might change, the nation, let my vanity feed unchecked on the president's unspoken approval. At about 3 A.M., Johnson rose from his chair and silently moved, swaying only slightly, toward his bedroom. I offered the assistant a ride, and, together, we left the White House.

Two days later, on March 18, the voting rights bill went to the Congress. Through the spring, congressional committees debated and revised, but did not weaken the bill, which was enacted on July 10, and signed into law on August 6. I still have, mounted on my study wall, the pen Johnson handed me on that occasion.

The act was probably the single largest and most enduring liberal accomplishment of the sixties. The Civil Rights Act of 1964, by ending segregation, had accelerated a process that was inevitable. Blacks had forged weapons — the boycott, pickets, the disruption of business — that could do economic damage to white-only establishments, could — in reality and in perception — disrupt the stability that a rapidly ascending white business community felt necessary for continued growth within a national economy. They had black power, and were learning how to use it. When it came to voting, however, blacks had little more than the moral force of their demand. Those who guarded the doors to the ballot box — elected and appointed officials alike — were white men, selected by a white constituency, whose own authority would be challenged by a change in the electorate. But now they had no choice. If local officials refused, federal officials would take over. And once the federal examiners entered the counties of the Deep South, the game was over. Registration of blacks was the only alternative to displacement.

In the next few years the shape of southern and national politics was changed forever. By August of 1966, a half million black voters had been added to the rolls, an increase of about 25 percent over 1964. In May of 1966, for the first time, blacks voted in large numbers in the primaries of the Deep South. In 1965 there were almost no blacks elected in the South; in 1968, 389 blacks held state and federal office. By 1980 ten million blacks were registered to vote, only 7 percent less than the proportion of eligible whites. And when the elections of that year were over, blacks had voted in about the same proportion as whites, and 684 blacks held elected office. And in 1984, the Reverend Jesse Jackson would become the first black to attain a position of national leadership through the political process.

Antistrophe

On March 18 — three days after the president's speech — as the Selma protestors prepared to resume their march, Johnson convened a meeting of his advisers in the Oval Office. "Now I want you to call Wallace," he instructed; "tell him to ask for assistance. But make sure you put in enough troops, and they have professional leadership. I want professionals there, not drugstore cowboys."

As his aide Buford Ellington moved toward the phone, the president said: "Now wait a minute. How do we explain the change in Wallace's attitude?"

"We can just say," Ellington answered, "that since your meeting he has confidence in you, and he needs help."

Johnson nodded, and Ellington placed the call: "He says he'll call you back in six minutes." The assembled advisers waited in silence, the phone rang, Johnson talked briefly to Wallace, then hung up. "Okay, let's get ready."

That evening Wallace sent a telegram explaining that, according to his Department of Public Safety, it would take more than six thousand men and 489 vehicles to protect the march, a far larger force than that possessed by the state of Alabama. The next day, March 19, Johnson received a copy of a telegram sent to Wallace by James Allen — lieutenant governor and presiding officer of the state Senate — informing him that although the state was willing "to call the National Guard to active duty to protect life and property," they didn't have enough money to "bear the expense . . . without jeopardizing the essential functions of the State of Alabama, and we respectfully request the Governor to inform the President of this fact."

On the morning of the twentieth, Johnson wired Wallace that, because of the governor's "strong feelings" that "responsibility for law and order rested with state and local governments . . . I was surprised . . . when you requested federal assistance," and "even more surprised that both you and the legislature, because of monetary considerations, believe the state is unable to protect American citizens . . . without federal force. Because the court order must be obeyed and the right of American citizens protected, I intend to meet your request by providing federal assistance to perform normal police functions."

The charade was over. The messages from Montgomery had left the president no choice, exactly as he had planned it. Federal troops were swiftly deployed, and around eight of a cold Alabama morning, the earth whitened by a heavy frost, hundreds of marchers, led by King and Ralph Bunche, walked slowly, singing "We Shall Overcome," over the tranquil Pettus Bridge on their undisturbed procession to Montgomery — a demonstration that was no longer a demand, but a display of moral support for the president of the United States.

And on the short stretch of Pennsylvania Avenue that fronts the White House only a few casual tourists could be seen. The pickets were gone.

18 / Beyond Civil Rights

IN LATE MAY, two months after the voting rights speech, Johnson summoned me to his office. As I entered, he was standing before the wire service teletype machine, installed so he could personally monitor press commentary on its way to a thousand city desks, and have his press secretary issue a rejoinder or correction that would arrive even before editors could digest and rewrite an offending report. He could not control the press — a secret yearning of all presidents — but he could compel the simultaneous publication of "his side" (usually referred to by all high officials as "the truth"). The president motioned me to a chair, then, with some slight reluctance, left the machine and sat behind his desk — our conversation accompanied by the unpleasant clicking of the mechanical printer.

"You did a good job on that voting rights," he began. It was his first overt acknowledgment of my authorship. (The White House staff had been instructed to assert that the president had penned it himself, presumably on the back of an envelope of incredible dimensions.) "A fine job."

"Thank you, Mr. President," I replied.

"Now, voting rights are important. But it's only the tail on the pig, when we ought to be going for the whole hog. During the depression I ran an NYA [National Youth Administration] project in Texas. All the boys, white and Negroes, were poor. But the poor Negroes were kept separate over in Prairie View, and always got the short end. They didn't even have a decent place to sleep. Now, the whole country's like one big Prairie View. Not everywhere, but most places. The problem's not just civil rights. Hell, what good are rights if you don't have a decent home or someone to take care of you when you're sick? Now we've got to find a way to let Negroes get what most white folks already have. At least the chance to get it. As I see it, the problem isn't so much hatred as fear. The white worker fears the Negro's going to take something away from him — his job, his house, his daughter. Well, we ought to do something about that." (About what? I thought — doctors, jobs, prejudice, terror?) "Now, we can't do everything at once, but we can make people feel a little guilty about not doing it. We've got the biggest pulpit in the world up here, and we ought to use it to do a little preaching. Why don't you see what you can do. You're my regular alter ego."

"I'll give it a try, Mr. President," still uncertain exactly what I was going to try.

"Fine." Then in a gesture of dismissal the president rose and returned to the endless fascination of the news ticker.

Clearly Johnson wanted to go beyond the traditional issues of civil rights — the subject of a multitude of protests, marches, and demonstrations — to discuss the denial of economic and social opportunity. Over the next few days, I discussed the substance and occasion for such an address with Bill Moyers and Jack Valenti. The president's scheduled commencement speech at Howard University on June 5 was, we agreed, the appropriate event. Research materials were accumulated and, late in the afternoon of June 4, I began to write, completing the draft just as the eastward-facing windows of the adjacent Executive Office Building began to mirror the dawn light. I did not often wait until the last minute to draft a speech, but deliberate delay was one of the tactics I occasionally used to keep other staff members, even cabinet officials, from trying to substitute their literary judgment for mine.

After writing a covering memorandum for the president, I took the draft to the mansion so that an attendant could show it to Johnson when he awoke. In the memo, I informed Johnson that I had shown drafts of the speech to Jack Valenti, Bill Moyers, and "Pat Moynihan of Labor," that Moyers and I felt it would be a "pathbreaking speech . . . will put us ahead of the trends," not merely a response, as were all previous civil rights initiatives, to the crisis of the clash between black demands and white resistance. "Coming now," we felt, "it could have a beneficial effect on the likelihood of violent demonstrations this summer." (A serious underestimation of the growing frustration within the northern ghettos.) Finally, spurred by a self-indulgent pride which was swollen by fatigue, in a brief thrust of grotesquely exaggerated rhetoric, I wrote: "You received almost all the Negro vote. You have fulfilled the expectations of that support. But both Bill and I agree that a speech like this might well help toward making you 'The Great Emancipator' of the twentieth century." Yet despite my present disclaimer, it might have gone a long way toward that end, had it been a prelude instead of an epitaph.

When I arrived at the second floor of the mansion with the draft and memo, I found Johnson already in the midst of breakfast. I entered his bedroom and handed him the speech, which he read silently, making occasional penciled amendments and inserts. Then, extending the manuscript toward me: "That'll do just fine, Dick."

"Don't you think I ought to check it out with black leaders?" I asked. "It goes a lot further than even the civil rights movement has gone, and I'd like to make sure it doesn't get us into trouble."

"If you'd like to," the president replied, turning toward his television sets. I took the draft and left. Johnson was unconcerned. It was what he wanted to say. Being more cautious or, perhaps, less attuned to the temper of the black movement, I spent the next hour or two reading the draft to King, Roy Wilkins of the NAACP, Whitney Young of the Urban League, and A. William Randolph of the Railroad Workers. They were all enthusiastic. (Stokely Carmichael, Rap Brown, and Malcolm X were not on my calling list; the establishment hadn't come that far.)

Later that day I accompanied the president on his ride across Washington to the campus of Howard University.

Standing at the foot of the temporary platform that had been constructed for the president's speech, I scanned the gathering of almost five thousand — nearly all black — faculty, visitors, and graduating seniors who occupied the spacious quadrangle facing the rostrum behind which hovered the large stone building named in honor of the heroic nineteenth-century leader Frederick Douglass. Johnson was introduced, acknowledged the applause, opened his notebook in a silence perturbed only by the gentle breeze rippling through the mild June air. The black faces were impassive, waiting. In many, especially the young, I thought I could discern a hint of skepticism. It may have been my imagination, but I didn't think so. For despite all he had done and said, despite the accolades of black leaders for the response to Selma, he was still a white man — the honkie intruder on black ground. What would it take, I thought, how many years of struggle and purgation before they could fully trust a white leader?

Johnson sensed it too, must have sensed it — an awareness bred of the experience of a southern lifetime — as he began to speak:

". . . American Negroes have been another nation: deprived of freedom, crippled by hatred, the doors of opportunity closed to hope.

"In our time change has come to this nation too," the president professed, citing the civil rights laws of recent years, including the voting rights bill then before the Congress. But these laws, he said, paraphrasing Winston Churchill, are only "the end of the beginning."

Admittedly "the barriers to freedom are tumbling down. . . . But freedom is not enough. . . . You do not," he explained, "take a person who had been hobbled by chains, liberate him, bring him up to the starting gate of a race and then say, 'You are free to compete with all the others' and still justly believe you have been completely fair. . . . It is not enough to open the gates of opportunity. All of our citizens must have the ability to walk through those gates. . . . Men and women of all races are born with the same range of abilities. But ability is not just the product of birth. Ability is stretched or stunted by the family you live with . . . the neighborhood . . . the school . . . and the poverty or richness of your surroundings. It is the product of a hundred unseen forces playing upon the infant, the child and the man."

I thought I could detect a turning of mood, respectful attention gradually charged with expectant intensity, the ritual applause gaining in vigor. Johnson looked sternly toward the capped-and-gowned graduates, acknowledged the achievement implicit in the growing number of black college graduates, but then reminded them that their accomplishments "tell only the story of a growing middle-class minority. . . . [F]or the great majority of Negro Americans . . . there is a much grimmer story. They are still another nation . . . for them the walls are rising and the gulf is widening." (They needed no reminder, but his words were addressed to a larger audience.)

The president recited the statistical litany, which revealed the mounting disproportions between white and black America, the staggering decline in relative employment, income, poverty, infant survival; the increasing isolation "as Negroes crowd into the central cities and become a city within a city."

Although the causes of this inequality are "complex and subtle," the president admitted, two are undeniably clear: "First, Negroes are trapped — as many whites are trapped — in inherited, gateless poverty — shut in slums, without decent medical care," where "private and public poverty combine to cripple their capacities." The eradication of these devastating conditions, Johnson said, was an objective of the War on Poverty and the Great Society.

"But there is a second cause . . . the devastating heritage of long years of slavery; and a century of oppression, hatred and injustice. Negro poverty," the president proclaimed, "is not white poverty" nor are the differences "racial," but "solely . . . the consequence of ancient brutality, past injustice, and present prejudice," which must be "overcome if we are ever to reach the time when the only difference between Negroes and whites is the color of their skin."

Responding to the subtle racism of those white politicians and social theorists who righteously invoked the successful upward climb of other American minorities, Johnson rejected the comparison: "The Negro, like these others, will have to rely mostly on his own efforts. But he cannot do it alone. For [other groups] . . . did not have a cultural tradition which had been twisted and battered by years of hatred and hopelessness, nor were they excluded because of race or color — a feeling whose dark intensity is matched by no other in society."

He had said it. I could feel, standing there, looking across the barrier of my own color toward the black multitude, a slight chill — not of pleasure, it was not a subject that permitted pleasure — but something like gratification. An American president — a white, southern American president — had acknowledged that racism which had joined the earliest colonists in their Jamestown settlement — the original sin of the American paradise — and which had endured, a dark stream etched along the margins of a white current, for over three centuries.

The disabling differences in the black experience, the president said, "are a seamless web" which "cause each other . . . reinforce each other." The achievement of Negro equality requires that we understand the mingled "roots of injustice": the isolation of Negroes in our cities, "a world of decay, ringed by an invisible wall . . . which can cripple the youth and desolate the man"; the "burden that a dark skin" adds to the search for productive employment — "eroding hope, which once blighted breeds despair." Added to this is the breakdown of "the Negro family structure" for which "white America must accept responsibility, having imposed the long years of degradation and discrimination which have attacked the Negro man's dignity and assaulted his ability to provide for his family.

"There is no single answer to all of these problems," the president admitted. But there are some answers, partial perhaps, but within our capacity to provide: "Jobs . . . decent homes in decent surroundings . . . an equal chance to learn . . . social programs better designed to hold families together . . . care of the sick . . . an understanding heart."

To these ends, Johnson pledged, "I will dedicate the expanding efforts of the Johnson administration." And because the problems and the means of resolution were not fully comprehended, Johnson announced his intention "this fall . . . to call a White House Conference of scholars, experts . . . Negro leaders . . . and officials of government. The . . . theme and title will be 'To Fulfill These Rights.' "

Old Tom Jefferson would have approved, I reflected, at this obvious play on phrases he had penned almost two centuries earlier. "To secure these rights" — the inalienable rights of man — was not only the purpose, but the soul of government. Jefferson had assumed that, given freedom, an abundant, unmastered continent would provide ample opportunity for fulfillment. And it had. For white men. Now the land was crowded, and strewn with new, unforeseeable obstacles to fulfillment by new claimants to the gifts of "the Creator." But Johnson's theme was always implicit in Jefferson's declaration — rights without opportunity were hollow deceptions, and to compensate the inadequacies of nature, governments were also "instituted among men."

From the Howard assembly I could detect an obscure modulation of mood: Surprise? Certainly. Hope? Perhaps.

"For what is Justice?" the president concluded. "It is to fulfill the fair expectations of man. . . . We have pursued it to the edge of our imperfections, and we have failed to find it for the American Negro.

"It is the glorious opportunity of this generation to end the one huge wrong of the American nation . . . to find America for ourselves with the same immense thrill of discovery which gripped those who first began to realize that here, at last, was a home for freedom.''

After the final enthusiastic applause had died down, Johnson turned and departed the rostrum, enveloped by blue-suited agents of the Secret Service, while I ran rapidly toward the gate and the waiting limousines. This time there would be no anecdotes and whiskey. It was midday and we both had work to do.

The next morning, the president received a telegram from Reverend King which crowned the almost universally favorable press comment. "Never before has a president articulated the depths and dimensions of the problem of racial injustice more eloquently and profoundly. The whole speech evinced amazing sensitivity to the difficult problems that Negro Americans face in the stride toward freedom. It is my hope that all Americans will capture the spirit and content of this great statement.''

That next month, July, the first American combat troops landed in Vietnam.

The August, the Watts ghetto in Los Angeles was set aflame by rioting black youths.

The conference "To Fulfill These Rights" was convened that fall, and, a few days later, adjourned — a total and irretrievable failure.

"It isn't the war," Johnson later said. "We're the wealthiest nation in the world. . . . We need to appeal to everyone to restrain their appetite, to stop running around after everything like dogs chasing their tails. We're greedy but not short of the wherewithal to meet our problems.''

But Lyndon Johnson was wrong. That understanding of men and events, at whose spaciousness I had so often marveled, had reached its limits.

It *was* the war.

19 / Digging the Ditch

> . . . What do you think of the ship *Pequod*, the ship of the soul
> of an American?
> Many races, many peoples, many nations, under the Stars and
> Stripes. Beaten with many stripes.
> Seeing stars sometimes,
> And in a mad ship, under a mad captain, in a mad fanatic's hunt.
> For what?
> For Moby Dick, the great white whale.
> But splendidly handled. Three splendid mates. The whole thing
> practical, eminently practical in its working. American industry!
>
> — D. H. Lawrence,
> *Studies in Classic American Literature*

IF YOU TAKE a great log and set in on end, and if you examine it very closely, you are apt to discover a slight crack across
the end grain, an incipient flaw, sometimes called the "stress point."
If you strike into this line, using a wedge or the beveled side of
sledgehammer, the log will split as if it were a twig.

In the mid-1960s the "stress point" was deep within the hith-
erto-secluded recesses of Lyndon Johnson's mind, the hammer
blow — not a single strike but a multitude of unremitting taps —
the determined ferocity of a multitudinous enemy concealed among
the villages and jungles of South Vietnam. What was broken was
Johnson himself, and along with him, the Great Society, the progress of a nation, the faith of a people, not only in their leadership,
but in the nobility of their destiny to lead a troubled world out of
the wilderness of war and the miseries of almost universal poverty.
For in the single year of 1965 — exactly one hundred years after
Appomatox — Lyndon Johnson reached the height of his leadership and set in motion the process of decline.

* * *

When I joined the White House staff in early 1964, I knew almost nothing about the situation in Southeast Asia, found it difficult even to identify the names of the principal actors in the turbulently shifting governments of Laos and Vietnam — Phouma somebody, Big Minh, Kahn, Little Minh, Tran Van Huong, General Ky — alien labels for men who, as coup followed coup, seemed to play a significant role in the formal governance of nations slowly disintegrating under insurgent assaults. Under Kennedy, my principal interest and concern had been the countries of Latin America. For Johnson I was almost wholly consumed with the development and articulation of domestic policies — the Great Society and civil rights. In 1964 and 1965, as I became the president's principal speechwriter, I did attend meetings of the National Security Council — primarily as an observer, in order to keep abreast of the policy decisions of presidential thinking that had to be accurately reflected in Johnson's addresses. What I did not fully realize, only later came to understand, was that NSC meetings were a charade, convoked to ratify decisions already made by Johnson and his steadily constricting inner circle, and that even this façade was partly fraud — significant information and intentions left undivulged. Thus my own attendance at the larger NSC meetings was of little import, as, even though only a silent onlooker, I became a receptacle of deception, and later, when I understood what was happening, an accomplice.

In the early spring of 1964, a new member of the Johnson "family," I sat alongside the modest swimming pool outside the Johnson home in Texas, accompanied by Valenti, Mrs. Johnson, Liz Carpenter, a secretary or two. (In the Johnson household there were no divisions of position and function in the conduct of daily life. Men of high government rank, secretarial help, family, occasional ranch hands and domestic servants mingled freely beside the pool, ate together at the family dining table presided over by the master of the house.) We watched the president as, borne by an inflatable, he idly drifted across the small patch of water already heated to the temperature of a lukewarm bath by the Texas sun, occasionally paddling toward one of several telephones strategically placed along the concrete sides. Lyndon Johnson was never far from a telephone, the essential instrument of his unremitting energies, to persuade, cajole, control the machinery of government — not as desirable as a face-to-face meeting where you "could look into a man's eyes, and tell what's in his heart," but the next best thing.

Pulling himself from the water, standing for a moment as the chlorinated liquid drained from the voluminous flesh, Johnson took a seat facing me, Valenti seated at his side, the others grouped at various distances, many within our hearing. He had just completed a phone call during which, uncharacteristically, he had listened without making a reply. Obviously disturbed, without preliminaries, he said: "You've got a top-secret clearance, don't you, Dick?" I nodded in affirmation. "Show him that document, Jack," he said to Valenti, who, without hesitation, pulled a memorandum of several pages from a briefcase and handed it to me. It was a report — or the summary of a report — from Robert McNamara, who had just returned from one of his frequent "fact-finding" missions to Vietnam. According to McNamara, the situation in the South Vietnamese countryside was deteriorating, the insurgent Vietcong guerrillas had up to 90 percent control in key Delta provinces, and South Vietnamese sentiment for some form of neutralization was rising. The report did not recommend that the United States bomb North Vietnam, but asked that the National Security Council continue planning for the "contingency" of future bombing. (What I did not know then, but later discovered, was that McNamara had talked with the president before drafting his report and was instructed not to include any bombing recommendation.)

In retrospect, I do not fully understand my lack of alarm at reading the grim report. Perhaps it was that Vietnam did not seem that important to my uninformed awareness. Since the Cuban missile crisis, we had taken important strides toward a peaceful accommodation with the Soviet Union — the test-ban treaty, the disappearance of danger to Berlin, the American University speech, a general lessening of Cold War tensions. I had seen the failure of the Bay of Pigs followed not by falling dominoes, but the gradual defeat of communist or anti-U.S. (it was often hard to tell the difference) insurgencies in Guatemala, Venezuela, and Peru by the indigenous governments and military forces of those countries, with only marginal assistance from the United States. South Vietnam was a troubled spot in a troubled world, and if things were not going well for "our" side there, we were, on balance, doing well in a world that I, and many others, no longer viewed as an arena within which the United States and the Soviet Union were engaged in a remorseless contest; having come to understand that most peoples would seek their own destinies in their own way.

Perhaps, also, my apprehension was dulled by my relative ignorance of Southeast Asia. I did recall, however, and with some puzzlement, that this was the same McNamara who, less than six months before, had returned from Vietnam to assure the American people that "everything was going fine"; that he would be able to withdraw a thousand American advisers by Christmas (that Christmas to come now having become Christmas past); and end the entire American commitment by the end of 1965, having reduced the Vietcong "insurgency to proportions manageable by the government of South Vietnam without the help of U.S. military forces." Wow, I thought, things have really changed.

Or had they? Or was it just the words that had changed?

I handed the document back to Valenti, conscious of the president's intense scrutiny as he searched my face for the reaction whose verbal expression was neither called for nor expected. "Let's go into dinner," he said, rising. "We've got a pecan pie you'll never forget."

I might have been more perturbed had I seen the National Security Action Memorandum (affectionately known as NASAM) based on the McNamara report. Intended as policy guide to carefully restricted departments of the government, the NASAM — undoubtedly drafted by McNamara and National Security Adviser McGeorge Bundy with, perhaps, some help from the ever-elusive Rusk — concluded that if we did not maintain an independent, noncommunist South Vietnam, then "all of southeast Asia" "would probably fall under communist domination (Vietnam, Cambodia, Laos), accommodate to communism" (Burma), "or fall under forces likely to become communist" (Malaysia to be taken over by Indonesia). "Even the Philippines," the memo concluded in language more resonant of rhetoric than analysis, "would become shaky and the threat to India to the west, Australia and New Zealand to the south, and Korea, Taiwan and Japan to the north and east would be greatly increased."

The attribution of such huge consequences to the possible "fall" of South Vietnam, when combined with the McNamara appraisal, conveyed the most ominous implications for future action. The authors, of course, were not simply setting forth the results of careful policy analysis. They were building a case for action founded on the most grotesque exaggeration; on fear, not understanding. At whom was this advocacy aimed? The president, of course. For Johnson had not yet decided how he would deal with the deteriorating situation in Vietnam.

Johnson had shown me — and others — McNamara's report as part of his normal technique of widening the circle of potential sympathy and support for future decisions — if and when they were forced upon him. "The thing in dealing with Congress," he once explained to me, "is to get as many of them as possible involved in making the decisions. If they're with you at the takeoff, they're more likely to be with you at the landing." However, when, much later, Johnson decided to escalate the war, there was almost no preliminary discussion outside a small circle of advisers, no sharing of memoranda, expression of doubts, open consideration of alternatives. Since this curtain of secrecy descended only after the crucial decisions had been made, the president's relative candor on this occasion, his expressions of uncertainty ("They're trying to get me in a war over there"), indicated that the future was still undecided.

Even before my poolside exposure to McNamara's doom-laden projections, on March 2, 1964, the president had called Senator William Fulbright, chairman of the Senate Foreign Relations Committee.

Receiving the president's call in his Senate office, Fulbright began by complimenting Johnson's performance in office. "You're bringing the country through a hard time. And you're doing it magnificently."

Johnson: "I appreciate that, especially coming from you, Bill. You know I told Kennedy you should be his secretary of state. No one better, I said, and history has proved me right." He paused. "Now if we can only get our foreign policy straightened out."

Fulbright: "The most important thing is to get that damn mess in Vietnam straightened out. Any hope?"

Having led Fulbright to initiate the discussion that was the purpose of his call, Johnson began, tentatively, in a lengthy almost-monologue, to lead Fulbright through the ambiguous maze of administration thought.

"Here is the best summary we have . . . the free world is facing an attempt by the communists of North Vietnam to overthrow the noncommunist government of South Vietnam. Our purpose is to help the Vietnamese by providing the training and logistic support they cannot supply themselves. . . . [A]s soon as our mission is complete our troops can be withdrawn."

Up to this point Johnson had merely restated the Kennedy policy. "But, unfortunately," he continued, "in the last four months there have been four changes of government in South Vietnam and the Vietcong have taken advantage of that confusion, and had some success.

"Now the way I see it," Johnson continued, approaching the objective of his call, "there are at least four alternatives open to us. We can withdraw from South Vietnam, and Vietnam will collapse and the ripple effect will be felt all through Asia, endangering independent governments in Thailand, Malaysia, and going as far as India and Indonesia and the Philippines."

("Ripples," which are vulnerable to changes of wind and current, had not yet been replaced by dominoes, whose fall, if they have been meticulously placed, is inexorable. Note also the comparative formality of Johnsonian expression — indicating that he was, in part, reading from a document.)

"Second, we can seek a formula that will neutralize South Vietnam à la Mansfield and de Gaulle, but that will only lead to the same results. . . . We all know the communist attitude that what's mine is mine, what's yours is negotiable . . . the communists would take over.

"Third, we can send in the marines and other U.S. forces against the source of these aggressions," (Did he mean North Vietnam?) "but our men may well be bogged down in a long war. . . .

"Or, fourth, we continue our present policy of providing training and logistical support for South Vietnamese forces. This policy has not failed. We propose to continue it." (Of course he was reading! It must have been some McNamara–Bundy memo, undoubtedly prepared for this very conversation; the language is stilted — the prose of the academic and the accountant.)

The president paused; there were a few moments of silence while Fulbright waited to see if the speech was over.

Fulbright: "I think that's right . . . that's exactly what I'd arrive at under these circumstances, at least for the foreseeable future."

Johnson: "Now I'm sending Bob McNamara over there to see how our policy is working. When he comes back, if we're losing, we've got to decide whether to send them in or whether to come out and let the dominoes fall." (The authentic Johnson was back, the carefully worded document put aside: *If* we're losing, Bill, you've got a choice: go to war or let Asia go to the communists. No "ripples" anymore, them's dominoes.) "That's where the tough one is going to be. And you do some heavy thinking and let's decide what we do." (Yet the McNamara document I had seen had already concluded that we were "losing.")

"Righto," responded Fulbright, ending the "consultation."

It would be a mistake to interpret this conversation as evidence that a decision had already been made. There was no mention of the bombing of North Vietnam, which was, the next year, to be the first major form of escalation. The dire vision of an entire continent, half a world, toppled into the eager arms of enemies by the collapse of the weak, incompetent, and insignificant leadership of a small fragment of Asian jungle was a rote repetition of lessons being taught by men who knew as little about Asia as Johnson himself. Moreover, the technique of argument was typical Johnson, a polemical device designed to make his own position — continuing to increase "advice and assistance" — appear the moderate course between two unacceptable extremes. We could let the communists take over Asia, or we could get into a prolonged land war against oriental multitudes, or we could just do what we were doing, only better — at least for now. If those were the choices, what sensible man would deny the president's wisdom?

Throughout the campaign year of 1964, Johnson resisted the insistent efforts of his foreign-policy advisers to escalate the war. It would, of course, have been bad politics. He was the man of peace in contest with a Republican candidate whose reckless rhetoric had made him appear dangerous — the kind of man who might actually get us into a war. Even McNamara and Bundy came to understand — or were directed — that Vietnam was to be kept under wraps until after the election; they were to plan, do the best they could within the restraints of existing policy, but do nothing to make it appear as if we intended to widen the war.

But it was not just politics, although politics was decisive. Lyndon Johnson honestly did not know what to do. He would not have the glory of his triumphant campaign marred by debates over the wisdom of conflict in Southeast Asia. He had seen the Korean war destroy the Truman administration, and knew, instinctively, profoundly, that his own Great Society — his hope for immortality — might well share the fate of the walls of Jericho assaulted by warrior trumpets.

In the campaign year of 1964 Vietnam was not an issue of any significance. I, and others, traveling with Johnson, drafted dozens of speeches dealing, in whole or in part, with the major issues of foreign policy. Not one was devoted to the conflict in Southeast Asia. The only mention of Vietnam was in occasional phrases or sentences that expressed determination to help our "allies in Southeast Asia" (and the Congo, and the Dominican Republic, and everywhere else) "maintain their independence against communist aggression." This had been our policy, Johnson asserted, since the end of World War II, and remained our policy — to help others help themselves. There was little sign in Johnson's speeches that, like the witches whose duplicitous ambiguity led Macbeth to his doom, McNamara, Rusk, and Bundy, their deliberations cloaked in secrecy, were concocting visionary projects to enlarge the war — revelations to be postponed until after the election. Indeed, the president's speeches were routinely cleared by the panjandrums of foreign policy and defense without the slightest hint that the words that we penned in all sincerity were, at the least, misleading and, in practical effect, a deliberate deception. Admittedly most of the prepared speeches were merely general exhortations on behalf of peace, unexceptionable in themselves, intended to contrast Johnsonian moderation with the reckless war-threatening policies of his opponent. (Of course, the omission of Vietnam was itself a deceit, since it was absolutely clear by mid-1964 that the newly elected president would, almost immediately, face decisions that could lead to a "wider war.")

On October 26, I stood in the audience outside the city hall in Macon, Georgia, as Johnson declaimed to an admiring throng of his fellow southerners: "I think there is but one real issue in this campaign. Who do you think is best able to secure peace in the world." The crowd broke into a spontaneous chant — "LBJ . . . LBJ." (Little more than a year later other crowds in other places would chant, "Hey, Hey, LBJ / How many kids did you kill today?")

In countless discussions with the president, reviewing speech drafts, conversing as we relaxed in the luxury of *Air Force One,* there was not a single word to give me, or others in the traveling campaign, cause to doubt that what we wrote and what the president said might not be a complete and accurate statement of his intentions. And perhaps they were. Certainly Johnson had no desire for war, and, in the complex chambers of his mind, desire and reality, wish and fact, often mingled, subtly interfused, the wish becoming father to the word.

However, those directly involved in the management of our policy in Southeast Asia had other wishes, saw a different reality.

On August 18 of that year, the campaign barely begun, Ambassador Maxwell Taylor, in a secret message to the president, after describing the deterioration in South Vietnam, had said that "something must be added in the coming months" and recom-

mended a sustained campaign of bombing against North Vietnam
to begin, conveniently, around January 1, 1965, after the election.
Undoubtedly Taylor and defense chief McNamara had been encouraged to urge this policy on the president by a recent incident
that had occurred in the Gulf of Tonkin close to the coast of North
Vietnam.

On the evening of August 4, I was working in my White House
office — there are no normal working hours during a presidential
campaign — when Moyers called to tell me that the president was
about to make an important statement. It was after 11 P.M. when
I rushed down to the "fish room" of the White House, where
technicians were already setting up cameras and microphones,
uncoiling the thick black coaxial cables that would transmit the
president's words to those citizens who had not yet gone to bed.

Two days before, on August 2, the president explained, North
Vietnamese PT boats had attacked the destroyer U.S.S. *Maddox,*
which was cruising in international waters close to the Vietnam
coast. Despite our protest, they had, this very day, done it again.
Upon hearing of the assault, and after conferring with his foreign-
policy advisers and congressional leaders, the president had ordered American planes to bomb the PT boat bases, and other
military targets in North Vietnam, in response to this "wholly
unprovoked" action against American ships. It was, he made clear,
a one-shot operation, not the beginning of more extensive bombing: ". . . our response *for the present* [my italics], will be limited
and fitting. We Americans know, although others appear to forget, the risks of spreading conflict. We still seek no wider war."
The president then announced that he would go to Congress for
a resolution retroactively approving his action, and allowing future reprisals against attacks on American forces. What he did not
say, what none of us then realized, was that the resolution would
amount to a virtual declaration of war against North Vietnam,
that its vague phrases would, as interpreted by the White House,
allow the president to do anything he wished in Vietnam without
further approval from either Congress or the people.

Just before his near-midnight appearance in the "fish room,"
Johnson had called his Republican opponent, Barry Goldwater,
and read him the statement he was about to make. "You've got a
good statement, Mr. President," Goldwater replied, "I don't know
what else you can do. I'm sure you'll find everybody behind you.
Like always, Americans will stick together."

"I appreciate that very much, Barry. I just wanted people to know that I had communicated with you on this. Not that you've given me any assurance of full support on my policies, but to make it sound like we're very much together, buddies, and agreeing on the bombing."

"You go right ahead," Goldwater replied, thus effectively taking the Tonkin incident out of the election, despite the fact he had absolutely no independent knowledge of the facts that had led to the reprisal, nor any awareness of these other circumstances in the Gulf of Tonkin, which were, in retrospect, to infuse the president's statement and action with considerable suspicion. But Barry was, as Johnson had often said, a most amiable and obliging man.

As I watched the somewhat frenetic late-night scene in the White House, I felt no sense of apprehension, no ominous forebodings, only a slight amusement at the entrance of Bundy and his aides, their faces and body language alive with a scarcely contained combination of tension and elation. Well, I thought, the old Harvard dean has finally got himself into the campaign. (Only much later did I realize that it wasn't the campaign at all; he'd finally got himself his war.) My reaction may have been unfair. Perhaps the obvious contortions of his lips in order to maintain an expression of appropriate grimness were not a struggle to hide other feelings, but merely a reflection of his indigenous difficulty in openly revealing any emotion at all. The man was a Lowell, after all — on his mother's side.

Like most of the American people, I accepted the occasion as it was made to appear. They had attacked us and we had struck back. Absent further assaults on our ships, the incident was over and the conflict would continue as before. As a politician, I also saw the advantage in Johnson's demonstration that, although he was a man of peace, a believer in negotiation with the Soviet Union, he was no weak, compliant, temporizing appeaser. He was willing to use strength if compelled by events, but not recklessly, not in a way to bring us to the brink of war. By calling Goldwater for approval, and asking for a congressional resolution, he would effectively destroy any Republican argument that he was "soft on communism." That the demonstration took place in the Gulf of Tonkin was, I thought, only adventitious. It could have been Panama or the Dominican Republic.

Although I was unwilling to believe that Johnson had bombed North Vietnam for political reasons, I admired the way he transformed the "necessity" for action into a political coup (in retrospect, a rather ignoble sentiment). My judgment of the politics was accurate (three weeks later, in his acceptance speech before the Democratic National Convention, Johnson did not even think it necessary to mention Vietnam). But the rest of my reaction was totally erroneous — the product of ignorance blended with wishful thinking and dulled perceptions. I didn't know the facts, and completely misunderstood the intentions.

My own failure of comprehension was extended to most of the country when, within forty-eight hours, Secretary McNamara went to testify in support of the Gulf of Tonkin Resolution. His calculated, egregious deception of Congress and, indirectly, the American people, makes the current circumlocutions and outright lies of Poindexter, North, et al. seem like models of honest witness — and on a matter of far greater import than their bungling effort to extricate both hostages and *contras* with a single intercontinental scheme.

First of all, contrary to McNamara's assertions, there was no clear evidence that in the shrouded evening hours of August 2 there had been any attack at all. At a news conference about six weeks later, on September 21, Johnson was asked if the "attacking boats had been torpedo boats." "I think you will have to stay with the announcement that Mr. McNamara gave," Johnson replied, "because . . . it reflects exactly what happened and is about all of the sure information they have. They saw unidentified vessels on their radar, and I don't think I can go beyond that. It is not because I don't want to, but I don't have any additional information." "Hell, boys," Johnson said later in private conversation, "for all I know they could have been shooting at whales out there." Thus Johnson, publicly and privately, distanced himself from the "facts" that had been the sole justification for our bombing. And today, a quarter century later, voluminous research has been unable to demonstrate that there was any "aggression" at all on the evening of August 2. McNamara knew this when he testified, and lied about what he knew — or didn't know. Then, heaping fraud upon fraud, he misrepresented the conditions of combat in the Gulf of Tonkin. Before and during the "attacks" on our destroyers, South Vietnamese PT boats — directed by McNamara and Bundy — had been conducting hit-and-run raids against the North Vietnamese coast. Admitting the raids (but not our direct involvement), McNamara told Congress that the U.S. destroyers, although cruising the same sea lanes as the South

Vietnamese boats, had nothing to do with the raids and the North
Vietnamese knew it. Yet our own radio intercepts, which Mc-
Namara had read, clearly revealed that Hanoi believed our destroyers were part of the combined commando attacks. And well
they might. What better reason for the unusual presence off the
shores of North Vietnam of American destroyers equipped to detect enemy radar?

Thus the "unprovoked" aggression seemed, to those in Hanoi,
a response to equally "unprovoked" assaults by American forces.
McNamara neglected to inform the Congress about the radio intercepts. Indeed, he implied the opposite and, by so doing, established a moral basis for our reprisal. It may well have been true
that the destroyers were not involved. But it didn't look that way
to Hanoi, and we knew it. Indeed, it is likely that the ships had
been sent to the gulf in order to create an impression of U.S.
aggression that would provoke a "counterattack." (Less than two
weeks before the Tonkin incident, Johnson had anticipated that a
"provocation" from North Vietnam might require a "response."
It could have been a rather remarkable coincidence, but it was
the only presidential reference to the possibility of a reprisal during the entire campaign.)

McNamara had a reason for his misstatements and omissions.
They provided the essential foundation for a much larger deception — that the resolution was merely designed to authorize the
president to respond against North Vietnamese attacks on American ships and bases; that it neither represented nor authorized
any significant change in American policy.

Asked by Johnson to manage the resolution on the floor of the
Senate, William Fulbright rejected a "clarifying" amendment by
Senator Gaylord Nelson limiting the American role to advice, support, and training. (In other words, the exact policy we had stated
and pursued for the previous ten years.) Fulbright responded that
he "agreed with Nelson's policy," and that he had talked with the
president and "I understand that's his policy too. But he's afraid
that if we allow one amendment, then we'll get more and more
changes and the whole thing will start to unravel, just when the
president needs an immediate demonstration of support." A not
totally reassured Senator Nelson dropped his effort and the resolution passed with only two dissenting votes.

"The President," the resolution declaimed, was "authorized to
take whatever steps he might deem necessary to combat aggression in Southeast Asia" — aggression to be defined by the president.

On August 6, returning from Capitol Hill, an exultant Mc-Namara called the White House: "On the whole the hearings were very satisfactory," he began in his customary analytical tones, and then, voice rising toward triumph, "it was just near-unanimous support for not only everything you've done to date, but everything you might do in the future, and generally a blank check authorizing any future action — except for this no-win group who doesn't want another Korea."

The calm restraint, the reassurances of peaceful intentions, with which McNamara had deceived the nation, were absent from his report to the president. Now the sky was the limit: bombing, troops, war, devastation, and more war — not yet decided but all possible, pursuant to an act of Congress. Indeed the resolution itself had not been produced by the Gulf of Tonkin. It had been drafted and kept in hiding for a propitious moment, a time when it could be made a test of national unity. There had been other attacks on American forces. Frogmen had actually blown up an American ship in the Saigon harbor less than three months before. But you couldn't bomb a frogman, not unless you were the Olympic champion of precision bombing. And so the resolution rested among the secret files, until, on August 2, 1964, something happened, might have happened, could be made to appear as if it had happened — and the planes flew, the bombs fell, and the Congress bowed.

Now Johnson had his blank check. But how was it to be used? It was one thing to fool the Congress. No one could do it better. But bombing raids and combat forces could not be hidden in a White House desk. Moreover, Johnson had not yet decided to act, was profoundly, justly afraid that escalation would only lead toward the wider war he so desperately wanted to avoid. Yet the time of painful decision was approaching. And he knew it. But not yet. There was still time. Saigon could hold out for a while. And there was a campaign to be fought, a clear path to the most glorious victory of a lifetime in politics. So he carefully folded up the check, put it in his back pocket, uncompleted, and took to the trail where the admiring love of millions awaited.

If Vietnam had been a minor issue before the Gulf of Tonkin, now it virtually disappeared from view. Those of us drafting speeches felt no compulsion to discuss it, nor were we encouraged to do so by the Panglossian memos that were wafted to the campaign entourage from the foreign-policy cabal in Washington. From mid-August to the end of October, in five different press conferences, Johnson was not asked a single question about Vietnam, and when, on October 3, we released a lengthy litany of accomplishments by the Eighty-eighth Congress, the Tonkin Resolution was not on the list.

There were a few exceptions: Occasionally Johnson, departing from his prepared text, would ad lib a minuscule dissertation — no more than a few sentences — concerning Vietnam policies. I did not hear these interpositions, being far too busy working on the next speech to listen to one already completed and approved. Nor were the president's remarks sufficiently significant to merit more than an occasional reference appended to the final paragraphs of daily newspaper accounts, being interpreted as nothing more than the reaffirmation of long-standing U.S. policy — which, indeed, they seemed to be, except for the unnoticed implication that far different policies already were being discussed in the high councils of government. Before a crowd in Stonewall, Texas, where he had gone to celebrate his birthday, Johnson told his fellow Texans that "I have had advice to load our planes with bombs and drop them on certain areas that I think would enlarge the war . . . and result in committing a good many American boys to fighting a war that I think ought to be fought by the boys of Asia to help protect their own land. And for that reason, I haven't chosen to enlarge the war." (Exactly the advice he would eventually follow and with the precise results he had verbally anticipated.)

On September 25, in Eufala, Oklahoma, Johnson told his audience, "There are those that say you ought to go north and drop bombs, to try to wipe out the supply lines, and they think that would escalate the war. We don't want our American boys to do the fighting for Asian boys. We don't want to get involved in a nation with 700 million people and get tied down in a land war in Asia. . . . [W]e are not about to start another war and we're not about to run away from where we are."

Nothing newsworthy in that. Although a few weary reporters, bent half-sleeping over typewriters and note pads, might have been shocked into more alert postures if they had known that "those that say you ought to go north" were not the nefarious Goldwater gang, but Johnson's own most highly placed advisers. As for the seven hundred million people, why there were nowhere near that many people in Vietnam. There was China of course; they had at least that many. And no one was pressing for a war with China.

But, after all, everyone knew that Lyndon was prone to occasional flights of hyperbole. And what difference did it make: seven million people, seventy million, seven hundred million? The point was clear enough. We weren't going to war with Asians. The exaggeration could be safely ignored.

Yet something was on Johnson's mind, something different from the reiteration of policy clichés, and, occasionally, it came to the surface. I didn't notice it at the time; neither did his audiences or the ever-attentive press. Only years later, reading the campaign transcripts as illuminated by the catastrophic events that were to follow, did I realize that Johnson, in his own obscure way, was trying to hint at the truth — not obviously enough to cause a political furor, but enough to make a record. Here are a few examples, with the significant phrases italicized to assist the reader who might not be as close a student of Johnsonian rhetoric.

In the middle of a news conference on July 24, following a lengthy reaffirmation of existing policy in Vietnam, just eleven days before our reprisal raid at the Gulf of Tonkin, this sentence appears: "It is true that there is danger and provocation from the North, and *such provocation could force a response,* but it is also true that the United States seeks no wider war."

On September 28, after Tonkin had, temporarily, passed into history, Johnson told the Weekly Editors Association in Manchester, New Hampshire, "Some of our people — Mr. Nixon, Mr. Rockefeller, Mr. Scranton and Mr. Goldwater — have all . . . suggested the possibility of going north in Vietnam." (Thus, by the simple expedient of listing the major Republican leaders — except Ike, of course, for Eisenhower paid attention to these things and might get mad — Johnson transformed the urgent, and still secret, counsel of his own advisers into bipartisan counsel.) "Well, before you start attacking someone," the president continued, "you better give consideration to how you are going to protect what you have." (Whatever that meant. But if the content is obscure, a non sequitur, the political logic was plain — the candidate of caution against the reckless.) "So," Johnson concluded his enigmatic syllogism, "*just for the moment* I have not thought we were ready for American boys to do the fighting for Asian boys. . . . We are not going north and drop bombs at *this stage of the game,* and we're not going south and run out and leave it for the communists to take over."

By the time of the Manchester speech, "this stage of the game"

was almost done. Indeed, reports to Johnson indicated that the
game itself was almost over as the Vietcong tightened their encir-
clement of major population centers in the south; while continual,
comic-opera overturns in the government of South Vietnam stripped
that doomed country of whatever political stability it possessed.
Taylor, followed by McNamara, and then, more reluctantly, by
Rusk and Bundy, joined in urging that something be done, anything — bombing, troops — to stave off collapse. The South Vietnamese could no longer fight their own war. They needed our
help, and more than help; they needed an ally to fight beside them.
And in all the world, we were the only candidate.

Decision could be postponed. The South Vietnamese could hold
out at least until the end of 1964. But not much longer. Thus,
Johnson, almost as soon as he was elected, would confront the
choice that both Eisenhower and Kennedy had considered and
rejected, that he himself had pledged to oppose, had not yet decided to make, but knew — even as he promised the electorate to
honor the carefully hedged commitments of his predecessors — he
must swiftly decide: Whether the war of the Vietnamese should
be transformed into an American war.

However, all this is the wisdom of hindsight. I had no forebodings of danger as I sat in my West Wing office at the turning of
the year preparing the 1965 State of the Union address for the
newly elected president. That speech was a spacious, unequivocal
call to a Great Society — the elimination of poverty, the movement toward an already visible "summit where freedom from the
wants of the body can help fulfill the needs of the spirit," which
"will require of every American, for many generations, both faith
in the destination and the fortitude to make the journey." In that
entire lengthy address, only 132 words were devoted to the conflict in Vietnam, and that was basically a boilerplate reiteration
of our commitment to "help against the communist aggression."
There was no note of alarm, no hint that a crucial decision to
enlarge the war was already on the president's desk, being ardently urged on the president by McNamara, Bundy, and members of the Joint Chiefs of Staff. Yet the speech had been seen and
approved without comment by State, Defense, and the national
security adviser.

After the president had delivered this hugely successful oration
to a cheering Congress, he, his staff, and the many guests invited

by Johnson to witness his moment of triumph went to the F Street Club for a celebration. As I walked up the steps toward the entrance, a towering Texan, resplendent in custom boots, specially acquired for the occasion from the famous Tony Lama, and wearing a white "ten gallon" hat, leaned down and touched me on the shoulder. "Great stuff, hey, boy, no more of that Ivy League stuff." Of course he didn't know me, was merely expressing his irrepressible ebullience at this ultimate triumph over the Yankee establishment. "That's right," I replied, "it's the real thing," my suppressed amusement accompanied by a sense of professional pride that my evocation of the "harsh caliche soil" and "angular hills" of Johnson's country which ended the speech (and would be referred to, somewhat sardonically, by my colleagues as the Pedernales peroration) had so effectively obscured the Boston-cum-Harvard origins of the author.

If in January of 1965 I knew almost nothing about the struggle in Vietnam, as the year progressed events compelled attention. But not enough. I was preoccupied with the formation of domestic policies, and much of my heightened awareness was distorted by the fact that my views were shaped from within the White House — attendance at high-level meetings, private conversations with Bundy, McNamara, et al., access to daily intelligence reports — where information as well as opinion was increasingly concentrated toward a single focus, where facts and analysis were shaped not to guide policy, but to justify it.

During this period I helped draft a few presidential statements concerning Vietnam, including one major address delivered at Johns Hopkins University on April 7, 1965. Those statements contained assertions of American interest and commitment stronger and more categorical than my own convictions. When drafting a speech, it was my job to give voice to the judgment of the president, not to substitute my views for those of the man elected to lead the nation. Writing a presidential speech is a political act, and like all politics involves the need for accommodation. Occasionally the discrepancy between administration policy and personal convictions may become so large that the dissident staffer feels compelled to resign. But such occasions are rare. As long as one is in basic sympathy with the goals of presidential policy, it is possible to serve loyally, even enthusiastically, despite differences on particular matters. In 1965, although increasingly restive at the course of events in Vietnam, I was engaged in the formation of those

Great Society programs in which I deeply believed, and which
were then the centerpiece and overriding goal of the Johnson administration. Thus, acting at the direction of the president and
those to whom he had delegated authority (McNamara, Bundy,
Rusk) I incorporated rhetoric into Vietnam statements which I
found excessively militant, extravagant in their assertion of the
American interest. I could, of course, have refused and made my
departure. But at this time — in the spring and summer of 1965 —
I thought the conflict in Vietnam a transient aberration, our military activities merely a prelude to some form of negotiated solution. Indeed, on occasion, in private conversations and in a few
memos, I told Johnson of my concerns about the escalation, suggested a diminution of our military effort and the more vigorous
pursuit of what then appeared a willingness by Hanoi to discuss
a peaceful negotiated solution. In retrospect, it became apparent
that my counsel was naïve, little more than wishful thinking; that
from midsummer 1965 forward we were bent on using military
force to impose a permanent division on that war-riven country.
But that course, and the plans for future enlargement of the war,
were known to only a handful. It certainly was not obvious, or
even visibly probable, in 1965. So I carried out my professional
responsibility to express the rationale for war, and our intention
to carry on the conflict until the freedom of South Vietnam was
secure — in terms framed by the president and his highest advisers.

Only after I left the White House, in the fall of 1965, did the
war become an increasing personal preoccupation, as I realized
that it was not only destroying the high promise of the early sixties, but wreaking perhaps irrecoverable damage on the fabric of
American society — assaulting not only our present but the future
as well. Liberated from the obscuring vanities and fears of power,
motivated by my own growing passions, I came to understand
what was happening in Southeast Asia — the appalling, self-
destructive futility of our actions.

"You know what the real problem is, Dick?" Johnson asked in
mid-1965 as criticism of his policies was mounting.

"No, Mr. President," I replied, "I don't."

"It's that everybody in America thinks they know everything
about everything, like Vietnam. They don't realize that the leaders are the ones who've got the secrets, and that's something they
should respect."

Later, having been driven from the presidency, Johnson told a friend that "sometimes I wish I was Catholic. I like the Catholics because they've got authority. They're never in doubt. They may be wrong but they're never in doubt. They accept direction. Not like America where the followers think they know more about important things than the leaders, the Catholic followers respect their leaders. Their leaders have the secrets and the followers respect the mysteries." It was, as Johnson must have known, a grotesquely idealized view of the Catholic faithful, the description of some medieval Vatican fantasy, but it was an accurate insight into the mind of Lyndon Johnson, where the claim that "leaders have the secrets" was readily transposed into "having secrets is necessary to leadership."

Both statements — that of 1965 and that which came later — disclose a crippling self-deception. There were no significant secrets in Vietnam, except for those the leaders chose to conceal from themselves. Once outside the White House, I was far freer to listen to the voices of informed and reasoned dissent, better able to form a clear picture of the historical realities and present conditions that were the confining matrix of our war in Vietnam.

20 / The Impossible War

Half a league, half a league, half a league onward.

— Alfred Tennyson,
"The Charge of the Light Brigade"

IT WAS CALLED "Operation Rolling Thunder." Initiated by Johnson within a month of his inauguration, the bombing of North Vietnam would be the largest sustained campaign of aerial attack in the history of warfare. For the United States it marked the entrance into a war that would widen to unforeseen, staggering dimensions. For the Vietnamese it marked another stage in a war that — with occasional interruptions — had gone on for almost twenty years.

The events in Vietnam that preceded the escalation of 1965 are not properly part of this account of my personal experience during the sixties. Yet a generation has passed since the bombs began to fall on North Vietnam. Many of the facts so widely known and discussed at the time — so firmly embedded in my own memory — might well be unknown or only obscurely recalled by the reader of 1988. Yet the events I witnessed, the opinions I formed, my own actions and response, cannot be fully understood without awareness of what preceded.

At the end of World War II, after the Japanese had been driven from Indochina, the French returned to reoccupy their former colonial possessions. In 1946 — three years before Mao Tse-tung had conquered China — Ho Chi Minh, himself a communist, organized and led the opposition to French rule. The war against the French lasted for eight years, until, in 1954 — with the collapse of the French stronghold at Dien Bien Phu — it culminated in victory for Ho Chi Minh. Twenty-five thousand Frenchmen had perished in the futile effort to maintain a colonialism that was being ended or destroyed throughout the third world.

On the eve of defeat, the French asked President Eisenhower for direct American intervention. He refused. "Ike sent General Ridgway and me to evaluate the situation on the ground," I was later told by General James Gavin, hero of the airborne assaults that preceded the Allied invasion of Europe. "When we returned, Ike asked us what we thought. Ridgway told him that intervention was a political decision, but he could give an opinion of the military situation. 'If we do go in, air strikes won't do the job. The war has to be won on the ground. To fight a ground war I would need to begin with a few divisions, building to a strength of several hundred thousand men fairly quickly. And even then I can't guarantee victory.' " If there had been any doubt in Eisenhower's mind, it was dissolved by this report from the general who had led our forces in Korea, and whose bravery, integrity, and honesty of judgment were beyond question.

"No one could be more bitterly opposed to ever getting involved in a hot war in the region than I am," Eisenhower said in February of 1954. "I could not conceive of a greater tragedy for America than to get heavily involved now in an all-out war in any of these regions, particularly with large units." Admittedly the United States had supplied the French with over 2.5 billion dollars of military and economic assistance, almost 80 percent of the French war effort. But the war was lost. Facts were facts. We would just have to write off our losses. Eisenhower was a realist.

In that decisive year of 1954, with the French approaching defeat and American intervention still a possibility, two men who were to direct the unfolding Asian drama of the sixties spoke in opposition to their country's involvement.

"No amount of American military assistance in Indochina," said Senator John Kennedy in April of 1954, "can conquer an enemy which is everywhere and at the same time nowhere, 'an enemy of the people' which has the sympathy and covert support of the people."

Around the same time, Senate Minority Leader Lyndon Johnson, summoned by John Foster Dulles in a frantic effort to assure bipartisan support for an American intervention, told the secretary of state that he could not support any military action that did not have the full support and assistance of our allies. It was, of course, an impossible condition. Our allies had no intention of companioning us into the Asian jungles. But it was shrewd politics. Johnson had not actually refused support, but he had avoided becoming an accomplice. The memory of Korea — the "Democratic war," which had helped elect Eisenhower — was still fresh. This time, if we were going to fight, he would let it be a "Republican war."

Once the possibility of U.S. intervention was foreclosed, the game was over for France. Ho Chi Minh could not be defeated. The best the French could hope for would be a long and probably losing war of attrition against Asian multitudes. Somewhat pompously we instructed the French that no military victory was possible in Vietnam unless a "proper political atmosphere" was established. "A proper political atmosphere!" Hidden in that abstraction, its inward meaning, was the key to French failure and to failures yet to come. Effective opposition to communist insurgency could come only from a people who had a stake in their own society, faith in their own future, a sense of allegiance, an identity of interests with their own government — enough so that they would fight and risk their lives for its preservation. The French commanded no such loyalty and belief, and neither, in the end, did we or the governments we selected and sustained.

A peace conference was called in Geneva to ratify the French withdrawal. Vietnam was "temporarily" divided in two at the seventeenth parallel, pending "elections of national unification" to be held in 1956. The elections never took place. According to a State Department White Paper of 1961, "It was the communists' calculation that nationwide elections scheduled in the accords for 1956 would turn all of South Vietnam over to them. . . . The authorities of South Vietnam refused to fall into this well-laid trap." The truth was probably not quite so bald; neither side trusted the other to conduct fair elections.

Now there were two Vietnams: the one in the north led by Ho Chi Minh, and that to the south under the noncommunist, but equally dictatorial, Ngo Dinh Diem. Over a million Catholics fled from the North to the protection of the Catholic Diem. Most of the southerners who had fought in Ho Chi Minh's war of liberation remained in their native towns and villages.

Immediately after the Geneva Conference, Eisenhower offered military and economic assistance to the Diem government, conditioned on the political and economic reforms that would create the elusive "proper political atmosphere." This was the famous "Eisenhower commitment" so often cited by Johnson. It contained no promise to come to the military defense of South Vietnam against any armed threat. Nor were the reforms made. The conditions of Eisenhower's carefully limited pledge were not met. Indeed, over the years that followed, the Diem regime became even more repressive. As late as 1966, 70 percent of the tenant farmers in the rich Delta area of the South were forced to pay more than half their rice crops to absentee landlords. Political opponents were persecuted, as were the institutions of the Buddhist faith held by a large proportion of the population. The South rapidly became a virtual fiefdom, run for the benefit of an oligarchy, its population and, ultimately, its government hostage to a military establishment fed and strengthened by U.S. aid.

In the late 1950s the insurgency began again, this time directed not against the French but the government of South Vietnam; and in 1960 the communists, henceforth referred to as the Vietcong, formed the National Liberation Front to "liberate" South Vietnam. Although Ho Chi Minh encouraged the front, offered it small amounts of assistance and undoubtedly provided considerable direction, almost all the Vietcong was initially composed of native southerners. Even as late as 1964, after large portions of the country had fallen under the rule of the Vietcong, the Pentagon itself estimated that only about 15 percent of the material needs of the Vietcong, and an even smaller proportion of the fighting forces, came from the North. (Although this estimate was probably no more accurate than other Pentagon assessments of enemy forces.)

Confronted by the growing communist insurgency in South Vietnam, Kennedy reaffirmed the Eisenhower "commitment," only on a larger scale. More money. More weapons. More "advisers." In addition, rejecting the uncreative lethargy of the Eisenhower years, we — i.e., we New Frontiersmen for whom "God's work on earth" would "truly be our own" — worked to develop new and innovative techniques of "nation-building." We would encourage or compel "liberal reforms," teach new techniques of "counterinsurgency," create "strategic hamlets" — fortified villages where the South Vietnamese could be protected from Vietcong attacks. The result of this monstrously misconceived policy was to disrupt the fundamental structure of village life — the backbone of Vietnamese life — and provide the communists with convenient and easily identifiable targets. However, although Kennedy dangerously increased the magnitude of American involvement, he did not change the nature and purpose of our commitment: to assist the evolution of a South Vietnamese society strong enough, sufficiently united in purpose, loyalty, and belief, to overcome the attack from within. In other words, to establish the "proper political atmosphere."

Admittedly the line between participation and assistance became thinner, more obscure, as the magnitude of our effort increased. But Kennedy was always careful to draw it. At the end of 1961 Maxwell Taylor, returning from a visit to Vietnam, urged the president to send combat troops — eight thousand at once, and more "if needed," to be accompanied by American bombing of North Vietnam, which "could be exploited diplomatically to persuade Hanoi to lay off South Vietnam." McNamara enthusiastically supported the Taylor report with the caveat that eight thousand troops would not be enough, but that we could "safely assume the maximum U.S. forces required on the ground will not exceed six divisions or about 250,000 men." (His estimate is an illustration of the wondrously alluring technique of giving a numerical value to a guess derived from speculation informed by ignorance and fueled by desire. But military men, like economists, are easily seduced by the security of statistics and, invariably, when the numbers don't "work" [i.e., halt or defeat the enemy], simply change their "quantitative estimates" without challenging the assumptions on which error was built, a technique that may be useful in the war games room of the Pentagon but is not so serviceable in a real war.)

Kennedy rejected the Taylor and McNamara recommendations: in 1961 when he received them, and later when they were renewed. He would increase "assistance," but he said, and repeated in the fall of 1963, "It is their war. They have to win it or lose it." Like Eisenhower before him, he was willing to help the South Vietnamese, but not to do their fighting for them.

The hope that our assistance might enable the South Vietnamese to defeat the communist insurgents was not wholly the delusory product of wishful thinking. Communist insurgencies in Greece, Malaya, the Philippines, and, later, in Venezuela, Peru, and Guatemala were beaten back by indigenous forces strengthened with U.S. aid. But this was South Vietnam — a war-torn, divided, impoverished country whose leadership was dedicated to its own power and wealth. The "proper political atmosphere" did not exist — as it had existed in other countries that successfully resisted communist overthrows — as it had not existed in Batista's Cuba or Somoza's Nicaragua. You can build up the strength of an undernourished, uncertain, but determined athlete. You cannot transform a hopeless cripple into an Olympic medal winner.

Kennedy's policy was doomed. And it was also dangerous. By increasing the number of American advisers from six hundred to around sixteen thousand, the Americanization of Vietnam was accelerated, the likelihood that Americans would come under attack was increased, and the credibility of the government in Saigon — the perception of its independence — was undermined, increasing the ability of the Vietcong to attract adherents for their "war of liberation."

Yet a mistaken policy is not a new policy. In later years Johnson and others in his administration would assert that they were merely fulfilling the commitment of previous American presidents. The claim was untrue — even though it was made by men, like Bundy and McNamara, who were more anxious to serve the wishes of their new master than the memory of their dead one. During the first half of 1965 I attended meetings, participated in conversations, where the issues of escalation were discussed. Not once did any participant claim that we had to bomb or send combat troops because of "previous commitments," that these steps were the inevitable extension of past policies. They were treated as difficult and serious decisions to be made solely on the basis of present conditions and perceptions. The claim of continuity was reserved for public justification; intended to conceal the fact that a major policy change was being made — that "their" war was becoming "our" war.

It is possible that Kennedy might have made the same judgments: No one can know that. But the fact is that he did not make them. The decision to transform the war would be President Johnson's decision, and his alone.

By the beginning of 1965, that decision had become urgent. Six months earlier, in June of 1964, George Ball had informed French President Charles de Gaulle that "the situation was clearly fragile and the government [of South Vietnam] weak. . . . If there was no improvement in the situation and the problem of insurgency was not resolved within a reasonable time, we would be required to bring increasing military pressures on Hanoi in order to change the communists' course of action."

"I take note of your hope," de Gaulle replied, "that you can suppress the insurgency by supplying Vietnam with arms, credits and military advice, but I cannot agree with it. I do not believe you can win in this situation. . . ." Then he added, prophetically, that even if we used our own forces, "The United States might maintain the struggle for an extended period of time . . . but you cannot bring the affair to an end."

Ball's report arrived at the White House, was read, scorned, and discarded. "Now, that de Gaulle," Johnson told a staff meeting in late 1964. "All we can do is turn the other cheek and say that the Good Lord forgive him for he knows not what he does." Yet de Gaulle had only said what American leaders had asserted for a decade, that without a "proper political atmosphere" in South Vietnam — an atmosphere that was, by now, impossible to create — the war would be lost.

Moreover, de Gaulle's judgment that no amount of assistance and advice, no new "counterinsurgency" techniques, would arrest the communist advance, was already shared by many among the inner councils of American strategy. And the events of 1964 strengthened that conviction, as the communists rapidly increased their hold on the country, encircled the urban centers. The South Vietnamese government was on the edge of defeat. Unless something was done, and quickly. (De Gaulle's equally accurate judgment that even the use of American combat forces would not result in victory was, as we all know, ignored or rejected.)

Sitting on the president's desk in January of 1965 were urgent recommendations that we launch large-scale air strikes against North Vietnam to prevent the imminent collapse of South Vietnamese resistance. Yet Johnson still hesitated. "I have never felt the war will be won from the air," Johnson cabled Ambassador Maxwell Taylor in January. "What is needed is more effective strength on the ground." Alone among the inner circle, Johnson was a politician. He understood that bombing North Vietnam, the unconcealable use of American military force, would have a large and unpredictable impact on American opinion, might even endanger the Great Society, which was to be his claim to historical greatness.

"I knew from the start," Johnson later said to Doris Kearns when he was working on his memoirs, "that I was bound to be crucified either way I moved. If I left the woman I really loved — the Great Society — in order to get involved with that bitch of a war on the other side of the world, then I would lose everything at home. All my programs. All my hopes to feed the hungry and shelter the homeless. All my dreams to provide education and medical care to the browns and the blacks and the lame and the poor. But if I left that war and let the communists take over . . . then I would be seen as a coward and my nation would be seen as an appeaser. . . . Oh, I could see it coming all right. . . . Once the war began, then all those conservatives in Congress would use it as a weapon against the Great Society. . . . Oh, I could see it coming. And I didn't like the smell of it. . . . I think the situation in South Vietnam bothered me most. They never seemed able to get themselves together down there. Always fighting with one another. Bad. Bad.

"Yet everything I knew about history" (which was very little) "told me that if I got out of Vietnam and let Ho Chi Minh run through the streets of Saigon, then I'd be doing exactly what Chamberlain did in World War II. . . . [T]here would follow in this country . . . a mean and destructive debate that would shatter my presidency . . . and damage our democracy. . . . And Robert Kennedy would be right out in front leading the fight against me, telling everyone that I had betrayed John Kennedy's commitment to South Vietnam; that I had let a democracy fall into the hands of the communists; that I was a coward, an unmanly man. Oh, I could see it coming all right."

Johnson was, of course, speaking five years after he had chosen the path of escalation, his description inevitably distorted by the deeply felt necessity of justification — the desire to make his decision seem the inevitable consequence of an irreconcilable dilemma. But even in 1965 he knew or believed some of this; realized that the war might endanger his presidency, although, then, unlike 1970, he undoubtedly hoped that the experts were right, that victory was possible, and that a triumph in Vietnam might leave him stronger, his prospects brighter, than before.

Robert McNamara had no such doubt. America was not his business. Managing the machinery of war was his business. "Bob's greatest concern at the beginning of 1965," one of McNamara's closest personal aides later told me, "was his fear that he might not be able to talk the president into the bombing. He spent all his time preparing arguments and lining up allies." McNamara also omitted — even from his memoranda to the president — discussion of the most unpleasant reality of all: that bombing would almost inevitably lead to the use of American troops in combat. Johnson didn't want to hear about combat troops — didn't want to be told that he might have to send American boys to fight for

Asian boys — and so, in deference to the president's sensibilities, McNamara struck from his analysis virtually all references to ground troops, even implied, falsely, that the bombing might reduce or eliminate the need for combat forces.

Yet the opposite was true. At a minimum American troops would be needed to guard the air bases and installations from which the raids would be launched. (It was inconceivable that the security of our air force would be entrusted to the unreliable soldiers of South Vietnam.) Moreover, the war was being fought and lost in the South, and no bombing of the North could — at least in the short run — stem the steady advance of the communists. Indeed, the CIA and military planners at the Pentagon had already concluded that if we bombed North Vietnam, the initial effect would be the movement of still more North Vietnamese troops into the South; thus increasing the need for American combat forces. Yet these "pessimistic" judgments were ignored or discounted by the advocates of bombing. Nor did McNamara incorporate into his flow of briefs a study by the policy-planning counsel of the State Department, which concluded that "bombing would not work; that Hanoi would not come to the conference table while U.S. bombs were falling on its territory; that the stakes would be raised making the conflict in South Vietnam a far larger and more important issue; and making the South Vietnamese government more dependent on the United States," thus weakening its hold on the society it purported to rule.

Rational and accurate analysis, however, had begun to dissolve under the corrosive reports of rapid deterioration in South Vietnam. The Vietcong were gradually swallowing up the countryside; the government in Saigon was virtually incapable of effective resistance or leadership.

On January 17, McNamara and Bundy joined in a memorandum to Johnson saying that "the time has come for harder choices." They admitted that Dean Rusk was still hesitant, that he had told them that the "consequences of escalation and withdrawal are so bad that we must simply find a way of making our present policy work." Having fairly stated this nonopinion by the secretary of state, Bundy commented, "This would be good if it were possible. Bob and I do not think it is." In other words, the Eisenhower policy, the Kennedy policy, and, until then, the Johnson policy had failed. (And Rusk would soon come to share this opinion, join in recommendations to escalate the war.)

In February, to give added weight to his already-fixed opinion, Bundy went to South Vietnam. While he was there, on February 7, the Vietcong attacked the American base at Pleiku. In a fifteen-minute assault nineteen helicopters and eight aircraft were damaged or demolished, eight American soldiers were killed and over a hundred wounded. Visiting Pleiku, McGeorge Bundy saw the face of war. From the tranquil, ordered offices in Washington, out of the polite debates around the highly polished conference table, had issued the carefully drafted directives that, upon arrival in Vietnam, were shockingly metamorphosed into real bodies, real blood, the audible moans of injured men. Bundy was horrified. We had to do something, he reported. We couldn't just sit by. Our boys were dying in their tents. "We had to do something."

"That Bundy," Johnson later said, "all it took was a little taste of blood to turn him into a real hawk." The president was being unfair. Bundy was already a hawk, but the sight of Pleiku had undoubtedly added a dimension of intensity to his convictions. No longer just a question of policy, it was a matter of honor and revenge.

One wonders what Bundy thought had been happening in Vietnam. For decades people had been dying in an interminable conflict; the entire country was one immense groan of pain. Could he possibly have thought that Americans who joined this struggle might be immune to its devastations? Almost twenty thousand U.S. troops were already in Vietnam. Their purpose was to help kill the Vietcong insurgents. The helicopters at Pleiku had already participated in combat missions against communist forces. Did he think — could anyone have thought — that the endangered enemy would not fight back?

On his way back from Vietnam, having recovered some of his composure, Bundy sent a calmer — but not more reasonable — message. He urged a program of "sustained reprisal" (i.e., the all-out, unrestricted bombing of North Vietnam). "We cannot assert," he wrote, "that [such] a policy will succeed in changing the course of the contest in Vietnam. It may fail . . . even if it fails, the policy will be worth it. At a minimum it will damp down the charge that we did not do all we could."

And so, because "something had to be done" so that, at the very least, we could avoid the charge that "we did not do all we could," on February 13, 1965, Johnson launched American crews into the dangerous skies, to begin the raids that would, before

they ended, drop more tons of explosives than the air armadas of
World War II.

When the raids began I did not foresee — perhaps no one
foresaw — that we had taken our first step toward a long and
bloody war. Had the consequence been known — that in three
years more than half a million Americans would be fighting in
Southeast Asia, that almost a hundred thousand would be dead
or wounded, and that we would still not be close to the end of
what was to be the longest war in American history — public resistance might well have forced a drastic reconsideration of our
commitments and policy in Southeast Asia. That, of course, is
exactly what Johnson and his inner advisers did not want. So they
refused to admit the possibility, the likelihood, of widening war,
even to themselves, as they took the gradual steps that led inevitably from a minor skirmish on the edge of American empire toward
a conflict that would transform Vietnam into a burial ground for
a multitude of Americans and Vietnamese, and for the soaring
hopes of the sixties.

Failing to perceive the bombing for what it was — a prelude to
a war on the ground — Moyers and I drafted a memorandum to
the president explaining that the most threatening consequence of
the bombing (for Americans, of course, not the Vietnamese on
whom the bombs were falling) was that it "had escalated the war
to the front pages of every newspaper," thus diverting public attention from the far-reaching programs of the Great Society,
threatening "to undermine the consensus on which domestic progress depended."

We received no reply. Ordinarily the president would take staff
memoranda to his bedroom in the mansion at the close of the day
in a folder marked "Evening Reading" and the next morning they
would be returned to the writer with a presidential comment or
order scrawled on the bottom of the page. With the memorandum
on the bombing, as with later expressions of opinion regarding
Vietnam (at least from me), there was no answer; the documents
simply disappeared: read, undoubtedly, but not answered. In April,
after the president delivered the speech at Johns Hopkins that I
had helped draft, I wrote additional memoranda to the president
suggesting that we should attend a scheduled conference on Cambodia, "and transmit to Hanoi privately the word that we come
prepared to discuss larger issues. . . . The basic assumption is
that we want to get the war to the conference table. We do not

know if Hanoi is willing to negotiate, but we want to make it as easy for them to do so as possible. . . . By slowing down the bombing you allow them to talk without looking as if they are being bombed into submission." It was not a "dovish" memorandum — advocated neither withdrawal nor complete cessation of air attacks — merely what I believed to be a practical approach to the quest for a negotiated settlement which I then mistakenly believed was the American goal. This memo, like the others, received no response. On this subject there was to be no exchange of views, no dialogue, as if the president had closed himself off from discordant thoughts, made of Vietnam a sacred subject whose discussion was limited to a tiny priesthood of the anointed participants in the mysteries of war.

Before "Operation Rolling Thunder" ended, thousands of raids were flown, hundreds of thousands were killed, villages destroyed, factories and power plants turned into rubble. And all to no avail. The stream of men and supplies from North Vietnam to the South increased, just as the CIA and the Pentagon had predicted. McNamara himself finally admitted the failure of his military policy when, in 1967, he told a congressional committee that "I don't believe that bombing . . . has significantly reduced, nor any bombing that I could contemplate in the future would significantly reduce the flow of men and material to the South."

Nor, as State Department policymakers had warned, did the bombing force Hanoi to negotiate a settlement. Quite the contrary. They had already fought for twenty years, sustained immense damage, would not now be forced into concessions under a rain of enemy bombs; especially after they had discovered that they could easily survive the bombing. Most of the country was rural, and craters blown into jungle and farmland were readily filled, while the destruction of some of their primitive industrial plants was more than compensated by increased aid from China and the Soviet Union. Before the escalation began, the fear of American power — the unlimited, advanced weaponry of the strongest nation on earth — might have persuaded Hanoi to make some kind of compromise. Once our power was loosed and survived, that possibility disappeared, destroyed by Hanoi's knowledge that they could endure and continue despite the American attacks. We had behaved like a kidnapper who shoots the hostage in order to prove he is serious about ransom.

* * *

Just nine days after the bombing had begun, Westmoreland asked for troops to protect the air bases, and, on March 8, two marine battalions — the first combat troops to arrive as units — began to wade ashore at Da Nang, arriving just seven days before Johnson was to proclaim "we shall overcome" to an admiring nation. The predictable, the foreseeable, the inevitable had begun. Now that the war was an American war, "American boys" would have "to do the fighting for Asian boys," because the Asian boys — the ones on our side — were losing, and now their loss would be our loss too. At least the president and his closest advisers thought so.

It was, as everyone knows, only the beginning. I was present at a National Security Council meeting on April 1, convened to consider Westmoreland's request for seventeen more battalions. He was given only two. But, far more importantly, the new troops were not restricted to guarding bases; they were authorized to go into the countryside after the enemy in what were called "search and destroy" missions. Americans would engage the enemy in the South. Although the numbers were carefully, arbitrarily limited and the scope of action confined, the decision had radically changed the nature of the American involvement. At the end of the meeting Johnson warned the participants that there was to be no public mention of our new strategy, that any leaks to the press would be severely punished. He had, as James Reston wrote two months later, "escalated the war by stealth."

The Vietcong response was predictable. They escalated in return, taking a provincial capital, throwing large, well-armed units into battle against the hapless South Vietnamese army.

And so, naturally, we responded in turn — not out of any rational calculation of risks and probabilities, but blindly, automatically, sending more and more of our soldiers into a battle where hope of success rested on nothing more than a wishful belief that somehow, in some manner, we could force a political or military victory from jungles already teeming with enemy forces, which could be readily augmented by troops that North Vietnam held in reserve. In 1954 General Ridgway had told Senator Aiken of Vermont that "even if two million men were sent to Vietnam they would be swallowed up." Ridgeway had fought in Korea, understood the hazards of Asian warfare. But he had been succeeded by a new generation of push-button generals who had unbounded faith in the high-tech military power they had so extravagantly nurtured, the accuracy of calculations provided them by the powerful computers that could — it was supposed — measure the strength of the enemy and the strength it would take to defeat them. Unfortunately technology had not advanced to the point where it could measure will, determination, courage, the strengths and weaknesses of entire societies. Nor were even more mundane calculations any better than the accuracy of the numbers on which they were based. And the numbers were not accurate.

After leaving the government, I was among the few laymen in a group of distinguised scientists — many of them Nobel Prize laureates — convened for a top-secret meeting at the peaceful Dana Hall School campus outside of Boston. McNamara had summoned this group for an "objective" appraisal of our war effort. Among the group was Murray Gellmann, co-discoverer of the elusive quark, then supposed to be the basic building block of all matter. Yet even his penetrating mind could not uncover some hidden coherence beneath our titanic effort to arrest the escalation of the war on the ground. The southward flow needed to sustain and increase the war was so small, could be sustained in so many ways — carried in trucks across pitted earthen roads, strapped to the backs of men walking through the jungles, tied to the bottoms of the small fishing boats that glided daily along the Vietnam coast — that no volume of airborne explosives could prevent it. The scientists were horrified to discover that we didn't know, that we couldn't know, the size and routes of infiltration. Along the Ho Chi Minh Trail, loyal South Vietnamese hid in the jungle counting the trucks coming from the North. Unfortunately the trucks were usually curtained, their contents invisible; and our observers were often forced by the passage of armed men to take refuge in the jungle, leaving the trails unwatched for days at a time. Yet they did the best they could; made estimates, sent them to Saigon where they were translated into "hard numbers" for transmittal to Washington. The possibility of error, the stunned scientists concluded, was not 20 percent or 30 percent — but 1000 percent or even more. In other words, we didn't know at all, could not even make an informed guess.

In April of 1965, Johnson sent forty thousand more troops to Vietnam, bringing the U.S. total to eighty thousand.

On June 22, Johnson instructed General Wheeler to cable Westmoreland: Would forty-four battalions be enough? For now, Westmoreland replied, but later more would be needed.

Again — gradually, imperceptibly, secretly — the issue was changing: It was no longer necessary to decide whether American troops would fight the war on the ground. That question had been resolved; although it was kept secret until inadvertently revealed at a State Department press briefing on June 8. At issue now was the scale of the American effort, whether we would send forces large enough to take over the principal responsibility for arresting the insurgency. A large change in the size of our commitment would mean a change in the nature of that commitment.

McNamara, Bundy, and Rusk, along with members of the Joint Chiefs of Staff, urged Johnson to go before the American people, proclaim that the country was in a full-scale war, and call up the reserves — thus reaching into every corner of America, plucking men from their jobs and families, a disruption that would mean openly disavowing the premise that the war in Vietnam was only a transient aberration.

In July, I was invited to attend a meeting of the National Security Council ostensibly convoked to consider the various proposals to increase our troop strength. I had been included — as an observer not a participant — because the agenda included the possibility of a major presidential speech, which I would be expected to draft, a task that would be somewhat eased if I had some idea of the president's purpose — not only in Vietnam, but toward the public he would address. Of course, the decision had already been made by Johnson and his minuscule inner council. The purpose of the meeting was not deliberation, but to enforce unanimity. And all the participants knew it, knew also that Johnson would let them know what "decision" they were supposed to make.

"This is how I see it," Johnson told the assemblage. "There are those who think we already have enough troops, and that I should turn Westmoreland down. The generals here," he said, gesturing toward members of the Joint Chiefs of Staff, "tell me that would let the Vietcong take over the whole country, killing a lot of American boys" (those he had already sent) "and losing the war. I don't know if they're right, but I'm not inclined to second-guess the experts. There are others, like Bob McNamara, who want me to declare war, call up the reserves, and just go all out, no matter what that does to our legislative program or to whatever support we now have in Congress. The third possibility is to do pretty much what we're doing, send Westy the troops he says he needs, and see how it works out." The president's statement of alternatives was an even clearer statement of his preference — the middle way, the moderate course. (Except, of course, moderation being a relative thing, there was no truly moderate course at all.)

The president paused, eyed his listeners sternly: "How many think that we should do nothing and just let the chips fall where they may?" No one moved. "Well, I agree with that. Now how many of you fellows think I ought to announce that we're now a war government, call up the reserves, and go full-scale?" Again there was no response; even McNamara, who had proposed the reserve call-up, remained silent. He knew what Johnson wanted, and he also knew that one thing he didn't want was disagreement. "Well, then," Johnson said, "I guess we're all in agreement." It was not a question. No reaction was called for. After all, there were only three choices, and two had been "unanimously" rejected. Then to protect against the possibility of discontents being muttered in the halls of the Pentagon and finding their way to the press, he looked directly toward the chairman of the Joint Chiefs of Staff, who was flanked by one or two of his colleagues: "You agree, don't you, General Wheeler?" The general nodded acquiescence. "And you too, General?" "Yes, Mr. President," came the obedient response. "Fine, then, it's all decided. I hope you fellows are right, but I'm willing to bet on you."

Although no specific numbers were discussed at this meeting, Johnson had privately committed 125,000 more troops. Despite this, he announced at the end of July that he would not call up the reserves and intended to send only 50,000 men to Vietnam — an understatement that amounted to a major deception of Congress, the country, and most of the government. And, for a moment, the political tactic worked. The *New York Times* responded to Johnson's announcement with a front-page article describing the relief expressed by many members of Congress at the president's decision not to call up the reserves. "An indication of the president's desire for peace," commented one senator.

Nor was the size of the commitment the only lie. At a press conference the day after his announcement, Johnson was asked whether the troop increase amounted to a change in the American mission, still publicly restricted to guarding installations and acting as emergency backup for the South Vietnamese army. "None whatsoever," Johnson answered. "It does not imply any change in policy or objective." But it did. American forces would now have the principal responsibility for fighting the war on the ground. Johnson had declared war in his own, idiosyncratic way: He didn't tell anyone.

The sequel was inevitable, and is well known. The 125,000 additional troops were not enough. "The ability of the Vietcong to

rebuild their units and make good their losses," remarked Maxwell Taylor as early as Thanksgiving of 1964, "is one of the mysteries of this guerrilla war. . . . Not only do the Vietcong units
have the recuperative power of the Phoenix but they have an
amazing ability to maintain morale." But it was no mystery at all:
They had plenty of men and arms; a belief in their cause, which
had now been transformed from national "reunification" to the
liberation of their country from a foreign power and its puppet
governments; and had been hardened by decades of war and deprivation. Americans were also willing to fight and die — even if
it was for a more ambiguous cause. But no matter how heroically
we struggled, how many men went into the bloody, flame-scorched
jungles and villages of a country now become one vast battlefield,
the Vietcong kept on coming.

How did you deal with a war like this? Why, you sent more
men out to die! American troops streamed into Vietnam. By April
of 1967 the number was well over half a million, slightly less than
the six hundred thousand Westmoreland wanted "for now." This
incompetent general, whose every estimate of his military needs
had been wrong, had only one answer for his failures: more men.
Later he would claim that we should have made a larger effort.
But no effort would have been adequate — not if we gave him all
he requested, and twice what he requested.

And the horror of it was that almost everyone knew that the
war was unwinnable — except for a president of the United States
and the few ambitious, limited men who shared and served to
fortify his disastrous self-deception.

"In framing a government which is to be administered by men
over men," wrote Madison, "the greatest difficulty lies in this: you
must first enable the government to control the governed; and in
the next place oblige it to control itself. A dependence on the people is, no doubt, the primary control on the government; but experience has taught mankind the necessity of auxiliary precautions."

Gradually, beginning in 1965, these "auxiliary precautions" were
dismantled: Congress — deceived and left in ignorance — was
rendered virtually impotent, no longer a participant, its debate
confined to a referendum on actions already taken by the president. The diverse instruments of the executive branch — cabinet
and security councils, advisers and ministers — were excluded from

the councils of decision, except for that handful who were already committed to the policies of war or could be counted on to follow — even support enthusiastically — the decisions of Lyndon Johnson. And finally the wisdom of Madison was wholly discarded for that far more ancient maxim of Saint Matthew's Gospel that "He that is not with me is against me," forgetting that an admonition to follow God through an act of faith had no relevance to mortal leaders whose acts are to be judged by reason and secular conviction.

In 1969 David Halberstam wrote a brilliantly assembled and accurate account of the making of the war, whose fairness was marred only by the title. He called it *The Best and the Brightest*, a reference to that luminous group of intellectuals, renowned public servants, noted academicians who had been assembled to staff the Kennedy administration in 1960. Yet as the escalation of the war continued, the best and the brightest disappeared from the ranks of advisers: Some resigned, others were fired, still others were excluded by presidential fiat or bureaucratic maneuvering from the inner circle. Robert Kennedy was gone, as were Ted Sorensen and Arthur Schlesinger. Adlai Stevenson was ignored — a "soft-minded liberal" safely confined to his luxury suite in the Waldorf Towers. Douglas Dillon, a Republican who had been one of the most important voices of liberal restraint, was no longer a participant. Averell Harriman, regarded as one of our leading experts on communist intentions, was stripped by Dean Rusk of his involvement in Southeast Asia and exiled as a roving ambassador to Africa. Roger Hilsman, who had served as the assistant secretary for the Far East, was summarily fired for his participation in the overthrow of the corrupt and rapidly deteriorating Diem regime, which, in President Kennedy's view, had become an insurmountable obstruction to any hope of strengthening the noncommunist forces in South Vietnam. He was replaced by William Bundy, who could be counted on to serve as his brother's faithful and obedient agent in the State Department.

Following the Bay of Pigs Kennedy had enlarged the number of his foreign-policy advisers. Now the opposite was done. Virtually the entire White House staff were simply omitted from the process of decision, and, for the most part, deprived of access to information that contradicted or cast serious doubt on the official line. Thus Bill Moyers and I, along with most other staff members, were ignorant of plans to escalate the war on the ground, to shift from a defensive strategy to direct assaults, of the hypocrisy of our impossible "conditions" for negotiation. At one point, the president cut off deliveries of all newspapers to members of the White House staff (although papers were available in the "fish room" as well as in every neighboring drugstore) as if he feared his own men might become contaminated by the published arguments of journalistic critics and dissenting congressmen.

We could not be wholly excluded, of course. Routine intelligence information crossed our desk; there were casual conversations in the White House mess with members of Bundy's staff; distressed and apprehensive foreign-service officers of subordinate rank would occasionally seek us out to voice their objections to the course of events, thinking, mistakenly, that through us they could reach the president. They were not wholly mistaken, of course. After all, we saw the president on an almost daily basis; indeed, much of what we learned about the war came from those late-evening sessions when Johnson, unwinding from the day's labor, would interrupt his flow of stories and discussion for brief monologues on his troubles in Southeast Asia. We would, on occasion, take advantage of these moments to voice our doubts about the course of the war. Johnson always listened — carefully, courteously — but then proceeded heedless of our unsought advice. After all, what did we know, how could we know of matters so arcane and complex?

And then there were only a few: Robert McNamara, McGeorge Bundy, and Dean Rusk, later supplemented by Walt Rostow and, of course, the Pentagon generals. These were neither the best nor the brightest. They were technicians, managers; men whose skill lay in their ability to carry out decisions, lacking the broader virtues of historical perspective, understanding of the legitimate forces of American democracy, knowledge even of Southeast Asia. "You know, Dick," McNamara said to me in 1966, "it might be a good idea if we had someone at these meetings" (i.e., the meetings where decisions were made) "who understood Vietnamese culture and politics." I was appalled at the implicit admission that no such person had participated; that we were fighting a war in a country we did not know against an enemy we did not understand. To me it was a moment of revelation, which on reflection — then and in the years to come — demonstrated the danger of policies conceived and carried out by a small group of men in virtual secrecy. They begin by lying to Congress and the public, all for the best of reasons; in this case the felt necessity of "containing" communism in South Vietnam. Next they lie to each other, concealing information and even private opinions that might introduce a note of discordant doubt. And finally they lie to themselves — having become so profoundly, psychically committed to the wisdom of their actions, having raised the stakes so high, that any admission of error would be a failure of unacceptable dimensions.

In order to strengthen his domination of the staff, in the spring of 1965, Johnson appointed a Texas businessman, Marvin J. Watson, as his appointments secretary, with a mandate to control all access to the Oval Office. A man of limited intelligence and little knowledge of public affairs, Watson's sole virtue was his willingness to carry out even the most casually expressed presidential directive without question or qualification.

For the most part I ignored Watson, as did Moyers, Jack Valenti, and others who, feeling secure in presidential favor, were not going to let this almost comically tough figure disrupt our normal relationships. Undoubtedly our conduct was a source of immense frustration to Watson, but there was little he could do as long as the president himself didn't object. But then he had a lucky break. On May 18, I received a letter from Watson, announcing that "Your file cabinet" (containing some secret documents among the littered collection of harmless memos and speech drafts) "was found open at 12:45 A.M. last night, May 17, 1965. Since this is the third time this has happened . . . I wish you would be good enough to talk to your fine secretaries and tell them it just causes so much concern for all of us when they fail to lock the safes."

Of course, Marvin knew it wasn't the secretaries, who had usually gone home long before I left my office. And admittedly I was a bit sloppy about "security violations," although it did occur to me that if the tightly guarded West Wing was not safe from intruders, a mere safe wouldn't stop them. I responded to Watson's letter with a memorandum that I circulated to every member of the White House staff.

May 19, 1965
ABSOLUTELY CONFIDENTIAL

Memorandum to Marvin Watson
From: Dick Goodwin

Perhaps due to inexperience you have rather clumsily spoiled one of the most skillful espionage operations in the history of the Amer-

ican government. Every few weeks a number of documents classi-
fied "top secret" are placed in my file cabinet. These documents
contain information which is deliberately misleading. (For example, before the Democratic Convention we had a memorandum
which said that President Johnson would not accept the nomination — which built up a lot of suspense.) Then I usually invite
someone from the Russian Embassy over for a nightcap. At an
appropriate moment (around 12:45 A.M.) I say I have to go over to
the mansion, and leave. The result of this has been a series of Soviet and Chinese diplomatic blunders of the first magnitude. However, I am afraid you have — inadvertently I am sure — destroyed
this ingenious offensive against the communists. Don't feel badly,
however, we'll find another trick.

In addition it is very rare that I am not here at 12 midnight and
later. Your security officer insists on coming in when I am in the
bathroom. In fact, I think they use that peephole over the second-
floor washbasin just so they can sneak in and find a security violation.

However, even though we are completely blameless, I have informed my secretaries of your wishes. They said: "If Marvin wants
it, we will do it." But don't worry, I won't tell your wife — it'll
stay a secret between the boys.
NEVER AGAIN.

Marvin didn't reply. In fact, except for amiable-enough greetings in the White House corridor, I never heard from him on any
matter of business, nor did he look up from his desk as I walked
past on my way to the Oval Office.

I include this incident in my narrative not to demonstrate a gift
for humor but to evidence that the White House in 1965 was not
yet a grim, beleaguered fortress. Bill Moyers was a habitual practical joker. Once, for example, he placed on the press-room ticker
a report of harsh, detailed criticisms of Johnson that I had alleg-
edly, after several drinks, made to a reporter, and he then sent
the teletype copy to my office with a note that "Dick, we'd better
get a denial ready before the President sees this. In his current
mood, I don't know if he'll believe you, but I'll do all I can to
help. I know you'd do the same for me." Shocked, virtually paralyzed, dire thoughts rushed through my mind — I couldn't recall
any such conversation; of course the president wouldn't believe
me; it would be seen as the ultimate act of disloyalty, a betrayal
of the man who had entrusted me with large responsibilities, etc. —
until I looked up and saw a grinning Moyers standing in the door-

way. Awareness was almost instantaneous — "You bastard, I'll get you back" — as we both began to laugh.

Not only was there room for humor, but we continued to develop domestic programs that we hoped would exceed the already impressive achievements of the early Johnson years. Although the war — no longer a distant, almost irrelevant cloud — was beginning to shadow Johnson's huge ambitions, we believed, naïvely, that it would soon be resolved like so many past crises, freeing the administration for the works of peace. It was a hopelessly misconceived assumption, but all we knew is what we were allowed to know — forecasts of optimism, promises of restraint.

At his height, Johnson had an appetite for information that was insatiable. Now, on the subject of Vietnam, the doors to debate were closing. Dissenting views were barred from the Oval Office, heard only on those rare occasions when voiced by a visitor from outside the government whose judgment, being uninformed, could be safely ignored.

For example, in 1966, Dick Daley, the mayor and boss of Democratic Chicago, visited Johnson to discuss certain federal projects of interest to his home state. It would not have occurred to the tough-minded but meticulously proper mayor to advise the president on foreign policy. But as Daley began to leave, the needs and politics of Chicago having been thoroughly canvassed, the president asked him: "Listen, Dick, I've got a lot of trouble over there in Vietnam. What do you think about it?" Daley paused for a moment. "Well, Mr. President, when you've got a losing hand in poker you just throw in your cards."

"But what about American prestige?"

"You just put your prestige in your back pocket and walk away."

"Thank you, Mr. Mayor. Now if you've ever got a problem you just pick up the phone and give me a call. Your president will always answer, hear."

"Thank you, Mr. President, I appreciate that, and if I can help you in any way, you only need to ask."

During 1965, Johnson was transforming the nature of the presidential institution, confining discussion and decision concerning Vietnam to the small secret council meeting each week at his Tuesday lunches, because, Johnson said, "Those men were loyal to me."

However, these men were linked not by simple loyalty to Johnson, but by their own profound involvement in the growing con-

flict. They had counseled, urged, the president toward escalation — phrased and even believed the falsely optimistic forecasts
that had been transmuted from estimates to dogma. We were going
to succeed. Had to succeed. If only we had the courage to stay
the course. They gathered weekly not to discuss Johnson's war. It
was their war too. And they had this in common: awareness that
their own ambitions, places of power, and distinction now rested
solely on the favor of a single man. And none of them knew much
about the United States — could not, did not calculate the impact
of the war on the material progress and moral cohesion of the
nation they were helping to lead; were unaware that to conduct a
major war in semisecrecy, abetted by purposeful deception, without public support and understanding, was a sure path to disaster. It was as if, every Tuesday, a small group of men gathered in
some space capsule, far removed from the turmoil and discords of
a distant earth, to deliberate the destiny of the troublesome planet
circling far below.

"A typical discussion of the Tuesday lunch," wrote a Johnson
biographer, "would begin with the alternative targets for bombing, continue with the lift capacity of the latest helicopters . . .
conclude with the production figures for waterproof boots, never
once calling into serious question the shared assumptions about
the nature of the war or its . . . importance to national security.
Someone once said as he watched Dean Rusk hurrying to the White
House . . . 'If you told him right now of a sure-fire way to defeat
the Viet Cong and get out of Vietnam, he would groan that he
was too busy to worry about that now; he had to discuss next
week's bombing targets.' "

The results of this narrowed focus were devastating. Within
government reasoned argument, the exchange of divergent views,
critical appraisal of fundamental policy, came to a halt.

It is a fearsome lesson in the potential power of the modern
presidency to ignore and override the process of democracy. We
have had other examples since: Watergate, the diversion of funds
to the *contras*. All illustrating the wisdom of Jefferson's counsel
that democracy does not depend "on confidence but on jealousy,"
that power alone can check power, and if the restraints, not of
men but institutions, are dismantled, then democracy is in mortal
danger. I have worked with many powerful men. They were all
convinced that their goals were righteous, that their sole objective
was the public good; and they all resented obstacles to their will.

Yet those obstacles are essential to preserve democracy, not against the depradations of the corrupt, but the deeds of those who believe their objectives benign or even, in Johnson's words, "essential to the security of the free world."

21 / Descent

Paranoiacs are so skillful at dissembling that many of them are never identified as such. The other characteristic is the urge to unmask enemies. These the paranoiac sees everywhere . . . he has the gift of seeing through appearances and knows exactly what is behind them. He tears the mask from every face and what he then finds is essentially the same enemy.

— Elias Canetti, *Crowds and Power*

I am not going to have anything more to do with the liberals. They won't have anything to do with me. They all just follow the communist line — liberals, intellectuals, communists. They're all the same. I detest the United Nations. They've tried to make a fool out of me. They oppose me. And I won't make any overtures to the Russians. They'll have to come to me. In Paris, Gagarin [Yuri Gagarin, Soviet cosmonaut] refused to shake hands with the astronauts. I sent those astronauts myself, and what he did was a personal insult to me. I can't trust anybody anymore. I tell you what I'm going to do. I'm going to get rid of everybody who doesn't agree with my policies. I'll take a tough line — put Abe Fortas or Clark Clifford in the Bundy job. I'm not going in the liberal direction. There's no future with them. They're just out to get me, always have been.

— Lyndon Johnson in personal conversation
(excerpt from my diary entry of June 22, 1965)

I FIND THIS part of my chronicle the hardest to write. Although I was, in 1965, to leave the White House, a year later to join the ranks of opposition, and, in 1968, to contribute to his downfall, I never lost my affection and admiration for Lyndon Johnson; a man whom I had served gladly, to the limits of my capacity, and who — until I became an ally of his enemies —

treated me with respect, dignity, and considerable warmth. Therefore, the more difficult it is to recount not merely the escalation of the war in Vietnam, which has been amply documented in many volumes, but the profound, if intermittent, instabilities of Lyndon Johnson, which made that war not just a mistake, which it was, nor a national tragedy, which it also was, but, in part, the consequence of a deterioration of the capacity to distinguish what was real — what his rational faculties knew to be real — from what he wished to believe.

During 1965, and especially in the period which enveloped the crucial midsummer decision that transformed Vietnam into an American war, I became convinced that the president's always large eccentricities had taken a huge leap into unreason. Not on every subject, and certainly not all the time. During this same period, Johnson was skillfully crafting some of the largest triumphs of his Great Society.

Nor do I mean that, from the beginning, the war in Vietnam was an act of unreason; still less that the most devastating event in American history since the Civil War was imposed upon an entire nation by the irrationalities of a single man. Too many people over too many years were involved to place the blame in any one place. At the beginning, the war seemed to many simply a continuation of that resistance to communist expansion which had been the centerpiece of American policy since the end of World War II. Even among those who thought the escalation an error, many felt — and I include myself — that our intervention was a temporary aberration, a mistake that would soon be corrected, leaving the nation free to pursue domestic progress. No one — except perhaps for Johnson himself — could foresee that the war would devastate not only Vietnam, but the hopes of the American nation. Yet despite these truthful disclaimers there is no question in my mind that both the atmosphere of the White House and the decisions taken until 1965 (the only period I personally observed) were affected by the periodic disruptions of Lyndon Johnson's mind and spirit.

I do not, in the brief description of this chapter, use terms such as "paranoid personality" or "paranoid dispositions" to describe a medical diagnosis. I am not Lyndon Johnson's psychiatrist, nor qualified to be. Within the world of professional psychiatry, those terms imply complexities of mental activity which have occasioned decades of debate among scientists. Yet, like the words "obsession" or "compulsion," they also imply, more or less accurately, a manner of behavior, a way of dealing with the world, that differs in rather specific ways from what we ordinarily regard as normal, rational conduct. Paranoia, Freud tells us, is a misuse of certain mental processes "for purposes of defense." Faced with painful and/or threatening experiences, the afflicted individual is urged, even compelled, to sustitute what he believes — what he wishes to believe — for reality. The ordinary critical and detached faculties of apprehension are suspended, allowing the individual to project his own needs — for justification, for self-protection — on the world around him. Unable to confront reality, he changes it; transmits it into more comforting beliefs which are then promoted to certain knowledge. As a consequence, those who oppose his wishes or his behavior are perceived as denying reality itself, something which can only be explained by impugning the motives of opposition. Thus Freud describes the "official who has been passed over for promotion [and thus] needs to believe that persecutors are plotting against him and that he is being spied upon. . . ." Or, the "litigious paranoiac [who] cannot bear the idea that he has committed an injustice. . . . Consequently he thinks that the judgment [against him] is not legally valid."

My conclusion that Lyndon Johnson experienced certain episodes of what I believe to have been paranoid behavior is based purely on my observation of his conduct during the three years I worked for him. The president's conduct — words and actions — during some of 1965 was, on occasion, markedly, almost frighteningly different from anything I had observed previously. Nor was this my conclusion alone. It was shared by others who also had close and frequent contact with the president.

I do not intend to indulge in conjecture about the source or intensities of Johnson's inner mental conflicts; but only to report what I observed, or what other people observed and reported to me, during the period I worked in the White House. I do not wish to impose on the reader my belief that such behavior was a consequence of sporadic paranoid disruptions. Rather I prefer to set forth some of the observations and events that led me to this conclusion, and let the reader make his own judgment. The story tells itself.

In April of 1965 the president of Pakistan, Mohammed Ayub Khan, and the prime minister of India, Lal Bahadur Shastri, were

scheduled to visit the White House. Both men had expressed opposition to our war policies in Vietnam. Both visits were abruptly
canceled. "We didn't cancel the visits," Johnson falsely stated at
a press conference, we just told them that since the president was
"very busy," this was not the most propitious time for a visit, and,
Johnson patiently explained, "when you put things that way, most
people want to come at the time that would be most convenient
to us, to the host . . . and the answer came back that they would
accept our decision."

The public pundits of foreign policy did not swallow the Johnson explanation. We had, they wrote, deliberately offended two of
Asia's most important leaders because they did not approve our
bombing of North Vietnam. A week later I sat beside Johnson as
Air Force One carried us from the Texas ranch to the White House.
Suddenly interrupting the silence, Johnson leaned over to me, looked
around, and speaking in tense, almost whispered tones, as if he
were confiding the highest secrets of state: "Listen, Dick, do you
know why there was so much trouble about Ayub and Shastri?"
"No, Mr. President," I replied. "Well you ought to know about
it, so you can keep on the alert. I had it investigated. Do you
know there are some disloyal Kennedy people over at the State
Department who are trying to get me; that's why they stirred things
up?" "I didn't know that," I answered. "Well, there are, and we
can expect to hear from them again. They didn't get me this time,
but they'll keep trying." In my diary entry of that date I noted
that "the president spoke in an intense low-keyed manner, characteristic of his most irrational moments."

The following day, I noted in my diary, "Hugh Sidey came to
see me. He said there was an increasing worry about the president
around town. A fear that his personal eccentricities were now af-
fecting policy. For example, he told me that in responding to criticism over the Ayub and Shastri affair, Johnson had said to reporters: 'After all, what would Jim Eastland say if I brought those
two niggers over here.' We agreed that it was such a stupid remark for LBJ to say — knowing that if it ever made its way into
public print, he would be severely damaged — that he had to be
a little out of control to say it at all."

A few days later Johnson received telegrams from our representatives in Saigon and in India suggesting a visit from Vice-President Humphrey as a demonstration that our goodwill toward the
nations of Asia remained unimpaired. Moyers and I were sitting

in the Oval Office when the telegrams arrived. Johnson read them, then, his face contorted in fury, rose and slammed them onto his desk. "I don't want telegrams like that," he almost shouted, then picked up the phone. "Get me Rusk. . . . Listen, *Mr. Secretary*," he began, softly sardonic, "you know those telegrams about Humphrey?" We couldn't hear the reply, but listened as the president suddenly raised his voice: "If they send me any more telegrams like that, I want you to call them back. Fire the bunch of them. I don't want any more telegrams like that." Then, without time for a reply, the president replaced the handset and turned toward Moyers. "You know what it is, Bill, don't you, it's those damn Kennedy ambassadors trying to get me and discredit me."

Yet even though there could be no real basis for Johnson's accusation, although there was no conspiracy of "Kennedy ambassadors" out to "get" him, on paper Johnson's remark might be regarded as a mere distortion, grotesquely exaggerated rhetoric. Yet the fierceness of expression, the lashing out of a man feeling beleaguered, left little doubt that he meant what he was saying. He knew it wasn't true. But he believed it. As later events would demonstrate, some obscure border was being crossed.

And it was expectable that the "Kennedy crowd," as Johnson called them, should be the prelude to that swarming crowd of "enemies and conspirators" that began to infect Johnson's mind. Not only had he felt humiliated — and with some cause — during Kennedy's presidency, but the enduring shadow of Camelot — glamorous, popular, intellectual, enshrined in steadily growing myth — seemed to him to obscure the achievements of his own presidency, preventing others from seeing how much more he was accomplishing than had his predecessor. The omnipresent ghost of that past was, for Johnson, reincarnated in the person of Robert Kennedy and his followers. However, understandable hostility would soon be displaced by the more ominous conviction that Robert Kennedy was not just an enemy, but the leader of all his enemies, the guiding spirit of some immense conspiracy designed to discredit and, ultimately, to overthrow the Johnson presidency.

"Why does he keep worrying about me?" Robert Kennedy once asked me. "I don't like him, but there's nothing I can do to him. Hell, he's the president, and I'm only a junior senator." "That's right," I replied, "that's the reality. But we're not talking about reality. In Johnson's mind you're the threat. If he had to choose between you and Ho Chi Minh" (to be his successor in office), "he'd pick Ho in a minute." An exaggeration, of course. Ho was not even constitutionally eligible. But uncomfortably close to a true description of Johnson's inward passions.

Johnson, whose unconscious mind was far closer to the surface of thought and speech than it is for most men, once explained why Fulbright and "all those liberals on the Hill" were squawking at him about Vietnam. "Why? I'll tell you why. Because I never went to Harvard. That's why. Because I wasn't John F. Kennedy. Because the Great Society was accomplishing more than the New Frontier. You see, they had to find some issue on which to turn against me, and they found it in Vietnam."

In May of 1965, I drafted a speech that Johnson was scheduled to deliver in San Francisco at the anniversary of the United Nations. Not limited to the standard plea for increased peace and understanding among the nations, it contained several tangible and far-reaching proposals for nuclear arms control. Johnson was delighted with the draft, approved it, and instructed that it be prepared for delivery. Then, shortly before the president was scheduled to go to San Francisco, Robert Kennedy addressed the Senate, calling for progress toward nuclear disarmament. The Kennedy speech, a somewhat academic utterance by a junior senator, received little public attention. But it infuriated Johnson. He called me in. "I want you to take out anything about the atom in that speech," he instructed. "I don't want one word in there that looks like I'm copying Bobby Kennedy." "But, Mr. President," I protested, "the Kennedy speech is very different from yours, and it's only his opinion. These are formal proposals from the president of the United States. The entire world will be listening." Johnson paid no attention; it was as if I hadn't spoken. He dropped his voice, picked up a newspaper. "Here's Reston's column on Kennedy's speech. You make sure we don't say anything that he says Bobby said. I'm not going to do it." Thus all the arms control proposals were excised, the speech becoming little more than a banal birthday felicitations to the other members of the United Nations.

Afterward, Johnson told Moyers, "I read the whole draft of that speech to some editors of the *Manchester* [England] *Guardian* who came to visit. They said it was great, one of the best speeches they ever heard. You know what I told them? I said I was glad they liked it, because they were the only ones that were ever going to hear it. I wasn't going to give one word of it."

Now the growing fears and suspicions, as they assumed increasing reality within the president's mind, crossed the line from irrational rhetorical outbursts to compel changes in policy. The American initiatives toward arms control were canceled — and never revived — simply because Bobby Kennedy had made a speech.

In the late spring of 1965, alarmed at what I perceived to be the president's increasingly irrational behavior, I began to study medical textbooks, talk with professional psychiatrists. I learned that the paranoid personality may pass relatively undisturbed through a long and productive lifetime, manifesting itself only in subtle traits of behavior: a somewhat excessive secrecy and suspicion, a need for control over the external world. Since particular displays of these traits nearly all have some basis in reality — there are real adversaries, real reasons for an ambitious man to seek control over people and events — they are ordinarily perceived more as personal eccentricity than as a failure of reason or a distortion of reality. To the gifted few they may even be a source of strength, increasing their ability to achieve mastery over that always treacherous world which they inhabit. The paranoid personality, for example, perceiving others as a potential source of opposition or even danger, is constantly on the alert — observing, listening — to discern the hidden intentions of others, thus sharpening skills that can give him a remarkable intuitive understanding of others — their concealed ambitions, weaknesses, greeds, lusts. The need to maintain control over otherwise treacherous surroundings may drive a man to the most productive endeavors, his energy heightened by inward need; aid him in the attainment of the highest ambitions — perhaps to lead a Senate or even an entire country.

"Because of the free aggression in the relatively un-neurotic representatives of this type," wrote Wilhelm Reich, "social activities are strong, impulsive, energetic, to the point and usually productive. The more neurotic the character is — or becomes — the more extravagant and one-sided the activities appear. . . . Between these actions and the creation of paranoic systems lie the many variations of this character type."

Yet there is always this danger. If control is threatened, mastery undermined, enemies increasing in number and moving beyond reach, then the mental apparatus so carefully constructed to transform potential weakness into external strength can begin to falter. The latent paranoia, liberated by the erosive pressures of misfortune and sensed helplessness, can take occasional control of the conscious mind, thereby transforming its strength into irreparable flaws; transforming the most highly developed faculties into instruments of willed belief, even delusion. But not completely. The victory is not total, the carefully nurtured and highly trained abilities to understand and manipulate the world are too strong to yield to total defeat. But this escalating combat of the mind can radically distort judgment and perception alike, transforming hitherto controlled suspicions into real and immediate dangers, the desire for protective secrecy into an urgent need of self-preservation, disagreement into personal attacks, rational opposition into the work of deadly enemies. And, should the paranoid episode be acute and long-lasting, all opposition congeals into a conspiracy led at first from many centers, then gradually perceived as the work of a single group of men or a single man: the communists or even Robert Kennedy.

It is as if amid the country of the mind stood a dormant but still active volcano, an impressive cauldron of turbulent heat and glimmering light. On its productive slopes, crops flourish, and around its base shining cities rise. Then subterranean, uncomprehended pressures begin to build, and the symbol of strength, the source of so much fertility, begins to overtop its rim, pouring the molten liquid of destruction over all that has been so carefully constructed over so many hopeful and impressive years.

Something like this began to happen to Lyndon Johnson during 1965 when he found himself — for almost the first time — encompassed by men and events he could not control: Vietnam and the Kennedys, and, later, the press, Congress, and even the public whose approval was essential to his own esteem. As his defenses weakened, long-suppressed instincts broke through to assault the carefully developed skills and judgment of a lifetime. The attack was not completely successful. The man was too strong for that. Most of Johnson — the outer man, the spheres of rationally controlled thought and action — remained intact, most of the time. But in some ways and on increasingly frequent occasions, he began to exhibit behavior which manifested some internal dislocation.

It was during this period, in the spring of 1965, that I first noticed that Johnson's public mask was beginning to stiffen. In his public appearances the face seemed frozen, the once-gesturing arms held tightly to the side or grasping a podium. Protective devices proliferated — TelePrompTers, special rostrums, the careful excision of colorful or original language — all, at least in part, I now believe, designed to guard him from spontaneously voicing inner convictions that he knew, in that part of his mind still firmly in touch with reality, would, if voiced, discredit him. "You know, Dick," Johnson once told me, "I never really dare let myself go because I don't know where I'll stop." I let the comment pass, not realizing the significance of his revelation, a glimpse at the protective shield so carefully constructed against threatening forces that he knew might overwhelm him.

In mid-June, Moyers entered the Oval Office to find Johnson holding a wire service report torn from the teletype machine that stood close to the desk. "Did you see this? Bundy is going on television — on national television — with five professors. I never gave him permission. That's an act of disloyalty. He didn't tell me because he knew I didn't want him to do it. Bill, I want you to go to Bundy and tell him the president would be pleased, mighty pleased, to accept his resignation." Johnson paused reflectively. "On second thought, maybe I should talk to him myself." (A not unreasonable judgment, given Bundy's rank and importance.) "No, you go do it." Then, as if responding to some sensed hesitation on Moyers's part: "That's the trouble with all you fellows. You're in bed with the Kennedys."

Moyers wisely ignored the president's order and left the White House to go home. "At midnight," I noted in my diary, "Moyers called me to talk about Johnson. He said he was extremely worried, that as he listened to Johnson he felt weird, almost felt as if he wasn't really talking to a human being at all."

The next morning when Moyers entered the Oval Office, Johnson looked up at him. "Did you speak to Bundy?" "No, I didn't, Mr. President," Bill replied. Johnson grunted, and returned his attention to the memorandum he had begun reading. Bundy was to last for another year.

My conversation that night with Bill was the first of many over the next few months, in which we tried to understand the irrational outbursts, the swift, unexpected, and unacceptable orders that came from the Oval Office. In most matters the president was as we had always known him, colorful, perhaps a bit eccentric, but very much in control of the skills that had produced six months of unprecedented achievements. Yet the aberrations came more often now, were more extreme.

A week or so later, on June 22, Moyers and I were talking with Johnson in the Oval Office when, provoked by nothing more than my comment that his federal aid to education bill had virtually complete support from liberal organizations — including hitherto hostile Catholic groups — Johnson proclaimed: "I am not going to have anything more to do with the liberals. They won't have anything to do with me. They all just follow the communist line — liberals, intellectuals, communists. They're all the same. I detest the United Nations. They've tried to make a fool out of me. They oppose me. And I won't make any overtures to the Russians. They'll have to come to me. In Paris, Gargarin [Yuri Gargarin, Soviet cosmonaut] refused to shake hands with the astronauts. I sent those astronauts myself, and what he did was a personal insult to me. I can't trust anybody anymore. I tell you what I'm going to do. I'm going to get rid of everybody who doesn't agree with my policies. I'll take a tough line — put Abe Fortas or Clark Clifford in the Bundy job. I'm not going in the liberal direction. There's no future with them. They're just out to get me, always have been."

I accompanied Moyers back to his office. "We were both shaken, alarmed," I noted in my diary, "not so much at the content of Johnson's statements — surely he didn't mean to halt all discussions with the Soviet Union or pull out of the United Nations — but at the disjointed, erratic flow of thought, unrelated events strung together, yet seemingly linked by some incomprehensible web of connections within Johnson's mind. He won't act on his words, but he believes they're true."

On June 28, I recorded in my diary that Johnson had "asked me and Bill if we thought Tom Wicker was out to destroy him, if Wicker was caught up in some sort of conspiracy against him. We said no, that he writes some favorable and some unfavorable stories, but we couldn't convince him. Then he suddenly switched the subject to say he thought Bobby Kennedy was behind the public assassination of Ed Clark — whom he had made ambassador to Australia. Without waiting for any reply, he went on to say that he had agreed to appoint Harlan Cleveland to the number-four job in the State Department but now he wouldn't appoint him dog catcher because he thought he leaked the story to Reston about the U.N. speech."

* * *

Gradually, as Johnson moved closer and closer to the fatal decision of July 28 when he would commit over one hundred thousand troops to Vietnam, circumstances of the kind he had sought to avoid and had mastered so brilliantly for most of his political life began to overwhelm him, elude his grasp. The decision to transform the war, which he knew was potentially fatal to his public ambitions, could no longer be evaded or postponed. Increasing opposition from the press and critics on the Hill could no longer be controlled by his hitherto almost irresistible power of persuasion. The somewhat frightening, always puzzling outbursts became more frequent. No longer isolated incidents in a pattern of largely rational behavior (although most of what the president did and said was rational, and even in the wildest of accusations and actions there was some seed of reality), they became more continuous, infecting the entire presidential institution.

No longer satisfied with impugning the motives of his critics ("That Fulbright," he told me after Fulbright had joined the ranks of dissent, "he never was satisfied with any president that wouldn't make him secretary of state"), or attributing his difficulties to "those Kennedys" or "those Harvards" or to the traitorous citizens who lived in seeming innocence along the banks of Boston's Charles River, Johnson began to hint privately (knowing that public statements of his convictions would discredit him, retaining always that measure of control) that he was the target of a gigantic communist conspiracy in which his domestic adversaries were only players — not conscious participants, perhaps, but unwitting dupes. It was a giant, if always partial, leap into unreason, an outward sign that the barriers separating rational thought and knowledge from delusive belief were becoming weaker, more easily crossed.

Sitting in the Oval Office on July 5, Johnson interrupted our conversation on domestic matters to confide: "You know, Dick, the communists are taking over the country. Look here," and he lifted a manila folder from his desk. "It's Teddy White's FBI file. He's a communist sympathizer."

Early that same month, I was sitting in Bill Moyers's office, awaiting his arrival for a conference to discuss the next year's budget, when Bill walked in, his face pale, visibly shaken. "I just came from a conversation with the president. He told me he was going to fire everybody that didn't agree with him, that Hubert [Humphrey] could not be trusted and we weren't to tell him anything; then he began to explain that the communist way of thinking had infected everyone around him, that his enemies were deceiving the people and, if they succeeded, there was no way he could stop World War Three." For more than an hour Bill and I discussed the intermittent, but clearly visible signs of Johnson's instability; the transformation of personality, which, far from total, was clearly accelerating.

"Suppose he really does go crazy," I said. And then, answering my own question: "I tell you what would happen if we went public with our doubts. They could assemble a panel of psychiatrists to examine the president, and he would tell them how sad it made him that two boys he loved so much could have thought such a thing, and then explain his behavior so calmly and reasonably that when he was finished, we would be the ones committed." Indeed, what could be done — what could anyone do — about a man who was always able to impose an immensely powerful and persuasive simulacrum of control to mask his growing irrationalities?

Shortly thereafter I consulted, privately and without informing Moyers, Dr. Paul Weissberg, a psychiatrist who was also a close personal friend. After he agreed to treat our conversation as privileged, I described the presidential behavior as I had observed it. Unknown to me until years later, Moyers took the same course, talking independently with two different psychiatrists. In all cases the diagnosis was the same: We were describing a textbook case of paranoid disintegration, the eruption of long-suppressed irrationalities. As for the future, it was uncertain. The disintegration could continue, remain constant, or recede, depending on the strength of Johnson's resistance, and, more significantly, on the direction of those external events — the war, the crumbling public support — whose pressures were dissolving Johnson's confidence in his ability to control events, that confidence which was his protection both against the buried cauldron of nonrational suspicions, and his fear of being left alone and helpless in a hostile world.

Johnson's formidable powers of resistance waged a heroic and often successful battle against the insistent, false beliefs which were displacing the knowledge derived from detached, rationally ordered perception. On July 14, Johnson walked into a staff meeting, took a seat, listened for a while, and then told us, "Don't let me interrupt. But there's one thing you ought to know. Vietnam is like being in a plane without a parachute, when all the engines go out. If you jump, you'll probably be killed, and if you stay in,

you'll crash and probably burn. That's what it is." Then, without
waiting for a response, the tall, slumped figure rose and left the
room.

If that's how he feels, I thought as I watched the door close
behind him, then why are we escalating the war; what's the point
if he thinks it's hopeless? Maybe he's going to end it. There was
truth — rational truth — in what Johnson had said, a moment of
illumination. Yet reflecting on the president's startling statement,
I realized that the seeming objectivity of his description also revealed the inward struggle: No matter what course he took, the
result would be disaster, total and irrevocable. He was trapped;
he was helpless — conclusions that were closer to a description of
his own fears than to external reality. Admittedly, there was, by
now, no easy way out. We had raised the stakes and increased our
commitment; American boys were dead and American resources
wasted. But still there were choices — to continue the unwinnable
war, to withdraw, or to seek some kind of jerry-built compromise.
These choices were all unpleasant, but they were not, equally,
disasters of fatal magnitude. Yet Johnson's assertion that there
was no escape from the doomed plane may well have been true —
for him, for that part of him already encircled by enemies.

Only weeks later, sitting around the pool at his Texas ranch,
talking with some members of the staff, Mrs. Johnson at his side,
Johnson gloomily proclaimed, "I'm going to be known as the
president who lost Southeast Asia. I'm going to be the one who
lost this form of government. The communists already control the
three major networks and the forty major outlets of communication. Walter Lippmann is a communist and so is Teddy White.
And they're not the only ones. You'd all be shocked at the kind
of things revealed by the FBI reports."

As the president spoke, his manner became more intense, his
body stiffened. Mrs. Johnson leaned over, tenderly patted his hand,
and, at her touch, tension seemed to seep from his body. "Now,
Lyndon," she said, "you shouldn't read them so much." "Why
not?" he asked. "Because," she replied, "they have a lot of un-
evaluated information in them, accusations and gossip which haven't
been proven."

"Never mind that," Johnson told his wife, "you'd be surprised
at how much they know about people. Why, that draft protest last
week that got everyone so excited. According to the FBI report,
out of the 256 who were supposed to have burned their draft cards,

a substantial number were crazy people who had a previous history in mental institutions. And most of the cards supposedly burned were xeroxed so that no prosecution would be possible. One of our informants in the communist party — we have them there, you know, just like in the newspaper city rooms — reported that the communists decided to do all they could to encourage demonstrations against the draft." Johnson removed his hand from his wife's grasp, leaned forward, the intensity returning: "Now I don't want to be like a McCarthyite. But this country is in a little more danger than we think. And someone has to uncover this information."

During the summer of 1965 Bill Moyers and I met every few days to discuss the president's increasingly vehement and less rational outbursts. We agreed that Johnson was changing, that some invasive inward force was distorting his perceptions, gradually infiltrating his actions, infecting the entire process of presidential decision. Although we were reluctant to acknowledge the possibility of a continued decline, refused to acknowledge it, the signs of aberration were too obvious to be ignored or rationalized as typical Johnsonian exaggerations.

In his book *Crowds and Power*, first published in 1962, Elias Canetti — among the world's most distinguished authorities on social psychology — writes: "[T]he paranoiac feels surrounded; his chief enemy is never content to attack him singlehandedly but always tries to rouse a spite filled pack . . . the piercing intellect of the paranoiac always unmasks them . . . the paranoiac exhibits a mania for finding causal relations. . . . Nothing that happens to him is chance or coincidence."

"It's all a few intellectuals and columnists," Johnson confided to a few members of the White House staff sitting with him in the Oval Office. "The people loved me, and they believed in me. You just go down to the White House basement. You'll see them. Boxes full of letters, all praising me for doing the right thing. They spread the doubt — every morning I wake up and see another column attacking me, or some professor on television. Naturally people get confused with all these voices shouting and hollering about how awful I am. Bobby saw his chance. He saw I was in trouble, so he put [Martin Luther] King on the Kennedy payroll to rile up the Negroes. That's why we had the riots. After all I've done for the Negroes. They never would have *attacked me* if they hadn't been put up to it.

"Bobby gave the communists the idea. Now, I'm not saying he's a communist, mind you. But they saw they might be able to divide the country against me. They already control the three major networks. So they began to complain that we were killing civilians, that we ought to stop the bombing. That got back here, and my critics took it up. Not just in the press. I was always getting advice from my top advisers after they had been in contact with someone in the communist world. Hell, you can always find Dobrynin's car in front of a columnist's house the night before he blasts me on Vietnam. Now we've got to get our own story out. Do a better job of letting people know what's really happening."

Later that summer the Senate Foreign Relations Committee was preparing to issue the report of its investigation of Johnson's intervention in the Dominican Republic the previous April. I had first learned of the precipitous and wholly unexpected invasion on April 28, when, working in my White House office, I received an urgent summons to attend an emergency meeting in the Cabinet Room. Hurrying, almost running, down the West Wing steps and along the corridor that led past the Oval Office, I encountered McGeorge Bundy, who told me that the president had just ordered marine contingents to be flown into the Dominican Republic. Appalled, I asked Bundy if it was too late, could anything be done to stop them. "They're already in the air," he replied. "

"But why the marines? Why not the army?" I said, my objection clearly futile, an absurdity misconceived from frustration and anger at this latest blow to the Alliance for Progress, whose steady dissolution I had helplessly observed for over a year. Still, behind my remark was an awareness that the marines were a vivid symbol of American intervention and occupation, not only of the Dominican Republic but of other Latin nations. Their appearance would be seen as a return to the worst days of gunboat diplomacy. I will never forget following Bundy into the Cabinet Room, observing him approach some of the other participants, laughing. "You know what Goodwin says? He wants to know if we can send someone else beside the marines." I felt a surge of anger; the decision may have been irrevocable, but it was no joke.

The intervention itself was one of the strangest episodes in Johnson's foreign policy, but, fortunately, being relatively peaceful and short-lived, was virtually without harmful consequence, although the storm of press inquiry and criticism which followed our mini-invasion did mark the end of Johnson's "honeymoon," elicited the first faint signs of his inability to cope with criticism. Nevertheless, the criticism died away as Johnson withdrew the marines and, over a period of time, the Dominican Republic returned to democracy.

In retrospect, one can see foreshadowings in the Dominican intervention of the conduct of the war in Vietnam: the decision to use force made suddenly, without discussion or debate, by Johnson and a small inner circle (Bundy, Rusk, McNamara) who were gathered in the Oval Office when a cable from our embassy arrived, recommending that we send in the marines; the action justified by undocumented (and untrue) intelligence reports that the "communists were going to take over."

Although I believed a mistake had been made, Johnson's explanations that April were rational, coherent, logically supportable. He had welcomed, at least in public, a full investigation by the Senate Foreign Relations Committee, under the chairmanship of Senator William Fulbright.

But now, in August, the committee having concluded its inquiry, Johnson's attitude had radically altered. Fulbright had become an enemy. Any criticism of Johnson's action in the Dominican Republic could only be a concealed attack on his policies in Vietnam — another attempt to stimulate the mounting, intolerable opposition. On August 23, Johnson called Senator Herman Talmadge, an old friend and ranking member of the Senate Foreign Relations Committee, to discuss the inquiry.

After Talmadge had picked up his phone to hear the White House operator announce, "Senator, the president is calling," Johnson began: "I want to talk with you in confidence, and I do not want anybody, not even your wife, to know I have talked with you. I went down on the boat last night" (the presidential yacht) "with our friend Fulbright. They're getting to him. The *New York Times* is determined to prove that we went off the deep end. You have two or three little Jewish boys up there that are — according to our phone taps and other sources of information — on the communist side of this operation. Herbert Matthews" (a *Times* editor) "says it would be better if every nation in Latin America had the Castro system."

"My God!" Talmadge responded.

"They all agreed — we have them on the record — that we're a bunch of plunderers and imperialists. Now they have used Bill's

[Fulbright's] picture in the papers now and then, and they write favorably of him as does the *Washington Post*. He is naturally human, just like when somebody in your state brags on you and you feel human and kind toward them. But these publications are out to destroy Bennett" (Senator Wallace Bennett of Utah, who had supported the Dominican action) "and to separate him from the rest of you fellows."

Talmadge: "Well, of course you know Fulbright, his country comes last."

Johnson: "Well, you and Russell are still up there, and you still have influence. You are just being too quiet about it."

Talmadge: "I don't think he'll ever bring a Dominican report out of committee."

Johnson: "He won't if you just hit him straight on and tell him that I say Bennett is 100 percent right, and the FBI says it, and so do Rusk and Mann; that the only ones that say Lyndon is wrong is Szulc of the *New York Times* and that other fellow from the *Washington Post*. Just say, 'Now listen, Bill, I don't know what's going on in this hearing, but if you all are trying to prove that Lyndon here is a blue blood and doesn't know what's going on — you're crazy.' Say the communists had this outfit in the Dominican Republic trying to take it over, and they would have had it exactly like they got Cuba, and the thing that stopped them were the U.S. Marines.

"And don't say I called."

Part of the conversation is vintage Johnson: sympathetic understanding of Fulbright's vulnerability to praise, flattering references to Talmadge's influence and superior powers of comprehension, the suggested design of arguments to be made. But there is also a more menacing tone, assertion and accusation that, by the time of this call, had come to characterize the president's discussions of Vietnam: communist agents on the *New York Times*, wire taps and informers, secret FBI reports, a media conspiracy to destroy a fellow senator and, by implication, the president himself.

Of course, Johnson was talking to a man he knew would be inclined to believe him; was careful, as he always was, even in the worse days to follow, to tailor his observations to his audience, always struggling to restrain the inner beliefs which, if revealed to the wrong people — those ignorant of the truth known to him alone — might destroy his credibility. Yet even if Johnson knew Talmadge would believe him, his slanders were not pure contrivance, an instrument of persuasion. Johnson believed it too. Every word of it.

At the beginning of June, I told Moyers in confidence that I intended to leave the White House later that year. "He won't let you," Bill responded involuntarily. "Why not?" I answered. Then we both began to laugh, recognizing the absurd outburst of some hidden perception that Johnson's will could not be denied. "Well," Bill said, in his more familiar calm and thoughtful tones, "you're probably doing the right thing. In fact, I've been thinking of leaving myself."

"You can't do that," I answered instinctively. "You're the only one who knows he's paranoid."

On July 5, I made a diary note: "It has been a wild and unbelievable week — dinner with Bill and his assistant and another long discussion of Johnson in which we agreed on his paranoid condition. I asked Bill if he thought I should talk to anyone before I left, perhaps to Bob McNamara, whose position might let him keep things from getting out of hand. Bill seemed to think that it might be a good idea, but made me promise to tell him first, before I did anything. I don't know if we can trust McNamara. He is intelligent and skilled, could understand our fears, but was also very ambitious and could let his ambition run away with him."

Three days later, on July 8, I noted that the "fact is that the disintegration is going on and it is unlikely that it will stop. I must put Moyers in touch with the psychiatrist." (Not knowing he had initiated his own discussions with medical professionals.)

In the long run all secrets which are confined to one faction, or, still more, to one man, must bring disaster, not only to the possessor . . . but also to all they concern . . . every secret is explosive, expanding with its own inner heat.

— Elias Canetti, *Crowds and Power*

Although disastrous in its consequences, Johnson's narrowing of debate and decision to a small inner circle was not, by itself, evidence of mental aberration. Other presidents — Kennedy and the Bay of Pigs, Reagan and arms to Iran — have fallen victim to the same temptations. Yet one can detect in some of Johnson's actions something different from an overzealous wish to protect important secrets. If the world was beginning to slip from his control, he would construct a tiny inner world that he could control, barricade himself not only from disagreement but from the need to acknowledge the very existence of disagreement except among the uninformed and the hostile. His acts alone do not prove this; it is a matter of degree and tone and intensity.

Johnson's conversations with the cabinet would begin with the question: "What are you doing here? Why aren't you out there fighting against my enemies? Don't you realize that if they destroy me, they'll destroy you as well?" The meetings themselves, no longer a forum for debate, were largely confined to reports by each secretary on the affairs of his department. Questions about Vietnam were discouraged, and, if asked, went unanswered.

Nor could the National Security Council be trusted. "Those National Security meetings were like a sieve," Johnson remarked. "There's that Arthur Goldberg" (the ambassador to the United Nations) "with a direct pipeline to the *New York Times*. You knew that after every meeting each of those guys would run home to tell his wife and neighbors what they said to the President. . . . And those fellows from Defense were the worst of all. Every Department of Defense official and his brother" (and, presumably, his sister, wife, and cousins) "would be leakers one time or another. You know how I could tell who it was? From the newspapers. Every time I saw some Department of Defense official's picture in the paper with a nice story about him, I'd know it was the paper's bribe for the leaked story."

And those who attended NSC meetings were sometimes told they should not use the occasion of those meetings to voice doubt or disagreement. The president didn't want to hear it. "I know how you feel, Arthur," the faithful McNamara told Ambassador Goldberg before an NSC meeting, "but it would be better if you didn't say anything. The president has already made up his mind and you would only embarrass him."

Gradually all meaningful discussion and decision were confined to the small, carefully chosen inner circle: Rusk, McNamara, the director of the CIA, the chairman of the Joint Chiefs, and, occasionally, others who could be trusted to maintain complete secrecy. And how were the "chosen" determined? Partly, of course, by office, but also, as Johnson explained, "That group never leaked a single word. I could control them."

Meanwhile, dissent from the outside — press or Congress or public — was discounted, rejected as the malignant issue of ignorance, political ambition, disloyalty, or even a multiplying conspiracy. The only effective restraints were Johnson's judgment of the limits of public and congressional tolerance, and his fears that the use of U.S. military force might precipitate Soviet and Chinese intervention.

Later, after he had left the White House, Johnson spoke of "secret treaties," formal documents committing Russia and China to come to the aid of North Vietnam should the United States transgress defined limits. "I never knew when I sat there approving targets one, two, three, whether one of those three might just be the one to set off the provisions of those secret treaties. I kept asking myself, what if one of those targets you picked today triggers off Russia or China?" There was, of course, no evidence that any such treaties existed. But Johnson needed them to justify his acts, and so he believed in their reality.

The incursions of paranoia — a kind of guerrilla warfare of the mind — are subtle, carefully establishing their chimerical, delusive outposts on still-firm remnants of reality. There was aggression in Southeast Asia, and opposition at home. These things were true. But the transformation of disagreement into disloyalty, political opponents into personal enemies, spreading dissent into a gigantic conspiracy, the rebels of Vietnam into the advance guard of world conquest, was the work of mental processes that bent and twisted the clay of reality into menacing fantastical shapes.

For much of the time, certainly during 1965, Johnson retained a large measure of control over his immense political skills. Congress, despite increasing dissent, never cast a single vote against the war or the money to fight it. Johnson not only defeated efforts to roll back the Great Society, but succeeded in enacting a dwindling flow of legislation. In Vietnam he could, at first, truthfully assert his consistency with the commitments of Kennedy and Eisenhower.

When, in 1964, Johnson took the presidential oath, behind him — securely lodged in the memory of a man who had first come to Washington during the administration of Herbert Hoover — was a century of American involvement with Asia, three Pacific wars, two decades of Cold War, and a belief, rapidly becoming a dogma, that the arena of confrontation was shifting to the "third world."

He inherited and adopted a world view that included criteria for American responsibility, principles of action, established standards for determining threats to American freedom. In Vietnam he had, at first, the support — and more than support, the persuasive advocacy — of that foreign-policy establishment which he secretly despised — thinking that they regarded him with contempt as the ignorant boy from a small Texas town accidentally come to power — but on whom he relied, believing their approval was a warranty that he was doing the right thing. And even as those who had guided and urged him on from the beginning reconsidered and fled, Johnson, finally almost alone among the powerful, never departed from the conviction that he was acting in fulfillment of his obligations to the country and the future of its freedom.

Yet the growth of dissent was not, as Johnson thought, "betrayal" or "cowardice," but a recognition that our actions in Vietnam had taken a giant stride toward irrationality. One could justify assistance to a beleaguered ally without acquiescing in actions that would thrust the United States into a major war, kill and maim hundreds of thousands, and tear the fabric of American society — dooming the poor to their poverty, leaving the black man immobilized along the still-untraveled path to justice, undermine the moral strength of an entire nation.

Johnson didn't want any of this to happen. Yet he made it happen; driven not only by his very real convictions, but by the uncontrollable compulsions of his own mind. He hoped, at first, to retain public support for his cherished Great Society by concealing the necessities of war, flourishing false estimates of rapid "progress" soon to be followed by "victory." In the side pocket of his jacket he carried cards on which were inscribed the latest "intelligence" — statistics demonstrating our accelerating control over the population, shrinkage of the Vietcong forces through death and rising desertions. It was, you see — couldn't you see? — only a question of time. He grotesquely understated troop commitments already made in secret, instructed McNamara to underestimate the cost of the war by a factor of at least 50 percent. This was not simply lying; although there were many lies. It was as if Johnson thought that by saying these things, then urging them upon others with his immense persuasive power, he could somehow transform his misstatements into truth; that his own fiercely terrible desire to believe would, through its own force, become an undeniable basis for belief by him as well as by others. "It is impossible to overestimate the importance of words for the paranoiac," Canetti writes; "perhaps the most marked trend in paranoia is that toward a complete seizing of the world through words, as though language were a fist and the world lay in it." And that grasp has a purpose — the reshaping of reality (an imagined reality) to conform to the beliefs which are the essential defense of the paranoid personality against external threats and internal doubts.

And, for a long time, Johnson succeeded: not in changing reality, but in deceiving much of the country and, perhaps, himself.

Because of the office he held, his access to media, his control over information streaming into Washington from Vietnam, Johnson was able to transmit his own confused — but never purposeless — distortions to the public. His optimistic public reports, the accounts of Hanoi's intransigent refusal to negotiate, were instantly and without qualification published and broadcast throughout the land. Many of the reporters, even some chieftains of the media, knew better, realized they were carriers of deception, but felt compelled to print and broadcast official public reports simply because they were official and public. "Theirs not to reason why." I do not intend this as a criticism of particular reporters or editors. It inheres in the nature of today's corporate media. Their own views and knowledge must be subordinate to the assertations — the declarations of fact or intent — by the president, unless, of course, some secret contradicting scandal is unearthed — Watergate or Iranscam. But Vietnam was not a scandal, it was a tragedy — a judgment, not a dramatic fact — and so the media had no choice. They would be Johnson's instrument and his accomplice in deception, until the accumulating evidence — the visibly increasing devastation — made denial impossible.

As he felt himself compelled to plunge even farther into the insatiable jungles of Vietnam, Johnson began to magnify the stakes of the war. "As for morality," he said to a small group of staff members, "why, I don't think there's a higher morality than protecting your brother from getting killed. Now, Fulbright and Mansfield and Lippmann and RFK don't see this because they think of the South Vietnamese as yellow people not worth protecting. Why, Ho Chi Minh and the communists in Southeast Asia are as much a threat to our national security as Hitler."

Later, after he had left the White House, Johnson expanded on the now almost obsessive theme — a besieged Johnson standing alone against the collapse of democracy and, ultimately, world-wrecking havoc. He told Doris Kearns, "I honestly and truly believe that if we don't assert ourselves and if Chinese communists and the Soviet Union take Laos, Vietnam, Cambodia, it seriously endangers India, Pakistan, and the whole Pacific world." (It was the domino theory running wild.) "Then we'll really be up for grabs. We're the richest nation in the world and everybody wants what we've got. And the minute we look soft, the would-be aggressors will go wild. We'll lose all of Asia and then Europe and then we'll be a rich little island all by ourselves. That means World War Three. And when that comes to pass I'd sure hate to depend on the Galbraiths and that Harvard crowd to protect my property or lead me to shelter in the Burnet caves" (a town near Johnson City whose caves were a local tourist attraction).

The wildly extravagant, often irrational Lyndon Johnson of the later years had not been metamorphosed by power and war from an earlier state of being, nor had he become merely a magnified version of what he had always been. The relentless inward enemies he had strived to master for his entire life, in a struggle that was the source of his energies, his most generously encompassing ambitions — those same hostile forces that we label, but do not describe, as "guilt," "fear," "need," the universal malignancies of existence — had finally penetrated his formidable armor, commanded the defeated provinces of his character with their strict captains — "depression," "delusion," "impotence" — turned inward those personal powers with which he had achieved extraordinary mastery over men and institutions until, become almost irresistible, they drove him from office and, finally, struck and halted his physical heart.

Yet it would be a mistake to attribute the man's poignant disintegration wholly to the inward disruptions of his mind. He also had the misfortune to be trapped between two Americas — the one in which he had grown up and the one he came to lead. He was fond of quoting Sam Rayburn saying "that a man who can't size up another person when he walks in the room had better be in another profession." No one could do that better than Johnson. His greatest gifts of leadership — the ability to understand, persuade, and subdue — depended on connections and relationships that existed on a human scale. "I always believed," he once said, "that as long as I could take someone into a room with me I could make him my friend. And that included anybody, even Nikita Khrushchev. From the start of my presidency, I believed that if I handled him right he would go along with me. Deep down, hidden way below, he too wanted what was good, but every now and then this terrible urge for world domination would get into him and take control and then he'd go off on some crazy jag like putting those missiles in Cuba. I saw all that in him and knew I could cope with it so long as he and I were in the same room."

The statement is, of course, a hopelessly simplistic view of world affairs, assuming, as it does, that the gigantic Soviet bureaucracy was the personal creation of Khrushchev, or that its course could be changed as readily as some senator might be persuaded to switch his vote on excise taxes. Nor would Johnson retain such an understanding, even sympathetic, view of communist leaders as the mysterious, seemingly inhuman persistence of the enigmatic Ho Chi Minh loosed forces that threatened to destroy him. Yet, even then, he remarked, "If only I could get Ho in a room with me, I'm sure we could work things out."

Nevertheless, it was true that there were few who could totally resist the influence of Lyndon Johnson's personal presence. "I can't stand the bastard," Robert Kennedy once told me after a private meeting with the president, "but he's the most formidable human being I've ever meet." Yet this man of such intensely personal gifts, who received understanding and transmitted influence through other men's eyes, was set at the head of a gargantuan bureaucracy, managed by people he could not know or observe; compelled to reach for his constituency while sitting in an empty office staring at the curved, blank lens of a television camera.

Often he would awaken in the middle of the night and — clad in pajamas, feet encased in thickly padded slippers — go down to the Situation Room of the White House, where he would sit for hours receiving the latest reports of bombing raids and missing planes, captured villages and fresh casualties, as if, somehow, in this way he could establish contact with the struggles, the secret desires, of living flesh. But it could not be done. Translated and addressed by Pentagon computers, decisions were electronically scrambled, hurled along invisible pathways through thousands of miles of space, setting machines and troops in motion against marks on a map. A master of men, the invulnerable genius of the small town had become the servant of technology; his perceptions confused, judgment distorted, no less enshackled because he believed in the power of that technology, the mathematical accuracy of transistor computation, even liked the machines with their illusion of control, but liked them as a small boy with a mechanical toy — never fully trusting, but with no other choice; his increasingly angry, increasingly baffling frustrations, a manifestation and metaphor for an aspect of America's own transformation.

Later I was to question my failure to disclose what I knew of Johnson's mental condition, inwardly speculating that through misplaced loyalty or personal cowardice I was betraying my obligation to the country. Yet such an act would undoubtedly have been disbelieved — what credentials did I have? — and later, after I joined the opponents of the war, regarded as politically motivated slander. I could not have proved my judgment then. Indeed, I cannot prove it now, although the history of the war in Vietnam has added testimony far more persuasive than my own observations of 1965. Moreover, after 1965 my personal witness to presidential behavior ended, and it is possible — given the nature of the affliction — that the paranoid disruptions diminished or even came to an end; although all the external evidence argues against such a salubrious conclusion. During the next few years, as I campaigned with McCarthy and then Kennedy, I never disclosed — even to my closest friends and colleagues — the wild surmise that had preoccupied my final days in the White House. But my own active, fervent opposition was always, in part, informed and motivated by the knowledge that Lyndon Johnson had become a very dangerous man. Still, to this day, I have never completely overcome the suspicion that my secrecy may have been a very large mistake of judgment or timidity.

22 / Leaving the White House

MY DECISION to leave the White House in the summer of
1965 was not motivated, at least not directly, by the war. I mistakenly felt then, and for some time after, that our involvement in
Vietnam was a remediable error; that diplomacy would find a
negotiated way out that did not require surrender on either side.
Certainly, I then thought, Vietnam did not outweigh Johnson's
large achievements and what I knew to be his future intentions.
It was true, however, that the progress of war, temporarily at
least, had immobilized domestic progress — not because of its financial costs, but its almost total absorption of the energies of
leadership required to move a reluctant Congress and an ambivalent nation.

"I believe we can do both," Johnson repeated over and over.
"We are a country which was built by pioneers who had a rifle in
one hand and an ax in the other. We are a nation with the highest
GNP, the highest wages, and the most people at work. We can do
both. And as long as I am president we will do both. I am tired
of people who talk about sick societies. Our country is being tested
with a war on two fronts — a war on poverty and against aggression."

He was right, of course. In the abstract. But in the real world
of fiercely clashing interests, the war became a weapon for those
who, as the price of their support of Vietnam, demanded a reduction, a virtual abandonment, of liberal reform. The increasing
withdrawal of public support deprived Johnson of the consensus
on which he had so skillfully built. "[T]here is not enough moral

energy, will and purpose and attention . . . to carry out the two conflicting tasks at home and abroad," wrote Walter Lippmann. From the floor of the Congress, Wilbur Mills, powerful conservative leader of the House Committee on Ways and Means, proclaimed with scantily concealed delight that "The Administration simply must choose between guns and butter," an admonition which, over the years, repeated from all sides, was distended to a metaphor for a turning point in American economic history. It was one of the most deceptively self-righteous slogans ever devised to mask the interests of the powerful. "Butter" was not the comforts of the wealthy, or the profits of the corporations, but expenditures for the poor and the blacks, the improvement of education, protection of the environment. Once Johnson's attempt to mask the true cost of the war was uncovered, the issue became — Who should pay? The answer was, as Johnson had anticipated, to exact sacrifice from the poor, the young, and the lower middle class; not from the wealthy or the corporate giants of industry and finance.

Yet even if the increasing sluggishness of domestic progress seemed temporary, it had reduced my role in White House policy to a virtual nullity. Admittedly I was the president's chief speechwriter, referred to by the press as a "top adviser," recipient of continual presidential attention, affection, flattery; trusted enough to be exposed to his lamentations and accusations. Still, the substance of authority was fading, my labors, once so productive, became a voluminous futility. Wanting to be a writer, I had become enmeshed in politics. Now it was time for a return to desires fixed from childhood.

In a memorandum to Bill Moyers — who had sought to persuade me to remain — I set forth some of my reasons for resigning. ". . . Having spent five years at this business I am tired. . . . All my inclinations — in fact my most ardent desires — are for a life where I can express and develop myself beyond anything I can gain from staying here. . . . Most of the stuff I am now doing is trivia. . . . True, in speechwriting I make a unique contribution, but this has become mostly image-making. In foreign affairs I have to write what Rusk, Bundy and others want to say; with little chance to reshape their views, or even to be heard on them. I have much more scope on domestic affairs, but as you know, that has come almost to a standstill. . . . Essentially I am not a word man — but an idea man — and one who wants to put those ideas into action.

"I know, better than anyone, that my departure will make no

difference to the acts or politics of the White House." (Not false modesty, but a coldly accurate judgment.) "It may have some slight effect on the image" (doubtful) "— but now that is in your hands.

"In a way difficult to explain, even to myself, my personal integrity — in the sense of personal wholeness — is on the line in this decision. I know I may be wrong about it. I know that it may be bad for my career." (And it was, at least for my public career.) "I know it may make Johnson an enemy" (which it did). "I hope these things won't happen. But I have to do it anyway. You ask how I can say no to the president" (who had asked me to withdraw my resignation). "Because I believe I should, and know I must. When you sum it all up, that's what it comes to."

On the bottom of my memo, the empathetic Moyers, wise beyond his years, a colleague become an intimate personal friend, inscribed a handwritten reply: "My personal integrity, what is left of it" (no man had more), "is also on the line; also something more important, my friendship with you, closer than a brother. So I simply have to say — I agree with you."

At the distance of almost twenty-five years, the exchange seems strangely overheated, the tone unnecessarily fervent (although I meant every word of it). After all, I was just quitting a job.

But the increasingly turbulent passions of the president — every act and word suffused with intimate personal import; are you with me or against me? — had infected the entire White House, which had now become a virtual projection of the president's own temperament. In this ambience, an ordinarily routine decision was permeated with emotions; confrontation with the president, especially defiance of his will, even on small matters, clouded thought with fear, doubt, regret, mistrust of one's own motives. It was, in this atmosphere, courageous of Moyers to ignore the president's instructions: "You're his friend, aren't you? Well, you get him to stay." Nor was it easy for me to leave Lyndon Johnson — a man I admired and even loved (cautiously, intermittently), who had elevated me to a position of considerable distinction and authority — never once violating my dignity, never demeaning or disrespectful. Moreover, the man, although often erratic, now manifestly troubled, had done great things. And I would miss the trappings of power: the limousine and White House phone, the public recognition, and the myriad of prerogatives that accrue to an important presidential assistant in official Washington.

And if my decision had cost considerable inward struggle, Lyndon Johnson wasn't going to make it any easier. In early June I wrote the president of my plans to leave in the fall. At first there was no response, no indication in our continuing encounters that anything had changed, or that he had even read my memo. But the hiatus was short. On June 14 he summoned Moyers to his office: "I've talked to Mrs. Johnson and told her that I don't intend to suck around you and Goodwin anymore. I told her if they want to go they can go." (Moyers had not resigned but had hinted at a desire to leave in the not too distant future.) "I told Lady Bird that I love these boys, and I'll do anything for them, but I don't intend to do that." As Moyers reported the conversation, for more than an hour Johnson alternated between cajolery and threat, appeals to interest and to fear. "I plucked both of you up from obscurity," Johnson said, "I made you and now you want to leave me, to walk out of a crisis when I need you." (Using the plural but meaning me.) "Let him go, if he wants to go. We'll get along. I've got Jack [Valenti] and Buzz [Horace Busby]. They're loyal."

A week later, around 10 P.M., I was working in my office, when the president called me to the mansion. I found him stretched out in bed in his pajamas, watching television. As I entered, he turned off the set, stared at me for what seemed an interminable interval, then: "I want you to know I've torn up your resignation," he said. "You can't go. I can't get along without you. The president of the United States, the leader of the whole free world, can't get along without you. I need you here and you're not going."

"Of course you can get along without me," I replied; "you got along without me before I came."

"That's not true. When are you supposed to go up there — in the fall? Well, you better call them up and give them plenty of notice because you can't go and you're not going to go."

I searched vainly for a reply. One could not argue with a command. I realized that my clothes were damp, that I was sweating under the formidable pressures of Johnson's adamant insistence.

"Do you want to live in the country, is that it?" Johnson continued. "Well, I'll get you a house in the country. Maybe you're not making enough money. Well, I can arrange for an extra payment from the Johnson Foundation. Whatever you need."

"Money is not a problem," I replied.

"Well, you have got to help pull me through this crisis. Bill and you are the only two I can count on."

The conversation was one of many. I quickly learned that it

was impossible to debate Johnson. Not only did he have an answer for every rational argument, but his own assertions did not allow for rebuttal — I owed it to him, to the presidency, to the country. It wasn't true, of course. I was only a small fragment in the pattern of presidential command. But how could I deny him? Could I accuse him of grotesque exaggeration; call him a liar? I realized the only sensible behavior was to listen in silence and then, shaken, often sweat soaked, return to my office and write still another memo reiterating my intention to leave.

A few days after that late-night conversation I walked alongside Johnson as he went from the Oval Office toward the mansion for his afternoon nap. As we moved through the corridor he turned toward me: "I'll tell you one thing, Dick. Either you stay here with me or go over to the Pentagon and get yourself a pair of those shiny black boots. There's a statute — McNamara and Vance sent it to me — which says we can draft specialists vital to the national interest. And that's what I'll do. I'll draft you."

"Will you make me a general?" I asked.

"You don't want to be a general, they'll be the first ones to lose their heads. You want to be a private."

"That doesn't seem fair," I replied; "when I was in the army I used to be a corporal."

"You'll be demoted," he answered, and departed for the living quarters.

He's just kidding, I thought. But to make sure I called McNamara and asked him if he had advised the president that I could be drafted. McNamara was evasive enough so that I was certain some such conversation had taken place. Although of course they weren't going to draft me. Were they?

During the weeks ahead, as I persisted somewhat shakily in my intentions, Johnson shifted tactics. I was no longer invited to meetings, close associates were told that my departure was an "act of disloyalty," that I "had decided that my future was with those Kennedys" (I had not told Bobby of my intention to resign or my future plans). Johnson even repeated the absurd rumor that I had consulted with the Soviet ambassador on the preparation of a presidential speech. (A tale whose origin was the presence of Dobrynin at Averell Harriman's swimming pool while a small group of us sought relief from the midsummer heat.) It was as if Johnson sought to combine in his single person the good-guy, bad-guy interrogation technique familiar to all readers of mystery fiction.

Although I was flattered at the intensity of Johnson's resistance to my departure, I was also puzzled. Other members of the staff were now playing a far more important role in the formation of policy. My own participation in matters of substance had dwindled. Reflecting later, I began to understand that he thought I alone could add to his glory: impart to his thoughts an eloquence of expression that might bring admiration from his most-feared critics, subdue the deeply founded fear that his own unpolished expression would draw contempt from the educated and worldly elite, and stimulate unfavorable comparisons with his predecessor. "I just won't give any more national speeches," he said to Moyers when discussing my departure. The irony, both poignant and self-destructive, was that Lyndon Johnson was a very eloquent man who, had he talked to the country as he spoke informally, would have won the admiring affection of his fellow citizens — at least until his actions began to speak louder than any words. But he was afraid.

Once it was clear that I was actually leaving, Johnson's mood softened, access to the Oval Office was restored. In August, while I was vacationing on Martha's Vineyard, he summoned me to draft the statement he was to deliver at the signing of the Voting Rights Act (dispatching a massive Coast Guard cutter to intercept my tiny Sailfish on the waters of Tashmoo Pond, to the startled amazement of my neighbors). He also exacted a promise that I would return in January to help write the 1966 State of the Union, and in September acknowledged my departure with a warm, positively flowery, exchange of letters.

"You have broadened my horizons," I wrote, "to include Texas, the land, and the America from which you come. Beginning in ignorance, I have ended in respect and affection. . . ." My departure was "an interruption and a change of direction in service to the country and to the ideals that you represent." I meant every word, and, indeed, would later try to continue my service; although I did not then suspect that I would pursue Johnson's ideals not as an ally, but as an adversary.

"Dear Dick," the president replied. "I read [your letter] with deep and mixed emotions — with intense regret for the decision it described, with gratitude for the affection it bears, and with a new appreciation for the extraordinary man who wrote it.

"I know that the unique opportunity to serve your country during these years has been a blessing to you, for it has given you the means of applying your brilliant talents to the problems that beset your fellow men. It has also been a blessing for the country — for within the high councils of government you have articulated with great force and persuasion man's hunger for justice and his hopes for a better life."

It was the most extravagant and eloquent tribute I ever received, before or since.

On September 16, excerpts from the letters, obtained from the White House press office, appeared in the *Baltimore Sun*. Although the communications were not confidential, presumably intended to be shown to my family and friends, the president was outraged. "I've learned my lesson," he said, holding up the Baltimore paper. "I'm never going to write another letter to anyone."

In 1966, as promised, I returned to draft the State of the Union address. I worked for over a week to compose a speech that would reconcile the war with continued progress toward the Great Society — "guns and butter." I reached the peroration at dawn of the day of delivery, having worked, without respite, for almost thirty-six consecutive hours. The typewriter keys were blurred, my mind in rebellion against the formation of coherent sentences. I called the White House doctor. "I only need a few more hours," I implored, "otherwise there's no way I can finish." A few minutes later the doctor appeared in my office, drew a hypodermic partially filled with an unnamed red liquid from his bag, and, as I continued to jab haltingly at the typewriter keys, never looking up, he injected the chemical into my shoulder. "Don't tell anyone," he requested. I nodded my thanks.

Whatever it was, it worked. By midmorning the speech was finished and sent to the president. Unable to sleep, I sat around the White House while the text disappeared into the Oval Office. No longer an insider, now a mere consultant, I was not asked to join the small group of editors gathered around the president. Yet, through reports from former colleagues, I became aware that the speech was being drastically altered, the pledges to domestic progress diluted, statements on the war made more militant.

At the end of the afternoon I returned to my room in the Mayflower Hotel and, frustrated, angry, exhausted, lay down fully clothed and fell asleep. About an hour later the phone rang. It was Johnson's personal secretary: "The president would like you to ride up to the Hill with him for the speech."

"I'll call you back," I replied.

For a moment, recalling the excitement of previous swift flights through the darkened Washington streets toward the crowded, noisy panoply of high occasions, I was tempted. Then I picked up the phone, instructed the operator to hold all my calls, and went back to sleep.

I was never to see or talk to Lyndon Johnson again.

Antistrophe

In the years that followed it became fashionable, even mandatory, to speak of the "failure" of the Great Society. But the Great Society did not fail. It was abandoned. The laws and messages of those first two years were intended as an experiment, the beginning of a quest whose direction would be altered as experience proved the worth of some efforts, discredited others.

Unfortunately the Great Society was so short-lived, Johnson's hold on the country so quickly eroded, that the process of experiment was frozen into immobility, mistakes and inadequacies left uncorrected, new initiatives swiftly aborted, often not even proposed. Moreover, Johnson's early emphasis on poverty, civil rights, and medical care led many critics to assimilate the Great Society to the goals of traditional, New Deal liberalism, and then to cite its failure in order to prove the obsolescence of the liberal tradition.

But the Great Society was not an extension of traditional liberalism. It was an expression of Lyndon Johnson's intention — his vision — to move progressive public policy into a new dimension.

After I left the White House, at the end of 1965, I compiled and edited, at Johnson's request, a volume of presidential speeches and messages delivered during 1964 and 1965. By the time that book had reached the galley stage, I had made a public break with Johnson on the issue of Vietnam. Immediately after my dissent appeared in the newspapers, Johnson contacted the publisher and asked to have my name removed from the book. That was impossible, the executives at McGraw-Hill explained. I had done the editing and written the commentary and could not be summarily obliterated. Whereupon the infuriated president canceled the book, repaid the publisher for all expenses incurred (including my fee), and found another editor to put together a different volume. A friendly editor inside the publishing house surreptitiously sent me a copy of the bound galleys, which now reposes in my personal library — the only copy of the book now in existence.

In that never-published volume I described the basic idea of the Great Society as the effort to improve the quality of American life. Since the New Deal, the dominant goal of liberal public policy had been equal opportunity in an economy of increasing abundance. Although a majority of Americans had achieved unparalleled standards of living, it had now become apparent that the much desired process of growth and industrialization had a darker side which threatened to diminish the life of the poor and the prosperous alike; that opportunity must be redefined to include not only higher living standards, but the chance for each person to realize the full potential of every aspect of his humanity.

This brief, rather leadenly abstract recapitulation is not a personal construct, but a distillation from a multitude of presidential speeches and messages, many of which now rest forlornly on the unvisited shelves of a thousand empty library corridors. They linger there as mute testimony to the possibility of devising a practical, tangible response to the most intractable difficulties of our society — those which have a moral and even spiritual dimension. Certainly it seemed that way to me, and to my companions, as we worked to draft the messages and laws that would begin to provide content for the Great Society.

Reading Lyndon Johnson's messages for the first time in decades, while seated at my typewriter writing this book, fresh from the morning newspapers laced with the latest episodes in the seemingly interminable litany of corruption, greed, indifference, and ignorance, I found my recollections obstructed almost to the point of paralysis — writer's block — by a pervasive melancholy — not at my own vanished power and position (although some of that), but at how well we had charted the course for a swiftly changing America: what might have been, what might still be, although the problems are greater now, more intricately woven into the fabric of American life.

After his departure from office had removed the unbearable pressures that fueled his mental agitation, Lyndon Johnson sank into a profound melancholy. He continued, often vigorously, to defend his policies in Asia. But his truest, most intimately sensed emotions were directed toward the failure of his ambitions for America, and the inability or unwillingness of others to understand how much he wanted to give, how much he had to offer.

"I just don't understand those young people," he told Doris Kearns. "Don't they realize I'm really one of them? I always hated cops when I was a kid, and just like them I dropped out of school and took off for California. I'm not some conformist middle-class personality. I could never be bureaucratized."

It was true. Lyndon Johnson was never the organization man, could never be blended into a homogenous mass, always stood alone even when he wanted most to belong — increasingly an anachronism among the plastic politicians of a plastic age. And he wanted most desperately to be understood by the young. For they, after all, were the future toward which he wanted to build.

Lyndon Johnson's war destroyed Lyndon Johnson's Great Society. The phrase comes easily, provides such a simple, facile explanation of the transformation of American life. And it is the truth, but not the whole truth. This formidable, brilliant, mad, tortured, lovable man did not, could not, wrench an entire nation from its course by himself.

At the beginning of his retirement, despite the steadily more corrosive onslaught of depression and melancholy, Johnson struggled to retain his native optimism. "Of course, I think the country's got problems," he told his dinner guests. "There's some danger to our safety and our future. But there's nothing we can't handle. We're more capable than any generation before us."

But it was too late. He knew it was too late; could not escape the feeling that he, personally, had failed and been rejected.

"I figured when my legislative program passed the Congress," Johnson said in 1971, "that the Great Society had a real chance to grow into a beautiful woman. . . . And when she grew up, I figured she'd be so big and beautiful that the American people couldn't help but fall in love with her . . . they'd want to keep her around forever, making her a permanent part of American life, more permanent even than the New Deal. . . . But now Nixon has come along and everything I worked for is ruined. . . . She's getting thinner and thinner. . . . Soon she'll be so ugly that the American people will refuse to look at her. They'll stick her in a closet . . . and then she'll die."

The metaphor is uniquely Johnson, as is the distortion of historical reality. The Johnsonian vision had begun to wither before the election of Richard Nixon. And so calamitous was the fall, that the retreat from ideals — the abandonment of shared responsibility for the well-being of our fellows, and for the enrichment of the American community — has endured for a quarter century. Only now, a generation later, can we detect a resurgence of discontent, a mild but swelling dissatisfaction with the arid, self-seeking complacency of the age. It is far too early to tell if this is an aberration, a meaningless blip — the result perhaps of a transient voltage surge — on the level brain trace of a mind-dead patient. But it might be more. It might even . . . But I fear confusing nostalgia with optimism. Yet the country has the capacities — resources, skill, freedom — which it had in the sixties. And perhaps the energizing essentials of will and belief are not dead at all, but merely dormant. Maybe if we open Lyndon Johnson's closet we will find not a corpse, but a sleeping princess ready to be restored. Of course she will need a new wardrobe. Styles have changed in twenty-five years. But not beauty. Not the ideal of beauty.

PART IV / THE INSURGENTS

The road is strewn with many dangers. First is the danger of futility; the belief there is nothing one man or woman can do against the enormous array of the world's ills. . . . Yet . . . each time a man stands up for an ideal, or acts to improve the lot of others, or strikes out against injustice, he sends forth a tiny ripple of hope, and crossing each other from a million different centers of energy and daring, those ripples build a current that can sweep down the mightiest walls of oppression and injustice.

— Speech delivered by Robert Kennedy
in Capetown, South Africa

23 / Bobby

AT DUSK of an autumn day in 1965 — having resigned but
not yet left the White House — I was sitting in the library of a
Park Avenue apartment having casual drinks with a woman who
had been associated with the Kennedy administration, when Robert Kennedy, wearing his worn leather flight jacket, entered the
apartment and walked into the library. He was slightly surprised
and somewhat suspicious. (We had seen each other only three or
four times since he had left the Justice Department.) I was still
with Johnson, whose hostility to him was widely known and discussed. What was I doing there? What did I want? In other words
he immediately proceeded to those internal calculations most natural to the politician. We shook hands cordially, I resumed my
seat and conversation while he wandered through the apartment
occasionally returning to the library where, on his third or fourth
appearance, he abruptly suggested, "Let's go ice skating." My
companion rose, as, more reluctantly, did I. As we stepped into
the building elevator, feeling my annoyance build toward anger at
his interruption — the assumption of authority it implied — I announced that "I don't know how to ice skate." "Well, you can
watch," he replied. "The hell with that, I'll give it a try," I grum-
bled.

Arriving at the ice rink in Central Park, I rented a pair of skates
and, gripping the outer rail with strain-whitened hands, began to
stumble around the perimeter, while my two companions skated,
conversing easily, across the scantily populated rink. However, I
did not spend much time observing them, being completely preoc-

cupied with groping along the rail, struggling to maintain my balance while, futilely, trying to achieve some appearance of unsupported movement. I fell three or four times, my ankles aching from the ill-fitting skates, when, after some interminable span, Bobby skated over to me and said, without comment on my performance, "Let's go for a drink." Was that a smile on the bastard's lips? I wondered. Probably.

The three of us walked to a small café in the Plaza Hotel, where, shortly after ordering, Kennedy launched into a semimonologue. He had been reading some works of popularized astronomy. "Do you know how many stars there are in our galaxy alone? How many galaxies there are?" he asked, expounding with that almost childlike delight at knowledge newly discovered, which I was later — not then — to regard as among his most admirable qualities. "And not only that," he continued, "but the stars are moving away from us at incredible speeds, some faster than the speed of light." Hurray, I thought, now I've got him on my turf. "That's impossible," I interrupted.

"It's true, just the same," he said.

"Impossible," I repeated. "Nothing can move faster than the speed of light," and then proceeded to an explanation (undoubtedly erroneous in detail) that Einstein's Special Theory of Relativity precluded any motion, relative to the earth, faster than light; that at such a speed the mass of a moving body became infinite.

"It's true," he repeated, obviously annoyed. "I don't know your theories" (they weren't mine), "but it's a fact."

"I'll bet you a bottle of champagne," I said, and with a nod of his head he acknowledged the bet. Soon thereafter we left, and parted, each to his own abode.

On my return to Washington the next day I asked the White House operator to set up a conference call with Robert Kennedy and Dr. Jerome B. Wiesner — former science adviser to President Kennedy, later president of MIT. "I'd like you to help settle a friendly dispute, Jerry," I said. "Is it possible for any object to move faster than light?" Bobby's curt greeting at the start of our three-way conversation had transformed his subsequent silence into an ominous, slightly unnerving presence. Wiesner, sensing he had been placed in a rather uncomfortable position, hesitated for a moment, then confirmed my argument. "Thank you, Jerry," Bobby said and then hung up. (Not a word for me.) I was content with my triumph, knowing that both Kennedy and I hated to lose — at anything.

I never got the champagne, even though I occasionally reminded Kennedy of his debt in the years to come. But from this
trivial encounter was to flourish the closest personal friendship I
ever experienced in politics, indeed, a friendship as important to
me as any I ever had. Even now, though much has happened,
many people passed from the ambit of my experience, he remains
an indissoluble presence in the recesses of my mind.

Many years later, Fred Dutton, a White House assistant for
John Kennedy, later traveling companion and principal assistant
in Robert Kennedy's presidential campaign, told a journalist who
was writing an article about me for *New York* magazine, "They
[Bobby and I] were remarkably similar men. They had the same
hostilities, the same awkwardnesses, the same introversions. I remember them walking on the wide expanse of lawn at the edge of
Hickory Hill deep in conversation. I remember them walking there
for an hour or two and no one felt they could interrupt them."

"Hostilities," "awkwardnesses," "introversions" — hardly terms
of praise, neutral descriptions of temperament, forming an elusive
bond distinct from the congruence of our public convictions. In
any event, it was true. We were, in many ways, some of them
quite obvious, very different persons, but there was also a likeness
which reinforced respect for those qualities we did not share.

Shortly after the astronomical dispute, I left the White House
for my new home on the Wesleyan campus in Middletown, Connecticut, where, the guidebook reads, an "extraordinarily wide Main
Street and the shaded campus of Wesleyan University give the
town a peaceful air. . . ."

Comfortable, even happy in my leisured retreat, I began to pursue my long-postponed ambition to write, beginning with a variety of articles on public affairs for the *New Yorker*, sketching out
plans for larger and more ambitious works. But those plans were
to be set aside for more than three years, as my thought and then
my energies were increasingly drawn back to the turmoil of public
events. Washington — the city's name a metaphor for public
events — was free of me, but I was not yet free of Washington.

In the mid-fall of 1965, I received a call from Robert Kennedy:
Would I like, he asked, to accompany him, some family, and friends
on a trip to South America, all expenses paid, and "you won't be
expected to do any work, just come along"? I accepted unhesitatingly. Although I had made three trips to Latin America with
President Kennedy, and traveled extensively through my favorite
continent, I had not been south since my ejection from foreign

policy in 1963. I was curious — more than curious — to observe the changes since President Kennedy's death and was excited at the chance to see old friends, revisit familiar places, the sites of remembered pleasures. I did not have enough money to make such a trip on my own, but if Kennedy was paying — hell, how could I let the chance go by?

It was decided in a phone call. Later, reflecting on my impulsive acceptance, I realized that Johnson, and my friends in the White House, would not regard me as the fortunate recipient of a wonderful opportunity. A trip to South America was understandable. But with Kennedy! The enemy, king of the enemies. That was something else. Later I found that Johnson had scrutinized the wire-service reports of Kennedy's trip, marking various sentences that, he triumphantly announced, "could only have been written by Goodwin." In fact, none of them was mine. I did no writing on the trip, speeches being left to the talented hands of Adam Walinsky, and Kennedy's own considerable capacity for verbal improvisation. (Indeed, the only speech I ever wrote for Robert Kennedy until we joined efforts on the Vietnam issue was delivered during a trip I did not make — to Capetown, South Africa, an excerpt of which is the epigraph to Part IV of this book.)

Although Kennedy had a serious interest in the continent that had been a principal concern of his brother's administration, the trip was also to be an adventure. Besides myself, the Kennedy party included his wife, Ethel, a few of his Senate assistants (speechwriter Adam Walinsky, and Tom Johnston, who managed the schedule of events), former associates such as John Siegenthaler, now editor of the *Nashville Tennessean*, who had worked for Bobby in the Justice Department, and a handful of friends including Bill vanden Heuvel (later to be ambassador to the United Nations), his wife Jean, and a few others who were friends of the Kennedy family. We were accompanied by a small band of friendly reporters whose editors felt compelled to cover a trip by a man who was already the second most important politician in the country, one whose ultimate goal, it was universally assumed, was the presidency.

In order to forestall any interpretation of his trip as a challenge to the president, knowing that the quest for confrontation was the animating spirit of all journalists, shortly after we boarded the plane Kennedy told the reporters, "I am not thinking of running for the presidency. I have a high feeling for President Johnson. He has been very kind to me. I would support his bid for reelection in 1968, and I strongly wish to campaign for him." Except for a few exaggerated phrases — "high feeling," "very kind," "strongly wish" — it was, in the fall of 1965, the truth. Bobby's seemingly inevitable quest lay in the distant future, 1972 or beyond.

The reporters accepted this disclaimer, as did the rest of us. No one could have conceived that within a year, Kennedy's mind would begin to nourish thoughts of a challenge which then appeared an evident absurdity. "Maybe I made a mistake," Kennedy told me. "Why should I deny something everyone knows isn't going to happen? It just encourages speculation. But I didn't want them to write this like some kind of a campaign trip."

As the plane approached our first stop, I looked down at the familiar, wondrous city of Lima, Peru — a mélange of old Spanish colonial structures set among crowded streets and often shabby shops which had been intruded on the more gracious loveliness of the past by the volcanic impermanence of our own century. Fronting the Pacific and the fecund fishing grounds of the Humboldt Current, the city — like all major Latin American cities — was ringed by slums of obscene poverty, the infamous *barriadas* where naked children, bellies swollen by hunger, played alongside open sewage ditches whose stink was almost unbearable to insulated, inexperienced Yankee senses.

As the plane slowed along the runway, I could see a small crowd gathered to welcome Kennedy's arrival. We followed Bobby out of the plane, and as I walked across the field toward the gate, I heard the shouts of waiting onlookers: "Viva Kennedy! Viva Kennedy!" Abruptly, I was brought to a halt, my luggage dropped from my hand. It was as if some nerve had been severed. I felt suddenly alone, an unanticipated melancholy isolating me from my enthusiastic companions. How many times in how many places had I heard that same rising shout — not from hundreds but from thousands, from hundreds of thousands, until the clamor "Viva Kennedy!" had overwhelmed all other senses. But he was dead. The cheer was appropriate enough. After all, it was Bobby's name too. Yet it was not because of him that they were shouting; but because he was the blood heir to someone admired almost to the point of reverence and, perhaps, out of some untested hope that certain bonds might be resurrected. I understood all this, of course, and, quickly restored, moved forward to join the party.

During the years that followed, as my understanding increased,

I would come to realize that Robert Kennedy had qualities of mind and temperament that, had he lived, might well have allowed him to transcend the achievement, the near-universal appeal, of the brother who had bestowed fame on the name he bore. But now, watching him walk past the armed security guards toward the wire fence holding back the hundreds of applauding Peruvians, stopping to exchange handshakes, greetings, and occasional banter, I realized that I did not know Robert Kennedy very well. I had worked with him occasionally during the Kennedy administration and found that we shared opinions on matters of my greatest concern. Although our infrequent collaborations were unmarred by conflict, I had observed in other contexts what seemed a somewhat enigmatic blend of fierce commitment to the most compassionate objectives with a somewhat less attractive self-righteousness. He displayed flashes of harsh, almost cruel anger toward those who seemed to obstruct or damage the goals or even the reputation of his brother's administration, along with a generosity of spirit, a gentle kindness, toward the errors and private difficulties of his colleagues. If he seemed to demand an almost unquestioning loyalty, he also returned it.

Once, in 1961, he received a letter from a major contributor who wished to impart his views on Cuba and Latin America to the attorney general.

"Dear Mr. Kaplan," Bobby replied, "I have spoken to Dick Goodwin at the White House who has the primary responsibility in this area and he will be happy . . . to talk with you. If you are in Washington . . . get in touch with me so I can set up an appointment . . . with him."

To which, Bobby told me, eight days later, a seriously irritated Jack Kaplan responded, "Young Dick Goodwin is less than half my age, and I doubt that he has had half my experience and knowledge of Cuba. . . . Would it not make sense for him to seek a visit with me, rather than to suggest merely that you . . . might set up an appointment with him? Of course I'll be glad to call on you . . . if that is your preference."

"We would be delighted to have your suggestions," answered an equally irritated and impolitic Kennedy. "It was with this in mind that I suggested you contact Dick Goodwin — or young Dick Goodwin, as you call him. I can believe that he is only half your age; however, I can assure you that the President has great confidence and trust in him. Young as he may be, he is the one who happens to have the responsibility at the White House at this time. As I said in my earlier letter, I am sure he would be delighted to see you."

The exchange may well have added at least one more to the ranks of those who thought him arrogant, but Bobby had won my heart.

Of course the denigrating reference to my age may well have annoyed Kennedy, who, himself little more than half Mr. Kaplan's age, was the second most important man in the administration, but it was also my first experience of that personal loyalty which overrode almost all other values. We were all in this together, "we band of brothers," the prase from *Henry the Fifth* that he took more literally than most of his associates, whose allegiances were more malleable (and who were not the president's blood brother). While campaigning for the Senate he insisted on attending — over the vigorous protests of advisers — a testimonial dinner for a now-discredited, about-to-be-indicted county politician. "He was there for Jack, when we needed him," Bobby replied, "now he's in trouble and I've got to be there." To those whose life is bounded by family, friends, close associates, such an act may appear a commonplace, but in the world of combat called politics, where expediency rules, it is a rarity. In Washington if you get out on a limb, you're out there all alone struggling to maintain balance while "friends" and "colleagues" watch in unmoved curiosity, waiting to see if you manage a safe return, but eagerly cautious to ensure that if you fall, you fall alone. I had experienced this constant of political life during my own period of decline from favor, when men I had naïvely regarded as "friends," social as well as business companions, totally disappeared from my life (with honorable exceptions, such as the large-spirited and generously loyal Arthur Schlesinger), only to reembrace me warmly at my resurrection.

It was, appropriately, during our trip to South America that the enigma began to dissolve, doubts gradually overcome by admiration. Ignoring the restraints of protocol, discarding the schedule of visits arranged by the embassy and the Peruvian government, Kennedy plunged, as if drawn by some compulsive inner magnet, into the wretchedness of the slums, lifting the hungry, naked children into a warm embrace, stepping across the foul sewage ditches to greet the occupants of crowded, flimsy hovels. His manner was warm, friendly, even gay, as if he were campaigning in some working-class neighborhood of New York. "It's so nice of you to have me," to the occupants of a tar-paper shack. "Do you think I could learn how to play this game?" as he kicked a soccer ball toward a group of children who could not, of course, understand his words, but whose warm laughter at the ineptness of his effort displayed comprehension of his almost familial tones. As crowds gathered around him, he stood on a stone wall, and exhorted them to "vote for Abe Beame" (then a candidate for mayor of New York). "Viva Kennedy!" they cheered, and as he climbed down, he whispered to me, "That ought to help old Abe." Carefully, he concealed his inward pity and anger, lest he appear condescending. But later, as we drove from the *barriada*, he said to me, "It's outrageous. Those people are living like animals, and the children — the children don't have a chance. What happened to all our AID money? Where is it going?" Then, sitting back in his seat, struggling with the images of his visit: "Wouldn't you be a communist if you had to live there? I think I would."

While in Lima, I arranged an informal evening for Bobby at the apartment of Fernando Seizlo, an artist and personal friend. The "off-the-record" meeting with a small group of artists, writers, and journalists soon became an outpouring of indignation at the State Department's recent decision to cut off all aid to Peru until they had settled a rather trivial dispute with the International Petroleum Company, a subsidiary of Standard Oil.

Kennedy had been outraged at the American decision. Earlier that day, I had accompanied him to the U.S. embassy, where he brusquely rejected all efforts at explanation. "Peru has a democratic government," he said. "We ought to be helping them succeed, not tearing them down just because some oil company doesn't like their policies. I'm not in the administration — *now* — but I am in the Senate, and you'll hear a lot more about this when I get back to Washington."

At the evening meeting Kennedy affirmed his disagreement with the American decision, then tried to turn the discussion to larger problems of poverty and social injustice. But he was unsuccessful. The evening became a series of speeches condemning U.S. imperialism, and Yankee business. Irritated by the attacks, Kennedy turned on his audience: "Well, if it's so important to you, why don't you just go ahead and nationalize the damn oil company? It's your country. You can't be both cursing the U.S., and then looking to it for permission to do what you want to do. The U.S.

government isn't going to send destroyers or anything like that. So if you want to assert your nationhood, why don't you just do it?"

The Peruvians were stunned at the boldness of Kennedy's suggestion. "Why, David Rockefeller has just been down here," they said, "and he told us there wouldn't be any aid if anyone acted against International Petroleum."

"Oh, come on," said Kennedy, "David Rockefeller isn't the government. We Kennedys eat Rockefellers for breakfast." The meeting ended in a rather jovial atmosphere. But, unknown to us, among the guests was a magazine writer who had a tape recorder hidden in his coat. Within a few days Kennedy's remark about the Rockefellers had spread throughout Latin America, and reached the American press. Fortunately, the report had become somewhat garbled in translation. When we arrived in Argentina, a reporter approached Kennedy and asked: "Tell me, Senator, is it true that you have breakfast with Rockefeller every morning?" "Not every morning," he replied.

From Peru we flew to Chile, where Bobby was to speak to about three thousand students at the University in Concepción, Chile's third-largest city. There was a strong communist faction at the university, however, which was determined to prevent Kennedy from speaking. A delegation called on him at the hotel. "We do not condemn you personally," the student leader told Kennedy, "but as a representative of a country whose hands are stained with blood."

"You describe me with blood all over my hands," Kennedy replied. "I haven't eaten you up since I have been here, have I? I haven't had a marine stick a bayonet in you, have I? I'll make you a deal. I'll speak, then one of your people can speak, and then I'll answer questions. If I don't answer the questions satisfactorily, then, hell, your position is much stronger."

"I'm sorry, Senator," the group's leader replied, "it's nothing against you personally. But you're a representative of U.S. imperialism, and you don't belong on our campus."

After the group had left, Kennedy turned to me: "Well I guess that's the ball game. Even if I go, I won't be able to speak. With a group that large making noise, no one will hear a word." Shortly thereafter a Chilean official told Kennedy that the university was legally off-limits to the police, and they could not guarantee his protection.

As we sat discussing the seeming hopelessness of the situation, two young students — representatives of the Christian Democratic party — entered the room. "If you don't come to speak to us, it will be a great victory for the communists. They're only a minority. But if they keep you from coming, they'll look like heroes."

Kennedy retired to his room. No decision had been made. In about twenty minutes he emerged, and seeing me still sitting in the suite, taking advantage of the brief interlude to consume a sandwich and a drink, he asked, "What do you think, Dick?" "I have an idea, Senator," I replied. "Since they object to you, why don't you just give me the speech and I'll go there and read it for you." A flash of anger quickly yielded to a smile as he realized I was joking. "It's nice of you to offer, Dick, but I think I better give my own speech. You can come along, though, I wouldn't want you to miss the fun."

As we entered the university gymnasium, we were bombarded with eggs and garbage. (Kennedy was not hit, while vanden Heuvel and I were stained with broken eggs.) Kennedy walked to the microphone and began to speak, his words totally inaudible over the shouts of the large communist contingent — "Kennedy go home!" "Kennedy to the wall!" Kennedy continued to read his speech, even though his words were smothered by the noise. Finally, having come to the end of his text, Kennedy walked over to the section of the hall occupied by the still-shouting communists. Looking up he saw the leader of the group that had come to the hotel, and extended his hand. The young man reached out for the offered handclasp, and then, as if realizing the import of the gesture, surprised by his instinctive impulse, he withdrew his arm. Kennedy smiled, gave a brief wave of the hand, and then departed.

"I guess we didn't accomplish much," he said, as we returned to the hotel. "You helped your friends," I said. "I suppose so," he replied, "but it's too bad. I would have liked to talk to them. We want to change the same things, but I don't believe the communist way is going to do it. Still, we're not so far apart as they think." Then, pausing: "Well that's over. Now on to another triumph."

As we moved from Chile to Argentina to Brazil, Bobby's statements became increasingly militant assertions of the need for social justice and democracy. "Every child an education!" he shouted to a crowd of over one hundred thousand in Natal, Brazil. "Every family adequate housing! Every man a job!" Speaking directly to a group of wealthy Brazilians, he warned that they were breeding their own destruction. In a Rio street appearance, he called on the military government of Brazil to grant democracy and complete political freedom. The government was outraged, but there was nothing they could do. After a dinner, a Brazilian minister whom I had known in Washington took me aside: "Can't you do something about this young revolutionary?" he asked. "He doesn't understand our problems at all." "I've already told him what I think," I answered ambiguously. "Why don't you talk to him yourself?"

On November 22 we went to mass in the small town of Bahia to commemorate John Kennedy's death. As soon as the mass was over, Bobby insisted on heading for the *barriada,* seeming to seek refuge for the pain of remembrance among the barefoot children who gathered around him as he walked through the mud.

Later that day, as we rode in a motorcade through the streets of Recife in Brazil's impoverished northeast, some among the jubilant crowd, in a gesture of celebratory welcome, set off a few strings of Chinese firecrackers. Hearing the sudden, sharp explosions cutting through the cheers, Bobby froze, hunched his body into a protective crouch, an expression of fear momentarily displacing the warmly responsive smile until, in some fraction of a second, realizing the sound was harmless, he stood erect and continued to wave enthusiastically at the dark-skinned masses behind the flimsy police barriers.

Toward the end of our visit to Brazil, I suggested a diversionary trip to the Amazon. We flew to Manaus, a city about a thousand miles from the river's juncture with the Atlantic Ocean. There, with over two hundred pieces of luggage, we boarded a white Dutch-built paddle-wheeler to take us along the river.

After a day or two on the Amazon, Bobby and I, along with a couple of reporters, boarded a 1936 single-engine seaplane, leaving the rest of the party behind, while we journeyed even farther inland, to a small Indian village located on the Nhamundá River, a tributary of the Amazon. "I must be crazy to get on this thing," Bobby yelled to Ethel as we climbed aboard. Flying for hours over dense jungle, the plane landed on a bend in the river near a group of thatched-roof huts that constituted a small Indian village. Aided by a missionary couple who had come to live in the village, whose

few hundred inhabitants spoke a unique language, we were able
to communicate. We asked them if they had ever heard of President Johnson or President Kennedy, and they said no. Then we
asked if they had heard of the United States, and one man said
yes. "What do you know about it?" we asked. He gestured to his
little village and said, "It's bigger than this place."

On the river we saw two men in a canoe drifting slowly over
the water, one man paddling while the other stood poised with a
bow and arrow, looking for fish. Pointing to the canoe, Bobby
asked if we could join the fishing expedition. Laughing, the Indians took us to the bank and called to the men in the canoe, who
approached the shore, allowing us to enter. As we cruised over
the water, Kennedy said to me, "You know, I'll bet there are
piranha in there." "Probably," I replied. "Would you dare go
swimming?" he challenged. "I'll go if you'll go, Senator!" I answered and then, without waiting for a reply, I jumped into the
water. Kennedy followed immediately, then paddling to keep afloat,
he loudly proclaimed, in an unmistakable imitation of Walter
Cronkite: "It was impossible to pinpoint the exact time and place
when he decided to run for president. But the idea seemed to take
hold as he was swimming in the Amazonian river of Nhamundá,
keeping a sharp eye peeled for man-eating piranhas." Then,
somewhat philosophically, he added: "Piranhas have never been
known to bite a U.S. senator."

"Well, I'm not a senator," I replied, "and I'm getting the hell
out of here," beginning to swim as swiftly as possible toward the
canoe, with Bobby following. "I wanted to keep swimming," Bobby
said as we climbed aboard, "but I didn't think you'd be safe alone
in the canoe. I mean, suppose it tipped over. You'd need me to
rescue you." "That's what I love about you, Bobby," I rejoined,
"you're always putting the other fellow ahead of yourself." "I can
tell you one thing," he said, "this is one of those things it's going
to be a hell of a lot more fun to talk about afterwards." And so
it is.

The trip to Latin America was the beginning of an enlarged
understanding, which would — over the next three years — continually evolve (as, in part, did the man himself) during innumerable conversations in his apartment at the United Nations Plaza,
over hamburgers and drinks at P. J. Clarke's on Third Avenue,
sitting on the Eastern shuttle as it interminably circled La Guar-

dia waiting for clearance, walking across the grass at Hickory Hill during intermissions from the touch football games in which I, clearly outclassed, refused to participate. The qualities of the man as I came to know him would most clearly manifest themselves in the events I am about to relate — the political and personal struggles that bridged the years between our return from Latin America and his death. Understanding of that journey and the man who made it might be illuminated, however, by some reflections from the vantage of a time two decades away from the end of a friendship.

Robert Kennedy, like most interesting people, was a constellation of contradictions. The man was a battleground where exuberance and the hunger for experience warred with melancholy touched with despair. He wished to master the complexities of an entire world, yet he was most comfortable with children and the oppressed and others whose wants were simple and direct. He believed in his powers almost to (sometimes past) the point of arrogance, but was haunted by apprehensions of failure.

I once asked him which of his older brothers — Joe Jr. or Jack — had most influenced his youth. "Joe," he replied without hesitation. "He was Dad's favorite and the model for all of us, except for Jack. I used to lie in my bed at night sometimes and hear the sound of Joe banging Jack's head against the wall."

"I suppose I was lucky to be so much younger and smaller," he remarked another time. "I was never involved in the rivalry, and Joe treated me nicely, almost like a mascot. Dad idolized Joe. We all knew he was the one. But I was closer to mother."

And there is little doubt that Bobby was Rose Kennedy's favorite, having arrived after their growing wealth and changing lifestyle had freed her for closer guidance of her children's upbringing. Joe and Jack were her husband's sons, free, with his approval, to depart from her own concepts of training and conduct (not without protest). Bobby was hers. The letters between them contain frequent, extravagant expressions of affection, love, and concern. Once when I was walking with then Senator Kennedy across the lawn at the Hyannis compound, we encountered Rose, who motioned us to stop, walked up to Bobby, and, pointing toward me, admonished him, "Now, Bobby, you listen to him. You can learn something." (I don't know what she had in mind. Bobby was offering to give me a sailing lesson at the time.) Though she hardly knew me, I had been categorized as a member of the species "intellectual," a group useless in itself, but from whom more practical men could extract information of value. Her remark, although I did not know it then, was a repetition of a familiar theme, an instruction in the importance of knowledge, which left him with a respect for ideas and enlightenment that in later years was to flower into a desire for understanding that led him to read not only astronomy, but Camus and Shakespeare, and the poetry whose anthologies became his constant companion on political travels.

The birth of four daughters separated him from Jack and Joe, leading his grandmother to express the needless concern that, surrounded by women, he might become "a sissy," an apprehension strengthened by the fact that he was short, the "runt" in a family of relatively tall men. In a fiercely competitive family, he had to battle more ferociously, recklessly, in order to hold his own. Although separated from his father's charmed circle — Joe, Jack, Kathleen — an outsider in this strange microcosm of the larger society, his confidence was preserved and fortified by his preeminence in his mother's affection, her willingness to forgive in him conduct for which she censured the older brothers. "Of course we need long-term programs," he once told me, "but it's also important to just give kids something to do. Hell, everybody gets into trouble between sixteen and twenty. I was always getting into trouble myself. We used to smash the streetlights in Hyannis, break windows. But Dad was always there to keep me out of real trouble, and Mother, although she didn't like it, never took it out on me. Those kids don't have that kind of support. So we have to support them, all us lucky ones."

It was all there: the battle against exclusion — to establish and define himself — mingling with gradually increasing confidence in his own capacities, a confidence whose fragilities were concealed, denied, by outward fervor, occasional bursts of temper, zealous (sometimes overzealous) insistence upon a code of "manly" conduct. Once, after his brother's death, he saw young John Jr., having taken a hard fall on the ski slope, crying as he sat on the snow. Skiing over to him, Bobby extended his hand and sternly admonished, "Kennedys don't cry." "This Kennedy cries," replied young John. And so did Bobby, although one rarely saw the tears. It was his most tenaciously maintained secret: a tenderness so rawly exposed, so vulnerable to painful abrasion, that it could only be shielded by angry compassion at human misery, manifest itself in love and loyalty toward those close to him, or through a revelatory humor. As I watched him play tennis at Hyannisport, rushing toward the net to smash the ball at his opponent, on returning to the baseline he saw me and grinned: "There, how do you like that. Now you see a really mean, aggressive personality at work."

After graduating from law school, he went to New York determined to establish an independent career, only to be summoned by the patriarch to manage Jack Kennedy's campaign for the Senate. He acquiesced obediently, but with great reluctance, apprehensive that a return to the family orbit would mean some indefinable diminution of self. He was wrong — mostly wrong. The relationship with his older brother would be the closest and most important of his life. As usual, once committed, all ambivalence disappeared in a total devotion of energies and skills to his brother's destiny. The subordination was also a liberation. For now the opinions of others, the perception of Bobby as "mean," "aggressive," or — as Tip O'Neill describes him — "pushy," didn't matter as long as his actions forwarded his brother's "cause." Once I was sitting on the White House porch while President Kennedy entertained a small group of southern senators. "I'm afraid, Mr. President," drawled a Georgia solon, "that I'm going to have to attack you on those civil rights."

"Don't do that," Kennedy replied. "Can't you just attack Bobby instead?"

Had Bobby heard the conversation — and it may well have been related to him by the president — he would not have been disturbed. (Although he probably wouldn't have been flattered.) That was his job, part of his job, to take the heat, do the dirty work, in order to protect his brother.

Bobby was also the point man for his brother's desire to construct an apparatus to counter what was then perceived as the newest technique in the communist arsenal — subversion, guerrilla armies, "wars of national liberation." (Not wholly an illusion, proclaimed by Chairman Khrushchev himself as the way to mastery of the third world.) Operation Mongoose, the virtual apotheosis of the Special Forces with their distinctive green berets, a strengthened capacity for covert operations — all these reflected the optimistic, unshakable confidence of the early Kennedy days that there was no difficulty that could not be confronted and overcome by men of determination and courage. (And why not? Had they not, against large odds, in defiance of "expert" opinion, taken the nomination and the White House?) To the extent this was a

misjudgment — an underestimation of the political and nationalistic component in third world upheavals — it was not Bobby's
alone.

Though he was not unwilling, personally fervent, he was also —
and preeminently — servant of his brother's purpose. By the time
of his death John Kennedy's perceptions, and thus his policies,
had been changed by an increased understanding of ambiguities
and limitations. We could not — should not — try to exert our
will on the teeming diversity of the continents. Not only impossible, it was not necessary, often not even important, to the pros-
pering freedom of America. And Bobby changed with him, that
change accelerating after John Kennedy's death, as, thrown back
on his own instincts, he came to believe that the most dangerous
and evil enemies of mankind did not carry guns, but more subtle
weapons, which stripped food and health, dignity and hope from
impotent masses.

Some have written that Robert Kennedy "grew" after John
Kennedy's murder, changed in some fundamental ways. It is true
that the irretrievably painful loss of the brother he loved so deeply,
served with such unquestioning faith, changed the course of his
life, modified his public purpose, altered his emotions and the
convictions founded on those emotions — his intensities, beliefs,
even his God. "Everyone is broken by life," wrote Hemingway,
"and afterward some are stronger in the broken places." Bobby
Kennedy, after November 1963, was like a landscape riven by an
earthquake, familiar landmarks shattered, displaced by novel contours. Yet the reconfigured land is composed of the same elements
of stone and soil that abided there before the earth shook. He
learned from experience and from books, found ambiguities in once
unquestioned truths, his sometimes frightening righteousness diluted by doubt — that awareness of uncertainty which, in large
men, breeds tolerance, even an empathetic sympathy, toward divergent beliefs and conduct. But the qualities that shaped him, on
which he built, were there from the beginning.

Once when I was having dinner with Bobby and his mother at
Hyannisport, Rose Kennedy reminisced of the time when, as a
teenager, her son had gone to hear the notorious Father Feeney —
a fascist sympathizer and fierce anti-Semite — deliver one of his
frequent diatribes on the Boston Common: "When he came back,
one of his friends told me that Bobby had interrupted the father,
and told him that what he was saying was wrong, that it contra-

dicted what he had learned from his own Catholic teachers. I was horrified. My own son arguing with a priest. But you know, Bobby was right. When the Vatican excommunicated Father Feeney, I knew Bobby had been right."

The confrontation with Father Feeney was a display not of religious doubts, but of the impulse toward defiance, the open rejection of what the youthful Kennedy thought a violation of Catholic morality. Most of us might think the encounter trivial, but not Rose Kennedy's favorite son, who had been taught that authority itself came clad in priestly robes. This was the same Robert Kennedy who, during the Cuban missile crisis, passionately rejected the proposal that we launch an air assault on the grounds that a surprise attack — a kind of mini–Pearl Harbor — was un-American.

The urge toward defiance is ethically neutral, impelling the terrorist and the saint. It can manifest itself as heroism or arrogance, commitment or ruthlessness — depending on the audience, the content, the purpose. In Robert Kennedy, especially the early Robert Kennedy, it took many of these forms; was sometimes tinged with a righteousness that allowed no contradiction. During the Kennedy administration, Bobby held occasional "seminars" at Hickory Hill, inviting distinguished intellectuals to address a small group of high officials and family friends. The impulse was beneficent, "self-improvement" being a typically American obsession, but the results were occasionally disastrous. At one time a nationally renowned psychiatrist explained the principal tenets of psychoanalysis to an increasingly restive audience. When he finished Bobby stood up. "That's the biggest bunch of bullshit I've ever heard. You're trying to tell us that people can't help being what they are." (Which is not what he was saying at all.) And then, interrupting her husband, came the indignant voice of Ethel Kennedy: "Everything isn't sex." The session came to an abrupt end, our "instructor" retiring in confused humiliation.

However, by the time I came to know him better, an expanding tolerance, nourished by both personal tragedy and sympathetic openness to his experience, had largely — not completely — drained the force from his less attractive certitudes. The line between right and wrong became blurred, erratic; even the noblest achievements had a price. The same impulse to defiance, given many names — passion, anger, commitment — became the source of his public appeal, his greatest strength, arousing the hopes and expectations of millions who felt themselves unfairly victimized by the ruling structure of wealth and power.

Bobby Kennedy rarely discussed death. What was the point? He had a life to live, large deeds to accomplish. And when the subject arose he dealt with it as the Irish — especially the black Irish, to whose tribe he belonged — nearly always do, not morbidly but with humor.

Shortly after returning from the funeral of one of his closest friends, Dean Markham, who had been killed in an airplane crash, we sat in a friend's New York apartment while Bobby explained that he and Dave Hackett (a friend since their years together at Milton Academy) "have so much experience at this kind of thing that we're going into business offering a special service for funerals. We'll select songs and readings, simple but moving. Then we'll pick out a cheap casket to save the widow money. You know how they always cheat you on the casket. Next we'll pick passages from the Bible, and use our contacts with caterers to do everything that is necessary to ensure an inexpensive funeral. This is the new service we can provide all our friends."

"Not only that," I joined in, "there's no reason a man in your position couldn't find a constituent to do the embalming for free. After all, every businessman knows he might need a favor from a politician. And you're a senator."

"But only in New York," he objected.

"Well, we could have it done in New York, and then get somebody to drive the body home."

"They always told me you were a good idea man," he replied, laughing.

There was no note of the macabre in our conversation — not to Kennedy and certainly not to me, who, being more of a pagan, free of the inward necessity to reconcile Catholic teachings with the realities of the world, had — since I broke with Orthodox Judaism in my teens — believed that life was a chance. I was afraid of death, still am, often marvel that I continue to work productively, enjoy my family, experience many of the same passionate discontents that moved me then, so long after so many of my past companions have been cut off. It just proves the point. You never know.

Not long after organizing the "Kennedy funeral business" (Bobby, naturally, would be chairman and CEO), the two of us were sailing just off the shore of Hyannisport. As we sat quietly, enjoying the warmth of unclouded skies and our slow progress across the tranquil blue-green sea, I broke the silence: "It's all so peaceful here. There are no signs of disaster, no way to tell if in an hour or a day the wind might rise or the boat sink, and you will be struggling hopelessly against the water. There is nothing in the sunlight to foretell the darkness."

"I know," he answered quietly. "It's hard, but sometimes you can tell."

Only that and nothing more. Later I wondered at his meaning. Was it that an experienced sailor could sense the approaching storm, or some more heretically prophetic claim? It was impossible to tell. Yet the tone — controlled, almost dismissive — hinted at something larger than nautical skills.

The death of his brother fortified his awareness that all lives were shaped by a certain inevitability; that one could not indict, try, and sentence a man for being what he was. "I like southerners," he once told me, "they just don't understand that their way of life, the way they treat Negroes, is unacceptable."

The reality, hitherto an abstraction, that life was so unpredictably tenuous made the alleviation of misery and injustice even more urgent. There was no time to wait, no right to sacrifice one generation for the sake of some utopian future. It had to be now. As a boy, he had been taught, in the words of Hamlet's father, that "heaven can wait." But that heaven became increasingly a receding abstraction, as did the omniscient God and the authority of his papal regent and attendant hierarchy. While he remained a good Catholic, he was freshly infused with a skepticism that loosened the rigidities of his belief and the personal moral code that had ruled his conduct.

Painful experience had drawn him closer to the Greek wisdom that a man's destiny was governed by an arbitrary, often whimsical fate; led him away from the loving protective God of his earlier, literal Catholic belief. Once, as we descended in the elevator from his apartment in the United Nations Plaza, accompanied by his wife and a few friends, Ethel turned to me, reporting, "My children came home from school the other day and told me that the world wasn't really created in seven days, that it was just an allegory. You're smart. How can I explain it to them?" I mumbled a few incomprehensible phrases, my discomfort quickly and thankfully interrupted when the elevator doors opened to the lobby. I saw Bobby looking at me and grinning. "You bastard," I whispered to him as we walked toward the street, "why don't you explain it? You're the one who went to Sunday school, not me." Yet not too many years before, Bobby might have asked the same question, although not of me, a friendly priest perhaps.

Now, without mentor or leader, the responsibility was his alone. He was driven to explore new worlds of thought and poetry, pleasures and the manifold varieties of human intimacy. Although I am sure he acted from deeply felt personal inclinations, it was almost as if he were deliberately equipping himself for a larger role, laboring to become worthy of succession to his romanticized vision of the fallen leader.

Once, as we rode together on the way to dinner, he opened a biography of John Jay and read aloud a passage explaining that new countries, born in turmoil, could not be expected to be tranquil and stable. "He wrote this almost two hundred years ago," Bobby marveled, "and it's just what's happening all around us today, in Latin America, Africa, everywhere. He understood it better than we do. We just get afraid, or look down on them. Why is it that we produced so many men of talent at one time, and don't have men like that today?"

"We have talented people," I answered, "but they don't have the chance to show it. That comes during times of rapid change. Now, to get ahead, it requires becoming part of the established order, part of a machine, learning how to please people, to keep things calm. That sort of discourages the kind of talent you're talking about."

Although my comment was clearly inadequate to explain the Founding Fathers, Bobby did not disagree. "It's tough in this country with all the newspapers and the big interests," he responded.

"He [Bobby] meant," I wrote in my diary, "that it was tough to run a revolution, since he is basically a revolutionary who has to work within a settled system." Later on that same ride he delightedly informed me that Congressman John Adams had obstructed a naval appropriations bill until the government had agreed to build some ships in Boston, in order to keep the Boston Navy Yard open. "That's the great thing about politics," he remarked, "some things never change. And that's why I'm going to force them to put some New York counties in the bill for Appalachia."

Long after John Kennedy's death, deeply engaged in his own political battles, he was concerned, almost obsessed, with the apprehension that his brother's place in American history would be diminished by the shortness of his rule, the achievements of Johnson. "All those things he's doing," he said to me as we sat in his apartment late one evening, "poverty, civil rights, they're things we had just begun. We just didn't have the time." In an effort, as a friend, to answer his concern — aware also that his brother's renown rested on something more profound, less determinate, than legislative enactment or tangible achievements, I walked over to the bookshelves and took down a volume of Shakespeare's plays. "Look at this," I said. "Julius Caesar is an immortal, and he was only emperor of Rome for a little more than three years." A grin shattered his melancholy expression. "Yes," he replied, "but it helps if you have Shakespeare to write about you." It is a measure of the man — of the changes in the man — that even though he loved his brother almost more than he loved himself, he would not permit the self-indulgent pleasure of that comparison.

Like all men, he had his fragilities, failures of understanding and awareness, but unlike many he could see many of these things in himself — at least he could now, after painful experience had shown him that, in a man's life, serious purpose commingled with absurdity. A contradiction which helps explain his fascination with the writings of Camus, who preached that "the acceptance of mystery and of evil" does not justify or permit the moral man to "accept history as it is." But even though Camus's work found a resonance in Bobby's own element of despair, he was not, in 1966 or later, crippled by pessimism, the sense of doom. He was exuberant, hungry for pleasure and experience, romantically resolved to master the miseries of the world, identifying himself with the man of La Mancha — a musical he saw three times — except that, for him, the windmills were real monsters and he was strong enough to strike them down. The man was a lover.

I did not, however, know at the beginning of 1966 that the "monsters" of imagination were soon to assume a more tangible shape; nor that we would fight them together.

24 / Joining the Resistance

IN LATE JANUARY of 1966, I went to Washington for an appointment with Robert McNamara. At that time we were amid one of several "temporary" halts in the bombing of North Vietnam. I had met with some of my fellow "liberals" — Schlesinger, Galbraith, et al. — and agreed that a continuation of the bombing halt might persuade Hanoi to negotiate. (It was clear by then that North Vietnam would not discuss a settlement while bombs were falling, or even during an intermission which had been officially described as "temporary," since they could not let it appear that American air attacks had forced them into negotiations.) My trip was in hope of persuading McNamara to this course. He was, after all, an appointee of John Kennedy, a close personal friend of Robert Kennedy, and, outwardly, appeared to be a man of reasoned and moderate judgment.

Entering the Pentagon, I gave my name to the guard and, almost immediately, with obvious deference (a pleasing echo of past glories), was escorted to the wood-paneled corridor on whose wall, stamped in letters of gold leaf, I read the imposing "Office of the Secretary of Defense." Quickly taken past the receptionist, then the personal secretary, I entered a door opening into a room two or three times the size of the Oval Office, furnished in the subdued splendor of fine, polished oak and mahogany, the walls and tables adorned with a sparse, meticulously arranged assortment of pictures, plaques, miscellaneous mementos. Behind McNamara's desk hung a map — at least eight feet in height — of all Southeast Asia from Malaysia to Vietnam. As I entered, McNamara rose, walked out from behind his desk to shake hands, exchange amenities, and offer me a chair, where I sat facing him as he remained standing, in shirtsleeves, behind his own mammoth desk.

"What can I do?" he asked.

Knowing my time was likely to be short — although McNamara never displayed the slightest sign of impatience — I made my case, emphasizing the argument that, "since we all know a negotiated settlement of some kind is inevitable, the sooner we move the better our bargaining position will be."

Without responding to my carefully prepared presentation, McNamara abruptly turned to the map behind him and, with one sweeping gesture of his arm across the entire panoply of Asian lands, asked, "Do you think it would make any difference to American security, Dick, if this entire place went communist?"

Surprised, I responded rather haltingly, inwardly searching for the import of his remark, "Well, that's another question, Bob . . . I haven't given it much thought . . . I'd like to consider it. But that's not why I came. It's Vietnam . . ."

"It wouldn't make the slightest bit of difference," he interrupted, and then sat down.

I remained silent, almost stunned into silence. If he meant that, then what was he doing? Why had he battled so fiercely — for the bombing, the troops, the mounting violence? What was it all about? Then momentary bewilderment yielded to awareness of some enormous gulf between this man and me — some huge disparity of perception or understanding or emotion, that reasoned discourse could not conceivably bridge, not in a hundred years. I had nothing left to say; my mission was hopeless. And a few minutes later, with the most cordial of farewells, I left, walked out across the broad Pentagon plaza, and, inhaling the damp cold air of a Washington winter, tried to understand the meaning of my experience. It was the beginning of awareness that neither I, nor anyone else, could influence the makers of this war; they themselves were almost out of control, as if caught up in some current which they had undammed but whose gathering momentum they could not resist.

On January 31, the bombing resumed.

Two weeks later the insistent, prolonged ring of a bedside telephone at my Middletown home awoke me at the unconscionable hour of 7 A.M., the midwinter dark still a translucent mantle for the cold illumination of approaching day. I'll let it ring, I thought, turning away from the infernally disruptive machine. But it kept on ringing, until, resignedly, I picked up the receiver. It was Bobby. Without apology for the hour (he hadn't been up writing until 3 A.M.), he asked, "Have you been following the Fulbright hearings?" I had, and with considerable interest, been reading the daily accounts of the Senate Foreign Relations Committee inquiry into the origins and conduct of the war in Vietnam, partially revealing a litany of administration lies and errors.

"I think he's done a pretty good job," I replied.

"Do you think there's anything constructive I can add?"

"I'm not sure," I replied groggily, "let me think about it and I'll call you back."

Hanging up, my futile efforts to return to sleep were defeated by the ideas, phrases, proposals tumbling chaotically through my mind. About an hour later I called Bobby back. "Everyone, even the administration, claims that the only solution is a negotiated settlement, but nobody's been willing to spell out what it would look like, what terms would be acceptable. That's something you could do."

"Would you try your hand at a statement?" he asked.

"I'll give it a shot."

It seemed obvious to me — logically self-evident — that any settlement with an enemy you couldn't defeat by force must be a compromise. If neither we nor the communists could impose a military solution, then any resolution must be political, governed by John Kennedy's pragmatic maxim that "in politics nobody gets everything, nobody gets nothing, everybody gets something." Just as we were unwilling to turn South Vietnam over to the communists, they could not, need not, accept an agreement that totally excluded them from the power they had, at enormous cost, struggled to acquire for almost a generation. During the day I sketched out this — to me — unanswerable logic, concluding that any negotiated settlement must give the communist National Liberation Front "a share of power and responsibility" in the future government of South Vietnam (carefully avoiding the scare word "coalition," with its resonance of communist coups in Eastern Europe). Late that afternoon I read my handiwork to Bobby, who agreed, suggested a few modifications, and asked me to send it to Washington.

My accompanying note of February 17 read, "Please protect me absolutely on this. Even from your notoriously discreet associates." (Irony.) "Say you wrote it yourself." (More irony.) Obviously I was still anxious to preserve my fast-dissolving bonds with Johnson, certain to be irrevocably ruptured by any hint of association with Bobby Kennedy on this subject. It was bad enough to go to South America, but Vietnam — a subject swiftly consuming the president's most intense fears and passions — would be an unforgivable breach.

"Second," I added in my note, "there is, of course, more to be said but I think this really reaches to the edge of political danger. . . ." I was wrong. It didn't reach "the edge." It leaped right off the precipice. After delivering the statement at a February 19 press conference, Bobby flew west for a skiing vacation with his family. And then the roof fell in.

In distant Australia, the peripatetic Hubert Humphrey, shown the Kennedy statement by reporters, denounced it as dangerous nonsense. It would be, he said, like "putting the fox in the chicken coop." Back in Washington an indignant but shrewdly calculating Johnson maintained a personal silence, but instructed those among his top assistants most closely associated with the late president to lead the attack. Appearing on "Meet the Press" the day after Bobby's statement, McGeorge Bundy decried the naïveté of the Kennedy proposal, and, with ultimate condescension, used as evidence President Kennedy's own statement, made in the unrelated context of European politics, that "I am not impressed by the opportunities open to popular fronts throughout the world." (Brother against brother — Bundy knew how to wound.) The same day, having requested an appearance on ABC's "Issues and Answers," the ever-compliant George Ball charged that "the step suggested by Senator Kennedy would mean creating a coalition government . . . and what we would have would be . . . in a very short time, a communist government in Saigon." (And this from a man who would, later, assert that he had courageously opposed our entire effort in Vietnam.)

Stunned by the ferocity of administration reaction, Bobby flew back to New York for a television appearance to "clarify" his remarks. Although refusing to abandon his position, he did introduce qualifications and cautions, spoke hesitantly, appeared to vacillate. It only made things worse. Those antagonized by his statement remained unreconciled, while those who had applauded his courage were filled with doubt. It was a painful episode. In the unanticipated furor of the moment, Kennedy thought that he had damaged, perhaps destroyed, his political future. And, sensing his distress, I felt terrible; guilty about my own participation. Although Bobby never mentioned it. It would not have occurred to him to reprove someone for a statement whose approval and delivery were his own responsibility.

Yet, although he regretted his statement and felt he had mishandled the consequent mini-crisis, Bobby Kennedy had taken the first step on the course that would, in the years ahead, make him a leader of the Democratic opposition. More than a year later, sitting together at some New York restaurant, I asked him — "What about the 'fox in the chicken coop' statement? We thought it would finish you. What do you think now? Was it a minus or a plus?"

"A plus," he replied. But by then the once-sparse ranks of opposition had become a national movement, had spread from the protesting young to the middle class and, decisively, to the business community.

On the Ides of March, less than a month after Bobby's statement, the foundation of the hopeful sixties — that compound of consensus, of hopeful protest, and of alliance (always partial) between the urge toward change and the guardians of power — began, at least symbolically, to crumble. For the second time in seven months, the Watts ghetto of Los Angeles was torn by indiscriminate fury. Black men burned black homes, looted black stores, and when the flames had resolved themselves into embers, two were dead and fifteen injured. The war had come home.

The fight for racial justice, which had been the initiating impulse for what seemed a new era of fulfillment, now signaled — not the end, not yet — but the beginning of the end. "April," Eliot wrote, "is the cruellest month / mingling memory and desire." But spring comes early to California, and the auguring season had reawoken the impassioned desire of the gateless poor, the memory of expectations and promises once seemingly within reach, now rapidly receding. The energy and resources committed to enlarging American life were being consumed in alien battles whose price could not be fully measured in dollars or even lives, but also by the political necessity to sacrifice the needs of the masses to ensure conservative support for the war in Vietnam. Black Americans were among the first to sense the change, understand that the days of achievement were coming to an end. Yet, they were also aware that, in America, one could influence the government, but not rebel against it — not successfully. So they rebelled against themselves, made gutted buildings and blood-streaked streets a monument to ungratified desire.

Martin Luther King tried vainly to arrest the tide, spoke against the war despite the counsel of his closest advisers, who did not share his profound intuition that it had become the greatest obstacle to his "dream." In May, younger blacks, impatient, aware that the persuasive force of nonviolence was weakening, elected Stokely Carmichael to lead the Student Non-violent Coordinating Committee on a platform that embraced the concepts of "black power" and "retaliatory violence." In June, a White House conference, which had been convoked to develop a program to increase economic opportunity for blacks, collapsed in rancorous, fruitless dispute over sociological abstractions, a debate that only masked awareness that Lyndon Johnson's summons "To Fulfill These Rights" was not to be answered, was doomed by the actions of the very man who had issued it. Later that same month, there began a summer of urban race riots. National guardsmen were sent to restore peace to Chicago's West Side; looting, fire-bombing, violence, and occasional death spread from San Francisco to midwestern Omaha and Cleveland, to Jacksonville in the South, and to the Brooklyn borough of liberalism's metropolis.

Lyndon Johnson, increasingly isolated in the White House, retained blindly, against all the realities of politics, his belief that "we can do it both, fight poverty at home and meet our obligations abroad." A man besieged, he saw the riots, the opposition of King, the mounting student protest against the war as a personal betrayal. "How is it possible," Johnson said after he left the White House, "that all these people could be so ungrateful to me after I had given them so much? Take the Negroes. I fought for them . . . I spilled my guts out in getting those civil rights bills through Congress . . . I tried to make it possible for every child of every color to grow up in a nice house, to eat a solid breakfast, to attend a decent school and to get a good job. I asked so little in return. Just a little thanks, just a little appreciation. But look what I got instead. Riots . . . looting, burning, shooting. It ruined everything. And the students. I fought to give them better schools, help them out with loans and grants. And look what I got back. All those ungrateful young people, deserting their classrooms, marching in the streets, chanting that horrible song about how many kids I had killed."

But by mid-1966 Lyndon Johnson the master politician — the

man uniquely gifted at understanding disagreement, reconciling differences — was gone; in his place a man enslaved by his own obsessions. Those who opposed his policies were now personal enemies, associates who diverged from his policies, who openly voiced disagreement, were traitors — not merely ungrateful, but treasonous to him and to the country whose surrogate, in his own mind, he had become.

Because of my experience in the White House, I understood — thought I understood — what was happening to Lyndon Johnson as, through the summer of 1966, I contemplated with increasing urgency my own act of "betrayal."

In his book on Robert Kennedy, Arthur Schlesinger reports that "in the late spring of 1966 Goodwin, Galbraith and I lunched in New York. 'It would be terrible,' Goodwin said, 'if, when the nuclear bombs began to drop on Peking or Washington, we had to reflect that all we did in the summer of 1966 was to rest comfortably on one or another beach.' LBJ, Goodwin said, was a man possessed, . . . impervious to argument. The only thing he understood was political opposition." (A mistake of judgment; Johnson's mind was already beyond the reach of adverse public opinion.) "We decided to do what we could to stir public opinion . . . discussed the idea of forming a national committee against widening of the war."

That spring, I wrote a long article for the *New Yorker,* which was later published as a book *(Triumph and Tragedy).* My analysis, although accurate, was incomplete, even a little timid. I did not call for an immediate end to the war (i.e., American withdrawal) nor avow that there was little, if any, American interest at stake. Rather, I argued against the continued bombing of North Vietnam and our increasing participation in the war on the ground. I asserted that ending escalation was an essential preliminary to a negotiated settlement, which would, by necessity, result in a coalition government. And I called for the varied voices of protest to coalesce their energies around the president's own campaign exhortation of "no wider war."

The book was not a personal moral declaration, an assault on the motives or rationality of the president. Nor did it reflect my apprehension — still uncertain — that things may have already gone too far, that peaceful compromise might no longer be possible now that the communists had discovered they could survive, even match, American military might.

It is difficult to recall with precision the mingled emotions and
calculations that persuaded me to such "restraint." To attack
Johnson directly would have been regarded by most of my fellow
Democrats as an unforgivable infidelity and meant a renunciation
of any future in politics (as, ultimately, it did). In 1967 I encountered McGeorge Bundy at a cocktail party. "It's a shame, Dick,"
he said, "a man like you with such great talent for public service.
You just didn't leave Washington in the right way." Meaning I
should have kept my dissent to myself. Averell Harriman was more
colorfully direct later that same year when, as we stood in Bobby
Kennedy's Hickory Hill dining room, he told me that "people like
you and Schlesinger are murderers, you're killing American boys."
Slightly surprised — not much — I retorted that we were trying
to stop the killing, not increase it. "You're just encouraging Hanoi," Harriman answered. "All this protest just makes them think
we're going to give up." And then he added, referring to Johnson,
"You're biting the hand that fed you." It was, I thought, a metaphor that would only occur to a man of inherited wealth, and
somewhat angrily I replied with the equally nonsensical observation, "He didn't feed me; I fed myself," reflecting my own, less
affluent origins.

I was not Johnson's servant, not duty bound to subordinate my
own beliefs to his, conceal private disagreement behind public approval or even silence. Yet Harriman's sentiment — stripped of
its arrogant condescension — had some force. Not when he said
it, long after I had crossed into open opposition — but in mid-
1966, when I was writing the article that represented my first halting
steps along that path. Johnson had given me an unexpected opportunity to help shape public policy. I liked and admired the
man, both his personal qualities and the sincerity and force of his
domestic ambitions. I still believed, hoped, that Vietnam was a
retrievable error, which, once recognized, would be corrected,
opening the way for a return to the Great Society. It was a delusion — partly self-serving (the urge to reconcile ambition with
conviction), partly wishful thinking (that rational reality would
dissipate the senseless, self-destructive pursuit of the unattain-
able), partly the pragmatic belief that a "moderate" position, if
transformed into a political force, might influence the warmakers.

The purpose of my writing as I did was a calculated effort to
strengthen the possibility of that influence. Experience had taught
me that the political force of language and ideas rested on their

consistency with the emerging doubts and aspirations of the times. And in mid-1966 a large majority of the American people supported the war in Vietnam, at least as they understood that war. Partly it was the natural and admirable instinct to rally around the flag. But the public support was also a tribute to the success of deception — partly self-deception — by the president and his small circle of advisers. Americans were being told, and many believed, that we could reconstruct a noncommunist South Vietnamese society able to defend itself; although those who promised it knew it wasn't true. They were being told, time and time again, that each fresh application of American military power would bring Hanoi to its knees; even though secret plans for further escalations were already approved. They were being constantly reassured that communist strength was waning, even though generals in the field and their commanders in Washington had overwhelming evidence that communist forces were increasing in size and firepower. They were being told that we were moving toward a negotiated peace, even though the conditions of negotiation — on both sides — were unacceptable, made compromise impossible. The cost of the war, its inevitable impact on domestic prosperity were deliberately understated. They were not being told what Washington knew: that military success would require a massive enlargement of the war — a half million troops and more, billions of dollars — and that, even then, prospects for success were uncertain.

Moreover, a fearful reluctance, imposed by the combined inhibitions of political regularity and misjudged public opinion, had rendered Congress and executive officials virtually impotent. Not one high official resigned in protest. Only a handful of congressmen spoke out against the president. And, until late 1967, no single major politician opposed Johnson's reelection on what inevitably would have been a platform of expanding war — a fight to the finish, at whatever cost. (By 1968 plans for the invasion of North Vietnam were already prepared — a million men or more to make a battlefield out of an entire country whose southern portion we were unable to defend.) Yet, in fairness, we must also remember that Congress was systematically and frequently deceived.

An unending stream of messages, reports, testimony inundated the chambers and committees of Congress, while groups of legislators were constantly summoned to White House briefings, usually presided over by Johnson, Rusk, and McNamara, illustrating their presentation with vividly precise charts and graphs. (The Pentagon's ability to graph the ungraphable is unmatched in the history of bureaucracy.) But they were not given some inside story. They were told what the rest of us were told — a compound of wishful thinking, numbers conjured from ignorance, ill-founded predictions, and lies. Yet even though many members knew it was a con job (such skill being the essence of the political profession), few challenged the accuracy of the presentations. Even as other officials spoke Lyndon Johnson dominated the room, his presence alone making the audience aware that to contradict his subordinates was to call the president a liar. And one didn't call Johnson a liar, not to his face.

"One time about seventy of us were asked to the White House for a briefing on Vietnam," Frank Thompson, a senior congressman from New Jersey, told me, "and after Rusk and McNamara had given us the usual on body counts and pacification, I stood up and asked, 'Now, is someone going to tell us the truth?' Johnson was standing at the side of the room, and when I spoke, he strode over, grabbed me by the arm, said, 'I want you out of my house right now,' and, never loosening his grasp, led me out of the room and down the corridor to the exit. As I walked out I said to him, 'It's not your house, Mr. President.' Two days later he called me: 'I want you to know that I was right in making you leave, but you were right that it's not my house.' He never talked to me again. You know," the congressman reflected, "I'm an inch taller than he is. But he seemed so big, I felt overwhelmed. God, he was a frightening man."

In retrospect, I believe it was the fusion of personal motives, political calculation, and my perception of the realistic possibilities of 1966 that persuaded me to confine my written opposition to further escalation, hoping to articulate a rallying point, a concrete objective, around which a substantial and coherent opposition might organize.

I had not consulted Bobby on the preparation of the article, as I would not, until mid-1967, discuss my antiwar acts and writing in advance. I was doing this on my own; was anxious that even the appearance of an anti-Johnson "cabal" be avoided. Still, shortly after the article appeared, while dining at a restaurant in Manhattan, Kennedy told me, "I read your piece. I agree with it. But what's your plan of action? There's no use coming up with an idea and doing nothing about it."

"The sit-in, teach-in crowd (academics, intellectuals, students) have just about exhausted their impact," I replied, "and all the riots and talk of violence is turning the country against the blacks." (A substitute word for Negroes recently introduced into the American lexicon by Stokely Carmichael.) "I'm going to try and get some solid establishment people lined up in opposition. It would be good to have some generals. General Gavin is against the war and so is Ridgway. No one can attack their patriotism. Hell, they've been there. And they won their wars. I'm not so sure about Doug Dillon. I think he may want to be secretary of state."

"That's wrong," he interrupted; "Dillon will do what he thinks is right. He's my friend." This assertion, coming from Bobby, ended debate — the integrity of friends, especially those who had served John Kennedy, was not to be doubted. He was right about Dillon, although a close personal relationship obscured his perception of McNamara's duplicity. "You might try General Norstad," Bobby continued. "I sat next to him at a lunch a few weeks ago and he thinks the bombing is a big mistake. But you're not going to find it easy to get these people into the open. They've been trained to stay out of politics, and they're not going to attack the commander-in-chief."

Knowing he was right, discouraged by that knowledge, I retorted gloomily that "I don't see any alternative to continued escalation, unless we're very fortunate."

"I don't think we're going to be fortunate," he replied, ending the discussion, which was edging toward the political conspiracy that neither of us wanted.

That same month — July of 1966 — I reviewed a book by Edward J. Epstein, *Inquest: The Warren Commission and the Establishment of Truth*. Until then, I, like nearly all of President Kennedy's family and associates, had accepted the Warren Commission's conclusion that Lee Harvey Oswald was a lone assassin.

The book was a stunner. In calm, analytical tones far more convincing than the shrill polemics of assassination buffs and conspiracy fans, it exposed the huge flaws in the Warren Commission Report; proved that it had been prepared in haste, based on a sloppy and superficial investigation. The Warren Report did not prove that Oswald acted alone or even that he was the killer — not beyond a reasonable doubt, not enough to get a jury to convict. Epstein did not provide an alternative. That was not his purpose; only to show that the case against Oswald was — in the verdict permitted a Scottish jury — "Not Proven."

In my review for *Book Week*, appearing on July 23, I wrote that Epstein's work "not only raises questions but demands explorations and answers. . . . I don't want to make the same mistake about the Epstein book that people made about the Warren Report, thinking it must be right because it sounds right. . . . It may all rest on quicksand, but we will never know that until we have made a much more extensive examination. . . ." And I proposed that an "independent group should look at [Epstein's] charges and determine whether the commission investigation was so flawed that another inquiry is necessary."

The next day, July 24, in a rather lengthy news story, the *New York Times* reported my review, commenting that "Mr. Goodwin is the first member of the President's inner circle to suggest publicly that an official re-examination be made of the Warren report."

The following evening, after dinner, I returned with Bobby Kennedy to his apartment, where I was to spend the night. He had never read the Warren Report (nor had I). The subject itself, accompanied by the dry anatomical depictions of bullets, wounds, and a shattered skull, was too painful, the scars too raw. We had lamented lost opportunities, but had never discussed the assassination itself. Aware of his sensibilities, the still-unhealed vulnerability, yet compelled by my own awakened necessities, I began cautiously, in subdued tones, to relate my reaction to the Epstein book. Bobby listened silently, without objection, his inner tension or distaste revealed only by the circling currents of scotch in the glass he was obsessively rotating between his hands, staring at the floor in a posture of avoidance.

After I completed my brief presentation, he looked up: "I'm sorry, Dick, I just can't focus on it."

Although aware of his pain, ignoring his response, I pressed on. "I think we should find our own investigator — someone with absolute loyalty and discretion. Marina Oswald must know something. He spent the last night with her. Maybe there's some way to find out."

"You might try Carmine Bellino," Bobby said. (Bellino had worked for Bobby on the Hoffa case.) "He's the best in the country."

He would not — could not — continue. I would have to act, if I did act, on my own. The conversation shifted, returned to problems of the present, becoming — as we entered the early-morning hours, listened to some music, sipped our whiskey — more pessimistic and philosophical.

"The worst thing about the war," he said, "is not the war itself, although that's bad enough, but all the great opportunities that are going down the drain. We have a real chance to do something about poverty, to get blacks out of the ghettos, but we're paralyzed. I don't like Johnson, but he was doing some good things. Now there's no direction."

"People are turning inward," I replied, "they're looking out for themselves."

"They're afraid. They don't understand the war or what's going to happen. The economy's shaky. They read about hippies and draft-card burners and riots. They feel something's happening to the country, something they don't understand or particularly like. They feel threatened, and if you're threatened, you withdraw. Did you ever see a turtle when you make a loud noise? He goes right into his shell." Of course, I had seen turtles, but turtles don't vote or pay taxes or send sons to war. However, it was too late at night to seek more appropriate metaphors.

"Sure, most people put their families first. We all do, even though most parents can't put their sons in the Senate. But it doesn't make them happy to see other people suffer. They're willing to give a little, to help the less fortunate. We proved that with the Peace Corps, the poverty program. People are selfish, but they can also be compassionate and generous, and they care about the country. But not when they feel threatened. That's why this is such a crucial time. We can go in either direction. But if we don't make a choice soon, it will be too late to turn things around. I think people are willing to make the right choice. But they need leadership. They're hungry for leadership."

"Well, Senator, what are you going to do about it? What's your plan of action?"

He grinned. "Why, I'm going to make speeches. That's what a senator does. I might even write a book. That'll show them. And tomorrow," he said, looking at his watch, "I mean today — Jesus, it's late — I'm going to meet with the Bronx County leaders. Now there's a bunch of crusaders for you."

Thus, with a flash of irony, the barely visible, but inevitably emerging question was postponed.

At 2:30 A.M., we arose from our chairs, set down our still half-filled glasses, and moved toward the hallway which led to sleep. Entering his bedroom, Kennedy paused for a moment, looked toward me, his eyes slightly averted. "About that other thing." I knew instantly he meant the conversation about the assassination that had begun the evening. "I never thought it was the Cubans. If anyone was involved it was organized crime. But there's nothing I can do about it. Not now."

Sleep came quickly. We never discussed the assassination again.

The first wave of "establishment" protest — including my own — against widening the war received a swift and decisive answer. On July 29 the United States, for the first time, bombed the North Vietnamese capital of Hanoi and the port of Haiphong, destroying, it was claimed, two-thirds of North Vietnamese oil supplies, and crippling the capacity to bring oil ashore from foreign tankers. As usual, the heralds of imminent triumph were stilled by events. The oil continued to flow, communist forces obtained fuel ample to all their needs, and the response to our attack was a "counterescalation" by North Vietnam.

Earlier that same month Robert Kennedy, dining with McNamara, had bet the secretary of defense five dollars that there would be at least one dramatic expansion of the war before the 1966 midterm elections in order to improve Democratic prospects. He had won his bet; indeed would win it several times over before November. It was McNamara himself — selflessly putting the national interest ahead of his own financial stake in the wager with Kennedy — who vigorously urged extending the air attacks. At a White House meeting to consider the bombing of Hanoi and Haiphong, McNamara had said — according to a former associate of mine who was present — "that bombing the Hanoi–Haiphong fuel dumps won't get us out of Vietnam, but they'll run us out of this country if we don't do it." Listening to this account I was horrified. To destroy lives in order to assuage public opinion was something more than a mistake; it verged on the criminal. In a diary entry of July 16, after noting the account of the meeting, I wrote: "He is even wrong about the politics. Of course, the polls go up when you bomb, but that is because people hope it will get us out, get it over. When that doesn't happen, disillusionment returns and people revert to their opposition." (And that is precisely what happened. By the end of 1966 less than 50 percent of the population supported the president, compared with 75 percent the year before.)

In retrospect the hope that protest, reasoned argument, organized public opinion could have influenced the course of the war seems foolish, even absurd. But not at the time. The progress of more than half a decade had been stimulated, given direction, by the collective action of the aggrieved and those who sympathized with their cause. The belief in that possibility was a dominant theme of the sixties, is, indeed, what distinguishes that decade. It was not yet clear that the doors were closing, the mass hardening, the once-receptive leaders of government building a wall between themselves and the nation, between their ideological obsessions and reality.

It was only slowly that I began to realize that Johnson would allow the war to swallow up all his most cherished dreams and ambitions, would even sacrifice himself — a martyr to the cause of freedom. Convinced that he was saving the world from destruction, he saw no return, no compromise. He had to win the war. And that compelled him to pursue the impossible dream — a military victory. I also believed what I could not reveal — not even to Bobby — that the mental aberrations I had witnessed, the encroaching paranoia, were winning their own fierce internal battle against his faculties of reason, judgment, and realistic calculation. The issue was not only the war. It was also Johnson. Through the late summer of 1966 I wrestled with this realization, tried to avoid its urgent implications, sought out and discarded alternative explanations for the president's conduct. But there seemed no possibility of evasion. Yet what could I do about it? My lone feeble voice — even the voices of millions — could not reach the shuttered mind. Still, even futility has its imperatives. I did know that I had only two choices. I could ignore the war, withdraw from debate, or I could go after Johnson directly. Any other course would be a deception, a lie to myself and those I addressed.

In the majestic world of affairs my actions were of trifling importance. I had no constituency, no following, no office. What I did or said mattered little to the government or the country. But it mattered to me. I accepted an invitation to address the National Board of the Americans for Democratic Action on September 16. The subject: The war in Vietnam.

The day after the speech, Max Frankel reported in the *New York Times* that "A former aide to Presidents Kennedy and Johnson condemned the Administration's conduct of the war in Vietnam today. . . . Richard N. Goodwin, once an adviser and speechwriter for both Presidents, combined his attack with a proposal for a national organization to unite all critics of the Administration's policy. . . . The address . . . surpassed in both intensity and scope the criticism previously made in public by Mr. Goodwin and other speakers before the A.D.A. . . . He has maintained good personal contacts both in the present Administration and with Senator Robert F. Kennedy. . . . Mr. Goodwin said he had not told the Senator about today's talk" (which was true) "which he regards as virtually burning his bridges to the Johnson Administration."

The White House refused comment. There was only silence. But I didn't expect or need a reply. I knew what was being thought and said. I was now an enemy — in the camp of the enemy — a traitor to the president who had lifted me to the highest levels, made me his "confidant," his "voice," his "alter ego" (Johnson's descriptions, not mine). In imagination I could hear Lyndon now: "After all I did for that boy. Then look what he does to me. He's climbed right into bed with those Kennedys, just like the rest of you would like to do."

I did not feel elated. Liberated, perhaps, but sad — at the loss of a relationship that had meant so much, at the knowledge that what I thought an act of integrity would, for a very long time, cause others to suspect that my convictions were shaped by personal expediency. But it was done. And rightly done. The bridges I burned were gone; their destruction setting me irrevocably on another course — one still undefined, ambiguous, precarious; the prospects of passage to be revealed only by events.

25 / "Bobby's Dilemma"

In THE MIDTERM ELECTIONS of November 1966, the Democrats lost forty-seven House seats, more than they had gained in the 1964 landslide. The liberal majority, which had made it possible to enact Johnson's program, was gone. In a single day of balloting, the conflicting opinions of commentators and pollsters were made irrelevant. There was still one power greater than the might of presidents. It was the only power we could hope to invoke. And those who wielded it were beginning to suspect their government, were becoming restless and discontented. It was a long shot. But the only one. Not for me, but for a restoration of that expansive national purpose which still lingered — in exile but very much alive — in the precincts of American desire.

Having made my "statement of conscience," broken with Johnson, I returned to my sanctuary in Middletown, where I could — surrounded by congratulatory friends and intellectuals — luxuriate in the vanity of vindicated virtue.

It would have been easier had the times been tranquil. But every edition of the morning paper stimulated those concerns which had consumed me for almost a decade. I was temperamentally incapable of ignoring the deterioration of my America, of confining my sentiments to private expression — over drinks, at dinner parties, in conversations with students. So in late 1966 and throughout 1967 I made speeches, wrote articles — mostly for the *New Yorker* — in opposition not only to the war, but to the intensifying concentration of power that stripped individuals of control over the public conditions of their private existence, leading, like all impotence, to withdrawal, division, anger, selfishness. But speaking and writing are riskless, a reality that is among the glories of American freedom, but also a sign that words and ideas have little impact on a nation that admires and honors successful action, practical achievement.

Even as I sat before my typewriter drafting still another polemic, I knew that words alone — mine or those of others — would not impede the course of events. Neither would protests, or marches, or the burning of draft cards, except to the extent they signaled a change in public opinion that might threaten the powerful. Yet because I knew Johnson so well — at least thought I did — I also believed that he was now probably beyond the reach of public discontent — perceived those who counseled against his policies in Vietnam as ignorant, deluded, or the victims of some nameless but traitorous conspiracy. As long as he was president, commanding the immense power for action and deception bestowed by that office, the war would continue to grow. The conclusion was as obvious as it then seemed improbable — Johnson must be removed from office. And in the America of the late sixties, that required his defeat in the presidential election of 1968.

At the beginning of 1967 there were very few among the influential members of the Democratic party — including those strongly opposed to the war — who shared this objective. With the exception of the "New Left" and its call for immediate withdrawal, the mainstream of "dove" opinion — itself a minority view in the nation — called for a halt to the bombing and for a negotiated settlement that would, of necessity, allow communist participation in South Vietnamese politics. It was a reasonable position — in the abstract. But it was an exercise in self-deception when addressed to a president who intended, as he told the troops on a visit to Cam Ranh Bay, to "come home with that coonskin on the wall." Johnson was not going to stop the bombing, but increase it. Nor would he settle for anything less than complete exclusion of the communists from political power. Since it was inconceivable that Hanoi would surrender at the bargaining table what we had been unable to compel on the battlefield, no negotiated peace was possible.

Yet the growing evidence of Johnson's determination not to compromise, but to win, was not, at first, translated into political opposition. No incumbent president of the twentieth century had been denied the renomination of his party. Only one — Herbert

Hoover — had failed of reelection. Opinion polls showed that a majority of the country still "supported" Johnson and the war. Yet behind the polls and precedents one could sense a growing discontent and frustration, a subtle but expanding change in the mood of the nation. Something was happening — not in Vietnam, but in America. Just as a faith healer cannot keep returning to the scene of a spreading epidemic, trust in the promises and predictions of the administration had begun to diminish — not temporarily but irrevocably. Americans were being lied to, deceived, and — even if most could not fully grasp the facts and arguments — they knew it. And they didn't like it at all. And whether they agreed with the government or attacked it, Americans — left or right, pro- or antiwar, impoverished black or middle-class white — were losing confidence in its integrity. The confidence of the early sixties, the belief in an inevitable destiny, the redress of old injustice and the attainment of new heights, was being displaced by insecurity; apprehension about the future; fragmenting, often angry, sometimes violent, division.

The "movements," which were the glory of the early sixties — the expression of aroused expectations for justice, relief from poverty, the triumph of more humane values — took a more ominous, ultimately self-defeating direction.

In 1967, the black poor, their hopes aroused by the early triumphs of the civil rights revolution and the now virtually abandoned War on Poverty, continued to express their frustrated anger in aimless violence. Through the summer of that year riots in Boston, Detroit, Spanish Harlem, Cambridge, Maryland, and Milwaukee took dozens of lives, left thousands homeless. For the first time since World War II, federal forces were used to quell civil disorders when Johnson dispatched over four thousand paratroopers to the flaming streets of Detroit. Few quarreled with the need to halt violence, but there was no justification — except the depleted sympathies of government and nation — for the refusal to address the grievances that had incited blacks to the destruction of their own neighborhoods. Now there was no call for compassion or understanding generosity, only a demand for more troops and police. In vain did the once-revered leaders of "nonviolent" protest call for restraint. Their authority over their own followers had been fatally undermined by the dissolution of their influence within the chambers of state power.

Many young whites — their somewhat romantic, somewhat

utopian desires once given outlet and direction by the Peace Corps, the civil rights movement, the desire to construct a nobler, less materialistic society — withdrew from social struggle, seeking fulfillment, or at least expression, in what was beginning to be called the "counterculture." If the larger society was hardening, more resistant to change, they would form their own mythical nations within the nation. They would "do their own thing," a deadly phrase that represented the abandonment of Plato's dictum that there is no greater good than "the bond of unity . . . where there is community of pleasure and pain, where all the citizens are glad or grieved on the same occasions of grief or sorrow . . . where there is no common but only private freedom a State is disorganized."

We heard about, discussed, praised or censured the emergence of hippies and love-ins, communes and the drug culture, the Woodstock Nation and the Greening of America. As 1966 moved into 1967 Timothy Leary founded the League for Spiritual Discovery, based on the sacramental use of hallucinogenic drugs. Scholars proclaimed that the emerging counterculture was the onset of an American redemption. It was, I wrote in 1967, "all a myth. There has been no genetic mutation, no psychic transformation. Today's youth are reacting to felt changes in the nation, their behavior — even in defiance — given form by the conditions and values of the time. They will discover there is no alternative to either changing the society or accepting it. There is no escape. No place to hide from the governing, pervasive values of the nation to which they are irrevocably bound."

Yet in 1967 the distinctive vitality of the sixties was still very much alive. Most people did not riot or join the counterculture; many refused to join the ranks of apathetic resignation or withdraw before the baffling confusions of unanticipated change. They still believed that committed, organized individuals could change America. Yet that belief — if it is not to remain a futile abstraction — needs a unifying objective, a cause. And many found it in the very circumstances that had arrested progress, crushed so many hopes — the war in Vietnam and the political structure that sustained it. The peace movement was the last surge of the sixties, embodying that decade's rare combination of idealistic hope and realistic possibility. It was to culminate in the tumultous events of 1968. But by 1967 its swelling force was already exerting significant pressures on the thought and decisions of political leaders.

Like other successful movements of the sixties it was not a monolithic organization, but a growing confederation of diverse groups
and individuals united, at first, in a common opposition to the
war, and, ultimately, in a common political objective. In that
sense — the true sense — I was part of the peace movement, as
were Senator William Fulbright, Eugene McCarthy, George
McGovern, Martin Luther King, Jesse Unruh (then the Democratic "boss" of California), and many others whose capacity to
influence events derived from experience or rank within "the system." This alliance of conviction between men of position and
popular protest was — as had been true of the civil rights movement — the vital ingredient of effective action.

At the beginning of 1967, many still hoped that public opposition, combined with the successful and mounting resistance of the
communist forces in Vietnam, would persuade Johnson to change
his course. Instead, the administration responded with increased
military force — the largest conventional bombing campaign in
the history of warfare, more men sent into battle (almost half a
million by year's end), and no end in sight. Those who criticized
the administration were met not with rational argument, but censure and condemnation; their motives impugned, their patriotism
doubted. Dean Rusk, at a private luncheon with *Newsweek* editors,
denounced "pseudo-intellectual" critics (meaning Galbraith,
Schlesinger, and maybe me) and claimed that the antiwar movement was "controlled by communists." Later in 1967 General
William Hershey, director of Selective Service, acting at the president's direction, ordered local draft boards to punish deferred
college students who interfered with campus recruitment by putting them at the top of the draft list.

Gradually, reluctantly, opponents of the war were compelled to
conclude that there was only one hope of success, one decisive
weapon — rejection at the ballot box. But one could not simply
vote against Johnson — an election is not a referendum. It was
necessary to oppose him with a candidate capable of unseating an
incumbent president. The hopes and pressures of discontent increasingly centered on the strongest among the Democratic leaders — Robert Kennedy. And he did not want to run, believing
that to lead a party revolt against the president would be a doomed
and quixotic gesture. Nineteen seventy-two — not 1968 — would
be his year of opportunity. The logic of this political calculation
was irrefutable. But events have their own logic, and were press-

ing him prematurely to a decision he did not want to make, had not anticipated, but could not avoid.

One evening toward the end of 1966, sitting with Bobby at our favorite, semiprivate table in P. J. Clarke's, I ventured: "I don't think it's impossible that you might have a real party revolt against Johnson in 1968. Especially if the Republicans have a strong candidate." Bobby did not reply. The slightest hint that he was contemplating the possibilities of 1968 would plunge him into a damaging two-year war of attrition with the White House and Democratic loyalists across the country; nor was he yet willing to contemplate so disruptive, potentially self-destructive a decision. "Isn't it fortunate," I said, in an ironic tone of withdrawal, "that you can't do anything about 1968 except what you're already doing — giving speeches, campaigning for other candidates, working on issues — and waiting to see what happens."

"It's lucky," he said, laughing. "How's your cheeseburger?"

That evening I recounted the conversation in my diary, commenting: "In fact there's a real chance for 1968. The White House expects him to make a move then, but you have to wait since it all depends on how drastically Johnson's fortunes have fallen by that time, and there is little that can be done to influence that. . . . I think," I confided to myself, "that the decline in Johnson fortunes is permanent, regardless of Vietnam, since it stems from a basic distrust of his integrity and intention which is rooted in reality — ineradicable flaws in his character — and thus cannot be reversed. I think it is already beyond the point where it can be covered up."

Believing that Kennedy would probably not run in 1968, I reflected bleakly: "It is very important to beat Johnson in 1968. I talked to Kenny O'Donnell, who is very perceptive, and we agreed that the country was in the most dangerous hands of its history. 'We'll survive it,' he said. Probably. But the man is unstable, with paranoid tendencies, capable of almost anything if there is a crisis which threatens to plunge us into a large war. I think he'll be much worse when he no longer needs to face reelection, free from the restraining fear of political defeat which now holds him back. I also think there's a good chance he may dump Humphrey, believing that Hubert, whom he doesn't like at all, can't beat Bobby in 1972. The only thing he really doesn't want is RFK's election. I think he'd stop at nothing to prevent that, even resigning before his term was over to let his appointed vice-president be his successor. Anyway," I concluded my secret nocturnal reflections, "it is too far into the future. The important thing is to defeat him in 1968 even if that means a Republican victory and damages RFK's chances for the future. It's just too damn important."

But the question Bobby did not want to contemplate would not go away. Instead it became more insistent, entered the realm of public debate, transformed his mind into a battlefield where instinct warred with reason, passion with ambition, moral certainty with moral ambiguity. Indeed, for Robert Kennedy — partly for me — the entire year of 1967 seemed one interminable debate, its terms continually shifting: would he or wouldn't he, should he or should he not run against Lyndon Johnson in 1968.

It was the year of what Arthur Schlesinger has called "Bobby's dilemma." It was not only a dilemma for him, but for his friends, political allies, and those multitudes for whom he embodied hope of a return to the glittering promise of the prewar sixties. In a speech delivered to a Boston audience in late 1967, I said, "In January of 1965 sixty million Americans watched as President Johnson stood before an amazed Congress and proposed a domestic program of immense scope and vision . . . yet within a year it was all gone . . . we reached out our hand for a new Age of Pericles only to draw it back scarred by the fire and agony of war." Yet for me, as for many others, that painful withdrawal was not irrevocable as long as Robert Kennedy stood at the center of political combat, ready, when the time came, to reach for the golden prize. I have long since abandoned my search for heroes — that deep-grained, erroneous American belief that a single leader might redeem, transform, the course of an entire nation. Still, there was something to it. The very existence of Robert Kennedy, the fact of his preeminence, was evidence that the conditions of possibility still existed, that the other America — expansive, just, adventurous — still survived, might yet be summoned to the ancient dream. Or was it? I didn't know then. I don't know now. But in the world of affairs uncertainty, although firmly grounded in true understanding, can also be a self-indulgence, allowing "conscience to make cowards of us all," and "enterprises of great pith and moment lose the name of action." The principle is unexceptionable; the difficulty inheres in distinguishing hesitation from wise restraint, impulse from impatience, courage from self-destruction.

Although friends and advisers put forth an abundance of arguments for and against Bobby's candidacy, at the core of "Bobby's dilemma" was a single issue. To run and lose in 1968, a defeated political renegade, would damage, probably beyond repair, his prospects for the future. Indeed, to oppose the president and fail would only leave Johnson stronger than before, appear to vindicate his policies. Even those of his friends and advisers who urged him to run did not want that. "You have to understand," I said to him as, in the fall, we drove to Hyannis for a long, lonely weekend of discussion, "I'm not asking you to be a profile in courage. I think you can beat him."

As 1967 progressed, it became apparent that there was no easy, riskless course — that inaction had its dangers. The war escalated, the peace movement grew, and Bobby's own opposition — expressed in Senate speeches and public meetings — mounted in scope and intensity. The war, he said, had grown "beyond any legitimate American interest," "was destroying our country's progress." He argued that "the destruction of Vietnamese villages" and the "sacrifice of American lives" in a "futile and unnecessary effort" was immoral. Yet at the same time he responded to questions about his political intentions with the litany of political boilerplate: "I intend to support President Johnson's reelection in 1968."

It is what politicians are expected to say: "I might differ with the president on some issues, but I agree with his basic direction, admire his leadership, believe that the country needs a Democratic president," etc. etc., etc. But the war was not just another issue. It was *the* issue. The contradiction between Kennedy's expressed conviction and his political position was too large, too blatant, led many to doubt the sincerity of his conviction, even to question his integrity. And the fiercest criticisms came from his natural constituency — liberals, blacks, the young.

Gradually his standing in the polls began to drop. His opposition to the war was controversial among the many who supported the administration's policies. His support of Johnson was controversial among those allied with the growing peace movement. The last thing this intense, polarizing man wanted was to add more controversy to his continued crusade for the oppressed and deprived. Yet for him there was no escape. He was trapped by the times, by an issue so immense that it allowed no evasion. He had taken a stand; his public discourse on the war was a reflection of intense inner conviction. But he was not a professor, he was a politician. And not just a politician, but the second most powerful leader of the Democratic party, uniquely required to accept or reject a direct challenge to the president.

In mid-1967, my fellowship at Wesleyan having expired, I returned to my native Boston and still another temporary position as a visiting professor at MIT. Shortly after my arrival I spoke to a group of MIT alumni. It seemed an unlikely audience for my antiwar message, being composed mostly of business executives and managing engineers — politically conservative and natural allies of the establishment. Yet, as I spoke, I became aware that the audience was listening to my arguments intently, with sympathetic interest. When I concluded, the applause was warm, even enthusiastic. As I stood at the lectern after the speech, several men approached me with congratulations or questions that reflected sincere doubts about the war. "I am a great fan of William Buckley," one said, "and I agree with everything you said." It was a non sequitur, but not without significance. As I drove home, I reflected that had I made the same speech to the same audience a year before, my words would have aroused hostility, evoked a barrage of objections, even censure of my motives or patriotism. If these men — not students or intellectuals, but masters of the marketplace — had turned against the war, then Johnson was in serious trouble.

This experience coalesced in my mind a pattern composed of a host of previously isolated observations — the appearance of querulous editorials in business publications, magisterial doubts by the *Wall Street Journal,* statements by bankers and business leaders — all questioning the conduct and course of the war. They were responding to an emerging awareness that we were engaged in the first unprofitable war of modern times; one that endangered the health of the economy. The longest sustained boom of the postwar period was coming to an end. Rising inflation was accompanied by a decline in the expected increase of income, profits, production. The national deficit was growing and, for the first time since the end of World War II, our supremacy in world trade was weakening. And the war was clearly the cause. Not the war itself, so much as the refusal of the government to admit its cost, to seek adequate financing.

In retrospect I was to see clearly what I then only barely perceived: The business community was turning against the war, and their opposition would be decisive. Now Johnson was threatened not from the fringes, but from the very heart of private power.

The next day I called Kennedy, related my experience. "Well," he said, "I'm glad you had a good time. I guess they like you more than they like me."

"That's not the point," I answered. "If these guys are turning against the war, then Johnson is really vulnerable."

"That's good news," Kennedy responded, "but aren't you calling the wrong fellow? I can have my secretary get you Nixon's phone number. I'm sure he'll be glad to hear from you."

We both knew that a shift in business opinion — if one had occurred, if I wasn't misreading the signs — meant something, but not how it should affect our own political calculations, not precisely. It was only a guess, an intuition in which it was impossible to disentangle wishful thinking from sober judgment.

Through the fall and into the winter the debate continued. "The professionals," Arthur Schlesinger writes (meaning Sorensen, Ted Kennedy, Fred Dutton, etc.), ". . . thought his entry would be an act of hara-kiri. The intellectuals who like to pose as professionals . . . thought likewise." Calls to antiwar Democrats — members of the Senate, political leaders, governors, mayors — revealed almost universal reluctance. Most vigorously opposed his entry, saying it would split the party and result in a Republican victory. After completing his canvass of fellow Democrats, a discouraged Kennedy reported, "No one was ready to stick his neck out. I was very much surprised. I expected a much better reaction."

The few of us who urged Bobby to run advanced our arguments uncertainly. Our difference with the opponents of his candidacy was not moral but political. No one wanted him to self-destruct just to make a point. We did not think that he was sure to win; but believed he had a substantial chance. And that's all you can ever hope for in a presidential campaign. That's all he would have in 1972. After several long discussions — at his New York apartment, in Hyannis, while walking the grounds at Hickory Hill — Bobby asked me to write out the case for his running. "But don't say you want me to run. Just say you're setting out the arguments for my benefit; to help me think. I might want to show it around, and it won't be helpful to you if I don't run and everyone thinks you wanted me to." It was a kind and generous precaution, but useless. The "secret" Kennedy meetings might as well have been conducted in the middle of Madison Square Garden. Those who followed the trail of political insiders knew of the debate, knew where the participants stood. Nor was I anxious for some inevitably flimsy cloak of self-protection. Whatever Bobby did, I was going to oppose Johnson. With no political future to destroy, I could afford the luxury of a futile moral gesture. Nevertheless, I followed Bobby's prescribed formula and, in a letter in November 1967, after a ritualistic disclaimer — "If you were to ask me 'should I try for it in 1968' I would say no" — I proceeded to set forth the arguments I really believed, had frequently made to him in person.

"Is there a chance?" I asked rhetorically.

> There are two aspects to this — your public appeal and the mechanics of the Democratic party. . . . Admittedly you are far from your height. In 1966 you had become a romantic figure. . . . [Y]our brand of mild disagreement suited the national mood which was, on the whole, still quite favorable to LBJ. . . . Now that has changed . . . you are down in the polls. . . . It is a mistake not to think that the deterioration of the national mood helps explain some of your decline. When people begin to lose faith, they lose it in *everyone*. . . . Your position has worsened because you can't say what you think . . . and people know it . . . and you necessarily share in the general disillusionment. *In a perverse way your own popularity has been tied to Johnson*. . . . Therefore, if you were to come out in open opposition . . . if you represent what the American people want — and I think you do — then they'll go for you. . . . If I am right about this, then you can win the primaries. I have, in fact, little doubt that you can beat Johnson almost everywhere.

Then I turned to some of the arguments that had been made against a Kennedy candidacy.

> A. *Johnson can't read you out of the Democratic party, even if he wanted to.* Four years from now it may well be an asset to have opposed LBJ. If the Republicans win, then the major thought in politicians' minds may well be that you could have made it. . . . B. *If you make it you will split the party.* There is no Democratic party in this sense. . . . If you can carry the convention, you will have carried the major states and their organizations. C. *It will wreck you publicly.* If people like you because of your independence, courage, idealism, etc., . . . it may build up real support. If you lose in the primaries, of course, you are really hurt. But if you can't beat LBJ in 1968, then whom can you beat? . . . You may well be hurt more by supporting LBJ, since you will have to say a lot of things you don't believe. . . .

D. *Are your chances better in the future? No one knows, of course, but the odds are against it.* If LBJ wins you can be sure he will devote all his attention to finding ways to keep you from the nomination. . . . If the Republicans win then you have to run against an incumbent. . . .

The future is unknowable. . . . So if you've got a chance (a) to make it, and (b) even if you don't, to try and not be destroyed, why not take it? . . . There are two basic assumptions to all this:

1. Your prospects rest on your own qualities; the less true you are to them, and the more you play the game, the harder it will be. . . . Unfortunately for you, you are not one of these bland neutral figures whose character is judged apart from their speeches and statements. You are a strong, well-defined, controversial politician whose views are regarded as a direct emanation of character and personality. Most politicians are like piano players, and when they strike a wrong note only experts know. But you are the guy in the back row with the huge cymbals and when you clang them at the wrong place the whole auditorium jumps.

2. The Democratic party is not a coherent sort of club whose members resent the guy who talks too loudly in the reading room. It is a diffuse, incoherent, disorganized and rapidly shifting jumble of disparate individuals. And when they do meet, they have tended to be much more responsive to popular sentiment, than to personal resentments or theoretical considerations about the properly demure behavior for potential candidates.

Bobby showed my letter to others, had me set forth the same arguments at still another meeting in New York on December 10, 1967. I made little impression on anyone. Except for one person, and he was moved more by a vaguely defined but urgent sense of obligation than by arguments. By now Robert Kennedy himself wanted to run, felt he should run; was restless, unhappy at the restraint imposed on him by the seemingly unanswerable arguments of the professionals, the lack of support among even the most friendly politicians.

In the fall, sitting in his apartment, I played the recorded score from *The Man of La Mancha.* As the strains of "The Impossible Dream" resonated through the apartment, Bobby's voice from the bedroom shouted: "Turn that damn thing off. If you keep playing it, I might run for president."

As fall became winter, I had dinner with Ted Kennedy in the Charles Restaurant at the foot of Beacon Hill, where a semiprivate enclosure provided the perfect place for private political discussions. Bobby had asked us to get together and debate the arguments. (Did he really think I would persuade Teddy?) After a long, inconclusive evening — wearily familiar arguments recited — we walked together up the steep slope of Chestnut Street, once home to the lordly brahmins of old Boston, where I lived in a rented house that faced across the narrow street toward three magnificent homes designed by Bulfinch. The Irishman and the Jew, new masters of Yankee turf. We had, naturally, a glass of brandy, and changed, by silent agreement, the topic of our conversation. There was nothing more to say. As Teddy left, I accompanied him out the front door to the cobbled sidewalk where his driver was waiting. He stood there hesitantly, looked at me, spoke: "Just the same, maybe he should do it. All his instincts tell him to go. And he's got good instincts."

I did not answer directly, asking instead, "What do you think your brother" (meaning President Kennedy) "would have done?" Teddy reflected for a moment and then grinned: "He would have advised against it. But he would have done it himself."

On November 30, Senator Eugene McCarthy announced his candidacy for the Democratic nomination, and his intention to enter the New Hampshire primary. Al Lowenstein, leader of the emergent "dump Johnson" movement — then largely composed of student activists, some academics, a miscellaneous handful of eccentric businessmen — had approached Bobby and then George McGovern in his efforts to find a candidate who could transform the objectives of the movement into a real political contest. Both men had refused to commit themselves. Bobby, though still undecided, would make the decision on his own, not in response to Lowenstein. McGovern concluded that he would be sacrificing a Senate seat for a doomed, purely symbolic, gesture of defiance. Consulting McCarthy at McGovern's suggestion, the anti-Johnson leaders found the enigmatic senator from Minnesota receptive to their arguments. Convinced that Johnson was not only damaging the country, but undermining the democratic process itself, McCarthy was willing — felt inwardly compelled — to enter the race, even if it was only to change the terms of political debate.

Although surprised by McCarthy's candidacy, the announcement had little effect on Bobby or his advisers. They did not consider him a serious candidate, "knew" he would move aside if Bobby entered, and, whatever his motivation, could provide Johnson with no serious opposition. Indeed, he merely added to the problem, making Bobby's continued public support of Johnson even harder to defend.

"I suppose what'll happen," Bobby had observed early in the fall, "is that we'll keep on talking and talking, and I won't do anything, and then it'll be too late to do anything, and I'll have made a decision without ever really deciding."

That's not what happened. Not exactly. But it came close. In reality Bobby was looking for a way to justify his candidacy — some support, some evidence of possibility, some tangible sign that he would not be destroying his hopes for future leadership in a self-indulgent display of moral righteousness. And he couldn't find it. At least not enough to change his political judgments.

In early January I was invited to Hickory Hill. There, in the mild chill of a Virginia winter, a small group retreated to the most unlikely of council chambers — the wood-framed bathhouse that adjoined the swimming pool at the bottom of the familiar grass slope leading from the house. Clustered around the plumbing were Bobby, his brother, Bill vanden Heuvel, Dave Burke — Teddy Kennedy's brilliant assistant — and me. The meeting was short; the cold did not encourage a lengthy gathering (perhaps that's why he picked the bathhouse). Bobby briefly summarized the arguments, concluded that "The support just isn't there. People will think it's a personal vendetta between me and Johnson, not the war. So," he concluded, "I guess I'm not going to do it." There was silence. Bobby was standing in the corner of the shower room, staring toward the floor, concealing of an expression of — was it pain? It seemed so. I felt it too — not because I had lost the argument, but from some indefinable poignancy in the moment. The helplessness of the strong. But it passed quickly. What the hell! He was young and rich and powerful. And his time would come. Now it was time to think about what I would do.

Bobby was scheduled to leave that same afternoon to attend Senate hearings on Indian problems in Oklahoma, and asked me to accompany him to the airport. The drive to Dulles was a long silence. When we arrived at the airport entrance, I walked with him to the gate, where he turned to shake hands. "I guess," I said, breaking the stillness, "I guess if you're not going, that I'll go up to New Hampshire and see if I can help McCarthy."

"That'd be helpful," he replied, and turned toward the waiting plane. He meant that having a "Kennedy man" in New Hampshire might help blunt accusations that he opposed McCarthy's antiwar candidacy. Thus, in even the most intimate connections of friendship, does the mind turn to its own concerns. That was not why I was going to New Hampshire. Not at all. I had no bright political future to consider. I wanted to go down fighting. And New Hampshire was the only battlefield left.

I returned to Boston, still uncertain about the McCarthy campaign. It looked hopeless. (In January polls showed McCarthy with about 15 percent of the New Hampshire vote.) Nor did I know much about McCarthy. At dinner a few months earlier in Washington he had asked me to work with him. I had answered, truthfully, that I could do nothing until Bobby made up his mind (which he had now done). I had liked McCarthy, his critical intelligence, subdued ironic wit, but I didn't know what he stood for, and — most important — how seriously he intended to campaign. I wasn't sure that I could contribute very much to such a clearly futile exercise — little more than a prolonged debate confined to the icy streets of New Hampshire. It was easier, for the moment, to do nothing, to slip back into my routine of writing and teaching.

But so much for reasoned calculation — within three weeks I was on my way to New Hampshire.

26 / The McCarthy Campaign

We're going West tomorrow, where the promises can't fail.
O'er the hills in legions, boys, and crowd the dusty trail.
We shall starve and freeze and suffer. We shall die and tame the
lands.
But we're going West tomorrow, with our fortunes in our hands.

— Folk ballad

THERE WAS LITTLE in the turning of the New Year to warn
of the tumultuous events that were to give 1968 a special place in
American history. One could not foresee that we were entering a
year that would be a historical divide, marking the end of the
sixties and, more fundamentally, the end of postwar America and
its soaring aspirations to lead itself and the world toward some
more golden promise.

It was a year when the New Politics emerged, but the Old Politics took all the prizes. It was a year that illuminated a national
desire for peace, yet ended with war still raging and the arms race
destined to continue for a quarter century and more. It was a year
that clamored for the new and produced the familiar — that offered the heroic and yielded the ordinary — that began with the
triumph of soft reason amidst New Hampshire tranquillity and
ended with the crash of the assassin's bullet and the policeman's
club.

There were some barely visible signs of the discontent that would
catalyze the clash of present and past, from which would emerge
a future that no one had clearly envisioned: that uncertain America — stripped of the unifying bonds of large purpose — in which
we now live. There was growing frustration with the prolonged,
enigmatically insoluble conflict in Vietnam, even more with rising
prices and economic uncertainty; one sensed a still-formless apprehension that the country was moving toward some new, un-

welcome though still-indefinable direction. The peace movement
was growing. Young people were smoking marijuana and wearing
long hair. But most of the country, even if they couldn't quite
understand the war and had lost confidence in the false reassurances of their government, still supported it out of rooted patriotism, and viewed both protesters and the "counterculture" with
suspicion, if not hostility. A woman in the Cheyenne, Wyoming,
tourist bureau, reflecting the sentiment of many Americans, told
a reporter that "kids don't appreciate what wonderful things
America has done for them . . . students shouldn't protest things
until they've made some sort of contribution to the country."

On December 31, 1967 — as I quietly celebrated the New Year
with my wife and friends at my Boston home — it seemed, to most
observers, that the war would continue, that Lyndon Johnson would
be reelected, and emergent new values would, somehow, be assim-
ilated into the old. There would be changes, but the world would
be the old world yet. That evening the traditional crowds gathered in Times Square; the White House tree still radiated its
multihued luminescence across Pennsylvania Avenue; at the
Polish-American clubhouse in Milwaukee, couples drank and sang
songs from the old country. In Waterville Valley, New Hampshire, as approaching darkness shadowed the slopes, skiers made
their last run; while farther to the north, in Berlin, New Hampshire, young men and women walked through lightly falling snow,
knocking on friendly rural doors, talking with cautiously modulated conviction about an unknown United States senator from
Minnesota.

> In restless dream I walked alone
> Narrow streets of cobblestone
>
> When my eyes were stabbed by the flash
>   Of a neon light
>   That split the light
> And touched the sound of silence.
>
> — Paul Simon, "The Sound of Silence"

Then, shattering expectation and belief — the guns of January.
Amid the Vietnamese Tet holidays in the final days of the first
month of 1968, explosions ripped through the streets of every major city in South Vietnam. A Vietcong squad blasted its way into

the "invulnerable" American embassy in Saigon, and then re-treated leaving death, damage, and recrimination. They came out of nowhere, from everywhere — the enemy we had thought half-defeated, exhausted, having been repeatedly told from the "highest sources" that the war was finally going well. A half million American troops, joined with the enfeebled forces of South Vietnam, had not stopped them. The most concentrated aerial bombardment in history had not stopped them. The American public was stunned. Their government, which had known of the enemy buildup for months, had concealed the rapidly growing communist concentration, its duplicity only intensifying the surprised shock.

Washington labeled the Tet offensive a victory, citing the inability of the communists to maintain possession of the South Vietnamese cities they had attacked. Robert Kennedy, speaking in Chicago on February 8 (a speech I had helped draft), rejoined that the offensive had "finally shattered the mask of official illusion about the war," demonstrating that no "part or person of South Vietnam was safe from attack. . . . It is time for the truth," he said. "It is time to face the reality that a military victory is not in sight and it probably never will come."

It was, the *New York Times* said, "the most sweeping and detailed indictment of the war . . . yet heard from any leading figure in either party." Yet Bobby was not a candidate, the condemnatory eloquence not intended to signal a change in his decision — now public — that he would not challenge the president's renomination. Instead, the *Times* reported, "sources close to Senator Kennedy said the speech . . . reflected his feelings that his refusal to run had set him free to speak his mind." On the contrary, it only demonstrated that his decision, made after such long, tormented debate, had not resolved anything — had widened the obvious contradiction between his actions and beliefs, between political withdrawal and rhetorical engagement. His "dilemma" was merely taking another form — would he support or oppose the McCarthy candidacy, a question that could be postponed only as long as a statement of support could be withheld as nothing more than a futile gesture.

Yet Bobby's dilemma was not mine. Not any longer. Sitting in the privileged sanctuary of an MIT seminar room, discussing the arid abstractions of foreign policy with a dozen half-interested students, I was restless, uneasy, apprehensive. The country was at war on two fronts — in Southeast Asia and in the streets of its cities. Leadership was in the hands of a man I knew had an uncertain, intermittent grip on reality, whose reelection would almost certainly enlarge the dimensions of conflict, unravel the hopeful progress for which so many of us had labored — none more diligently than Johnson himself.

I read and believed the poll-studded newspaper accounts, which reported that McCarthy's campaign was going nowhere, that he had no chance for anything more than a nominal vote of 10 or 15 percent and was headed toward a humiliating defeat that would only strengthen Johnson's position. I consulted with friends from the political world, men whose judgment I respected, and found unanimous agreement that the McCarthy effort was doomed. Clearly Johnson and his advisers thought so too. Believing wrongly that McCarthy was a surrogate for Robert Kennedy, the president, whose name was not on the New Hampshire ballot, recklessly mounted a write-in campaign, organized the entire political establishment of New Hampshire — governor, senator, mayors — for a contest whose decisive outcome would drive the Minnesota pretender from the scene, keep Kennedy on the sidelines, and eliminate all further obstructions to his renomination.

Ironically, had Johnson refused to engage in New Hampshire, instructed his supporters not to campaign, and disavowed all efforts on his behalf, he might well have been renominated. But he believed what all "informed" politicians believed, what they all told him: that it would be an easy and decisive conquest.

I believed it, too. Yet judgment could not close my mind to the unremitting torrent of television pictures and news accounts portraying the fierce agony of the fighting that followed Tet — villages destroyed, cities in flame, and everywhere the dead and crippled; roadways indiscriminately strewn with the bodies of Vietnamese and Americans, companions in death as they had been enemies in life. In less than three weeks of battle, the once-majestic city of Hue, the ancient capital and traditional center of Vietnam's intellectual and religious life, was almost totally destroyed.

One morning in late February I sat at breakfast with my wife and read aloud the *New York Times* account of Hue's devastation. "It is not only the loss of our buildings," a young medical student, Nguyen Van Chu, said, "it is the loss of our spirit. It is gone. My Hue is gone. I loved my city, but all gone." The impression, the *Times* reported, "was of a city about to lie down and die." A "truckload of bandaged, weary and muddy marines rolled through cratered streets, past shattered houses. . . . Vietnamese on the route stared sullenly. . . . A marine wounded in the arm and grimacing every time the truck jolted said, 'They all blame us.' "

In an adjacent story on the same page the *Times* reported that "nuclear weapons are available for immediate use in Vietnam."

It was madness. And there seemed no limit to the reach of that madness. We were destroying the country we fought to save. And that wounded marine was a young man sent out to die by old men trapped in their own grotesque errors, a soldier in an army without a mission except to kill and be killed.

I put down the paper, ceased my reflections, then said to my wife: "The hell with it. I'm going to New Hampshire. Maybe it's hopeless, but it's better than sitting on your ass in Boston. It's something."

That afternoon I abandoned my teaching job. ("You don't have to quit," the president of MIT told me, "we'll give you a leave until the New Hampshire primary is over.") I put some clothes and an electric typewriter in the trunk of my car and called McCarthy's office. "The senator is campaigning in Berlin, New Hampshire," I was told. "Please tell him I'm coming," I said and, finding Berlin on a road map, began to drive.

The winter sun had already descended as I rode past the scattered clusters of light that disclosed the towns of New Hampshire's populous southern tier — Nashua, Manchester, Concord — headed northwest, the calm oceanic white obscuring the contours of hills and forests broken by an occasional yellow gleam from an isolated farmhouse or huddled rural village, passed the White Mountain National Forest toward Berlin — the northernmost citadel of Democratic voters encircled by Republican farms. Gradually my inner reluctance dissolved under the stimulus of the Bob Dylan tapes — "the losers now will be later to win" — which were my only companion; and I reflected — not on my decision, that was made — but on strategy, tactics, and, most of all, what I would find when I arrived. I knew little about the McCarthy campaign; the newspaper accounts had been infrequent and sparse. (When Ned Kenworthy, the *New York Times* reporter, later asked why his stories from New Hampshire were not printed, he received word from the august chambers of his Manhattan editors that "McCarthy was not a candidate." Presumably the senator from Minnesota was merely on a prolonged lecture tour of New Hampshire.)

It was midnight as I drove into the Perkins Motel, where, I had been told, the McCarthy "staff" was staying. My first concern was to avoid members of the press corps, who would know me and certainly report my arrival as news, until I had a chance to talk with McCarthy, establish that my presence was desired, and that a working relationship was possible. Getting out of the car I edged up to the entrance of the hotel bar — the logical place to find reporters, especially at midnight in Berlin, New Hampshire. From a distance I scrutinized the room, saw no familiar faces, asked the desk where Seymour Hersh, McCarthy's press secretary, was staying, and walked outside to the door of Sy's room, which opened to my peremptory knock. Characteristically disheveled, the interior of his room cluttered with papers, Sy greeted me warmly, enthusiastically. It was my first encounter with a man who would be my constant companion for almost three months, whose frenzied energy, stimulated by profound commitment, was to provide the McCarthy campaign with much of its driving force. Later, as we all know, Sy would go on to become one of America's most respected and honored investigative reporters, but now, age thirty, he had put aside his own ambitions for this seemingly chimerical crusade against the war; would, despite continual frustrations from a barely cooperative candidate, often work through the night typing press releases and drafting statements that he knew might never see print.

"First tell me," I asked Sy, "what reporters are covering us."

"None," he replied.

"None," I repeated. "Not a single one?"

"Not here; there were a few down in Manchester.'"

Subduing my astonishment — a presidential campaign without a press corps! — I reflected for a moment before responding: "We've got to make some news. If we make news then the reporters will come. Fulbright is having hearings." (The Senate Foreign Relations Committee was conducting an inquiry into the Gulf of Tonkin incident.) "McCarthy is on that committee, isn't he?"

"Yes," Sy answered.

"Then let's draft a couple of statements on the Gulf of Tonkin. We can show them to McCarthy in the morning and if he approves we'll put them out. That'll make news, and bring the reporters."

"Sounds like a good idea," Sy replied.

"Good. Get a secretary and a typewriter and we'll get started."

"We don't have a secretary."

"Just a typewriter then."

"We don't have a typewriter."

Already beyond surprise, I motioned to Sy: "Come over here," walked to my car and opened the trunk, where, shivering in the northern wind, we both stared down at my small Smith-Corona portable. I turned toward Hersh. "You, me, and this typewriter, Sy; together we're going to overthrow the president of the United States."

It was bravado, a leap of arrogance intended more as a morale builder than as prophecy. But it all came true, except it was not just me and Sy, but McCarthy and the thousands of young volunteers who had already begun to infiltrate past the somnolent sentinels of traditional politics.

Finishing the statements at about 3 A.M., and after a few hours sleep, we took our drafts to the breakfasting senator, who gave his approval and promised to use them in his scheduled luncheon address to the Berlin Chamber of Commerce.

Returning to the motel, I told Sy, "You're the press secretary. Call every network and major newspaper and ask them why they're not here to cover McCarthy's statements on the Gulf of Tonkin. Don't tell them nobody else is up here either, just imply they're the only ones missing the boat."

Sy picked up the phone, dialed the Washington bureau of the *New York Times*, and asked for the "city desk."

"Hang up," I interrupted. Sy looked at me in surprise. "Just hang up," I repeated. Putting the phone down, Sy looked to me for an explanation. "Now, call them again," I instructed, "and this time ask for James Reston" (then the bureau chief). "Your employer is running for president of the United States. You have the right to speak to Reston directly, and he's more likely to pay attention than some reporter who happens to pick up the telephone. Hell, this is the highest office in the country, and you don't ask for the city desk. Pick the top guy and ask for him."

It was, of course, too late for reporters to come to Berlin, but several asked that McCarthy's statement be read over the phone. The next day the *Boston Globe* reported that "Senator Eugene McCarthy . . . charged in Berlin that the Administration had 'deceived' Congress and the American public about the Gulf of Tonkin incident, which triggered the first U.S. bombing raids against North Vietnam." Most major news outlets ignored the statement, but it was a beginning, the first slim stream of a swelling flood of coverage that would transform the campaign into what it deserved to be — what it was — a major political story, finally the most important political event in America.

During the entire weekend of campaigning in Berlin, McCarthy saw little more than a hundred people. Returning to Manchester, McCarthy and I entered the dining room at the Sheraton–Wayfarer Inn — then the largest restaurant in the state. The room was crowded with skiers returning from the weekend, local residents, tourists. Yet not a single head turned as we walked toward our table. With the primary only a few weeks away, no one appeared to recognize McCarthy. Not a single person came over to our table as we ate. As we left the dining room, McCarthy put his arm across my shoulder — "Dick, as St. Augustine said, 'When one person goes across the fence to steal a pear, he is filled with weakness and fear. But when two people go across the fence to steal a pear, they feel assured of success!' "

It was the only time I ever heard an expression of gratitude from McCarthy. It was more than enough. He and I were in New Hampshire for the same reason — at least the principal motive was the same: to arrest, if we could, the monstrous folly of Vietnam. I had as much, more, reason to be grateful to him than he to me. He, not I, had made it possible to submit Johnson's record, his conduct of office, to the judgment of voters, a goal I had struggled futilely to attain for over a year.

Acres of print have been expended describing the McCarthy campaign and the man who led this extraordinary movement of the young and inexperienced to momentous victory. Once, sitting next to his then wife at dinner, I remarked that "I have worked with Irish Catholic politicians all my life, and Gene is totally different from all of them."

"You don't understand," she replied, "he's not Irish, but German." By birth he was both, but had grown up in the German Catholic provinces of Minnesota; combined the natural gifts of the Irish bard — poetic, acutely intuitive — with the fierce, withdrawn melancholy of the forested German soul. He was a reverential Catholic, but not in the way most Irish are Catholic. He responded to priestly authority not in dread of eternal damnation, but in the more intellectual, ideological — not less fierce in belief — manner of the educated European. Having abandoned early thoughts of the priesthood for a twenty-three-year career of public service, McCarthy frequently revisited the Benedictine monastery from which he drew lifelong solace and renewal. Committed to the moral ambiguities of politics, something in him longed for the purifying possibilities of religious life, which, later, he would seek in its only secular counterpart — the austere discipline of poetry.

As a candidate he was often eccentric, his behavior frustrating to his most loyal adherents. More than once, sitting late at night with groups of his young volunteers, I would listen to their complaints — how he had been late to appearances, refused to make statements that politics required and expected. ("I didn't say I want to be president," he told an interviewer on national television, "I'm willing to be president.") After patiently hearing out their lamentations, I would say: "Your problem is that you've never been in a political campaign before. All candidates are difficult, all good candidates. They've got opinions and personal inclinations of their own. The trick is not to try to change the man, but to work with him on his own terms. You've got to accept that. And I don't want any more of this talk about McCarthy. It's bad for morale. He's our candidate, and if you keep on with this gossip we'll end up with stories about discontent in the McCarthy camp. That's not going to be helpful to him or you, not if you want to beat Johnson. Remember you're here because of him, not the other way around."

I did not say what I was coming to realize, that McCarthy was compelled to battle with an inward self-hatred that would, much later, lead him to destroy the immense future possibilities that remained to him after the 1968 campaign was over. Had he simply stayed in the Senate, spoken out on the issues, made some effort to cultivate the political establishment, then he and not McGovern would have been the party's nominee in 1972. But maybe that's not what he wanted.

In the years that followed, McCarthy has given some accounts of campaign incidents that tend to aggrandize the solitary heroism of his effort. But none of that really matters. It is even possible that he remembers things that way. For when all the debris of discussion and dispute is cleared away, one solitary, overwhelming reality remains: He ran. When no other politician would take on the president, offer the voters an alternative to the policies that were unraveling the hopes of a nation, Eugene McCarthy came to New Hampshire. The man was a hero, and achieved heroic results. After his campaign was over, it was no longer possible to escalate the war, which meant, inevitably, eventually, that it must come to an end. And the power of political bosses over the presidential nomination had been irrevocably shattered.

But the doubts, recriminations, amateur psychoanalysis all came later, after the buoyant hopes of New Hampshire began to crumble. In quoting St. Augustine, McCarthy was saying that he was glad I had come; that a fellow professional had joined him. For among the thousands who rallied to his cause, McCarthy and I were the only two people who had been in politics more than six weeks (a vivid proof of how much political experience is overvalued). In the following weeks I found him not only personally amiable, often hilariously witty, but easy to work with, amenable to suggestions, receptive to advice, willing to delegate authority. He was not only an ideal candidate, but the most original mind I had ever known in politics. He understood the issues, and the politics that could transform popular discontent into votes. Later, although his political insight was acute, he was not able to act — perhaps did not want to act — in conformity with what he knew. (He told me, for example, that the Indiana primary between him and Robert Kennedy was the crucial test of his presidential hopes — which it was — and then virtually abandoned the field to Kennedy on the pretext that he preferred to wait for the contests in the West — Oregon and California.) But in New Hampshire, insight and action were blended into a powerful appeal. He did then what he later failed to do. He matched his personal conduct to the necessities of politics; perhaps because, in New Hampshire, his cause was pure, the issues cleanly drawn and unstained by personal ambition. It was easier to justify the raucous brawlings of politics for a cause than for himself.

As we made that first ride from Berlin to Manchester, our desultory conversation — of politics, Johnson, and poetry — concealed a certain dejection on my part, and probably on his. The gatherings had been small, courteous but not enthusiastic; there were few signs of an effective campaign organization; the candidate himself — although forthright, occasionally eloquent in his presentations — did not radiate confidence. How could he? There was little reason for confidence. Admittedly, I had not expected much more, had come to New Hampshire on impulse born of anger and frustration. Yet once there my natural competitive instincts took command. The purpose of a campaign was not to make debating points, but to win; not to discuss events, but to change them. McCarthy, too, although he did not expect to win, was apprehensive of a defeat so humiliating that it would make his courageous action appear a fool's errand. As we sat in the rear seat, passing through the serene winter countryside, I had a swift, subliminal vision of Don Quixote and Sancho Panza moving across the plains of Madrid, with the terrifying distinction that we were both perfectly sane and aware of the roles we were playing.

"I think I first decided to run," McCarthy told me, "when [Attorney General] Katzenbach testified that the president didn't need congressional approval to make war, that the congressional power to declare war had been made obsolete, and therefore irrelevant, by the changes in technology and the new postwar responsibilities of the commander-in-chief. The war itself was bad enough, but these fellows were threatening to undermine our whole system of government. I walked out of the hearing room determined to do something about it." In other words, the prescribed order of things, the process of democracy itself, was threatened.

A week or two later, as the McCarthy movement was gaining visible, unanticipated momentum, he told me, "You know the first time I thought Johnson might be beaten was when I realized that you could walk into any bar in America and insult Lyndon Johnson, and no one would punch you in the nose." Similarly, in an article written a year before, I had said that "people don't like Lyndon Johnson and they don't trust him. And anyone whom people don't like or trust can always be beaten."

The first hint that my despondency might be unjustified, the first slim gleam of possibility, came the evening of our arrival in Manchester's Sheraton–Wayfarer Inn, after I left the restaurant and walked toward my room in a corridor of the hotel crowded with young volunteers, laboring at tables and typewriters, looking up to greet me enthusiastically, their manner a contagious ebullience; the fiery innocence of that first wave in the McCarthy army that would conquer New Hampshire and topple the imperial president from his seat.

The first to greet me, her raucous voice silencing the corridor, was Mary Lou Oates (now a columnist for the *Los Angeles Times*). "You're Dick Goodwin," she shouted. (I was soon to learn that Mary Lou spoke softly only when conditions demanded, in the middle, for example, of a funeral mass.) "Come on in and meet the teeny-boppers." Ushering me into a large room from which all the standard hotel furniture had been removed and replaced by tables and chairs, she proudly displayed her gaggle of young men and women who made up the press operation of the McCarthy campaign. Mary Lou was Sy Hersh's assistant, and not just his assistant — she was his confidante, therapist, and guru. She and her crew kept up the continual flow of statements, press releases, and position papers to the continually swelling press corps that gathered around the New Hampshire primary, nearly all of whom stayed at the same hotel.

Transcending the normal duties of an assistant press secretary, Mary Lou made sure she knew every reporter personally, talked with them in the hotel bar, scooped them up to join her at irregular meals as they aimlessly wandered the lobbies. Her candor and bluntness made her credible, while her passionate, nearly coarse, humor-tinged enthusiasm endeared her — and the campaign she represented — to reporters who realized that they were dealing with a rare blend of idealism and toughness.

It was Mary Lou who gave me the title, adopted by many of the volunteers, and which I bore with proud pleasure — "Che Guevara of the teeny-boppers."

There were others I met on that first day who were to accompany me through the campaign. The redoubtable Steve Cohen, a college student who had been among the charter members of the "Dump Johnson" movement, and who concealed behind a mild innocence of manner and mien an ability to penetrate barriers of security and opposition vigilance that Willy Sutton might have envied. He was a constant visitor to the Johnson headquarters, his reports over the coming weeks confirming our own sense that fear was infecting the establishment ranks. Once, in Milwaukee, Steve, at my request, assembled a crew which, on a moonless night, scaled the Republican billboard whose slogan, "Nixon's The One," dominated the main thoroughfare, and meticulously painted over the word "The," so morning communters were startled to see the message "Nixon's One" as they drove to work. But Steve was much more than a prankster. Like all the young people at the heart of the McCarthy "organization" he was a true believer, not only in the terrible wrong of Vietnam, but in the possibility that he — joined by thousands of others, led by McCarthy — could use the political system to alter the course of American history.

And even that first day in the Manchester headquarters, as I listened to Steve and Mary Lou and others, as we talked far into the night, I began to feel ashamed of the large doubts that had infiltrated my mind on the long drive from Berlin. With people like this, why couldn't it be done? For over a year I had said and written that Johnson could be beaten; but that he couldn't be beaten with nobody. Well, this wasn't nobody. This was an army, not a Kennedyesque "band of brothers" but a congregation of brothers and sisters willing to work any hours, undertake any task, give any effort to win an election that might end the war. And this army had a leader, a candidate fully capable of representing their cause, of providing a choice — not among competing views, but in the more decisive forum of the ballot box. Unlike every other campaign, the workers were not in the field because of the candidate. He was there because of them. It was a unique departure from political orthodoxy, and it was to prove uniquely powerful.

That first night in Manchester and over the next few days as I inspected the volunteer field operations, I began to change, not my mind so much as my heart. Maybe I was wrong. Maybe we could win. One thing was sure. We were going to run — I was going to run — as if victory was within our grasp. There is no other way to do it. So I put aside the secret enemies of hope — rational calculation, experienced judgment — said farewell to the ordered bodily regime of adequate sleep and regular meals. I'd give it the best shot I had. And I did so knowing I would have plenty of company among comrades I had just met, would soon leave, but with whom I felt more closely bonded in friendship and in love than I ever had or ever would again.

A few days later I visited the headquarters of the McCarthy volunteer organization. What was intended as a tour of inspection became a voyage of amazed admiration. I had never seen anything like it in politics. It was the biggest and best field organization ever assembled for any political campaign, before or since. Captained by men such as Sam Brown and Curt Gans who had come out of nowhere to assume responsibilities that, in conventional campaigns, would be delegated only to skilled and experienced politicians, the volunteers were impressed into a disciplined, systematic effort to bring McCarthy and his message to every Democratic household in the state. They were coming now by the thousands, from all parts of the country; on weekends, when classes were not in session, their numbers rose to four or five thousand. Every week, every day of every week, they came — from as far away as Michigan to the west and Virginia to the south; in buses and cars, by prearranged transportation, or by hitchhiking. Some stayed a few days at a time, others had dropped out of school for full-time service. The volunteer leaders had established a system that told them each time a substantial group had left for New Hampshire and the approximate time of arrival. They arranged accommodation — in friendly homes, the basement shelters of churches and convents, empty schoolrooms and gymnasiums; wherever a sleeping bag could be spread or an empty bed was found. Our wing of the Sheraton–Wayfarer was continually crowded with young, unfamiliar faces looking for a place to rest, sleeping four and five to a room. I would often return to my own room in the early-morning hours to find young strangers sprawled out on the floor, slumped in the chairs, occasionally occupying my bed, from which I — using the prerogative of age — promptly evicted them, occasionally with profound regret as I awoke some uncommonly attractive young woman whose charms stirred fatigue-smothered desires. (Or perhaps I didn't always evict them. I can't remember.)

The headquarters building itself had been divided into a series of briefing stations where arriving volunteers would be assigned specific targets, given street and precinct maps, along with bundles of pamphlets and broadsides that detailed McCarthy's background, the reasons for his candidacy, the sins and failures of the Johnson administration. They were told how to approach New Hampshire voters — politely, deferentially, in a low key — instructed to present their case, not to argue, and never to lose their temper. "Just knock on the door and say you'd like to talk to them about Gene McCarthy. If they say they're not interested, ask if they would like to have some of the literature and, if so, give it to them and leave. Never try a hard sell. Never try to push your ideas on unwilling listeners. But if they do invite you in for a talk, remember it's their home and you just sit and discuss the campaign as long as they are willing to listen. A minute or an hour, it's up to them, and you must not make them feel you're anxious to move on, even if you're way behind schedule."

Volunteers with long hair or beards were asked to cut their hair or shave, or both (a barber was usually available) and, if they refused, were assigned to basement rooms where literature was being folded, envelopes stamped and addressed. This was no alien hippie invasion, but the boy or girl next door come to call. Their slogan was "Neat and Clean for Gene" (later abbreviated to "Clean

for Gene") and many who had not seen the inside of a barber-
shop, or even a razor, for many months compliantly consented to
be shorn for the "movement"; while young women searched their
duffel bags or neighboring stores for long skirts to replace the un-
acceptably provocative miniskirts in which they had arrived. (And
which, in New Hampshire, constituted not only a cultural affront
but a danger of frostbite.)

"Who the hell is organizing all this?" I asked Sam Brown, realizing that systematically tracking the arrival and assigned destination of such unpredictable numbers was, in those precomputer
days, a formidable task well beyond my own powers. Sam pointed
toward two young men sitting on a corridor floor, insulated from
the bustle by their own intense concentration on the slide rules
they were manipulating with obvious dexterity. "They're graduate students in physics from Cornell," I was told. I walked over
to introduce myself. "It's great to meet you, Mr. Goodwin"; welcoming hands outstretched from their positions on the littered floor.
"You're doing a fantastic job," I responded. "It's not as hard as
it looks," said one of the young men, "our system is to —" "Don't
explain," I interrupted. "Just tell me one thing. Do you know
what you're doing?" "Of course we do," he answered. "That's
wonderful, just keep doing it." And, giving a V-for-victory sign, I
proceeded with my tour.

I left the building aware that this component of the campaign
had no need of my "professional expertise." They did know what
they were doing and they were doing it well. If their organization
was like nothing I had ever seen in politics, I knew, instinctively,
that it was sure to be effective; that any imposition of more traditional order and hierarchy would only disrupt or retard the enthusiastic labors that were at the heart of the McCarthy campaign.

By election day the volunteers had managed to canvass almost
all the homes of registered Democrats in the state of New Hampshire. Their reports, tally sheets of sympathizers and opponents,
were given to a team of volunteer statisticians for an analysis that
would pinpoint areas of strength and weakness, keep track of shifts
in the mood of voters. Our poll was not derived from a "scientific
sample," but from the entire electorate; with the result that our
own predictions were to prove more accurate than those of the
professional pollsters who flocked to New Hampshire as the primary neared. "You'll be lucky to get a quarter of the vote," Richard Scammon, then polling for one of the networks, told me in a

hostile tone the night before the election. "Shit, Dick," I replied, "you don't know what you're talking about. We're going to get forty percent, and maybe more." He turned away angrily, almost with contempt. (He was not only a Johnson supporter, but regarded me as an opportunistic renegade.) "Just remember, Scammon," I called after him, "your polls are just wishful thinking. You're telling your bosses what they want to hear. I know what's going to happen. The kids told me."

Returning to the hotel after my tour, I had been impressed, even elated at the blend of enthusiasm, commitment, and tough-minded organization I had seen. Professional politicians and renowned commentators had predicted that New Hampshire residents would be repelled by the invasion of young men and women from other states. They were wrong. This was not the Woodstock Nation, carriers of the drug-infested "counterculture," but clean-cut young men and women, polite, well spoken, much like the children of New Hampshire. The New Hampshire winter nights were long; conversation with such bright, eager young people a welcome break in the enforced indoor routine.

But I knew that an army of spirited volunteers would not be decisive. The young people weren't running for president. Gene McCarthy was. And on election day voters would cast their ballots not for that pleasant young man who stopped by the other night — but for the senator from Minnesota; a person they hardly knew. Their decision, the outcome of the primary, would depend on what they thought of him as a man and potential leader. There I could be of help.

"I saw him as a candidate," wrote Al Lowenstein, an early leader of the "Dump Johnson" movement. "He saw himself as a moral protester for a cause. That was where the early trouble lay." True, but only partly true. Morally offended, not only by the war, but by the undermining of democratic institutions that accompanied it, McCarthy had come to New Hampshire in search of a platform to raise these exigent issues; knowing that the only way to accomplish his purpose was to enter the primary against Johnson. Yet that necessary act transformed the nature of the contest. No longer a debate, it was an election. No referendum statement would appear on the ballot, only the name "McCarthy" printed under the word "President." People don't vote for a symbol but for a man, not an issue but a candidate. Yet McCarthy — perhaps thinking that opposition to the war was stronger than support for him, perhaps fearing that a defeat on the issue would be more honorable than a personal humiliation — had been telling audiences that they were choosing not a president, but a policy. It was a potentially disastrous error. Americans — most Americans — are not attracted to philosophical or ideological debate, but to conflict: team against team, man against man, winner and loser. The most persuasive arguments of statisticians do not resolve the outcome of a World Series. It is inconceivable. The games have to be played.

After returning to the Sheraton–Wayfarer, I met with McCarthy to try to persuade him that he would achieve more as a traditional candidate — asking people to support him not because of his principles, not just because of his principles, but as the man best qualified to be president. "That's how I'm listed on the ballot," he replied; "when people get into the booth they'll know." "That's too late," I answered, "we want them to make that decision before they go to vote." McCarthy's resistance, whatever its motivation, was light, his acquiescence swift. He was, after all, an accomplished politician with a long history of successful elections, understood that not only was I right, but it was his only chance. Maybe he had just been waiting for a companion to help point the way to that particular pear. In all that followed — speeches, radio, television, and press interviews — we stressed not just the issues, but the man and his capacity to occupy the office.

One of the less thrilling joys of the McCarthy campaign, yet revelatory of its uniqueness, was that it was not enough to persuade the candidate of changes in strategy. You had to persuade everyone; at least explain it to everyone. It was a participatory election, with McCarthy on the ballot, but a thousand candidates. "It's my judgment," I told Sy while the others listened, "that people will only vote for a man they think is serious about being president. They don't have to think that he's going to win — that's what professional politicians worry about — but that he's a respectable candidate, and they don't have to feel foolish if they vote for him. That's one of the reasons George Wallace declined even among people who shared his views: They just couldn't see him in the White House. McCarthy is no Wallace — hell, he's a goddamn midwestern conservative. It's up to us to help let people know it."

There was scarcely any response, absolutely no disagreement. A tribute to my manifest wisdom, I thought, deference to my su-

perior knowledge — until I saw among my auditors an expression
not of awed respect, but slight bewilderment. What was this all
about? They had been running for president all along.

Later that day Sy and Mary Lou showed me some material for
newspaper, radio, and television ads, which had been prepared by
a New York advertising agency. I was appalled. There were pictures of freshly fried Vietnamese babies, advertising copy that assailed American "aggression," clips of bombs tumbling from the
swollen bellies of American planes into jungle hamlets, protesters
being dragged from the Pentagon steps. The campaign was designed to appeal to Manhattan's Upper East Side. It would be a
disaster in New Hampshire. "We can't use this stuff," I said. "In
fact, except for the candidate's own speeches, I think we should
forget about the war, drop it from our advertising and literature,
not completely, but just one issue among many," and was rewarded, for my comments, with my first look of surprise. I could
sense their thoughts: Drop the war? Why the hell does he think
we're here? Why is he here? Maybe he is some kind of Kennedy
spy.

I went on to explain, not just then, but several times over the
next few days, that "the people who are against the war are already for McCarthy. They know where he stands, and what brought
him here. You don't need to persuade them. And you know how
many that amounts to? Maybe twenty percent. Hell, you can get
twenty percent just by putting your name on the ballot." (The
number was not chosen at random. A recent "peace referendum"
in Concord, New Hampshire, a liberal, middle-class town, had
received 20 percent of the vote.) "People aren't against Johnson
just because of the war. They don't trust him; they don't trust the
government; and they don't like the way he's leading the country.
But, they're not going to respond to an attack on America. These
people are patriots. It's because they're patriots that they don't
like the direction of the country. Shit, we're the patriots, not Johnson; we want this country to be great again, and he's dragging it
down. That's what our campaign is about, and that's the message
we're going to deliver.

"And the toughest part of our job is that we've got to get
McCarthy's message to the whole state in less than a month. The
volunteers will help, if we can get them the right kind of literature.
But there's only one really effective way to do the job — television. We're going to need a lot of television. And that costs. Tell
me who's got the money; who's financing this campaign?"

I was directed toward the far end of the "McCarthy corridor" to Arnold Hiatt, president of the StrideRite Shoe Company, and the most generously gentle, self-effacing man I ever met in politics, or anywhere else for that matter. Temporarily abandoning his business, Arnold had come to New Hampshire impelled by deeply felt opposition to the war. Not only did he contribute from his own resources, but he was to prove an uncommonly skillful fund-raiser and, later, became the official treasurer of the campaign. In those freewheeling days before campaign "reforms," there was no limit to individual contributions. A handful of wealthy individuals could cover much of the cost. Since men of means are little inclined to throw their money away on a hopeless cause, we had to depend upon that scarcest of all breeds — the romantic rich. (Under present limitations — i.e., one thousand dollars per person — it would have been impossible to finance our New Hampshire insurgency.)

A day or two later, a volunteer leader informed me that a Mr. Howard Stein was calling from New York. "Who the hell is Howard Stein?" I asked. "He's a contributor," I was told. With my well-honed sense of political priorities, I abandoned my typewriter for the telephone. After long-distance introductions, Stein told me that the New York advertising agency, whose services he had enlisted, was upset at rumors that we did not intend to use their creative work, that we were revising a strategy carefully designed by men who were "advertising geniuses," that the war was the only issue that mattered. As I listened, my annoyance mounted to the edge of anger, until, finally, I interrupted: "Listen, Mr. Stein, you don't know what you're talking about. And you certainly don't know a damn thing about politics. There's no way you can direct a New Hampshire campaign from New York. The action is here, the voters are here, and the work is here. If you're serious about wanting to help, why don't you just get in your car and drive to Manchester where you can find out what's really going on." On that disagreeable note the conversation ended. Guess I blew that one, I thought as I hung up. But two days later Howard Stein, accompanied by his wife and a trunkload of New York delicacies to supplement the drab hotel menu, arrived in New Hampshire, took a room, and went to work. President of the multibillion-dollar Dreyfus Corporation, and one of McCarthy's largest contributors, Stein merged swiftly into the volunteers corps. He manifested no sense of injured dignity, no air of self-importance. Spending most of his time working with Arnold and others trying to raise money, he was also willing to undertake the most menial campaign tasks. Shortly after his arrival I looked across the corridor and saw Howard working his way through the tangled chaos of Sy Hersh's room, meticulously placing discarded underwear, shirts, and jackets into bureau drawers and closets. "Good work, Howard," I shouted through the open door, and felt an admiring warmth, which Stein's unostentatious and untiring labors through the following weeks were to confirm and fortify.

Asked to meet with Hiatt, Stein, and a few other "money people," I was informed that my plans for an intensive radio and television campaign would exceed their New Hampshire budget, leaving no funds for future primaries. "It doesn't matter," I said. "But we'll be broke," one replied. "No we won't," I rejoined. "If we get murdered in New Hampshire, we won't need money. There'll be no other primaries. And if we do well there'll be plenty of money. It'll pour in. This is an all-or-nothing shot for McCarthy, and so we better put everything we've got into the pot."

And so we did, spending about $150,000 — almost all our liquid assets — on the New Hampshire primary. And after it was over, and it was "on to Wisconsin," the money came in.

Although we had modestly adequate resources to buy air time and newspaper space, the medium was not the message. The message was the message. With only about three weeks remaining before the election, it was essential to modify and expand the theme of the McCarthy campaign. The virtual anonymity, which helped explain McCarthy's low, almost nonexistent standing in the polls, was also his most important asset. (In late February a volunteer, returning from canvassing, told me that two people had told him, "I liked his brother Joe [McCarthy] and I'm going to vote for him." What should he say? he asked me. "Tell them you appreciate their support and move on," I instructed.) The minority of voters who were paying attention to this seemingly meaningless contest knew that McCarthy opposed the war. Beyond that their impressions — if they had any — were vague, undefined. It was an enormous advantage. It is far more difficult to modify fixed impressions than to shape still-unformed opinion.

Large numbers — not only in New Hampshire, but everywhere — remembered that halcyon time, only a few years earlier, when we were riding an economic boom straight toward a Great Society. Suddenly that direction had begun to change: The economy was shaky, inflation rising, the protests of black Americans transformed into urban riots, young people turning toward drugs and embracing life-styles offensive to most Americans. Most important of all, people felt that things were getting out of their control; that their own poor power to influence change was being drained into the remote and increasingly hidden offices of executive government. They sensed that their own leaders were not to be trusted, were seemingly impervious to popular will, indifferent to opinion. This underlying discontent — undefined, inarticulate — was so powerful that many who would have been willing to "bomb 'em back to the stone age," if they thought it might end the war, would ultimately vote for McCarthy. It was the task of the campaign to tap this impotence-fueled discontent, to persuade voters that McCarthy was offering an alternative, that, win or lose, his candidacy gave them a chance to express their desire for a change, or for a return to a different America.

"Find me a picture of McCarthy and President Kennedy together," I instructed Mary Lou. It wasn't easy. The two men had not liked each other, were rarely, if ever, found publicly wrapped in warm embrace. But politics is a profession conducted in front of a camera and finally a picture was uncovered. Kennedy and McCarthy weren't hugging each other: they weren't even shaking hands, but walking side by side in some unknown setting outside the borders of the photograph. And, miraculously, they were both smiling. It was enough. Beneath the martyred hero and our candidate for heroism, we constructed a newspaper ad — one of many — that proclaimed the theme of our campaign:

> In 1960 we started to get America moving again. Today, eight years later, the fabric of that great achievement is unraveling.
>
> In 1963 the economy was booming, taxes were being lowered, prices were stable. Today our prosperity is slowing down, prices are going up, and we are being asked to pay higher taxes.
>
> In 1963 our greatest cities were relatively tranquil. Today we look upon a period of virtual civil war.
>
> In 1963 our children in colleges and universities were concerned with the Peace Corps and Civil Rights. Today it is marijuana and draft protests.
>
> In 1963 we were at peace. Today we are at war.

We bought a full-page for the ad in local newspapers, and, proud of my clichéd effort, I sent a copy to Bobby Kennedy. When he received it, according to Bill vanden Heuvel, his only comment was "Gene must have a lot of money, he's only using one side of the paper." (I had neglected to inform him it was not a pamphlet but advertising copy.)

McCarthy knew, better than I, that discontent with Johnson and the state of the country was his greatest asset. Yet newspaper ads, pamphlets, literature, even speeches reach only a tiny fraction of the electorate. In America few people read anything serious, even fewer anything political, and almost no one who is not already convinced is transformed by the written word. But everyone watches television, or listens to the radio as they drive to work. Almost all our money (in fact, as our creditors would later discover, more than our money) was used to buy television and radio spots. We spent far more on New Hampshire media than did the overconfident Johnson campaign. And McCarthy was masterful.

We used no elaborate production techniques. McCarthy would simply go to a studio, sit behind a desk facing the camera, and talk. And he did it without a script; the first and last candidate I had ever worked with who could speak coherently, even eloquently, for thirty or sixty seconds and, with the help of cue cards, end his presentation on a perfectly rounded paragraph. But he had that rare command of language — a poet's gift — which allowed him to amend his sentences even as he spoke, compressing ideas into the the strict, inflexible parameters of the television commercial.

Although his presentations were extemporaneous, they were not impromptu. Before each taping session we would go over a prepared list of topics. We would discuss each of them in some detail — the points to be covered, suggested language, and so forth. And if one of the spots didn't turn out well, we would do it again. But whatever the specific topic, they were all related to the emerging theme of the campaign. "The issue in this campaign," McCarthy would say, "is not Vietnam or the economy. The issue is leadership. It is the direction of the country — where we are going and where we want to go. It is whether you will be satisfied with four more years of national decline and increasing division, or whether we will return to the forward progress which seemed to be our direction only a few short years ago. I am running for president to give you that choice." In other words, McCarthy was running for president because the country was going to hell; and he opposed Johnson because it was Lyndon who was leading us into the flames.

Although McCarthy was effective — increasingly so as we

reached larger and larger audiences — our effort was given an enormous boost by the amateurish, misguided, totally incompetent Johnson campaign. Although every major — and most minor — politicians in New Hampshire endorsed Johnson, the direction of their campaign came from Washington, where Marvin Watson, his desk guarding the gateway to the Oval Office, sat in the glory of his unrelieved ignorance. Knowing nothing about politics when he came to Washington, Marvin had miraculously succeeded in reducing his political skills to below zero.

Thank God for Marvin, and for the New Hampshire politicians, many of whom knew better but felt they had no choice but to follow their candidate's direction. "A vote for McCarthy is a vote for Hanoi," proclaimed the Johnson ads. "Ho Chi Minh is watching New Hampshire" (unlikely). The administration message was lucidly simplistic, unperceptive. To support McCarthy was to encourage communist aggression and to betray our boys in Vietnam. By implication, McCarthy himself was perhaps the unwitting dupe of subversive elements. We did not answer these slanders. McCarthy himself was the answer.

Day after day, in personal appearances and on television, voters could see this calm, unthreatening midwesterner, quietly rational in his presentation. Clearly the man was no radical. His entire manner revealed him to be a moderate, even a conservative, especially on economic issues. The administration had made the classic mistake of politicians — underestimating the perception and intelligence of the voter. Its shrill assaults had little impact. The failure to address any issue but the war, the absence of any response to the multibranched theme of McCarthy's campaign, discouraged, even repelled many who were inclined to support the president. Several important New Hampshire political leaders called the White House to advise a change in strategy. But to no avail. The beleaguered, incestuous band of Johnsonian insiders had reinforced the walls of the fortress, raised an impenetrable barrier to criticism from friends as well as adversaries. The belief in one's sole possession of the truth, a unique comprehension of both reality and virtue, was like a cancer that had spread from alien Asian soil to the towns and countryside of New Hampshire.

Two weeks before the vote, *Time* magazine published a poll that showed McCarthy with only 11 percent of the vote. The poll was wrong. And I knew it. Just as in the last days of the 1960 campaign we could feel John Kennedy's victory slipping away, as

February yielded to March of 1968 I could sense a gradually mounting transformation: Voters beginning to realize that support for an incumbent president was not mandatory, that McCarthy offered them an opportunity to express their discontent. There were a hundred scattered signals — growing crowds, the warmth of people greeting the candidate on streets he had once walked almost unnoticed, the arrival of reporters who, still skeptical, had come out of a sense that something newsworthy might be happening in New Hampshire, the excitement of volunteers who returned to headquarters late at night with stories of friendly conversations and promises of support.

"I have seen the winter go all down hill / In waters of a slender April rill," wrote Robert Frost. The New Hampshire winter was not yet over. It was only March. But as if swept by some premature spring, the hard-frozen power of the president had begun to thaw, the slim liberated streams converging toward a widening surge.

McCarthy felt it too, as did some of the more perceptive among the New Hampshire politicians. About ten days before the election, Bill Dunfey — New Hampshire's leading Democrat, who had run John Kennedy's primary campaign in 1960 — asked me to a private meeting in an empty suite of his Sheraton–Wayfarer Inn. A passionate opponent of the war, Dunfey was in no position to openly defy the leadership of the party he had helped create; yet he was sympathetic to McCarthy's cause (had hoped Bobby would run) and was helpful whenever honor permitted. Closing the door behind me, I listened as an outraged Dunfey told me of a White House plot to discredit the McCarthy volunteers by planting marijuana in some of the rooms (a plan that evaporated after I leaked my knowledge of the intended trap to members of the press). "You know something else?" Bill said. "I've been hearing a lot of people talk favorably about McCarthy. And almost no one likes Johnson. I think you people might do better than anyone expected. You might go as high as thirty percent."

"We're going to do a hell of a lot better than that," I replied, smiling, my confidence fortified by Dunfey's appraisal. "Now, wouldn't that be a shocker."

Although I had not talked with Robert Kennedy since arriving in New Hampshire, I was certain that Dunfey and his many other friends in that "Kennedy state" were keeping him fully informed. On Wednesday — six days before the election — Bobby called me. "I just wanted you to know," he began tentatively, cautiously probing for my reaction, "that I'm still considering getting into this thing, and I'd like McCarthy to know this now, so he doesn't think my decision has any relationship to whatever happens in New Hampshire."

Right, I thought, and maybe you can make him think that you stayed out as a special favor so he could have a place in the history books, or that the moon is made of Camembert. But I remained silent. I had heard only a desire, not a request.

"I asked Teddy to pass the message along to McCarthy," Bobby continued, "but he hasn't done it. Is there anyone he's close to who I could ask to do this for me?"

"He's not close to anyone," I replied.

"Then will you tell him?"

"I can't do that, Bobby. I can't act as your messenger. I'm working for McCarthy now. I'm committed to him and he trusts me; and not just him, but all the kids. They've got faith in me and I love them. I won't give anyone a reason to think I'm a kind of double agent. Some people have thought it all along, but it didn't bother me because they were wrong. I've worked my ass off for the guy, and I've got to keep the relationship pure."

Bobby did not reply. Swiftly, my own annoyance, almost anger, began to dissolve. The man was my friend, and he was in a difficult, perhaps painful position. He had cut the Gordian knot of his "dilemma" by deciding not to run, and now the severed ends were beginning to regenerate themselves, fusing into a tighter and more intricate tangle.

After a few moments, the telephone silently linking two men struggling to resolve very different puzzles, I said, "I'll tell you what I will do. I'll do what any other staff member would do. I'll say that you called and left a message for him, and tell him what the message is. I won't act as your agent, or confidant, but as his representative bringing important information."

"Suppose he asks you if you think I'm going to do it?"

"I'll tell him I don't know. Because I don't. Do you?"

Not answering, Bobby asked, "What if he asks your advice?"

"I'll tell him what I think is best for him. That's what I have to do, Bobby. You know that. Hell, you're the one who taught me about loyalty."

"Okay," Bobby replied after a thoughtful pause. "I guess that's good enough." Then, the transaction completed, he asked, "How do you think you're going to do?"

Relieved, the sense of excited anticipation returning, I answered: "We're going to get at least forty percent, and if we had ten extra days we'd be over fifty."

"How would I have done?"

"You would have won sixty–forty."

The call was over. Bobby, who had phoned from his New York apartment, turned to some friends, reported our conversation, and mused, "He's right. I would have won it."

As I sat on the bed, staring at the phone, I reflected on Bobby's call and the wisdom of my response. Were my distinctions too subtle? Would I be misunderstood? Should I say anything at all? Then Sy Hersh burst into the room, holding the draft of a statement that, he told me, had to be released in a few hours. The call from Bobby instantly obliterated from thought, I turned my full concentration to the pages Sy handed me, made some slight revisions, smoothed out the prose, added a phrase or two, and, most important, tested each sentence for the possible slip-up, the incautious misstatement that could undo not only a single speech, but an entire campaign. (Remember the Cuban "freedom fighters"?) It was only after two more days of frantic labor, interrupted reluctantly for occasional hours of compulsory sleep, that I finally walked over to McCarthy's suite to deliver Bobby's message. McCarthy was alone, his room an oasis of relative tranquillity in the maelstrom that had once been a carefully ordered hotel.

"We're doing well, Senator," I said as I entered.

"It's looking better," McCarthy replied.

"I just wanted you to know that Bobby Kennedy called me," I began, and then repeated the substance of the phone call as McCarthy listened in unrevealing silence. Manifesting neither surprise nor indignation, he waited until I had finished, then: "Why don't you tell him that I only want one term anyway. Let him support me now, and after that he can have it."

The comment may sound strange, even grotesque — two renegades on the farthest fringes of empire already dividing the throne. We both knew that the path was difficult, perhaps impassible, the odds too long for any reasonable gambler. But despite our inner knowledge, the prospect of victory was the only allowable assumption of conversation. It is the natural condition of an occupation in which talk of defeat is likely to prove self-fulfilling. And anyway, we both believed in miracles, my faith of more secular origin than his.

"You don't mean that, Senator," I replied to his suggestion, "and even if you think you believe it now, once you're in there you won't want to get out after four years. There'll still be too much you want to do."

"I do mean it," McCarthy interrupted, "I'm quite serious. I've given it a lot of thought, and it has nothing to do with Kennedy. The presidency should be a one-term office. Then the power would be in the institution. It wouldn't be so dependent on the person."

He really does mean it, I thought. And, in truth, it was a concept wholly consistent with McCarthy's belief in process and institutional relations as the essence of democracy; a healthy fear of entrusting men — any man — with untrammeled power. But did that mean he would be the first president since George Washington to forgo reelection in obedience to an abstraction of ideal government? We'll never know.

Then, in a rare moment of disclosure, a brief glimpse beneath the shielded reticence of this uncommonly complex man, McCarthy remarked: "You know why I don't get along with the Kennedys? They never appreciated me." Only this. And the curtain closed. But it was enough to reveal the resented years of rejection and indifference while the Kennedys dominated the stage of national life. And it was true. They hadn't appreciated or understood the remarkable qualities of a person whose subtle understanding of public issues was more acute, more spacious than that of almost any man of his time. But the failure of appreciation was also McCarthy's fault, as, with a few illuminating exceptions — e.g., his eloquent speech nominating Adlai Stevenson at the 1960 convention — he preferred virtually silent withdrawal to the empty boredom of his secure Senate seat over active participation in the momentous public conflicts of the sixties. Until, that is, he went to New Hampshire.

"I'll tell him what you said," I replied, and left the room to call Bobby, whose only response to my report was a groan of disbelief. I did not try to convince him of McCarthy's sincerity. The two men inhabited irreconcilably different worlds of action and belief.

That same evening, the Saturday before election, I was summoned to an urgent meeting with the members of McCarthy's finance committee. "I have bad news, Dick," Arnold Hiatt told me. "The radio stations are going to cancel all our spots. They want cash payment in advance and we've run out of money." "Do you mean," I replied, in feigned indignation, "that you called me away from some really important work just to talk about money? How much do they want?"

"Twenty thousand dollars," Arnie replied.

"Fine," I said, withdrew my checkbook from an inside jacket pocket, and began to write, looking up to ask: "Who do I make it payable to, the campaign or the advertising agency?" Arnold gently reached out and took the pen from my fingers. "Don't worry about it, Dick. We'll take care of it."

"Good," I replied, "then I can get back to work," returned the checkbook to my pocket, and left abruptly to conceal my relief, lest they suspect — and I think Arnold did suspect — that I had only six hundred dollars in the bank. Within a few hours I was told that the money had been "found," and the radio campaign would go ahead. (I have little doubt that the campaign funds had run out, and that Arnold paid for the radio spots with his own money.)

With less than seventy-two hours to go, the shift toward McCarthy tangibly accelerating, I withdrew all our radio spots that addressed a multiplicity of issues — domestic priorities, civil rights, leadership, the environment, the war — and replaced them all with a single spot, which was to be played repeatedly on every major radio station in the state for the final two days. "Think how you will feel if you wake up Wednesday morning to find that Eugene McCarthy has won the New Hampshire primary and New Hampshire has once again changed the course of American politics."

Shortly after midnight on Monday, the citizens of Waterville Valley assembled for the honor of being the first community in New Hampshire to vote. All thirteen registered Democratic voters were there. McCarthy's name was checked off on eight ballots while Kennedy and Johnson each received two or three write-in votes. The *Boston Globe*, which was widely distributed in southern New Hampshire, rushed into print with a special late-night edition whose front page carried the banner headline "McCarthy Takes Early Lead," over a story that did not mention that the only returns were from Waterville Valley until the careful reader had reached the continued text on an inside page. The papers were already at the factory gates and newsstands when workers left for home the next afternoon. Better one friendly headline writer, I exulted, than a thousand editorial writers, and directed a sym-

bolic gesture of gratitude toward Boston-bound Tom Winship, the
fiercely antiwar editor of the *Globe*, who had supported Mc-
Carthy's campaign where it counted — in the headlines.

Election Tuesday: The bitter winter dark had not yet begun its
sullen withdrawal before encroaching dawn when they began to
come: the sleepless old/young women halting at polling places on
their way from labors at all-night diners, heavy-jacketed workers
carrying lunch pails. From Keene and Nashua, Concord and
Manchester, distant Berlin and academic Hanover, as the russet-
hued steeples and chimneys were whitened by the mounting sun,
the first reports began to arrive. The voting was heavy, a welcome
signal that indifference had yielded to interest, apathy to engagement. As I looked through the lobbies of the Sheraton–Wayfarer,
wandered the corridors, I recalled that first visit only a few weeks
before when McCarthy and I had dined unnoticed amid a crowd
of skiers, and local families on their weekly break from the routine
of an evening at home. Now the hotel was crowded with men and
women gathered to observe, report, perhaps celebrate the warrior
from Minnesota. Television networks had commandeered the hotel meeting rooms; one could hardly traverse a corridor without
stumbling over a thick coaxial cable, the umbilical that linked the
candidate and his tiny headquarters on the outskirts of a New
Hampshire town to the country and to the world. Newspaper reporters crowded the corridors, interviewing staff members and
volunteers, gathering material for a story which had not yet unfolded. And in every vacant space, sitting against the walls, standing in crowded rooms, were the young volunteers — McCarthy's
legions — having made their way along snow-flanked roads from
every part of the state to share in the moment.

I felt both excited and emptied of excitement. There was nothing more to do. Nothing that could be done. I wandered restlessly,
talking to friends, thanking strangers, giving nonsensical interviews in response to nonsensical questions. Waiting. Just waiting.
It was a little over three years since the first American bombs had
exploded in the villages of North Vietnam. It was more than two
years since the movement toward a Great Society had come to a
halt and begun to crumble. In that time, America's course had
been debated interminably, fiercely, on the Senate floor, from the
White House, among the diverse participants in Washington power.
There had been protests and counterprotests. Journalists, editors,

television commentators had pronounced on the wisdom of the war, described the growing divisions of American society, authoritatively assessed the public mood, somberly transmitted the false certainties of statistics that pretended to measure public feeling. And now it was all irrelevant. No exercise of the president's awesome power, no act of Congress, no authority of analysts and experts could prevail over the thousands of people who were streaming toward the polling places to shape the final, unappealable judgment of democracy. What a great country, I thought, when on a March Tuesday, the fate of the leader of the free world was in the hands of denim-clad workers, high-booted farmers, housewives stopping on their way to the supermarket. "The tumult and the shouting" had died, the captains and the kings not departed, but their authority suspended, vulnerable.

Toward the end of the afternoon, our excitement mounted as early returns showed that anticipated Johnson strongholds in Nashua and Keene and Dover were crumbling; that the McCarthy vote was exceeding our own expectations in places, like Portsmouth, where we had expected to do well. Before the evening ended, as returns became final, McCarthy had received 42 percent of the vote, Johnson 48 percent. (Later, after the McCarthy write-ins on Republican ballots were counted, he would come within 230 votes of defeating the president.) Twenty of the twenty-four elected delegates to the national convention were McCarthy men. We had not won the election. Not technically. We had achieved a far more significant victory — unmasked the subterranean discontent with the president and his policies, revealed how intense and widespread was the desire for change, transformed a Minnesota senator into a national political leader, a hero. I was now certain that whatever McCarthy's personal destiny, Lyndon Johnson would not be the next president of the United States.

At midnight, McCarthy strode into the main hotel ballroom where a dozen television cameras were stationed to record and report his statement to the jubilant mob of young volunteers who packed the room, overflowed into the corridors. As I watched him mount the podium, move confidently toward the microphones, I could detect a physical change in the man. His cheeks, which that morning were pale with exhaustion, had drawn on some adrenaline-fed reservoir of vitality, filled with color. No longer the scholar-senator, he waved happily to the crowd, let the cheers and applause wash over him, exulting in the moment before beginning to speak. Always distinguished in appearance, tonight he was something more. The man was presidential.

"People have remarked," he told the crowd, "that this campaign has brought young people back into the system. But it's the other way around. The young people have brought the country back into the system."

With his extraordinary acuity, McCarthy had accurately discerned the meaning of the day. The ideals of the sixties, withering under assaults from a hundred hostile strongholds, had been resurrected. At least for the evening. America had changed many times in many ways since that day in 1956 when Rosa Parks had refused to go to the back of a Montgomery bus. For over half a decade, pride and aspiration had been in the air. Black was "beautiful"; Martin Luther King had a "dream"; John Kennedy sought a New Frontier; Lyndon Johnson, a "war to the death against poverty"; and Robert Kennedy wanted "to seek a Newer World." Then the world shifted, and change, once so welcome, had taken a darker direction. But now for a moment, it seemed as if McCarthy, his colleagues, and, especially, the young men and women — "Clean for Gene" — walking the streets, peaceful and persuasive, disarming the fear of those to whom youth had seemed an alien force, might herald a restoration, allow us to break clear of the deepening morass of national frustration.

We did not know, could not have suspected, that the sense of renewed hope, of enormous possibilities, would survive only three more months.

Long after the television cameras had been disassembled and stored, the ballroom lights darkened, the wonderful people of New Hampshire consuming the sustenance of slumber for the next day's work, bands of McCarthy workers mingled in the corridors and rooms — talking excitedly, telling war stories, laughing. No one wanted the night to end. We had stunned the country. We had stunned ourselves. The faithful had been justified, the doubtful cleansed. We stood on Nebo, astride the promised plains of Canaan. We were not to reach that sought-for land. But the tumult and tragedy of the months to come, the long descent of future years into mediocrity and self-absorption, could not take the exultant promise of that night from those of us who shared it, nor obliterate the hope that some day, somehow, it would come again.

Admittedly McCarthy had won only twenty delegates of the hundreds that would assemble for the Chicago convention; had come close, but had not won the popular vote. Yet the strength of his achievement — the little-known senator without a chance, so far behind, his presence barely visible, coming so swiftly, so great a distance — had shattered Johnson's most formidable protection: the myth of invincibility, the belief that an incumbent could not be denied. Voters had been dramatically reminded of their power to express protest, to make themselves heard. That accomplished, I was convinced that the floodgates would open; that New Hampshire would prove only a feeble augury of larger defeats to come. Johnson would almost certainly lose every primary in which his name was entered; his refusal to engage in other states interpreted as a fear of defeat. The next few months would be one long humiliation, rejection following rejection. And by the time the party assembled in Chicago, it would be clear that Johnson could not be reelected; that his nomination would mean a certain Republican victory. In 1968, the great majority of delegates were selected and controlled by governors, bosses, confederations of county leaders, and so forth. Those political leaders who wanted him — and there were many — would be compelled to deny him the nomination in response to the inevitable pressures from their own constituencies, and from candidates for office — governors, senators, congressmen — who would anticipate their own defeat in a Republican landslide. They might like Johnson, even agree with his policies, but they would not go down with the ship. "Women and children second" metaphorically expresses the first, overriding law of political behavior. The Democratic leaders in Illinois and Pennsylvania, Ohio and New Jersey would not throw their hard-won power on the sacrificial pyre.

And because Johnson would soon foresee the same course of events — his political judgment shocked back into lucidity by the early primaries and, most decisively, by an event I had not anticipated, the long-feared candidacy of Robert Kennedy — in about three weeks from that transforming New Hampshire day, Lyndon Johnson would no longer be a candidate for the office of president of the United States.

Twelve days before the New Hampshire primary, the Kerner Commission, established by the White House to investigate the causes of urban violence, concluded that America was in danger of becoming "two societies — one white and one black, separate but unequal." From the White House, where Lyndon Johnson had once, such a very short time before, asserted that "for one hundred years emancipation has been a proclamation, now it must be a fact and result," there was only a sullen silence, almost resentment, as if the commission's truth was a betrayal of presidential trust.

And on the Wednesday morning after the election, the same front pages that blazoned the stunning triumph of McCarthy also noted that Richard M. Nixon, back from the dead, had won an overwhelming victory in the Republican primary, and had followed his victory with the statement that "the American people do not want four more years of Lyndon Johnson in the White House." It didn't take a man of principle to discover the issue of the day. Political insight was enough. And Richard Nixon had plenty of that.

Thus, even as we prepared to continue our own battle for control of the Democratic party, the forces that would ultimately contend for the soul of the nation were beginning to reveal themselves, assemble, gather strength.

27 / The Last Crusade

With rue my heart is laden
    For golden friends I had,
For many a rose-lipt maiden
    Any many a lightfoot lad.

By brooks too broad for leaping
    The lightfoot boys are laid;
The rose-lipt girls are sleeping
    In fields where roses fade.

— A. E. Housman

On ELECTION EVE in New Hampshire, as I sat in the press room monitoring returns, a volunteer entered to inform me that I had a call from Robert Kennedy. "Tell him I'll call back," I responded, totally absorbed in the calculations that revealed the dimensions of McCarthy's achievement. Three hours later, close to midnight, I called Bobby and, before he could talk, launched into a jubilant monologue: We had done it. Johnson was on the ropes, this election might — would — change the direction of the country; it was more than we had hoped, et cetera. Bobby listened patiently for a few minutes, then asked: "Well, what do I do now?" I halted, poised silently between the elation of the evening and the implications of Bobby's question. It was not a surprise, not wholly. He had already told me and McCarthy that he might run. But on that night of a victory he had not shared, my emotions were not prepared for the tough-minded calculations of politics. I could not advise him to run against McCarthy, the man whom I had served with immense labor, and who had returned my efforts with his trust. Yet I could not refuse to answer, or lie. Bobby was my friend and, more than friend, the man I thought best qualified to the president. So cautiously, somewhat evasively, I replied: "I don't know what you should do. But there's only one sure thing, Bobby. You can't keep saying that you're neutral. You could only be neutral on the premise that McCarthy wasn't a serious candidate. Now he is. That leaves you two choices. Either you run or you support McCarthy."

"What would happen if I support McCarthy?" Bobby asked.

"He'll be president."

The conversation over, Bobby replaced the phone in his Virginia home, turned to a companion: "I think I blew it."

I returned to the celebrations, joined by my wife, who had driven up from Boston for the occasion. All thoughts of Bobby's call were swiftly dissolved in the loud ambience of exhilarated comradeship. The sun was beginning to rise as I finally went to bed, staring for a moment at the lightening snow, indulging the ironic thought that yesterday at this time I didn't know what was going to happen, and today, after twenty-four of the most eventful hours in my political life, I still didn't know what was going to happen.

Around midday, I was awakened by Blair Clark, McCarthy's national campaign manager, who burst into my room asking, "What are you going to do about Kennedy?" "Do?" I responded sleepily. "What are you talking about? What's he done?" His tone slightly suspicious, only half-believing my ignorance, Blair explained that Bobby, walking through the Washington airport on his way to the New York shuttle, had been spotted by reporters and asked his plans. "I'm reconsidering my decision," he had replied. It wasn't much. But it was enough. A public statement of "reconsideration" was almost an announcement.

"I don't know what he means," I said to Blair, concealing my inner realization that a Kennedy candidacy now seemed virtually inevitable. "It's just what he told McCarthy last week." (But not publicly.) "I know what he means," Blair answered. "What are you going to do?" "I'm going back to sleep," I replied, and did, until an hour or two later, I received a call asking me attend a Kennedy council in New York hurriedly convoked to discuss his possible candidacy. "I can't go to any such meeting," I replied. "I'm working for McCarthy." Then, thoroughly awakened, I left the comforting precincts of the Sheraton–Wayfarer and flew to Washington, where the McCarthy staff was preparing for the Wisconsin primary.

Later, I was told that when Kennedy arrived at Steve Smith's apartment that afternoon, Steve asked him, "Why are we having this meeting? You've already announced." "No, I haven't," Bobby said somewhat defensively. "I had to tell them something, and I couldn't say I wasn't going to do it."

The next day Kennedy called me at my room in the George- town Inn and asked me to his home for a drink. "It's not a meet- ing?" I asked. "No," he replied, "I just want to talk."

Driving through the familiar landscape of McLean, into the driveway toward the large house, walking past the huge recum- bent dog Brumus, I felt, for a moment, as if I was returning home. How many nights had I slept there on my visits to Washington, the setting for so many events, conversations, exchanges imbued with tragedy, hope, ambition. As I entered, Bobby silently indi- cated the stairway to his upstairs bedroom and study. On the first floor a group of New York journalists was already gathering for a long-planned dinner. Immediately sensing my apprehension, Bobby said, "I know you're in a difficult position. I didn't ask you to come here for a commitment. I haven't made one myself. But you're a friend, and I'd just like some advice." Relieved, but not surprised, by his sensitive awareness of my own dilemma, I sat down, sipped my scotch, and listened as Kennedy initiated an almost exact repetition of our last phone conversation, finishing, once again, with the question "What happens if I support Mc- Carthy?" "He'll be president," I repeated. "I agree with you," he said, then paused. "Well, I guess I better get downstairs to my guests. I'll be in touch." I left, only slightly puzzled. Bobby wasn't asking for a commitment, but he was waiting to see if I would take some initiative on my own.

I left Kennedy's home for McCarthy's headquarters, returning to my hotel at around 3 A.M. to find that Bobby had called me three times during the evening. It was too late to return his calls, but the messages were enough. Bobby Kennedy had not called me three times, long after his usual bedtime hour, to let me know that he was still undecided, or that he would concede the nomi- nation to McCarthy. At 6 A.M. the phone rang. "Well," Bobby said, "I'm definitely going to run."

"Okay," I replied.

"I'd like you to be with me."

God, was I tired. I felt as if I hadn't slept for a month; was incapable of concentrating my thoughts. "We'll have to talk about that" was all I could say, and then I returned to sleep.

At 10 A.M. on Saturday, March 16, in the same Senate Caucus

Room where, eight years before, John Kennedy had announced his presidential candidacy, Bobby formally entered the race. I did not hear his announcement. My resistance lowered by fatigue, I had acquired a short but miserable influenza, and lay feverish and alone in my hotel bed. For the first time in my life I was almost glad to be sick. At least I didn't have to do anything, had time to reflect, could count on my highly contagious condition to forestall visitors. But there was always the telephone. Bobby called me, as did other members of the family, including Jacqueline Kennedy — Could I? Would I? When? Ted Kennedy, characteristically reckless, braved the germ-contaminated air to pay me a solicitous visit, to tell me how much his brother loved me, how much he loved me, what a rare and precious talent I possessed, that I and I alone could smooth Bobby's path to the White House. I was only slightly flattered, knowing from years of observation that when the Kennedys wanted something, restraint of word or deed would not be allowed to blunt the force of pursuit. (The same, of course, was true of Johnson; except that he would have installed a private nurse, drowned my room in flowers, perhaps have moved me to Walter Reed Hospital where "you can get the best care this country has to offer; the care you deserve.")

It wasn't easy. For much of the decade my personal history had been linked to the Kennedys and, in recent years, especially to Bobby, with whom I had formed so many bonds. "I hope you'll be able to join me," he said in a conversation that week; "the chemistry is right." "Chemistry," a synonym among the inhibited Irish for sympathy, affection, tacit understanding. And I felt the same way about him. He possessed, I knew, extraordinary qualities, which with luck, under favoring circumstances, if the country was ready, could make him the Joshua of that arduous, often thwarted, march that America had begun more than a decade before.

Yet I could not leave the McCarthy campaign. Not now. Not on the brink of that Wisconsin primary which might transform the swift, successful foray of our New Hampshire guerrilla band into a decisive overturn. Much of the McCarthy campaign — press, media, issues, speeches — had been built around my direction. To abandon it now would necessitate a large alteration of responsibilities, the recruitment of new skills. And the election was little more than two weeks away. And even if I overestimated my importance to the McCarthy campaign — a possibility that fre-

quently occurred to my fever-plagued mind — there was no doubt
that I had formed a special attachment to the dedicated, joyously
devoted young volunteers. More a romantic rebellion than the traditional political combat in which I had been trained, the "movement" was wonderfully matched to my own temperament. In this
movement I was a leader — a leader by default, perhaps — and I
njc ed the responsibility and the authority to shape strategy and
decisions.

All these thoughts and more coursed randomly through my mind
as I lay, alternating between sleep and congested wakefulness,
waiting for my trivial but disabling illness to pass. Finally, decisively, I knew that my precipitous departure would be viewed as
betrayal — might actually constitute a betrayal — by those with
whom I had shared the labors of New Hampshire, and by Mc-
Carthy himself. I also knew I was exaggerating the importance of
my decision; that the events of 1968 would take their fateful course
unmoved by my personal powers. But it was important to me. To
resolve in action the mingled ambiguities of conscience and reason
is to define the man, and self-definition, in our secular age, is the
only alternative to the servitude of self-denial. This truism is, of
course, the solitary reflection of an aging writer; then I only knew
that I should do what seemed right — not for Bobby or Mc-
Carthy, but for me.

I called Kennedy and told him I was going to Wisconsin. "Look,
Bobby," I explained rather feebly, "you're not on the ballot in
Wisconsin, and a defeat for Johnson is as important to you as to
McCarthy." "If that's your decision," he replied, obviously an-
noyed. "That's it," I said, "good luck," and painfully replaced
the receiver. The next day I flew to Milwaukee.

Kennedy did not keep his annoyance to himself. Over the next
few weeks he told friends and staff members that I had personally
been responsible for at least 10 percent of McCarthy's vote in
New Hampshire, and was now trapped, intoxicated by the very
momentum I had created. He referred to me as "His Nibs." Yet
there was more puzzlement than anger in his attitude. He had
fully expected me to join him immediately, a belief that reflected
a far larger misconception. He failed to realize that the triumph
in New Hampshire had transformed McCarthy into a national
figure — fresh, attractive, with a powerful hold on the imagination of the electorate — a shining knight from Minnesota assaulting the battlements of established power. By making his an-

nouncement only days after the New Hampshire primary, denying
the McCarthy workers time to savor their victory, to let their sense
of invincibility fade in the light of political realities, Bobby had
incurred a harsh, hostile resentment among McCarthy's legions.
To them it appeared that Bobby had stepped in to reap the rewards of McCarthy's courageous battle. Their judgment was unfair, of course. McCarthy might topple Johnson, but Kennedy was
far more likely to carry the fallen standard to the White House.
Yet it was unreasonable, foolish, to expect the McCarthy supporters to let such calculations overrule their passionate ebullience.
They had made history, and would make it again. Murray Kempton, the country's most skilled and intelligent columnist, a Kennedy friend and admirer, declined an invitation to a party hosted
by Ted Kennedy with a telegram reading, "Sorry I can't join you.
Your brother's announcement makes clear that St. Patrick did not
drive out all the snakes from Ireland."

Over the next few months the anger would fade as it became
apparent that Kennedy was the only antiwar candidate with a
chance for victory. But never completely. And the clumsiness of
timing would, until the end, make Kennedy's course more difficult.

But all that lay in the future as I entered Milwaukee's Sheraton–Shroeder hotel, headquarters of a McCarthy campaign that
was, as McCarthy speechwriter Jeremy Larner later wrote, "heady
with history." There was none of the uncertainty that had greeted
my arrival in New Hampshire. Volunteers were everywhere, rushing through the crowded corridors, jammed into hotel rooms,
sleeping on cots, in sleeping bags, or on the uncovered floor.
Through long nights of work, sustained by soft drinks and peanut
butter, they labored to produce transcripts of speeches, pamphlets
and posters; rushed their product to the volunteer headquarters
where every day hundreds of young people arrived, received their
instructions, and boarded buses and cars to carry the McCarthy
message to every corner of the state. Before the campaign ended
we had canvassed one million three hundred thousand homes in
the state of Wisconsin, which meant that we had reached, personally, almost every voter. And as the reports began to flow back
into headquarters, were examined and calculated by our resident
statisticians, the results defied expectation and belief. There were
entire towns in rural Wisconsin where volunteers were unable to
find a single Johnson supporter. We were headed for a landslide.

Meanwhile, the White House, startled out of complacency by the New Hampshire results, brought all its dwindling political resources into combat. An experienced campaign manager set up headquarters in every substantial city. Members of the cabinet were dispatched to speak in support of Johnson. Television and radio time was purchased. The vice-president, an admired citizen of neighboring Minnesota, descended on Wisconsin with his customary energy and eloquence only to find his audiences, even in districts he had taken from John Kennedy in the 1960 primary, more dutiful than enthusiastic, more anxious to see him than to hear about Johnson. It was all in vain. It was too late. Returning to Washington, the administration campaigners reported what they had sensed — the smell of defeat. Johnson's campaign manager left the state almost a week before the election, saying, "We've done all we can do." Larry O'Brien, then postmaster general, told the president that the outlook was far more bleak than he had anticipated. An NBC poll, confirming our own unscientific tallies, predicted that McCarthy would get well over 60 percent of the vote, that Johnson's total might dip under 20 percent with the rest going to an assortment of write-in candidates. Late at night, seeking a short break from the continual labors, the cacophonous intensity of the McCarthy hotel, I would walk through the silent Milwaukee streets to the Johnson headquarters where, through the glass front, I could see two or three middle-aged women typing letters, or folding pamphlets into envelopes, surrounded by an acre of empty tables.

As the weekend before the primary approached, Lyndon Johnson was confronting the largest, most humiliating defeat in modern presidential history. And he knew it. Men whose judgment he trusted — Clark Clifford, Larry O'Brien — informed him that the tide could not be arrested, that he had a decision to make. That Sunday, the primary little more than two days away, the White House announced that the president would, that same evening, make a major address to the nation.

Sunday night I sat in a hotel suite with Blair Clark and Teddy White — in Wisconsin pursuing his third *Making of the President* — watching as the television announcer intoned: "Now, from the White House, the president of the United States." I was stunned at Johnson's appearance. Leaning forward against the table, manuscript in his hand, he seemed not subdued but drained, as if the life force had been dissolved, his face pallid, lined, aged. As he began to talk about Vietnam, I felt somber, sorrowful. I had worked against him, wanted to keep him from the presidency, but not this: this beaten, melancholy, man, so little like the massive, unquenchable figure I had served. "Look at him," I said to Teddy, "he looks terrible. You won't believe this, but I feel sorry for him."

After a boilerplate repetition of American policy, Johnson announced that he was "taking the first step to deescalate the combat," had "ordered all our aircraft and naval vessels to make no attacks on North Vietnam." Then, his address seemingly concluded, he looked down at the pages in front of him, paused, looked toward the camera. "This country's ultimate strength lies in the unity of our people. There is divisiveness among us all tonight. . . . With America's sons in the fields far away, with America's future under challenge right here at home . . . I do not believe that I should devote an hour or a day of my time to any personal partisan causes. . . . Accordingly, I shall not seek, and will not accept, the nomination of my party for another term as your president."

Stunned, then exultant, I leaped from my chair, rushed over to the television set, pointed directly at Johnson, saying, according to White's account (my own recollection dissolved by the intensity of the moment), "I thought it would take another six weeks." Outside, the corridors of the Milwaukee hotel were instantly thronged with hundreds of young volunteers shouting, chanting ("Hey, hey, LBJ . . ."), cheering ("We did it!" or, from their own childhood, "The witch is dead, the wicked witch is dead"). For them faith had been justified, labor rewarded, right had prevailed. As they crowded the corridors, overflowed into packed rooms, spilled out into the chill Milwaukee streets, the entire decade seemed to come alive, the frustrated hopes undammed, the sense of impotence released, in one gorgeously climactic moment. You could go home again: back to an America that after a few short years of vitality had seemed to have receded into history.

My own reaction, after the initial excitement, was muted, uncertain, more a sense of relief as if a door had been unbolted from within a fortress, opening to new but ambiguous possibilities. And I could also remember what they did not recall — that the man whose departure had ignited the celebratory flames had, not long ago, been the formidable, courageous leader of the most progressive forces of the decade: dragon and St. George fused in one tormented flesh.

Directed by an instinctive, almost involuntary, political impulse, I began to discuss with McCarthy the actions he should now take to maximize the rewards of his unanticipated triumph. I suggested he call Johnson, which he did, and McCarthy's wife spoke with Lady Bird. Naturally the conversations were brief, distant, cold. Johnson was in no mood to pretend geniality toward the man who, as he thought, had cleared the way for his greatest enemy. I advised him to call other political leaders — Daley in Chicago, Governor Lawrence in Pennsylvania, Governor Hughes in New Jersey — to ask their support, not because they were likely to accede to his request, but to help dissipate, through this enactment of a traditional political ritual, the hostility that McCarthy's candidacy had aroused among party leaders. He had campaigned against the establishment, attacked "boss" control. The assault had been productive, but now he needed them if he was to have any hope of nomination. (Although Humphrey would not announce his candidacy until April 27, allowing an appropriate interval of lamentation for his fallen leader, I did not doubt, nor did McCarthy, that he would soon be in the field, the president's chosen successor.)

McCarthy went into a private room to make his calls. At least I think he did, although he might also have retreated to contemplate, or to immerse himself and his emotions in a volume of Yeats or even Robert Lowell. Returning to the sitting room, McCarthy sat facing me, and said quietly, "Indiana will be decisive." I knew immediately that he was right. The Indiana primary was only a month away. It would be a contest not against Johnson and the war, but between McCarthy and Kennedy. A Kennedy loss would probably end his chances for the nomination, which rested on the premise that he alone possessed the personal appeal necessary to defeat the Republican nominee. McCarthy would have slain both the giants of the party. On the other hand, a McCarthy defeat would end his own already-slim hopes. It would be a crucial confrontation between the pretenders. And I was on the wrong side.

That same evening, in a distant state, amid the evening's respite in his own barely begun campaign, Bobby Kennedy watched, said little, and almost immediately turned to a discussion of future strategy. Things would be different now. The knights were still in the field, but the dragon had slain himself. And it was not his moment. It belonged to the Minnesota senator and his triumphant companions; although it was his own candidacy, as much as anything, that, for reasons deeply embedded in Johnson's mind, had helped turn the balance of decision. Kennedy was aware that his own course was now more difficult. Would McCarthy withdraw? Improbable. So he would have to be beaten. It would not be easy. The man was a hero, regarded as an exemplar of political purity and principle. And Bobby also knew that while he was absorbed in combat with McCarthy, all the formidable power of the White House would be directed toward the nomination of Hubert Humphrey.

The mold had been shattered, with consequences no one could then foresee. We only knew that the gargantuan figure who had dominated American public life for half a decade, and who, only thirty days before, had seemed certain to be nominated and, more likely than not, to be president for another four years, was now a lame duck. Only a few short months of dwindling power remained.

> All at once, the moon clouded over
> We heard gurgling cry
> A few seconds later, the captain's helmet
> was all that floated by.
> The sergeant said "turn around men
> I'm in charge from now on"
> And we just made it out of the Big Muddy
> With the captain dead and gone.
>
> — Pete Seeger

But the route out of the Big Muddy was to prove longer and more arduous than anyone had imagined. And it would not claim only the captain.

On Wednesday, April 3, I flew from Milwaukee to Washington, the morning newspaper resting on my lap, unread, as I struggled with the decision I knew I would now have to make.

On April 4, Martin Luther King — the Gandhi of his people, the largest figure of the age — was killed by an assassin's bullet on the balcony of his Memphis hotel. The murder of John Kennedy was stupefying, an eye-scorching blast from a cloudless sky. A grieving country had halted for a moment, then moved toward the destiny he had come to represent — more, perhaps, in death than in life. The New Frontier had been followed by the Great Society, the War on Poverty, large advances in civil rights, the emergence of a half-dozen liberating movements. But this murder was different. Martin Luther King's death did not pour fresh energy into black demands, arouse the accommodating sympathies of a country. It left only an emptiness — the failure of the Poor People's Campaign, federal forces dismantling the Resurrection City which had been assembled on the margins of Washington to dramatize the horrifying injustices of black poverty. It is not that Kennedy was white and King was black, although one would have to ignore American realities not to realize that was part of it. But more important were the times. It was 1968 not 1963. We had already begun to shatter that collective self— the bonds of American community — and move toward the self-regarding individualism that would dominate approaching decades. On March 31, the spirit of the sixties seemed to have renewed itself, resurrection at hand. On April 4, it began to die.

That night, in over a hundred cities, blacks poured into the streets, their frustrated outrage — "the Man, baby, the Man" had killed him — loosing flames into the urban skies, destroying, looting, burning. Some invisible assassin from some invisible land had struck down the hope of his people — and the enemy, the murderous enemy was everywhere, unidentifiable, concealed behind every white face, behind the stores and apartment buildings, on the asphalt streets and in the shabby wooden homes. So it was "burn, baby, burn," violate and shatter. It would lead nowhere, would create nothing, transgressed the principles that the martyred King so steadfastly, with waning persuasion, had preached to his people and to the country they inhabited — neighbors and aliens. But it would, they must have felt, accomplish one thing: It would prove they were alive. They were there. You couldn't kill them all.

It was the next morning before the flames began to subside. I looked out from my hotel room over debris-strewn streets that resembled the films I had seen of bomb-shattered English neighborhoods during World War II. Federal troops patrolled the streets, as if Washington was under martial law. The shrill discord of the evening had been replaced by an incredible, unprecedented silence. Barricades blocked the movement of traffic, and I had to receive a special pass to leave my hotel, drive through the desolate boulevards, across the bridge spanning the Potomac (had not armies assembled here once before?) to Hickory Hill where Robert Kennedy was waiting, first stopping for a visit with Gene McCarthy to tell him of the decision that had been forming since the night of Johnson's withdrawal.

"I would have liked to stay with the McCarthy campaign," I explained in an oral interview for the McCarthy archives made shortly after the presidential election of 1968. "I enjoyed the McCarthy campaign, working with the kids, the whole atmosphere, open, freewheeling, relatively free of the usual infighting, maneuvering for position. I knew I would like it more than the Kennedy campaign — not because of Kennedy, but because I would be surrounded by all the old professionals. And I had great respect for McCarthy, had no hesitation about working for him. But my whole life up until then, almost since I graduated from law school, had been tied closely to the Kennedys. I had become a personal friend of Bobby's, knew how much he wanted to do for the country, believed in his abilities, shared many of his passions. And there was another thing. I thought if I stayed with McCarthy I might be able to help beat Bobby Kennedy. He was beatable. Oregon proved that. And McCarthy had a real chance to beat him in Indiana. McCarthy was very tough and very smart . . . and Indiana was a pretty conservative state. So I just couldn't do it. That was all. It was a purely personal, internal thing." But it was also more than that. McCarthy would be a good president. Bobby, I believed, had the possibility of greatness.

As I drove up to McCarthy's house, the senator was sitting outside, tranquilly absorbing the soft air of the Washington spring. After greeting me, he sat silently, knowing the purpose of my visit. "I'm sorry, Senator, more than you know, but I just can't be part of a campaign whose purpose is to end the political career of one of my best friends."

"Well," he said, "that's the kind of campaign it has to be."

"That's right, that's how I would have to advise you. And that's why I can't do it."

McCarthy sat silently for a moment, lifted his face to receive the calming sunlight breaking through the overcast, then said, "Maybe we'll meet again." Without responding I turned, infinitely sad, infinitely certain I had made the only possible choice, and drove to McLean.

I was not in a genial mood as I entered the Kennedy house,

where Bobby greeted me with "Well, it's about time." "Listen, Bobby," I exploded, "it's not my fault you didn't run. You're the one who put me in this position." He did not argue or show resentment, gently took me by the arm and guided me into a sitting room where much of the Kennedy inner circle had assembled — the bright and idealistic new men, Adam Walinsky, Jeff Greenfield, and the old guard resuscitated for this replay of past glories, Sorensen, Salinger, O'Donnell.

My former colleagues looked toward me without enthusiasm; I could sense their disapproval: just another player in an already-crowded game. "Listen you bastards," I said as if responding to a slight that no one had offered, "I'm the only one of you who did the right thing, and I'm the only one who's going to suffer for it."

I spent the next couple of weeks assembling a media crew, which, fortunately, was augmented by John Frankenheimer, a brilliant Hollywood director who volunteered his services to Kennedy, and who would work tirelessly on the television campaign until the end. Once organized, my personal "production company" traveled to Indiana, where, for the first time, Kennedy and McCarthy would be on the ballot. Johnson's withdrawal had virtually eliminated the war as an issue. This, together with McCarthy's decision not to wage an active campaign in Indiana, transformed the election into a battle where Bobby Kennedy himself became the principal issue — his qualities, his temperament, his beliefs. Southern Indiana, bordering the South, had voted heavily for Nixon in 1960, and had been an early stronghold of the Ku Klux Klan. The industrial cities of northern Indiana contained large numbers of ethnic workers, many of Slavic descent, who were fiercely hostile to what they saw as the threatening encroachment of that black America with whose cause Kennedy had become so firmly identified.

Confronted with the menacing contradictions of the state, Kennedy found his theme. It was not a contrivance, not a formula derived purely from political calculation, but a manifestation of his most deeply held convictions. He would be the "tribune of the underclass," not just the blacks or the impoverished but all those who sensed that their needs, their desires, were disdained or denied by the ruling forces of American life. For behind the varied problems of the day was a single issue — impotence; the sensed helplessness of citizens to shape the conditions of their own life and that of the country. "The purpose of my campaign," he said, "is not simply to do things for others, but to show individuals that they do count, to give them the opportunity to change their lives, to be heard on the direction of America."

Watching Bobby tour a black ghetto was to see into the man himself. His evident passion evoked an equally intense response, as if he had come as liberator. "Who do you want for your president?" he would shout to the black throngs who crowded around his motorcade. "You," they would respond, "we want Kennedy." They didn't care about his policies, the programs that — for campaign purposes — had been so carefully crafted to meet the needs of the poor and dispossessed. They knew he was on their side. And that was all that mattered.

Among the blue-collar workers of the industrial states, although the words were different, the references to racial injustice omitted, the message was the same. "This is your country. You have a right to work, to be cared for. And I'm not going to let them take it away." His inner urge toward defiance — of unjust privilege, indifferent power, concentrated wealth — which provoked so much fear and even hatred among some, was also the source of his greatest strength, arousing the hopes and expectations of millions who felt themselves victimized. Many of the same workers in Gary, Indiana, who later became supporters of George Wallace also voted for Bobby Kennedy. They did not accept Kennedy's embrace of the "black revolution," but his racial convictions were far less important than their rightly sensed belief that he stood for those who were disadvantaged — not so much economically — they were not poor — but because their opportunities were unfairly limited, their way of life held in disdain, barricaded by the affluent middle classes.

During the campaign Kennedy told me of a speech that Jacqueline Kennedy's brother-in-law, Prince Stanislas ("Stash") Radziwill, a man descended from Polish nobility, had delivered to an auditorium filled with workers of Polish descent. After Radziwill had finished his campaign exhortation, one of the workers stood and said, "We believe you, Prince Radziwill, but what about the blacks?" "Better to be in America living next to a thousand blacks," Radziwill replied, "than in Poland living next to one commissar." The hall broke into prolonged applause. Telling me the story, Bobby laughed. "It was a complete non sequitur," he commented, "but it worked." Then, speaking more soberly: "That's what I've got to do. Convince them that blacks aren't the enemy. They're being discriminated against too. Not because of race. But

because the people at the top don't care about them. They need
what the blacks need — a decent home, medical care. If they waste
their energy fighting against blacks, they're only going to sink
themselves. But it's not easy."

Of course it wasn't easy. Words and arguments wouldn't convince them. But there was in Kennedy's intensity, the passion of
his concern, something that compelled belief. And for a very good
reason. He believed it himself. If elected, he would fight for it.
Kennedy was a militant. And they were militants, too. And in
politics, as in life, human bonds rest less on a congruence of ideas
than a sense of shared sensibilities, emotions, trust. He alone among
white American politicians might have been able to heal the widening divisions between black Americans and lower-income whites,
between the hopeful young and a middle class that was turning
away from hope.

As I listened to him campaign, and even more in private conversations, I realized that Kennedy, like me, was a born outsider,
but one compelled to seek power through the hazardous, intricate
maze of American politics. Once, at lunch, he asked me to describe my impressions of Che Guevara. When I had finished, he
thought for a moment, then said, "You know, sometimes I envy
the bastard. At least he was able to go out and fight for what he
believed. All I ever do is go to chicken dinners."

Naturally, the envy, though felt, was a barren sentiment. This
was America. To lead America one did not captain a guerrilla
army or organize a coup. So he set out to master the maze, made
the necessary compromises, tailored his rhetoric to his audience
as all politicians must. He talked of the need for law and order in
a society increasingly streaked with lawlessness and disorder. He
meant it, of course. No politician, no rational citizen, would advocate crime or violence. But he also knew that to many in his
audience the phrase "law and order" was a code phrase for opposition to black protest. It was not what Kennedy intended. It
was not what he said. But if some of those listening gave it that
interpretation, then the mistake was theirs.

Few things in the campaign bothered him more than the defection of the young. One late night we walked past McCarthy's
headquarters and saw a group of young volunteers sitting on the
stairs outside the building. Kennedy turned and walked toward
them. They watched him silently as he approached. "Mind if I sit
down?" he asked. A young man on the bottom stair moved aside

and indicated a space beside him. Sitting, Kennedy smiled. "I know why I'm here. I'm running for office. Why are you here?" His good humor dissolved the tension, brought forth a torrent of replies. "We're campaigning for McCarthy." "We're here to try and end the war." "But I'm against the war," Kennedy interjected softly. There was no disagreement, only puzzled whispers — What did he want? Finally, one young woman, whose tailored suit would not have raised a questioning eyebrow in all of Indianapolis, spoke above the murmurs. "I've been part of the peace movement for more than a year. McCarthy gave us a chance. I joined his campaign in New Hampshire to fight against the war because he was there. And you weren't there. And as long as he continues to fight I'll be with him." Ignoring the implied criticism, Kennedy asked, "How many of you left school or good jobs to work in the McCarthy campaign?" Almost every hand went up. "How many of you are going to stick with it to the end, even if it goes all the way to November?" Again, nearly all the hands were raised. "I know some of you might not like me," Kennedy continued, "think I just jumped in to take your victory away. Well, that's not quite the way I see it. But it doesn't matter what you think of me. I want you to know that you make me proud to be an American. You've done a wonderful thing. I'm only sorry we couldn't have done it together." With that Kennedy got up to leave, and, as we began to start down the street, he turned and waved. Every person on the steps waved back. "Thanks for talking to me," he called, "maybe we'll meet again."

After a few minutes of silence he turned to me: "Damn it, damn it all, those are my people. I'd give anything . . ." His voice trailed off. "Well, it can't be helped. If I blew it, I blew it." And with that we reentered the hotel and went to bed.

Although Kennedy was a skilled politician, was tireless in pursuit of victory, he never lost — as most politicians do — the capacity to detach himself intellectually from his goals. One evening, long after midnight, as we sat drinking in an Indianapolis restaurant, unwinding from a long day of campaigning, he commented: "Suppose I do make it. Suppose I really do get to be president. Will it be worth it? With Congress and the press and business pressing down on me all the time, how will I be able to accomplish what I want?" He spoke, of course, from an insider's knowledge of the limits of presidential power. But there was something else, a clarity that managed to pierce the overwhelming fa-

tigue of the day. He really did want to help the blacks and the
poor and the children; he remained as he had been when the sixties began — a true believer who wanted to change the country.
Once it had all seemed possible. But the country had changed.
Maybe it couldn't be done. Maybe it was too late. Kennedy's
doubt was well founded. He loved America, but he also knew it —
knew it couldn't be moved against its will, and that it would be
difficult for him, even as president, to restore that will. But the
question was inadmissible, could not be discussed in the middle
of a campaign lest it blunt the single-minded effort required for
victory. So I said nothing, and, shortly thereafter, we left for a few
hours sleep before another long day of campaigning. First we would
win, and then, only then, look for an answer.

The heart of the Indiana campaign was not money or organization. It was sheer energy and personal drive. Campaigning
eighteen hours a day, Bobby personally visited every town with a
population of more than five thousand. He acted as if he intended
to see every Democratic voter in the state. Their response came
on election day, May 7. Kennedy won the Indiana primary with
43 percent of the vote. McCarthy received 27 percent, with the
rest going to a slate of uncommitted delegates.

That same night Kennedy defeated Humphrey by a margin of
62.5 percent to 37 percent in the District of Columbia, whose large
black population gave Kennedy an overwhelming victory. Shortly
thereafter, Kennedy beat both McCarthy and Humphrey in the
Nebraska primary.

Up to then McCarthy had seemed curiously withdrawn from
the race, did little personal campaigning; although he had kept
his campaign structure intact, and even strengthened it with the
addition of some professional staff. But as the campaign moved
into Oregon, McCarthy's seeming casualness disappeared. He
campaigned hard, and he campaigned effectively. He attacked
Kennedy's refusal to enter the presidential race until after he had
shown the way. "We began this campaign against the war when
no one else would touch it. We are not just running a political
campaign, we represent a movement — a movement for peace in
Vietnam, a movement for reconciliation at home. We must not let
Kennedy's personal ambitions halt that movement. And I don't
think he can. Certainly he's not going to beat me here in Oregon
by traveling around with an astronaut" (John Glenn) "and a dog."
McCarthy continually challenged Kennedy to a debate, which

Kennedy mistakenly declined, yielding to the accepted political counsel that a front-runner never debates a lesser-known opponent.

Kennedy knew he was in trouble in Oregon. "If only we could move a ghetto up here, just for a day, then I know I could win it." But there were no ghettos in Oregon. Minorities made up only 2 percent of the population. The entire state seemed like one sprawling suburb.

Late on election day, May 28, as the polls were closing, Kennedy and I, along with other staff and family members, boarded a plane in Los Angeles for the flight to our Oregon headquarters. When we took off, the outcome was still uncertain. But before we arrived, reports radioed to the airplane indicated that defeat was almost certain. As the news circulated, the cabin became silent. Sitting near Kennedy, I heard him say, "We frightened them," then relapse into thought.

Arriving at Portland, we rushed to our hotel headquarters. The election had ended in defeat. The final result would show McCarthy with 44.7 percent of the vote, Kennedy with 38.8 percent. It was the first election any Kennedy had lost. The day's work was not over. Kennedy and a handful of staff members, including faces familiar from past Kennedy campaigns — Larry O'Brien, Bill vanden Heuvel — went to a rear room of our hotel suite to discuss and prepare Kennedy's concession. "He beat us," Kennedy instructed, "and he beat us fairly. It's my own fault. I could have done a better job. You might point out that our combined vote is an overwhelming rejection of the war." Kennedy sat back in a chair as his staff members worked over the draft. I watched him from across the room. His head was slightly bent, his features a model of sober thoughtfulness, then he looked up and our eyes met, locked from across the room, and there was, for only an instant, a glimpse of ineffable pain. We both looked way.

That same night we returned to Los Angeles. The California primary was only a week away. "I've got to debate him," Kennedy told us on the ride back. "I'm not in much of a position now to say he's not a serious candidate. Hell, if he's not a serious candidate after tonight, then I'm not a candidate at all."

The campaign in California had already been long and tumultuous. Kennedy was mobbed by admirers in Watts, spat upon by enraged students at San Francisco State. ("Not as bad as Chile," he told me.) But even in those last hectic days, with his entire political future on the line, Kennedy's sense of the ambiguities of politics, of life, never left him. Riding in a motorcade through the cheering streets of a California ghetto, he turned to me: "Suppose we do succeed, and the whole country becomes just one big middle class, do you know how much we'll lose?" He did not intend the remarks as a justification of poverty or bigotry, but as an apprehension that the distinctive richness of black culture, which he loved, might be swallowed up in a homogenized America. But that was a problem for the distant future; present injustice was his enemy. "You know," he said later during the same ride, "if anything happens to me, there'll never be another white politician they'll trust." (In 1984, while traveling through Mississippi with Jesse Jackson, I repeated Kennedy's observation to a local black leader, a minister. "We never trusted him either," he answered, but he laughed, almost remorsefully, blunting the thrust of his own healthy defiance.)

Early polls of the California electorate had shown Kennedy well ahead. But after Oregon, that lead was beginning to crumble. I was receiving calls from a personal network of young volunteers working in the valleys around Los Angeles. "People are beginning to change their mind"; "They're turning against Kennedy"; "There's a lot of talk about McCarthy." From dozens of similar calls I reached the conclusion that Kennedy was slipping badly. How much and how fast? It was impossible to know. I did not talk to Kennedy about the information I was receiving or what I thought it meant. It was my obligation to reveal bad news that might be corrected. But it was too late for changes. There were only a few days of compaigning left. Our television and radio commercials had been completed. Kennedy had done everything he could. We all had. The Kennedy–McCarthy debate, which took place on June 1, had either arrested the slide or not. There was no point in guessing, I told myself. We would soon know . . . in just a few days, on . . . I looked at my calendar . . . on the fourth of June.

The sixties came to an end in a Los Angeles hospital on June 6, 1968.

Two days before, election Tuesday had begun for me in the middle of the morning as I struggled for consciousness against the weight of the oppressive weariness built up over the previous five months of campaigning. It was now almost summer, and the long, swift days of activity, interrupted by only four or five hours of sleep, had begun in the middle of New Hampshire's winter. Campaigning finally becomes all fatigue, and stamina and instinct become more important than thought, policies, or convictions.

Today, however, would be almost a vacation, a liberating respite from deadlines, as we waited for the primary results, while the discussion of strategy and the clipped political humor would mask the unspoken awareness that, in hours, the future could collapse. Had we reached enough of them, and what were they thinking? And, knowing the intensities Kennedy aroused, how many hated him or were afraid? Not enough, surely, I told myself, to outweigh the passionate of the ghettos.

During breakfast, I talked with a few friends from the McCarthy campaign. They were disturbed by the thought that a large Kennedy victory might leave Kennedy the one candidate able to defeat Hubert Humphrey, thus trapping them between their personal commitment to Eugene McCarthy and the convictions that had drawn them into the campaign. There was no easy answer unless McCarthy provided it by withdrawing, and that seemed remote. After breakfast, Bobby called to say he was spending the day at John Frankenheimer's Malibu Beach home. Would I come and join him?

The living room of the Frankenheimer house and the adjoining dining room were divided by a glass wall from a swimming pool and a broad patio. Beyond was the gentle-surfed beach. Ethel Kennedy was seated, talking with Teddy White and Mrs. Frankenheimer, but the candidate was not there. Going into the next room for the buffet lunch, I turned casually toward the pool.

Robert Kennedy was stretched out across two chairs in the sunlight, his head hanging limply over the chair frame; his unshaven face was deeply lined, and his lips slightly parted. There was no movement. I felt a sudden spasm of fear. But it swiftly receded. He was sleeping, only sleeping. God, I thought, reaching for the food, I suppose none of us will ever get over John Kennedy.

By the time the telephone brought the first tentative vote projections, Kennedy and Fred Dutton had joined the group in the Frankenheimer living room. One of the networks, having surveyed voters in key precincts as they left the polling places, was now predicting a 49–41 victory over McCarthy. (About 10 percent was conceded to an independent slate of delegates.) "They were pretty accurate in the other primaries," Kennedy remarked.

"But not in Oregon," said Dutton.

"We lost all the undecided there," Kennedy replied, then added, "Maybe they won't break away from us here. If only we can push up our percentage a point or two."

It seemed then that the extra point or two would make all the difference. We all believed that it was not enough for Kennedy to win in California. In order to soften the blow of his Oregon defeat, we felt he had to win big, and that meant more than 50 percent of the vote, with 40 percent or less going to McCarthy. Still, 49 percent was close to the target, and enough to ease the remote apprehension of an actual defeat. ("If I lose?" he had answered a reporter. "Well, if I lose, I'll just go home and raise the next generation of Kennedys.")

We talked idly, reminisced, discussed future strategy, as if the big victory were already in — not because we were sure, but because that's the only way politicians can talk.

But Kennedy was so tired that even the easily familiar shoptalk came haltingly, and he soon went back to the bedroom for a nap while I drove to my hotel to draft the victory statement.

That evening, the dozen or more rooms in our corridor of the Ambassador Hotel were filled with friends, relatives, and a few journalists discussing our "decisive" California victory with the euphoric wishful thinking of the amateur. Some, however, knew that outside the hotel, and beyond California, the Humphrey campaign, propelled by the single-minded power of Lyndon Johnson, was moving from state to state, persuading, coercing, calling in old debts and creating new ones, progressing toward control of the Chicago convention.

Still, no one was immune to the building excitement as the networks began projecting well over 50 percent for Kennedy. Only Jesse Unruh, the ultimate professional, was not smiling. "They're wrong," he said softly. "Those are our votes coming in now. It won't be that good." Jesse was right, of course. The final result was 46–42. But Kennedy was never to know how close it was.

Bobby motioned to me, and we walked from room to room looking for a private place. Finding none, we went into a bathroom and closed the door. With victory now assured, we went over the familiar ground with new urgency. "I've got to get free of McCarthy," Kennedy said. "While we're fighting each other, Humphrey's running around the country picking up delegates. I don't want to stand on every street corner in New York for the next two weeks." (The New York primary was two weeks away, and the McCarthy forces were strong there.) "I've got to spend that time going to the states, talking to delegates before it's too late. My only chance is to chase Hubert's ass all over the country. Maybe he'll fold."

Ted Sorensen had joined us, and the reports from New Jersey and Ohio were grim. It looked as if both delegations would go to Humphrey, maybe in the next week.

"Look," said Kennedy, "even if McCarthy won't get out, his people must know after tonight that I'm the only candidate against the war that can beat Humphrey. That's what they want to do, isn't it, to end the war?" He spoke as if rehearsing the argument he would use with the McCarthy supporters, but behind it was an unspoken awareness that the passionate hostilities engendered by a bitter campaign might make even so powerful a view inadequate. Still, there had been enough contact with McCarthy supporters in the past week to convince us that if Kennedy alone emerged from the California battle, many of them would come over.

Taking me aside, Kennedy whispered, "I think we should tell him if he withdraws now and supports me, I'll make him secretary of state." I had suggested this earlier, and Kennedy had rejected the proposal. But now McCarthy could prove a fatal obstacle. The goal was well worth the price.

Moving into the crowd, Kennedy accepted congratulations, usually with a quip that turned aside any obvious compliment, talked with a friend or two about skiing or the ghettos with a casualness that was instantly suspended when a political detail was brought to him for comment or decision. A television network wanted to put Larry O'Brien on for an interview. "What about Steve?" Kennedy asked. (Kennedy's brother-in-law, Stephen Smith had been as close to a primary manager as the intricacies of California politics had allowed.) "He deserves it. People think of him as a back-room type, and he's one of the best men we have. It'll be good for Steve."

A group sprawled over a double bed to discuss the victory statement. "It says how great the McCarthy movement was," commented one participant. "I'd like to say something nice about him personally," Kennedy said.

Kennedy left the room for a scheduled television appearance. We watched as he was interviewed by a network correspondent. The change in Kennedy was startling. The frantic sense of the

early campaign, the harsh, punched lines, defensively seeking assurance in assertion and command of fact, were gone. There was
now an easy grace, a strength that was unafraid of softness. For
the first time since he had announced his candidacy, Robert Kennedy reminded me of his slain brother. If he looks like that for the
rest of the campaign, we might win, I thought. It wasn't the victory or confidence in the political future that had brought about
the transformation. For he was not very confident. It was more as
if the defeat in Oregon had freed him from the entangling pressures of his past, and now this victory was not just a Kennedy
victory, but his and his alone. Whatever the reason, he looked like
a president. And once a man had begun to look like a president,
he had doubled his chances to be one.

Although the returns were still incomplete, Kennedy decided to
go downstairs and make his victory statement. If he waited much
longer, everyone in California would have gone to sleep, and, anyway, it was only the size of his margin that was in question, not
the fact that he had won. I had intended to accompany him, but
as he was preparing to leave, I received a call from a prominent
McCarthy supporter who we hoped might help persuade Mc-
Carthy to withdraw. It was more important than watching the
victory statement. I was on the phone as Bobby left. He touched
me on the shoulder and said, "I'll go downstairs and do this, then
we can talk some more over at the Factory" (a local discotheque).
I didn't look up, sensing only the casual pressure of my friend's
hand.

Several minutes passed, then there were shouts and screams in
the corridor. I cut the call short, rushed into the bedroom, and
sat beside Ted Sorensen, paralyzed, listening to the dread inevitability unfold from the television set. "Who was it?" "They don't
know." "It can't be him." "Somebody's been shot." I watched,
silently clutching at hope, yet knowing in some inadmissible portion of my mind that it was Bobby and that he was dead.

Then we heard the confirming tones of Steve Smith's voice —
"The senator is hurt. Is there a doctor here?" On the floor of the
hotel kitchen Robert Kennedy lay, a slowly spreading pool of blood
underneath his head. The assassin's first bullet, a chance shot from
a feeble .22 round, had entered the brain from behind the right
ear.

The senator's lips moved. A friend leaned over to listen. "Jack,
Jack," he murmured, and then lapsed into unconsciousness from
which he never recovered.

He was taken to a nearby hospital, then moved to the Good Samaritan Hospital, where, through the long night, we sustained the hope of his survival. At dawn, Steve Smith emerged from a meeting with the assembled physicians and surgeons, walked down the corridor toward the impromptu waiting room. "Come on, Steve," I said. "Let's go down to the cafeteria and get some breakfast." He nodded in acquiescence. We entered the elevator. Steve's face was immobile, features rigidly set, his struggle for control poorly concealed. One look and I knew. "It's over, isn't it?" I said. He nodded briefly, stiffly. We entered the cafeteria, ate in silence, returned to the hospital corridor.

We waited through the morning, aware that the activity of that spacious, generous mind had ceased; that his life was now being maintained by a network of machines that pumped the lungs and circulated the blood. This man whose passions had been so fiercely directed at the basic needs of human existence was now sustained only by the most sophisticated contrivances of advanced medical technology.

I felt helpless, sad, angry. I cried a little, then, denying grief, hurled silent, defiant curses at fate, at God Himself. Then when it seemed I was too tired to feel anything, I sensed the dampness of unanticipated tears. McCarthy came for a brief visit and I sat with him in the lobby. None of the family wanted to see him. "Sirhan Sirhan," McCarthy reflected somberly, "It's just like Camus's the Stranger, the first name the same as the last name." The president called. "From now on," he said, "I'm going to provide Secret Service protection for all the candidates." It was a Johnsonian condolence. At least, I thought, he hadn't pretended to false affection. But it didn't matter. They didn't matter. What mattered was gone.

Sometime in the early afternoon, Kennedy's friend from prep school, Dave Hackett, touched my arm and whispered, "You better go in now if you want to see him." I entered the hospital room, saw my friend lying on the bed, his chest moving in electrically stimulated regularity. Teddy knelt praying at the foot of the bed. Ethel lay beside her dead husband, her body expressing a grief words could not convey. Other members of the family — Pat Lawford, Jean Smith, Steve, Jacqueline — stood silently, their gaze or their prayers or some unknowable mixture of grief, fear, emanation of their own mortality focused on the figure beneath the sheets, attached to life, a semblance of life, by wire and cables and pumps.

God, I thought, he looks so small. Then, as the doctors began
to turn off the life-mimicking machines, I cried again, then trem-
bled in grief, in fear of my own mortality, but most of all, in anger.

I left the room, and, without a parting word, departed the hospital for my hotel. I made love. Then I slept.

Postscript

NOW THE GHOSTS DISSOLVE. The tumult and the speeches fade into silence. The great leaders are tucked away. The impassioned, mildly eccentric protagonist of this story has moved toward the final stretch of years. Only memory remains. That and a seemingly unquenchable recurrence of desire that denies silence, death, defeat, years, all the realities of existence in inexorable history. Not just my personal existence, but that of the country to whose story I am inseparably fused. And for which I have written this book because it shows signs of a most troublesome decay.

I do not, like some athlete reflecting upon his bemedaled appearance in an ancient Olympiad, remember the sixties as the high point of striving and achievement. Admittedly, I have missed the occasional exhilarations of public life, but that lack has been more than compensated by the absence of the horrors that companioned them.

If that is so, you may well ask, why do I write about the past? It is a question best answered after, in briefest outline, I bring my personal narrative up to the present.

The year after Bobby was killed, I moved to a small house on Freeman Ridge in the township of Freeman, whose open, uncultivated fields and quiet woods were surmounted by the mountains of west central Maine. I went, not just as a retreat from the wounding blows of declining fortune, but to write; believing only distance and solitude could free me from addiction to the world of public action. And it worked. For the next five years in Maine and during the fifteen years after my return to Boston, I wrote —

a book, a play, many shorter pieces. But not about my experience of the sixties.

I was not, consciously or from some concealed impulse toward forgetfulness, rejecting that experience. But that time was over — for America and for me. When I reflected, which was rarely except to tell old war stories to new friends, I thought that in time others would come to pick up fallen standards and resume the American journey. They always had, I knew, for two centuries.

I am no longer quite so confident. Nor is my uneasiness a natural symptom of advancing years. It reflects a clearly observed, widely noted, two-decade departure from pursuit of the American dream. That dream is a simple one, at least it can be simply stated: a society in which all would have a chance to share in growing abundance; a land without huge inequalities of wealth or fixed class divisions, a nation that promised each individual not a certain income, but the opportunity to achieve to the limits of his capacities.

During the twenty years since the events I have described, we have abandoned this pursuit, preferring instead to fortify the barriers — of race, of class, of income — against which the fair expectations and "inalienable rights" of millions are dashed. There is not, as John Kennedy reminded us, a wall around America "to keep our people in." But we have built a multitude of walls along the contours of our inner landscape to hold our people back.

Today the clamor from the streets and public platforms, which marked the sixties, is gone, replaced by a strangely muted discourse. It is not an improvement. For the silence only masks the widening ruptures within the nation, hides the swelling ranks of distress, conceals the decline of American strength and purpose.

Our whole history argues that the conditions of this present are transitory. But history is an enigmatic teacher, a trickster whose only certain lesson is that the future cannot count on the past, that what has "always" been true may become irrevocably false. And there are now plenty of voices to tell us that the time of glory is gone, that muscle and bone are aging, and exploits of the past cannot be exceeded.

I do not believe it. I refuse to believe it.

The sixties, after all, were not a unique and isolated episode in the American chronicle. At our very beginning, Washington admonished that the fate of liberty and democracy were "deeply . . . finally staked on the experiment intrusted to the hands of the

American people." America as "experiment" — the guiding theme of two centuries, has recurred to dominate the life of the nation during every shaping period of our history. The sixties were the latest stage in that great experiment. Turbulent, violent, laced with corrupting digressions, it was also a time when most Americans felt the future could be bent to their wills. The large public events of the time cut deeply into our personal lives: the civil rights movement, the sit-ins, the beginnings of the women's movement, the War on Poverty. It was the time of the New Frontier and the Great Society and the dream of Martin Luther King.

And then, the experiment barely begun, it collapsed in the voracious terrain of Vietnam. The sixties, so filled with promise, came to an end. Not a failure, but abandoned. Never given a chance.

We cannot, of course, go back to the sixties. Nor should we try. The world is different now. Yet, two decades have passed since that infinitely horrifying day in Los Angeles which closes this book. And a new generation is emerging. They can pick up the discarded instruments and resume the great experiment which is America. There is no question of capacity, only of will. And I see — compel myself to see — a country that, like the waning March days in frozen Concord where I write, is teeming with the still-ambiguous signs of renewal. If this book has any purpose at all, it is not to impose a guide on that future, but to remind that men and women can live as if their world was malleable to their grasp; and that, true or false, to live in this belief is to be most authentically alive.

— Concord, Massachusetts
March 1988

Index

Hyannis, Massachusetts, 131, 446–447, 477

Indiana primary (1968), 528–529, 532
Inquest: The Warren Commission and the Establishment of Truth (Epstein), 462–463
Institute of Urban Development, 291

Jackson, Jesse, 339, 534
Jackson, Robert, 29
Jacobs, Jane, 285
Jeffers, Robinson, 164, 273
Jefferson, Thomas, 390
Johnson, Lady Bird, 350, 404
Johnson, Lyndon Baines, 6–7, 33, 72, 139, 227, 243–244, 256–427 *passim*, 457, 525, 539; and civil rights, 257–258, 287, 294, 310–341, 457; and Congress, 260–266, 269–270, 312–315, 353, 369–370; early career, 259, 260–261, 270; and Great Society, 271–272, 273, 275, 277–281, 364, 424–427; and 1960 presidential campaign, 78–79, 89, 100–101; and 1964 presidential campaign, 243, 247, 261, 283, 293–309, 355–357, 522–524; and 1968 presidential campaign, 469–470, 473, 486, 505, 512, 514, 522–523; and "Panama affair," 250–253; personal style of, 251, 252, 254–255, 258, 281, 414–415; psychological state of, 392–416, 457–458, 466, 473; and Robert Kennedy, 101, 244, 248, 261, 295–296, 298, 375, 396–397, 401, 405–406, 415; as senator, 72, 369–370; and tax cut bill, 261–266; as vice-president, 100–101, 260, 293–294, 302; and Vietnam war, 38, 271, 351–364, 366–367, 369–370, 373–391, 393, 403–404, 412–416, 455, 461, 466, 469, 522–523; and War on Poverty, 248, 257, 286–287
Johnston, Tom, 434
Jordan, Hamilton, 78
Josephson, Bill, 220

Kaplan, Jack, 436–437
Kaplan, Sumner, 24, 25
Katzenbach, Nicholas, 320, 493
Kearns, Doris, 374, 414, 425
Kefauver, Estes, 79
Kempton, Murray, 521

Kennedy, Edward, 6, 479–480, 519, 521
Kennedy, Ethel, 434, 447, 449, 535, 539
Kennedy, Eunice (Shriver), 114
Kennedy, Jacqueline, 111, 156, 222, 224, 228, 230, 519, 539
Kennedy, John Fitzgerald, 3–4, 25, 133, 140–143, 155–156, 233–238, 247, 259, 261, 443, 445–446, 454, 503; and Bay of Pigs, 125–126, 150, 152, 172, 174, 180–184, 185–186, 315; and "Catholic issue," 77, 83–84, 85, 87–88, 109, 110–111; and Cuban missile crisis, 218–219; death of, 226–232, 462–464, 526; debates with Nixon, 102, 112–116, 123–124; and Latin American trips, 214, 221; 1960 presidential campaign, 3, 69–70, 72–90, 91, 98–99, 100–132; as senator, 24–25, 40–41; and Vietnam, 369, 371–373; Warren Commission Report, 462–463
Kennedy, John, Jr., 444
Kennedy, Joseph P., 24–25, 41, 77, 82, 122
Kennedy, Joseph P., Jr., 443
Kennedy, Robert, 30, 65, 72, 78, 88, 89, 92, 114, 122, 186–187, 230, 244, 246–248, 254, 298–299, 385, 431–451, 463–464; as attorney general, 153, 224, 246–248, 436–437, 445–446; death of, 5, 538–540; family background, 443–444; and John Kennedy, 187, 446, 450–451, 463–464; Latin America trip, 433–435, 437–442; and Johnson, 101, 244, 247–248, 261, 295–296, 298, 375, 396–397, 401, 415, 431, 451, 464, 481; and 1964 election, 261, 295–298; and 1968 California primary, 5, 533–538; and 1968 presidential campaign, 472–481, 492, 503–504, 506–509, 516–521, 525–526, 528–538; personality of, 436–437, 443–448, 530; and religion, 299, 446–447, 449–450; as senator from New York, 248, 297, 464; and Vietnam war, 454–456, 461–462, 464, 465, 475, 485
Kennedy, Rose, 136, 443–444, 446–447
Kennedy Library, 246, 299
Kenworthy, Ned, 487
Kerner Commission report, 514–515
Kerouac, Jack, 93
Khan, Mohammed Ayub, 394–395